Scenes of Writing

Strategies for Composing with Genres

Amy Devitt
University of Kansas

Mary Jo Reiff
University of Tennessee

Anis Bawarshi
University of Washington

PEARSON
Longman

New York   San Francisco   Boston
London   Toronto   Sydney   Tokyo   Singapore   Madrid
Mexico City   Munich   Paris   Cape Town   Hong Kong   Montreal

Senior Vice President and Publisher: Joe Opiela
Senior Acquisitions Editor: Lynn M. Huddon
Development Editor: Karen Helfrich
Executive Marketing Manager: Ann Stypuloski
Senior Supplements Editor: Donna Campion
Production Manager: Charles Annis
Project Coordination, Text Design, and Electronic Page Makeup: Pre-Press Company,
    Inc.
Cover Design Manager: Wendy Fredricks
Cover Designer: Maria Ilardi
Cover Photos, Left to Right: © Ryan McVey/Getty Images, Inc.; © Tim Hall/Getty
    Images, Inc.; and © Anthony Marsland/Getty Images, Inc.
Manufacturing Manager: Lucy Hebard

For permission to use copyrighted material, grateful acknowledgment is made to the
copyright holders on pp. 571–574, which are hereby made part of this copyright page.

Library of Congress Cataloging-in-Publication Data

Devitt, Amy J.
    Scenes of writing : strategies for composing with genres / Amy J. DeVitt, Mary
Jo Reiff, Anis Bawarshi.
    p. cm.
    Includes index.
    ISBN 0-321-06111-X
    1. English language--Rhetoric. 2. Report writing. 3. Literary form. I. Reiff,
Mary Jo. II. Bawarshi, Anis S. III. Title.

PE1408.D4757 2004
808'.042--dc22
                                                                    2003064690

Please visit our Web site at http://www.ablongman.com

ISBN 0-321-06111-X

Dedication

To Jim, Dan, and Amy, for making our scenes so rich

Brief Contents

Detailed Contents

Preface to Instructors

Overview of *Scenes of Writing*

Our goal in this book is to help students write more effectively, knowingly, and critically in different writing contexts—what we call scenes of writing. Our approach teaches students how to become more agile and astute writers, writers who understand how and why to make writing choices as they negotiate among and participate in various scenes of writing.

To help students see and understand their possible choices, we teach students strategies for observing and analyzing writing scenes, and we show them how the kinds of writing done in those scenes reflect various situations—their readers and writers, purposes, subjects, and settings. Our understanding of scenes, situations, and kinds of writing draws on the best of rhetorical theory, especially recent research in rhetorical genre theory. That theory reveals genres not simply as types of texts but as forms of rhetorical action that are intimately related to forms of social organization and action. Understood in this way, genres are kinds of texts that help writers gain access to and participate in the scenes in which they are used.

Building on this research, *Scenes of Writing* teaches students how to gain knowledge of scenes and genres and how to use that knowledge to make more critically informed and effective writing decisions within various scenes. We hope that learning such strategies will enable students to write wherever and whenever they need to—in college and in the rest of their lives.

Features of *Scenes of Writing*

EMPHASIS ON TRANSFERABLE SKILLS

Throughout *Scenes of Writing*, we offer guided questions for analyzing scenes and opportunities for writing within multiple scenes and genres. Our approach emphasizes transportable skills that teach students how to use genre knowledge to read and write their way into different situations inside and outside of a writing class. Students learn how to read contexts and then turn that reading of context into their writing in context.

INTEGRATION OF WRITING AS A RHETORICAL AND SOCIAL ACTIVITY

After introducing students to our key terms—*scene, situation,* and *genre*—in Chapter 1, we use these terms throughout as we teach students to move from observation of the writing scene and its shared goals, to the rhetorical interactions that make up the situations of this scene (the readers, writers, purposes, subjects, and settings), to the genres used to participate within the situations and scenes. Students examine how the shared objectives of groups within scenes shape rhetorical situations. They also examine what textual patterns of genres (content, appeals, structure, format, sentences, words) reveal about the people who use the genres, the scenes in which the genres are used, and the activities that take place there.

GUIDED ANALYSIS OF WRITING WITHIN SCENES/GENRES

Specific guided questions throughout help students identify and analyze newly encountered genres. We include guided questions for observing scenes (Chapter 1), for analyzing genres and patterns of communication within scenes (Chapter 2), for making effective writing choices within scenes (Chapter 3), and for critiquing genres and their scenes (Chapter 4). These steps of observing scenes, analyzing scenes and genres, and writing within them are then followed and enacted throughout the remaining chapters.

EMPHASIS ON ACADEMIC WRITING

Part II of *Scenes of Writing* explicitly discusses the expectations and values of writing classes, college, and the academy. It enables entry into, participation in, and critique of academic situations and genres, from writing courses (the focus of Chapters 5, 6, and 7) to other discipline-specific courses (the focus of Chapter 8).

A FOCUS ON WRITING IN MULTIPLE SCENES

Scenes of Writing examines writing in academic, workplace, and public scenes. Part I illustrates its concepts with a variety of genres from everyday life as well as school and the workplace. Following Part II's emphasis on writing in academic scenes, we show students (in Part III) how they can use their knowledge of academic situations and genres to participate in scenes beyond the writing classroom. To that end, the book includes coverage of a wide array of genres, from first-year writing genres (analysis papers, argument papers, and researched position papers) to proposals, reports, complaint letters, editorials, and letters to the editor. Writing projects at the end of each chapter also allow students to gain experience writing both in traditional academic genres and a range of genres not typically found in the writing classroom.

A Situated View of Writing Processes

Chapter 3 of *Scenes of Writing* treats writing processes as specific to various genres and situations and helps students develop more effective processes for the different situations that they encounter throughout the book.

Integration of Critical Reading and Writing

Chapter 2 offers an overview of critical reading strategies and explains how writers' analytical readings of genres can help them access, understand, and participate effectively within scenes of writing. Chapter 5 includes guidelines for critical reading. Throughout the book, students are asked to consider critically various sample readings and genres and to participate in activities that ask them to respond as critical readers.

Emphasis on Critique of Genres

Scenes of Writing incorporates critique of genres (introduced in Chapter 4) and encourages genre change. The book supports critical thinking and works against treating genres as static models.

A Focus on a Range of Research Projects

Chapter 7 treats a range of research projects in addition to researched position papers and supports a wide range of types of research assignments. The chapter includes explanation of primary as well as secondary research.

Treatment of Civic Discourse in Public Scenes

Chapter 10 guides students through understanding and writing in public scenes and genres, including editorials and letters to the editor. The chapter discusses explicitly the role of the individual in public scenes and the contested nature of the public.

ATTENTION TO SENTENCE-LEVEL WRITING CHOICES

The discussion of each genre in Parts II and III includes discussion of expectations for sentences and words as well as organizational structures, formats, and rhetorical appeals.

NUMEROUS AND FULL-TEXT SAMPLES OF GENRES

Throughout the text, samples of a wide range of genres appear in full. The genres range from editorials to menus, patient medical history forms to letters to the editor, genre analyses to argument papers, ethnographic observations to proposals.

READINGS FROM STUDENT AND PROFESSIONAL WRITERS

Readings include student papers written for first-year composition classes as well as professionally written articles. The topics of readings vary, including studies of specific scenes, analyses of visual rhetoric in popular culture, and arguments on a variety of topics.

NUMEROUS INDIVIDUAL AND COLLABORATIVE WRITING ACTIVITIES

Every chapter provides opportunities for both individual and collaborative activities that ask students to apply and build on principles. A number of these activities ask students to explore and evaluate electronic communication.

Structure of this Book

Scenes of Writing is divided into three parts:

- Part I: Writing within Scenes, Situations, and Genres
- Part II: Reading and Writing within Academic Scenes
- Part III: Reading and Writing Beyond Academic Scenes

Part I establishes the structure and logic that guide the book and that are later applied in Parts II and III. As such, Part I provides students with transferable strategies for reading and writing within scenes, which students then apply specifically to academic scenes and then to workplace and public scenes. Structurally and logically, then, the book moves in both a centrifugal and a centripetal direction: it invites students to apply the skills they learn in Part I to increasingly expanding scenes—the college or university writing course and then courses in other academic disciplines in Part II and workplace and public scenes in Part III—at the same time as it encourages students to reflect on those skills through the optics of these scenes.

The four chapters that comprise Part I introduce students to the idea of "scenes of writing" and teach them strategies for understanding how to read and write within them.

- **Chapter 1: Understanding Scenes of Writing** describes the key terms of the book—*scene, situation,* and *genre*—and teaches students how to identify and describe scenes so that they can locate themselves as participants and writers within them.

- **Chapter 2: Using Genres to Read Scenes of Writing** helps students gain access and insight into a scene of writing by teaching them how to read critically its different kinds of writing—its genres—which function as textual maps of the scene.

- **Chapter 3: Using Genres to Help You Write** shows students how to use their knowledge of a scene and its genres in order to begin making more informed and effective writing choices—to turn, that is, their *reading of* a scene into their *writing in* a scene.

- **Chapter 4: Critiquing and Changing Genres** teaches students how they can use that same knowledge of scene and genre to write creatively within, critique, and change genres and their scenes.

The four chapters that comprise Part I—observing a scene, analyzing it through its writing, making writing choices within it, and working critically and creatively within it—serve as the foundation for the rest of the book, where students repeat and apply these strategies as they encounter and learn to write within academic, workplace, and public scenes.

Part II examines the ways in which genres can give students access to academic scenes and can help them perform successfully within various academic situations, foremost among those the first-year writing course.

- **Chapter 5: Understanding Academic Scenes and Writing Courses** situates the particular scene of the college writing course within the broader academic scene of the college or university. Moving from the overarching scene of the college or university to the more particular scene of the writing classroom, it explores

    The shared goals of writing courses (and how these goals reflect the larger shared goals of the college or university)

The rhetorical interactions that make up the situations in the writing class scene

The genres used to interact within the situations of the writing class scene

■ **Chapter 6: Writing Analyses and Arguments** focuses on two important genres used in the writing course: the analysis paper and the argument paper. It guides students through the process of analyzing the patterns and assumptions of these genres so that students can write them more meaningfully and effectively.

■ **Chapter 7: Writing Research-Based Genres** examines the role of research in academic scenes. It teaches skills students can use to conduct various types of research and write various research-based genres in writing courses and beyond, including the researched position paper.

■ **Chapter 8: Writing in Unfamiliar Academic Scenes and Genres** invites students to look beyond the writing course to examine and write within various disciplinary scenes, using the skills they learned in Part I and their knowledge of academic genres as their guides.

The two chapters in **Part III** allow students to extend and practice the skills they have acquired for scenes beyond the academy. In the same way that they have used genres as rhetorical maps to help guide their exploration of academic scenes, they will now have an opportunity to use their genre knowledge to travel beyond academic scenes and navigate the terrain of workplace and public scenes.

■ **Chapter 9: Reading and Writing within Workplace Scenes** applies genre analysis and writing to workplace scenes and situations. It helps students inquire into the nature of workplace scenes and to examine workplace genres as part of that inquiry. Then it invites students to use their knowledge of workplace scenes, situations, and genres to make more critical and informed writing choices.

■ **Chapter 10: Reading and Writing within Public Scenes** applies genre analysis and writing to scenes and situations in the world outside of work and school to see how people use a range of genres to communicate information to broad audiences and to influence public actions. After examining the nature of this public, the chapter looks at a range of public genres and analyzes them for what they can tell us about how and why people communicate and behave in public scenes of writing. It then invites students to use their knowledge of these genres in order to participate as writers within these public scenes.

Resources for Teachers

The Instructor's Manual to *Scenes of Writing* is designed to guide and support teachers as they develop their writing courses using this textbook. It describes the book's approach and its grounding in genre theory, helps teachers design their schedules and assignments, and provides practical strategies and examples to help teachers use each chapter. The Instructor's Manual describes the book's organization and presents chapter-by-chapter overviews, highlighting each chapter's main goals and key concepts, providing suggestions for using the chapter activities and writing projects, and suggesting topics for journal writing and class discussions. A distinctive feature of the Instructor's Manual is its extended discussion of how *Scenes of Writing* works with the Council of Writing Program Administrators (WPA) Outcomes Statement for First-Year Composition and how teachers can use the book to help students meet these objectives. To help teachers design courses to meet their own program's objectives, The Instructor's Manual identifies and explains the logic of various pathways through the book, each with a different course emphasis. Then it provides several detailed syllabi that add to and exemplify some of these pathways. For further reading, the Instructor's Manual also includes a selected bibliography of genre scholarship.

Acknowledgments

This book is the result of an abiding commitment to an idea and the shared vision that has sustained and developed it. We may not have known what we were getting into when we began, but what we have gotten out of it is a deep appreciation for collaborative work. Without the three of us working together, this book would not be possible. Likewise, over the years, we have learned a great deal from our students, some of whose work we reprint in this book. We are grateful for their patience and goodwill as we worked through some of the ideas that inform this book. We would like to thank our editors at Longman, Lynn Huddon and Karen Helfrich, for their good advice, expertise, and shepherding through the long process of bringing this book to light.

We would also like to thank our reviewers, many of whom reviewed the manuscript in more than one version: Ellen Barton, Wayne State University; Bill Condon, Washington State University; Ruth Fischer, George Mason University; Susan Marie Harrington, Indiana University Purdue University–Indianapolis; Gary L. Hatch, Brigham Young University; Ted E. Johnston, El Paso Community College; Marshall Kitchens, Oakland

University; Carrie Leverenz, Florida State University; Barbara Little Liu, Eastern Connecticut State University; Rita Malenczyk, Eastern Connecticut State University; John David Moore, Eastern Illinois University; Randall Popken, Tarleton State University; Katrina M. Powell, Louisiana State University; David R. Russell, Iowa State University; Eileen E. Schell, Syracuse University; Christopher Schroeder, Northeastern Illinois University; Lucy Schultz, University of Cincinnati; Penelope L. Smith, Gannon University; Mary L. Tobin, Rice University; Mark L. Wiley, California State University–Long Beach; and Janet Zepernick, University of Missouri–Rolla. All of our reviewers provided thoughtful and helpful commentary, offering suggestions in a kind spirit and with generosity. We incorporated much of their advice, though of course any flaws that remain in the book are our responsibility alone.

Finally, we must thank our families. They endured years of our obsession with "the textbook" and provided help and sustenance through many flurries of activity as we finished one more round of work. We thank them for their time, their patience, and their encouragement.

AMY DEVITT

MARY JO REIFF

ANIS BAWARSHI

* * *

All the world's a stage,
And all the men and women merely players.
They have their exits and their entrances,
And one man in his time plays many parts . . .

Shakespeare, *As You Like It*, 2.7.139-42

Writing within Scenes, Situations, and Genres

I

Understanding
Scenes of Writing

1

You are an actor. Each day of your life you play a variety of roles or "parts"—as son/daughter, sibling, friend, student, teammate, employee—and you act out these parts in a variety of scenes, whether at home, in school, in the gym, in the workplace, or in your neighborhoods or communities. As in the scenes of a movie or a play—where actors take their cues from co-actors and directors, the stage and surrounding sets, and the time and place of the action—you take your cues for how to act from the scenes you act within. As students, you constantly negotiate among scenes: from dorm room, apartment, or home to cafeteria, classes, or work; from meetings of clubs or organizations to dinner with friends; from a date on Friday night to a party on the weekend, to the football game on Saturday, and to visits with your extended families on occasion.

Each of these scenes is different; each requires you to play a different role, which involves different strategies for acting and communicating within it. How you dress, how you present yourself, how you interact with others, what you talk about—all these behaviors depend in large part on the scene in which you find yourself. You are constantly coordinating how you act with the scenes in which you act. Within familiar scenes, this coordination becomes so habitual that it seems intuitive and effortless. When you enter new or less familiar scenes, however, you need to make more conscious, less automatic decisions about how to act.

Entering New Scenes

Think about what you do when you enter the scene, say, of a social get-together at your college or university and you do not already know the people attending. What do you do as you walk into the room? How do you decide where to go in the room and what to do there? In all likelihood, one

3

of the first things you do is look around. As you begin to observe the room, what do you look at? What do you look for? You might pay attention to what people are wearing. Are they dressed formally? Are they dressed to impress? You might also take in the way the room is structured. Are people standing around? Is there space to walk, or is the room set up in such a way that forces people to sit? You almost certainly would focus on how people are interacting with one another. Is the room buzzing with conversation, or are people shyly avoiding one another? You might discover that some are talking in groups while others are engaged in one-to-one conversations.

READING SCENES

You might notice these things and others as you begin to look around the room. But you don't just passively absorb these images; chances are you also begin to analyze or "read" them to help you decide how to act. That is, you begin to think about what these images tell you about this scene, how people are acting within it, and how you might act. For example, what people are wearing and how they are interacting can tell you whether the scene is formal or informal and whether you will fit in comfortably. (Did you wear the "right" thing? Will you be able to tell raucous jokes or have intellectual discussions?) Drawing from your past experiences with how people present themselves on various occasions and how they interact, you begin to form assumptions about what sort of scene you have entered and how best to position yourself and act within it.

Say, as you make your way around the room, that you decide to join a group conversation. Once again, you probably begin by observing or "reading" the group. You might observe the group dynamic: Is everyone engaged in the conversation or is one person dominating the conversation? Are people interrupting one another or are they taking turns talking? Is it women or men who are interrupted most frequently? You surely also pay attention to the topic of conversation: Is it a topic you know something about? Is it something you are interested in? Is it a topic that must be treated seriously, or is there room for joking and banter? How far along is the conversation? Has it just begun, or has the group already covered much of the topic? Should you listen, or can you contribute something to the discussion? And if you can contribute, when would be the best opportunity to do so?

Timing may not be everything, but it does count quite a bit, as the ancient Greeks understood well. They referred to this notion of rhetorical timing and opportunity in communication as *kairos*. If you want to get people's attention—if you want to persuade them of something, or get them to cooperate with you, or have them identify with you or something you believe in—your timing must be right *given the conditions in which you are operating.* Have you ever known someone whose timing was off, who always made comments a topic behind or leaped ahead to new topics when others were still discussing something introduced and "covered" earlier? In order to get the timing right, you must be able to read the scene effectively.

In addition to paying attention to the group interaction and its topic of conversation, you might also observe *how* the group is handling the topic: What is the style of conversation? Are people having a calm discussion, or is their tone animated? What kind of language are they using to discuss the topic? Is their language elevated or full of jargon and expressions that only they would understand? Are people making declarations, or are they hemming and hawing, qualifying what they say? Are some asking questions? What sorts of things are people using as evidence to support their views in this group: facts, citation of authority, personal experience, gossip, etc.? These are just some of the questions you could, and probably often do, ask unconsciously in order to make effective decisions about how to communicate and behave in an already existing scene.

Writing Activity 1.1

Describe the scenes you experienced yesterday. What different places were you in, who did you interact with, and what roles did you play?

Collaborative Activity 1.1

Make a list of all of the different scenes that you participate in at college. Compare your lists in small groups, and select one scene to analyze or read, as in the example of the social get-together we "attended" earlier in this chapter. Describe the various clues to how participants are expected to behave and interact within the scene your group selected. You might consider the kinds of clues we observed in our social get-together:

How the place or setting of your scene is structured

Who is participating and how they present themselves

What style of communicating is common

What people are communicating about

How people are timing their contributions

Any other elements especially important to the particular scene you are analyzing

MAKING RHETORICAL CHOICES

Observing a scene and reading it by the process described above help you make more effective choices about what to say, how to say it, to whom, and when. Scholars who study the art of communication refer to these choices as rhetorical choices. **Rhetoric** is the use of language to accomplish something, and **rhetorical choices** are the decisions speakers and writers make in order to accomplish something with language. Rhetorical choices include

What sort of tone and language to use;

How to engage and address others;

How to develop, organize, and present one's ideas so that others can relate to them;

What kinds of examples to use when communicating;

When and how to start talking and when and how to stop.

The more appropriate your rhetorical choices, the more likely you are to communicate effectively.

The scene in which you participate helps determine which choices are appropriate. Whatever their writing tasks, writers are always making rhetorical choices as they ask themselves questions such as

"What should I write about?"

"How should I organize it?"

"What should I include?"

"How should I begin?"

In fact, "How should I begin?" is perhaps the most significant—and challenging—question a writer can ask himself or herself. Yet answers to this question and others like it do not need to be as mysterious or elusive as they are sometimes imagined to be. Imagine how differently you would answer such questions if you were in your home writing in your diary rather than in a classroom writing an essay examination. You can develop answers to such questions by examining the context of your writing, what we in this book are calling **scenes of writing**.

Just as you make decisions about how to act based on your knowledge of the social scene you are acting in at any given time, so too writers make decisions about how and what to write based on their knowledge of the rhetorical scenes they are writing in. *The more effectively you understand the scene you are writing in, the more effectively you will com-*

municate. Working from this premise, our goal in this book is to teach you how to make more effective writing choices as you function within and move from one scene of writing to another.

Writing Activity 1.2

Begin keeping a list of all the things you write in a day, including such small texts as notes or e-mails as well as longer texts like letters or reports. For each thing you write, describe the writing scene in which it functions—the location or context (workplace, classroom, academic discipline, dorm room, etc.), your role as a writer, your reader(s) and your relationship to them, and your purpose for writing it (what you were trying to accomplish/respond to).

Defining Scene, Situation, Genre

The four chapters that make up Part I of this book introduce you to the idea of "scenes of writing" and teach you strategies for understanding how to read them and how to write within them. Before we show you how to analyze and then write within different scenes of writing, we begin by defining what we mean by the word *scene* and identify its key components, *situation* and *genre*. These three terms—scene, situation, and genre—figure prominently throughout this book. Indeed, they are the building blocks of all that follows.

Each of these terms receives explanation and examples in what follows, but here are brief definitions of each concept. A *scene* is the overall setting, a place where communication happens among groups of people with some shared objectives. A writing classroom is a scene; so are a restaurant kitchen, a chat room, and an editorial page. A *situation* is the rhetorical interaction happening within a scene. For example, students and teachers discuss readings and respond to each other's writings, cooks and servers discuss food orders, chatters explore topics that interest them, and editorial writers convey their opinions on current issues. A *genre* is a common way of responding rhetorically to a situation, including class discussions and writing prompts, restaurant meal orders, chat room postings, and editorials.

We begin with **scene** because it is the overarching term. *Scene is a place in which communication happens among groups of people with some shared objectives.* Examples of a scene range from a large tax accounting firm to a small business, from a classroom to a sorority house, from a doctor's office to a peace rally, from a baseball game to a bar to a criminal trial—to name but a few. In this book, we will help you explore the way communication happens in a variety of scenes, from academic scenes to workplace scenes to public scenes.

Certainly, not all scenes are so obviously physical as a doctor's office or a ball game. The "place" of a scene can extend across well-defined physical spaces. For example, the college or university you are attending is one scene, a clear physical place. But it also participates in a larger **academic scene**, a "place" of academia that reaches across colleges and universities throughout the world. Within the larger academic scene, there are a number of different disciplinary scenes, such as English, history, geography, and chemistry. These scenes consist of groups of people who have their own bodies of knowledge, facts, and theories; their own research methods; their own ways of communicating with one another—all of which reflect their shared objectives: to advance and convey understanding of a subject matter. You may learn to write case studies in your psychology class, lab reports in your biology class, and profiles in your sociology class. Each piece of writing will reflect its scene and should meet special expectations in terms of use of evidence, special terminologies, special styles and formats.

To illustrate, suppose you are taking a class in architectural history. This class will familiarize you with a specific subject matter: styles of architecture throughout the ages, landmark buildings, and ideas of influential designers like I. M. Pei and Frank Lloyd Wright. You will also gain knowledge of the economic and social forces that have shaped architectural structures—as well as the beliefs and values of architects and others who participate in the larger architectural scene, such as their struggles with the social and ethical issues of preservation. In order to feel comfortable in this scene and function effectively in it, you will need to become familiar with the participants' language—their use of terms such as *rectilinear design* or the distinctions between concepts such as *shingle style* versus *stick style*. Finally, you will need to become familiar with the methods of communicating within this scene—perhaps by writing architectural descriptions of buildings, following guidelines set by the National Register of Historic Places. To participate effectively in this academic scene, you must participate in its **rhetorical practices**—practices which reflect the group's shared objectives.

Like the academic scenes with which they overlap (as students move from architecture classes, for example, to architecture firms), **workplace scenes** are also places where communication happens among groups of people with some shared objectives. Your ability to succeed in the workplace depends on your ability to use the language of the scene in *appropriate ways,* to achieve its shared objectives—whether you are asked to write an e-mail to your coworkers to promote the company picnic or a sales letter to clients to promote a new product.

As in academic scenes, with their specialized disciplines, workplace scenes are also made up of smaller scenes: various departments and social organizations whose specialized ways of communicating reflect their own shared objectives. An engineering firm, for example, represents one workplace scene; its departments (human resources and design, for example) represent smaller scenes. (The profession of engineers represents another, larger scene.) With engineers' emphases on form, precision, and technical detail, an employee in an engineering firm will need to know how to produce an organized and detailed technical report—with title sheet, table of contents, list of figures, definition of the problem, design presentation, letter of transmittal, and closure—and will need to be familiar with the information that should be contained within each section of the report. As we saw with the language of architecture, the shared technical knowledge of engineers is expressed through a shared language. A mechanical engineer is likely to be familiar with a *gear box design,* which may involve terms meaningful to other members of this scene (terms such as *input/output RPM, torque,* and *HP capacity*) but mostly meaningless to those of us outside this scene.

Outside of and often interacting with academic and workplace scenes, groups exist at various levels in civic or **public scenes** to achieve different kinds of shared objectives. If you have ever observed a criminal trial, for example, you would have seen a scene that involves a place (a courtroom) in which communication happens among groups of people (judge, jury, lawyers, defendant(s), plaintiff(s), witnesses, court reporter, bailiffs, and observers) with some shared objectives (most generally, to reach some kind of verdict and, more ideally, to seek justice through a fair trial). The combination of the courtroom, the participants, and the shared objectives is what *constitutes,* in general, the criminal trial as a scene. In other public scenes, political groups, such as the local branch of the Democratic Party, work to elect their candidates and to achieve their agendas by using pamphlets, news releases, fund-raising letters, and other kinds of texts, to spread, in their own language, information about pertinent political issues. Other community action groups, whether created to stop the closing of a local elementary school or to promote the use of the public library, exist in particular scenes and use language in particular ways to achieve their particular objectives. At times, such public scenes can be quite large. City inhabitants may share a common newspaper, with its editorials and letters to the editor addressing local issues, and people may share some regional objectives. Even larger groups like Amnesty International have branches across the nation but still share common objectives and use their newsletters, Web sites, and other ways of communicating to reach their goals.

In this book, we distinguish between academic, workplace, and public scenes in order to help you identify different types of scenes. Actually, these categories may not be clearly distinct. Quite often, scenes overlap. For instance, the trial scene is both a public scene and a workplace scene: a public scene for observers, defendants, plaintiffs, and jurors and a workplace scene for judges, lawyers, court reporters, and bailiffs. Similarly, you likely inhabit multiple academic, workplace, and public scenes, often simultaneously.

ACTING WITHIN SCENES

We have seen that, just as understanding a scene helps an actor act within it, understanding scenes is an important first step in learning how to write within them. But the writer does not just passively sit by while the scene creates a piece of writing. Instead, the writer actively makes rhetorical decisions. The individual writer acting within a particular scene has a range of choices to make—choices regarding what information to include, how to organize that information, and how best to present it. And to make these decisions well the writer must analyze and interpret the scene. The writer has the very important role of constructing a text that is appropriate in terms of content, organization, format, and style. Writers draw on their knowledge of a scene, especially on how others have responded similarly within that scene, in order to develop strategies for how best to respond.

Imagine, for instance, that you have an item that you would like to sell—a bike, for instance. You might choose to post a flyer at the grocery store, send an e-mail to everyone in your address book, or create a listing for an online auction service like eBay. Another option is to write an ad that will appear in your local newspaper's classifieds section. If you decide to write a classified ad, how will you know what to do? You will have to familiarize yourself with the scene of the classifieds within the newspaper. You might start by defining the groups of people involved in this scene and their shared objectives. One group involved includes the subscribers to the newspaper who come to this place where communication happens (the classifieds section) with the shared objectives of looking for a product/service to buy or sell. Another group of people in this scene is the newspaper's classifieds staff, whose shared objectives are to sell advertisement space and to compile all of the necessary information for selling the product (name, price, contact number) or service while maintaining the newspaper's policy of brevity and space for other ads. The group of those (including you) who *place* ads may even share some objectives with the classifieds staff, such as the objective of brevity, since the cost of advertisements is per word.

Such knowledge of the scene is critical because it helps guide your rhetorical choices regarding content, language, length, and format. For example, knowing that the classified staff needs to pack many ads into a small space and that they charge by the word, you will understand why your ad must be so short. Knowing that some readers come looking for specific items to buy, you will understand how important it is to highlight what kind of thing you are selling. To decide exactly how to achieve your purpose of selling your item, you will likely draw on what you already know about the classifieds from having used them in the past and on the knowledge available in the classifieds section. In the section itself, you would find, first, examples of ads, such as the ones shown here.

CLASSIFIED ADVERTISING WEDNESDAY, DECEMBER 11, 2002

414 Collectibles	431 Computer/Software/ Accessories	440 Appliances, Household	441 Furniture/Furnishings/ Carpets	441 Furniture/Furnishings/ Carpets	452 Tools and Shop Equipment
Comic Book Collection (Large)	*Duel P3 Server*	*ESPRESSO MACHINE*	*Bedroom Set*	*Rossezzi Farm Maple youth BR set*	*Craftsman bandsaw 12" pedestal*
415 Estate Sales	**437 TV, Radio, Home Stereos**	**441 Furniture/Furnishings/ Carpets**	**Leaving Country**	**442 China/Glassware/ Tableware**	
417 Jewelry			**ACCENTS/FURNISHINGS**		

By looking at these examples you can see how people describe their items, the sort of language they use, what information they include and do not include, how they organize the ad, and so on. Observing these features of ads is like observing the kinds of conversations people are having at the party we described earlier. Your second source of information about the scene of classified ads is the explicit guidelines the newspaper staff includes, usually printed at the beginning of the classified section. Looking at the newspaper's policies regarding ads (cost per line, deadlines, and so forth) will tell you how to get your ad placed. By combining your observations about what ads look like and your reading of the newspaper's rules, you can write an ad that effectively participates in this scene—and achieves your goal of selling your bike. So writing a classified ad involves more than just knowing something about the item you are selling; it involves knowing how to develop strategies for presenting that item within the classifieds scene. Such strategies are learned through understanding the scene itself, whatever that particular scene might be.

Of course, even though your knowledge of the scene helps you frame your classified ad, there is still room for individual interpretation and choice—decisions on exactly how much and what information to include, how to balance the item's defects (if any) and its strengths, and how vividly to describe the item. The scene acts on you as an individual writer, but as a participant in that scene you also act on (and within) it.

Collaborative Activity 1.2

Write a classified ad for an item you wish to sell or can imagine selling. In small groups, share your ads and note similarities and differences in responses. What accounts for the similarities? Speculate also on the reasons for any differences in the ads. To what extent were the content, format, language, and tone influenced by the scene of writing? What part did individual choices and decisions play in the differences among your ads? Explain.

INTERACTING WITHIN SITUATIONS

When you need to write a classified ad, you encounter not just the large scene of classified ads but also the particular *situation* of writing *your* ad. *Situations, as we define them, are the various rhetorical interactions happening within a scene, involving participants, subjects, settings, and purposes.* In other words, each situation represents a specific rhetorical interaction that involves certain participants who are using language to engage with a certain subject in certain ways for certain purposes. A closer look at the scene of a criminal trial (as described on p. 9) for example, reveals that this scene has many situations in it. A few of the situations—the rhetorical interactions—that together make up the scene of the criminal trial include making opening statements, swearing in witnesses, testifying, cross-examining witnesses, making closing statements, instructing the jury, deliberating, reading the verdict, and sentencing. In each of these situations, a specific group of people is engaged in a specific rhetorical task, which requires them to relate to and communicate with one another in certain ways—to use language to accomplish something specific within the overall scene.

Not every participant within the scene of a criminal trial is or needs to be involved in all its situations, of course. For example, the lawyers, defendants, court reporter, and observers do not participate in the jury deliberations. Only jury members are engaged in the rhetorical interactions of that situation as participants dealing with a specific subject (the facts presented at trial) in a specific setting (behind closed doors at the end of a trial) for specific purposes (to come to a consensus about whether the prosecution has proven guilt beyond a reasonable doubt). In another situation within the scene of a criminal trial—the situation of cross-examining witnesses—a different rhetorical interaction takes place, involving a different group of participants (most immediately, a lawyer and a witness, while judge, jury, and other lawyers observe). In this situation, a lawyer and a witness are usually engaged in a more "aggressive" interaction, with the lawyer perhaps trying to expose or discredit a witness. The situation of cross-examination, then, engages the participants in a specific rhetorical interaction, involving a specific setting (the witness in a chair, the lawyer standing before the court), a specific subject (testimony), and a specific purpose (to test whether the witness's testimony might prove incorrect or unreliable).

Because situation involves rhetorical interaction, it is often referred to by teachers of writing as the **rhetorical situation.** Within a rhetorical situation, how participants communicate about a certain subject will depend on **who** these participants are, what **setting** they are in, and what their **purposes** are in communicating. For example, a writer's purpose (what he or she wishes to accomplish) will influence his or her approach to the **subject,** suggesting what information needs to be included and how the subject might be presented. The writer's understanding of audience and the setting will, likewise, shape how the writer approaches the purpose and subject and will also influence the writer's **tone** (the attitude that comes through the writing) and the writer's **persona** (the image presented, the character of the writer that comes through). *These elements—the participants, subject, setting, and purpose—interact within rhetorical situations.*

Consider the scene you are in while taking this writing course and the rhetorical situations it includes. Within the broader academic scene, you are in the scene of a writing class, and within the classroom you participate in many interactions, from chatting with a fellow student to listening to a lecture to contributing to a class discussion or working on a group task. Even though all these *situations* exist in the same scene of your writing class, they differ in exactly who is participating and in what ways, what subjects they address, and the purposes people have for participating in them. Even the setting varies a bit, with the group work occurring in a small circle of desks rather than the larger classroom of a lecture. Any differences of participants, subjects, settings, or purposes from one situation to another influence how you act within the larger class scene. When listening to a lecture, you probably take some notes for yourself, while in a group activity you might record the group's responses or complete a form for your teacher. You probably use more formal language when contributing to a class discussion than you do when you work with your peers in a group. The persona or image you project when speaking with classmates without the teacher present may differ from that you project when your audience includes your teacher.

Writing Activity 1.3

One situation in this writing class is responding to the Activities in this textbook. You have already seen in this chapter two other Writing Activities and may have responded to one or both. You have also encountered two Collaborative Activities. Select any one of those four Activities and consider its rhetorical situation. Identify the participants, subject, setting, and purpose in this activity. Explore how each of those elements might affect what you would do in responding to it.

Writing Activity 1.4

Looking back on the classified ad you wrote for Collaborative Activity 1.2 (p. 12), use the terms you have just learned to describe its rhetorical situation within the scene of the classifieds section: Who are the participants in this situation? What are they interacting about (subject), where (setting), and why (purpose)?

ANALYZING THE SITUATIONS OF THREE EDITORIALS

The following three editorials, which are on the topic of drilling for oil in the Arctic National Wildlife Refuge (ANWR), exemplify three different scenes and rhetorical situations, each with its own interaction of subject, participants, setting, and purposes. The first editorial is written by the vice president of species conservation at Defenders of Wildlife; the second editorial is written by a student and native Alaskan; the third editorial is written by the chairman of the International Association of Drilling Contractors (IADC).

As you read the editorials, consider the different scenes of writing (a national conservation organization, a university, and a corporation), and try to identify the various elements of the rhetorical situations within these scenes:

- *Who* the participants are, especially writer and readers
- *Where* the interaction is taking place (the setting of the interaction, which in this case has to do with where the editorial appears)
- *What* the subject of the interaction is
- *Why* the writer is presenting the subject in this way (what purposes seem to be driving the interaction)

Notice how, even though the editorials address the same topic, they address it differently based on their rhetorical situations. As you identify elements of each rhetorical situation, pay attention to how they affect how the writers of the editorials present themselves, describe ANWR, and characterize the oil companies.

※ ※ ※

New Technologies But Still the Same Messy Business

Bob Ferris

Bob Ferris is the vice president of species conservation at Defenders of Wildlife. This editorial appeared in TomPaine.com, an online journal of progressive opinion.

Each time an argument for oil drilling in the Arctic National Wildlife Refuge is analyzed and rebutted, a new one emerges. President Bush suggested that drilling would help solve California's energy woes, but that makes as much sense as filling up a car's gas tank because its pistons don't work. Others have argued that ANWR could help us become independent of OPEC, but in the unlikely event that there's enough oil in Alaska to make a difference, trade regulations under the World Trade Organization would prevent keeping all the oil for domestic use.

Now the oil industry is touting advances in technology that would let them drill with minimal environmental impact. They are using this new technology to paint a very pretty, almost clinical picture of petroleum extraction. In recent weeks, a number of media outlets, including the *New York Times* and *60 Minutes* have run stories heralding the new technology.

Yet this pristine view is strongly at odds with experience. Oil extraction, much like open heart surgery, is a very messy business.

Of primary importance is not fancy technology, but whether we should trust oil company claims of cleaner, more ethical behavior. Incredibly, they are projecting this newly sanitary image at the same time they are reporting an oil or chemical spill every eighteen hours on Alaska's North Slope. Then there's the case of BP-Amoco—one of the most likely refuge lessees. The firm must be seriously hoping that their $22 million settlement with EPA for dumping toxic chemicals in Alaska (not to mention the potential congressional investigation of its business practices) will somehow not make it to the public's radar screen before Congress votes on whether to open up the refuge to drilling.

That point aside, while improved technologies can certainly lessen the impact of major surgery or oil drilling, neither is easy on the patient. And the scars—whether on flesh or land—never do disappear. Period.

Conservationists favor technologies that lessen the impact of necessary resource extraction. But all of these technologies have both pros and cons. Using the "targeted drilling" featured in the news reports, drill heads can steer through the rock laterally deep below the earth's surface.

The benefit is indeed a reduced drilling footprint, but the trade-off is a need for dramatically more detailed seismic data, derived by blasting dynamite and by even more intrusive and extensive seismic testing than ever before. This seismic testing is not benign and visitors to the refuge can still see evidence of testing that is nearly two decades old.

The oil industry also boasts of ice roads "harmlessly" made out of water that protect the delicate tundra. They fail to simultaneously mention that the vast volume of unfrozen water they use to make those roads is rare in the arctic. And it is much needed by fish that often get pumped up with the water and become part of these harmless roads.

Drilling and seismic activities comprise just a small percentage of the total extractive insult to land, water and wildlife from oil development. Behind the drillers come the legions of roads, water use, pipelines, garbage dumps, worker housing and a host of associated infrastructure problems that even the most gee-whiz drilling practices cannot eliminate. As the *New York Times* noted in a January 30, 2001 editorial, imposing this industrial sprawl on the pristine coastal plain of the Arctic National Wildlife Refuge is an unconscionable price to pay just to roll the dice on six months worth of oil.

The new technology is promising, but it will never mean that drilling can occur without serious environmental consequences. Defenders of Wildlife would rather see the country's technological elbow grease applied to energy conservation, which would have the same result as drilling, but with less cost to people and the environment.

If we truly need the oil we could extract it from the plugged and abandoned wells that dot our country's mid-section and which contain many billions of barrels. In fact, two areas in north and east Texas contain roughly 7 billion barrels of oil—more than twice the mid-range estimates for the Arctic National Wildlife Refuge. If the president and vice president are so gung-ho to drill why don't they look a little closer to home?

Americans love the promise of having their cake and eating it—the seductive voice that says we can have oil development and an Arctic Wildlife Refuge. We can't, and no amount of oil company advertising will alter the laws of physics and biology to make it so. ▦

※ ※ ※

My Opinion: The Shortsightedness and Exploitation of Oil Drilling

Elizabeth Morrison

Elizabeth Morrison is a senior majoring in general arts and sciences and a Penn Collegian *columnist. This editorial appeared in the* Penn Collegian *newspaper.*

In a national news magazine recently, I saw an advertisement: "Alaskans support oil drilling." It was an ad picturing smiling (presumably) Alaskan people, grinning in agreement with the oil industry, who (obviously) paid for the ad. I've seen this ad now in the *New York Times, Newsweek* and *Time*. The advertising campaign is an effort to convince the continental United States that because Alaskans support yet more oil exploration, they should also.

I've certainly never polled the 450,000 people who live in Alaska, but I know absolutely that I am not the only Alaskan who is against the opening of the Arctic National Wildlife Refuge for oil drilling.

For those who don't know, there is an ongoing battle between boom and bust oil developers and environmentalists about whether to open up ANWR for oil exploration and drilling, or to keep the land protected.

Situated on Alaska's North Slope, just west of the Canadian border, the 19 million acre refuge is home to several thousand indigenous peoples, grizzly bears, musk oxen, wolves, migratory birds and a herd of 180,000 caribou. But to the oil industry—and those who benefit from it—the refuge is nothing but a potentially profitable lode of black gold.

This battle tipped for a brief period in favor of drilling opponents after the *Exxon Valdez* oil spill. But in the three years since the Persian Gulf War, the political mood has changed drastically. Once purely a state issue, it has now been brought to national attention, and opinions have swung in favor of drilling. Even the change of presidential administration last November did little to stop the tide of opinion. In fact, shortly before the election, the Democratic Party took its opposition to oil drilling in ANWR out of its platform. Since then, a tide of senators and members of Congress have flown in their private jets to the middle of ANWR, looked at the tundra and proclaimed it not worth saving.

Of course, drilling may have seemed logical after the emotionally frenzied aftermath of the Gulf War. Why should we be dependent on foreign oil, politicians asked, when there is oil waiting to be tapped in our own backyard?

I think there are an awful lot of reasons. First, contrary to what developers and oil companies publicly say, there are innumerable variables and guesswork involved in oil drilling—and absolutely no guarantee that oil will actually be found, much less be actually exploitable. Although developers and those opposed to drilling agree that there is indeed oil under the plain, the size of the oil deposit is a mystery.

The U.S. Interior Department's estimates range from 600 million barrels to as much as 9.2 billion barrels. Even the highest estimate, an almost unimaginable amount to most of us, is only the amount of oil the United States uses in just one year. In addition, the department puts the odds of actually finding a commercially exploitable oil field at just one in five. Assuming (and this is a major assumption) an oil field is found, as long as 10 years may be needed to gear up before major production could begin.

Compounding the logical inconsistencies and practical fallibility, opening up the refuge to oil drilling would be a gross intrusion on one of the last untouched wilderness areas in the United States. Politicians and oil men who advocate drilling argue that it would create thousands of jobs and billions of dollars in tax revenues.

In reality, drilling would only be lucrative to certain people, namely those mentioned above. However, those who would not profit and who would be most adversely affected are, ironically (but not surprisingly), those with the least voice in whether the refuge is opened. This includes the indigenous peoples who have lived in what is now ANWR for thousands of years. To advocate drilling is to blatantly disregard the Native Alaskans who bitterly oppose the rape of the land and intrusion on their way of life.

Last summer, at an open forum on this issue, Sarah James, a tribal leader of the Gwich'in Indians said, "This is a simple issue. We have the right to continue our way of life. We are caribou people."

To open the refuge for drilling is also to virtually ignore the environmental effect oil exploration and exploitation has on the animals who live there, and on the land itself. The most-often-cited example is the caribou. The herd that makes its home in the refuge represents the largest migratory pattern in the

United States, and it would be in danger of disruption and displacement, as would other birds and animals.

Oil is a non-renewable energy source; a fact that advocates of drilling conveniently neglect to address. Opening ANWR for oil drilling would only act as a short-term drug for a chronic ailment. It would succeed in putting off, yet again, the urgent need to find alternative energy sources. It would be folly to count on any oil in the refuge to fuel our gas-guzzling lifestyles for long. The contribution to U.S. petroleum needs would be small compared to other means of reducing demand and finding alternative energy sources.

The billions of dollars squandered in oil exploration, oil drilling and oil production is money not spent on potentially more-beneficial activities. Most importantly, it compromises the inherent value of the land, the animals and the people who live there. The proposal to open the ANWR for oil drilling is an attempt at a short-term solution to a problem that requires careful long-term management.

This is no longer a state issue; as I said above, it has long been a national one. We are all dependent on oil, and we all suffer, sooner or later, from the environmental consequences. In our increasingly global economy, the use of one of our greatest natural resources—land—is all of our responsibility. 🔳

🔳 🔳 🔳

Alaska Environmental Bugaboos

Bernie W. Stewart

From Bernie W. Stewart, chairman of the International Association of Drilling Contractors. This editorial appeared in the IADC corporate magazine, Drilling Contractor.

As IADC chairman this year, one of my most rewarding activities has been the opportunity to travel to our Chapters and visit with contractors in a variety of markets, both geographical and operational. Most recently, I was the guest of our IADC Alaska Chapter. In addition to participating in a well-attended Chapter meeting, **Doyon Drilling, Nordic-Calista Services** and **Pool Arctic Alaska** graciously hosted me to the North Slope. I was very impressed by how the North Slope drilling contractors and operators conduct their business. Through close cooperation, the industry has developed ingenious adaptations for this very difficult environment.

Speaking of the environment, much is made over the allegedly deleterious effect of drilling on the Alaskan ecology. I'm here to tell you that drilling operations are in no way going to harm the environment in Alaska. Industry's environmental precautions in Alaska deserve tremendous applause.

Technology has been used to great advantage in Alaska. Despite the field's vast area, the Alaskan industry has been miserly when it comes to generating footprints of drilling operations. They have done their utmost to minimize the number of well pads through the canny use of horizontal drilling and offset wells.

The caribou are among the most visible source of nervous anxiety. The fact is that these magnificent animals graze unconcernedly around the drilling rigs. The scene is little different than cows munching pasture around a rig in Texas. One experience was particularly striking. In Alaska, the buildings stand 7 ft off the ground to avoid damaging the permafrost. At one site, a mother caribou stood with her calf in the shade of such a building. So much for our industry's threat to the caribous!

This brings me to the great Alaskan environmental bugaboo— the Alaskan National Wildlife Refuge. The US Congress regularly denies drilling access to ANWR. From the hype, one might conclude that allowing drilling on this frozen wilderness is to invite an environmental disaster on a par with Chernobyl. In all this, one gets the notion that ANWR is a pristine Eden of scenic proportions equal to Yellowstone or Yosemite.

From "A" to "Y," ANWR couldn't be more different from Yellowstone. There are no sweeping forests and grand roiling rivers, all teeming with wildlife unknown in modern society. ANWR is a barren and empty place. It is a land of endless tundra where no vegetation stands taller than 6 in. The principal wildlife is the migratory Porcupine Caribou Herd. Having observed the aplomb with which caribou react to drilling activities elsewhere on the North Slope, I have no doubt that this 150,000-animal herd would be similarly unaffected.

Part of the reason is there's plenty of room in ANWR. Out of the refuge's 19 million acres, 17.5 million acres are permanently off limits to exploration. Development would be confined to only a small fraction of ANWR's coastal plain. Estimates are that this field could reach a peak output equal to 10% of total current US production. Developing ANWR would create jobs, enhance national security and lower consumer costs, all at an extremely remote environmental risk in a forbidding area of the US. In a cost-benefit analysis, it's easy to see the logical solution.

Collaborative Activity 1.3

Working with classmates, select one of the three editorials and describe in as much detail as you can the rhetorical situation to which it is responding. Who are the likely participants in this situation? What purposes seem to be driving these participants? What's the setting in which the editorial appears, including the date of its publication? And how does the interaction between the participants, the purposes, and the setting affect how the subject of the editorial is treated and presented? Describe some of the choices that the writer makes regarding kinds of organization, examples, style, tone, and persona as a result of his or her situation. Then explain how these rhetorical choices were shaped by the situation of writing.

Writing Activity 1.5

Keeping in mind their different rhetorical situations, compare how the three editorials treat the topic of oil drilling in ANWR. (For example, even though the first two editorials take a similar position on the topic, they differ because of where and when they were published, who wrote them, and who would be reading them.) How do the shared objectives, beliefs, and values of the differing scenes (the national conservation organization, the academic scene, and the corporate scene) affect the rhetorical choices? Look back over the editorials and compare how the writers present themselves in each, the ways they treat ANWR as a place, and how they describe the oil companies. Once you have described the differences, speculate on the effects these differences might have on readers of the editorials.

As the three editorials exemplify, each time we communicate, we act within a rhetorical situation. When we write, we perform a rhetorical action—an action shaped by the situation we are responding to. As you discovered in the previous activities, this action involves all sorts of strategic decisions and choices, choices regarding vocabulary, sentence structure, tone, persona, organization, and supporting evidence. These choices are guided not only by the situation—the participants, subject, setting, and purposes—but by the chosen type of writing (in the case above, an editorial). The type of writing chosen guides decisions about such elements as the use of examples, length (fairly brief for an editorial), tone, and persona (the editorials chosen as examples are informal). The next section will focus further on this key component of scene, the type of writing or genre.

ACTING WITH GENRES

We know that each of the various situations that make up a scene represents a specific rhetorical interaction taking place within that scene. As participants find themselves in these situations over and over, they develop habits or rituals of interacting within them. In the case of the criminal trial, for example, participants have developed typical rhetorical ways for dealing with such situations as swearing in witnesses, delivering the opening statements, or presenting evidence to the jury. In each of these repeated situations, participants draw on a pattern of action that is already in place, widely accepted by participants in the scene to guide them as they act in that situation. They do not need to invent everything anew. Some of these patterns are more flexible than others (the conventions for the swearing-in of witnesses are more strict than the conventions for opening statements, for example), but all involve certain conventions for using language to accomplish efficiently and effectively certain tasks within the situation. This is where genre comes into play. *Genres are the typical rhetorical ways of responding to a situation that repeatedly occurs within a scene.*

You may already be familiar with the term *genre*, which literally means "type," as in genres of books (mystery, science fiction, autobiography, textbook), genres of music (classical, country, alternative), or genres of movies (action adventures, romantic comedies, "slasher" movies, or thrillers). But genres are more than just categorizations. Genres carry with them certain expectations—expectations that a romantic comedy will end happily or that an action adventure will incorporate high-tech special effects. Where, you might ask, do these expectations come from?

Your expectations of genre are based on your participation in scenes that repeat themselves and your prior experiences with reading, writing, and using genres. For example, how do you know how to respond to the Writing Activities in this textbook? Much of your knowledge comes from having written such classroom activities before, in other classes with other textbooks and teachers. While the details of this particular set of activities and your teacher's use of them probably vary somewhat from your past experience, you know from your past experience what to expect in them and how to respond appropriately, to meet your teacher's expectations.

You might be surprised to realize that most of our spoken and written communication operates within generic conventions. Some of our generic responses, our responses to situations that repeat themselves, are automatic. When the phone rings, you know, without even thinking about it, to answer "Hello" or "Smith residence" or maybe even "Bob [your name] speaking." Any response that varies too much from these typical responses might confuse the caller at the other end. Similarly, when you write a personal letter to a friend, you know to begin by addressing the recipient ("Dear Sue") and greeting him or her (usually with "How are you?" or "How's it going?" or even "What's up?"). How do we automatically know how to act within these situations? We know because these are situations that have been played out many times, and we are familiar with our roles as communicators within these scenes. You are not the first to have answered a phone call or written a personal letter. These generic conventions have arisen in response to a situation that has been repeated. Without these generic responses to situations that repeat themselves, we would have the almost impossible task of inventing new ways of communicating each time we confronted a rhetorical situation.

In the next two chapters, we will teach you how to analyze genres in greater detail so that you can turn your understanding *of* genre into your writing *in* the genre. And then in Parts II and III of the book, you will have the opportunity to apply your genre knowledge to write more effectively in academic, workplace, and public scenes.

Writing Activity 1.6

To illustrate how genres arise based on rhetorical situations that repeat themselves, consider the genre of the postcard. (If you've never written or received a postcard, answer the following questions for the genre of the greeting card.) What repeated situation does it arise from? What is its purpose? What are the expectations of the readers of postcards? What relationship with readers is established? What are the particular features or textual regularities that make up the postcard? For the next class meeting, bring in a postcard that you or someone you know has received and compare your findings.

Writing Activity 1.7

Read back over the editorials presented earlier in this chapter. Despite their differences, what do they share in common that defines them as editorials? What makes editorials different, say, from a newspaper article, an advertisement, or even an argument paper you would write in your writing course? What do editorials allow their writers to accomplish that these other genres may not?

Putting Scene, Situation, and Genre Back Together

Let us summarize the key terms we have been describing and then return to the scene you are now becoming more familiar with, that of the writing course, to show how they work together:

- **Scene:** a place where communication happens among groups of people with some shared objectives. Think of the scene as the overarching site that frames the action.

- **Situation:** the rhetorical interaction happening within a scene, involving participants, subjects, settings, and purposes. Scenes often have multiple situations within them, each with its own specific participants (who), subjects to deal with (what), settings in which they interact (where and when), and purposes for doing what they do (why). Together, the participants, their subject, setting, and purposes combine to create a specific rhetorical situation.

▥ **Genre:** the typical rhetorical way of responding to a repeated situation within a scene. As situations within a scene repeat themselves, participants develop rhetorical conventions for interacting and getting things done within them—typical ways of using language to accomplish certain actions in a situation. Genres are these typified rhetorical actions.

The typical writing class, likely similar to the one in which you are currently enrolled, is a scene. It is a place where communication happens among teacher and students who have some shared objectives. These objectives, which are frequently outlined in the course syllabus, vary from institution to institution and teacher to teacher, but, generally, they could include something like "teaching students to write effective academic papers" and "encouraging students to read and write critically." (We will discuss the objectives of the writing class with more complexity in Part II of the book.)

In this scene, and working to accomplish its shared objectives, are a number of situations, each of which involves teacher and students (who) in specific rhetorical interactions: certain ways of interacting with one another in order to engage in a specific subject (what), in a specific setting (where), for specific purposes (why). Situations in a writing class scene might include peer review workshops involving students, in groups, as they exchange, read, and respond to each other's writing in order to help their writing improve; student-teacher conferences, a different rhetorical situation, as student and teacher meet in the teacher's office to discuss a student's progress on an assignment or in the class in order to help the student make better progress; and class discussion, yet another rhetorical interaction. In each of these situations within the scene of the writing class, students and teachers make different rhetorical choices as they interact with each other on different subjects, in different settings, and for different purposes.

To help them function effectively in these and other distinct situations, teacher and students use various genres, each of which enables them to respond in typical rhetorical ways to these repeated situations. To respond to the situation of evaluating student writing, for instance, teachers use the genres of margin comments and end comments. To respond to the situation of peer-review workshops, students often use the genre of peer-review sheets as guidelines. To respond to the situation of generating ideas, students use the genres of freewriting, clustering, and brainstorming. To respond to the situation of explaining common concepts, teacher and students use the genre of textbooks. These, as well as other genres such as the syllabus, assignment sheets, class journals, paper outlines, final drafts, and others all help teachers and students function effectively in the various situations of the writing class scene.

Collaborative Activity 1.4

Working in groups, use our key terms—scene, situation, and genre—to describe your own writing course scene. What makes your writing course a scene (a place where communication happens among groups of people with some shared objectives)? Describe a particular situation or rhetorical interaction within your writing course, and define the subject, the setting, the purpose, and the roles of the participants. What genres are used to interact within this repeated situation? Generate a list of your answers, and compare it with the findings of other groups of your classmates.

Learning Strategies for Observing and Describing Scenes

Scenes fill our lives. Any given culture is defined by the combination of its many scenes, some of which are more powerful than others. Not all members of a culture, of course, interact within or even are aware of all its scenes. Some scenes require certain credentials from their participants and are therefore more exclusive (such as certain workplace scenes like law firms or social scenes like sororities and fraternities), while others are more public (such as the scene of a peace rally or protest). As we mentioned at the beginning of the chapter, you already interact within numerous scenes and most likely are able to navigate between some of them with more ease than others. You also are just in the process of getting to know some new scenes, scenes such as your academic major and other college or university scenes. And, of course, there are various scenes you probably hope one day to join, including workplace scenes. Observing these less familiar scenes can help you eventually participate in them more fully and more effectively.

If a culture is defined by its numerous scenes, then your role and place in the culture will in part be defined by your participation in these scenes. This is, in fact, one reason sociologists and anthropologists give for why it is important to observe scenes: Observing scenes can tell us things about how a culture works, how people interact, and why people do what they do. By studying the scenes in which we participate, we can learn something about ourselves.

Ethnography is the sociological term for studying a scene from an insider's perspective. One gains access to the scene and then conducts field-work by immersion into that scene over a period of time, sometimes lasting years. An ethnographer carefully collects data by observing what happens within a scene: the actions and interactions taking place, the daily routines of people within that scene, who does what, when, and why. He or she collects these observations in field notes. The ethnographer also supplements observations by interviewing participants within a scene and collecting artifacts from the scene, such as written documents used by participants within it. In short, ethnography allows a researcher to observe how individuals interact, behave, and think in specific settings.

Observing scenes is a particularly relevant activity for writers since effective writers are mini-ethnographers of sorts. They observe scenes in order to understand how and why individuals communicate within them. Such observation enables writers to access and begin to identify the various situations and genres contained within these scenes so that they can more effectively participate within them.

You probably already use various strategies for observing scenes. We all constantly observe our worlds in the process of making decisions about how we should act within them, whether we are entering a party or deciding whether to speak up in class. In this section, we will build on this ability so that you can apply it to your acts of writing. We will also help you expand on this ability by guiding you from observation to *analysis* of how and why people do what they do within a scene and the underlying reasons and beliefs that shape people's behaviors and interactions. You will be able to use this knowledge to participate more meaningfully and critically as writers within different scenes.

For example, notice how the following sample ethnography by Stephanie Smith of a greyhound racing track helps to bring the scene to life through close observation and description. Smith's ethnography was written for an anthropology course and appears in a book called *Field Ethnography: A Manual for Doing Cultural Anthropology*.

The study by itself is interesting for the access and insight it gives into people who participate in this scene. But as you read it, pay specific attention to the scene itself and try to identify some of the situations and genres found within it. From what Smith writes, what do you think makes the greyhound track a scene? In what ways are the three areas Smith describes smaller scenes that make up a larger scene? What are some of its situations and what are the components of these situations? And what genres do you notice participants using in this scene? Also, as you read, think about how this knowledge of the scene could help you participate within it. What do you learn from the observation, for example, that might help you figure out how to act in this scene?

※   ※   ※

Ethnography of a Greyhound Track: A Study on Social Stratification and Diehards

Stephanie Smith

When I thought about taking on the Rocky Mountain Greyhound Park as the subject for my ethnographic study, I had some preconceived notions about what it would be like. I wanted to study the "type" of person who participated in the dog races. I was assuming there was one type of person I could classify and study, no problem. I imagined this seedy place with lots of middle-aged down-and-out loners, placing bets with money they hocked their TV to get. I was convinced I could construct a model of this type and fit all of my informants into the mold.

Then I went out to the track. My first thought was, "Oh S——!" as I looked around at the crowds of senior citizens, young couples, business types, and even families with four children. A two-second look around at the track will clue in any moron to the fact that the crowd is a diverse mishmash of every type of person. I had a lot of work to do.

Along with the physical and age diversity was the difference in intentions. Not everyone goes out there just to bet. Some go for the entertainment with the kids or the food. Some go for the novelty of betting, picking dogs for their names, or look at the minimum $2 bet. Others are more serious, studying the dogs and placing big bets. The more I studied, the more I began to see an underlying social structure. This structure is determined by the three areas from which the public can watch the races. Although the focus of my study is not the actual greyhound race, that is the reason everyone is there. I think it is important to understand what the races, the park, and wagering, are all about.

The Common Denominator: The Setting

The Rocky Mountain Greyhound Park opened in 1949, a few months after the first track in Pueblo started. Located in the north-central part of Colorado

Springs, it sits on approximately 25 acres off Nevada Avenue. The elevation is over 6,000 feet, and to this day RMGP remains the highest greyhound park in the world. It is a part of a nationwide system of 57 tracks. Until this year the racing season at RMGP had been three months in the fall. Due to a recent court decision in which the state of Colorado approved tracks to operate live racing six months a year, the season has been changed to April through September. (Although not publicized, gambling or wagering occurs all throughout the year via closed circuit television. People gather at the park and wager on live races broadcast from other parks.)

The RMGP consists of a racing track, spectator stands (indoor and outdoor), an administrative building, and an immense parking lot (see map). Spectators have three areas to choose from: the Grand Stands, the First Turn Tavern, and the Cloud 9 Restaurant. Admission to each area is $1, $2, and $3, respectively. Race programs sell at $1.25. The park and all areas are opened to the public one hour before the program begins. The program is a set of races, usually 13, that take place one or two times a day. Matinees take place at 1 P.M. Wednesday and Saturday; evening performances take place at 7:30 P.M. A typical 13-race program will last three and a half hours. Most of my work was done during the evening programs.

Procedure of a Race

Many people arrive as the park opens an hour before the first race. I had even seen a small group waiting for the gates to open one Friday evening. I noticed that the majority of people who arrive at the park early come to figure out their bets, study the night's dog selection, and to view the previous night's replays on the many TVs that cover every nook and cranny of the place.

About fifteen minutes before post time the dogs are paraded before the spectators. There are eight dogs per race, each one wearing a numbered blanket and a muzzle. (The muzzles are worn only to determine the outcome in photo finishes.) They come out single file in numerical order led on a leash by official handlers. Each dog is subject to an inspection; the muzzle and blanket are pulled and tugged. The purpose is to show each dog and its statistics up close on the TV screens. The dogs are paraded up and down the length of the track for all the spectators to see. During this time the people can change or confirm their choices and place a bet. When the scoreboard says "0 min to post," the dogs are placed in the gate according to their numbers. At the announcer's last call the handlers leave the gates and the lights are turned out in the spectator areas. An Aldritt mechanical lure they call "Rocky" then pops out of its gate making its way to the dogs' gate. The announcer does a Johnny Carson type "HERERRRRRRRRR's ROCKYYYYYYYYYYYYYY!" at the end of which the gate to the dogs is opened, and the dogs are off.

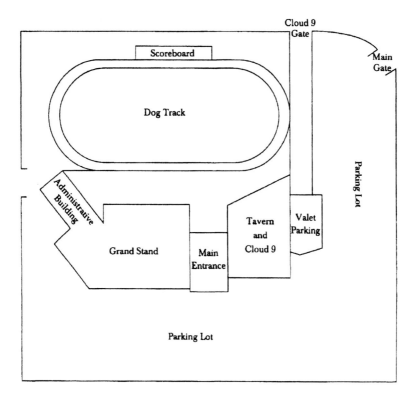

The greyhounds take off from the gate chasing the lure, reaching speeds from 25 to 40 mph. The general speed of the race is determined by the class, "A" being best, "E" and "M" being the lowest ranked. The first turn is usually the deciding factor in the race. The best dog can easily trip or be knocked out on the first turn. After the dogs come out of this turn, the leading two or three dogs are apparent. Of course this can always change, which is what people are literally betting on. When the dogs have gone three-quarters of the track, a light shines on the finish line. The dogs pass the line and a picture is taken. If the 1st, 2nd, and 3rd places are obvious then the paybacks are listed on the scoreboard and TVs right away. If there is any doubt, the picture is analyzed and scores held back until the judges reach a conclusion.

Meanwhile the dogs are stopped by a net farther down the track. The dogs are herded into one area and the handlers scramble to get their dogs back on the leash. The dogs once again are led single file in numerical order back to their respective trainers. The next batch of eight dogs take their place in the lineup to be paraded. This exact procedure is followed for every race I saw. It was pulled off smoothly even in inclement weather and as it says at the bottom of the race programs, "strict post time observed."

Grand Stand Area

The Grand Stand area holds the largest number of people, 3800, and at $1 is the least expensive to gain entrance to. It is a huge indoor structure with three levels that look out a wall of windows onto the track. The first level is primarily food and betting windows. The entire north wall is dedicated to betting windows (and one information booth), 34 total. There are two bars and concession stands on the south side. The food consists of hot dogs, hamburgers, chips, popcorn, nachos, candy bars, and such. The bars offer beer, wine, and mixed drinks. There are many doors leading to the patio on this side. Scattered all over are TVs. Between the two main stairways are rows of chairs facing large TVs.

The second level is tucked under the main Grand Stand area, above the first level. This is similar to the offerings of the first level. It has 20 windows, one food stand, and one bar. A large-screen floor TV dominates the attention around the tables and rows of chairs. The third level is where most of the seating is. It is just like Grand Stand seating, with reams of seats, one flight next to the other, sloped toward the event. Seating right in front of the window is divided into boxes. It costs $2 to sit in a box seat. Box seats offer a better view of the track, cushioned seats with arm rest/drink holder/ash tray, and separation from the general crowd. The range of people that attend the races, especially in the Grand Stand area, is extremely diverse. The dress is casual—jeans and more jeans, I estimate the percent of whites who attend runs about 60 percent. The other 40 percent consist of mostly black, then Hispanics and Asians. There are couples, families, groups, and "solos." The couples range widely in age and race. The elderly couples usually settle in the box seats close to the window. Usually the man gets up and down, presumably to bet, while the woman sits in her seat. Young couples sit in the Grand Stand area toward the window and bet together. Then there are the buddy couples. Quite a few male duos hang out there, of either the same age or father/son type, I saw very few female duos.

I was surprised to find so many families. The families tend to favor the box seating. Many couples bring their children out to the track, and extended family groups, with grandparents, cousins, and so on, are not uncommon. Children under 18 are not allowed to place bets but they can be in certain areas. The next classification, the solos, were the most interesting to me. This is the type I expected to dominate the scene at the track. The solos are people who hang out at the track alone. My own stereotype for a solo is a 40+ male who hangs out in the upper section of the Grand Stand away from other people. He bets on every race using a system he invented. Since this characterization is a stereotype, I found exceptions to it but not many.

One of my informants who frequents the Grand Stand area is "Flamingo," a 35-year-old black man with a granddaughter. He likes to come to the track by himself, claiming "I'm a loner, I cook for a living. I see [enough] people." He plays the dogs every day the track is open but does not consider himself a "diehard." Diehards are "the ones you can't see. They hang out in the Cloud 9 Room. Instead of work, they are here all the time." Flamingo uses a system of betting that allows him to stay away from the track. He comes up with three numbers and then plays the trifecta (see "wagering") with the same numbers the whole night. He does not know statistics or other information about the dogs like some diehards do; he just plays the numbers. Usually he bets in the future for a whole program. This means he will pick his numbers and place his bets for say a Friday night program on Thursday. This way be does not have to be at the track during the races. "This is not exciting to me! I don't have time for this s———! I look in the paper [the next morning] like a kid at Christmas to see if I won." If he wins he can collect the money the next day.

Flamingo claims to do quite well at the track. He uses the winnings as a supplement to his job income. "I could take a second job, but I take a chance on this." I saw him win with this method. Apparently on one Friday he won $130, Saturday night, $106, and Monday, $480. All of these paybacks were off $2 bets. "I've made about $800 in the last three days out of 48 bucks. I expect more but I settle for this." When Flamingo told me these figures I just kind of nodded my head thinking "yea, RIGHT!" However I saw him win $130 from only $2. Something in his method works.

First Turn Tavern

The First Turn Tavern is located on the first level in the building west of the Grand Stand area. The tavern has two entrances, one from the main gate and another on the west side of the building. This entrance is exclusively for the tavern and the Cloud 9 Room. Access to the Tavern cost $2 and no one under 18 is allowed. The price includes the use of a table for the duration of the program. The decor of the room is in oak, brass, etched glass, and maroon plastic tabletops.

The Tavern has a capacity of 300. There are four tiered levels of tables and chairs all facing the track. Each table has a small TV that operates for an extra $1.50 and broadcasts network TV as well as the greyhound information. The Tavern offers food and beverages in a bar-type atmosphere. The foods offered are various appetizers, burritos, deli sandwiches, salads, cakes, and ice cream. The bar serves beer, wine, and mixed and blended drinks. The food and drinks are pricier in the Tavern than the Grand Stand, and everything is served to the tables by a waitperson. The only reason to get up from your table is to bet (or go to the bathroom). The Tavern has 17 betting windows.

The first thing I noticed when I walked into the Tavern was a sign that said,

AVOID INCONVENIENCES
BY REFRAINING FROM EXTREMES
IN CASUAL DRESS

I suppose "extremes" is the operative word in that request because the dress of Tavern patrons is quite casual. As in the Grand Stand area, the main trend is jeans. For men, shirts tend to be short-sleeve Izod types, and button-up cotton shirts, a step above the T-shirt. The women are just as casual in printed shirts and blouses.

Another major difference about the Tavern people is their age. The 18-and-over policy no doubt raises the average age. Interestingly there are more young-to-middle-aged people than anything else. The proportion of whites in the Tavern rises to about 80 percent, the other 15 percent black and 5 percent Hispanics and Asians. The ratio of elderly persons seems low in comparison to the Grand Stand area, and there are no families. The majority of types in the Tavern are groups of three to five. There are mostly men, but women are definitely an active part of the Tavern scene. The solos who do hang out in the Tavern either do so in the very front, where no one else can see them, or in the back standing at the counter.

The social atmosphere is similar to that of a bar. The low ceiling imposes an air of intimacy not found in the Grand Stand area or the Cloud 9 Room. Everyone has a drink at their table. The waiters and waitresses socialize with the customers and know a good many of them on a first-name basis. The table seating arrangement causes people to look at each other and interact more than if they were sitting shoulder to shoulder in rows of seats. By the same token people do not walk around to other tables and mingle as often as in the Grand Stand area. The wagering seems to be taken quite seriously. Many tables are crowded with various racing papers. Reams of notes are being taken and lots of bets are made.

Mark jokingly refers to himself as a "degenerate gambler." He says, "True pros will sit in the Grand Stand." But Mark is a pro; I consider him a diehard. He hangs out in the Tavern just about every night the track is open. He is a white male in his late thirties (his age is a guess because he would not tell me), has a mustache, wears glasses and dresses in short-sleeve polo shirts and jeans. "Professionally I'm a U.S. Merchant Marine. On my time off I play the dogs [to support myself] until I run out of money."

Whenever I see him he is always very friendly and willing to talk to me, but 95 percent of the time his eyes are on the TV screen. He carries around a spiral book of notecards, which he constantly writes on. I have seen the cards a few times, but I cannot make any sense out of his diagrams and figures. Like most diehards he has a method for betting but he is not eager to reveal it to me. I am not sure I could even understand it. I can say it is extremely analytical. Unlike Flamingo, Mark is definitely interested in what the dogs look like, their weight, present and past performance, and other statistics. Unfortunately, he would not give me exact figures on his paybacks, and he placed future bets so that I never saw the amount of money he bet with. But I can only assume, given Mark's serious dedication and attention, that his bets average much more than the $2 minimum.

Cloud 9 Room

The Cloud 9 Room is a restaurant located above the First Turn Tavern. It is structured similarly to the Tavern. The Room has four tiered levels of tables, a full bar and food selection, a capacity of 300, and its own betting windows, 11 total. The decor is dark wood, brass, glass, carpeting, and linen tablecloths and napkins. The ceiling is quite high and every table seems to offer a good view of the track.

The restaurant has its own gate to the park (although it can be easily reached by the main gate) and one entrance to the building. Valet parking is offered at $1 to patrons. Upon entrance to the building you must stop at a hostess booth to pay the $3 cover charge and to confirm your reservation; there is no admittance to the Cloud 9 without one. At the bottom of the escalator that whisks you up to the restaurant is a sign that says,

IMPORTANT NOTICE TO CLOUD NINE PATRONS
Proper attire must be worn for admittance
to the Cloud 9
Body Shirts, frayed jeans, tank tops, shorts
and similar styles are not accepted

At the top of the escalator is another hostess booth. A host in a tuxedo takes your reservation slip, checks it against his records, then leads you to your table. Each table has a number, which is given to you in case you want to request that table again. It is just like the procedure at a fine restaurant. The menu has appetizers, steak, seafood, pasta entrees, ice cream, cheesecake, coffee/tea, and vintage wines. There are many servers around to cater to your needs. The waitpersons are very friendly and attentive. Like the Tavern servers, many of the Cloud 9 servers know their customers by name.

The crowd was about 95 percent Caucasian, 5 percent Asian on the night I went to the Cloud 9 Room. The dress varies from nice casual to dressed up. The standard dress for men is a clean short sleeved polo shirt and slacks. Some wear sport coats, suits, or designer sweat suits. It is similar for the women, who wear mostly slacks and blouses, some dresses and some designer sweat suits. Couples dominate this scene. I took a census at one point and out of 30 occupied tables, all were mixed couples or groups except one. That table had two men.

Socializing is the key theme in the room. It is not the milling and mingling around type of interaction characteristic of the Grand Stand area. Socialization occurs at the tables. It does not take long to figure out it is a highly social atmosphere within the table unit. There is much laughter and conversation in the air. Most people have smiles on their face directed at the person across from them instead of the track below them. There is not a dominant preoccupation with betting that is characteristic of the Tavern and among the Grand Stand diehards.

"This is the only place to be," said Mary, an elderly woman who is a regular with her husband Jim at the Cloud 9 Room. They frequent the dog track circuit, which runs from Pueblo to Denver (Cloverleaf). Although the drive from Canyon City is a pain, Mary and Jim do it every weekend to have dinner and bet on the races. To Mary the Colorado Springs track is her favorite because apparently the other tracks do not offer good dining rooms to hang out in.

Mary does not do any betting; she leaves it up to her husband. "I don't come here for the gambling. . . . I like to watch the dogs run. I'm a ranch girl." Jim has the concentration of a diehard. With pen in hand and eyes on the TV screen, he is constantly scribbling on his program and putting his hand on his forehead to think. He keeps himself much too involved to ever talk to me. I can sense he does not want to tell me anything. Mary is quite happy to converse, since she is just there for the entertainment. When I finally asked Jim about the amount he spent on each bet he muttered, "Oh not much, certainly not much for this room." Then Mary piped in, "Oh pooh. You spend about $20 on each bet; I'd say that was a lot of money." After that Jim told me he usually manages to pay for dinner, traveling expenses—he breaks even.

Analysis/Interpretation

There are so many intricacies at the dog track it is difficult to define the whole "culture" of the place. What makes the culture of the track is the people. The diversity of people is immense and what keeps them coming back is the entertainment, the social opportunity, and of course the wagering, that "$2 dream." At the risk of sounding like a commercial, it truly has something to offer everyone. Because of this the track draws from every social stratum of the city. I found on any given night that the track has a cross section of society in attendance. But the different social classes are not interacting together. The diverse appeal would not be there if everyone were meant to mingle.

A social hierarchy exists, which is staked out quite clearly by the three rooms. The Grand Stand represents the working class, the Tavern is the middle class, and Cloud 9 is the upper class. This structure is supported and perpetuated mainly by the diehards, who maintain myths and preconceived notions about the different sections.

The administration for the dog track has handled this situation quite shrewdly. The Tavern and Cloud 9 Room did not exist until 25 years ago. Before then both the buildings were Grand Stand areas. Stacie Taylor, head of promotions and publicity, acknowledges that there was a need for the type of services that the Tavern and Cloud 9 offer. She says they have served most successfully as facilities for group parties and fund-raiser benefits.

Whatever the intentions of the administration, the different rooms make it possible to separate oneself from others. This is an idea more appealing to the upper class, so it makes sense that the areas reserved to them have restrictions in dress, high prices, and an emphasis on service. It is also no surprise that whites dominate the scene. It is all a reflection of the social hierarchy that exists in the community.

But the nicer areas are not inaccessible to the everyday Joe. It is not like a club where you have to "belong" and be voted on to gain entry. Admittedly, the signs concerning dress code in front on the Tavern and Cloud 9 do have a deterring effect. Any sign indicating some restriction immediately sets off a signal in a person's head that there is some type of assumption about the customers and the atmosphere. I felt some trepidation when I first walked up the ramp toward the hostess booth at the Tavern. Was I dressed OK? Will I stand out too much? But other than fitting in in a superficial sense, I had no worries. If you have the money, entry to the Tavern or Cloud 9 only takes a little planning ahead.

Interestingly, the diehards all have their theories about one another, according to the room. Flamingo told me that the real hard-core diehards were the "ones you can't see" in the Cloud 9 Room. If I were to believe his theory, Cloud 9 would be a place full of solos in suits calmly smoking cigarettes and placing thousand dollar bets. In reality I found the Cloud 9 Room to be a highly social place, with no solos. In fact the crowd would get extremely rowdy during a race, more so than in the Tavern, yelling for their dog to win. My informant Mary, a little old lady going blind in one eye, even started yelling, "Go baby go!" at one point.

The high-rolling diehards that Flamingo imagines *do* exist in the Cloud 9 Room according to Lissa, my waitress one night. I never had the opportunity to speak to them. They either pretended they didn't know what I was talking about, did not want to talk, or really were not diehards. Lissa told me, "I've worked here two years . . . you see a lotta lotta money. I've talked to a couple people here, asked if they had day jobs and they said no. They just follow a win-ner around [the circuit] and make their money." When I asked her how much a "lotta" money is she told me about $2,000 to $5,000 a bet. Mark thinks that the pros are really in the Grand Stand. I could never quite get to the bottom of his reasoning for this, but he seemed pretty sure about his opinion.

Jane, a cocktail waitress in the Tavern, told me, "There is a different crowd here than at the Grand Stand. They spend money to come in and sit. [People in the Tavern] are willing to spend money in here, there is nicer dress in here. Plus there are no tabs, so I make more in tips. People come in here holding a lot of money."

Crossovers into different areas happen often; the culture does not demand that you stick to one room. But the social stratification between the rooms is so obvious it is hard not to notice it. The mobility among the rooms exist in a downward direction, much more than upward. Nonetheless, the spectrum of intentions from the little old lady who bet $2 on a dog because of the name, to the diehard 30-year-old with reams of notes placing $2,000 bets to pay the rent, all exist at each level. The ratio of the types in each room varies, but they are all in there. The main difference is appearance and bank account. This is obvious from the similarity of offerings in each area. The basics are the same for every room: food, drinks, bathrooms, a view of the track, a place to sit, betting windows, TVs, and people.

I also believe the track is a great service to the people of the community. There are many benefits for the large number of senior citizen patrons: free admission for 60+ and nighttime escorts to cars. Families may bring their chil-dren so they do not have to find a babysitter or stay home. On a more subtle social level, as one informant said, "It's a good place to learn about people—lots of weirdos." Perhaps "weirdos" is pushing it, but I think she was right in her assessment of the situation at the Rocky Mountain Dog Track. It is a good place to learn about people and provides a perfect model of how social stratifi-cation works. And hopefully make a buck or two in the process.

Collaborative Activity 1.5

Working in groups, use our key terms—scene, situation, and genre—to describe the scene of a greyhound track. In what ways is a greyhound track a scene (a place where communication happens among groups of people with some shared objec-tives)? Are there smaller scenes within this larger scene? If so, what are they? What are some of the situations we find within this scene (rhetorical interactions involv-ing particular participants, subjects, settings, and purposes)? And what genres (the typical ways of interacting within the repeated situations of the scene) are used in this scene? Generate a list of your answers, and compare it with your classmates' findings.

Writing Activity 1.8

Smith describes the overall scene of the greyhound track as well as three smaller scenes within it (the Grand Station, the Tavern, and the Cloud 9 areas). Based on her observations of this general scene and its constituent scenes, situations, and genres, explain to a newcomer in this scene how he or she might act within its different smaller scenes. What from the observations help you determine how someone might act in these scenes?

You can use ethnographic techniques like the ones Smith employs to observe and describe scenes of writing, including their situations and genres. Such techniques can allow you to find out what sort of "place" the scene is, what sort of communication happens within it, who participates in this communication, and what objectives participants share. In addition, such techniques will help you to discover and describe some of the situations that happen within the scene, including who participates in these situations, what subjects they engage in, the specific settings where they interact, and the purposes for their interacting. Finally, by using such techniques, you can also identify what genres participants use to interact typically within the situations of a scene: Through observations and interviews, you can find out what patterns and rituals participants have developed to interact with one another in the situations that make up a scene.

Before you begin your first observation, you should know a few things about how to observe scenes ethically and responsibly. Scholars conducting ethnographic research submit their research plans to review boards, who check that they are following accepted practices for protecting the people and places they observe. Although your observations will not require such review, you should make sure you follow some of the same practices as you observe a scene:

- If someone is in charge of the site you want to observe, ask his or her permission.

- If observing a private group or a stable group of people, one whose participants you can identify, let them know what you are doing with your observation, what your purposes are, and how you will use what you observe—that you will share findings with your teacher and classmates.

- Ask for their consent to your recording their participation.

- Especially when you are observing a private group, whose interactions would usually not be open to public observation, assure them that you will hold what you observe in strictest confidence except for those purposes you've told them about. Never reveal what you observe to anyone outside of your original purposes—in this case, those connected to your writing class assignment.

Following such practices will help ensure that you observe a scene without damaging it or its participants.

We will now guide you through some strategies for observing scenes, moving from the scene itself to its situations and genres. Once we have described these strategies, we will list them as guidelines for observing scenes in Box 1.2 (pp. 44–45). By the end of the chapter, you will be able to practice using these strategies to observe, describe, and then reflect on a scene you participate or have participated in. In later chapters, you will be able to use these strategies to gain access to less familiar academic, workplace, and public scenes.

STRATEGIES FOR DESCRIBING THE SCENE

Place

One of the first things you can identify, when observing a scene, is what the scene "looks" like. Since a scene is a place where communication happens, ask yourself these questions:

What sort of place is this?

How is it organized?

What are its parameters?

At this point, rather than observing specific interactions within the scene, you are focused on identifying the larger environment in which these interactions are happening. Once you have described the environment of the scene, you can then start to identify what is generally happening within it.

The Group's Activities

Here you will be observing what is going on within the scene:

Who is taking part?

What are they doing?

Keep track of the activities you observe and how groups of people are interacting/communicating while performing these activities. Try to separate what you have observed from what you think about what you have observed. One effective way to record your observations involves using a **double-entry notebook**. This type of notebook divides your observation notes into two parts. After drawing a line down the middle of each page of the notebook (or using a notebook with two facing pages), you write on one side your direct observations of the scene as they happen. On the other side you note your questions about and your reactions to what you have observed, either while you are observing the scene or during later reflection.

Writing Activity 1.9

To begin practicing observing scenes, record and gather observations during a half-hour of an ordinary scene in your day, such as having dinner with your family or friends; chatting in your dorm lounge, coffee house, or restaurant; studying in the library or the student union; or discussing topics at a meeting. Describe both the setting and the participants and their activities in the setting, recording details of place and perhaps even sketching out the space or mapping it. In addition to describing the participants and their activities and interactions, be sure to add your own reflections on anything interesting or unusual about the interactions.

Shared Objectives

Once you have observed the environment of the scene, its participants, and their activities, you need to try to identify the participants' shared objectives so that you can see how communication, including writing, helps them achieve their objectives. Here, you are trying to get a general sense of *why* people are doing what they are doing in this scene. Try to figure out why people are participating in the scene. Ask yourself these questions:

What is it that brings people together in this scene?

What overarching objectives do they share?

What are they trying to do or accomplish?

The Need to Interview

Sometimes the shared objectives might be fairly obvious, but often the objectives go deeper than an observer might be able to see. For example, the objectives of a criminal trial might seem obvious—to come to a judgment about a defendant's guilt—but participants might also have deeper or multiple objectives like securing justice, protecting the public, or even pushing a prosecutor to offer or a defendant to accept a plea bargain. All these objectives will affect how people interact within the scene.

Since you might not be able to observe deeper objectives, you might need to supplement your observations with interviews of people participating in the scene. It might not be evident just through observation what people are doing, but by asking them, you would get an insider's knowledge about what is going on. Since you are looking especially for *shared* objectives, try to ask as many participants as possible so that you can find commonalities among their answers.

To help you conduct interviews, consult the interview guidelines in Box 1.1 below. You might need to refer back to these guidelines in later chapters when you observe academic, workplace, and public scenes.

Box 1.1 *Interview Guidelines*

1. Contact the interviewee, preferably in advance, by phone or e-mail and set up a day, time, and place for the interview. Be sure to explain the purpose for the interview and how much time it will take. Ask permission to tape record the interview if that becomes necessary. (Test your equipment before going to the interview.)
2. Prepare interview questions in advance, but be willing to remain flexible if the interviewee would like to bring up additional issues that might be of interest.
3. When formulating questions, avoid "closed" questions that can be answered with a short response (like "yes" or "no" questions), and instead frame questions that elicit more detailed responses. For example, instead of asking "Is your purpose to convict the defendant?" (a yes/no question), ask "What do you see as your main purposes in conducting a trial?"
4. During the interview, take notes by hand or recorder. For shorter interviews, note-taking should be sufficient, but you might want to develop a shorthand of sorts—notations that can be made quickly as the person is talking but that you can go back to and decipher later.
5. Thank the interviewee for his or her time, and ask if he or she would like to see the final version of the writing project you are working on.

Writing Activity 1.10

To practice interviewing, interview a classmate on the topic of what the person hopes to achieve by attending college. Formulate at least five open-ended questions. Then interview the classmate, and write a paragraph that collects and synthesizes your findings. In another paragraph, answer the following questions: What was the most difficult part of the interview and the write-up? Were some questions more effective than others? Why? Did any information come up that you didn't ask about, and how did you handle that? Did you revise any of your questions during the interview or add any questions? Did you encounter any problems with recording and then transcribing the information? In your write-up on the classmate, how did you decide what to include and what to leave out?

Collaborative Activity 1.6

Compare the results of your interview with those of some of your classmates, and try to discover some shared objectives that people have for attending college. Look for both the most general objectives and the ones some sets of people might share. Prepare to share your discoveries with the class.

STRATEGIES FOR OBSERVING AND IDENTIFYING SITUATIONS

Observing and identifying the environment of the scene, its participants, and their interactions and shared objectives allow you to sketch the general outline of the scene. But because a scene is also made up of various situations—each with its own specific participants, interactions, subjects, settings, and purposes—observing some of these particular situations will give you a more in-depth understanding of the scene. This section outlines some strategies for observing the situations within a scene.

Situations, remember, are the specific rhetorical interactions happening within a scene. A typical scene will include multiple situations, some more visible than others. For example, the scene of a baseball game includes such visible situations as fans buying food, fans cheering the team in the stands, and the home plate umpire calling balls and strikes. But there are also less visible situations that involve coaches relaying signs to catchers, reporters interviewing players after the game, and players meeting in the locker room. As an observer, you may not have access to all these situations, but you can at least try to identify as many of them as you can by looking for different interactions that are happening within a scene. To identify situations, ask yourself questions such as the following:

What types of interactions can you see happening?

What different groups of people might be interacting?

Are there less visible settings where interactions might be occurring?

Once you have identified the different situations within a scene, you can begin observing some of them more closely. In your notebook, try to describe the following:

Who is participating in the situation?

What are people doing, and how do they seem to be relating to each other?

Where are their interactions taking place, in what specific setting?

What is the nature of their interaction? For example, are they engaged in conversation, or are they placing orders, or are they asking questions? What sort of language are they using? What words do you hear? Is the language formal or informal or somewhere in between? What sort of tone do they use?

What subjects are they interacting about?

What is it that brings them together? What are their purposes for interacting?

Here again, you can supplement your observations with interviews (see guidelines for interviewing in Box 1.1, p. 40). By asking yourself and the participants some of these questions, you can begin to identify some of the situations within a scene and better understand how to act within it.

STRATEGIES FOR IDENTIFYING GENRES

Earlier in the chapter we discussed how, as situations reoccur, participants develop typical ways of interacting within them. That is, they develop habits of communication that help them interact in these situations in fairly recognized and predictable ways. For example, coaches give umpires lineup cards to announce the starting players. Pitchers and catchers have developed signals for communicating to each other different pitches, pitch outs, and so on. Fans and vendors have developed typical ways of interacting, with vendors calling out "programs, get your programs" and fans signaling their interest and passing money down the aisle. These typical rhetorical ways of interacting in repeated situations are all genres. In a more academic scene, the genres might include essay examinations instead of lineup cards, the syllabus instead of the program, and literature reviews instead of pitching signals. Within the multiple situations of a scene, participants will use a variety of genres, both written and spoken, to help them interact efficiently.

One way to identify genres when observing a scene and its situations is to look for patterns or habits in people's interactions. Look for similarities in how people talk within a situation. Look for any written documents that typically appear in that situation. For example, in an office scene you might notice spoken genres such as the hallway greeting, the work request, the delivery of completed work, or the phone call with a client; and you might notice written genres such as message slips, e-mail announcements, employee time sheets, business letters, memos, budget reports, order forms, newsletters, and so on. Each genre is used in a different recurring situation. To connect a genre to its situation, try to pay attention to who uses the genres in each situation and for what purposes.

Because it may not be clearly visible what genres are used in a situation, especially written genres, another way to identify genres is again by asking participants in that situation—the users of the genres. Since they may not know what the word *genre* means, especially as we use it, ask them what kinds of things they typically write in that situation. Ask them also to describe these kinds of writing and to tell you what they call them. If possible ask if you could have or borrow some examples of the genres. Finally, try to find out why they use these kinds of writing: who uses them, when, where, and why. Be sure to record your findings in your notebook for later reference, when you want to understand better how to act in that situation yourself.

We will discuss genre in much greater detail starting in Chapter 2 and then throughout the book.

Describing a Scene You Participate In

Now we invite you to practice using the strategies we have discussed above to observe and describe a scene in which you participate. Being able to map a familiar scene and its situations and genres will serve you well when you begin to observe and write in less familiar scenes later. As you perform your observations, consult Box 1.2 (pp. 44–45), in which we compile the strategies that we have discussed so far for observing and describing scenes.

Writing Activity 1.11

Using the strategies outlined in Box 1.2, observe and describe a scene in which you already participate. Address the following questions: What makes it a scene? Who are its participants? What are their shared objectives? Then identify some of the situations within that scene. What kinds of rhetorical interactions happen within each of these situations? Who participates in these interactions and in what settings? What subjects do they engage in, and for what reasons do they engage in them? Finally, try to identify the genres participants use to respond to these situations. How do these genres help participants act within the situations? Be prepared to share your observations with your teacher and classmates, and be sure to keep a record of your findings because you might need to refer back to them in Writing Project 1.1.

Box 1.2 *Guidelines for Observing and Describing Scenes*

1. Select and Gain Access to a Scene.

Once you have selected a scene, determine how you will gain entry into it. Whenever possible, ask for permission from somebody in that scene with the authority to grant it (the manager of a supermarket or office, for example, or an owner of a small business or a teacher of a classroom). Tell him or her what you are doing and why you are doing it. Ask also if you could get permission to interview participants in the scene (refer to Box 1.1 (p. 40) for interview guidelines).

2. Observe the Scene in General.

With a notebook or voice recorder in hand, you are now ready to begin your observations. Begin by describing the scene in general terms. Ask yourself and, whenever possible, ask the participants in the scene the following questions:

- What sort of *place* is this scene?
- What *activities* take place within the scene? *Who* participates in these activities?
- What is it that brings people together in this scene? What are the participants' shared *objectives*?

3. Identify the Situations of the Scene.

To identify the situations within a scene, use the following questions:

- What *sorts of interactions* do you see happening in this scene?
- Are different interactions occurring in different *settings*?
- Do different *people* participate within these different interactions?
- Are different *subjects* discussed within these different interactions?

4. Observe and Describe the Situations of a Scene.

Once you have identified some of the situations within a scene, you can begin observing some of these situations more closely in order to describe them more fully. In your observation notes, try to describe the participants, setting, subject, and purposes of the interaction for each situation. Keep these questions in mind: *(continued on next page)*

- *Who* is participating in this situation? How do the participants seem to be *relating* to each other?
- *Where* exactly is their interaction taking place within the scene? *When* does this interaction typically take place?
- *What* are they interacting about? And what is the *nature* of their interaction? What sort of *language* are they using? What sort of *tone* do they use?
- *Why* do they need or want to interact? What is the *purpose* of their interaction?

5. Identify the Genres in the Scene.

To identify the genres of a scene, look for patterns or habits in the interaction within a situation. Ask yourself:

- What *patterns* of speaking do you notice in those situations?
- What *written documents* typically appear in and are used repeatedly in those situations?

Because you might not be able to observe all of the genres in action, interview participants in the situation about their genres, and, if possible, collect samples. Try to get responses to the following questions:

- What *kinds* of writing do the participants typically write in that situation?
- What are these texts *called*?
- What do these texts *look* like?
- *Who* uses these texts, *when, where,* and *why*?

Writing Projects

Writing Project 1.1

Based on your responses to Writing Activity 1.11, write a self-reflective essay (4–6 pages) in which you examine your experiences with writing in a scene you have participated in. You might describe your transition from outsider to insider in this scene, the struggles and rewards of participating in this scene, and your adaptation to language and writing in this scene. You might also reflect on how this scene has shaped and perhaps continues to shape who you are as a writer, including what you have learned about writing as a result of participating in this scene. Use the following questions to guide your reflections:

- How did you feel about the scene in which you wrote? Were you comfortable or uncomfortable interacting within it? How? Why?
- Did the objectives of that scene suit you well? Were you able to achieve those shared objectives? Did you struggle with those objectives?
- What subjects did you write about? Were these subjects easy for you? Why or why not?
- For what reasons did you write? Did you have multiple purposes? Where you able to achieve those purposes?
- In what ways did your participation in the scene shape the way you wrote within it?
- In what ways did your participation in the scene shape the way you write outside the scene?

Writing Project 1.2

Many scenes—whether academic disciplines or organizations, social organizations, political organizations, professional groups, or even hobby groups—have their own electronic forums for discussing issues of interest to them. These electronic discussion groups are known as **listservs** or **newsgroups**. A listserv is an electronic mailing list in which a computer (called a list server) distributes mail sent to people who subscribe to the list. Messages sent to the list are received by all subscribers and are delivered to their private e-mail boxes. A newsgroup is an electronic discussion group in which messages are collected on a system called a news server, where anyone with access to the Internet can retrieve them. Newsgroups are types of "bulletin boards" where, unlike listservs, individual messages are posted for participants to retrieve rather than stored on their computers. The following directories can help you search for discussion groups that focus on a variety of topics such as business, health, music, science, the arts, computers, humanities, nature, politics and religion.

> **Directories of Listserv Lists:**
> http://tile.net/lists
> http://www.liszt.com/
> http://www.nova.edu/Inter-Links/listserv.html
> http://n2h2.com/KOVACS/ (a directory of scholarly discussion lists)

> **Directories of Newsgroups:**
> http://www.dejanews.com
> http://sunsite.unc.edu/usenet-i/home.html
> http://www.liszt.com/news
> http://woodstock.stanford.edu:2000/

Join a newsgroup or subscribe to a listserv group related to a hobby or field of interest. After monitoring their messages for some time, use the guidelines in Box 1.2 (pp. 44–45) to identify and define the scene of the electronic discussion group that you joined: Who are the participants on this list? What seem to be their backgrounds? What shared subject or body of information does the group discuss?

What seem to be their shared objectives? What language, style and conventions are used? What opposing theories or conflicts exist within the online group? Drawing from the information you have gathered, write a guide for new participants in the group. What should a new participant know in order to participate effectively in this listserv or newsgroup? Use dialogue or quotations from the discussion list or newsgroup to give a clear sense of the scene, including its members, style of communication, and shared objectives.

Writing Project 1.3

As we mentioned earlier in the chapter, there are various genres available to help people sell used items, the classified ad being one of them. Other ways include posting a flyer at the grocery store, sending an e-mail to everyone in your address book, or creating a listing for an online auction service like eBay. Select a genre other than the classified ad, and use it to sell the same item you were trying to sell in Collaborative Activity 1.2. (p. 12) In making your decision about what genre to use, think about the scene in which you wish to sell your item. Before you start writing the genre, think about the situation of the genre: the setting in which it is used, the people who read it, the purpose embedded within it. Use your knowledge of the scene, situation, and genre to produce a piece of writing that most effectively presents the item you wish to sell. When you are finished composing, write a cover letter to your instructor explaining the choices you made in writing the genre.

Writing Project 1.4

In the course of studying this chapter, you have heard about or encountered many different genres. Select any one of those genres that you might enjoy writing, and write your own text within that genre. Be sure to consider the scene and situation in which the genre is to be used, including what subjects are most appropriate for the genre, who reads the genre and why, and what your purposes are for writing the genre. When you are finished composing the genre, write a cover letter to your instructor explaining the choices you made in writing the genre.

Writing Project 1.5

Visit a scene on your campus where individuals meet to discuss issues or to accomplish some shared objectives. Drawing on the questions in Box 1.2: Guidelines for Observing and Describing Scenes (pp. 44–45), describe this academic scene. Remember to keep a notebook in which you collect your observations and to supplement your observations, if needed, with interviews with participants in the scene. Address the following questions: What brings these people together? What is special about the place? Who is typically involved? What is the nature of their interactions? What rules or conventions (either formal or implicit) govern the interactions? Write 4–6 pages as a detailed description of the scene for your teacher and classmates.

2

Using Genres to Read Scenes of Writing

*R*eading is not just deciphering words on a page—the typical definition of the activity—but also, in a larger sense, observing and
making sense of a scene by examining its language, both oral and
written. Reading and writing are interconnected activities that depend on
their scenes, situations, and genres—the concepts Chapter 1 introduces.
This chapter begins to explore that interconnection and focuses on the concept of **genre**, which we defined in Chapter 1 as *the typical rhetorical ways of
responding to a repeated situation within a scene.* You will learn in this chapter
how to read and analyze genres in order to access and understand scenes
and situations. You will then practice using that analysis to make informed
choices in your writing, a process we take up in more detail in Chapter 3.

Reading Scenes, Situations, and Genres

Chapter 1 explored how writing is enmeshed within scenes and the specific
situations within them. Reading, too, is enmeshed within situations and
scenes. When you pick up a book to read, you usually know already what
genre the book is: mystery, romance, biography, or textbook, for example.
The same is true for shorter kinds of texts, whether letters from friends,
sales letters, application forms, or e-mail messages. Your knowledge of the
genre provides you with a mental framework for how to read it; it gives you
a set of guidelines, what reading specialist Frank Smith calls "specifications," for how to approach and make sense of a text. Because you know the
genre, you are already on your way to knowing how to read the text.

You know a great deal about many scenes and situations as well as about
the expectations of the genres involved. If you pick up a sales letter, for
example, you know these elements of the scene and situation: The writer is
acting as a sales agent, not as a friend or colleague; the subject of the letter
will be some product; the writer's primary purpose is to sell you something;

and you are being treated as someone who is in a position to buy the product. Because you know the scene of sales letters, you know that someone thought you would share the writer's interest in the product, but you also suspect that the information in the letter will not necessarily be unbiased or fully accurate.

You probably do not think about this knowledge consciously, but you reflect it in your decisions about how to act in response to the text: You might scan for the nature of the product and, if you do not in fact share the writer's interest in the product, you might throw it away without reading further. Similarly, when you pick up a textbook, you know some things about its scene and situation as you begin to read. The *scene* of an assigned text for a course requires that you at least pretend to share the teacher's interest in the subject and that you read the entire text whether that interest is real or feigned. The *situation* places you as a seeker of knowledge and the textbook author as expert, and you read accordingly, highlighting key points, studying definitions, and accepting the information you find in the textbook as accurate. When you read, then, you act on your knowledge of the genre, situation, and scene of the text. *You not only process the words inscribed on the page; you also read the situation and scene inscribed in the genre.*

People adjust their ways of reading texts to the genres, situations, and scenes that those texts involve. For example, as you have been reading this textbook, you have been acting differently as you read the various genres within it, even though you are probably not aware of those shifting habits. The whole book represents the textbook genre and the scene of a writing class; within it are certain genres of communication which reflect their own scenes and situations. You read the body of this textbook for its information, perhaps highlighting important points or new terms, but you read the Writing Activities differently, perhaps waiting for your teacher to assign them before you consider their content seriously and looking for what you are supposed to do rather than what you are supposed to know. You read the Table of Contents differently again, just seeking page numbers or topics, and you read the Index with yet another approach. *This process of negotiation, of repositioning ourselves from one scene to the next and at times within multiple scenes at once, is not the result of guesswork; it is not a random process. Rather, it involves a complex, active process of reading.*

Sometimes, though, we get it wrong. In Chapter 1 we learned about what the ancient Greeks called *kairos*, the art of timing communication correctly. Imagine someone who always misreads scenes, who is constantly saying the wrong thing at the wrong time, like a character in a *Saturday Night Live* skit whose contributions to a conversation are always two topics behind the rest. When others have moved on from discussing the boss's hairpiece to discussing an upcoming concert, the misreading character chimes in with, "And it doesn't even match his hair's real color!" Misreading a scene leads to gaffes and ineffectiveness (in less extreme ways probably) for each of us. We may make a joke in class that a classmate finds offensive, or we might request something of a boss in a way that gets an immediate denial. Sometimes, we misread a scene on purpose, trying to find a way to get other people's attention or to protest accepted behavior. A protester can shout out during a lecture, or a student can refuse to follow a paper assignment (turning in a collage instead of a history paper). Sometimes, though, we are just so unfamiliar with a scene that we fail to read it accurately or completely. The first time we go to a formal party, we may not know what to expect, how to dress, or what kinds of conversations we will have. Learning how to read formal invitations, though, can give us some clues that will help us prepare. Similarly, the first time we want to join a public discussion about a current issue, we can begin more effectively by learning how to read such public genres as editorials and letters to the editor. In both cases, the genres, as typical ways of communicating and acting in their scenes, contain clues about how we can communicate and act effectively in these scenes. Learning how to analyze genres will help you read unfamiliar scenes as well as to think consciously about familiar scenes so you can choose how to act in them as writers.

Writing Activity 2.1

List at least 10 different genres you read, including if possible at least one genre that you read on a computer. Remember to include not just formal or school genres and not just literary genres but also the everyday genres you read, like the backs of cereal boxes. Then pick three of these genres and write a paragraph describing how differently you read each of them. How does your reading of a cereal box differ from your reading of textbooks and sales letters, for example?

Writing Activity 2.2

Think of five different genres you have written, including one you write on a computer. How do you think you learned to write each one? Have you read examples of those genres written by other people? If so, how do you think that influenced your writing of them? If not, how do you think you learned to write a genre without reading it? Do you feel more confident writing some of these genres than you do working with others? If so, do you think that confidence is related to how you have learned them? Write a paragraph or two describing your experiences with at least three of these genres and speculating about how you have learned to write them.

Reading the Language of a Scene

To see how you can read scenes and situations through genres, you first need to see how language—words, sentence structures, forms—can reveal more than just the content of what people have to say. The language people use can reveal who they are, who they are trying to be, who they are communicating with, and what they are trying to achieve. Just as we can learn something about a scene by "reading" the way people dress and behave in it, we can also learn something about a scene by reading the way people communicate in it. The language of a scene tells us a great deal about the scene, about the people in it, even about their values, goals, and beliefs.

Patterns in the language people use are as visible in scenes as are patterns of social behavior such as certain rituals, habits of interaction, ways of dressing, and so on. But you are probably better at reading social behavior than you are at reading rhetorical behavior because you have had more experience learning to read social behavior. For example, you probably are very good at reading the meaning and effect of a facial gesture (a blush or a wink) or other form of body language, but you may struggle with trying to explain the meaning and effect of, say, a passive sentence, subordinate clause, or a strategically placed sentence fragment. Without necessarily knowing any of these grammatical terms, people *choose* these linguistic forms, just as they choose to wear a certain style of dress or other behaviors. So learning to read people's language choices, though it takes some practice, can help you read people's situations and scenes. You can then use that reading to make effective linguistic choices in your own writing; you will be able to communicate effectively with other participants in your scene of the moment.

THE SIGNIFICANCE OF WORD CHOICES: *BED* VERSUS *RACK*

Think about the word *bed*. When we say "bed," we usually think about a place where we go to sleep. The **connotation** of the word (what the word implies) suggests something positive: A place to rest, a place of comfort and warmth. The Marines, however, use a different word to refer to the object on which they sleep. Instead of "bed," they say "rack." Is this merely a difference in word choice? Is "rack" just another way of saying "bed"? Not really. Even though the two words refer to the same thing, the word *rack* connotes something different from *bed;* it implies something hard and cold, something on which we store objects such as merchandise.

Why would a Marine use the term *rack?* There are probably many reasons. One reason, though, is very likely that the word *rack* reinforces the toughness Marines are taught to develop. To be an effective soldier, one has to depersonalize oneself to some extent. To fight in battle, a soldier has to become more like a machine than a human with feelings; otherwise, he or she might not be able to perform under the horrible conditions of war. The word *rack* facilitates this process of dehumanization by influencing the way that Marines think of themselves more as objects than as persons. This process of depersonalization is a necessary part of a Marine's socialization into and eventual success within the military scene and its various situations.

For a Marine, learning to say "rack" is very much like learning how to clean a gun or how to navigate a minefield. It is part of a Marine's training. The word is part of the military *script* a person must learn in order to act and communicate as a Marine. By critically reading the language of this scene we, as outsiders, gain insight into both behaviors and values of the participants in the scene. We start becoming aware of the scene's implicit script, which is an important first step in helping us make effective choices about how *we* could behave and communicate within this otherwise unfamiliar scene.

In the following essay, Perri Klass reads the medical community's language in order to reveal something about its underlying script. As you read "Learning the Language," pay attention to the language that doctors and nurses use to communicate, and consider what that language reveals about the medical scene and those who participate in it. Part of what makes this essay interesting is that it is written from Klass's experience. Think about what it meant for Klass to "learn the language."

Learning the Language

Perri Klass

"Mrs. Tolstoy is your basic LOL in NAD, admitted for a soft rule-out MI," the intern announces. I scribble that on my patient list. In other words, Mrs. Tolstoy is a Little Old Lady in No Apparent Distress who is in the hospital to make sure she hasn't had a heart attack (rule out a Myocardial Infarction). And we think it's unlikely that she has had a heart attack (a *soft* rule-out).

If I learned nothing else during my first three months of working in the hospital as a medical student, I learned endless jargon and abbreviations. I started out in a state of primeval innocence, in which I didn't even know that "s̄ CP, SOB, N/V" meant "without chest pain, shortness of breath, or nausea and vomiting." By the end I took the abbreviations so much for granted that I would complain to my mother the English professor, "And can you believe I had to put down *three* NG tubes last night?"

"You'll have to tell me what an NG tube is if you want me to sympathize properly," my mother said. NG, nasogastric—isn't it obvious?

I picked up not only the specific expressions but also the patterns of speech and the grammatical conventions; for example, you never say that a patient's blood pressure fell or that his cardiac enzymes rose. Instead, the patient is always the subject of the verb: "He dropped his pressure." "He bumped his enzymes." This sort of construction probably reflects the profound irritation of the intern when the nurses come in the middle of the night to say that Mr. Dickinson has disturbingly low blood pressure. "Oh, he's gonna hurt me bad tonight," the intern might say, inevitably angry at Mr. Dickinson for dropping his pressure and creating a problem.

When chemotherapy fails to cure Mrs. Bacon's cancer, what we say is, "Mrs. Bacon failed chemotherapy."

"Well, we've already had one hit today, and we're up next, but at least we've got mostly stable players on our team." This means that our team (group of doctors and medical students) has already gotten one new admission today, and it is our turn again, so we'll get whoever is admitted next in emergency, but at least most of the patients we already have are fairly stable, that is, unlikely to drop their pressures or in any other way get suddenly sicker and hurt us bad. Baseball metaphor is pervasive. A no-hitter is a night without any new admissions. A player is always a patient—a nitrate player is a patient on nitrates, a unit player is a patient in the intensive care unit, and so on, until you reach the terminal player.

It is interesting to consider what it means to be winning, or doing well, in this perennial baseball game. When the intern hangs up the phone and announces, "I got a hit," that is not cause for congratulations. The team is not scoring points; rather, it is getting hit, being bombarded with new patients. The object of the game from the point of view of the doctors, considering the players for whom they are already responsible, is to get as few new hits as possible.

This special language contributes to a sense of closeness and professional spirit among people who are under a great deal of stress. As a medical student, I found it exciting to discover that I'd finally cracked the code, that I could understand what doctors said and wrote, and could use the same formulations myself. Some people seem to become enamored of the jargon for its own sake, perhaps because they are so deeply thrilled with the idea of medicine, with the idea of themselves as doctors.

I knew a medical student who was referred to by the interns on the team as Mr. Eponym because he was so infatuated with eponymous terminology, the more obscure the better. He never said "capillary pulsations" if he could say "Quincke's pulses." He would lovingly tell over the multi-named syndromes—Wolff-Parkinson-White, Lown-Ganong-Levine, Schönlein-Henoch—until the temptation to suggest Schleswig-Holstein or Stevenson-Kefauver or Baskin-Robbins became irresistible to his less reverent colleagues.

And there is the jargon that you don't ever want to hear yourself using. You know that your training is changing you, but there are certain changes you think would be going a little too far.

The resident was describing a man with devastating terminal pancreatic cancer. "Basically he's CTD," the resident concluded. I reminded myself that I had resolved not to be shy about asking when I didn't understand things. "CTD?" I asked timidly.

The resident smirked at me. "Circling The Drain."

The images are vivid and terrible. "What happened to Mrs. Melville?"

"Oh, she boxed last night." To box is to die, of course.

Then there are the more pompous locutions that can make the beginning medical student nervous about the effects of medical training. A friend of mine was told by his resident, "A pregnant woman with sickle-cell represents a failure of genetic counseling."

Mr. Eponym, who tried hard to talk like the doctors, once explained to me, "An infant is basically a brainstem preparation." The term "brainstem preparation," as used in neurological research, refers to an animal whose higher brain functions have been destroyed so that only the most primitive reflexes remain, like the sucking reflex, the startle reflex, and the rooting reflex.

And yet at other times the harshness dissipates into a strangely elusive euphemism. "As you know, this is a not entirely benign procedure," some doctor will say, and that will be understood to imply agony, risk of complications, and maybe even a significant mortality rate.

The more extreme forms aside, one most important function of medical jargon is to help doctors maintain some distance from their patients. By reformulating a patient's pain and problems into a language that the patient doesn't even speak, I suppose we are in some sense taking those pains and problems under our jurisdiction and also reducing their emotional impact. This linguistic separation between doctors and patients allows conversations to go on at the bedside that are unintelligible to the patient. "Naturally, we're worried about adeno-CA," the intern can say to the medical student, and lung cancer need never be mentioned.

I learned a new language this past summer. At times it thrills me to hear myself using it. It enables me to understand my colleagues, to communicate effectively in the hospital. Yet I am uncomfortably aware that I will never again notice the peculiarities and even atrocities of medical language as keenly as I

did this summer. There may be specific expressions I manage to avoid, but even as I remark them, promising myself I will never use them, I find that this language is becoming my professional speech. It no longer sounds strange in my ears—or coming from my mouth. And I am afraid that as with any new language, to use it properly you must absorb not only the vocabulary but also the structure, the logic, the attitudes. At first you may notice these new and alien assumptions every time you put together a sentence, but with time and increased fluency you stop being aware of them at all. And as you lose that awareness, for better or for worse, you move closer and closer to being a doctor instead of just talking like one. ⬤

Collaborative Activity 2.1

After reading "Learning the Language," work with classmates to describe the language doctors and nurses use to communicate. Why do doctors and nurses use the language that they do? What does the language they use tell us about the medical scene and the beliefs, assumptions, and objectives of the participants in that scene? In addition, what happens to Klass as she begins to learn the language? Why do you think this happens? Can members of your group relate to her experience? That is, have any of you had occasion to learn a new way of communicating, and if so, what kind of effect did that acquisition have on you? Be prepared to share your responses with the class.

Writing Activity 2.3

Think of some group to which you belong: Perhaps a volunteer organization, an online discussion group, a fraternity or sorority, a club or team, or even a group of friends. What words do members of your group share that are not used the same way by other groups? Look at those words to see if you can discover reasons your group has chosen them. Do the reasons have something to do with the values, beliefs, and objectives of the group? What do the words mean to your group? Write a paragraph reporting your thoughts about the words and your group.

THE SIGNIFICANCE OF SENTENCE STRUCTURES: PASSIVE VERSUS ACTIVE SENTENCES

Not only choices of words but also choices of sentence structures can reveal different points of view. In the same way that we can read the language of the medical and military scenes in order to learn something about the way people within them communicate and act, we can also read the language of

the various academic scenes that we encounter in a college or university in order to communicate and act more effectively within them.

A great deal of writing in the sciences, for example, uses passive sentence constructions, such as "Twelve samples were studied," "The investigation was focused on the transmission of HIV," or "The ozone has traditionally been viewed as a protective layer." In each of these examples, the person or people performing the action—studying the samples, focusing the investigation, and viewing the ozone layer—are omitted so that the action seems to have occurred somehow on its own. The writer has constructed the sentence to eliminate reference to who is doing the action. You might recall English teachers who warned you against using the passive voice in your writing, preferring instead active sentences, such as "Professor Miller studied twelve samples" or "The team of scientists from MIT investigated the transmission of HIV." Participants in the humanities prefer the active voice because they believe **agency** (who is doing an action) is significant and because they focus on the human and the subjective. Their language reflects these values. In the sciences, however, different values and assumptions prevail.

In the sciences, the passive voice reinforces a scientific belief that the physical world exists objectively, independent of human intervention. A scientist traditionally assumes the role of someone who observes and records what happens, and the use of the passive voice reflects this process. Passive sentences suggest that actions occur mainly through their own accord, with the scientist simply *describing* them. Passive voice also allows the scientist to emphasize the physical world, the object of investigation, rather than the scientist, whose agency is less important. For the scientist who writes, "Five ounces of nitrate were added to a solution," it does not matter who actually added the nitrate; what matters is how the nitrate behaved after it was added to the solution. The passive voice not only linguistically reflects the objectivity that scientists desire; it also gives readers the impression that the action occurred on its own, free of human bias. This perspective is an important one for scientists to convey.

The difference between the active and the passive use of language enables us to recognize some of the differences between the scientific and the humanistic academic scenes. The active is not more effective or "better" than the passive; each just represents a different way of thinking, behaving, and communicating in different scenes. Similarly, "bed" is not better than "rack," and a medical student's vocabulary is not worse than a funeral director's. *As we learn to recognize the different uses of language in different scenes and situations, we can start to read the significance and meanings of those differences.* We come to realize that these differ-

ent linguistic habits are not arbitrary or artificial; rather, they are adapted to and reflect their social scenes quite well. By learning to recognize and read the linguistic habits of each scene, we also learn how to position ourselves within it as social actors and as writers. In this way, the process of reading and the process of writing are dramatically connected.

Writing Activity 2.4

Think of a scene in which you are currently participating and, using some of the observation strategies we described in Box 1.2 (pp. 44–45), observe the language used within that scene. For example, note the language used during a course you are currently taking; spend an hour in your workplace (when you are not working) and record the language you hear your fellow workers use; print copies of all the exchanges on your class electronic discussion list for a day; or observe the language used at a meeting of volunteers for a nonprofit agency for which you volunteer.

1. Record not just the specialist vocabulary of the participants but also how they use more ordinary words.
2. See what patterns you can recognize in the language you have recorded.
3. Speculate about what those patterns might mean, how they might reflect the values or goals or activities of the scene you observed.

Write for your teacher and classmates a one-page summary of your findings, including what scene you described, what language patterns you observed, and what their significance might be.

Writing Activity 2.5

Study two Web sites from two different organizations. You might pick organizations having some common ground but different perspectives, like sites of a Republican and a Democratic organization, or sites of an animal breeding organization and an animal protection organization, or sites of a community college and an elite university. Look for different forms of language used on the two sites. Write a paragraph discussing how the different uses of language reveal the different perspectives of the two scenes.

Collaborative Activity 2.2

You may already have begun to see the differing values and expectations among academic scenes. In small groups, trade textbooks that each of you brought in from a class in a different department, and compare these with this textbook. What

different uses of language do you recognize in these two texts? Can you see more than just differences of technical or specialist vocabulary? List some examples of different language use, and speculate why these differences might exist.

Reading Scenes and Situations through Genres

The language that people use reflects not only the scene but also the situation and genre within the scene. People adjust their language to the particular situation (involving certain participants, subjects, settings, and purposes) and the particular genre (the typical way of responding to the situation) in which they are participating. For example, scientists usually do not *speak* in passive voice no matter what situation they are in and what genre they are using. If they are instructing students how to perform an experiment, they will more likely use the imperative, saying "Pour the chemical into the beaker," not "The chemical was poured into the beaker." Passive constructions are prominent instead, as we've seen, in such genres as lab reports and research articles associated with a more reportive communication situation within the scientific scene. Similarly, medical students do not use the language Klass describes in all situations, but mainly when they are speaking with other medical personnel. And even Marines may shift from "rack" to "bed" when speaking to their families.

Once you learn to recognize how different situations and genres encourage different uses of language, you can use your understanding of these differences to make more effective writing choices within different situations and genres. In the remainder of this chapter, we will show you how to recognize and interpret features of genres; at the end of this chapter and then in the next one, we will show you how to turn that social understanding into making your own writing choices.

GENRES AS SOCIAL SCRIPTS

As typical rhetorical ways of acting in different situations, genres function as social **scripts**. For instance, when you attend the first day of a typical college course, say this writing class, the first things you probably do are look around at the other students, check out the layout of the room, try to figure out what the teacher is like, and so on. In other words, you begin to read the scene in order to decide how best to act within it. But perhaps the best indication you will get about the nature of this scene is through the syllabus that the teacher distributes. As you know, the syllabus is a genre, one that teachers typically distribute on the first day of class. Beyond containing impor-

tant information about the course goals, policies, and expectations, it helps *set the scene* of the course. By reading it carefully, you not only learn what you have to do in order to succeed in the course, when assignments are due, what the course policies are, and so on; you also learn something about how to behave in this scene; what kind of role your teacher will play and what kind of role she or he expects you to play; and what values, beliefs, and goals guide this course. The syllabus, in short, gives you early and important access to the "script" of the course. How well you read this script will impact how effectively you will act within the scene of the class and its various situations.

Writing Activity 2.6

Select a course other than this one for which you have received a syllabus. Before looking back at the syllabus, describe the "personality" of that course—the nature of the course that is conveyed through the class structure, activities, assignments, teacher-student interactions, student-student interactions, etc. Now look at the syllabus for that course: Does the syllabus share any "personality traits" with the course? Could you tell from the syllabus what kind of course it is turning out to be? If so, find some features of the syllabus that reveal that personality. If not, find some features of the syllabus that suggest a different personality.

Collaborative Activity 2.3

In a group of three or four other students, revise the syllabus for this writing course to create a "personality" quite different from the one the actual syllabus describes. Think about how different the role of students might be, what different kinds of information might be conveyed, how different the persona of the teacher might be. Your new syllabus should not change the requirements of the course, but it should significantly change the nature of its scene. Depending on what your teacher requests, write your new syllabus on an overhead transparency or your computer or post it to your class's Web site, and be prepared to explain to your classmates what aspects of the course's scene you changed by changing the syllabus script.

READING THE PATIENT MEDICAL HISTORY FORM

For another example of how the language of genres reflects their situations, think about the scene of the doctor's office. Most of us can readily picture this scene, with its seating area, its coffee table piled with magazines, its

reception desk, and its small examination rooms with health posters hanging on the walls. It is a familiar scene. What may be less familiar, however, is the role that genres play in scripting this scene.

The Patient Medical History Form (PMHF) is one such genre. You might recognize the form as the genre patients have to complete prior to meeting with the doctor on their initial visit to the doctor's office. The PMHF asks patients to provide critical information regarding their age, sex, weight, and height as well as their medical history, including prior and recurring physical conditions, past treatments, and, of course, a description of current physical symptoms. These questions are usually followed by a request for insurance information and then a consent-to-treat statement and a legal release statement that a patient signs. With these components, the PMHF is both a patient record and a legal document, helping the doctor treat the patient and at the same time protecting the doctor from potential lawsuits.

The PMHF does more than convey information from patient to doctor. In its content and visual design, it also tells us something about the scene that the patient is entering. Reading the genre, for instance, we notice that most if not all of its questions focus on a patient's physical symptoms. The genre is designed in such a way that there is very little space in which patients can describe their emotional state. The genre's focus on the physical reflects Western cultural views of medicine, which tend to separate the body and the mind. The medical assumption seems to be that doctors can isolate and then treat physical symptoms with little to no reference to the patient's state of mind and the effect that state of mind might have on these symptoms.

The attitude reflected in the language of this form resembles the description in Perri Klass's article earlier in this chapter of how doctors and nurses talk. As a genre, then, the PMHF reflects and preserves the habits of the medical community. It functions as one of the scripts by which the actors in this medical scene perform their roles and interact with one another. By completing the PMHF, an individual begins to assume the role of patient, one who has certain physical symptoms. And when the doctor meets the patient, the doctor will likely relate to the patient that way (it is not uncommon, for instance, for doctors and nurses to refer to patients by their physical symptoms, such as "I treated a knee injury today" or "the ear infection is in Room 3").

The Patient Medical History Form, thus, is one of the scripts that underwrites the scene of the doctor's office. Other genres within this scene (prescription notes, referral letters, patient files, letters to insurance companies, to name a few) set up other relations (between doctors and pharmacists,

PATIENT HISTORY (Please Print)

THIS INFORMATION BECOMES PART OF YOUR CONFIDENTIAL MEDICAL RECORD

NAME _____ PRIOR PHYSICIAN _____

            LAST   FIRST   MIDDLE INITIAL

ADDRESS _____ TODAY'S DATE _____

              CITY   STATE   ZIP

TELEPHONE # (DAY)_____ (EVENING) _____ AGE _____ SEX M F

Chief Complaint and/or reason for visit _____

History of Present Illness - describe in detail _____

_____

_____

Medical Conditions (Give names and dates)	Personal	Date	Family	Date		Personal	Date	Family	Date
Hypertension	❏	____	❏	____	Anemia	❏	____	❏	____
Diabetes	❏	____	❏	____	Blood Disorders	❏	____	❏	____
Lung Disease	❏	____	❏	____	Obesity	❏	____	❏	____
Heart Disease	❏	____	❏	____	Ulcers	❏	____	❏	____
Cancer	❏	____	❏	____	Intestinal Disorders	❏	____	❏	____
Stroke	❏	____	❏	____	Jaundice	❏	____	❏	____
Chest Pain	❏	____	❏	____	Infertility	❏	____	❏	____
Abdominal Pain	❏	____	❏	____	Ear/Nose/Throat	❏	____	❏	____
Arthritis	❏	____	❏	____	High Cholesterol	❏	____	❏	____
Back Pain	❏	____	❏	____	Kidney Disease	❏	____	❏	____
Osteoporosis	❏	____	❏	____	Bladder Infections	❏	____	❏	____
Mental Disorders	❏	____	❏	____	TB Skin Tests	❏	____	❏	____
Phlebitis	❏	____	❏	____	Sleep Problems	❏	____	❏	____
Migraine	❏	____	❏	____	Alcoholism	❏	____	❏	____
Alcohol/Drug Abuse	❏	____	❏	____	Hepatitis C	❏	____	❏	____
Tobacco Abuse	❏	____	❏	____	Hepatitis B	❏	____	❏	____
Hereditary Disorders	❏	____	❏	____	Hepatitis Non A, Non B	❏	____	❏	____
Thyroid Disease	❏	____	❏	____					

Surgical Procedures (Give names and dates) _____

Blood Transfusions (Give dates) _____

Hospitalizations (Give dates) _____

Injuries/Trauma (Give type and dates) _____

Allergies _____

Immunization History

Influenza yearly ❏ Y ❏ N   Pneumonia ❏ Y ❏ N   Tetanus ❏ Y ❏ N   Hepatitis ❏ Y ❏ N

Social History

Marital Status _____ Occupation _____

Education _____ Housing/source of drinking water _____

Status of immediate and extended family _____ Number living in the household _____

Coffee/Tea intake?	❏ Y	❏ N	Amount? _____
Difficulty sleeping?	❏ Y	❏ N	
Wear seatbelts?	❏ Y	❏ N	
Do you have a Living Will?	❏ Y	❏ N	
Do you have a Durable Power?	❏ Y	❏ N	

Social History (continued)

Cigarette use?	❑ Y ❑ N	Amount? _____	Number of years? _____
Pipe? Cigars? Chew?	❑ Y ❑ N	Amount? _____	Number of years? _____
If you smoke, do you want to stop?	❑ Y ❑ N		
Alcohol use?	❑ Y ❑ N	Amount? _____	Number of years? _____

I.V. drug or intranasal cocaine use, even if only once, at present or in the past? ❑ Y ❑ N
Have tattoos or extensive body piercing? ❑ Y ❑ N
Multiple sex partners (now or in the past?) ❑ Y ❑ N

Have you ever:

Had blood transfusions or any blood products? .... ❑ Y ❑ N
Been rejected for trying to donate blood? .... ❑ Y ❑ N
Been told that your liver function tests were elevated? .... ❑ Y ❑ N
Been stuck with a needle or had an exposure to blood?................... ❑ Y ❑ N
Had any sexually transmitted diseases (i.e. syphilis, chlamydia, gonorrhea)? ... ❑ Y ❑ N
Do you use condoms? .... ❑ Y ❑ N

Family History

	AGE IF LIVING	AGE AT DEATH	PRESENT CONDITION/CAUSE OF DEATH
Father			
Mother			
Children			

DRUGS FREQUENTLY OR PRESENTLY USED (CHECK ALL THAT APPLY)

❑ Aspirin	❑ Decongestants	❑ Hormones	❑ Diet Pills
❑ Vitamins/Minerals/Herbals	❑ Antibiotics	❑ Diabetics	❑ Antidepressants
Over the Counter Meds	❑ Laxatives	❑ Insulin	❑ Sedatives
❑ Water Pill	❑ Antacids	❑ Birth Control Pills	❑ Sleeping Pills
❑ Blood Pressure	❑ Antihistamines	❑ Heart	❑ Cortisone
❑ Asthma	❑ Thyroid	❑ Nitroglycerin	❑ Anti-inflammatory Pills

Other _____

Symptom and System Review

❑ Headache	❑ Shortness of Breath	❑ Hemorrhoids	❑ Muscle Cramps
❑ Dizziness	❑ Coughed up Blood	❑ Abnormal EKG	❑ Varicose Veins
❑ Fainting	❑ Night Sweats	❑ Abnormal X-ray	❑ Phlebitis
❑ Seizures	❑ Cough	❑ High Blood Sugar	❑ Goiter
❑ Numbness	❑ Wheezing/Asthma	❑ Low Blood Sugar	❑ Hot Flashes
❑ Nervous	❑ Loss of Appetite	❑ Skin Rashes	❑ Fluid Retention
❑ Irritable	❑ Indigestion	❑ Dry Skin	❑ Tired
❑ Depressed	❑ Heartburn	❑ Heart Murmur	❑ Trouble Sleeping
❑ Ear Trouble	❑ Nervous Stomach	❑ Palpitations	❑ Kidney Trouble
❑ Sinus Trouble	❑ Abdominal Pain	❑ Irregular Heart Beat	❑ Difficulty Urinating
❑ Stuffy Nose	❑ Diarrhea	❑ Enlarged Heart	❑ Urinary Burning
❑ Nosebleeds	❑ Constipation	❑ Tire Easily	❑ Frequent Urination
❑ Vision Trouble	❑ Change in Bowel Habits	❑ Ankle Swelling	❑ Middle of Night Urination
❑ Nasal Allergies	❑ Gall Bladder Trouble	❑ Back Pain	
❑ Hoarseness of Voice	❑ Swallowing Trouble	❑ Neck Pain	MEN - ❑ Impotence
❑ Swallowing Trouble	❑ Yellow Jaundice	❑ Arm Pain	MEN - ❑ Loss of Libido
❑ Sore Throat	❑ Vomiting of Blood	❑ Bursitis	WOMEN - ❑ Loss of Libido
❑ Chest Pain/Pressure	❑ Passing Blood by Rectum	❑ Arthritis	WOMEN - ❑ PMS

Activity Level

❑ Sedentary life with little exercise   ❑ Mild exercise with job, house, or recreation (i.e. climb stairs)
❑ Occasional vigorous activity with work or recreation   ❑ Regular vigorous exercise program or heavy manual work

---

FOR WOMEN ONLY

Date last menstruated _____	Any menstrual problems?	❑ Y ❑ N
Period every _____ days	Heavy periods	❑ Y ❑ N
Number of pregnancies _____	Infrequent periods	❑ Y ❑ N
Number of miscarriages _____	Irregular periods	❑ Y ❑ N
Birth control method _____	Painful periods	❑ Y ❑ N
Date of last pap smear _____		

Check if you have had: ❑ D&C   ❑ Toxemia   ❑ Hysterectomy   ❑ Ovarian Failure
                                    ❑ Difficulty with pregnancy   ❑ with labor   ❑ with delivery

doctors and other doctors, etc.), other actions, and other social roles. Together, the genres provide a kind of rhetorical map that we can read in order to chart how people behave and communicate within this scene.

Collaborative Activity 2.4

Working with classmates, examine the visual elements of the sample PMHF we have included. Pay attention to the design of the document: The use of borders, boxes, headings and subheadings, font shape and size, color, etc. What else do these elements tell us about this genre and the scene in which it is used? In what ways do the visual elements support the claim we have been making about the PMHF?

FROM READING TO ANALYZING GENRES

What we just did in reading the Patient Medical History Form to determine what it can tell us about how people behave and communicate in the doctor's office is called **genre analysis**. Genre analysis involves the close and critical reading of people's patterns of communication in different situations within scenes. As a process, it involves collecting samples of a genre, identifying patterns within it (recognizing, for example, that PMHFs focus almost exclusively on physical symptoms), and then drawing conclusions about what these patterns reveal about the situation or scene in which it is used. *By doing this kind of genre analysis, you will gain access to the patterns of communication that will enable you to write more effectively within different situations and scenes.*

Genre analysis involves close reading and some observation by

1. Collecting samples of a genre

2. Finding out where, when, by whom, why, and how the genre is used

3. Identifying rhetorical and linguistic patterns in the genre

4. Determining what these patterns tell us about the people who use it and the scene in which it is used

You might want to review our discussion of observing scenes in Chapter 1, especially Box 1.2 (pp. 44–45).

In order to demonstrate how genre analysis works, we will now move from our relatively informal reading of the PMHF genre to the formal process of analyzing the genre of the business complaint letter. After you practice analyzing genres yourself, we will show you how you can use your analysis of genre to make your own writing choices.

A Sample Genre Analysis of the Complaint Letter

We have chosen the complaint letter as a model for our genre analysis in part because it is a genre you might have some experience with, and because it is short enough that we can include several samples (pp. 67–69). As noted above, the first step in doing genre analysis involves collecting samples of the genre. There are several ways to collect samples. You can ask participants in a scene you have been observing for copies of the genre they have been using. If the genre is a more public one, as in the case of greeting cards, classified ads, menus, Web sites, wedding announcements, etc., you can readily find samples of the genre. You can also collect samples from books about the genre. For the analysis that follows, we collected complaint letters from several business-writing textbooks that included examples of the genre.

The second step is to start collecting information about the genre's situation and scene. Before you look at the samples we have included, consider what you already know about the complaint letter as a genre:

* Who uses the genre?
* What is it about?
* Where is the genre used?
* When is it used?
* Why is it used?

There are several ways in which you can answer these questions before doing the deeper analysis of the genre samples. One way is to draw on what you already know about the genre. Another way is to observe the scene and situation in which the genre is used (see Box 1.2, pp. 44–45). The observation could include interviewing users of the genre, watching people use the genre, and observing what the genre does. In the case of the complaint letter, we know that, unlike a syllabus, a lab report, or a patient medical history form, the complaint letter is not solely used in just one concrete scene (a classroom, a lab, or a doctor's office, for instance). Individuals may write complaint letters from home, or an employee in a company's purchasing department may write a letter of complaint from the office. However, the general scene of this genre involves a group of participants (consumers) who have the shared objective of seeking restitution for a defective product or inadequate service.

Once we have identified the scene, we can consider the elements of situation (setting, subject, participants, purposes) that prompt and define complaint letters. Drawing on prior knowledge, we know that complaint letters are letters written in any setting, mailed or e-mailed, about some sort of problem that has arisen, be it a billing error, poor or inadequate service, a defective or falsely advertised product, and so on. We also know that a complaint letter is often written by someone who has been either directly affected by the problem or represents an organization that has been affected by the problem in some way. In turn, readers of complaint letters are ideally people who are in a position to address the problem, ranging from the owner of a small company to the consumer affairs department of a large organization. Finally, we know that the purposes of the complaint letter are to bring the problem to the attention of the person or organization responsible for it, to convince them that the complaint is justified, and to request some sort of fair settlement or correction, which, if settlement is reached, often arrives in the form of a related genre called the adjustment letter. Gathering information about use of a genre (in this case complaint letters), either through your prior knowledge, interview, or observation, is the second step, after collecting samples, in performing a genre analysis.

The third and fourth steps in genre analysis are a little more challenging. They involve identifying a genre's linguistic and rhetorical patterns and determining what these patterns reveal about the people who use it, including their behaviors and activities, and the situation and scene in which it is used. You are probably already familiar with most of these patterns from past English courses in which you practiced doing textual criticism and analysis of works of literature.

To begin identifying the rhetorical and linguistic patterns of a genre, we need to read it closely, looking for any recurrent features that all samples of the genre share. In identifying recurrent features, it is best to move from the general to the specific:

- Identify content
- Identify the appeals to the audience
- Identify the structure used
- Identify the format used
- Identify choice of sentence style and words

We begin by looking at the **content**, at the information that is typically included and excluded in the samples.

Then we look at the types of **rhetorical appeals** that are used. Rhetorical appeals are ways of trying to persuade an audience, the names of which—logos, pathos, and ethos—are based in the classical study of rhetoric in ancient Greece. *Logos* is appealing to an audience's rational mind, to the persuasiveness of logical and reasoned arguments and evidence. *Pathos* is appealing to an audience's emotions, persuading readers by making them feel the writer's position, whether through sympathy, compassion, anger, or any other emotion. *Ethos* is appealing to an audience's belief in the personal qualities of the writer, persuading the readers that the writer should be believed or agreed with on this subject. For example, writers may try to convince readers they are credible because of their expertise, sympathetic because of their experiences, or believable because they are in positions of power.

After the largest elements of content and rhetorical appeals, we look at the largest **structural patterns** (What are the various parts? How are they organized? In what order do they appear?) and then **format** (the layout of the sample texts, their appearance, length, etc.). Then we focus on the more specific linguistic features, on the **syntax** or sentence structure and the **diction** or word choices. Syntactic choices include sentence length and complexity and other patterns in sentence style, such as using the passive or active verbs, as we discussed earlier. We also look at the kinds of words that are used within the samples: What kinds of words are used to convey the subject matter? Are they mainly words used by specialists (jargon) or slang? What do the words connote? Recall our earlier discussion of the difference between the connotations of the words *bed* and *rack*. How would you describe the writer's voice (the personality or presence of the writer that is conveyed through the words)? *Everything from the content to the structure to the word choices within a genre makes up its rhetorical patterns.* With this brief overview in mind, we will now walk you through the process of identifying rhetorical and linguistic patterns typically found in complaint letters. As you read the samples on pages 67–69, see what rhetorical patterns you can identify.

IDENTIFYING CONTENT

Beginning with content, we see that each complaint letter describes a specific complaint, something that went wrong or did not work as promised. The letters also include detailed information about the products or services that are the cause of the complaint, often listing invoice numbers, purchase dates, model numbers, etc. And each letter makes some request of the reader: Asking for a new product, a repair of the old product, or compensation to the writer for the bad service or product.

Sample Complaint Letter 1

Rudi's Country Store
R.D. 1
Ft. Mark, PA 15540
August 22, 19

Mr. Franklin Morrison
American Paint Company
537 Schoolyard Road
Messina, PA 15540

Dear Mr. Morrison:

I am writing to you because I have been unable to reach you by phone, even after leaving messages on your machine. Your painting crew just finished painting my store and I am not entirely satisfied with the job or the bill.

Your workers tended to arrive late, about 9:30 a.m., and leave early, about 3:30 p.m. Once they missed a whole afternoon because, according to the foreman, they had another job to do. As a result, they were on site for four days instead of the estimated three.

The crew's behavior on the job was also unnecessarily disruptive. They worked with no shirts on and yelled to each other. My store stays open until 10:00 at night, and I would have appreciated it if they had cleared away their empty paint cans and other paraphernalia from around the front and sides of the store after work every day, but instead they left each afternoon without cleaning up.

I also seem to have been billed for a can of paint that the workers overturned, staining the parking lot. I fixed the stain, but I would like my bill adjusted accordingly. I hope you will pass these complaints on to your foreman. Because you are a successful company, I am sure that these practices are not normal. Your bid was low, and the paint job looks good. I look forward to doing business with you again, if you can assure me that the problems I mentioned will not arise.

Respectfully,

Sample Complaint Letter 2

1390 Southwest Twentieth Street
Davie, FL 33326
22 September 2000

The Doubleday Store
Customer Service Department
501 Franklin Avenue
Garden City, NJ 07769

Re: Account #96-299-38934

Gentlemen:

Please review my account for a credit. On 12 July 2000 I received the Pierre Cardin canvas luggage set from your company which I ordered on 15 June 2000. When I received the luggage from your company, it was on a trial basis for 60 days. After examining the luggage, I determined that it was not substantial enough for my needs, and I returned the entire set on 12 August 2000.

The charge of $279.95 has continued to be shown on my last two monthly statements. I wrote a note on the statement each time indicating the date and return of luggage and sent the statement back to your company. Copies of these notes are attached to this letter. To date, I have not received an adjusted statement.

Would you please credit my account for $279.95 and send me an adjusted statement?

I will appreciate your prompt attention to this matter.

Very truly yours,

Ruth Burrows

Sample Complaint Letter 3

ROBBINS CONSTRUCTION, INC.
255 Robbins Place   Centerville, MO 65101   (417) 555-1850

August 19, 19XX

Mr. David Larsen
Larsen Supply Company
311 Elmerine Avenue
Anderson, MO 63501

Dear Mr. Larsen:

As steady customers of yours for over 15 years, we came to you first when we needed a quiet pile driver for a job near a residential area. On your recommendation, we bought your Vista 500 Quiet Driver, at $14,900. We have since found, much to our embarrassment, that it is not substantially quieter than a regular pile driver.

We received the contract to do the bridge repair here in Centerville after promising to keep the noise to under 90 db during the day. The Vista 500 (see enclosed copy of bill of sale for particulars) is rated at 85 db, maximum. We began our work and, although one of our workers said the driver didn't seem sufficiently quiet to him, assured the people living near the job site that we were well within the agreed sound limit. One of them, an acoustical engineer, marched out the next day and demonstrated that we were putting out 104 db. Obviously, something is wrong with the pile driver.

I think you will agree that we have a problem. We were able to secure other equipment, at considerable inconvenience, to finish the job on schedule. When I telephoned your company that humiliating day, however, a Mr. Meredith informed me that I should have done an acoustical reading on the driver before I accepted delivery.

I would like you to send out a technician—as soon as possible—either to repair the driver so that it performs according to specifications or to take it back for a full refund.

Yours truly,

Jack Robbins, President

IDENTIFYING RHETORICAL APPEALS

Second, we look for the kinds of rhetorical appeals the writers use. The writers of these complaint letters use a variety of rhetorical appeals to register their complaints in a forceful yet restrained and reasonable manner. They use *logos,* approaching the subject logically and treating the reader as a rational person who will surely see the problem and try to correct it. The writers offer facts and details about the situation and evidence of the problem to appeal to the reader's logical mind and to demonstrate that the writers are also rational and credible individuals. In order to create a credible and sympathetic *ethos,* or image of the writer, the letter writers portray themselves as reasonable people, who did what they should have done and yet encountered difficulty. Although the complaint letters rarely show anger (which might harm their sympathy or credibility), they do indicate how troubling or inconvenient the problem was, what pain and suffering was caused, appealing to *pathos* or to the reader's emotions for sympathy. In order to create sympathy between reader and writer, complaint letters often end on a note of optimism, suggesting that the writer believes the reader will respond conscientiously ("I will appreciate your prompt attention to this matter"). These complaint letters use logos, pathos, and ethos to try to persuade the reader to do what the writer is requesting.

IDENTIFYING STRUCTURE

After describing what we can of the content and rhetorical appeals of the genre, we turn to describing the structure of the complaint letter—its parts and their order. We notice first that, for the most part, writers begin the genre by identifying themselves as customers of the company or organization being addressed. The first part of the complaint letter also sometimes includes the specific product or service that has caused the complaint, which the company or organization will need in order to issue repairs or refunds. The second part of the complaint letter provides a specific description of the nature of the problem. Included here is a description of what happened, especially what went wrong. This section does more than just describe, however; it also tries to convince the reader that the product is defective or the service is inadequate by giving detailed examples, primarily through personal testimony but sometimes supported by more objective data. The final part of these complaint letters usually proposes or requests some kind of action, solution, or adjustment in relation to the problem. Some conclude with a curt request; others conclude with a more courteous optimism, signaling the writer's hope that the reader will respond fairly and promptly.

IDENTIFYING FORMAT

In terms of format, layout, and appearance, these complaint letters generally follow standard business letter format, with a heading that includes the writer's address or letterhead as well as the date, an inside address with the name and address of the recipient, a salutation ("Dear Ms. Webber"), the body, the closing ("Sincerely" or "Respectfully"), and the signature. Although they are not represented among our samples, we have seen complaint letters that have been handwritten as well as typed, but even handwritten letters tend to follow the standard business letter format.

IDENTIFYING SENTENCES, WORDS, AND TONE

On the sentence and diction levels, we notice that complaint letters tend to be slightly formal and often direct. The writers of these letters use mostly active sentence constructions, such as "I ordered," "We have used your product for years," "Your workers arrived late," and "I think you will agree we have a problem." Writers of the complaint letters periodically use sentences that begin with introductory phrases, such as "As steady customers of yours for over 15 years, we came to you first . . . ," "On July 9, I ordered . . . ," and "Because you are a successful company, I am sure that . . ." These introductory phrases provide background to the claim that is about to be made in the sentence. As such, they serve as a way to create a narrative, a sort of cause-and-effect relationship that leads up to the point the writer is making. At the same time, they also help justify the credibility of both the writer and the complaint.

Because the complaint letter refers back to an event that already occurred, writers mostly use the past tense when describing the nature of the problem. In the final paragraph, however, when the writer shifts from a description of the problem to a request for settlement, the tense shifts as well, signaling future or conditional action often with the use of the auxiliary verb *would*. Overall, the sentences in these complaint letters tend to be slightly long and embedded, using a variety of transitions such as coordinating conjunctions (*and, but*), subordinating conjunctions (*because, after, though*), and interrupting phrases (phrases that add information or explanation such as "we were able to secure other equipment, *at considerable inconvenience*, to finish the job on schedule"). Such embedding creates a **narrative effect,** helping the writer describe a chain of interconnected events and their effects. Indeed, it seems that one of the rhetorical functions of the interrupting phrases in particular is to allow the writer to insert his or her feelings of annoyance into the description without drawing explicit attention to the annoyance.

A calm and rational tone, even when the writer may be annoyed, is perhaps the most typical feature of complaint letters, and it is evident at both the word and sentence levels. While moments of anger do appear, they are usually embedded within the larger description of the problem, as we saw in the embedding of "at considerable inconvenience." Even though first and second person pronouns (*I/we* and *you*) are primarily used—reflecting the relationship between writer and reader—the writers of these complaint letters temper this directness by depersonalizing the *you*. Rather than pinning the blame directly on the reader personally, writers instead often identify the reader as a representative of the company or organization or even the product that is to blame, hence we see phrases such as "because you are a successful company," "your Vista 500 Quiet Driver," "your painting crew," "your Newark, New Jersey parts warehouse," etc. Other examples of restraint and calmness include the selection of more formal words such as *informed* instead of *told, telephoned* instead of *called, arise* instead of *come up, paraphernalia* instead of *stuff, indicating* instead of *saying*, and so on.

INTERPRETING GENERIC PATTERNS IN THE COMPLAINT LETTER

Now that we have described rhetorical patterns in the complaint letters, genre analysis turns to the *significance or meaning of those patterns:*

> What do these rhetorical patterns tell us about the genre of the complaint letter and the situation and scene in which it is used?
>
> What can we learn about the actions being performed through the genre by observing its language patterns?

These questions mark the final step in performing a genre analysis.

There are, of course, many ways we can answer these questions and many conclusions we can make and support. One argument we can make—our **thesis**, if you will—is that the genre of the complaint letter tries to create a situation that depersonalizes the relationship between the writer and the reader. In a relatively uncomfortable situation of complaint, the complaint letter genre enables the writer to complain without it "being personal." The writers present themselves not as the managers and company presidents that some of them are but as "customers." We see this especially at the beginning of the complaint letter, where the writer assumes the role of customer: "On July 9, I ordered nine TV tuner assembly units," "Your painting crew just finished painting my store," or "As steady customers of yours for over 15 years, we came to you. . . ." In this role of customer, the writer then presents his or her complaint in fairly *objective terms*. That is, he or she mainly describes how the service was inadequate or the product was defective rather than how he or she felt about the service or product. By couching any personal resentment or anger in a less emotional, relatively objective description of what happened to him or her as a "customer," the writer achieves credibility in the complaint letter. Likewise, the reader is also depersonalized. Rather than being addressed as personally responsible for the problem, the reader is addressed as the company or organization. This way, the reader is less likely to become defensive.

In mainstream U.S. culture, there are various "scenes" in which we can communicate our complaints. Some of them include genres with more emotional expression than others—for example, when a baseball player complains to an umpire about being called out. People in other cultures may treat complaints differently, and the genres that respond to their problems will reveal different attitudes and relationships, through different rhetorical patterns. When we write a complaint letter that reflects the habits and patterns that we have just analyzed, we probably are not even aware that the scene of writing is being shaped in a way that maintains a delicate and distancing relationship between the writer (customer) and the reader (company or organization). How we write about the problem and the sort of demands we make are all partly shaped by the genre we are using.

Sample Genre Analysis

So that you can see an example of genre analysis, we include below an analysis written by a student, Nicole Rebernik, who here compares menus from two Italian restaurants to show how differences in their linguisitic and rhetorical patterns reveal differences in their customers. As you read this sample, note how the author discovers things about the genre by doing an analysis of the genre's patterns.

Note also how the author presents this interpretation in the form of some kind of argument about what the genre tells us. Such claims that focus a paper are called in academic writing a thesis or controlling idea.

The **controlling idea** is the main thing a writer wants to say, the point of the paper, the primary claim the writer wants to convey. The controlling idea controls the paper, working within a particular genre to help the writer determine what content is relevant and needed and how that content should be organized. The nature of the controlling idea varies in different genres, of course. As we will see in more detail in Part II, on academic genres, different kinds of ideas are important in different genres. In genre analyses, the controlling idea makes a **claim** or interpretive statement about the significance of the genre patterns. For example, the student who analyzed the PMHF (p. 60) claimed that the genre emphasizes physical symptoms to the exclusion of the whole patient. If we were to write a genre analysis paper based on our analysis of the complaint letter, we might construct a controlling idea that complaint letters depersonalize the complaint situation, making it easier for people in U.S. society to register complaints. Genre analyses result in claims about the genre, situation, or scene that become controlling ideas when written up in academic papers.

As you read Nicole's analysis, pay attention to how she *supports her claim with evidence* from the menus. Think also about any additional claims you could make based on her analysis.

Rebernik 1

The Genre of Restaurant Menus: A Comparative Analysis

Nicole Rebernik

College students have many options throughout the city when it comes to Italian dining. One popular spot near campus is BelaRoma Pizza and Pasta, which caters to a college crowd and advertises on its menu the restaurant's goal of "Satisfying Your Cravings." Located further from the campus strip is another Italian restaurant, Sicily's, that caters more to the larger community and offers a more formal dining experience. On its menu, you will find a different advertisement: "Silver Platter Award Winner for Best Italian Food." The differences in the implications of these quotations taken from the menu covers show the differences in the communities these restaurants are trying to create and the customers they are seeking to serve. BelaRoma's main purpose is to serve takeout and delivery food to on-the-go students, while Sicily's restaurant serves a sit-down clientele. Though Sicily's Italian Restaurant and BelaRoma Deli are both restaurants that offer Italian style dining, as demonstrated by their menus, the fact that they represent different communities is evident in the layout, items, pricing, and language of their menus.

Sicily's and BelaRoma, while being very different types of restaurants, share some basic similarities in their menus, reflecting the shared goals of the restaurant business. Each of the menus clearly displays the restaurant's name in large letters, with a graphic underneath the title to catch the customer's attention and to make the restaurant memorable to the customers so that they will keep coming back. When the customers first open the menus, a variety of food options are revealed, conveniently following the order that they usually are consumed, with appetizers listed first, followed by main dishes and then desserts. Each variety of food is broken down under different headings, such as "Appetizers" or "Pasta," thus making the menu easier to read and helping to guide customers as they make their choices.

Upon further examination, each of the food items then becomes a subheading, such as "Veggie Pita" or "Spinach Lasagna," with a description of the item underneath it; this is done so that the customers know precisely what they are ordering. The descriptions usually include vivid details and adjectives that try to sell customers on a particular dish with descriptions such as, "The lasagna is cooked until crusty brown and bubbling hot." The menus also include graphics throughout to make them more pleasing for the customer to peruse. The graphics include pictures of certain delectable food items that persuade customers to order that item. Finally, under each of the food descriptions is the price that the restaurant charges for the item, which is included after the description to downplay the cost as compared to the

Rebernik 3

deliciousness of the entrée. The menus also include payment options that the customer may use.

All of these similarities reflect the purposes and audiences of the genre being utilized. Each menu is trying to
attract a certain customer base. The purpose of the restaurant menu is to make the food presentable in a way that customers will want to order the offered menu items. The menus
need to explain the food that they are serving so that the customer will have an understanding of what they are ordering
and what it costs. The audiences that the restaurants are trying to attract and their purposes are similar in the sense that
they want to attract people who want the convenience of
eating out instead of preparing food themselves. They also
want the service and good food that goes along with this. All
of these strategies are reasons for the similarities in the
menus of Sicily's and BelaRoma.

Although the similarities in the menus reflect the
broader goals of restaurants to attract, serve, and maintain
customers, the differences in the menus reflect different situations. For instance, differences in the layout and organization of each menu become obvious just by looking at the
cover of each of the menus. BelaRoma's inexpensively
printed, flyer-like menu is printed on bright yellow paper
to attract the customer's eye when placed with other
takeout menus and is meant to be picked up or attached to
takeout orders so that customers can keep the flyer. "Free
Express Delivery" is displayed in bold lettering along with
BelaRoma's phone and fax numbers, hours of operations,
payment options, and location all on the cover of the
menu--all of which fits with their emphasis on takeout
business. The restaurant needs to make it as easy as
possible for the prospective client to find its phone number
and location; otherwise they could easily move on to

another takeout menu that more readily provides this information.

Sicily's restaurant's menu, on the other hand, is slicker and printed on heavier, more expensive paper and is colored in a somber dark green and red coloring of Italy, giving the feeling of a more formal eating environment. Sicily's does allow takeout ordering, but does not state this anywhere on their menu, which is meant only for in-restaurant use. The payment options, phone number, hours of operation, and location are all listed on the back cover of the menu in contrast with BelaRoma having all this on the front cover, demonstrating their different purposes. While BelaRoma has coupons for menu items such as pizza on the back of its menu, Sicily's lists the numerous awards it has received such as the Metro Weekly Award for "Best Italian Food" and "Most Romantic Restaurant." These differences in the cover layouts of the two menus reflect the differences between the communities in which Sicily's and BelaRoma participate. BelaRoma provides delivery services and takeout foods for a mostly campus clientele. The Sicily's menu reflects that they are looking for a more sophisticated clientele and not one that is looking for a fast takeout solution. Sicily's primary business comes from sit-down dining, and that is reflected in the more artistic and elaborate looking menu. Sicily's lists its awards on the back cover to give eating at the restaurant an aura of prestige and attract diners that are looking for quality food.

The menu items themselves are an accurate depiction of the differences between the two restaurants. Sicily's concentrates mainly on gourmet Italian food while BelaRoma offers Italian-type foods and also a wide variety of American fare. This is demonstrated by the statement on the front cover of BelaRoma's menu, "The diversity of our menu

enables us to cater to a wide range of tastes and cravings."
There is everything from Alfredo Pasta to a Mushroom
Swiss Burger on the BelaRoma menu. Sicily's offers a wine
list and champagne, while BelaRoma offers Coca-Cola
products. The differences between the items Sicily's and
BelaRoma carry reflect the different communities they are
trying to create. BelaRoma is trying to market a variety of
foods so that it can please almost everyone in a large group
of people, such as a large group of college students. Sicily's
has narrowed the group towards whom it is marketing its
items to a smaller demographic group that only wants
higher-quality foods.

The price differential between Sicily's restaurant's menu
and BelaRoma restaurant's menu further reflects the different
aims and audiences of the menus. The most expensive item
on BelaRoma's menu is $15.00 for a large pizza that will
feed a few people on average--perfect for college students
who don't have a lot of money--while Sicily's most expensive
item is an entrée entitled Filet Chianti at the cost of $19.99
and is meant to feed one person, a bit more out of the college student's range. A traditional Italian entrée of Lasagna
at BelaRoma costs $5.99 while at Sicily's restaurant it costs
the customer $9.99. The more expensive foods that are
served at Sicily's restaurant, along with the atmosphere and
service, justify the differences in prices. Sicily's offers more
select Italian foods than BelaRoma. The quality of ingredients
that go into making the dishes are part of the higher pricing
as is the preparation and artistry involved. BelaRoma is
focused on college students who would be more interested
in the types of food that they serve--pizza, quick pasta
dishes--and therefore need to price their items so that
the average college student would be able to afford
them.

Rebernik 6

The language on the menus fit the different price ranges and different clienteles of each restaurant. The use of elevated language in the Sicily's menu reflects the higher prices of its items and the more formal dining experience they provide. There are entrées on the menu at Sicily's such as "Zuppa del Giornio" and "Chicken Saltimboca." Most of the items on BelaRoma's menu consist of more familiar names like "Spaghetti" and "Reuben." This reflects the difference in types of food and claims to authenticity or ability to specialize in Italian food that-each establishment offers as well as the different customers they are trying to attract. Sicily's restaurant is looking for more serious diners who would be interested in trying a menu item named "Linguine Pescatore" while BelaRoma is trying to attract customers-- most likely college students--who want to be able to order a "Bacon Swiss Burger" or "Cheese Sticks," in addition to Italian fare. The language of the menus, like the prices, lends a particular atmosphere to the foods offered by each restaurant.

The differences in the menus of BelaRoma Pizza and Pasta and Sicily's Italian Restaurant reflect the fact that these eateries belong to different communities of eating establishments. Each is using its menu to try to attract and appeal to a specific clientele: Sicily's is trying to attract a smaller group of people who are more selective and who only want Italian food while BelaRoma is trying to appeal to their diverse clientele of mostly college students with many different eating habits and tastes. While they share the similar goal of trying to get people to eat at their establishments and order their food, their strategies in menu layout, pricing, language, and menu items reflect differences in target customers.

Collaborative Activity 2.5

Drawing on the sample menus reproduced here and your reading of the sample student paper, discuss with your classmates how you might extend the analysis. Note the visual elements of the menus and point out additional features of format as well as content, language, and structure that aren't mentioned in the sample paper. What other examples can be used to support the writer's claims? Next, compare and contrast the ways in which the two menus appeal to ethos, logos, and pathos. Then discuss with your group what other conclusions you might draw about the significance of the menus. What might your analysis of these menus (along with Rebernik's) lead you to conclude about the image of college students that the owners of BelaRoma appear to have, for example? Or what might you conclude about the larger scenes of these two restaurants?

Collaborative Activity 2.6

Bring to class a copy of a sample menu (many of which can be found online) from the community in which your college/university is located and share the menus in your small group. Notice the visual elements of the menus as well as the other kinds of elements—content, structure, format, sentences, words. How do the menus reflect similar or different purposes and define similar or different roles for the restaurant and the customer? Based on the similarities and differences you found, what conclusions might you draw about menus as a genre? For example, what might you conclude about the role that menus play in setting the tone of a situation? Or in establishing behavior in a scene? Finally, based on your analysis of various menus, what might you conclude about the larger scene of restaurants in your college community?

Practicing Genre Analysis

Having studied how genre analysis works and seen it in action in a couple of samples, you now have the opportunity to practice doing genre analysis yourself, using the guidelines for analyzing genre summarized in Box 2.1 on pages 93 and 94. The three activities that follow will guide you, individually and in groups, through the steps involved in analyzing genre. Then, in Writing Activity 2.8, you will have a chance to carry out a genre analysis on a genre of your own choosing, possibly one which you will then write about in Writing Project 2.1.

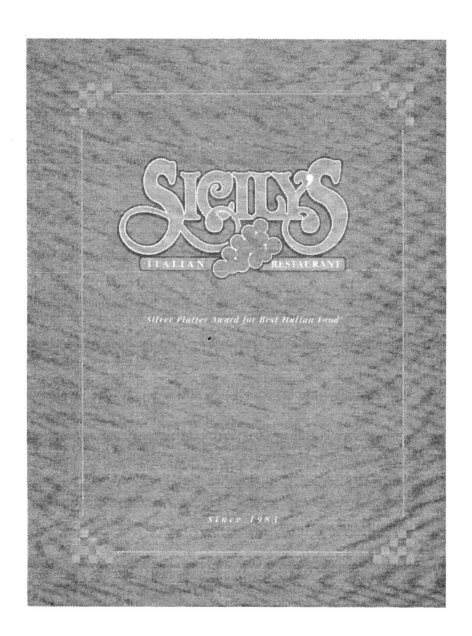

SICILY'S

ITALIAN   RESTAURANT

"Silver Platter Award for Best Italian Food"

Since 1983

"Silver Platter Award for Best Italian Food"

SOUPS

Zuppa del Giornio - Soup of the day, a fresh daily choice 3.25
Minestrone - Hearty broth with fresh vegetables 3.75
Seafood Soup - Hearty broth with mixed seafood 5.25

APPETIZERS AND SALADS

Bruschetta - Toasted bread topped with diced tomatoes, garlic & fresh herbs 3.59
Roasted Garlic - Garlic roasted in olive oil and served with toasted bruschetta 6.79
Baked Clams - Clams stuffed with homemade stuffing and herbs 7.59
Stuffed Mushrooms - Fresh mushrooms stuffed with bacon, cheese & onion 7.59
Fried Calamari - Deep-fried calamari served with a spicy tomato sauce dip 7.99
Sicily's Salad - Fresh romaine with shrimp & tomatoes in oil vinaigrette 6.59
Caesar Salad - Romaine lettuce, bacon, cheese, croutons in chef's special blend 4.79
Tomato Salad - Fresh tomatoes with onions dressed in oil & vinegar 5.29

PASTA

Fettucine Alfredo - Fettucine in a rich cream and parmesan sauce 12.59
Rotini alla Maria - Pasta tossed with fresh broccoli and chicken in white wine garlic sauce 10.59
Gnocchi - Homemade potato dumpling in a rich, creamy basil cream sauce 10.59
Linguine Pescatore - Pasta mixed with seafood and a "spicy" tomato or olive oil white wine sauce . . .12.59
Tortellini alla Pesto - Tortellini tossed in an olive oil and pesto sauce 9.79
Lasagna - Old country recipe, cooked until crusty brown and bubbling hot 9.99
Spinach Lasagna - Filled with spinach and 3 cheeses, cooked until crusty brown and bubbling hot 9.79

ENTRÊES

Veal Parmigiana - Veal cutlet topped with ham, cheese & tomato sauce 15.59

Chicken Parmigiana - Tender breast of chicken topped with tomato sauce and melted mozzerella 14.99

Chicken Rustico - Pan-fried chicken in a "mouth-watering" rosemary, mushroom cream sauce 14.99

Chicken Saltimboca - sauteed with Marsala wine, prosciutto ham, mozzarella, atop spinach 12.99

Veal Marsala - Pan-fried veal sauteed with Marsala wine & mushrooms in a cream sauce 16.79

* All of the above entries are served with pasta *

HOUSE FAVORITES & SPECIALTIES

Risotto Seafood - Italian rice sauteed in white wine garlic & herbs mixed with fresh seafood 13.99

Spaghetti alla Sicily's - Pasta tossed with sun-dried tomatoes, olive oil, garlic & cheese 11.59

Filet Chianti - 10 oz. cooked to perfection with wine sauce, served with rice and salad 19.99

Pasta Primavera - Linguine with vegetables and fresh tomatoes sauteed in a white wine garlic sauce ...16.99

Ravioli alla Bolognese - Fresh pasta filled with veal in homemade tomato meat sauce 11.29

DESSERTS

Tartufi - frozen Italian chocolate mousse 4.59

Cannoli alla Sicily - pastry shell filled with ricotta, cream cheese and chocolate chips 4.99

Spumoni - Italian chocolate, cherry, and pistachio ice cream, served with a cookie 3.99

Torta di Formaggio - Cheesecakes:

    Light Chocolate Cheesecake - topped with peanuts and chocolate 4.99

    American Style Cheesecake - topped with spiced apples and caramel sauce 4.99

    Peanut Butter Pie - layered with Reese's chocolate peanut butter and chocolate chips 4.59

Tiramisu - lady fingers soaked in coffee and liqueur, layered with marscapone cheese 4.59

Select a "dolce delizioso" from our delectable daily dessert specials

Ask your server about our extensive wine list

Satisfying Your Cravings

We at BelaRoma are committed to the preparation of, presentation, and consistency of our products, and to the finest service possible. The diversity of our menu enables us to cater to a wide range of tastes and cravings. We are always open to any suggestions that could help us better serve you. And we always expedite your order with fast, free delivery.

Free Express Delivery

522-1234

Or fax your order to 522-5221

OPEN
Sunday–Thursday 11a.m.–2a.m.
Friday–Saturday 11a.m.–4a.m.

CATERING
Box Lunches • Coffees • Parties • Meetings • Groups

PAYMENT OPTIONS
Cash • Check • Visa • Master Card

We will be glad to accept your local check with proper I.D. and two phone numbers. There is a fifty cent (.50) charge for each check or credit card transaction. There is also a $20.00 returned check charge—no exceptions.

---

715 17TH STREET, KNOXVILLE, TN 37916
Cumberland Avenue at 17th Street (In the lower level beneath Threds)

SPECIALTY SANDWICHES

PHILLY STEAK & CHEESE
Three-flavored sirloin steak, grilled with bell peppers & onions, topped with provolone cheese, and served in a french roll with a side of lettuce and tomato. $5.49

GYRO (HERO)
Thin slices of beef and lamb, lettuce, tomatoes and onions, served in a warm gyro loaf with garlic cucumber sauce. $3.95

STEAK IN A SACK
Grilled sirloin steak with onions, seasoned to perfection, and served with A-1 sauce, lettuce and tomato on the side. $5.49

VEGGIE PITA
A variety of garden fresh vegetables. Lettuce, tomatoes, onions, spinach, bell peppers, cucumbers, black olives and carrots. served in a pita bread with balsamic oil and vinegar **V** $3.50

FAJITAS (STEAK OR CHICKEN)
Your choice of steak or chicken grilled with bell peppers, onions, herbs and spices, topped with spicy cheese and stuffed in a pita bread. Served with a side of lettuce, tomato, sour cream and guacamole. $4.99

CHICKEN SALAD
Made from scratch, topped with provolone cheese, and served on a croissant with a side of tomatoes and sprouts. $5.49

HEALTHY CLUB
Sliced ham, turkey, bacon, swiss and american cheeses piled high with lettuce and tomato on whole wheat slices. With mayo and mustard on the side. $4.95

THE ITALIAN SUB
Ham, salami, pepperoni, swiss and provolone cheeses, all stuffed in a french roll and topped with lettuce, tomatoes, onions, herbs and spices. $4.50

MEATBALL SANDWICH
Italian meatballs stuffed in a sub roll with marinara sauce and melted cheese. $5.49

REUBEN
Lean corned beef, sauerkraut, swiss cheese and dressing served on a pumpernickel bread with a pickle on the side. $4.49

LITE TURKEY
Served hot or cold. Gourmet turkey breast on a french roll with lettuce, tomato, mayo and mustard on the side. $3.99
Add cheese $.50

ROAST BEEF (HOT OR COLD)
Roast beef slices in a french roll with lettuce, tomato and onions on the side. $3.95
Add cheese $.50

HAM & CHEESE
Served hot or cold. Lean ham with your choice of american, swiss, or provolone cheese served in a french roll with sides of lettuce, tomato, onions, mustard and mayo. $4.49

SALADS

ROMA SALAD
A bed of mixed greens with tomatoes, cucumbers and carrots topped with croutons and served with garlic bread sticks. **V** $3.50

LA PETTITE SALAD
A smaller version of the Roma salad for the smaller appetite. **V** $1.75

CHEF SALAD
Ham, turkey, bacon, mozzarella and cheddar cheeses on a bed of mixed greens with tomatoes, cucumbers and carrots $5.99

CAESAR SALAD
Romaine lettuce and croutons with Caesar dressing **V** $3.50

GRILLED CHICKEN SALAD
Grilled chicken breast strips seasoned lightly a top our Roma salad. $5.99

FRIED CHICKEN SALAD
Lightedly breaded chicken breast filets deep fried then chopped a top our Roma Salad. $5.99

CHICKEN CAESAR SALAD
Grilled chicken breast strips atop our Caesar salad garnished with tomatoes, olives, and mild krino peppers. $5.99

GREEK SALAD
Mixed greens with feta cheese, black olives, krino peppers, red onions. tomatoes and anchovies with balsamic oil and vinegar **V** $5.99

HUMMUS
Garlic and chick pea dip served with olives, peppers and pita bread. **V** $3.95

Dressings
Lite Ranch, Honey Mustard, Lite Italian, Bleu Cheese, Caesar, Thousand Island, Balsamic Vinegar and Oil, and Cholesterol and FAT FREE Honey French

V = Vegetarian   **LF** = Low Fat

BELA ROMA PIZZA

Your Choice—Deep Dish or Regular Crust

LOW FAT CHEESE	Medium - 12"	DEEP DISH PIZZA
Available Upon Request	Large - 15"	For Large, Add **$1.50** For Medium, Add **$1.00**

SIGNATURE GOURMET PIZZAS

SEAFOOD PIZZA

Shrimp and crabmeat in a light creamy white sauce with a secret seasoning and topped with parmesan, jack and mozzarella cheeses.

Large $12.99
Medium $9.49

BBQ CHICKEN PIZZA

Grilled bbq chicken breast with onions, jack and gouda cheeses and bbq sauce.

Large $12.99
Medium $9.49

VEGETABLE PIZZA

Broccoli, Zucchini squash, onions, mushrooms, artichokes and mozzarella and jack cheeses. **V**

Large $10.99
Medium $7.99

JAMAICAN PEPPERED BEEF PIZZA

Lean ground beef, onions, spices, mozzarella and hot pepper cheese.

Large $10.99
Medium $7.99

ROMA DELUXE CHEESE PIZZA

In a white sauce with hot peppered cheese, mozzarella, provolone and jack cheese. **V**

Large $9.99
Medium $7.99

VENUS PIZZA

Vine ripened tomatoes, fresh basil, garlic and oregano with mozzarella cheese. **V/LF**

Large $9.99
Medium $6.99

HOT CHICKEN PIZZA

Select chicken breast marinated in a blend of spicy herbs topped with green onions, spinach, carrots and mozzarella and peppered cheeses.

Large $11.99
Medium $8.99

FETA SPINACH PIZZA

Spinach, feta cheese, mozzarella cheese, sundried tomatoes, onions and spices. **V**

Large $11.95
Medium $8.95

GARDEN PESTO PIZZA

Broccoli, carrots, mushrooms, tomatoes, basil pesto, parmesan and mozzarella cheeses. **V**

Large $11.00
Medium $9.00

MEATBALL PIE

Sliced Italian meatballs with mozzarella cheese.

Large $9.95
Medium $7.99

ROMA DELUXE PIZZA

Your choice of any 8 toppings

	Medium	Large
Regular	$9.50	$13.00
Gourmet	$12.00	$15.00
1/2 & 1/2	$10.75	$14.50

SPINACH ARTICHOKE PIZZA

Spinach and artichoke in a light, creamy white sauce, topped with provolone and mozzarella. **V**

Large $11.99
Medium $8.99

CREATE YOUR OWN PIZZA

	Cheese Pizza	Regular Items	Gourmet Items
Medium	$5.99	$.75	$1.00
Large	$7.99	$1.00	$1.50

BELAROMA'S POOR MAN'S PIZZA

When you have scraped up all your change and you only have a couple of bucks, don't worry. Just come on down to BelaRoma's and we'll feed you. Get a medium pizza with one regular topping for just **$3.99**. You can't take it with you, and we won't deliver it. But you're more than welcome to eat it here.

TOPPINGS

Regular Items

Cheese • Mushrooms • Bell pepper
Tomatoes • Black olives • Jalapenos • Bacon
Beef • Ham • Pepperoni • Onions • Anchovies
Green olives • Italian sausage
Banana peppers

Gourmet Items

Artichokes • Pesto • Genoa salami
Smoked gouda • Canadian bacon
Sun dried tomatoes • Pineapple • Broccoli
Feta cheese • Fresh spinach • Shrimp

CALZONES

MEAT CALZONE

Ham, pepperoni, bell peppers and onions with ricotta and mozarella cheeses. Marinara sauce served on the side. $5.95

VEGGIEZONE

Spinach, mushrooms, tomatoes, artichokes and onions with ricotta and mozzarella cheeses. Marinara sauce served on the side. **V** $5.95

CHICKEN PARMESAN CALZONE

Tender fried chicken, garlic, herbs & spices with fresh parmesan and mozzarella cheeses. $6.50

MEATBALL CALZONE

Meatball slices with special spices served with ricotta and mozzarella cheeses. ..$5.95

CHEESE CALZONE

Mozzarella and ricotta cheeses with marinara sauce... ....$4.00

PASTA

SPAGHETTI

Thin Spaghetti with our own marinara sauce and parmesan cheese served with garlic bread. $4.79

With chicken or meatballs $5.99

LASAGNA

Traditional old world style lasagna with marinara and parmesan cheese. Served with garlic bread

Meat $5.99

FIVE CHEESE LASAGNA

Our five cheese lasagna is low in fat only 6 grams per serving. Served with hot garlic bread. $5.99

RAVIOLI

Tender stuffed pasta covered with marinara sauce and served with hot garlic bread. Meat or Cheese **V** $5.99

ALFREDO

A mixed blend of spinach and egg fettucini made from scratch with fresh sweet basil, oregano, swiss cheese and herbs and spices in a creamy alfredo sauce. Served with garlic bread sticks. $4.95

SEAFOOD ALFREDO

Shrimp and crab meat in a creamy alfredo sauce made from scratch with fresh sweet basil, oregano, swiss cheese and herbs and spices. Served with garlic bread sticks. $6.49

CHICKEN ALFREDO

Grilled chicken breast strips in our creamy alfredo sauce. Served with garlic bread sticks. $6.49

PRIMAVERA

Zucchini squash, broccoli, carrots, mushrooms, peppers and onions in our creamy alfredo sauce. Served with garlic bread sticks. **V/LF** $5.99

BURGERS

THE BELAROMA BURGER

100% lean ground beef cooked to perfection with all the trimmings. Served with lettuce, tomato, onion, mustard, ketchup and mayo all on the side. $2.49

MUSHROOM SWISS BURGER

The BelaRoma Burger with mushrooms and swiss cheese, served with all the trimmings. $3.49

Add bacon   ....$.50

BACON SWISS BURGER

The BelaRoma Burger with bacon and swiss cheese, served with all the trimmings. .$3.49

Add mushrooms . ...$.50

GARDEN BURGER

The original GardenBurger made with whole grains, nuts and mushrooms. Served with lettuce, onion, tomato and pickle with our chutney yogurt sauce on the side. **V** .$4.95

WESTERN BURGER

The BelaRoma Burger with southwestern flair. Served with chili, onions and cheddar cheese. All the trimmings come on the side. $4.95

APPETIZERS & SIDES

LOADED POTATO SKINS
Crispy potato skins loaded with cheddar and mozzarella cheeses, bacon and topped with chives served with sour cream on the side. $4.99

FRENCH FRIES
Skin on fries seasoned with our own special spices. **V**..................$1.50

LOADED FRIES
Our fries topped with bacon and chives and served with sour cream and melted cheese on the side. $3.00

CHEESE FRIES
Our seasoned fries served covered in melted cheese. **V** $2.00

BEER BATTERED MUSHROOMS
Deep fried battered mushrooms served with honey mustard sauce. **V** $2.75

BEER BATTERED ONION RINGS
You gotta try these! **V** $3.25

ARMADILLO EGGS
Not really, they're just jalapeno peppers stuffed with cream cheese or cheddar cheese, then battered and deep fried. Served with honey mustard. **V** $3.99

BAKED POTATO
Baked Idaho Potato $1.49.**V**
Get it loaded $2.49.

BUFFALO WINGS
BelaRoma's nearly famous buffalo wings served with celery, hot or mild sauce, and your choice of bleu cheese, ranch, or honey mustard sauce.
10 for $3.99
20 for $7.49

NACHOS & CHEESE
Nacho chips served with cheese and sour cream. **V** $2.99

CHEESE BREAD STICKS
Garlic bread sticks topped with lots of mixed cheeses. Seved with a side of marinara sauce. **V** $3.99

BREAD STICKS
Garlic bread sticks served with marinara sauce. **V** $1.99

CHEESE STICKS
Mozzerella cheese sticks served with marinara sauce. **V** $3.75

CHIPS
By the bag. Choose from a variety of flavors. **V**.. ....$.99 each

CHILI OR VEGETARIAN CHILI
Hearty homemade chili with ground beef, beans, olive oil, herbs and spices. Vegetarian chili is meatless, but with cracked wheat. Each bowl is served with cheese, onions and crackers. **V** $2.95

FRESH CHICKEN SANDWICHES

MESQUITE CHICKEN SANDWICH
A plump chicken breast grilled to perfection then served with lettuce, tomato and mayo on the side. $4.99

CAJUN CHICKEN SANDWICH
A plump chicken breast grilled to perfection with rich cajun spices then served with lettuce, tomato and red onion.........$4.99

BBQ CHICKEN SANDWICH
A plump chicken breast grilled to perfection with bbq sauce then served with lettuce, tomato and red onion. $4.99

CHICKEN QUESEDILLAS
Chicken strips grilled with peppers, onions and mushrooms then served with lettuce, tomato and sour cream in a flour tortilla. $5.99

CHICKEN TENDERS BASKET
Chicken tenders fried golden brown and served with our seasoned fries. Served with honey mustard sauce on the side. $5.99

CHICKEN TENDER SANDWICH
Chicken breast filets lightly breaded then deep fried golden brown. Topped with hot pepper cheese and all the trimimngs on the side............................$4.99

BUFFALO TENDER SANDWICH
Chicken breast filets light breaded then deep friend golden brown, dipped in our special wing sauce. Topped with hot pepper cheese and served with ranch or blue cheese dressing. $5.49

BEVERAGES

Coke	$.95
Diet Coke	$.95
Mellow Yellow	$.95
Dr Pepper	$.95
Iced Tea	$.95
Water or ice cup	$.25
Mountain Valley water, 1 litre	$1.29
2-litre Coke	$1.99
Fresh lemonade	$.95

Beer
(No Beer Delivery)

	EACH	BUCKET(6)
Rolling Rock	$2.00	$8.75
Budweiser	$2.00	$8.75
Bud Light	$2.00	$8.75
Miller Lite	$2.00	$8.75
Michelob Light	$2.00	$8.75
Heineken	$2.50	$11.25
Samuel Adams	$2.50	$11.25

DESSERTS

Chocolate Suicide Cake	$3.50
Apple pie	$2.00
French silk pie	$2.25
Vanilla ice cream	$1.35
Gourmet cookies ...$.50 ea. ...$5.50 dz.	

(chocolate chip, white chocolate macadamia nut)

Brownie supreme with lots of ice cream and fudge	$3.50
Carrot cake	$2.25
Cheese cake	$2.25
Brownies	$1.35 ea.

Toppings

Strawberry, Chocolate	$.50
Hot Fudge	$.60

DRUG STORE

Bayer Aspirin 24 tablets
Nuprin 24 tablets
Tylenol 24 tablets
Rolaids 12 tablets
Alka Seltzer 12 tablet box
Alka Seltzer Plus 12-tablet box
Robitussin DM 4 oz. bottle
Gillette Razors 3 pk.
Band-Aids 10, 3/4" strips
No-Doz 16 tablets
Crest Toothpaste 2.7 oz.
Tampons regular, box of 8
Children's Bayer 36 tablets
Midol max. strength, 8 tablets
Goody's Powders 6 pieces
Pepto Bismol 4 oz. bottle
Toilet Tissue 1 roll

Nyquil 6 oz. bottle
Playing Cards Aviator
Shaving Cream 11 oz. can
Visine regular, 1/2 oz.
Deodorant Sure, 1.7 oz.
Tooth Brush Oral-B
Condoms lubricated, 3 pk.
Knoxville News Sentinel daily or Sunday

Tobacco Products

Marlboro	Mkt Price
Marlboro Mediums	Mkt Price
Marlboro Lights	Mkt Price
Camel, Camel Lights	Mkt Price
Disposable lighters	$1.99
Cigarette papers	$2.49
Cigarette tobacco, pouch	$2.99

FREE EXPRESS DELIVERY

Yes, we do deliver, and we will be happy to bring you any of the non-food items that we carry in our drug store. However, without a food order, a $10 minimum order is required for delivery.

ITS THE LAW: You MUST be 21 to purchase alcohol products! You MUST be 18 to purchase tobacco products!

Collaborative Activity 2.7

This next set of three activities is your opportunity to work with classmates to conduct a genre analysis of a genre of your own choosing. First, collect and review samples of the genre. Then list everything your group can think of that you might know about the scene in which this genre is used—where it is used and the beliefs, values, assumptions, and objectives of the people who use it. (For guidelines about how to study and describe a scene, refer back to Box 1.2, pp. 44–45.) Then list everything your group knows about the situation of the genre, using the questions on situation in Box 2.1, Step 2. What do you know about the setting, subject, participants, and purposes of the genre?

Writing Activity 2.7

For this next step, work individually before sharing your results with your group so that you learn how many patterns in the genre you can in fact see on your own. Reread samples of the genre, looking for patterns in the genre's features. For this activity, work your way methodically through the list of features in Box 2.1 Step 3, from content through diction. List any patterns you see in these samples. Be prepared to share your results with others in your group.

Collaborative Activity 2.8

Share your list of genre patterns with the group, adding to your list the patterns others saw that you did not. After compiling a group list, your final task is to analyze what the patterns you noticed might tell you about the situation and scene in which the genre is used. Again for this activity, your group should work methodically, writing down answers for each of the questions we suggest for analysis in Box 2.1, Step 4: From what the participants have to know through what attitude is implied. Remember, you are working to discover what might be significant about these patterns, what they might reveal to you about what the genre, situation, and scene is about and what people within it are trying to do. There is not only one good answer to these questions. Different analysts will discover different things, so explore all the different interpretations your group members suggest. Be prepared to share your discoveries with your teacher and other groups.

Writing Activity 2.8

Choose a genre that you would like to know something about, perhaps one that is related to your academic major or your future profession or one you encounter in your job, in volunteer work, or in other parts of your life outside of school. Then perform a genre analysis on it, following the guidelines and questions in the preceding activities and Box 2.1 (pp. 93–94). In the past, our students have chosen such genres as the lab report, the resumé, the psychology research paper, the graduate school writing sample, the sweepstakes letter, the wedding invitation, the personal ad, the petition, and the school yearbook. In fact, this chapter's analysis of the Patient Medical History Form is based on the analysis work of one of our students who was preparing to be a doctor. If you want to analyze a professional genre but are uncertain about what genres are used in your academic major or future profession, we encourage you to ask a professor or a graduate teaching assistant, an upper-division student in the major, or a professional in that field.

Whatever genre you choose, make sure to keep track of your findings—either in your class journal or notebook. You might need to refer to these notes later, when you translate your analysis into writing for Writing Project 2.1. For now, though, concentrate on trying to learn as much as you can about your genre. When your research is complete, be prepared to report and discuss your findings with your teacher and classmates.

When you learn to perform a genre analysis, you are not just learning how to read a piece of writing. You are also learning how to read people's activities and behaviors within a scene. By doing the kind of genre analysis you practiced in the preceding activities, you are, in a way, uncovering the script of a scene; you are using the language of a scene to examine how people interact, think, and communicate within it. You are, in short, reading a scene through its patterns of writing.

Turning Reading into Writing

Now that you have practiced doing genre analysis, how can you use what you know about genre to make more effective writing choices? Chapter 3 explores this key question fully. Identifying a genre's patterns and analyzing what they mean does not give writers a ready-made syllabus or complaint letter. Just as readers bring their own knowledge and beliefs to their reading and can choose to resist the roles defined for them by genres, writers also do more than just copy these patterns. Unlike a script for a play, where actors have all their lines written and need to choose only how to perform those lines, a genre's pattern or "script" does not tell us, as writers, exactly what actions to take, what roles to perform, or what sentences and words to use. What it does give us is a *general* sense of the scene and situation and some general rhetorical patterns, and we can use this knowledge of the scene and people's rhetorical behaviors within it to make more effective and informed writing choices.

Box 2.1 Guidelines for Analyzing Genres

1. Collect Samples of the Genre

If you are studying a genre that is fairly public, such as wedding announcements, you can look at samples from various newspapers. You can also locate samples of a genre in textbooks and manuals about the genre, as we did with the complaint letters. If you are studying a less public genre, such as the Patient Medical History Form, you might have to visit several doctors' offices to collect samples. If you are unsure where to find samples, use our strategies for observing scenes in Chapter 1 (p. 25) to ask a user of that genre for assistance. Try to gather samples from more than one place (for example, wedding announcements from different newspapers or medical history forms from different doctors' offices) so that you get a more accurate picture of the complexity of the genre. The more samples of the genre you collect, the more easily you will be able to notice patterns within the genre.

2. Identify the Scene and Describe the Situation in Which the Genre Is Used

Following the guidelines in Box 1.2, Step 1 (p. 40), try to identify the larger scene in which the genre is used. Seek answers to questions about the genre's situation. Consider:

- **Setting:** Where does the genre appear? How and when is it transmitted and used? With what other genres does this genre interact?
- **Subject:** What topics, issues, ideas, questions, etc. does the genre address? When people use this genre, what is it that they are interacting about?
- **Participants:** Who uses the genre?
  Writers: Who writes the texts in this genre? Are multiple writers possible? What roles do they perform? What characteristics must writers of this genre possess? Under what circumstances do writers write the genre (e.g., in teams, on a computer, in a rush)?
  Readers: Who reads the texts in this genre? Is there more than one type of reader for this genre? What roles do they perform? What characteristics must readers of this genre possess? Under what circumstances do readers read the genre (e.g., at their leisure, on the run, in waiting rooms)?
- **Purposes:** Why do writers write this genre and why do readers read it? What purposes does the genre fulfill for the people who use it?

(continued on next page)

3. Identify and Describe Patterns in the Genre's Features

What recurrent features do the samples share? For example:

- What **content** is typically included? What excluded? How is the content treated? What sorts of examples are used? What counts as evidence (personal testimony, facts, etc.)?
- What **rhetorical appeals** are used? What appeals to logos, pathos, and ethos appear?
- How are texts in the genres **structured**? What are their parts, and how are they organized?
- In what **format** are texts of this genre presented? What layout or appearance is common? How long is a typical text in this genre?
- What types of **sentences** do texts in the genre typically use? How long are they? Are they simple or complex, passive or active? Are the sentences varied? Do they share a certain style?
- What **diction** (types of words) is most common? Is a type of jargon used? Is slang used? How would you describe the writer's voice?

4. Analyze What These Patterns Reveal about the Situation and Scene

What do these rhetorical patterns reveal about the genre, its situation, and the scene in which it is used? Why are these patterns significant? What can you learn about the actions being performed through the genre by observing its language patterns? What arguments can you make about these patterns? As you consider these questions, focus on the following:

- What do participants have to know or believe to understand or appreciate the genre?
- Who is invited into the genre, and who is excluded?
- What roles for writers and readers does it encourage or discourage?
- What values, beliefs, goals, and assumptions are revealed through the genre's patterns?
- How is the subject of the genre treated? What content is considered most important? What content (topics or details) is ignored?
- What actions does the genre help make possible? What actions does the genre make difficult?
- What attitude toward readers is implied in the genre? What attitude toward the world is implied in it?

Rather than staring at a blank page or screen and guessing about how to begin writing or what to write about, you can turn to your knowledge of genres. Writing becomes choosing, not guessing. By analyzing any given genre, for example, you can make choices regarding major rhetorical elements:

Your purpose as writer

Knowing what genres are available in a given scene and how and why they are used will help you decide which one can best accomplish your purpose in writing. On the other hand, if you are *assigned* a genre to write and are not sure about your purpose for writing it, studying the genre can show you the purposes other writers have pursued with that genre. In either case, purpose and genre are interrelated: Your purpose for writing affects your choice of genre and your choice of genre affects your purpose.

Your role as a writer

Your role as a writer has to do with the kind of persona you choose to present in order to be persuasive as a speaker or writer. For example, should you be aggressive, soft-spoken, excited, subdued, or confident? The persona you choose will have a great deal to do with how effectively you write within a specific scene, as we saw in the example of the complaint letter. The patterns of behavior and communication within a genre will help you choose the role within that scene that will be the most appropriate in fulfilling your purpose.

Your readers

Certain genres are geared toward certain readers (the syllabus is geared toward students, the resumé toward an employer). By analyzing the genre, you learn something about your readers even though they may not be physically present. What do readers *expect* from the genre? For instance, do they expect to be treated with respect? Do they expect you to assume authority? Do they expect to laugh or cry or both? Do they expect you to be detailed, technical, and complicated, or do they expect simple and direct communication? Knowing something about your readers as revealed through the genre will help you "see" your audience, much like we began to "see" the audience during our analysis of the complaint letter. Such knowledge will help you decide what genre most suits your purpose.

Your subject matter

Any given subject can be treated in different ways depending on the genre used. A writer who analyzes the genres first is in a better position to decide which genre to write and then how to treat the subject matter. Using your knowledge of these genres, contemplate your subject matter: How should you introduce it? Should you treat it objectively or personally? Do you need to explain it in detail or is such explanation unnecessary? Should you present it logically or emotionally or sarcastically, etc.? Do you need to provide examples? Should you be descriptive, argumentative, or both? Should you present both sides of the subject? Do you need to quote experts on the subject or can you depend on your own authority? And so on. Knowledge of the genre will help you make some of these decisions about what and how to write.

Your format and organization

On a very obvious level, knowledge of a genre's patterns will help you decide how to format your writing. A resumé, for example, is formatted differently from a complaint letter. Knowing this, you begin to conceptualize the appearance of your text so that what may have begun as a blank page or screen suddenly has a shape. You can decide if you should present your content in the form of tables and charts, graphics, lists, prose, or poetry. The structural features of a genre will help you decide not only how to format the physical appearance of your writing; they will also help you decide how to present and organize your ideas. For example, by learning the patterns of a genre, you can decide what to mention first, second, third, and so on. You can learn whether the main ideas are stated at the beginning or at the end, whether to move from generalities to particularities or from particularities to generalities. You can also decide what kinds of transitions, if any, to use between different sections of the text. In short, not only will your genre knowledge help you approach your subject matter, but it will also help you present your subject matter in certain ways.

Your sentences and word choices

Having read samples of your genre should have given you a sense of the typical style used in that situation, a feel for what texts in that genre sound like. You can imitate that style, trying to make your text sound like the ones you studied. As you revise your draft and take a more explicit and conscious approach, knowing something about the genre's sentence and diction patterns will help you decide, for instance, whether to use active or passive sentences. It will also help you decide how long your sentences should be and what kind of complexity and variation is expected. In the resumé, for example, sentences often begin with a verb rather than a subject and need to be consistent ("Managed the sales department," "Served as liaison between employer and employees"). In other genres, of course, different sentence styles are preferred. The same applies to word choices. In scientific research articles, for example, the people being studied are often referred to as "subjects" while the pronoun "you" appears frequently in business letters. By looking at the patterns in word choice within a genre, you will be able to make more effective decisions about what words to use and why.

What we have just presented is meant only as a set of guidelines for using your knowledge of a genre to make more effective writing choices within that genre. There is no exact formula. The more you practice genre analysis, the more skillful you will become at reading genre scenes and situations. The better you are able to read and understand the patterns of a genre, the better you will become at knowing what purpose these patterns serve and how to make use of them in your writing. The next chapter will expand on this initial list and help you develop strategies for turning your reading of a genre into your writing of a genre.

Writing Activity 2.9

Review the genre you analyzed collaboratively in the last sets of activities or the genre of your choice in Writing Activity 2.8 (p. 91), including the samples you collected, your notes, and your conclusions. Based on your analysis, describe what a writer needs to understand about the scene and situation in order to write that genre. Use our suggested guidelines in Box 2.1 (pp. 93–94) and be as specific as you can. As a writer of this genre, what choices would you make regarding your role as writer, your readers, your subject matter, your format and structure, and your sentences and word choices? Record your responses and be prepared to share them with your teacher and classmates. Think of this activity as an exercise in prewriting, planning, and invention. You will be able to use this work as you proceed through the next chapter.

Writing Projects

Writing Project 2.1

To demonstrate to your teacher and classmates your understanding of genre analysis and to share your perspective on a particular genre, write your own genre analysis paper, either of the genre which you studied in Collaborative Activities 2.7 and 2.8 (p. 91) or of the genre you chose to study in Writing Activity 2.8 (p. 91). Much of this chapter has been teaching you how to perform a genre analysis. Now you have a chance to write a paper based on that analysis (we recommend you review the sample genre analysis paper and our discussion of it in this chapter). For this assignment, write a paper (4 to 5 pages) for your instructor and class-mates that makes a claim about what the genre you have chosen tells us about the people who use it and the scene in which it is used. Be sure that your paper makes a claim and has a controlling idea about what you think the genre reveals about some aspect of the situation or scene: How people behave, their goals and beliefs, or the actions they perform. (You might wish to review the description of control-ling idea and how the sample genre analysis paper used its controlling idea, pp. 73–74.) Your controlling idea will also need to be supported by specific examples and explanations taken from your analysis of the genre.

Writing Project 2.2

Write a complaint letter of your own. First, select a subject (an actual problem you have had with a product or service). Then decide on an audience (someone who can address your problem, perhaps researching the name of the head of Customer Service for a specific company or the boss of someone whose service was inade-quate—checking a company's Web site is a good starting place for researching such information). Drawing on the analysis of the complaint letter and the sam-ples in this chapter, write your own complaint letter. Finally, write a cover memo (a brief, straightforward description) addressed to your teacher that explains what choices you had to make about such things as your letter's content, appeals, struc-ture, format, sentences, and words and how your choices reflected your particular situation and scene.

Writing Project 2.3

As we mentioned earlier in the chapter, there are various ways to register complaints, the genre of the business complaint letter being one of them. Imagine a situation in which you wanted to register a complaint within the scene of your college or university, say about the availability of parking on campus or the cost of tuition or the lack of funding for student activities, etc. First identify an actual complaint and then decide to whom and where to address the complaint. Then choose a genre that would best accomplish your purpose for your situation and compose that genre. When you are finished, submit the genre along with a cover memo to your teacher explaining why you chose the genre you did and how it is an effective response given the scene and your purpose, audience, and subject.

Using Genres to Help You Write

3

For many people writing is a mysterious and often difficult process. People who usually have no trouble talking to others in groups or individually sometimes feel stumped when they are asked to write. You might be one of them. If so, what do you think makes writing so difficult?

For many, the difficulty is not just with the "skills" of writing—such as grammar, punctuation, and spelling conventions—critical as these are. Rather, the difficulty lies in knowing what to write about and how to write it, when to begin and how, what sort of tone and style to use, when to explain ideas and why, when to move from one part to the next, and so on. There is no exact formula you can memorize to help you make these choices. And so many inexperienced writers feel as though they are wandering in the dark when they write. They recall the popular image of the writer sitting alone with a piece of paper or in front of the computer, writing away effortlessly, and they feel as though they can never live up to that image.

Part of the reason writers can never live up to this image is that this image is, by and large, a myth. Very few, if any, writers write completely on their own—that is, without drawing on any other writers or readers. Just as few write without a deep understanding of the scene in which they are writing. In fact, writers rarely start from scratch. Rather, they start with some kind of purpose related to a scene they are in, and then they choose a genre to help them achieve this purpose. Depending on the scene and situation, they may want to report on an experiment, complain about a faulty product, investigate a human behavior, celebrate their friends, express themselves, pass on office information, plan a course, and so on. With those purposes in mind, they may decide to or be asked to write a lab report, a complaint letter, a research paper in psychology, a toast, a novel, a sonnet, a memo, a syllabus, and so on. By making a choice, as we have been discussing in the first two chapters, writers realize they are in a scene that is already crowded with patterns of communication, behavior, and action—patterns that in turn affect the ways they present and achieve their purposes. *Good writers use patterns to make informed and meaningful decisions about how and what to write*—about the structure and tone they should use, about the role they should assume as writers, about how they should relate to their readers, about what they should include and what they should exclude. As we saw in Chapter 2, genre knowledge demystifies writing, making writing very much like playing a part in an already existing scene with a script or map in hand.

In this chapter, we will explore the components of writing:

* Planning or inventing
* Drafting
* Revising
* Presenting

Then we will describe various writing processes that writers use when writing different genres in different scenes and situations and invite you to practice them. By the end of this chapter, you should have at your disposal various strategies you can use in order to make more effective writing choices within different scenes of writing. You will have a chance to further practice using these strategies in Parts II and III of this book.

The Roles of Genres in Writing Processes

Genres not only adapt to and shape our *purposes* for writing; genres (and the situations and scenes they participate in) also guide our writing *processes*. Sometimes people talk about "the writing process" as if there were only one way to write, or at least only one "good" way to write. *In fact, just as there are many kinds of writing and many kinds of writing situations and scenes, there are many kinds of writing processes.* What writers do when they write varies depending on the scene, the situation, and the genre. Although each writer may have a favorite way of writing, writers must *choose* strategies depending on what they are trying to accomplish.

In some writing situations, the typical way of writing is so quick that you would barely notice that a process actually occurred. For example, when we write a grocery list, an observer would see us pick up a scratch pad and pen, jot some words down in rows, and our grocery list would appear to be done. The full process is a bit more elaborate than that observation would reveal, however. It begins Saturday morning when we ask our housemates—the people who share our scene—what they want from the grocery store; we generate part of a list that we then keep in our heads until we have the opportunity to write it down. It continues later that morning, after the first draft of our list has been written, when we check our coupons to see what particular brand we might want to add to our list. Even a quick writing process requires more planning and revising than it might at first appear.

Some writing situations call for much more elaborate writing processes. To write a scholarly article, for example, we may spend many months reading books and journal articles, writing notes, talking with academic colleagues, and even conducting independent, primary research before we are ready to draft very much. We may spend a week drafting a section of the article, pausing along the way to reread others' research or to go back and revise earlier paragraphs. Once we have a draft done, we may ask two or three colleagues to read it and tell us what they think of it, and then we could spend weeks more revising the draft in response to their comments. The writing process for an article does not even end at that point. After we submit the article to a journal, the journal's editor will probably send us still more readers' responses and suggestions for change, which we will need to consider as we revise yet again. By the time the journal article is published, our writing process has become very elaborate and involved.

The writing situations we probably think of most often call for writing processes somewhere between that of the grocery list and the journal article. Many writing situations lend themselves to spending some time coming up with ideas, some time drafting, and some time revising the draft before calling it done. Many writers of academic papers, for example, spend some time coming up with ideas, perhaps including some library research or study of textbooks, spend time drafting, and finally go over the paper a few times to improve it before turning it in to the teacher. Writers of business letters often think about what needs to be accomplished in the letter, write a first draft, then revise it until it seems all right. A writer of a letter to the editor might decide to write about an issue that has been troubling him or her, generate a draft, then fine-tune it until it is time to put it in the mail.

Writing Activity 3.1

Think of a genre you already feel comfortable writing (perhaps e-mail messages, personal letters, class notes, research papers, Web sites, lab reports, or letters of application). Describe how you go about writing that genre. As you share your observations with the class, compare the different ways of writing different genres.

ANTICIPATING THE PROCESSES BEHIND DIFFERENT GENRES

Since writing processes differ for different genres, you might, when you begin to write something new, want to ask yourself: What is the writing scene and situation behind this kind of writing and how will they affect how I write it? Considering your scene and situation will lead you to more specific questions:

- How much time do I have to spend on this writing task?
- Is this the kind of text where I already know pretty much what I want to say, or will I need to gather a lot of information?
- Is this a text that could have results that would make a big difference in my life or that of someone else?
- Will the reader of this text fill in any gaps or ambiguities I might leave, or will the readers expect me to fill any potential holes?

The situation of a complaint letter, for example, requires responding quickly to whatever has caused your complaint; you need to complain about the bad product or service while the event is still fresh or the product still new. So you will not have much time to think about or craft your letter. Anticipating the process of the complaint letter, then, can encourage you to move quickly and direct you to the most important research you will need to do. Thinking about your audience will remind you that you need to learn the name and address of the appropriate person to whom to write, a task that might take some digging. Considering the kind of process that the writing task seems to require can save you time and effort, not to mention produce better results.

Particular genres tend to encourage or even demand particular ways of writing. One or more of the components of the writing process (see p. 100) may be emphasized or some may be combined. Grocery lists tend to encourage specific ways of planning or deciding what to say, called *inventing* (recalling from memory, asking housemates, checking refrigerators and cupboards, checking coupons, and for some people imagining moving around the grocery store). *Drafting* grocery lists tends to go along with *inventing* and *revising* them, as you keep adding to and changing a running list. Complaint letters, on the other hand, might require relatively little separate *invention* since the nature of the complaint is so clear in the writer's mind, but such letters might require careful *drafting* and *revising* to control tone since the writer is often angry or frustrated.

Once you become truly familiar with a particular genre, then, you also become familiar with a particular way of writing that

genre. You don't even have to stop and think about how to write a letter to a friend now, but you may recall yourself as a child asking your parent what to say after you had written "Dear Grandma, How are you? I am fine." You may also have a familiar process for writing academic papers. The ways you already have developed for inventing ideas to write about and for drafting and revising papers will probably benefit you as you write papers for other college contexts. Some academic genres in college, though, may call for writing processes that you are not so familiar with, so you will want to add new strategies. It also pays to become as flexible as possible in your writing processes, so you can handle any kinds of writing processes that seem to be appropriate. When you encounter new kinds of writing tasks in your life, both in college and after, one of the things you will want to learn is what kinds of writing processes that task calls for and learn whatever new strategies you need. In the rest of this chapter, we will help you develop such strategies.

Writing Activity 3.2

Can you remember a time when you learned how to write a new kind of text or piece of writing? If so, describe how you figured out what you needed to do. Could you learn about a new text the same way now? If not, why not? If so, how? If you can't remember such a time, think about a new writing task that you have encountered recently. How does it seem the same as what you've written before? How does it seem different?

THE DYNAMICS OF WRITING PROCESSES

We opened this chapter with a list of the parts of writing processes: planning or inventing, drafting, revising, and presenting. **Inventing**, or coming up with a plan and what you want to say, can include such hidden acts as thinking about a writing task, such visible acts as freewriting or keeping a journal, and such collaborative acts as group brainstorming or team research. **Drafting** can include composing titles in your head, writing down especially effective words and phrases or a section that will be combined with others, and, of course, writing a complete draft. **Revising**, too, includes a variety of actions, including changing specific words, moving sections around, deleting parts, or adding new material.

None of these parts of writing processes is really as distinct as this division makes it appear, though. They do overlap. When you add new material during revision, you are drafting anew, and while you draft you usually discover new ideas to include. Even while you are planning, you may well write down ideas that become part of a draft, and invention you do later in a project may well lead directly to new revision. Remember that inventing, drafting, and revising interact when you write, even though the rest of this chapter will discuss these activities separately.

Another part of what people do when they write is to prepare the text for others to see—to focus on what we in this book will call **presentation**. Presentation includes choosing *layout* features like columns or tables, a *medium* like handwritten or digitized, and other aspects of the *visual* appearance of the document. Presentation also includes *editing*—choosing a set of conventions or styles appropriate to the document. Therefore presentation includes correcting punctuation, spelling, and grammar when the text needs to follow the conventions of Standardized Edited English (SEE)—the name for the more formal written English of schools, workplaces, and government. Presentation includes following formatting conventions like those for citing research sources that we describe in Chapter 7. But presentation also includes adding frames and graphics to a Web page or emoticons, such as the sideways smiley face :) in an e-mail message to a friend.

Naming these parts of writing processes—inventing, drafting, revising, and presenting—describes what is common to writing acts. These names can disguise, however, the fact that writing processes differ for different scenes, for different situations, for different genres, and for different people. We might prefer to think, read, and talk our ideas out with others before we draft, for example; we might prefer to draft a whole text on the computer; we might prefer to have a trusted friend read and respond to a draft before we revise further. But we do not write that way every time. Think about the process of writing a grocery list, which most people would never write on a computer. When a business executive writes a memo, he or she tends to handwrite it as soon as the need for it occurs, read it over once and, unless it addresses a very sensitive subject, give it to a secretary to type and distribute. When you write a letter to a friend, you may do both your invention and your revision as you draft. After all, the situation of a friendly letter includes a reader predisposed to like what you write, a comfortable relationship between writer and reader, and a primary purpose of keeping that relationship strong—all features that usually make the writing task and the process of writing a letter more relaxed. A college application, on the other hand, involves unknown readers and a high-stakes situation, so you would likely go through many drafts and spend a lot of time deciding exactly what to write. Each different scene and genre can encourage quite a different writing process.

Collaborative Activity 3.1

In groups, compare your preferred writing processes to those of your classmates. Are there preferred processes many of you share? If so, what are they? Do any of those common processes come from writing the same genres (for example, did you share processes for writing school papers)? In what ways do people's preferred processes differ most? How much did those differences result from different kinds of writing tasks and genres? How much from individual personalities?

Inventing with Genres

Inventing is coming up with all the things you want to say in a text and all the ways you want to say them. As we have mentioned, inventing is not something a writer finishes completely before drafting; writers invent throughout the writing process. In many scenes and their situations, though, writers do some invention first in order to find a starting place for a writing project. In some writing scenes, inventing comes easily, especially when you are writing something that matters to you or something relatively simple—an impassioned letter to the editor or an e-mail message to a friend, for example. In other writing scenes, even ones that you care a great deal about, inventing is hard work. It helps to have learned how to use as many different invention strategies as possible—whether freewriting, brainstorming, outlining, talking with friends, or other invention strategies—so that you have a range of strategies to choose from and to try.

Paying attention to the genre being written can help a writer select an effective invention strategy. In fact, as you saw in Chapter 2, learning something about the genre is itself an invention strategy. A writer who knows how to recognize the rhetorical situation embedded within a genre will be better able to produce (invent) the kinds of information called for by the genre. Each genre includes specific kinds of information about the writer's rhetorical situation:

what kind of role or persona the writer should play;

how a writer should frame his or her purpose for writing;

who the readers are, what they expect, how best to relate to them;

how best to present and treat the subject matter.

Let's look at a simple example. A letter to a friend typically begins with a form of address ("Dear Sam") and ends with a closing ("Cheers"). Knowing this convention of the genre, a writer does not have to spend a great deal of time *deciding* how to begin; instead, he or she can immediately begin to choose an appropriate strategy that suits his or her purpose and relationship. For instance, a thoughtful writer considers what form of address would be most appropriate in each particular letter. Should I write "Darling Sam" and close with "Love"? Should I write "Dear Mr. Adams" and close with "Respectfully"? The exact form the greeting and closing will take depends on the scene of writing and its particular situation—on how the writer and reader relate to one another in that situation: as friends, lovers, business partners, colleagues, and so on; on the specific subject; and on the purposes that the writer and reader are trying to accomplish.

Inventing what the genre seems to call for can sometimes lead a writer into offering what readers expect more than what that writer thinks, so don't become too locked into a plan. It would not be honest to write "Love" in signing a letter just because the reader might expect it; the reader's feelings can still be spared and the writer can remain honest by signing "Cordially" or "Fondly" or "With affection." In the same way, it would not be honest to write that *Hamlet* is a great piece of literature if the writer has carefully and critically assessed it and decided that the work is overrated, even if the literary analysis assigned seems to expect the writer to praise the work. *As you use genre to guide invention, keep a careful eye on what you want to say in addition to what the genre and reader want you to say.*

INVENTION STRATEGIES FOR THE COMPLAINT LETTER

For a more specific example of how genre guides invention, consider again the genre of the complaint letter that we analyzed in Chapter 2. Complaint letters are written to companies or organizations to complain about a service or product that did not fulfill what it promised. For example, one might write a letter to an airline complaining about being bumped from a flight involuntarily, or write to an electronics manufacturer complaining about a cordless phone that has needed repeated repairs, or write to a concert promoter complaining about the way lawn seating was handled at a recent concert.

Knowing the genre of the complaint letter, you are in a better position to know what kinds of information you need to develop. For instance, you need to discover who your audience will be—that is, who is most capable of addressing your complaint. Then you need to gather all the specific details of the incident about which you are complaining—specific identification of the product or service, exactly what happened when, who was involved. You also need to decide what you want your audience to do in response to your letter, what redress you are seeking.

By knowing the genre of the complaint letter, you know what kind of invention you need to do, even if you don't yet know exactly what your letter will request. You also know something about the rhetorical strategies you will select. Knowing that successful complaint letters use a matter-of-fact tone and make direct statements of the problem and desired solution, you will know to begin your letter succinctly and directly, to treat the occurrence as a mistake rather than a willful attack, not to embellish with emotional outrage, and to treat the audience as a reasonable person who of course wishes to maintain your goodwill and the good reputation of the company. When you know the genre you are writing, you are well on your way to knowing how and what to invent for that text.

Below is the brainstorming list one person wrote when preparing to write a letter complaining about a recent airline trip. Notice how the writer, knowing the complaint letter genre, lists many of the kinds of information that complaint letters typically include.

—Atlanta to Asheville, #7805L, 9:05

—flight canceled cuz of mechanical problems

—new flight next morning (8:25)

—no hotel offered, left on our own

—all hotels booked cuz of weather probs

—terrible taxi ride across town, awful traffic jam, took an hour to get there, $50

—no restaurants open, ordered pizza

—slept only a few hours, then taxi back to airport

—everything expensive

—got to airport, found out airline had shuttled others to a hotel, but not us

—what do we want? Give us back our money. Give us free tickets. Apologize.

Notice that the writer's invention list includes details about the flight number as well as a chronology of events. At the end, the writer lists what she wants from the airline. Generating such an invention list comes more easily because the writer knows the genre of complaint letter and understands what kinds of information she needs to have at hand.

INVENTION STRATEGIES FOR OTHER GENRES

More complex and academic genres prompt invention in a similar way. Research-based genres by their nature require writers to conduct research in the library or on the Internet, a particular kind of invention. Personal narratives require the choice of a specific incident and details from personal

experiences to develop the writer's ideas, so invention from personal memory will be required. Literary analysis papers typically require response to a
set of readings, so invention will involve careful reading and interpretation
of other texts. Lab reports of course require laboratory experiments to be
conducted as part of invention, but they also encompass specific topics in
different sections, indicating what kinds of information and results need to
be discovered. Remember: Whenever you begin working on a writing project, first examine the genre you will be working in to see what kinds of
information, ideas, and approaches you will need to develop.

Writing Activity 3.3

Consider a writing assignment you have been given for this class, and write a paragraph or two describing what inventing you think will be necessary to complete
the assignment successfully. Use Box 3.1 below to guide your response. If your
teacher asks you to, share your response with others in your group, and discuss any
differences in your expectations. How can group members help each other with
the invention that seems most difficult?

Box 3.1   *Questions for Inventing*

1. What genre am I writing? What is the scene of writing behind this
   writing task? What is the nature of the situation I am writing in?
   What do I want to accomplish in this text?
2. What are the first thoughts that occur to me about what I want to
   say in this text?
3. What kinds of information do this writing task and genre ask for?
   What do I already know about this topic? What do I know I need to
   discover, learn, or develop?
4. How can I invent the kinds of information needed? How much of
   what I need can I develop from my own memory? From talking
   with others? From reading? From doing research?
5. Which invention strategies can help me develop the kinds of information I need for this genre? Try different strategies that seem
   most helpful to the particular writing task.
6. Am I still saying what I want to say? Check periodically to make
   sure you are writing something that is honest and true, not just
   convenient or expected.

In college and beyond, successful writers will have learned to use a variety of strategies so that they can adapt to any writing situation, even as they continue to use their favorite strategies whenever they are appropriate. For example, a student in one of our classes told of how she had to learn a new way of inventing when faced with writing a *longer* paper for one of her classes in her major. She had previously always invented *through* drafting, seeing what she had to say about a subject by writing a first draft, then doing research on specific gaps she had discovered. Faced with a 15-page paper, though, she could not draft the whole thing before she had done any research, so she had to learn how to anticipate what she would need to know.

As you become familiar with new genres, you will need to learn new writing processes, including new ways of inventing that you can combine with your preferred or customary ways of writing. Some people find commonly used invention strategies—especially the strategies of freewriting, brainstorming, and clustering—helpful in a variety of situations. (These strategies are described in more detail in Chapter 5, in case you do not yet know them.) Keep in mind, though, that no strategies apply in every situation. You will always need to adapt your inventing strategies to the particular scene and situation in which you are writing.

DISCOVERY DRAFTS AS AN INVENTION STRATEGY

Some writers, like our former student, discover what they think about a topic by writing about it, drafting full paragraphs and texts as a way of thinking through their ideas. However, drafting is one of the more time-consuming methods of invention. The draft written for invention is not a draft that becomes the final text. Instead, writers read what they have written to find the most promising ideas, the things they felt most passionate about, the trains of thought that might lead somewhere, and the gaps in what they have to say. Much if not all of that **discovery draft** will be discarded in favor of a newly written draft.

For example, writing a discovery draft of a complaint letter can allow you to vent your anger or frustration and discover what you want as recompense, but mailing such a draft is not likely to get you what you want. Below is the discovery draft written by our traveler stranded in Atlanta.

This draft was written before the brainstorming list we saw earlier in this chapter (p. 107), and the writer's purpose was to exhaust some of her anger before drafting the actual letter. Discovery drafting also allowed her to see what mattered most to her. After writing this draft, though, she threw it away and began on her invention list, separating what information would be useful and appropriate for the actual complaint letter from what she needed to write in her discovery draft.

Dear Whoever:

We have just had the most horrible experience flying on your airline. When we got to Atlanta, we were told that our flight was canceled, supposedly because of mechanical problems. Then we were told we couldn't get there until the next morning, and that we were on our own finding a hotel for the night. I was very upset. We spent a long time in baggage claim calling every hotel, but every single one was booked up. Finally, we begged one hotel person to suggest where we might be able to get a room, and she suggested the Marriott and gave us the number, so we called there and fortunately the nice person said they had a room. We got a taxi to get to the hotel, which was a long way from the airport, and then it got stuck in a terrible traffic jam so that we just sat there for ages. We were beat and exhausted, but the taxi driver didn't seem to know what he was doing so we were stuck in traffic forever. Finally, we got to the hotel, only to find that no restaurants were open that late and our only chance for any food was to order in pizza. It was food, but it tasted pretty awful. Finally, we fell into bed, got a couple hours sleep, and took a taxi back to the airport in time for our flight.

Imagine our anger when we heard from other passengers waiting there that they had been bused to a hotel near the airport by the airline. They had had all their expenses paid and were bused back in time for the plane. That wouldn't have been great, but at least it would have saved us all that aggravation and we probably would have gotten more sleep. We were furious. We asked the ticket agent why this happened and to pay us back for all our expenses, but she insisted we had to write to the airline to ask for what we so obviously deserved. At last, we got on the plane and made it to Asheville, no thanks to you or your airline.

We had a terrible experience because of you. We want you to reimburse us for all our expenses, plus give us free tickets to wherever we want to go. It doesn't make up for what we endured, but at least it's some recompense for what you put us through.

Sincerely,

Some writers make the mistake of writing a discovery draft but treating the result as a final draft. That is, they begin to write without doing any invention work, yet they expect the resulting text to serve as a finished draft rather than as an aid to invention. That kind of drafting is not an effective use of drafting for invention. Teachers often recognize it because the best idea turns up in the final paragraph. For important pieces of writing, drafting works as an invention strategy only if the writer intends to begin drafting anew once the discovery draft is done.

The exceptions are genres of writing that commonly merge drafting and invention: informal and less public genres—like letters to friends, casual e-mail messages, routine memoranda—or genres whose *purposes* are to discover what the writer thinks: journals and diaries, reading-response notebooks, even the genres of freewriting and brainstorming. Some teachers encourage such writing by asking for brief, in-class writings that will not be read for anything other than their initial ideas. Inventing and drafting at the same time is appropriate for these genres since that process suits the situations (the participants, the subject, the setting, and the purposes) of those genres.

Collaborative Activity 3.2

Discuss with a group your own use of invention strategies. When have you drafted as a means of inventing (appropriately and inappropriately)? What genres do you write that seem to call for drafting and inventing at the same time? What circumstances lead you to draft too quickly? What have been the results and consequences of drafting before inventing? What ways do you have of inventing that have worked for you? What ways used by your group seem most promising?

Drafting with Genres

Writers draft their texts differently in different scenes and for different situations and genres, just as they invent differently and, as we will see, revise differently. Drafting this chapter involved many days and even weeks of sitting in front of the computer, in addition to the time spent inventing and revising. Since this book is co-authored, drafting this chapter also involved later drafting, as each co-author read the first draft and contributed new sections. In contrast, drafting the grocery list required only a few minutes of writing things down. Drafting a job application form may take only several minutes in the employer's office. On essay exams, drafting is deliberately limited to a set time, place, and manner (handwritten rather than typed or word-processed). The scene of a complaint letter allows more time for drafting, yet it needs to be written soon after the event prompting the complaint in order to be most effective. Many writers, like our stranded traveler in the last example, draft an initial complaint letter in the heat of the moment and then write a second draft after their anger or frustration has cooled. (You will see her draft in the next section, when we will also see how she revised that draft.) Drafting varies in time, location, and manner, depending on the genre, the particular situation to which it is responding (who will be writing and reading it, what the subject is, the setting in which this interaction is taking place, and the purposes for the response), and the individual writer's preferences.

Since some genres, like essay examinations, can require particular methods of drafting, successful writers learn how to write under different circumstances. Writers tend to have favored ways and places to draft. One of us prefers drafting on a computer in the home study, with a cup of coffee nearby. Others prefer drafting on legal pads in coffee shops. Many writing situations, though, do not allow the luxury of choosing the manner and place of drafting. A manager may need to dictate a memo while standing at the typist's desk. A petition may need to be drafted collaboratively in someone's living room while a recorder copies down the group's composition onto scratch paper. A novelist may need to jot down the perfect title on a napkin in a diner. Flexibility again is an important goal for writers who wish to be able to write successfully in a range of genres.

To some extent, writers can prepare for different ways of drafting if the scene, situation, and genre are known ahead of time. If you know you are visiting a potential employer, for example, you know that a job application may need to be filled out. Knowing what the genre of job application is like, you can gather the kinds of information often asked for on applications (inventing) and write it down carefully, deciding on such issues as official titles of past jobs (drafting). You can even draft descriptions of job duties, in case they are needed, and draft career objectives and reasons for wanting the particular job with the particular company. Then the drafting required in the employer's office has a better chance of going smoothly. Similarly, if you know you are going to write an essay examination, you can study hard and anticipate the kinds of questions that might be asked (inventing), and you can practice composing good responses to those questions (drafting). You can prepare similarly to write an in-class theme for an English class, especially by doing as much invention as possible beforehand so that you can be ready to draft when you see the specific writing prompt.

Writing Activity 3.4

Write a paragraph describing how you deal with drafting under time pressure, as in essay examinations or in-class writings. What strategies have you used to try to draft effectively in such situations? What gives you the most difficulty? How might you prepare to draft more effectively?

Collaborative Activity 3.3

Share what you wrote for the previous activity with a group of classmates, looking for strategies that have worked for some people. As a group, write a few paragraphs for this textbook suggesting how writers can deal more effectively with time-pressured writing tasks. (If you wish to send your material to us in care of the publisher of this textbook, we will consider incorporating it in later editions.)

DRAFTING COLLABORATIVELY

While some genres like poetry and personal letters are most often written individually, other genres call for more collaborative drafting. Some scenes of writing, especially workplaces and scientific disciplines, often use multi-authored genres such as reports and research articles. Such collaborative writing projects may still involve individual drafting, if the writing team has decided to draft different sections separately first. For instance, for an assignment to write a business proposal, one group of students divided drafting duties based on the various sections of the proposal, with one student writing the background, another defining the problem, another laying out the plan, etc. Another student group chose to assign drafting roles based on their own interests and areas of expertise, with artistic students creating the graphics for the proposal and business students drafting the budget section, for example. These longer, more complex genres are well suited to such **collaborative models**, in which each writer contributes to the development of a single text.

In many ways, technology has changed the scene of collaboration, allowing writers who are separated in time and space to share drafts more easily. Writers can transmit files electronically, attaching a file to an e-mail message. They can also interact asynchronously (with time lapses in between) through e-mail messages and postings to Internet bulletin boards or newsgroups, or synchronously (in real time) in Internet chat rooms or MUDs or MOOs (places or "rooms" on the Internet where live, online chats occur). Students working on group projects may have conflicting work schedules or may not live on campus or near one another, and for them electronic collaboration can be extremely useful. It enables people from different locations to interact without having to meet fact to face—to meet instead in cyberspace.

Collaborative drafting, electronic or otherwise, requires some special strategies and carries its own difficulties and rewards. Perhaps most importantly, as we mentioned above, collaboration can build on the diverse knowledge and expertise and talents of the group members as well as their wide-ranging interests and particular strengths and talents. The diverse backgrounds of group members result in richer feedback during the drafting process and a more critical process of inquiry and response. With the input of several people, there is a better chance of catching inconsistencies and problems with reasoning. Finally, with shared responsibilities and writing tasks, working as a team also increases the confidence and morale of writers.

However, despite all of these advantages, you have no doubt worked as part of a group that did not function effectively. Perhaps members did not equally contribute to the writing project. Or maybe you ended up with an uncohesive document, with ideas that never really came together. There might have also been a breakdown in communication among group members or some sort of interpersonal conflict. It's no secret that drafting as a team can be a slow process at times, if people debate each word. The best strategy for collaborative drafting may be to generate as much text as possible first without censoring or editing, and then to revise that draft extensively. That way, the group might not get bogged down in local decisions before the larger structures and arguments have been determined. The following activities are designed to get you thinking about guidelines for effective collaboration, including collaborative invention as well as drafting.

Collaborative Activity 3.4

Imagine the following scenario. A new president will be joining your university next fall, and you have been assigned to a task force (along with three other students) to determine the most significant issues facing students. Your group is to prepare a report that prioritizes and ranks the top five issues as well as proposes guidelines that the new administration might put into practice.

After three heated meetings, the group is divided. Two of you argue for making rising tuitions the top-ranked issue, while the other two think parking should be the top-rated issue. The group can't even reach consensus on the top five issues, with individual lists focusing on issues as diverse as overcrowded residence halls, lack of adequate lighting on campus, inadequate advising, an outdated system of registering for classes, and inadequate dining hall services. The group is further divided on proposed solutions to these problems: For instance, some group members are in favor of building more residence halls to deal with overcrowding, but the others believe this would mean fewer parking spaces for students, overall.

Your group has reached a deadlock and will be unproductive as long as these conflicts go unresolved. Based on the above scenario, how would you respond? What strategies would you use to work through the deadlock? How would you begin to draft the report—as a group or by assigning individual roles? Be prepared to share your responses with the rest of the class.

Collaborative Activity 3.5

Since you are spending quite a bit of time working with each other and responding to each other's writing, work in groups to formulate a set of guidelines for group work. Consider your own experiences with collaboration—particularly peer group responses to drafts—both positive and negative. What factors led to some of the most productive feedback you've received on papers, and what factors led to less helpful feedback? What made the group interactions work effectively, or what could have been done to make these interactions more effective? What responsibilities should the individual have to his or her group members? What guidelines are needed to ensure that the group functions well and acts efficiently on the tasks before it? Once you have drafted your guidelines, your instructor might choose to compile and synthesize your responses, adding his or her own thoughts and then distributing the guidelines for use throughout the class and for the many collaborative activities still to come in this textbook.

Collaborative Activity 3.6

Try collaborative drafting with members of a group. Work together to write a summary of Chapter 1 or 2 of this textbook. (If you have not yet studied those chapters in your class, write a summary of this chapter instead.) A **summary** selects and restates the major points of a text, using your own words. When you are finished drafting your summary, describe your experience. What process did your group follow for collaboratively writing the summary? How did the group ensure that all members had a role in the writing? Was the process effective? Why or why not? What would you change for the next time you work on a collaborative writing project?

DEALING WITH DRAFTING DIFFICULTIES

When a genre is one that is familiar to you, you may choose your preferred ways of drafting: at your desk or in the coffee shop, on a legal pad or computer, in all-night marathons or daily bursts. When it comes time to draft less familiar genres, though, the writer may feel left alone with the blank page. It might help to remember, however, that the page is not really blank, that the writing scene, situation, and genre have already inscribed the page with a purpose, a relationship between writer and reader, a particular way of addressing the subject, and, as we will learn more in coming chapters, with certain structures, style, even particular language.

No doubt, though, some genres seem to create more drafting blocks than others. If you do encounter difficulty drafting, you might return to invention strategies, to see if you can become more comfortable with what you want to say. Freewriting—writing your thoughts down as quickly as you can, without rereading or editing what you write—can help you get past a writing block, as can doing more research if your genre requires it. Discussing your idea with a teacher or a trusted reader might help you articulate orally what you are having trouble putting down in writing.

The genres that often seem easiest to draft, like grocery lists and complaint letters, have a strong and focused sense of purpose. Since all genres, from the most thesis-oriented to the least, are driven by some kind of purpose, one trick for effective drafting is to make sure that your purpose for writing matches the purpose embedded within the genre. ***Keeping the controlling purpose in mind when drafting keeps the writer's attention focused on the primary goal of the drafting.*** In fact, research has shown that successful experienced writers focus on their primary purpose and refine their goals as they draft. **Attending to purpose** means not focusing too much, while drafting, on sentence-level concerns like precise wording, spelling, grammar, or punctuation. When you draft, keep your main goal, your main readers, and the main genre you are writing in mind first. Remember that you can revise once you have a draft, even in situations where you have very little time.

Writing Activity 3.5

For the same writing assignment to which you responded in Writing Activity 3.3, describe your drafting process. Use Box 3.2 below to guide your reflection before and while you draft. If your teacher asks you to, share your reflections with others in your class. How can working collaboratively help you with parts of the drafting that seem most difficult?

Revising with Genres

The kind of *revising* a writer does depends, not surprisingly, on the kind of *writing* being done. In some writing scenes, the situation and genre both call for extensive revising. In others, minimal revising is either necessary, appropriate, or possible. Of course, the importance of the text to the writer and reader always weighs heavily in deciding how much revision is appropriate. The more important the consequences of the text, the more important it becomes to revise thoroughly and carefully.

Even genres that seem to allow for limited revising entail some reworking, though it might be nothing more than a quick rereading to catch any

Box 3.2 *Questions for Drafting*

1. Given what I know about the scene, situation, and genre, what strategies for drafting will be most effective?
2. What is my controlling purpose, and how does it relate to the purpose embedded in the genre? That is, what am I trying to achieve in this text, and how does this text help me achieve it?

    If possible, write that controlling purpose somewhere where it will be in front of you while you are drafting. Return to it any time you get stuck.
3. What parts will I need to include to conform to the genre and to achieve my purpose?

    If you have a plan or an outline of needed parts, keep it in front of you while drafting.
4. Who will read this text? What role does the genre define for the readers? What kind of relationship do I want to establish with the readers? What do they know already?
5. What should my text look and sound like to fit the genre I am writing?

    As you write, ask periodically whether what you are writing seems similar to the texts you have seen of the genre you are writing.
6. Am I saying what I wanted to say? If not, have I discovered a better idea so that I need to begin inventing and drafting anew?

    Ask yourself these questions periodically to help keep you on track before you get too far off track. Ask these questions also any time you feel stuck, when every word comes only with difficulty.
7. Am I worrying about wording too much?

    Especially when drafting with others, try to get a draft of the text out before searching for the best words to achieve your purpose. You can concentrate on words during a round of revision.
8. Am I editing too much?

    Try not to edit as you draft if editing interferes with your progress in drafting; do not stop to check spelling, correct punctuation, or look up a grammar issue in your handbook. Work to get your ideas out first. You can edit later.

major problems. Rereading a grocery list reveals forgotten items to add. Even when writing privately about personal experiences, thoughts, and feelings, most writers would reread their diaries and journals, perhaps adding forgotten experiences or ideas afterwards. Revision occurs throughout the drafting of a text-in-progress, too, as writers reread paragraphs and sections as they write and make changes before going on. Rereading is the beginning of revising, for you have to read your own text to be able to re-see it as others would.

But what do you look for when you reread to revise? What are you trying to see? Revision is actually a complex process itself, with several parts:

1. The writer first must gain distance from the text.

2. The writer must recognize problems or gaps in the text.

3. Even after recognizing that something is not quite working right, the writer has to decide what the source of the problem is and how to fix it, what to change.

Some inexperienced or unconfident writers may make seemingly random changes in a draft, trying to improve it without really knowing what might not be quite right. Effective revising is not just changing a text; it is changing a text in ways that make the text better. That statement may seem obvious, but it can be difficult to achieve. The difficulty, of course, involves knowing how to define "better." *Better* can mean different things in different scenes, situations, and genres. For example, a better research paper might need to include more examples, while a better memo might need to be more direct. Likewise, a better letter might conclude with "Love" in one situation but "Sincerely" in another.

Improving a text will vary in different scenes, but in all cases learning how to revise a text to make it better involves learning how to gain distance from the draft, learning how to recognize what is not quite right in that draft, and learning how to make appropriate changes.

Writing Activity 3.6

Write a paragraph describing your usual revision strategies for revising important texts. How do you go about reviewing your draft? How do you decide what to change? What works especially well for you; what gives you trouble in revising?

Collaborative Activity 3.7

In a group, compare your responses to the previous activity. Did you describe revising different kinds of texts, or did you all describe revising academic papers? If you all described the same kind of writing, generate lists of how revising other genres differs from revising the one you already described. If you described different kinds of writing, discuss how similar or different it is to revise in different genres.

GAINING DISTANCE

Writers have many strategies for gaining the needed distance from a draft, depending on individual preferences as well as situational and generic differences. *Time* almost always helps. Setting a draft aside for a day or more allows the writer to separate from the drafting process, though it requires careful time management. Not all writing situations allow the luxury of time, though, and spending a lot of time on a text is not always appropriate. Groceries may need to be bought that day, for example, and waiting a day to send out a memo might delay transmitting news too long. When the text you are writing matters to you, though, and you have enough time before it must be completed, taking time before revising helps enormously in gaining distance and perspective on what you have written.

With less time, simply *reading aloud* can help the writer hear the text anew. Hearing rather than seeing the text gives a different perspective, which can reveal especially effective sections and rougher patches. Read with a pencil in hand to mark spots that seem to need work. Printing out a hard copy of an electronic draft is also a good idea. It not only gives you distance but also allows you to mark the draft without deleting the original draft, in case you want to try several versions before picking one or even returning to the original.

Another way of gaining distance and objectivity is *asking for response from readers*, whether members of a writing group, friends, a teacher, or an assistant in the writing center. Take care with choosing a responder, since that person will need to be able to read the draft *as* a reader involved in your writing situation. It doesn't help to have your roommate tell you a draft of your history paper is great if he doesn't know what historians—the readers in your writing scene—think or expect. Your fellow traveler on the disastrous airline trip might not be the most levelheaded reader of your complaint letter to the airline and might not be able to read it from the airline executive's perspective. Skillful readers of drafts—well-trained writing assistants, your teacher, and often your writing group—adopt the role of the readers in your scene of writing.

Some of the most helpful responses are **guided responses**, where the writer asks the reader to attend to particular aspects of the draft. When one of us asks for response to a draft of an important memo or business letter, the question often is "Is the tone of this all right? Do I write anything that might offend someone or give the wrong impression?" Those questions work especially well because they target what a reader should focus on—possible problems an outside reader can spot more easily than the writer can—and they reflect what is critical to the particular genre being written. When asking for a response on a scholarly article, a writer might be more likely to ask whether the argument is clear or whether important ideas or objections are being neglected rather than whether the tone is right.

The questions, then, should reflect the kind of writing scene, the particular situation, and the most important or difficult elements of the genre being written. In the early revision stages on a draft in a less familiar genre, the writer might ask simply what stands out as the draft's major strengths and weaknesses. It is important to see the strengths as well as the weaknesses in order to know what qualities to keep as well as what to change. As the writer gets farther along in the process, the questions can become more specific, asking about aspects of the draft that the writer is most insecure about or that the writer knows do not match well with what the genre requires or what the writer is trying to achieve.

Writing Activity 3.7

Find out what writing assistance is available at your school. Is there a writing center? Other sources of help? How do they operate? Do you have to make an appointment or can you drop in? What kinds of assistance can they provide? What is their approach to working with student writers and their texts? What is their philosophy toward revising? Are they experienced in addressing all kinds of texts, or will their help be limited to academic writing? How could you make use of the services now for any writing project you are working on? Write a one-page description summarizing your answers to the above questions.

Writing Activity 3.8

Return to the writing assignment for which you began inventing (Writing Activity 3.3, p. 108) and drafting (Writing Activity 3.5, p. 116), and write out a set of questions for your current draft that you would like a reader to respond to in order to help you revise. Find an appropriate reader (perhaps a classmate or a writing associate at the writing center), and ask for responses to those questions. Then find another reader and ask for responses to the same questions. Notice the differences in how various readers respond.

DETECTING DISSONANCE

After gaining distance from a draft, you will have some ideas of places in the draft that need improvement. To detect additional opportunities to improve, you will need to examine your draft even more carefully and methodically. What you are seeking is **dissonance**—aspects of the draft that do not match what you are trying to achieve. *Such gaps between your goals and your draft can be filled through revising.*

Dissonance can take many forms:

An example does not illustrate well

An explanation does not clarify

An attention-grabber bores.

You recognize dissonance whenever what you intended and what you achieved differ. Much of what you are trying to achieve will be established by the genre you are writing. Remembering the genre you are writing in, then, can remind you of what you intended and can help you perceive dissonance between your text and others of your genre. Remember the scene behind what you are writing, especially the situation (the readers, subject matter, setting, and purpose) behind that genre. Remember, too, your own individual goals for drafting the genre.

Large sources of dissonance (the situation and your response to it) can be particularized, brought down to the level of a text, partly by comparing your draft to others of its genre. Since genre responds to common situations, you can examine your draft's response to its situation through examining its similarity to others of its genre. Where does your draft seem most like others of its genre? Where does your draft seem not to be like others of its genre? Where you detect dissonance between your draft and its genre, you can consider more closely whether your draft is different because you are trying to do something a bit different or because you have not yet achieved what the genre is designed to do.

If you are writing a complaint letter, for example, your choice of genre suggests that you want to describe your experience to someone in a position to recompense you in some way. Your goal is to get the reader to give you what you request. Dissonance in a complaint letter, then, appears wherever part of your draft seems not to encourage the reader to give you what you want. Below is the draft of the complaint letter written by our stranded traveler. Highlighted in italics are parts of the draft that the writer noticed and underlined after she had put it away for an hour, parts she thought might need rewriting.

Dear Mr. Knight:

When my husband and I flew from Kansas City to Asheville, *you abandoned us* in Atlanta and forced us to find our own hotel and pay for all our own expenses. We *need you* to reimburse us for all of these expenses immediately and to send us free tickets for our next flight.

Flying on States Airlines to Atlanta, we were supposed to connect to your airline to fly to Asheville. When we got to Atlanta, we were told that your airline had canceled our flight due to mechanical problems and that we were rebooked on your flight leaving the next morning. We were also told that we had to find our own hotel room for the night and were directed to the hotel courtesy phones in the baggage claim area. After calling *every single* hotel in the vicinity of the airport and being told there were no rooms available (there were weather problems in Atlanta that night), the only room we could find was at a Marriott well across Atlanta. Since we could find no other room, we took a tax to that Marriott. *The taxi took forever because we hit a traffic jam on the interstate, and our driver didn't seem to know any ways around the mess.* By the time we got to the hotel, we were exhausted and starving. We ordered pizza *that was barely edible.* Exhausted, we fell into bed for a few hours and took another taxi early the next morning back to the airport.

We were *horrified* to discover, when we arrived at the airport, that you had shuttled some passengers to a hotel for the night, *but not us!* We would gladly have accepted it over the *nightmare* of trying to find a hotel room in an unfamiliar town when all the airport hotels were full. We asked at *your ticket counter* to reimburse us right away, but all three agents we *argued* with insisted that we had to wait and write to customer service later. *That's you,* and so that's why I'm writing.

You treated us very badly and made our travel experience a nightmare. We *demand* that you reimburse all our expenses and give us two free tickets *to anywhere we might want to go.*

Sincerely,

You might notice, as the writer did, that the tone is a bit snippy and overly outraged, so the reader might be offended—and not eager to help. The writer noticed especially the direct assaults on the reader, where she had accused him of harming her directly ("You treated us very badly," for example). Knowing the genre of the complaint letter, she knew that effective letters treat the reader as a reasonable representative of the company who intends no harm and wants to make things right. She also thought she had gotten lost in irrelevant details about the experience (the quality of the pizza, for example, that the reader could not have helped). And she noticed she left out some details usually included in complaint letters, including the details of exactly what flight she was on so Mr. Knight could check the details of her experience. The request she made in the end, she thought, might be asking for too much, for she knew the most effective complaint letters asked for recompense directly related to the harm, and she had, after all, gotten to her destination eventually.

Since every genre is different, revising a genre involves attending to different textual qualities—qualities that are specific and significant to that genre. The quality of controlling ideas is critical in revising academic papers, for example, but not relevant when revising memoranda. A personal voice is essential in personal essays but not in lab reports. The best revision, then, targets the particular qualities of the particular genre.

When you detect dissonance between your text and the genre you are writing in, you may or may not want to make a change. You may prefer your way of doing things to the genre's expected ways. The next chapter of this book takes up questions of adopting genres to better meet certain goals. For now, aim for becoming aware of the traits of different genres so you can choose when you revise whether to conform to or break those traits. Based on general elements of genres and situations, Box 3.3 below can serve as a rough guide to detecting dissonance in a draft. Once you have analyzed your genre, as we demonstrated in Chapter 2, you can specify the most likely sources of dissonance and examine your draft more precisely.

Writing Activity 3.9

Return to the writing assignment for which you began inventing (Writing Activity 3.3, p. 108), drafting (Writing Activity 3.5, p. 116), and revising (Writing Activity 3.8, p. 120). Examine your draft more precisely by detecting dissonance between it and the genre you are writing in. Use Box 3.3: Questions for Detecting Dissonance Based on Genre to help you. Record your responses to the questions since you will likely be using them to make final revisions of your draft.

Box 3.3 *Questions for Detecting Dissonance Based on Genre*

1. What am I trying to achieve? What is this genre designed to achieve? Does my purpose fit with the purpose of the genre I am writing? How well does my draft achieve my controlling purpose? Where does it fail to achieve that purpose?
2. What kinds of people read this genre and for what purposes? Does my draft give them what they need and expect?
3. Does my draft offer the kinds of information usually supplied in texts of this genre? Does it cover appropriate topics at an appropriate level of detail?
4. Is my draft structured like others of its genre? Does it have all components that the genre requires? Does it include components that are unnecessary in this genre? Have I structured the draft in a way that supports my controlling purposes?
5. What kinds of language do texts of this genre usually use? How simple or complex are the sentences? How varied in structure? What specialized vocabulary is appropriate? What kinds of words are favored? Does my draft sound like other texts of this genre?
6. What conventions do texts of this genre usually follow? Is Standardized Edited English expected? Is slang allowed? Are particular formats followed for citing sources or for other specialized information? Does my draft follow those conventions fully and carefully?
7. Am I saying what I want to say, even if it does not match the genre? If it does not match the genre, how am I helping readers to accept my text?

MAKING CHANGES

Using questions like those in Box 3.3 (for yourself or for use in a guided response), you will find aspects of a draft you want to improve; you might, for example, find it lacking in terms of items 2 and 3 in the checklist above. You will need to draw on all your skills as a writer to make appropriate changes. **When revising, writers make changes by adding, deleting, and reordering things in the draft.** *Adding* to sections that inadequately develop or refine your controlling purpose may well require further inventing and drafting. We needed to create new examples to illustrate many points, including many of the examples in this paragraph, in response to readers' questions. You might need courage to *delete* words, sentences, and whole sections that do not contribute to your goals. When revising this chapter, for example, we found the courage to delete 15 pages from the original manuscript that we decided were not relevant. The chapter is better for that deletion. We also deleted repetitious sentences and wordy structures. *Substituting* one example, one word, or one topic for another combines the courage to delete what you have drafted and the creativity to discover something better. In revising this textbook, we substituted readings and switched sample situations and genres to make them more interesting to readers. *Moving* sections around can sometimes rescue a faltering argument, and an organizational pattern might become clearer if the sentences in a paragraph were *reordered.* We reordered whole chapters and many sections and sentences in this book. When you detect a spot that needs improvement, then, you might try asking whether you should add something to it, delete part or all of it, or move it or parts of it around.

Sometimes, making changes involves choosing an entirely different genre for communicating about a certain subject for a certain audience. In the following example, one of our students, Cathleen Ceremuga, decided to write what she called an "informative paper" to tell other students about the benefits of working as an intern at the Philadelphia Children's Zoo. Here is her analysis of the writing situation for the informative paper:

Writing Situation Analysis
(for informative paper, "Meeting Spindles")

Topic Area: The Philadelphia Children's Zoo

Message:
The Internship Program at the Philadelphia Children's Zoo offers a variety of opportunities for college students to gain experience working with animals and educating the public.

Audience:
I think the people who would benefit the most from this paper are college students, specifically those with backgrounds in the biological sciences and those interested in dealing with animals. This paper may also be helpful to those that really want some sort of job experience but do not know where to go.

Purpose:
My main purpose is to inform. After reading the paper, students might be interested in applying for a position at the Children's Zoo, or at least be more educated about what goes on at a Children's Zoo. I plan to describe the internship program in detail and to draw on my own experiences from the summer of 1998 there as examples. Certainly the last part of my paper will focus on the question "What's in it for me?" and describe the benefits of the internship.

Persona:
I will speak from my own knowledge of and experience with the Children's Zoo. My goal in this paper is to open college students' eyes to one of the possibilities for gaining job experience. I will be honest and give a straightforward account of what should be expected of an intern. I will not neglect the drawbacks of the program (e.g., no pay, a lot of manual labor, etc.), but I will try to put the program in a fair light. To give the paper some character, I'll even detail some of my own experiences. I want my tone to be helpful and credible.

Based on her analysis of the situation, the student, Cathleen Ceremuga, then drafted the following informative paper, which she titled "Meeting Spindles, or Interning at the Philadelphia Children's Zoo."

Ceremuga 1

Meeting Spindles,
or Interning at the Philadelphia Children's Zoo

"Will she bite me?" I asked, eyeing the buck-toothed South American porcupine with suspicion. The Lead Keeper shook his head, a smile on his face, and unlocked the giant cage door. Spindles and I stared at each other warily until I took a deep breath, gathered my courage and walked in the cage. Following the keeper's instructions, I held out my right hand and gently grabbed Spindles's thick, prickly tail. As if on cue, she immediately spun around and felt with her human-like hind paws for my outstretched left hand. The porcupine slowly backed up onto my arm, and I felt a joy and amazement at the trust which this gentle creature had shown me. From that moment on, I realized how much new knowledge and fulfillment I had gained from my internship at the Philadelphia Children's Zoo as well as the unique situations I had never dreamed I would ever experience.

The Philadelphia Children's Zoo was the country's first Children's Zoo and houses over 30 species of domestic and exotic animals. As an essential part of the Zoo's Education Department, it works to educate the public about the intrinsic value and protection of all animals. In doing so, the Children's Zoo offers various demonstrative programs, hands-on exhibits, and interactive areas. The Children's Zoo also boasts an extensive internship program for high school graduates, which I took advantage of last summer. This internship program targets college students who have an interest in pursuing a career in the biological sciences, especially those with a background in biology or wildlife management. Three seasonal internships are offered: Spring, Summer, and Fall, with each requiring at least 16 hours per week for 12 weeks. Of these, the summer session is usually the most popular, and thus the most competitive. In fact, during my internship at the Zoo, I worked with 11 other interns, but usually the number at a given time is much smaller. Overall, the internship provides an excellent opportunity to gain experience working with animals and educating the public.

Ceremuga 3

Responsibilities of Interns

Two types of interns work at the Children's Zoo— Animal Program and Animal Care. Duties of these interns differ and require distinct skills and qualities. For instance, Animal Program interns are mainly involved with educa- tion—they present animal programs and perform specialized animal care duties, such as maintenance of the hatchery. Animal Care interns, however, perform the daily cleaning of the Children's Zoo and are under the direct supervision of the Lead Keeper and the Foreman.

In general, the Animal Program internship is a more specialized program than the Animal Care internship. While Animal Program interns may be asked to help out with the morning cleaning duties, they mostly deal with presenting animal programs to the public. For this reason, Animal Program interns should be comfortable talking to large groups of people and be able to develop new and creative educational demonstrations. Furthermore, since anything can happen when handling wild animals, Animal Program interns should be able to deal calmly with unexpected situations.

Animal Program interns present a variety of programs for the public. Most are held in the Amphitheater, while oth- ers take place at the various exhibits. One of the most popular is the Cow-Milking Demonstration, where an Animal Program intern interacts with the audience while an Animal Care intern milks the Jersey cow, Moonlight. Another popular program is the Hawk Talk, a demonstration that involves an intern presenting one of the raptors to the audience. Other presentations include Live Animal Demonstrations, Good Pet/Bad Pet, Reptile Raps, Turtle Talks, and Animals of South America/North America.

Although they are not as involved as the Animal Care interns in the care of the animals, Animal Program interns

Ceremuga 4

also have husbandry duties. One of the main responsibilities is cleaning of the Hatchery, where the incubating eggs as well as the newly hatched chicks are displayed to the public. In addition, Animal Program interns clean the silky chickens' pen and are in charge of filling all of the feeders in the Barnyard (the Zoo's petting area) and the duck pond. On days when the Children's Zoo is understaffed, however, Animal Program interns will help with the daily cage cleanings in the Animal Room or Bird of Prey Barn.

Animal Care interns, while not as involved in presenting animals to the visitors as Animal Program interns, mainly perform basic husbandry duties. Besides cleaning cages and yards, Animal Care interns prepare the animals' daily diets, deliver food, and administer medication. They also take part in general upkeep tasks, such as trimming branches and raking the grounds. Animal Care interns should possess a strong love for animals as well as a strong stomach and not mind performing a fair amount of manual labor.

My Summer Experience

I spent my summer at the zoo as an Animal Care intern and, as such, had a variety of daily duties. For the Children's Zoo Animal Care interns, each day was divided into a morning session and an afternoon section. The morning half of each day generally involved cleaning of the animals' habitats. First, we fed the pigs, goats, and sheep in the Barnyard and changed the hay in their yards. Then we raked the yards of the other animals, such as parrots, rabbits, ducks, and turtles. Depending upon the day, we drained, scrubbed and refilled the turtle and duck ponds-- Monday for turtles, Tuesday for ducks. Finally, we cleaned the cages in the Animal Room and Bird of Prey Barn. These two facilities housed such animals as ferrets, porcupines, parrots, and chinchillas in the Animal Room, while the armadillos and raptors resided in the Bird of Prey Barn. At this time, we recorded the weight of the ferrets' remaining food, as we were changing their diets and observing how much new food they consumed. One of my favorite duties was bathing the armadillos, especially one named Brillo, while their cages were cleaned.

After lunch, the afternoon duties commenced, which varied for each intern according to the daily schedule. Usually, however, the duties included feed preparation and delivery. Two interns prepared the diets for all of the Children's Zoo animals each day, a project that took about 1-2 hours, depending upon the interns' knowledge and swiftness. I thoroughly enjoyed this time in the kitchen once I learned each animal's diet. Afterwards, we fed the raptors in the Bird of Prey Barn as well. Sometimes, to the delight of the young audience, the Animal Program interns would feed the terrapins during their Turtle Talk. After that, the Animal Care interns presented an animal in the Play Yard; monitored the Parrot Yard, Barnyard, or Backyard Bugs, the arthropod exhibit; presented a hands-on Activity Table full of animal skins and antlers; and/or performed a Cow-Milking Demonstration at 12:30 or 3:30 pm. The interns also assisted the Lead Keeper with general maintenance, such as trimming branches and refilling food supplies. Often, the Director had assignments for the interns as well, such as taking surveys of the visitors and other special tasks.

Internship Benefits

Internships at the Children's Zoo provide many benefits to the participants. One benefit includes the knowledge and experience gained through working at the zoo. Animal Care as well as Animal Program interns gain training in handling a variety of domestic and exotic animals, from sheep to armadillos. Specifically, Animal Care interns learn the animals' diets and how to administer medication to sick animals. While I was at the zoo, we had a sick ferret which

we treated with medication each afternoon as well as a pig
with a scratched eye that we anointed with ointment at the
end of each day. We also had three chinchillas that were
infected with a parasite, so we had to learn how to properly
sanitize their dishes and cages. Animal Program interns may
gain more experience speaking formally to large groups,
and in doing so, learn many general facts about the animals.

Aside from gaining knowledge about the animals,
interns learn how to better deal with people. In the summer
especially, patience and politeness are a must. Interns learn
how to react in all sorts of situations, from escaped goats to
missing children. During this time, interns also form valuable
connections. In fact, the internship program is a valuable
source of references since the end of the internship calls for
evaluations made by the Children's Zoo Foreman. On this
paper, he rates each intern's performance with animals as
well as with other staff and visitors. This evaluation is then
kept on file and can be used as a reference by the Foreman.
Moreover, since the program involves much cooperation
between interns, the staff, and the volunteers, friendships are
relatively easy to make. In fact, I still e-mail one of the other
Animal Care interns on a regular basis.

I thoroughly enjoyed my summer as an Animal Care
intern at the Philadelphia Children's Zoo. Although I did a lot
of manual labor and received no stipend, the knowledge and
friendships I gained more than compensated for these drawbacks, Even now, more than 5 months after the end of my
internship, I can still feel the grip of Spindles's paw around my
fingers and see the sleepy, contented expression on Brillo's
face as I scrub his back during his daily bath. I cherish these
memories and am grateful for all that my internship taught
me. I highly recommend this internship to any college student
interested in caring for animals, gaining job experience, and
making new friends. Of everything that can be said of the

Ceremuga 6

program one thing is certain: the experiences gained through working at the Philadelphia Children's Zoo are not easily forgotten.

After drafting the informative paper and then gaining some distance from it, the student decided that the informative paper was not the most effective way for her to communicate to other students about the internship. She decided to choose a genre more appropriate for her subject, purpose, and audience and to revise the paper into a brochure. The writer explains her decisions in the following revision plan:

Revision Plans

(for revising paper "Meeting Spindles" into brochure, "Internships at the Philadelphia Children's Zoo")

Overview:
I am going to alter the purpose of my writing situation. Instead of being informative, I am going to make my paper more persuasive. I am going to try to convince students to actually intern at the Philadelphia Children's Zoo, not just tell them about it. In doing so, I will change the format--I will make it into a brochure, which is more reader-based. I imagine I will also need to eliminate some of the more specific details, especially the unsavory ones, and include more detailed benefits of the internship.

Evaluation of Focus, Content, and Organization:
Focus: I believe in my first paper I focused more on informing the audience than persuading the audience. I've communi-

cated the idea clearly--presented the information--but I feel the paper does not aim to "sell" students on the idea of an internship at the Philadelphia Children's Zoo. I may need to revise the main idea to concentrate on the benefits of the internship, rather than so many specific examples of duties. I want less of an "I" focus and more focus on the reader.

Content: My supporting evidence is adequate for informing students about the internship itself, but in order to persuade students, I'll need more information and details about the benefits and will need to trim any irrelevant material. I will also need to decide what information is most crucial to include.

Organization: My organizational strategy for the informative paper uses regular paragraphs divided into sections by sub-headings; this will need to be revamped in the revision, which will follow a brochure format. I'll need a central focus on benefits of the internship, in order to sell readers on the idea, and I will need to highlight these benefits. I will probably also have to redo the introduction and conclusion and will need to end with information about applying for an internship. The organization should reflect less of an "I" focus and more focus on the reader.

Revision Goals:
—Focus on benefits of the internship
—Add more detail to the benefits
—Take out some personal experiences without losing the tone
—Persuade the readers to become interns at the zoo
—Rework into brochure format

Notice how once she chooses this new genre, the brochure, the student re-evaluates her writing situation. Her choice of a new genre helps shape a new purpose and guides her decisions about changes in focus, content, and organization. Based on the new writing situation and her revised goals, the student wrote the brochure reproduced here.

Internships at the Philadelphia Children's Zoo

What are *you* doing this summer?

What are Internships at the Philadelphia Children's Zoo?

- Have you ever thought about working with exotic animals?
- Do you like to work with children?
- Do you like to teach people?

If you answered yes to these questions, then an internship at the Philadelphia Children's Zoo may be what you're looking for.

The Children's Zoo boasts an extensive internship program for high school graduates. This program targets college students who have an interest in pursuing a career in the biological sciences, but there are a variety of internship programs available, ranging in type from animal husbandry to education to public relations.

Besides the Summer term, the Children's Zoo offers internships in the Spring and Fall, with each requiring at least 16 hours per week for 12 weeks. Of these, the Summer session is usually the most popular, and thus the most competitive.

Since the Animal Program and Animal Care programs are the most popular, this brochure will detail only these positions. Descriptions of the other programs can be found on the Philadelphia Zoo's Web site, which is listed in the How Do I Apply? section.

What's So Special About the Philadelphia Children's Zoo?

The Philadelphia Children's Zoo was the country's first Children's Zoo and houses over 30 species of domestic and exotic animals. As an essential part of the Zoo's Education Department, it works to educate the public about the intrinsic value and protection of all animals. In doing so, the Children's Zoo offers various demonstrative programs, hands-on exhibits, and interactive areas.

Some of the unique features of the Children's Zoo include:

- **Amphitheater:** the central structure of the Children's Zoo, where various programs and demonstrations take place.
- **Backyard Bugs:** a pavilion that houses the Zoo's extensive arthropod collection. Always staffed, it encourages hands-on learning and questions.
- **Barnyard:** the most popular part of the Children's Zoo, it houses the domestic and farm animals, such as goats, sheep, calf, and turkeys. Part of the Barnyard is also a petting zoo.

| Front Cover | Panel 2 | Panel 3 |

Collaborative Activity 3.8

Working in groups, examine the changes the student made as she revised the informative paper into a brochure. How does the change in genre (from informative paper to brochure) affect the changes that she made? To what extent do the changes accomplish what she set out to do in her revisions? What is the effect of these changes? Do you agree with her reasons for changing genres? Explain, and then share your responses with the class.

REVISING FOR STYLE

Once you have addressed and are satisfied with the more substantial changes to a text, you can begin to focus on **stylistic revision**. For instance, the writer of our complaint letter chose language—words and sentences—that established an appropriate tone, conveyed a certain directness, and presented her as an aggrieved, determined, yet reasonable customer. She

What Will Be My Duties as an Intern?

Two of the most popular internships at the Children's Zoo are the Animal Program and Animal Care positions. While both work with the animals, duties of these interns differ and require distinct skills and qualities.

Animal Program interns are mainly involved with education—they present various animal programs and demonstrations to the public. Such programs include the handling of exotic as well as domestic animals. They also perform specialized animal care duties.

Animal Program interns should be comfortable talking to large groups of people and be able to develop new and creative educational demonstrations. Since anything can happen when handling wild animals, Animal Program interns should be able to deal calmly with unexpected situations.

Animal Care interns mainly perform basic husbandry duties. Besides cleaning cages and yards, Animal Care interns prepare the animals' daily diets, deliver food, and administer medication. They also take part in general upkeep tasks, such as trimming branches and raking the grounds.

Animal Care interns should possess a strong love for animals and basic knowledge about handling various animals. They should also have a strong stomach and not mind performing a fair amount of manual labor.

What's In It For Me?

Internships at the Philadelphia Children's Zoo provide many benefits to the participants. One benefit includes the knowledge and experience gained through working at the zoo. Animal Care as well as Animal Program interns gain training in handling a variety of domestic and exotic animals, from sheep to armadillos.

Knowledge. Specifically, Animal Care interns learn the animals' diets and how to administer medication to sick animals. Meanwhile, Animal Program interns may gain more experience speaking formally to large groups, and in doing so, learn many general facts about the animals.

Service. Aside from gaining knowledge about the animals, interns learn how to better deal with people. In the summer especially, patience and politeness are a must. Interns learn how to react in all sorts of situations, from escaped goats to missing children.

Connections. The internship program is a valuable source of references since the end of the internship calls for evaluations made by the Children's Zoo Foreman. This evaluation is then kept on file and can be used as a reference by the Foreman when needed.

Friendships. An internship is a great way to make friends, since the program involves much cooperation between interns, the staff, and the volunteers. Because of this constant interaction, many of the friendships formed at the Children's Zoo turn out to be long-lasting.

How Do I Apply?

To apply for an internship at the Philadelphia Children's Zoo, just send a resume, copy of a current college transcript, and cover letter. In the letter include the program for which you are applying, why you are interested, and dates you are available.

Send these materials to:

Human Resources
The Philadelphia Zoo
3400 W. Girard Avenue
Philadelphia, PA 19104

Deadlines for applying are December for Spring, March for Summer, and September for Fall.

*Note: For the Summer positions, paid positions in Guest Relations are also available.

Any questions?
Contact the Philadelphia Zoo:
Call (215) 243-5326
or visit the Web site at
www.phillyzoo.org/intern.htm

Panel 4	**Folded Overleaf**	**Back Cover**

achieved that tone and persona (image of the writer) partly through her choice of style.

Style includes the structure and length of your sentences, the particular words you choose, and the persona and tone you create. Because different kinds of texts make different stylistic demands, you will again want to work for flexibility, to be able to adjust your sentences and words for different effects in different situations. Although a literary, essayistic style is common in English classes, no one style is the best style for all circumstances. Descriptive images would bog down and potentially mislead readers of a lab report, for example. Passive voice helps lab reports stay focused on the experiment rather than the experimenter, but active voice keeps essays more engaging. Later chapters will examine different stylistic expectations for different genres in different scenes. When you are working with an unfamiliar genre, try reading examples of that genre to capture the flavor and tone of it; then work to create a comparable flavor and tone in your own draft.

Examine the sentence level changes our stranded traveler made in her complaint letter. Deleted text is bracketed, new text italicized.

Dear *Mr. Knight*:

When my husband and I flew from Kansas City to Asheville, *North Carolina, your airline stranded us overnight* [you abandoned us] in Atlanta and forced us to find our own hotel and pay for all our own expenses. *I am enclosing copies of all of our receipts, and I ask that* [We need] you [to] reimburse us for all of these expenses *as soon as possible.* [immediately and to send us free tickets for our next flight.]

Flying on States Airlines to Atlanta *on March 7*, we were [supposed] to connect to your airline to fly to Asheville—*flight #7805L, leaving Atlanta at 9:05 pm to arrive in Asheville at 10:03 pm.* When we [got to] *arrived in* Atlanta, we were told *by two of your agents* that your airline had canceled our flight due to mechanical problems and that we were rebooked on your flight leaving the next morning. We were also told that we had to find our own hotel room for the night and were directed to the hotel courtesy phones in the baggage claim area. After calling every [single] hotel in the vicinity of the airport and being told there were no rooms available (there were weather problems in Atlanta that night), the only room we could find was at a Marriott well across Atlanta. Since we could find no other room, we took a taxi to that Marriott, [The taxi took forever because we hit a traffic jam on the interstate, and our driver didn't seem to know any ways around the mess. By the time we got to the hotel, we were exhausted and starving. We] ordered pizza, [that was barely edible. Exhausted, we] fell into bed for a few hours, and took another taxi early the next morning back to the airport. *Receipts for our hotel room, food, and two taxi fares are enclosed. These are the expenses we need to have reimbursed.*

We [were horrified to] discover*ed*, when we arrived at the airport, that *your airline* had shuttled some passengers to a hotel for the night, but *that offer had not been extended to us.* [not us!] We would gladly have accepted it over the nightmare of trying to find a hotel room in an unfamiliar town when all the airport hotels were full. We asked at your ticket counter to *have this problem resolved right then,* [reimburse us right away,] but all [three] agents [we argued with] insisted that we had to wait and write to customer service later. [That's you, and so that's why I'm writing]

[You treated us very badly and made our travel experience a nightmare. We demand] *Although we do not believe that we were treated well by your airline, we are most concerned right now* that [you reimburse all] our expenses *be reimbursed.* [and give us two free tickets to anywhere we might want to go.] *I appreciate your help in resolving our problem.*

Sincerely,

You can see the changes our writer made in response to the dissonance she had perceived between her draft and the genre of complaint letters: She removed many of the emotionally laden and accusatory words and substituted less pointed phrasings, adding details about the flights and removing details about the quality of meals and taxi rides. She even changed her request to a more moderate stance, one she hoped Mr. Knight would more likely approve. And she added language at the end to project her reader as a reasonable and helpful man. Knowing how her genre works and why—knowledge gained through genre analysis—enabled her to make decisions about how to change her draft once she had perceived the places of dissonance. Our suggestions for using genre to guide revision are summarized in Box 3.4: Questions for Revising below.

Writing Activity 3.10

Return to the text you were working on in Writing Activity 3.9 (p. 123), in which you identified places you might want to revise based on dissonance between the text and the genre. Using Box 3.4, revise that text, adding, deleting, moving, or substituting things in ways that you think bring the text closer to achieving your controlling purpose and the target genre. Try to explain what elements of your genre you were trying to match better with your revisions.

Presentation

How your text looks reflects on you. It forms a first impression with the reader, one that may incline the reader favorably or unfavorably toward you. *Presentation,* the physical appearance of a text, is a part of every genre,

---

Box 3.4   *Questions for Revising*

1. What kind and amount of revising is appropriate for this writing task?
2. How can I gain distance from this draft, given my writing situation?
   - Do I have time to leave it for a day or two?
   - What rough spots do I hear when I read it aloud?
   - Who might understand the writing situation well enough to serve as an effective responder for this draft?
   - What guided questions can I ask that responder; what do I want to know?
3. What dissonance do I detect between my draft and the genre?
   - Does my purpose fit with the purpose of the genre I am writing? How well does my draft achieve my controlling purposes? Where does it fail to achieve those purposes?
   - How would the readers of this writing scene and situation respond to this text? Where would they be likely to respond differently from how I intended?
   - In what ways is my draft similar to others of its genre? In what ways does my draft seem different from others of its genre? Are those differences deliberate ones, due to differences in my situation? If not, how can I change my draft to fit the genre more closely and better achieve the goals it is designed to achieve?
4. How well does my style suit my genre? Have I achieved a tone and persona I want?
5. What additional inventing might be helpful? Do I need to do more research? Are there facts or details I need to generate? Do I need more ideas or information?
6. What do I need to add? What needs to be deleted? What can be improved by being moved to a different place?

---

though its importance varies from one genre to the next. When you are writing a letter to a friend, you might take care to choose the stationery you think your friend will like best; that's attending to the presentation of your letter. When you send an e-mail, you have probably already chosen a default font, spacing, and margins, and you may end with one of two or three signatures. Those elements of form are part of presentation. Even writers of personal journals, which would seem to require little presentation, attend to the type of paper they use, whether the pages are bound or not, and often to the type of pen used. They also often develop conventions, such as dating each entry.

Other genres may have more extensive expectations for how they are presented. The use of visuals, for example, plays a particularly important role in workplace genres—such as instruction guides or procedures manuals—where graphics and pictures can help communicate complicated technical concepts or large amounts of technical information. Furthermore, the visual presentation of a text in a workplace scene can be crucial not just to the reader's comprehension of information but to his or her safety. Safety warnings in some technical documents are often visually represented in a contrasting color or larger type size or using a graphic ⚠ so that readers can easily access this information. The visual characteristics or design elements of a text can be crucial, then, in conveying information to your readers and are an important part of presentation in many genres. In the sections that follow, we will highlight the main elements of presentation:

- **Visual presentation**, which includes page layout, typography, and graphics
- **Editing** for stylistic conventions and Standardized Edited English (SEE), including punctuation, usage, and spelling

To better understand how to revise for presentation, consider the complaint letter below, whose process we have been following in this chapter. The letter has been formatted and edited as part of the revision for presentation.

2306 Rhode Island Street
Richardson, Missouri 77055
March 19, 2001

Dan Knight
States Airlines
200 Marchfield Avenue
Atlanta, Georgia 30355

Dear Mr. Knight:

When my husband and I flew from Kansas City to Asheville, North Carolina, your airline stranded us overnight in Atlanta and forced us to find our own hotel and pay for all our own expenses. I am enclosing copies of all of our receipts, and I ask that you reimburse us for all of these expenses as soon as possible.

Flying on States Airlines to Atlanta on March 7, we were to connect to your airline to fly to Asheville—flight #7805L, leaving Atlanta at 9:05 p.m. to arrive in Asheville at 10:03 p.m. When we arrived in Atlanta, we were told by two of your agents that your airline had canceled our flight due to mechanical problems and that we were rebooked on your flight leaving the next morning.

We were also told that we had to find our own hotel room for the night and were directed to the hotel courtesy phones in the baggage claim area. After calling every hotel in the vicinity of the airport and being told there were no rooms available (there were weather problems in Atlanta that night), the only room we could find was at a Marriott well across Atlanta. Since we could find no other room, we took a taxi to that Marriott, ordered pizza, fell into bed for a few hours, and took another taxi early the next morning back to the airport. Receipts for our hotel room, food, and two taxi fares are enclosed. These are the expenses we need to have reimbursed.

We discovered, when we arrived at the airport, that your airline had shuttled some passengers to a hotel for the night, but that offer had not been extended to us. We would gladly have accepted it over the nightmare of trying to find a hotel room in an unfamiliar town when all the airport hotels were full. We asked at your ticket counter to have this problem resolved right then, but all agents insisted that we had to wait and write to customer service later.

Although we do not believe that we were treated well by your airline, we are most concerned right now that our expenses be reimbursed. I appreciate your help in resolving our problem.

Sincerely,

Dana Feldman

Since complaint letters follow conventions of other formal business letters—including the use of spacing to highlight formal elements such as addresses, dates, salutations, and signatures—our writer added this formatting in her revised draft. She also adjusted the paragraphing in her letter to create the shorter paragraphs expected in a business letter, while continuing to use the visual cues of line spacing to indicate new paragraphs and to help break up or "chunk" information for readers. In addition, the writer of the complaint letter checked her text to make sure it followed stylistic conventions, such as using a colon after the salutation, and the conventions of Standardized Edited English (SEE); doing that reduced distractions for readers who expect certain conventions, allowing them to concentrate on what the writer has to say. While the writer's observance of the conventions of SEE creates clarity and correctness, which add to the writer's professional ethos, this professionalism is further enhanced by the writer's use of the conventional business letter format. The visual presentation of the letter, meeting the standards of formal business correspondence, makes the writer more likely to be taken seriously and to prompt action on the part of the reader.

VISUAL PRESENTATION

As the letter above illustrates, ***the effectiveness of your text depends not just on what it says but how it looks.*** Think, for example, of the effect that a text full of dense type has on you as a reader. What is your first impression of a page full of lengthy paragraphs with no breaks and with no white space? If you are like most readers, it can both intimidate you and turn you away. Using visual cues and paragraphs to break up the information into smaller units or chunks makes a text not only easier to read but also easier to comprehend. If Dana Feldman's letter was all one paragraph, it would be difficult to follow the sequence of events and to comprehend and recall all of the details. The writer chunks the information for easier comprehension and uses visual features to present a hierarchy of information that helps readers understand and navigate the text.

Visual presentation includes physical as well as visual elements:

* The size of the document (such as $8\frac{1}{2} \times 11"$ vs. legal size)
* Type of paper (such as recycled vs. glossy coated paper)
* Binding of a text (stapled vs. spiral bound)
* Page layout: white space, margins, line length, columns, placement of headers, footers, and page numbers, use of lists (numbered, lettered, or bulleted), use of headings and subheadings
* Typography: typeface (such as Arial or **Palatino Bold**), type size (10-point vs. 14 point), type styles (**bold**, *italics*, underline, SMALL CAPS), line spacing (single or double spaced)

▓ Graphics: drawings, maps, photographs, diagrams, charts, graphs, tables; letterheads and logos; boxes; use of color

Consider, for example, how the student brochure on "Internships at the Philadelphia Children's Zoo" (pp. 134–135) uses the visual presentation of the text, especially the use of headings ("What Are Internships at the Philadelphia Children's Zoo?" or "What Will Be My Duties as an Intern?"), to organize information for readers and visually alert readers to new ideas. The writer makes it easier for readers to find those headings by using a larger type size and boldface type to make them stand out visually—to announce to readers that she is beginning a new idea. These and other visual cues are like road signs that a writer leaves for readers to help them navigate through the text.

Collaborative Activity 3.9

Look back at the informative paper "Meeting Spindles" (p. 126) and the brochure on "Internships at the Philadelphia Children's Zoo" (pp. 134–135) and, in your small group, discuss how the differing visual presentations of the same subject matter have differing effects on you as readers. Then examine the page layout: What are the differing effects of the use of white space, margins, and line length? What other layout features (headings, subheadings, lists) are used, and what is their effect on your processing of information in each of the documents? Do the texts use a legible, functional typeface that is appropriate to the message? How is type size and type style used to organize and highlight information in each of the texts? Is the line spacing (the amount of white space between lines of text) effective? What is the effect of the photographs included in the brochure? How do they reinforce the writer's message? Be prepared to discuss your group's findings and to share strategies for how each of the texts could improve its visual presentation.

Today, the use of technology in writing is making visual presentation a more important part of the content of all kinds of text—not just in workplace genres but even in more traditional genres such as argument papers in English courses. More and more teachers are inviting students to include visual elements such as photographs, text boxes, and graphics in their writing (see, for example, the sample student brochure on pages 134–135, or the student Web site (pp. 433–438) or student newsletter (pp. 425–428) in Chapter 7. These visual elements do not just create a visually attractive text; they actually *contribute* to the argument the writer is trying to make. As such, these visual elements deserve the same strategic attention that a writer would give to paragraph organization, word choice, and voice.

Attention to the visual is referred to as **visual rhetoric**, which suggests that the visual and other design elements of a text contribute to the way that the text communicates. Effective Web sites, for example, depend as much on their visual presentation as they do on their content. How the writer—or, more commonly, the writers—of a Web site structure the home page, what colors and fonts they use, where they mark links, and so on affect the meaning they are trying to convey. These visual rhetorical choices also affect how readers of the Web site negotiate the links between the pages. As such, when you are writing a genre that involves a strong visual impact, be sure to examine similar genres to see how other writers have used *presentation* in the service of their writing. When preparing your text for presentation, think about how visual elements might help you achieve your purpose for writing, and consult with your teacher and classmates about how best to use these elements in your writing. Be prepared to make a case for how the use of visuals will enhance your text.

Collaborative Activity 3.10

In groups, find a Web site and analyze its presentation, looking to see how the visual aspects of the text (layout, typography, graphics) work with or do not work with the written aspects. What makes the site effective? What does not? How would your group revise and edit the Web site to make it more effective?

EDITING

Editing a text for its presentation should come last, after all other revisions are completed. Fixing the format of a table that will be revised or correcting the punctuation in a sentence that will be deleted in revision wastes time, so save all editing and presentation tasks until last. Editing is an essential part of the writing process, though, one not to be skipped. For most formal texts, editing requires checking your text carefully for conformity to SEE, including spelling expectations, grammatical expectations like subject-verb agreement, usage expectations (for example, do you need to say *affect* or *effect?*), and punctuation expectations such as apostrophes. Editing also includes checking the formatting conventions of such elements as source citations. Before you give a completed text to someone else, then, be sure you have constructed its presentation thoughtfully. Look at other texts of the same genre and make your text look like those texts, whether that means enclosing it in a binder, using graphs and charts, adding images, or including a Works Cited page. *The way your text looks makes a statement. Make sure it says what you want it to say.*

Take advantage of tools that exist to help you as you write, especially with visual rhetoric. A variety of software programs help create tables, graphs, and charts or insert graphics into text. Word processing programs have various templates to help with presentation, though they are often too general to fit many genres. Dictionaries, handbooks, spell checkers, thesauruses, and computerized style checkers can all help as you edit and revise for style, though use them as guides only since no machine can know what you intend to say. Word processing itself now allows much easier drafting and especially revision. Writers can make changes, then cancel them, can try out several different wordings and choose the best, can move around single words or whole sections to see what makes the most sense. To take advantage of the flexibility of word processors, writers need to be careful not to let the beauty of an apparently printed page lure them into thinking the text is finished. Just because it's neat doesn't mean it's good. Technology can even help with invention. Internet and online catalogues, indices, and databases have made it easier to do thorough research or to find some specific facts.

Writing Activity 3.11

In a paragraph or two, describe how new computer technologies (word processing programs, electronic tools like spell checkers and grammar checkers) have influenced your writing processes. Which tools do you use, and which do you choose not to use? Why? How does your use of tools differ in different writing situations? In what ways have these technologies enhanced your writing processes (particularly drafting and revision)? In what ways have they made your processes more difficult or less effective?

Writing Activity 3.12

Now that you have revised your draft in response to Writing Activity 3.9, page 123, you are ready to prepare the text for presentation. Use Box 3.5 to guide you as you make final revisions.

Box 3.5   *Questions for Presentation*

1. Does my text look like others of its genre? Have I formatted the text appropriately (margins, length of paragraphs, typeface, etc.)? Have I labeled and bound the pages appropriately?
2. Have I included any expected visual elements (graphs, images, figures)? What other visual and formatting elements would be appropriate given my situation—my purpose, subject, audience, and setting?
3. Have I followed all the expected conventions for my genre? If Standardized Edited English is expected, have I edited carefully for spelling, punctuation, grammar, and usage? Have I followed appropriate citation systems?

Putting Writing Back Together Again

Fortunately, writing is not Humpty Dumpty. Even after we have taken the process of writing apart as we have in this chapter, writing always goes back together again. The act of writing moves in an intricate dance of inventing, drafting, and revising. It may start slow, change its tempo, stop suddenly, or glide smoothly across the floor. The explanation and advice offered in this chapter may help when part of the writing bogs down or when you reach a stage that always gives you difficulty or when you encounter a new writing situation and must expand your skills.

We all encounter new situations within new scenes as we go through life, and writing often helps us meet those situations. With new situations come new genres, all with their own scenes and appropriate writing processes. The more aware we are of how others have responded to those situations and the more we have learned to adapt our favored writing processes to different genres, the better prepared we will be to join the scene of writing as effective, successful participants.

Writing Projects

Writing Project 3.1

Having invented, drafted, revised, and presented the text you first began in response to Writing Activity 3.3, collect your final draft along with all previous drafts and responses to the activities you produced along the way and submit them as a writing portfolio for your teacher. As part of the portfolio, write a cover letter in which you reflect on your process of writing this paper, including the changes you made along the way, the reason you made these changes, and the results of these changes.

Writing Project 3.2

Using the interview techniques you learned in Chapter 1 (see Box 1.1), interview several people who all have experience writing the same genre, to learn how they tend to approach writing that genre. What processes does each use for inventing, drafting, and revising? How do those processes differ from one writer to the next? Do differences exist between the writing practices of people who have been successful users of that genre and those who have been less successful? What parts of inventing, drafting, and revising seem to matter most in creating effective texts in that genre? Write a summary of your findings for novices who will need to write in that genre.

Writing Project 3.3

For the next edition of this book, we would like to add new sections to the chapter on writing in workplace scenes (Chapter 9), and are seeking your assistance. We would like to know more about the processes of writing that people use in particular situations in workplace scenes. Using the interview techniques you learned in Chapter 1 (Box 1.1), interview a professional in the workplace (perhaps in a field or profession that you are interested in entering), and ask about his or her writing process for a specific kind of writing done on the job. How does he or she gather information, think through ideas, draft documents, get feedback, and revise? Are these individual or collaborative processes or both? Do the parts we have described in this chapter—inventing, drafting, revising— capture accurately the processes your interviewee uses? How do they differ and why? How do the processes used reflect the workplace scene, situation, and genre? Based on your interview findings, write your contribution to this new section of our textbook, which we would entitle "Writing Processes in Workplace Scenes."

Writing Project 3.4

Based on a genre of your choosing (or one that we worked with in this chapter or previous chapters), write instructions for writing the genre for writers who are new to the scene. What do writers of this genre need to know about the scene and the rhetorical situation? How can they use this information to make more effective writing choices? For example, you might include instructions for how to write a syllabus that meets student expectations without sounding overly formal or distant, a description of how to write an effective laboratory report or in-class essay that will get a good grade, or suggestions for how to write a good advice column. It is up to you to decide how to present your instructions, given the task at hand. Think about what genre would be most effective in allowing you to fulfill this task, whether it is a Web site, a brochure, a handbook, etc.

Critiquing and Changing Genres

In the previous chapters, we have asked you to analyze genres for what they can tell you about the communication and behavior of participants within scenes of writing, and we have encouraged you to apply your genre knowledge in order to make more informed and effective choices as you begin to participate as writers within these scenes. In short, we have described strategies for using genre to make sense of and function effectively within various scenes of writing. In this final chapter of Part I, we will take up the question of how genres can also be used to critique and change not only how participants communicate but also how they behave within some of the scenes making up our lives.

Because genres carry with them particular strategies for writing, you might assume that, as writers, you have little say in creating new genres or changing scenes of writing. However, since we are always making choices as we write within a genre, we are, in a sense, always being creative. An appropriate analogy would be actors on a stage. Even though they are given a script from which to perform, different actors will necessarily perform the same script differently. The constraints of the script would be the same, but different actors will make different choices about how to present the personality of their character, how to interact with others on the stage, even how to read their lines. Although a dramatic script is much more limiting than a genre script, the kind of creative control that exists for actors is available to writers. Different writers will make different writing choices within the same genre. The degree of variation depends on the genre, of course. There is more room for choice in the free-verse poem, for example, than there is in the sonnet, more room for individual creativity in an e-mail message to a friend than in a message to a newsgroup or discussion list. Nevertheless, within the patterns of each genre, writers always have to make choices, and *all* of these choices are creative.

How do writers make creative choices within genres? Writers' creativity depends in large part on their knowledge of the existing conventions. This assertion may sound like a contradiction, especially since we tend to think of creativity as being the opposite of conventionality. But in a very important sense, *writers cannot resist or modify conventions unless they know what these conventions are and what they do.* We can recognize an innovative mystery only if we know the conventions of a traditional mystery. We recognize that a Web site is especially well designed only if we can see how well it works compared to others we have visited. In this way, the constraints that already exist within the patterns of a genre and which limit the writing choices we can make are also what enable writers to be creative.

Writers are not creative by accident, nor do they make creative writing choices simply for the heck of it. Very often, their choices are informed and purposeful. They have a reason for making the choices that they do, and, what is more, they know which patterns within the genre they can modify and which ones they had better not. This knowledge is important since, if writers modify too many essential elements of the genre at once, the audience will no longer be able to recognize the genre at all, defeating the purpose. That strategy might also backfire since users of the genre would likely reject such a wholesale revision of their habits of communication and behavior. Consider, for example, the French artist Marcel Duchamp, who in the early twentieth century submitted a porcelain urinal for an art exhibition, titling it *Fountain.* While this innovative act challenged the conventional understanding of what constitutes art—resisting the traditional presentation of genres and the conventions of "good taste" and aesthetic beauty in art—it also stirred a great deal of controversy and led to the rejection of his "art" in the exhibit and his ensuing resignation from the Society of Independent Artists. This example illustrates the need to examine the patterns of a genre and the scene itself in order to gauge how far you can expand your choices without losing your credibility. But the example also demonstrates how resisting the expectations of a genre can lead to genre change. While not everyone begins with the credibility of a Marcel Duchamp—who, despite the controversy (or perhaps because of it), has become associated with the transformation of art in the twentieth century—his example nevertheless illustrates how you can use the conventions of a genre and your variations from those conventions to make a statement about and to critique existing conventions.

While the previous chapters have shown you how learning to read a genre is an important first step in gaining the experience to write it effectively and creatively, this chapter will explore further how the genres we read and write might fail to serve the goals of a situation and, consequently, might need to be revised. You will have an opportunity to revisit and critique some of the genres we have examined in previous chapters, including such genres as the Patient Medical History Form, the complaint letter, the syllabus, or any of the other genres you have explored so far. We will examine several approaches to genre critique:

- What a critique of genre might look like
- How some genres may not work equally well for everyone within certain scenes
- How genres change as the needs of their users and their scenes change
- What happens to scenes of writing when we change the genres that exist and are used within them

From Thinking Critically to Critiquing Genres

Because genres can give us access to how people act and interact within scenes of writing, they serve not only as sites for **thinking critically** about these scenes, but also as sites for **critiquing** them. Although the words *critically* and *critiquing* are related, each represents a different level of engagement.

The strategy for performing genre analysis (see Box 2.1, pp. 93–94) that we have described and practiced so far in this book asks you to read genres critically. *Critically* in this case means looking below the surface to identify the patterns of various genres and then to use these patterns to gain insight into the scenes in which they are used—using these patterns, in other words, to uncover what they can tell us about some of a scene's assumptions, values, beliefs, and goals. *Critiquing*, however, asks you to do something more. It asks you to *question and evaluate* assumptions. To critique means to engage in **judgment**, to examine and then determine the strengths and shortcomings of certain genres. As such, critiquing genres enables you to examine not just how genres function within their scenes, but also how they might support and/or fail to serve the needs of their users within these scenes. This is the kind of critique that we will now examine in more detail.

As an example of the difference between critically reading and critiquing a genre, let us return to a genre we examined in Chapter 2: the Patient Medical History Form (PMHF). (See pages 61–62.) The PMHF is a commonly used genre in the scene of the doctor's office, a genre that you yourself have probably filled out on your initial visit to a doctor's office. As you might recall from our earlier discussion, the PMHF asks patients to describe their physical characteristics such as age, sex, weight, height, etc.; their medical history, highlighting prior and/or recurring physical conditions; and, most importantly, their current physical symptoms. In performing our critical reading of the PMHF, we noted that a prominent characteristic of the genre is that it focuses mainly on a patient's physical symptoms, while soliciting very little, if any, information about the patient's emotional state. Based on this critical reading, we concluded that the PMHF as a genre reflects Western views of medicine, views that tend to separate the mind from the body in treating illness. The use of the PMHF, then, reveals something about how doctors treat patients by focusing mainly on their physical symptoms, the assumption being that doctors can isolate and then treat physical symptoms with little to no reference to the patient's state of mind. This critical reading of the PMHF helps us describe how the PMHF as a genre reflects the ways doctors and patients communicate. Through our critical reading (which Chapter 5 will explore in greater detail), we come to see how the PMHF acts as a kind of social script for how patients and doctors typically act and communicate within the scene of the doctor's office.

Critiquing a genre takes the above critical reading of the PMHF one step further. It also allows us to *question the practices* that the genre reflects and enables. For example, a **genre critique** might draw attention to the fact that the PMHF actually reduces patients to physical objects in a way that limits the extent to which they can be treated. In other words, by discouraging patients from describing their emotional states and how these emotional states might be connected to their physical symptoms, the PMHF could very well encourage doctors to ignore the full extent of a patient's physical symptoms. In this case, the critique of the PMHF becomes a part of *a larger critique of the medical community* and its typical assumptions, beliefs, and practices. Such a critique involves pointing out the PMHF's shortcomings, especially the ways in which it fails to represent the patient fully and, therefore, fails to serve more completely the needs of the patient (as well as the doctor, perhaps).

On the other hand, a critique of the PMHF might also explore how in fact the PMHF does indeed work effectively in the scene of the doctor's office. You could argue, for example, that by separating the patient's physical symptoms from his or her emotional state, the PMHF actually enables doctors to treat patients more effectively. Reducing the patient to a physical object allows the doctor to keep an emotional distance from the patient, a distance that is necessary, some would argue, for the doctor to maintain objectivity. In this case, the critique reveals the PMHF's positive effects for the doctor.

Genre critique, thus, can take many forms. It can examine whose needs a genre serves or does not serve within a specific scene. It can also question the ways that a genre or genres might fail to serve the objectives and practices of a scene—how, that is, a genre or genres might limit what individuals can and cannot do within certain scenes. Whatever argument you might choose to make about the effects of a genre, keep in mind that a critique of a genre must be based on a critical reading of a genre; the two go hand in hand. As our above example of the PMHF indicates, you need to know how a genre works and what it reveals before you can examine its effects, including its strengths and weaknesses.

WHY IT IS IMPORTANT TO CRITIQUE GENRES

Since genres reflect the typical strategies for communicating and behaving, we might be tempted to assume that this means genres reliably and equitably serve the needs of all their users. This in fact is not always the case. Some genres privilege the needs of some users over the needs of other users. In supporting some of the values, beliefs, and assumptions of members of a scene, genres may limit other possible values and beliefs. Sometimes, people misinterpret or misuse these generic strategies. Furthermore, not everyone within a scene of writing will always agree on these strategies, especially when such strategies may not serve their needs. As a result, genres do not always operate smoothly or effectively within their scenes of writing. They do not always communicate what we intend or expect them to, or we may not want to communicate what genres encourage us to.

Critiquing genres and the scenes in which they are used helps us detect any dissonance between a genre's purposes and the objectives and assumptions of the scene it functions within. For instance, a writer may choose an inappropriate genre for a given occasion, or in some cases someone might confuse one genre for another. Sweepstakes companies use such genre confusion to their advantage by sending sweepstakes letters that look temptingly like legal documents telling us that we have "won" 25 million dollars or a fancy car or a 10-day vacation. Banking on the fact that we will be fooled by the legal-sounding language, such companies try to convince us to take their offers seriously. So well can the sweepstakes promoter make the genre of the sweepstakes letter resemble a legal document that some recipients have responded as if they indeed have received notification of their winnings: Recipients have undergone hardship and expense to claim their prizes and, when the truth is discovered, have filed real lawsuits against the sweepstakes promoters. The strategy of this sweepstakes letter genre is based, in part, on its misuse of another genre and on the recipients' misrecognition. A critique of genres can work to expose such misuse and misrecognition.

Critiquing genres can also help explain how and why some genres might fail to function effectively in a scene of writing. One of us, for example, has studied why jurors might have trouble following jury instructions given them by the judge. Among other things, she discovered that the language used in these instructions was written by and between lawyers and judges to specify legal details to achieve shared objectives of *their* professional legal scene. As a result, the jurors, who were not members of that professional scene, could not fully understand the legal nuances of terms such as *mitigating* or the responsibility implied in a use of passive voice. The genre of jury instructions in this case worked for lawyers and judges but failed to function effectively for those who relied on it most, the jurors. Genre critique can help explain why certain genres fail to produce their desired effects or achieve their writers' purposes.

Writing Activity 4.1

Think about a time when a genre has either failed you or failed to function effectively in one of your scenes of writing. For example, you might have expected a genre to help you communicate something but then you found that it could not (such as the use of the five-paragraph essay in your college-level writing courses). Or perhaps your use of a genre did not produce the desired effect, or your or someone else's use of a genre created controversy within a scene of writing. As you reflect on this occasion, think about how the genre failed. Was it a failure of the genre to meet the needs of its scene and situation; or did you mistakenly choose an inappropriate genre for your situation? What do you think may have contributed to this failure?

EXAMPLES OF CRITIQUING GENRES

Genres, then, can reveal how people communicate and behave within certain scenes, but they can also reveal the potential—and sometimes less obvious—tensions and limitations within certain scenes; such tensions and limitations can lead to misrecognition, miscommunication, and unequal practices. By becoming aware of and then examining these tensions and limitations as they are revealed through genres, you can begin to develop possible strategies for revising genres and changing the scenes in which they are used. Before we describe such strategies for revising genres and changing their scenes, we will now provide some examples of genre critique: one from a student and one from a genre scholar. In both cases, the genre critique functions as a precursor for changing the genre and its scene.

What follows is an analysis paper, an academic paper that breaks something into its parts and examines how those parts relate (for more about the analysis paper, see Chapter 6). This paper was written by a student who identifies and examines tensions within the genre of the wedding invitation. In it, the student writer performs what we have been calling genre critique. The paper is by no means flawless, but it does serve as a helpful example of what a genre critique might look like written by a student who, perhaps like you, is attempting a genre critique for the first time. As you read it, notice how the writer employs a critical reading of the genre in order to critique the genre. That is, she first describes how the genre works and then evaluates its effects—both in terms of what the genre does and in terms of the effect it has on those who use it.

Devine 1

For the Bride or Groom?

Theresa Devine

Invitations are used for a variety of events such as a birthday, christening, anniversary celebration, party, and, in my case, a wedding. Each event brings with it a different kind of invitation with its own set of conventions. For each of these invitations a different genre exists, each being a written form of the American culture. Since an invitation is a written representation of the American culture, it can tell us about our culture. The genre I would like to discuss is the genre of the wedding invitation.

A major decision that a bride and groom face to initiate the first step toward their big event is choosing the wedding invitations. There are many issues a couple has to consider when deciding upon the perfect invitation. For example, what kind of pattern should they pick? What color should be used? What type of writing? And what should the invitation say? All of these questions contribute to the genre of the wedding invitation. However, who does the genre of the invitation usually appeal to most? Are the invitations really appealing to both the bride and groom? Wedding invitations are looked at as an invitation that represents a joint union between two people. But when analyzed, wedding invitations seem to represent an unequal union. The invitations themselves are more appealing to the bride than the groom. And when the invitation arrives at a couple's house, who is more likely to look at it and view the invitation, the man or the woman? By examining such questions, I have come to the conclusion that the genre of wedding invitations is gender biased through the colors, patterns, writing, and dialogue displayed in it.

To begin supporting this claim I would like to examine the colors of wedding invitations. By looking at invitations in the catalogs "Wedding Treasures," "Now and Then," and "Rexcraft," the predominant colors appear to be soft feminine pastels like: pink, green, and blue. Other colors displayed in the catalogs are vibrant, bright, and shiny, for example hot pink, silver, teal, and red. It is hard to find invitations that could appeal to a man using masculine associated colors like: navy blue, forest green, and maroon. The colors used are colors that are directed to the eyes of most women. The colors are soft and bright, not bold and dark. The softness of the invitations is made to appeal to women and not to many men. The colors used on the majority of the invitations and displayed in these catalogs supports the claim that the genre of wedding invitations is gender biased.

Next, I would like to draw attention to the patterns or drawings used on wedding invitations. Drawings that predominantly appear on the invitations are flowers, bows, roses, small children, a fairy tale castle, a dancing man and woman, and hearts. Almost all of the invitations that I viewed contained at least one of these drawings or symbols. As a woman, I've been taught to find these symbols cute, pretty, and feminine. What symbol here could possibly be considered appealing to a man? How often in our culture do men recognize the beauty of flowers, or ask for them as a gift? Who always dreams about the fairy tale castle? There is not much to be found as masculine in the form of a wedding invitation. The simplest, and I would consider most appealing invitation to a man, is found only five times throughout the wedding catalogs. The detail on the invitation is just a silver outline around the invitation, with no patterns or pastel colors. This invitation is in the middle of most of the catalogs. This invitation will be easily missed and overlooked among the flowers, colors, and bows, once again reinforcing the gender bias within the genre of wedding invitations.

The lettering and the content of the invitations also support their gender bias. Cultural views of women generally perceive them as writing a soft flowing bubbled yet clear print. The writing on each and every invitation used in the wedding catalog is very similar to most writing styles of women. In fact, out of twenty and some odd types of writing styles to choose from in the different catalogs, only four of them are in a traditional print that could be considered as unisex writing. Likewise, looking over the dialogue used in invitations, again it can be seen that wedding invitations are gender biased. I have gone through the different catalogs and found that the majority of the invitations use fairly similar dialogue. Within three catalogs averaging fifty-eight pages and displaying approximately four types of invitations a page, only seven in each book were worded differently than the following:

Devine 4

Mr. And Mrs. Benjamin Sharpe
request the honor of your presence
at the marriage of **their daughter**
Michelle Louise
to
Mr. Christopher R. Botham
on Sunday the fifth of October
nineteen hundred and ninety-seven
at twelve noon
St. Etc . . .

Just by looking at the above example it can be seen that this invitation clearly represents the bride. Look at the bolded letters **their daughter**. What about the other parents' son? The groom is briefly mentioned with no long introduction like the bride and right after his name is the date, time, and place. So I ask, who is the invitation really appealing to and who does it represent? I clearly see the answer to be the BRIDE.

What does this say about our culture, values, and the way that we view this announcement? As a culture we see this event as a moment where the bride, or "their daughter" is giving up a part of her identity. "Their daughter" is giving up a name that has represented her over the past eighteen years or more. The value of that name and change of names is extremely important to the bride and her parents. The bride mentioned on the invitation will always be "their daughter." However, the bride's name is most likely changing and she will no longer be recognized as "their daughter" just by looking at her name. More information needs to be known about this woman in order to find out who her parents are. A wedding invitation allows parents to formally recognize their daughter through this type of dialogue before she then gives up her name.

Devine 5

Also, the dialog often represents who is contributing a lot of time and effort in this event. Recognizing the parents of the bride and their daughter first reflects that they have built on the initiation of this event (the engagement) and see this as the moment in which they give away their most precious gift of all, their daughter. As such, the invitation remains gender biased.

Our culture seems to view this event as a feminine and traditional celebration. The genre of the invitations represents the femininity of the occasion. I am not saying that the groom is not important and not involved in this process of choosing an invitation. However, I am saying that the female usually does play more of a role in this process. When asking five future spouses, "Who generally initiates the planning and decision making in the wedding, you or your fiancé, the answer is a unanimous me (the bride) or me and my mom (the other woman).

I recognize that there are other styles of writing on invitations and not all women like the flowers, bows, and heart patterned invitations; and in some situations the groom plays an equal role in deciding on wedding invitations. However, I am making the claim that the majority of wedding invitations are gender biased and are more appealing to the female eye. Invitations display this feminine bias using the types of colors, patterns, style of writing, and dialogue displayed on them. As a result of my analysis of wedding invitations, my fiancé and I have chosen to use the single male-appealing invitation using a feminine style of writing-- just so that we can balance the gender inequality a little.

Writing Activity 4.2

In "For the Bride or Groom?" distinguish between the parts that perform a critical reading of the genre and the parts that perform a critique of the genre. Give examples of each and explain how they differ.

Because genres, as Theresa Devine observes above, are indeed reflections of our culture, they can be critiqued in order to expose some of the entrenched cultural assumptions and practices they reflect. In the case of wedding invitations, in addition to making the assumption that weddings are for the bride and her parents, we notice a cultural irony at work, an irony the student critique points out but does not fully address. The irony goes something like this: The wedding invitations are meant mainly to appeal to the bride, yet it is ultimately the bride's self-interests that are least served by these invitations since these invitations reduce the bride to a piece of property that is being transferred from parents to husband. In this case, the student critique suggests that the genre of wedding invitations not only reflects but reinforces gender inequalities. *Genre critique can help reveal shortcomings in the ways we communicate and act in our various scenes. Such critique can also potentially lead to changing the genre to make it more equitable.*

Collaborative Activity 4.1

Working with classmates, think about how the wedding invitation could be changed to address the critique that "For the Bride or Groom?" raises. What would it take to correct the inequality between bride and groom? Write a wedding invitation that reflects this equality.

Genre scholar Randall Popken has performed a similar critique of another popular genre, one we will describe further in Chapter 9: the resumé. In his scholarly article "The Pedagogical Dissemination of a Genre: The Resumé in American Business Discourse Textbooks, 1914–1939," Popken traces the evolution of the resumé from its beginnings to the present. In its current state, he argues, the resumé works to erase the presence of the individual who writes it. By downplaying the voice and persona of resumé writers, the resumé depersonalizes job seekers, portraying them as commodities that can be sold. To prove his claim, Popken turns to the genre itself and its rhetorical patterns. The following patterns, he argues, all help erase the presence of the resumé writer, thus limiting his or her ability to present a personality:

- The use of subjectless sentences to describe a person's work history, sentences such as: "managed a large budget" instead of "I managed a large budget," etc.

- The physical constraints of the resumé, which is usually limited in length from one to two pages.

* The overall structure of the resumé and its prescribed categories such as "career objective," "work experience," "education," etc.
* The kind of "acceptable topics" the resumé writer can include, which tends to be limited to his or her previous positions, educational accomplishments, and career success, while excluding topics such as the writer's home life, nonwork interests, or philosophy of life.
(Popken 92–93)

The above characteristics all contribute to the exclusion of personality in the resumé. This exclusion reveals a possible shortcoming in the way that individuals communicate and interact within business scenes of writing, reinforcing an artificial and potentially detrimental split between the personal and the professional. Such a split also contributes to the reduction of individuals to the sum of the work they do, a reduction that in some cases helps turn employees into commodities that can be bought and sold.

PERFORMING YOUR OWN GENRE CRITIQUE

To perform a genre critique like the ones we describe above, first follow the guidelines for conducting genre analyses we outlined in Box 2.1, pp. 93–94. These guidelines will help you identify the scene or scenes in which the genre is used, the key patterns within the genre itself, and what these patterns tell us about the scene or scenes. After you have completed the above analysis, you are ready to determine what you see as the effects of the genre, including its strengths and weaknesses. Keep the questions in Box 4.1 in mind as you consider the effects of the genre.

Box 4.1 offers just a sampling of the possible questions you could ask to help you gauge a genre's effects. Notice how the questions invite you to engage the genre not so much on its own terms (by describing its features and explaining how and why they function within a scene of writing) but rather on *your* own terms. That is, the questions lead you to look beyond how and why the genre works so that you can assess how well it works based on standards you hold. For instance, someone else might agree with Popken that the resumé indeed does depersonalize its writer, but that same person might not agree that such depersonalization is necessarily a limitation of the genre. When you are critiquing a genre, then, you need to be sure to make compelling **arguments**—specific claims, supported by reasons and evidence—about how and why the genre does in fact fail or succeed in some way.

Box 4.1 *Questions for Critiquing Genres*

- What does the genre allow its users to do and what does it not allow them to do?
- Whose needs are most served by the genre? Whose needs are least served?
- In what ways does the genre succeed the most? In what ways does it fail?
- Does the genre enable its users to represent themselves fully?
- Does the genre effectively accomplish what its users intend it to do?
- Does the genre limit the way in which its users can do their work?
- Does the genre create inequalities among its users that lead to imbalances of power?
- Do the assumptions that the genre reflects privilege certain ways of doing things?
- Do those privileged ways of doing things run counter to the supposed objectives of those who use it and the scene in which it is used?
- Does the genre allow its users to do certain things at the expense of others? And if so, at what cost?

Writing Activity 4.3

Choose a new genre or look back on a genre that either you or we have analyzed in an earlier chapter. For example, this can be the genre you analyzed in Chapter 2 (Writing Activity 2.8, p. 91, and Writing Project 2.1, p. 97) or any of the genres we have analyzed throughout the book so far, such as the syllabus or the complaint letter. Your teacher might assign one of these genres. Whatever genre you choose or are assigned, carefully examine its features and, using some of the questions we listed in Box 4.1, work to develop a critique of the genre. In the process of developing your critique, identify those features of the genre that support your critique, much like Popken identified those features of the resumé that limit the expressions of the writer's personality. Keep careful notes of your findings as you might need to use them to develop your argument in Writing Project 4.1 (p. 182).

Having described what we mean by a genre critique and having invited you to practice doing such a critique, we will now further address what is gained by doing such a critique. Critique even for the sake of critique can be enlightening since it exposes some of the entrenched and sometimes hidden limitations within a genre and its scene of writing. Indeed, as the above examples of the PMHF, the wedding invitations, and the resumé demonstrate, genre critique can reveal how genres do not always function smoothly or effectively for all their users—how, in fact, genres can be sites of controversy as much as sites of communication. *If you understand a genre's limitations when you write it, you might be able to resist its embedded assumptions.* In addition to exposing some of the limitations and complexities of genres, however, a genre critique can also serve as the starting point for changing already existing genres and developing new genres. The next section will describe how genre critique can lead to such potential genre transformation.

Changing Genres

Genres are not static entities. At times, they may appear to be unchanging, especially when they become entrenched in how and why people act and interact within certain scenes. But the reality is that genres do change as the people who use them and the scenes in which they are used change. *As attitudes, ways of knowing, and goals change, people revise already existing genres and sometimes develop new ones that more effectively reflect these new attitudes, ways of knowing, and goals.* Likewise, as the technologies for communication change, new genres emerge to accommodate them (for example, personal computer technology has enabled writers to incorporate more design and images into their writing, leading to such genres as Web pages). In this way, genres *evolve* over time, so that, by tracing the evolution of a genre within a certain scene, scholars can actually trace the evolution of people's assumptions within that scene.

For instance, one such genre scholar, Charles Bazerman, has traced the historical evolution of the genre of the experimental report in the first English scientific journal, the *Philosophic Transactions of the Royal Society of London*. In his book *Shaping Written Knowledge: The Genre and Activity of the Experimental Article in Science,* his research shows how the experimental report genre, which began as an informative letter exchanged among scientists, developed and changed between the years 1665 and 1800 as a result of changes in assumptions regarding what nature is and how it can be studied. For example, Bazerman observed that the genre developed over the period of those years, from being a way of simply describing an unusual phenomenon (for example, how mercury expands when heated) and, in some cases, showing readers how to re-create the phenomenon; to being a more conscious investigation of phenomena that involves some manipulation of the phenomena (for example, testing how mercury reacts under different conditions); to being more driven by a specific goal, such as the testing of a hypothesis or the resolving of a debate. The changes in the genre during these early years, Bazerman explains, reflect changing attitudes about nature, from a view of nature as a "given" to a view of nature as a subject of contention. In other words, in the earliest stages of the experimental report, "nature was portrayed as speaking for itself" and so the report was simply a way of describing nature and telling readers what happened (Bazerman 77). Later, as assumptions about nature changed, so too did the way scientists report their experiments. As Bazerman explains,

> experiments stop being a clear window to a self-revealing nature, but become a way of tying down uncertain claims about an opaque and uncertain nature. The meaning of an experiment is no longer the simple observation of what happens. An experiment is to be understood only in terms of the ideas that motivate it, for nature is no longer considered to be so easy to find. (67-8)

So what we recognize today as an experimental report with its testing and proof and description of methods and results is a reflection of our current attitudes about what nature is and how it can be studied. Each genre contains ways of thinking that have evolved over its history.

FROM CRITIQUE TO CHANGE

Genres are always changing as the assumptions and needs of their users change. Genres do not change magically on their own; *people* change genres, usually slowly and imperceptibly, as they begin to recognize the ways in which genres no longer fully serve their needs. The genre of the experimental report, for instance, did not evolve overnight into the genre we recognize today. It took nearly 150 years to do so, and it in fact still continues to evolve with the influence of new scientific technologies and greater knowledge about nature. In each stage of the experimental report's development, some scientist or group of scientists would likely have encountered and identified a limitation caused by existing genre conventions and attempted to revise the genre. While they may not consciously have performed a genre analysis and decided on a needed change, their actions in writing the genre differently created changes so that the genre would accommodate their new perspective. In this way, genre critique and genre change work hand in hand.

We can observe how genre critique might lead to genre change if we look once again at the genre of the Patient Medical History Form (PMHF). We discussed one possible critique of the PMHF earlier in this chapter. If enough patients and doctors begin to complain about the PMHF's limitations, then it is quite possible that the American Medical Association will recommend revising the genre so that it solicits more information about a patient's emotions, especially in terms of how the patient's emotional state might affect his or her physical symptoms. Such changes might occur slowly at first, with a few doctors adding questions that ask patients to describe their state of mind. Eventually, these changes, especially if they are sanctioned by the AMA, could become new conventions.

The following student's researched position paper, an academic argument based on the writer's research (a genre we discuss in detail in Chapter 7), provides a real-world example of how a new genre evolves from an already existing genre to meet new conditions and needs. The student, an education major, chose to examine how the report card as a genre has changed over the years as assumptions about how students learn have changed. In particular, she explores how a new genre of student assessment, the grade continuum, is emerging to reflect these new assumptions. As you read her researched position paper, think about what it teaches us about how and why genres change and what such generic change means for the people and scenes that use them. How, for example, do changes in the genre reflect changes in education philosophies? What reasons does the writer give for supporting these changes?

Weishaar 1

Changing Forms

Amy J. Weishaar

What is the purpose of attending school? One might answer that the ultimate goal of education is to promote the intellectual, social, physical, and even spiritual growth of an individual to achieve at least a minimum set of criteria in order to maximize the individual's personal quality of life and contribution to society. Assuming that this type of response is accurate, how does the education community formally communicate, to the individual as well as to society, an evaluation of the individual's progress and achievements? In America since the late 1800s, the answer has been the almighty grade

Weishaar 2

card. The grade card, also referred to as a progress report, is a
genre, the "typified response" of the education community
to the "recurring rhetorical situation" of reporting a student's
progress in education. Currently the traditional grade card
evaluation practice is undergoing revision throughout the
United States. In particular, Quail Run Elementary School in
Lawrence, KS, is leading the reform of this genre in the
Lawrence Public Schools. What do the changes being made
to this genre tell the public about the education community?
This reform reflects the education community's commitment
to continually revise and implement educational strategies in
order to maximize the quality and effectiveness of student
instruction.

In each decade it seems that the government and educators come up with a new emphasis for education. For
example, in the late 1950s and 1960s the educational push in
America was to emphasize mathematics and science in order
to compete in the booming field of technology such as space
exploration. Then came the segregation of students with like
abilities or disabilities (i.e., learning disabled, behavior disor-
ders, educable mentally handicapped, gifted/talented/
creative) in order to give individualized, specialized attention
to each child. What led to changes such as these? The
answer is assessment of students. Assessment influences and
often changes instruction. Assessments such as state-required
proficiency tests, "multiple choice" in design, as well as the
individualized grade card show that students are not measuring up to the set standards of the state, the schools, or the
teachers. Test scores measuring American students' intellectual development are constantly being compared to that of
Japanese children. The results rarely seem promising.
Observations such as these lead educators to wonder: Are we
evaluating students fairly? Are our assessments constructed

Weishaar 3

to give a fair analysis of students' performances? Do our current forms of evaluation influence teachers' means and emphases of instruction so that student work and progress can easily be converted to a weighted measure required by the grade card genre? The grade card, due to its physical and textual form, presents those reviewing a child's progress with a concise list of the skills which the child should acquire in each particular grade level. This genre reflects the assessments of the educational community, pre-constructed ideas which are considered most important in a child's education. The feedback that students and parents receive about the student's performance is contained within the grade card genre, and unless a parent-teacher conference is held, the grade card is solely responsible for reporting the child's educational progress. Thus, the grade card genre is a powerful instrument. What exactly does it tell the reader?

Currently the standardized report card for elementary schools utilizes the seventy-nine-year-old A, B, C, D, and F grading scale in conjunction with symbols (i.e., +, –) and/or other terms such as satisfactory and unsatisfactory to report student achievement. These forms subdivide the curriculum by subject, and assign a letter grade or symbol to each subject. The graded subjects include math, language arts, reading, writing, social studies, science, music, art, physical education, and behavioral attributes. Subdivisions for each of the categories include more specific statements about the curriculum of the subject (i.e., "The student knows addition facts through 100"). Blanks next to the more specific statements are checked with a "+," indicating that the child has mastered the skill, or a "–" indicating that the child needs to improve or has failed to learn that knowledge. Students are then placed into categorical grades such as A--outstanding effort, B--above average, C--average, D--below average, and

Weishaar 4

F--failed; other categories might include a less-harsh wording system such as satisfactory or unsatisfactory. What meaning do these terms actually hold? Is the student's performance average when compared to that of her peers, or is the student failing to meet the state and school criteria of achievement for that grade? Does "average" achievement for one teacher translate to "above average" achievement for another teacher in terms of expectations? Does the student's grade reflect the information that he/she has actually learned, or is the grade a type of punishment, a reflection of a lack of responsibility on the student's part to turn in assignments? With the current type of report card assessment, educators, parents, and students cannot be sure.

Assessment, especially the genre which presents the assessment, influences and often changes instruction. The standard type of report card fails to explain exactly what is expected of the students and what the degrees (i.e., +, −, average, etc.) of a child's performance actually mean. Assessment is being altered so that it is reflective of the curriculum which is to be taught. The genre is being altered to communicate a more thorough evaluation of a child's development, accomplishments, and goals. Thus, the means of instruction are changing to complement the new evaluation. The products and specific skills which teachers require students to master are geared toward meeting the requirements of the new genre of evaluation.

This is not to say that because student performance is not skyrocketing the charts of our current forms of assessment, that educators are changing the way they assess in order to make our students appear more intelligent. Instead, educators are asking, "Do our forms of assessment (genres) accurately measure the knowledge that our students have mastered?" For example, does a multiple-choice test

Weishaar 5

necessarily reflect a child's ability to write a well-developed paragraph, or even ask a child if he or she can explain how he or she interprets a concept? If the answer is no, then a grade drawn from a multiple choice assessment is equally lacking in accurately reflecting a child's knowledge. Furthermore, assessment should not just be a measure of what the student can memorize for a test and then forget ten minutes later. Instruction today is valued as it applies to the student's application of knowledge, skills, and understanding in important, real-world contexts.

One of the newest forms of assessment, called Performance Based Education, measures what really counts-- it measures how students apply their knowledge, skills, and understanding to real-world contexts. What is assessed should be what is important to learn. Principal Harold London of Ridgewood High School, Norridge, Ill., in an article in the NASSP Bulletin of May 1996, writes that: "Our purpose for grades is to communicate progress to students and parents. If we want to communicate accurately, we need to expand the choices available for teachers to use [for giving assessments, the genre used] so the purpose can be realized. If we have high expectations for our students, we need to establish the expectations early and demand that students meet the expec- tations" (119).

Because education is turning toward Outcomes Based/Performance Based Education (P.B.E.), the methods of assessment, and therefore the genre of reporting these assessments, must be reformed. Why? One of the greatest flaws of assessments such as the standardized report card is that these types of assessments often provide an evaluation of a student's achievements without any documentation of the achievements. P.B.E. calls for educators to define content standards and learner outcomes and then to make these con-

Weishaar 6

tent standards and learner outcomes available to the public. Along with this documentation of what students will be expected to learn, a criteria and high standards must be established to measure the student's performance because the student's achievement will be assessed on his or her performance. This type of assessment also demands that schools develop a curriculum and instruction to fit the content standards.

Obviously, the current standardized grade card cannot accurately reflect or give a documentation, an ongoing flow chart, of the student's achievements. Therefore, schools like Quail Run Elementary are reforming the traditional grade card, the genre of student assessment. Currently Quail Run teachers are perfecting a new type of "grade card," specific to general subjects (for now writing and reading), called continuums. A continuum is unlike a traditional grade card in design, content, and even in its range of function.

The continuums are divided by general subjects such as writing and reading which overlap many content areas. With the new push for measuring a student's application of his or her knowledge to real-world situations, many subject/content areas overlap. For example, writing ability might be measured in a social studies unit which might also include scientific investigation and mathematical problem solving. Standard grade cards do not facilitate the combining of subject areas because a grade must be given for each area. Continuums are designed in levels of development; each level of development has content standards and objectives which a student must demonstrate a command of before moving to the next development category. In the writing continuum, for example, the categories include: (For Primary students) Pre-Emerging Writer, Emerging Writer, Developing Writer, Expanding Writer, and Accomplishing Writer; (For

Weishaar 7

Intermediate students) Expanding Writer, Accomplishing Writer, Maturing Writer, and Distinguishing Writer. These categories are laid out horizontally across an 8" × 14" page. Under each development category are the criteria for assessment.

With this change in assessment, new criteria and scoring tools have been developed which allow teachers to evaluate a student's performance based on his/her application of his/her knowledge, The new scoring tools reflect the real-world idea that there is not necessarily one correct answer (a concept which was not enforced in the standard grade card genre). Grading rubrics, rating scales, and performance lists are scoring tools composed of the criteria which list the qualities educators consider to be most significant in student work. In the Quail Run writing continuum, the criteria are based on the Six Trait Writing model. This model measures the quality of a student's work by looking for six writing traits: Idea, Organization, Voice, Word Choice, Sentence Fluency, and Conventions. The new continuum also explains this model of evaluation on the backside of the continuum. Also, teachers are required to keep a portfolio of each student's work. As projects, papers, etc. are completed, the student along with the teacher selects pieces to be placed in the portfolio. Through these writing pieces, the teacher documents examples of a child's ability or difficulty with meeting a listed criteria. The portfolios, although not attached to the continuums, are used in direct conjunction with the continuums. They are the documentation of the student's progress. The continuum genre demands that instruction be geared towards the standards of the continuum and that examples of the students' applications/demonstrations of these specific skills be documented. Portfolios, because of the function of the genre, are now a necessity in evaluation. They back up everything that the new genre, the continuum, reports. In fact, this reformed genre does not limit what we ask or learn about a student to the simple question and measurement standard of "what grade did I get?" The continuums, instead, call upon other sources, such as the portfolio, to prove the report.

The continuums hold teachers accountable for giving accurate, detailed evaluations because they must keep an up-to-date portfolio of each child's work. Parents and students are exposed to a clearly defined curriculum early on, and because the development levels are laid out, they are aware of not only what the student has already accomplished but also where the student is heading. The continuums have a "time line" of sorts running horizontally across the top of the development categories. At each marking period, after determining the category of development that the child falls under as demonstrated by his or her performance recorded by the portfolios, the teacher will mark an approximate place of current development status. This mark, if found to remain in the same area over several grading periods, will indicate to the teacher that this student could need specialized attention in a specific area.

With the movement towards the inclusion of all learning abilities within one classroom, the continuum in this way fills the need for individualized attention or a way to check on student progress. The development categories of the continuum, along with the rubrics used as scoring tools, provide a flexibility within this genre that allows teachers to give a personalized critique of individual students in what could pose to be a class with extremely diverse learning abilities. This flexibility was not found in the old genre of report cards with a rigid five-category letter grade approach. The continuums do not end with a development level anything less than the

Weishaar 9

abilities of an adult writer. Thus, students and parents are asked together to write goals for improvement at each marking period, and because of the "continuous" format they always have an idea of what goals are appropriate to aim towards.

Furthermore, the continuums generate flexibility among schools to accommodate new students. In this highly mobile world, students often transfer schools throughout districts and across the country. The continuum not only is designed to travel with the student from year to year, but in the case of a transfer, the new school and teacher will be able to see how the student has progressed, the curriculum he/she studied (from portfolios), and will immediately be able to tell the student's current learning state.

Educators, in their commitment to maximize the quality of student instruction, are developing a tool for evaluation, a genre which sets clear educational standards and requires that students demonstrate that they have met these standards. The revision of the standard, limiting grade card genre has evolved into a flexible form of communication which enhances student performance and does not just measure it.

Weishaar 10

Works Cited

Goodrich, Heidi. "Understanding Rubrics." <u>Educational Leadership</u> (Dec. 1996/ Jan. 1997): 14-17.

Guskey, Thomas R. "Making the Grade: What Benefits
Students?" Educational Leadership (Oct. 1994): 14-19.

Hartenbach, David, and Joan Ott, and Sue Clark.
"Performance-Based Education in Aurora."
Educational Leadership (Dec. 1996/ Jan. 1997): 51-55.

Kirby-Linton, Kate, and Nancy Lyle, and Susan White.
"When Parents and Teachers Create Writing
Standards." Educational Leadership (Dec. 1996/ Jan.
1997): 30-32.

Claffidge, Pamela Brown, and Elizabeth M. Whitaker.
"Implementing a New Elementary Progress Report."
Educational Leadership (Oct. 1994): 7-13.

London, Harold. "Do Our Grading Systems Contribute to
Dumbing Down?" NASSP Bulletin (May 1996):117-
121.

McTighe, Jay. "What Happens Between Assessments?"
Educational Leadership (Dec. 1996/ Jan. 1997): 6-12

Meisels, Samuel J. "Using Work Sampling in Authentic
Assessments." Educational Leadership (Dec. 1996/Jan.
1997): 60-65.

Wiggins, Grant. "Practicing What We Preach in Designing
Authentic Assessments." Educational Leadership (Dec.
1996/ Jan. 1997): 18-25.

Collaborative Activity 4.2

Think about what the above researched position paper—as well as our earlier discussions of the PMHF and the experimental report—teach us about how and why genres evolve or new genres emerge. What factors seem to encourage genres to change? How does that change come about? As a group, generate a list of your findings. Be prepared to share and discuss your findings with your classmates.

As we observe in the examples of the experimental report, the PMHF, and the report card, the new genres that develop out of new conditions and/or needs are most often revisions and refinements of already existing genres. This is the case even with genres that seem to be completely "new" such as the various kinds of e-mail that have emerged as a result of Internet technologies. Although the medium for communicating in e-mail might be new, the genres of e-mail that are developing—such as messages to friends, shared jokes, office communications, and spam or unsolicited e-mail advertisements—are themselves revisions of more traditional, already existing genres. Language scholars are beginning to study the characteristics of e-mail writing, and, in the future, we might be able to characterize its genres more fully.

Even now, however, we know that some e-mail messages combine characteristics of speaking and writing, giving them somewhat of a conversational quality. Messages in an e-mail thread are often responses, sometimes with the previous message included in the response, making such messages resemble conventional turn-taking conversations. However, unlike face-to-face conversations, the technological medium of e-mail—quicker than sending a letter to someone but slower than a face-to-face conversation—results in some written genres that use abbreviated language and shorthand (such as "BTW" for "By the way" or "IMHO" for "In my humble opinion") or symbols known as "emoticons" such as smiles :), frowns :(, or winks ;) that convey missing visual cues, tone, and body language. At the same time, e-mail genres draw on a variety of already existing written genres, such as memoranda, business letters, personal letters, reports, and so on. As such, we notice how some e-mail messages begin and end with greetings and salutations much as traditional letters do, while others use the subject line and memo headings as reports do.

Writing Activity 4.4

Think about the ways that you write e-mail messages. What genres do you find yourself drawing on, even unconsciously, as you compose your messages? How would you characterize your e-mail writing style, and how does this differ as you write in different e-mail genres? How many different kinds of e-mail genres do you think you write? What characteristics distinguish those different e-mail genres? In what ways do you find yourself writing differently when you write in e-mail genres (such as a note to a friend) as opposed to when you write more traditional genres (such as snail-mail letters to friends)?

REVISING OLD GENRES TO DEVELOP NEW ONES

There are reasons that new genres usually develop as revisions of previous ones. Genres reflect habitual ways of communicating and behaving in various scenes, and habits, as we all know, are difficult to break, especially when we rely on them to function in various scenes. If a completely unprecedented genre were to emerge, people would simply not know how to engage with it. And, even if people *were* able to make sense of a completely new genre, the question remains, can someone actually create a completely new genre without borrowing from other genres? Scholars who study the development of genres claim that it is unlikely. In fact, even genres that appear to be radically different from those that preceded them often result from combining already existing genres with a new scene or medium, just as we saw in the case of e-mail genres.

The genre of the resumé provides a case in point for how genres change. Earlier, we discussed how Randall Popken has argued that the resumé depersonalizes its writers, turning them into commodities that can be sold. As Popken explains, this was not always the case. Originally, job seekers relied solely on letters of application, which allowed them to write in full prose paragraphs about themselves and their qualifications. When the earliest versions of the resumé began to appear between 1914 and 1924, they were embedded in these letters of application. Popken refers to them as "resumé-in-letter." Here is an example of one such "resumé-in-letter." As you read it, notice how the "resumé-in-letter" is different from and similar to today's resumés.

X462 Tribune,
   Chicago.

Dear Sir:
   This is in answer to your advertisement for a stenographer:
   My education experience and qualifications, briefly, are: I am a graduate of the shorthand department of Brown's Business College, Peoria, and also of the Peoria High School, a school that is on the accredited list of the State University. I can take dictation rapidly and transcribe it quickly and accurately—spelling correctly, and placing the punctuation and capitals properly.
   I know how—
To arrange a letter tastefully on the letterhead.
To file a letter properly—or to find one that has been filed.
To use the mimeograph and other duplicating devices.

To fold a letter.

To make out a bill correctly.

To meet callers.

To keep the affairs of the office to myself.

To attend to the mailing so that the right enclosures will go with the right letters.

I fully understand the uses of common business papers, such as drafts, checks, receipts, invoices, statements, etc.

I am twenty years old and live at home.

I have no experience, but my course of training has been thorough and has duplicated as closely as possible actual business conditions.

May I not have an opportunity to demonstrate my ability? The salary question we can safely leave open until you have had a chance to see what I can do.

Very truly yours,

From Randall Popken, "The Pedagogical Dissemination of a Genre: The Resumé in American Business Discourse Textbooks, 1914–1939" *JAC: A Journal of Composition Theory* 19.1 (1999): 91–116.

Notice how in the above example, the list of facts about the applicant is embedded within the sentence framework of the letter, thereby giving the applicant an opportunity to at least present himself or herself as more than just a list of facts. Popken notes that by 1924, the resumé begins to appear as a separate genre, one not embedded within an application letter. This separation reduced the self that could be presented more fully in the letter mainly to a set of facts that are depicted in the resumé. Here is a version of an early freestanding resumé from 1924. Notice how the genre has changed from the earlier version of the resumé-in-letter:

Qualifications of Mr. Samuel Crompton

Personal:

Age, 25; unmarried; height, 5ft. 7in.; weight, 156 lbs.

Habits: good; does not drink; smokes moderately; likes outdoor sports.

Associations: member of St. John's Episcopal Church; active in the Elks and Odd Fellows, and a member of the Arts Association.

Health: very good, rarely sick.

Personality: see photograph attached.

Education:
Textile Arts School, graduated, 1917.
Temple College, attended night sessions, winters, 1913, 14, 16, 18.
Massachusetts Institute of Technology, finished night course in design, 1915.
Home Study Course, Correspondence Institute, pursued courses in carpet designing, show card writing, textile weaves and design, 1912-16.

Experience:

General Design work,	The Textile Mills,	1917-23	$2500
Asst. Carpet Designer,	Frankford Mills,	1915-17	1800
Ornamental Designer,	Clay Pottery Works,	1914-15	1500
Architectural Drafting,	Christopher Wren Co.,	1912-14	1400
Teaching and Drafting,	Christopher Wren Co.,	1910-12	1000

References:
Mr. Theodore Lee, General Manager, Textile Mills, Philadelphia
Mr. John Mercer, Ass. Supt., Frankford Mills, Philadelphia
Mr. Joseph Aspdin, Pres. Clay Pottery Works, Philadelphia
Mr. Richard Artwright, Instructor, Drexel Institute, Philadelphia
Rev. Samuel Benedict, Philadelphia
Address: 19752 Gloucester Avenue, Philadelphia; Telephone, 469J, Germantown

From Randall Popken, "The Pedagogical Dissemination of a Genre: The Resumé in American Business Discourse Textbooks, 1914–1939" *JAC: A Journal of Composition Theory* 19.1 (1999): 91–116.

In this early precursor of the modern resumé, we notice features that we recognize in today's resumé, including the subjectless sentences and the categories of education, experiences, and references. We also recognize the list of facts and dates, arranged in an outline format. Today's resumé, however, generally allows even less personal information. It is not common for applicants to disclose their health, personality, height, weight, or even personal hobbies. Yet in the evolution of the genre from a letter, to a resumé-in-letter, to a free-standing resumé that allows some personal information, to the present-day resumé that allows less personal information, we can see a chain of interconnections that link each new genre to a prior one. And, even today, the genre of the resumé is undergoing more changes as new technologies allow more creative use of design and visuals and Internet technologies allow applicants to create online resumés with links to other sites, such as their professional portfolios.

Collaborative Activity 4.3

Working with a group of classmates, find a sample contemporary resumé, either one of your own or one from someone you know (or refer to one of the samples in Chapter 9, or find one on the Internet), and compare its features to that of the early resumés we described above. What strikes you as being similar and different? What might account for these differences?

Collaborative Activity 4.4

This activity invites you to change an already existing genre. In your group, and while working with the same contemporary resumé that you examined in the previous activity, try to revise the resumé in ways that make it more reflective of its writer's personality as you imagine it. What changes would you make? What would you add and/or delete? How creative can you be without risking the effectiveness of the resumé in helping its writer get the desired job? After making your revisions, reflect on them. What strategies did you use? What risks did you take and what risks did you avoid? Why? What do you think will be the effects of your revisions?

Using the Power of Genre for Change

As we have demonstrated with our ongoing example of the PMHF, genre critique can lead to genre change. But this is not all genre critique can do. Genre change can, in turn, lead to changes in the ways that people communicate and interact. For example, the new questions added to the PMHF, which ask patients to describe their mental state in relation to their physical symptoms, would change the genre; they might also change the ways doctors treat patients and what patients feel comfortable discussing with their doctors. Changing the genre *reflects* but can also *affect* changes in assumptions and practices. This is what we mean when we say that genres have power. Genres are not just sites for communicating and acting within scenes of writing; they are also potentially sites for changing the scenes themselves.

The emergence of Web sites and other hypertext genres in the last couple of decades shows how the power of genre can affect how people communicate and interact. James Sosnoski has studied these effects, focusing in particular on how genres written in hypertext, such as Web sites, are changing the way people read and interact with texts. He describes eight characteristics that define what he calls "hyper-reading." They are:

1. Filtering: a higher degree of selectivity in reading

2. Skimming: less text actually read

3. Pecking: a less linear sequencing of passages read

4. Imposing: less contextualization derived from the text and more from readerly intention

5. Filming: the ". . . but I saw the film" response which implies that significant meaning is derived from graphical elements as from verbal elements of the text

6. Trespassing: loosening of textual boundaries

7. De-authorizing: lessening sense of authorship and authorly intention

8. Fragmenting: breaking texts into notes rather than regarding them as essay, articles, or books

> From James Sosnoski, "Hyper-readers and their Reading Engines." *Passions, Pedagogies, and 21st Century Technologies.* Eds. Gail E. Hawisher and Cynthia L. Self. (Logan, UT: Utah State UP, 1999, 161–77.)

Sosnoski argues that these new characteristics of reading and interacting with texts mark a departure from more traditional ways of reading in that they shift authority from the writer to the reader. As a result, reading a Web site becomes a more constructive act than, say, reading a magazine article: Readers pick and choose different portions of text, and they "create" the texts as they select and navigate through various links. The reading of and interaction with texts becomes less linear and more three-dimensional, so that the dividing line between image and text as well as between reading and writing begins to blur. Eventually, Sosnoski argues, these hyper-reading characteristics will not be limited to hypertext genres. As children grow up internalizing these ways of reading, they will transfer them to the reading of other, nonelectronic genres, thereby changing the ways we use and interact with a great many genres.

The power of genre to enact change, however, does not have to be as dramatic as what Sosnoski describes. We see people using the power of genre to effect change without having to depend on major developments in technology. For example, people use genres like petitions to gain support for new policies and write letters to the editor to try to change public opinion (the letter to the editor will be discussed more fully in Chapter 10).

People can also add genres where they didn't exist before to effect change. For example, a teacher who is having difficulty getting the parents of her students involved in their education might decide to create a newsletter that the students help to write and that parents can then read in order to stay connected to their children's learning. The presence of this new genre, the classroom newsletter, might facilitate better interaction between parents, students, and teacher.

In a similar gesture, two students in one of our advanced writing courses decided to use the power of genre to create a more balanced relationship between the needs of learning-disabled students and their parents, and the needs of the teacher and the school. To create such a balance, the two students modified an existing genre called the Individual Education Plan (IEP). Signed into law in 1975, the IEP requires that learning-disabled students who are mainstreamed into traditional classrooms must have an individual education plan drawn up for them that is appropriate for their learning abilities and needs. At the start of each school year, the classroom teacher, special education teacher, parents, school principal, and other specialists meet to develop the student's individual education plan. As a result of their critique of the IEP, the two students in our class concluded that these IEP sessions were mainly one-sided, with parents playing a small role in developing the IEP and the students themselves (who have the most to gain and lose) playing no role at all. To address this lack of participation, our two students created an extra dimension to the IEP, a friendly-looking form (unlike the very institutional-looking IEP) with the heading: "This Year I Would Like To:" followed by enough space for the learning-disabled student to list five personal goals. As stated in their rationale for this addition, our two students hoped that such an inclusion might allow the student's voice and goals to play a part in the IEP.

Writing Activity 4.5

Think about a time when either you or someone you know used the power of genre to make a difference, great or small. If you cannot draw from an immediate experience, then think about a time in history when a genre was used to make a difference. How was the genre used? What difference did it make? Why?

Writing Activity 4.6

Think about how the genres that you use might be changed to suit you better. Consider genres you use at work, in school, in your public life, or in your private life. Select one that you would most like to see change and briefly describe how the genre works currently, the specific changes that might make the genre work better for you, and what these changes could achieve.

We end this chapter by describing an incident in which the power of genre actually did make a difference in the world—and in the process ignited a large controversy around the power of genre.

In 1983, Rigoberta Menchú, with the assistance of anthropologist Elizabeth Burgos-Debra, published her memoir called *I, Rigoberta Menchú*. A "memoir," as the name suggests, is a genre based in "memory"—a recollection of past lived experiences that hold some significance for the present. In her memoir, Menchú recounts her struggle as a Mayan peasant growing up in war-torn Guatemala, including her father's battles with oppressive landlords, the murder of members of her family, and the peasants' courageous attempts at resistance. The power of Menchú's memoir drew the world's attention to the suffering of Guatemalan peasants and won her critical acclaim as a human rights advocate. The memoir itself became an international best-seller and, in 1992, won the Nobel Prize. More significantly, by bringing attention to the suffering of poor Guatemalans, Menchú's memoir did something even more powerful: It helped force the Guatemalan government to sign an agreement to stop violating human rights.

The story does not end here, however. In 1999, David Stoll, an anthropologist, published a book called *Rigoberta Menchú and the Story of All Poor Guatemalans*. In the book, Stoll proves that many of the incidents Menchú recounts either did not actually happen to her or have been exaggerated for effect. The human rights violations that Menchú describes did occur, but not always in the versions she tells them and not always to her or her family. As you can imagine, Stoll's book ignited a controversy, with some people calling for a ban of Menchú's memoir from college reading lists and others hailing her work for its literary strength and ability to create change in the world. This controversy will not likely be resolved anytime soon, but what we do know is that Menchú's memoir *did* make a difference in the world. It helped bring attention to a people's suffering in a way that other attempts had not been able to accomplish, and it ultimately helped to curb the Guatemalan government's human rights violations. And it could be argued that it made the difference it did in part because it *was* presented as a memoir and yet did not remain true to all the expectations of a memoir.

This argument, however, raises the question of what it means to change genre conventions. Because they touch us on a personal level, memoirs can have a great effect on us, much like Menchú's did. At the same time, we expect that memoirs should depict events truthfully, and, when we find that they do not, we feel cheated, as many readers of Menchú's memoir did. Some could argue, though, that Menchú used the genre of the memoir because she knew it would make a powerful impact, but that she stretched its boundaries because she had to tell a powerful story, one more powerful even than her own story. In this, we could see Menchú using the power of genre (a genre that already has certain power in our culture) by adapting it to fit better her purpose and ultimately change her scene: to change the horrible conditions in which poor Guatemalans live.

We leave it up to you to decide where you stand in relation to this controversy. But most of all we hope that you find evidence in this controversy of the power of genre. Indeed, as we argue throughout this book, genre can give us access to the world in which we live and the various scenes of writing we participate in and negotiate. At the same time, genre can also enable us to critique the world in which we live while holding out the possibility that, through such critique, we can change the ways people communicate, interact, and live in the world. As you study the situations and genres of other scenes, keep in mind the power of genre not only to limit what you can communicate but also to critique those limitations. As you perform your critical reading of various genres in your life, take the time also to perform a critique of those genres, to reflect on their power over you and how you can use their power.

Writing Projects

Writing Project 4.1

Write a critique of the genre you have begun to examine in Writing Activity 4.3 (p. 161), with your classmates and instructor as your audience. Make sure to state and then develop a **claim** that evaluates some aspect of the genre's effects. Then support your claim with **evidence** taken from the genre, evidence that you have already identified in Writing Activity 4.3. In the process of developing your claim, keep in mind that you will need not only to describe the effects a genre has, but also to evaluate the strengths and/or limitations of these effects. To help you get started, read again the sample student paper, "For the Bride or Groom?" (p. 154), which performs a similar critique to the one we are asking you to perform.

Writing Project 4.2

Using the list of findings about generic change that you developed in Collaborative Activity 4.2 (p. 173) as your guide, trace the development of some genre for your teacher and classmates. You can investigate a genre you have already analyzed in earlier activities and assignments or a genre you have not examined yet but which you would like to learn more about. Try, if possible, to determine how the genre came into existence, and then explore how and why it has evolved over the years. In order to research your chosen genre, you might gather samples of the genre used in different periods of time, interview long-time users of the genre, or find books/articles written about the genre and its development and use. When your research is complete, choose what you consider the most effective way to present it (given your subject matter, purpose, and audience). Various genres lend themselves to such a presentation of research, including a poster board, a Power-Point presentation, a Web site, or a researched position paper (discussed in Chapter 7). The genre you use to present your research will affect how you organize and describe your research; it will also affect how your audience relates to the research; take some time to consider which genre to use.

Writing Assignment 4.3

Find a genre that you are familiar with and that usually is no longer than one page. Various forms fit this specification, but so do everyday genres like bills, obituaries, party invitations, and flyers. After analyzing how this genre operates, write your own version of the genre so that you change its conventions (as the students rewrote the IEP or the teachers rewrote the grade report). Write a cover letter to your teacher explaining what conventions you changed and how you think those changes have altered the genre's situation (subject, participants, setting, purposes) and scene.

Reading and Writing within Academic Genres

II

Understanding Academic Scenes and Writing Courses

5

Among the recurring roles you have played in a variety of scenes as a writer are the multiple performances that have taken place within academic scenes and against the backdrop of the classroom setting. Some of you may even recall your debut performances as writers in this scene—forming your first letters and words or writing your first "story" in elementary school—and gradually moving to more challenging roles, like writing book reports in middle school and term papers or literary analyses in high school. All of your writing experiences over the course of your academic career, but particularly your more recent high school experiences, have served as rehearsals of sorts for the college or university scene.

Anytime you enter new scenes of writing, like the university and its various disciplines, you are likely to experience some uncertainty about how to communicate within them. You may feel a little like an outsider, out of place in an unfamiliar setting. The way people interact within these academic scenes, the choices they make when they speak and write, and their habits of mind may seem mysterious at first because you do not really know the reasons they are making the choices they are making. Academic writing does not need to be this mysterious, however. This chapter and the following three in Part II will help you become more familiar with academic scenes, the rhetorical interactions or situations within those scenes, and the academic genres that frame those scenes.

The first four chapters of this book taught you to define and observe scenes of writing (Chapter 1); to analyze the genres or patterns of communication within scenes in order to gain access to scenes of writing (Chapter 2); to use your knowledge of scenes and genres to make effective writing choices within those scenes (Chapter 3); and to use that same knowledge of scene and genre to write creatively within, critique, and change genres and their scenes (Chapter 4). In Part II, we will draw on what you have learned in the previous four chapters about communication within scenes and apply it specifically to reading and writing within academic scenes and academic genres, especially those that you will most likely encounter in your first-year writing course. This chapter will situate the particular scene of the college writing course within the broader academic scene of the college or university. We will explore the shared goals of the writing course (and how these goals reflect the larger shared goals of the college or university), the rhetorical interactions that make up the situations in this scene, and the genres used to interact within the situations of the writing class scene. In later chapters of Part II, you will be able to use your knowledge of academic scenes and genres to participate more effectively in your writing course and, building on that experience, to read and write your way through other scenes in the university or college more effectively and confidently.

The Objectives of Colleges and Universities

In Chapter 1, *we defined scene as a place where communication happens among groups of people with some shared objectives.* The college or university is a scene that involves a place (a campus) in which communication happens among groups of people (students, faculty, staff, administrators) with some shared objectives (to facilitate the pursuit, production, and exchange of knowledge). While colleges and universities are diverse, with differing traditions and missions, they share essential overarching objectives. Colleges or universities generally encourage the pursuit of knowledge (its creation and application), critical inquiry and research, and openness to diverse experiences, worldviews, and values. Underlying the pursuit of knowledge is the shared idea that knowledge is not something that one can find simply by looking, and not something one can achieve alone. Rather, knowledge is something *constructed,* most often through a process of social interaction and collaborative inquiry.

The shared objectives of higher education thus go beyond career preparation or job training to include the teaching of habits and strategies for working with others to acquire, create, and apply knowledge. Many university mission statements, for example, contain language referring to "a lifetime of learning" or to making students "lifelong learners." Most higher education institutions see their mission as preparing students not for one career but for a multiplicity of potential careers as well as preparing them to play critical and thoughtful roles as citizens in a complex, changing society.

This vision of a "well-rounded" education that shapes a responsible, reflective citizenry dates back to classical Greek and Roman times and the earliest models of an educated society. In *The Republic*, the ancient Greek philosopher Plato argued that a good education combines intellectual development with spiritual, social, and artistic growth, laying the foundations for what we have come to know as a "liberal arts" education. While there are a number of liberal arts colleges that make this their sole mission, many universities try to integrate the breadth of the liberal arts with the depth of specialized training. These shared goals of professional training combined with the development of "lifelong learning" are even reflected in the organization of institutions of higher education, with their separation into Colleges of Arts and Sciences and Colleges of Law, Agriculture, Business, Engineering, etc. Even the physical layout of a university campus—often with separate buildings for different disciplines (such as the "Humanities Building") or separate floors/offices for individual departments (such as the English Department or the Psychology Department)—reveal this attempt to provide "coverage" of a wide array of disciplinary knowledge while also allowing concentration in a particular major.

Within this overarching scene of shared goals and systems of organization that carry out and reflect these goals, different colleges and universities, of course, form their own distinct scenes. Some colleges, for example, which began as teaching colleges, continue strongly to emphasize teacher training. Other regional schools may have programs tailored to meet the particular needs of citizens in that area—for example, strong agricultural programs in schools in solidly agricultural regions. Religious colleges or universities may highlight moral or religious values in their mission, while technical colleges may emphasize the development of technical skills over a "liberal arts" background. And although all universities and colleges share in the pursuit and production of knowledge, some may highlight the application of knowledge over its production, while others may highlight different aspects of knowledge and specialize in different kinds of knowledge making.

Writing Activity 5.1

Check your university or college's Web site or catalogue for a statement of the mission and goals of your college or university. Based on the stated goals/objectives, how would you describe the scene of your institution? Which statements seem like goals that could be met by institutions anywhere, and which seem specific to the particular scene of your university/college?

Multiple Scenes within Colleges and Universities

While a university or college is itself an overarching scene—a place where communication happens among groups of people with some shared objectives—it is also made up of multiple scenes that both share in the overarching objectives and have their own more particular objectives. The various administrative offices, the different schools, disciplines and departments, and the multiple curricular and extracurricular organizations and clubs are all *scenes,* because they each involve a place in which communication happens among groups of people with some shared objectives. For example, members of English departments are likely to pursue knowledge as it is produced and interpreted in texts, while members of sociology departments are likely to pursue knowledge as it takes place within social groups and cultures. Each department thus becomes a more particular scene within the larger academic scene.

Even within the more particular scenes of disciplines and departments, there are more specific scenes such as specializations, tracks, and courses. In the department of English, for instance, there may be specialized tracks and courses in literature, rhetoric-composition, technical writing, creative writing, or linguistics. As we mentioned in Chapter 1, each course you take is its own scene in that it, too, involves a place in which communication happens among groups of people with some shared objectives. In the department of English, each course, while sharing the objectives of the larger department, has its own more specific objectives, which are often outlined in the course syllabus.

As you make your way through the multiple scenes of your university or college, try to identify and define the particular scene you are in, but also remember that the scene is itself part of a larger scene which might very well be part of an even larger scene. The more you can situate the scene in which you are participating within the larger scenes that influence it, the more fully you will be able to understand and carry out its objectives.

Writing Activity 5.2

Log on to the Internet, and visit the home page of your college or university. What do the features of the Web site indicate about the overarching scene of the college or university and the multiple scenes within it? How are different scenes indicated (through different kinds of links, for example, or other kinds of structures)? What are some of the various scenes that you can identify?

Multiple Situations within Colleges and Universities

Each of the multiple social and academic scenes within a college or university has its own particular *situations,* defined in Chapter 1 as *the rhetorical interactions happening within a scene, involving participants, purposes, subjects, and settings.* Each course, in fact, is a scene made up of multiple situations, so that in any given course you will find students and teachers engaged in different types of interactions. Examples of these situations, as we described in Chapter 1, include class discussions, students working in peer groups, student and teacher engaged in one-on-one conferencing, students writing in-class papers, etc.

You have probably already encountered a variety of academic situations, where participants are discussing a variety of subjects and are using language to accomplish various purposes in various settings. While walking to class you have probably observed a variety of situations, from students gathered on the quad chatting about the band that is playing on Saturday night to students sitting in hallways reading the student newspaper or studying class notes. Or you might have passed classrooms where teachers are giving a class lecture as students furiously scribble notes or where students are gathered in a science laboratory taking notes on an experiment. Or maybe you have passed a professor's office and found him or her conferring with a student.

The multiple situations taking place within academic scenes are too numerous to mention here and may range from situations outside the classroom (students filling out financial aid forms or registering for classes, fans cheering at a basketball game, or students debating a proposal before the student government), to a multitude of academic situations that vary according to different disciplines and departments. Whether theater majors rehearsing on a stage in the university auditorium, computer science students working collaboratively to write new software in a computer lab, faculty and deans from the school of business gathered in a conference room to discuss new internship requirements, or students and faculty gathered in an auditorium to hear a poetry reading or political lecture, these rhetorical interactions accomplish some shared objectives and carry out the actions and activities of various university scenes.

Writing Activity 5.3

Drawing on Box 1.2: Guidelines for Observing and Describing Scenes (pp. 44–45), choose a situation within an academic scene and write a one-page description of the situation. You might observe a situation in a class you are taking, such as a lecture, class discussion, group work assignment, or oral presentation. Or you might observe a group of students studying in the library, a meeting of a student group or organization, or a group of fans at a sporting event. In a paragraph or two, describe the participants in the situation, the setting of their interaction, the subject of their interaction, and their purposes for interacting and the type of language and tone used. What is the nature of their communication, and how is it shaped by the situation and scene?

Academic Genres

In order to carry out their shared objectives within an academic scene or to accomplish a particular purpose within an academic situation, participants draw on genres. *Genres are the typical rhetorical ways of responding to a situation that repeatedly occurs within a scene.* Within academic scenes that share the overarching missions of cultivating learning and gauging the effectiveness of that learning, teaching situations and evaluation procedures tend to repeat themselves semester after semester, year after year, leading to typical responses. For instance, teachers—regardless of discipline—rely on certain typical rhetorical interactions to carry out their instructional goals, whether through the genres of assignments, lectures, class discussions, visual presentations (such as overheads), conferences with students, or even textbooks such as this one. In addition, to gauge whether they are effectively transferring this knowledge, teachers ask students to participate in proven patterns of action such as oral presentations, journals, quizzes, term papers, tests, and exams. Because educational institutions at all levels participate in a scene that increasingly values accountability, you, as student have no doubt become more than familiar with the many genres of testing, whether true/false, multiple choice, or essay exams. Analyzing the genres used in the college or university scene is one strategy for better understanding that scene and learning how to participate in it. Here, we will focus on two genres that are used across multiple academic scenes: the syllabus and the writing assignment.

THE SYLLABUS

As writers, we can begin to understand and communicate in different academic scenes of writing by identifying their central assumptions. Since assumptions are embedded in the genres people use within these academic scenes, we can use genres not only as scripts, but also as maps for gaining access to these academic scenes. The *syllabus* is one such map. One immediate way to begin navigating new academic landscapes is by carefully reading your different courses' syllabi, which help frame each course's scene of writing. Doing so will help you identify some of the assumptions that shape the values and goals of these courses, knowledge that will help you start making more informed choices as a writer when it is time for you to perform within these different scenes of writing. Following is a sample syllabus from an advanced writing course, which we will use to illustrate how this genre can help you uncover the assumptions and expectations of a course.

English 355: Rhetoric and Writing

COURSE GOALS

English 355 is an advanced writing course designed to develop your writing proficiency and to further refine your writing skills, with emphasis on development of ideas, analysis of style, and clarity of thought and expression. Through analysis of the rhetorical situations that motivate your writing and roles as writers, you will learn to adapt and adjust your messages to particular audiences, purposes, and contexts for writing. You will plan, draft, and revise papers that address a variety of situations within academic, professional, and public contexts. In addition, you will critically read and discuss both published texts and the writing of your peers and will learn to analyze and evaluate writing based on its appropriateness to the rhetorical situation (audience, purpose, persona) and to guide its revision.

COURSE ORGANIZATION

Based on the principle that writers learn to write by writing, the class will be organized as a writing workshop, with a large portion of our class periods spent on in-class writing projects, discussion of works in progress and planning, drafting, and revision of written assignments. In addition, because writing is a dynamic social process and learning to interact with other writers is central to every writer's development, you will also collaborate in small-group workshops as well as participate in full-group workshops and discussions. As a writer, you are responsible for bringing copies of your paper for each member of your group on the class period scheduled. As a responder, you will be responsible for carefully and critically reading and commenting on your classmates' papers. All response sheets will be handed in with final drafts of papers.

WRITTEN WORK

You will plan, draft, and revise four papers and will complete a final revision project, in addition to peer responses (both written and oral) and other informal in-class writings and style exercises. You will choose your own topic areas and will determine the genres that would be most appropriate (for example, a letter, proposal, report, editorial, article, newsletter, brochure, etc.). For each assignment, you will develop an analysis of the writing situation (both the social and the rhetorical situation) surrounding that piece of writing and will target a specific audience and forum for publication. That analysis will be submitted with each paper. At the end of the semester, you will revise some aspect of your rhetorical situation and will rewrite a fitting response for this new situation.

COURSE POLICIES

Since English 355 will be conducted as a writing workshop, its success depends upon active and informed involvement and participation. You are expected to submit rough drafts for peer response on time. Written and oral responses to the writing of others are significant components of this course—activities for which you will receive credit. As a result, regular attendance is necessary in order to perform successfully in this course.

GRADING

Paper 1—10%	Paper 3—20%	Revision Project—15%
Paper 2—15%	Paper 4—25%	Workshop Grade—15%

ENGLISH 355: DAILY SYLLABUS

Wed.	1/10	Introduction to Course
Fri.	1/12	In-class Writing: Writing Background Analysis
Mon.	1/15	Martin Luther King Day: No Classes
Wed.	1/17	Ch. 1 "Writing in College" & Ch. 2 "What Is Good Writing?"
Fri.	1/19	Ch. 3 "What Happens When People Write?"; Assign Paper 1
Mon.	1/22	Ch. 4 "What Is your Writing Situation?"; Rhetorical Situation; Appeals
Wed.	1/24	Ch. 5 "Drafting Your Paper"; Writing Situation Analysis Due
Fri.	1/26	Ch. 7 "Holding Your Reader"; Bring draft-in-progress
Mon.	1/29	**Draft Due: Paper 1;** Ch. 8 "Writing Clearly"
Wed.	1/31	Draft Workshop (Bring copies for small group); Ch. 6 "Revising"
Fri.	2/2	Style Workshop (Bring copies—small group); Ch. 9 "Crafting Paragraphs"
Mon.	2/5	**Final Due: Paper 1;** Prewriting for Paper 2: Exploratory Paper
Wed.	2/7	Planning/Drafting: Paper 2

Fri.	2/9	Writing Situation Analysis: Analyzing the Rhetorical Situation/Social Community
Mon.	2/12	Group Troubleshooting Workshop: Paper 2; Voice: Ch 1–2
Wed.	2/14	**Draft Due: Paper 2** (Bring copies for full-class workshop); Ch. 3
Fri.	2/16	Draft Workshop: Full-Class Discussion
Mon.	2/19	Draft Workshop: Full-Class Discussion
Wed.	2/21	Draft Workshop: Full-Class Discussion
Fri.	2/23	Draft Workshop: Full-Class Discussion
Mon.	2/26	**Final Due: Paper 2**; Prewriting for Paper 3: Rhetorical Analysis
Wed.	2/28	Doing Nonlibrary Research
Fri.	3/2	Analyzing Communities/Rhetorical Actions
Mon.	3/5	"Learning the Language" (handout)
Wed.	3/7	Sample Analysis: Political Speech
Fri.	3/9	Planning/Drafting: Paper 3
Mon.	3/12	Group Troubleshoot: Paper 3 (bring intro, tentative thesis, rough outline & questions)
Wed.	3/14	**Draft Due: Paper 3**; Draft Workshop (bring copies for small group)
Fri.	3/16	Conference on College Composition and Communication; Coherence: Ch. 6
Mon. Fri.	3/19– 3/23	Spring Break: No Classes
Mon.	3/26	Draft Due: Paper 3; Style Workshop; Structural Variety: Ch. 10
Wed.	3/28	Editing Workshop; Ch. 10
Fri.	3/30	**Final Due: Paper 3**; Prewriting for Paper 4: brochure/magazine article
Mon.	4/2	Planning/Drafting: Paper 4
Wed.	4/4	Writing Situation Analysis
Fri.	4/6	Sample Genres
Mon.	4/9	Bring in draft in progress; Actors and Actions: Ch. 9
Wed.	4/11	Bring in draft in progress: Word Choice: Ch. 4–5
Fri.	4/13	Easter Break: No Classes
Mon.	4/16	**Draft Due: Paper 4** (bring copies for full-class workshop); Ch. 11
Wed.	4/18	Draft Workshop: Full-Class Discussion
Fri.	4/20	Draft Workshop: Full-Class Discussion

Mon.	4/23	Draft Workshop: Full-Class Discussion
Wed.	4/25	Draft Workshop: Full-Class Discussion
Fri.	4/27	**Final Due: Paper 4**; Planning for Revision Project
Mon.	4/30	Workshop: Revision Project
Mon.	5/7	Final 8–10 a.m.—Turn in Revision Project

The syllabus is a genre that not only contains helpful information about the course policies and schedule; it also contains important information about the course's underlying logic—information that frames the course's scene of writing. What, for instance, are the stated objectives of the syllabus? How does your instructor describe these objectives? You can usually find these statements at the beginning of the syllabus, where the instructor often includes a description of the course and its goals. The sample syllabus begins with a section called "Course Goals," which mentions specific objectives, such as development of writing proficiency and style, practice with writing processes, and awareness of rhetorical situations.

Next, you can examine the syllabus in order to identify how your instructor plans on accomplishing these objectives. You might look at the daily assignments and readings as well as any writing assignments or major projects for clues to this. Do the assignments and activities outlined in the syllabus build on one another? If so, how? If not, then how do they relate? What does your instructor expect you to practice and learn in each assignment and activity? In the syllabus, there are several clues to how the objectives will be carried out: assigned readings, papers, and class discussions that develop critical thinking skills; various workshop activities such as "planning/drafting" and "draft workshops" that emphasize writing processes; and oral responses, writing assignments, and collaborative activities that ask students to implement rhetorical strategies. The reference to revision projects under the heading "Written Work" as well as the many references to planning and drafting on the daily schedule emphasize the instructor's expectation that students will develop processes for writing and will spend a significant amount of time revising their work. In addition, the fact that each writing assignment is weighted more heavily than the one preceding it (see "Grading") indicates the increased complexity of assignments as well as the underlying belief that student writing will improve throughout the course.

As you continue to uncover the underlying assumptions and expectations of the course in your analysis of the syllabus, look for key words and phrases, words and phrases that might be underlined or repeated often. Think about what these words reveal about how the course will treat the subject of study. In the sample syllabus, there are repeated references to "process," "workshops," "peer response," "rhetorical situations," and to the stages of "planning," "drafting," and "revision." These terms reflect the course's focus on learning to write by writing (rather than by lecturing about writing) and the expectation that students will actively participate in the learning process through their participation in the writing process activities and collaborative activities of peer review.

Learning to analyze your syllabus in this way is a first step in becoming an active academic participant rather than a passive receiver of information, and it is a first step in beginning to make more effective learning choices in the academic scene. Of course, the syllabus alone does not contain all the answers, but as a genre that reflects and reveals the goals and objectives of a course, it does offer a map of the course scene that can help you begin navigating the class and locating yourself in this scene.

Collaborative Activity 5.1

Bring in sample syllabi from courses that you are taking, and share these syllabi in small groups. Drawing on the Guidelines for Analyzing Genres in Box 2.1 (pp. 93–94), *identify* the rhetorical patterns of the syllabus genre (content, format, language, tone, organization). Then *analyze* what these patterns reveal about the academic scene and the roles of participants within this scene. What is expected of students in college courses, for example? How are they expected to behave, according to the syllabi's assumptions? What kinds of roles are teachers expected to take, as reflected in the syllabus genre? What kinds of things do the syllabi seem to stress, and what does that say about the expectations within the academic scene?

Next, drawing on the Questions for Critiquing Genre in Box 4.1 (p. 161), *critique* the genre of the syllabus. What does the genre enable its users (both teachers and students) to do, and what does it not allow them to do? Whose needs are most and least served by the genre? What limitations does the genre place on participation in the writing course scene and the larger academic scene? Be prepared to share your responses with the rest of the class.

Collaborative Activity 5.2

In small groups, share the syllabi you collected for the previous activity, but this time analyze the differences among the different versions of the academic scene. Note not only the variation possible in the syllabus genre, since every genre allows variation, but attend also to how those differences may reflect disciplinary differences. Do the syllabi from the humanities (like English, history, philosophy) differ from those of the sciences or social sciences? How does the general academic scene vary in different disciplines?

Box 5.1   *Questions for Analyzing Writing Assignments*

1. *Setting:* What kind of course is this assignment for? Does this kind of course or this field have expectations I can anticipate? Is this one of a set of assignments? If so, how does this particular assignment fit in?

2. *Subject:* Does the assignment specify a subject? If so, what is it? If not, what subjects are most appropriate? Whatever subject I choose, how am I being asked to treat it? What does the assignment want me to do with the subject—describe it, analyze it, argue about it, research it? What should my goals be in addressing the subject?

3. *Writers:* What kind of role does the assignment ask me to play as a writer? What sort of stance should I take? (Should it be critical, questioning, accepting?) What kind of tone shall I present?

4. *Readers:* Who should I assume will be my readers? What kind of information does the assignment provide about the readers? What else do I need to know about the readers for me to address them effectively? What are my readers' expectations—of me and the subject matter?

5. *Purposes:* Other than to get a grade, why am I writing this assignment? What does the teacher want me to gain from this assignment? What do I want to gain?

6. *Genre Features:* Are there certain expectations about organization and format? If so, what are those? If not, then where can I go to find out? What about style? Does the assignment specify a certain style or am I permitted to choose a style? Given the role I will be taking on, my readers, and the subject matter, what style will be most appropriate?

THE WRITING ASSIGNMENT

While the syllabus helps frame a course's general scene of writing by containing some of its basic objectives and assumptions, writing assignments are genres that specify some of the situations that will occur in the course's scene. Writing assignments help to frame the situation for writing by specifying, to some extent, the subject, setting, audience, and purpose for writing. So yet another way to access and participate effectively in academic scenes is by identifying the expectations regarding subject, setting, audience, and purpose for writing that are embedded in your assignment.

The first and most important step you can take as a writer is to position yourself within the assignment as a reader, to make sense of the writing assignment. "Reading" an assignment is just like reading other genres that we described in Chapter 2. Before you decide how to act in a situation, you need to read what the genre tells you about that situation. The more you can figure out what the underlying assumptions and expectations are, the more likely you will be able to make informed writing choices.

When you are given a writing assignment, try to identify its expectations and assumptions by asking yourself the questions in Box 5.1, which are based on our analysis of situations in Chapter 1.

By asking yourself such questions before you begin writing, you not only begin to understand your writing situation better, but you also begin to situate your writing choices more knowingly within it. (Chapter 8 will focus further on academic writing assignments and will explore several specific cases of assignments from different courses or scenes of writing in the university.)

Writing Activity 5.4

Take a writing assignment, either from your current writing course or from any other course, and analyze it using the questions in Box 5.1 as your guidelines. What do you learn about your writing situation as a result? What kinds of writing choices would be most appropriate for you to make as you begin to write?

The Objectives of Writing Courses

Like many new college students, chances are you might have had some trepidation about writing in college, especially as you entered your first-year writing course, which is an unfamiliar scene. You might have heard horror stories about the required writing course (or courses): how it is a "weed-out" or "boot camp" course, how its teachers' standards are so much higher than those you encountered before in school, how it is a course you just have to get out of the way before you get to the "real" classes that have "real" subjects, and so on. College-level writing courses really do not deserve such stigmas. Indeed, by the time they are ready to graduate, an overwhelming number of surveyed students consistently single out their first-year writing courses as being among the most beneficial and rewarding of their college experience. These students cite the small class size, the opportunity to receive one-to-one instruction as well as to work collaboratively with peers, the close attention to their writing, and the transferable writing skills that they can use throughout their college careers and beyond as contributing to the positive experience. In fact, when they reflect back on their writing courses, most students realize what we hope to convince you of here: That writing courses like the one you are taking are in fact not "weed-out" but "weed-*in*" courses; they introduce you to and help you learn how to function more effectively as readers and writers within the scene of the university.

In many ways, college writing courses are transitional courses. They function in part as "ports of entry" into the ways of thinking and interacting that are common in the university, with its emphasis on critical analysis, inquiry, and research. You already possess—and have most likely practiced—some of the thinking and interacting skills that are valued in the university, and writing courses such as the one you are currently taking help you build on and refine these skills so that you can function more effectively as college writers. Thinking of writing courses metaphorically as "ports of entry" can be a helpful way of imagining how such courses let you develop the rhetorical skills that will enable you to move with more agility and awareness through the various scenes of writing that await you.

If writing courses are ports of entry, then language use and genre knowledge are kinds of passports for entering into and navigating these often unfamiliar landscapes of the college and university scene. In addition, the metaphor of passports—which entitle their bearers to participate in the scene they are entering as well as the scenes they leave behind—suggests that you enter the writing class with a knowledge of language and of genres already in place and don't just show up to your college writing course as blank slates.

Writing researcher and college professor Anne DiPardo, in her research study entitled *A Kind of Passport*, uses this passport metaphor to describe students' struggles with writing as they move from the scene of their home cultures into academic scenes, particularly the scene of the college writing classroom. In the reading that follows, DiPardo—drawing on some of the techniques for observing scenes that we discussed in Chapter 1—closely observes and interviews students as they adjust to the academic scene of "Dover Park University" (DPU). The following excerpt from DiPardo's study focuses on how one writer, "Sylvia," uses language to negotiate multiple situations and rhetorical interactions within this scene. As you read, consider the nature of the struggles that Sylvia faces as she attempts to adjust to the demands of college life, particularly her struggles with communicating within unfamiliar academic scenes.

░ ░ ░

Sylvia

Anne DiPardo

Cultural and Linguistic Background

Sylvia's family immigrated from Mexico when she was eight months old, settling in a prosperous, traditionally Anglo farming community that was then in a process of demographic transformation. While Sylvia recalled that some of the local Anglos "began to hate the idea that Latinos might take over," the town gradually became a place where families from widely varied backgrounds peaceably coexisted. She seemed particularly eager to dispel any suspicion that it was an impoverished ghetto:

> The town where I live is an urban area, and it's middle class, upper-middle class. There is the lower class, but I mean, I don't see it, because I'm not around it all the time and stuff. It's not *that* bad. I grew up with, I don't know, a variety of people, you know, Mexicans, blacks, Asians, whatever.

Sylvia's parents had never become fully proficient in English, and Spanish remained the language of home: "they've picked up a little English here and there," she explained, "but like fluently, no." Although both held relatively low-paying jobs—her father working in the fields and her mother doing housecleaning and childcare—they had managed to purchase some lucrative farmland, send money home to relatives, and save for Sylvia's education.[1] Still, as Sylvia explained in an essay entitled "My Dream," she "felt sorry" for her parents, who "didn't have the opportunity to make choices" that she now possessed:

> When they were my age, times were hard for them and life was pretty much planned out for them . . . Well, in this day and age I have choices. I can go to college, or I could quit school altogether and work. It is my decision. I also have the choice of the field to go into. I could be an engineer, a teacher, or a mathematician. It is entirely up to me. The jobs are out there, I just have to choose which one I will pursue.

Elsewhere in the essay, Sylvia explained that while her own life was already rather different from her parents', she would always share their commitment to family: "my family would be the most important thing in my life," she wrote, "because they will always be there for me, and they will always stand beside me."

But already, Sylvia's dual commitment to family and worldly achievement was fraught with paradox. Even as her parents boasted of their daughter's presence at a four-year college, they worried that she was losing touch with her roots; and even as Sylvia was trying to recapture an earlier sense of ethnic identity, she longed to break away from the typecasting that had long plagued her, to be perceived "just like any other American." In one of her essays she described the "many barriers" that she had crossed, the "many negative messages" that she had overcome:

> . . . my family back in Mexico is proud that I am going to school, but some members put me down. They can not understand that I am doing something worthwhile with my life. They feel that I should do things the traditional way, which is to stay home until I get married. My family sees me as an independent woman that left home and will never get married.

Although Sylvia's parents had helped force her to take the first big step into the Anglo world—when they sent her, then a five-year-old girl who could speak only Spanish, to a local kindergarten—they had ample cause to regret her cultural and linguistic estrangement. The problem first became evident during Sylvia's second-grade year, when she made an abrupt and disruptive switch from a bilingual classroom to an English-immersion program. For a time, she was gripped with "the fear of speaking in either English or Spanish," and had trouble communicating at home and school alike:

> So by the time they said, "Well, here's English," I was like, "Whoa, wait a minute, slow down here!" It was just like a big switch, it was kind of hard for me. And ever since then I've had that [writer's] block kinda thing . . . I didn't even know the basics of my own language, you know, when they said, "Boo, here's English." You know. And the funny thing is, I *lost* my Spanish. I couldn't speak it no more. And you know, my parents, it was a really . . . *[exasperated sigh]* it was so tough to communicate.

"I lost it," she repeated softly, as if still amazed that such a thing could happen. "I could have lost it completely," she added, "and not even speak Spanish right now, and really be called 'coconut.'"?

Deeply concerned, Sylvia's parents arranged a month's stay in Mexico between her second- and third-grade years—this in the hopes that she might recover the ability to speak her native language, and might also realize the link it represented to her extended family. Sylvia found the experience disorienting and somewhat disturbing: even as she basked in the warmth of her relatives' hugs and eager chatter, she was literally speechless. At first, her brother was her translator and emissary—then, as Sylvia recalled, "reality hit. I said [to myself], 'You've gotta learn it.'" At first, she was halting and awkward, but by the end of that pivotal month she was once again comfortable speaking Spanish to relatives and Hispanic friends. Even as Sylvia approached young adulthood,

Spanish remained the language spoken at home, especially when one of her parents was present—"to show respect," as her father had always said.

Sylvia remained apprehensive, however, about her ability to communicate in Spanish with strangers: "My fear," she explained, "is that I cannot pronounce the words and they won't know what I'm talking about." While she felt somewhat uncertain about her English writing, she was even more insecure about composing in her native language: "I just can't write it properly," she maintained. Flicking aside playful criticism from non-Spanish-speaking friends, she had futilely scanned the schedule of classes for a course that would help her speak and read her native language with renewed confidence. Sylvia spoke longingly of her nine-year-old sister back home: "she can speak better Spanish than I can," she explained, "and that's because they speak it in the house all the time."

Sylvia felt fully competent in neither language—in both, she was keenly aware of her foreigner's accent and uneasy about her abilities as a writer. It would be inadequate to say that Sylvia had made an incomplete transition from Spanish to English, the reality being vastly more complex, more tangled with dilemma. As Sylvia described her sense of being caught between languages, she inevitably described her sense of being caught between cultures as well: "It's funny, because like when I go to Mexico, I don't feel I'm part of them. I don't feel any less, either. It's just like I have two different cultures in me, but I can't choose."

While she felt more at home in the States than in her native Mexico, Sylvia was as concerned about recovering a sense of her family's culture as she was about retaining her first language: "I don't know my culture that well, to tell you the truth. I know more American culture than I know about my own. But everyday I'm learning, you know, and I like it . . . my friend is always joking with me, saying, 'You're not a real Mexican.' I say, 'But a proud one, though.'"

Although Sylvia's path had been far from easy, she was pleased with her progress, and quick to point out that her experiences in two worlds had helped her toward a number of important realizations. She had begun to see her bilingualism as a resource, and was fast overcoming her habitual shyness about speaking Spanish in public: whenever she overheard someone struggling to assemble fragments of broken English, she explained, "I see myself when I was a kid," and she was stepping in to help wherever she could. She had also acquired a certain easygoing open-mindedness, an ability to consider diverse perspectives but ultimately chart her own course—this from growing up in a multiethnic, multilingual community, and from her struggle to come to terms with the assumptions and values of her extended family back in Mexico. Finally, her own experiences in school had convinced her of the value of bilingual education, a topic that she took up in her last essay of the semester:

My opinion for bilingual education is that there should be programs funded by the government . . . How is a student going to be able to comprehend a second language, if the student has not had a strong foundation of his first language? By studying and understanding the basics such as grammar and structure, the student will be able to switch to another language.

Sylvia's argument was informed by knowledge of Cummins's (1979, 1981) "interdependence hypothesis," and by an abiding belief that she was living evidence of its truth. With her family's support, she had long struggled toward an "additive" bilingualism, toward a facility in two languages that would empower her in new ways without diminishing the importance of the old. Only as an insightful and ambitious young woman was she beginning to grasp the full complexity of that struggle, and to cast a discerning eye upon the lingering effects of what had happened to her—to her sense of linguistic competence, to her sense of identity—in second grade.

Adjustment to DPU

When asked if she were happy at DPU, Sylvia was decidedly upbeat: "I'm *very* happy here," she assured me; "I'm glad that I came, and for many reasons." Her father, she explained, had always wanted her to learn to be independent, and the experience of being away gave her a newfound confidence in her ability to get along on her own. While she admitted to fleeting moments of homesickness, Sylvia also boasted of her 2.9 G.P.A. and her ambition to "really push," to become a "better person," to fill in deficiencies in her academic preparation and build from existing strengths. If her glowing score on an initial placement exam was any indication, some of her greatest strengths were in mathematics, which she was "looking into" as a possible major. "Ever since I was a kid," she explained, "mathematics came easy to me—I get a thrill doing math." She could see herself going on for graduate work in math or engineering and possibly teaching at the college level.

Sylvia often spoke of the need for equity students to "get out of their cliques," noting that her upbringing in a multiethnic community had provided the sorts of experiences that were allowing her to thrive at DPU. Of Sylvia's closest friends on campus, two were Mexican and two African-American: "We can joke about race and not get offended," she emphasized, noting that she had learned much from their many discussions "about who we are and where we come from." Although her membership in M.E.Ch.A. initially opened a number of important doors, she had recently distanced herself somewhat from the organization. She was, however, continuing to serve as a DPU recruiter under the auspices of M.E.Ch.A.—leading campus tours and talking to local high school students "about what it's like to be away from home, in college." Sylvia spoke of this community service with particular pride, reporting that these highly positive experiences were helping to banish her lifelong fear of public speaking.

On the one hand, Sylvia felt a strong need to spend time with other Hispanic students—to speak Spanish ("music to my ears," as she described one recent conversation), and to reflect together upon the rewards and challenges of life at DPU; on the other hand, she worried that campus Anglos might regard her close association with the Hispanic community as a sort of protective cocooning, a shield that she insisted she neither wanted nor needed. Having grown up among people of many backgrounds, she was untroubled to find herself the only non-Anglo student in many of her classes. In a beginning-of-term interview, Sylvia flicked aside the many complaints she heard from others: "Sometimes if they feel that they're a minority," she speculated, "they feel real low or, like, low self-esteem. Who knows, you know? I'm a minority, I don't have a problem."

By the end of the semester, however, Sylvia's perception of ethnic relations at DPU had shifted somewhat. In an initial interview, she had insisted that she saw no signs of prejudice on campus, emphasizing that she refused to "look for trouble"; in a final interview, however, she noted that one of the most important lessons she had learned during her first year at DPU concerned the reality of discrimination. When an article in the county newspaper included the accusation that DPU equity students were recruiting for inner-city street gangs (see chapter 3), this young woman who liked to avoid "trouble" joined the protest march downtown. In the attitudes of security personnel and newspaper staff, Sylvia saw undeniable evidence of the same entrenched biases displayed in the article. This new awareness was, she admitted, initially shocking:

> I wasn't aware of what's out there when I was in high school. And then when I come here, it was a whole new world for me, you know, and I've never really been—well, I've been discriminated, but not to my face . . . and for me to actually see something like that, the first time it was really shocking to me. I thought, "damn," you know?

While Sylvia saw community attitudes as part and parcel of what she had observed on campus, she was especially disturbed to find DPU students—particularly students of color—discriminating against one another: "I thought we were all here to do something for ourselves," she mused, "not to put someone else down." Too many students, she observed, "see the outside first," missing the person within:

> I don't see the color. I mean, I can see the color, but I don't use it, like, "Oh, okay, she's white, she's this and this and this," or "She's black, she must be this and this and this," you know what I mean? I just look at them as the person.

Sylvia continued to regard racial prejudice as a hallmark of ignorance, of a failure to understand that human destinies are inextricably interwoven. Sobered by what she had observed during her year on campus, she was neither dejected nor sorry. While she had had to "cross many barriers," her ethnic identity was not associated in her mind with disempowerment or disadvantage. As far as she was concerned, her people were—like Sylvia the individual—up and coming:

> Like they say, "minorities." But I heard in the year 2000, that minorities are gonna be the majority, okay? Then why are we still being called "minorities"? Why can't we be called underrepresented"? I like that better, you know, than "minority." I am not no minority. I am not in one of those little groups—I'm *underrepresented.*

Struggles with Writing

On the basis of her low score on an initial placement test, Sylvia had been assigned to a two-semester basic writing course. Impressed by her early work, course instructor Susan Williams gave Sylvia the option of moving into fresh-man composition after completing only the first semester—an offer Sylvia declined, electing to enroll in Williams's English 90 course. Although Williams saw Sylvia as the strongest writer in the second-semester class, she complained that Sylvia "doesn't go as much into depth as she needs to," and, lacking con-fidence in her writing ability, "sticks to real simple forms." Sylvia seemed well aware of these weaknesses, and spoke often of her desire to move beyond the five-paragraph essay, which she had first encountered in a writing workshop for Hispanic high school students; she also explained that while she had been influ-enced by her father's frequent reminders to "hurry up and get to the point," "writing teachers always want more detail."

When Williams asked for a written description of the "basic ingredients of an essay," Sylvia gamely recited the well-worn precepts she had heard again and again:

> The three basic ingredients of an essay are thesis, sufficient support for the the-sis, and logical arrangement of that support. The thesis is the main point that the author wants to get across to the reader. Sometimes the thesis is mentioned, somewhere in the essay or the reader has to determine what it is from the read-ing. Sufficient support for the thesis is giving backup evidence to the thesis. The support could be factual or not. Logical arrangement is how the author wants to arrange his thoughts. The arrangement makes the paper flow.

But as the semester drew to a close, Sylvia was still somewhat unsure of how to offer "sufficient support" or to make her papers "flow." Here, for instance, is a paragraph from a five-paragraph essay on "stereotypes" that she turned in during the final weeks:

> Society has stereotyped Latina women through the use of the media in television shows and movies. Sometimes the media shows Latinas as hookers that the white men prefer because they think that the women can give the men "good sex". Young Latinas have also been portrayed as being pregnant with two kids. The young women are also shown as having an abusive husband that beats her for the smallest reason, like a spot of dirt on the wall. Latinas are rarely cast into the roles of college students or graduates. I am a Latina woman who is in a four-year college, making something of my life. I don't have an abusive husband or children, but I am still fighting these stereotypes.

As with most of Sylvia's work, Williams felt that while this piece was adequate, it seemed a bit lackluster, as if she had stopped short—short of the livelier way with words that seemed well within her grasp, and short of expressing the vital emotions that lay just beneath the surface.

When asked on a beginning-of-term questionnaire if she liked to write, Sylvia had replied, "Not much. When I feel like writing, I write about things that interest me." But even when writing about matters of profound personal concern, Sylvia tended to rush, hurrying through the gist of a story or argument rather than providing the sorts of detail that her writing teachers always seemed to want. This tendency was evident in an essay describing her mother's battle with cancer, which began with stage-setting realism, but soon sped through long and significant stretches of time:

> Seven years ago a major change came into my mother's life and swept the family with her. One day I arrived at home after dance practice. I walked in the house, it was pitch dark, there were no lights on. Usually the stove light is on, but not this day. As I walked into the house, I got a strange feeling in my body. My mother was in her bedroom asleep. When she woke up, she looked as if she had seen a ghost. She was yellow, and her eyes were blood shot from crying. She did not want to tell me what was wrong. Eventually, she told me she had cancer. My mother said she had to make a decision whether to get an operation or not. She decided to go through with the operation. After the operation, my mother had to go through chemotherapy. The first day after chemotherapy, she came home all drained out. She felt as if her spirit was sucked out by a vacuum cleaner. I felt as if I also had cancer because I was defenseless to help or stop her suffering.

In an interview, Sylvia traced her struggles with writing to her troubled linguistic background—to the fact that she had first learned to write in an atmosphere of linguistic conflict and confusion, and at a time when she was being prematurely immersed in an all-English classroom environment. Written words came forth more easily in English than in Spanish, but somehow her composing still felt hidebound and unnatural; somehow she had never come to visualize the reader over her shoulder, to see composing as an opportunity to express or convey meanings. "I was always ashamed of my writing," she recalled. "My writing experiences are not as vivid as it might be to other people," she wrote in an in-class paper. "Ever since a kid, I did not like to write much. I would only write papers because they were assign to me." Only once, when a high school teacher had carefully led her step-by-step through a term paper assignment, had she felt both engaged and accomplished: "for the first time in a long time, I had confidence," she recalled. An ambitious paper which involved drawing upon secondary sources to compare three American writers, the assignment was more rigorous than anything Sylvia had yet been asked to do in college.

Describing Sylvia as a "very, very bright young woman," Williams remained puzzled by her acceptable but undazzling performance as a writer, surmising that Sylvia had developed "a little bit of a negative attitude about writing"; since "everything else comes pretty easily to her," Williams speculated, perhaps Sylvia was "a little upset that the writing doesn't." While Williams believed Sylvia had problems with "second language input," she held that "it's more in her case just a kind of a lack of interest in writing," since "her language interference problems aren't that severe." "I'd love to see something she's written in Spanish," she added hopefully.

Meanwhile, Sylvia's description of her enduringly troubled relationship with both English and Spanish belied the assumption that her writing was plagued by a clear-cut case of first-language "interference." Although Sylvia believed that her struggle to bring forth words in written English was rooted in the trauma of her early schooling, she only dropped hints to that effect in the presence of her teacher or group leader. Her written words remained mere kernels, the germs of ideas that might be encouraged to grow in the warm light of conversation and engaged feedback, but Sylvia was not particularly eager to move in that direction. When asked if her writing had improved over the semester, she replied, "not what I was looking forward to, or hoping. But that's only because of myself, because I brought it upon myself."

Group Leader's Response: Morgan

Morgan saw many similarities between herself and Sylvia—in their shared struggle against those who would accuse them of ethnic disloyalty, and in their propensity for stubborn resistance. While Sylvia's small-group attendance was about average for the class as a whole (she was present for twenty sessions and missed thirteen), Morgan considered her absenteeism excessive. Even when

Sylvia was present, Morgan was often frustrated at Sylvia's level of participation—at her frequent reluctance to share writing and, occasionally, to participate in group discussions. One morning, as Morgan struggled to generate a brainstorming session, she paused to meet Sylvia's gaze: "You're giving me a bored look," Morgan observed; "You've got an intimidating look—I thought I was the only one with that took." At the last session of the semester, Morgan was a bit more direct: after Sylvia declined to read aloud the essay that she had been scanning silently, Morgan observed, "You're so feisty sometimes, I just want to, like, grab you by that hair." Unperturbed, Sylvia explained that she had a lot on her mind. "I'm teasin' you," Morgan quickly explained, if somewhat unconvincingly.

On those rare occasions when Sylvia brought in rough drafts of her essays, Morgan was an engaged and inquisitive reader, playing back her understandings of the text and encouraging Sylvia to extend her ideas. Late in the term, for instance, Sylvia handed Morgan a rough draft of an essay about her mother and asked her to read it silently. Sensing Sylvia's dissatisfaction with the piece, Morgan asked Sylvia what she felt was wrong. When Sylvia replied that it "wasn't balanced," Morgan worked to describe what she saw as the essay's controlling theme, and then asked a series of questions to help Sylvia clarify her purpose. Having agreed that the piece would contrast the mother's and daughter's differing aesthetic sensibilities, Morgan and Sylvia brainstormed details that would help bring alive these differences. Although they sometimes seemed to be lapsing into informal banter, Morgan periodically brought their conversation back to a focus, reminding Sylvia that the instances she was bringing up needed to illustrate a larger point: "What's the significance of that?" she asked repeatedly.

More often, however, Sylvia brought in only preliminary ideas, and they lapsed into mutually supportive discussions about life, often with no direct reference to writing. As she began to brainstorm an essay about stereotyping, for instance, Sylvia observed that many of her Latino friends back home "kind of feel jealous," openly criticizing her decision to go to a predominantly white college; "I'm doing something for myself and they're putting me down," she asserted. This struck a responsive chord in Morgan, who went on to describe her own struggle to overcome the conception that she was somehow "not black enough." The discussion continued in a later group, when Sylvia described how relatives back in Mexico often assumed that she was leading an Anglicized existence of ease and wealth, and Morgan spoke at length of how estranged she would feel in the presence of African natives. Both displayed a sense of pride at the people they were becoming, at the paths they were pursuing, at their defiance of cultural conventions that both found rigidly prescriptive. One morning, when Sylvia was to speak to a group of Hispanic high school students, she noted that she "didn't care who was out there," that her goal was simply to communicate that she was happy to be pursuing an education. An appreciative Morgan literally cheered.

At other times, however, Morgan's strong identification with Sylvia interfered with her understanding of how their backgrounds diverged, and possibly impeded her efforts to help Sylvia formulate her own thoughts in writing. When Sylvia began brainstorming ideas for her essay about her mother's battle with cancer, for instance, Morgan mistakenly assumed that Sylvia's mother, like her own, had died of the disease: "My mom had cancer and died, too," she said, adding that when she tried to write about the experience for a timed essay exam, she had felt "too emotional" and found she "couldn't do it." "Oh, she didn't die!" Sylvia quickly explained, adding that while she might feel somewhat emotional about the subject, she was sure she could write about it. "Always be that critical writer," Morgan warned, "the objective writer . . . try to put yourself outside of the situation and look at it in terms of writing a story." In an interview, Sylvia explained that she found the cautionary note unnecessary; she, too, was a private person, she maintained, but before she could write on a subject, she had to feel personally connected to it.

In a final interview, Morgan observed that Sylvia seemed more receptive to her comments and a bit more open about bringing in her work. Still, Morgan shared Williams's feeling that although Sylvia had "complex ideas," she was readily frustrated by the effort it took to express them in writing:

> She tends to be a perfectionist. And so, when her writing isn't really, really good, uh, her writing is simple in a lot of ways, very simple. And it's, she doesn't like anybody to see it, you know, until it's really perfect. And then, I, I think that's her roadblock—she likes to do something, put it out and it's done, and it's nice and it's set out. And she looks nice all the time—her hair's always done nice, her makeup's always on, you know. And I think with her writing, she wants to do it once and here it is, it's nice and it's all done, and it's all wrapped up and it's tidy. It bothers her that, you know, she doesn't have it down the first time.

There's "something in her personality that comes out in her writing," Morgan observed—a tendency to "just present things," to forego "a deeper analysis." Morgan saw something of this same "black-and-white" approach in Sylvia's attitude toward the group:

> She doesn't worry about anybody else's trips, you know. We've had conversations before on tapes where she's like, oh, when we were talking one time about the students not showing up, she's like, "It doesn't bother me if they show up or not, I'm still gonna get ahead, I'm still gonna do my own thing," you know? So it's very clear: "These are my goals, these are what I'm doing, it doesn't bother

me if anybody else does or not." She doesn't feel a need to bring the whole group along—if she's getting along, then that's fine.

Operating under the assumption that Sylvia was a native speaker of English, Morgan's analysis did not include attention to how Sylvia's linguistic background might play into her present difficulties with writing. What Morgan and Williams suspected was probably true to a point: embarrassed that her writing was not stronger, Sylvia was reluctant to share her preliminary efforts, and admittedly spent inadequate time revising her essays. An understanding of the psychological and linguistic reasons behind this behavior might have helped Morgan provide more consistently engaging and appropriate help; but such insight proved elusive, as Sylvia remained in Morgan's mind an intellectually gifted young woman whose problems with writing could be ascribed to a perfectionistic slant of character and, perhaps, a touch of basic laziness.

Perspective on the Adjunct Sessions

Sylvia began the semester with buoyant optimism, glad that Morgan was so much more personable than the critical, often-patronizing group leader that she had the previous semester. "I know I need help with my writing," Sylvia wrote in her journal after an early group session; "I feel this class is going to help because there is more of an individual help . . . the group leaders here are willing to help the students, if the students want help." The possibility that the adjunct sessions might foster peer response and discussion did not seem to occur to Sylvia, who described the small groups as a cost-effective but somewhat inefficient means of providing one-on-one assistance:

> I think one-on-one you get more out of it. Because you can spend an hour and go through a lot . . . and with a group, a small group, you could only get to two or three people, and the other two or three are left. And they need, they might need more help, or less help, or whatever.

When asked about the effectiveness of group sessions, Sylvia's answers always focused upon her perceptions of her relationship with Morgan. In the beginning, Sylvia explained that especially since Morgan did not assign grades, she seemed less threatening and therefore more approachable than Williams: "I see her as a friend, but with the skills of a teacher," she explained, "and I'm not afraid of asking her, 'Morgan, what do you think of this?'" While Sylvia believed that she would ultimately have to overcome her writer's block on her own, she thought that her group leader could help by "having patience" and by understanding the source of her seeming resistance. It is important, she emphasized, that both teachers and group leaders "don't give up on the students—'cause that's what I think a lot of teachers do, just give up on the student, and say, 'Well, they're not gonna do it, or they don't wanna do it.'"

In a final interview, Sylvia admitted that she had not attended the small groups as often as she had initially thought she would, explaining that she had gradually "lost interest." When I asked why, she began by assuming full responsibility ("I wasn't taking advantage of it, when I should have"), but she soon confessed her disappointment in Morgan's shifting attitude:

> I don't know, I mean, I guess because the leaders lost the interest—not to all of us, but kind of lost the interest in working with some of us. And so, I mean, we're not that blind, if we see, if I see that Morgan's not that interested that day, you know, we'll just talk about things, you know. And I guess that's what happened.

Morgan's enthusiasm was "really off and on," Sylvia observed, noting particularly Morgan's tendency to get frustrated when the group seemed unresponsive: "Sometimes she would come to the group all pumped up and ready to go, and we wouldn't be all pumped up with her, but that's how reality goes." Although Sylvia felt that she understood Morgan's reaction to the group, she was still troubled by it:

> I think she had high expectations of all of us in the beginning. But then when she got to know us, I guess through our writing and through our discussions, she, I don't think she had high expectations. I mean, I don't know—to me, when someone has high expectations and the person doesn't please them, or whatever, then the other person will be all, like, down and, like, "I didn't do my job right," or whatever.

Although Sylvia sometimes enjoyed the group's talks about issues and assigned readings, she generally preferred whole-class discussions, noting that they encompassed more perspectives. When it came time to share writing, however, Sylvia found even the small group a daunting audience:

> I'd rather have one person criticize me, and I know I can take that, than on a group basis. Because I remember in the beginning we would do, like, freewrites or whatever, and Morgan would want us to read them out loud, and I would, I would not like that. I mean, that sounds kind of strange, I mean, to, for me to say something like that, because I like to see myself as an outgoing person, that, "Hey, go ahead, read my stuff," you know. But I'm also that private person that I can only let one person read it at a time.

Sylvia traced the emergence of this fear to negative classroom experiences in elementary school:

> You know, because of the barrier of coming from a Spanish-speaking home to, going to a school and have English. Because I have the accent and stuff—but I didn't get laughed at, it's just that the teachers sometimes would say it in a nice way but I would take it as a negative way, you know. They would try to say it in a nicer way and I would get offended. That's just something I have.

Although Sylvia had initially looked to the small-group sessions as an oppor-tunity to receive friendly, but expert, advice from a quasi-teacher, she eventually found that she preferred going to friends for assistance: "I get a lot of help on writing through my friends. I have friends that help me, and I always say, 'Here, check it for me, please' . . . And then when she would be finished, she'd go, 'Okay, what are you trying to say here?' and she'd help me that way." Sylvia had several friends whom she often approached for help: one who was enrolled in a basic writing class, another in freshman composition, and a third who was majoring in English. She explained that she felt more comfortable with them than with Morgan: "Because, well, because I know the kids, I know the students in my group, but I don't know Morgan that well . . . We've talked on a group basis and stuff about our experiences growing up and stuff, but I still don't have that personal touch."

On the other hand, when I played back taped segments of her work with Morgan, Sylvia seemed to realize that her feelings about the groups were somewhat more mixed than she had first allowed. Sylvia smiled, for instance, as she listened to the group brainstorm papers on stereotyping—a discussion dominated by herself and Morgan, both of them describing what it was like to be accused of "acting white." Morgan did most of the talking at first, but then Sylvia jumped in:

> I remember once, it was so funny to me, because I come from a middle-class background—although we're not white, we still come from the middle class and all. And this family, this guy, he's all, "You're white." I'm all, "No, I'm not" . . . Then he's all, "Why do you try to be, why do you try to act white?" And, well, I'm not, I know who I am and stuff, you know. It was when I was, like, in twelfth grade or something like that. And then he's all, that I was calling him a wetback and stuff, and I'm all, "No, I would never use that against my own race, I would never use it as a negative way. Joking around with friends I would."

Somewhat uncharacteristically, Sylvia had spoken at length in several instances on the tape, her words punctuated only by an occasional "Right" or "Uh huh" from Morgan. Sylvia seemed pleased to listen to her own words played back, but I was also interested in what she thought of Morgan's end of the conversa-tion. Morgan had, after all, both begun and ended the discussion by talking about her own struggle against those who would call her "not black enough," and I asked Sylvia if she felt connected to this, if it helped her reflect upon her own situation. Sylvia responded:

> Well, I see it as kind of similar. We're going, like, we're in the same boat on that. Because when her friends tell her, "You don't act black," to me, what is "acting black"? Because you can dance, or you can sing, or whatever, you know? And when they tell me, "You're not Mexican," what is that? Just because I can't eat hot, spicy stuff, or I can't speak Spanish properly, or whatever? . . . I'm getting her

input, and I'm getting her viewpoint. I mean, she has more experience than I do, and I can learn from her. You know, and how she has accepted it from society, and it hasn't brought her down.

When I asked if the conversation helped her gather ideas for the essay, Sylvia enthusiastically replied, "Yeah! . . . Because I did use some of the ideas that we talked about in my essay . . . it helped out, it really did." Sylvia saw the session as typical of Morgan's teaching style: "Not formal, very informal—not very, but informal. Laid back, almost—she talks about her experiences all the time."

On the other hand, Sylvia found the next tape that I played back to be representative of something that she did not particularly like about Morgan's approach. The group was brainstorming descriptive essays, and although Sylvia volunteered only that she was thinking of writing about her mother, she was in fact mulling over memories of her mother's battle with cancer. Feisty and demanding, Morgan provided questions intended to nudge Sylvia toward greater specificity:

MORGAN: Um, okay, are you, like, thinking of any characteristics you wanna, like, throw out back and forth, that you want to talk about? How would you approach writing about this person?

SYLVIA: *[pause]* Uh, I don't know. *[laughs]*

MORGAN: You're a college student, you *should* know, that's why you're here . . . *[pause, then Sylvia starts to say something]* Any possible approaches?

SYLVIA: Just the way she has influenced me in my life.

MORGAN: What ways has she influenced you? Positive, negative? Let's start from there.

SYLVIA: Both.

MORGAN: Both?

SYLVIA: I mean, mostly positive.

MORGAN: Mostly positive?

SYLVIA: Yeah.

MORGAN: Influenced what about you?

SYLVIA: Um, well, like never to give up.

MORGAN: Okay, so if you put it under *[Sylvia starts to add something, but Morgan continues]*, if you put it under a broader, um, definition, what would you say, never to give up, never to, what would you call that, what she taught you, how she influenced you?

SYLVIA: What would I call it?

MORGAN: Yeah, what did she influence you, what did, what, what did she teach you? If you called it a whole body of things . . . *[pause]* So I guess what I'm driving at, what I'm trying to get to, is like values, morals, beliefs, ambitions.

SYLVIA: Oh, okay.

MORGAN: You know? Okay. So while we're talking, why don't you, uh, make notes about things you could possibly approach about it, not saying that you have to. Let's start, you know, getting that together.

When asked for her response to the session, Sylvia filled in some of what was left unsaid in the rapid-fire exchange of questions and answers:

I did write an essay about my mother, about not giving up. And that to me was of value. I talked about her experience with cancer . . . *[softly]* and, um, how she had cancer twice, and she had just had, uh, my little sister. She had cancer the first time, it was about a year and a half after my sister was born, nearly two, And so, uh, I just saw how the . . . that was the first time, and the second time was about another year and a half, and that's when she got into chemotherapy and radiation and all that. And how the chemicals wore her down, and I would see her come home like a rag doll, almost. And how, one of my cousins was helping her into her bed, and stuff, that was in the beginning of the treatment. And how she had one of her breasts was taken out, and—I mean, just a lot of these things, like her body was taken, and it would bring her down physically, but not mentally. It would bring her up. She would look at us and cry and stuff, but then she would say, "No, I've gotta do it for them, I gotta keep on for them." I admire my mother a lot, I mean.

She said some of this in the paper that she wrote about her mother; why, I asked Sylvia, did she not talk about it in the small groups? She replied:

Because at the time Morgan asked me, and I wasn't ready for this, I wasn't ready for, to be asked all these kind of questions and stuff. And it was just that we were brainstorming, and I was just, that just popped into my head, afterwards . . . it wasn't personal because I talk about that experience a lot. And so . . . in the beginning, when she did have cancer, I would talk about it and I would cry. But I have gotten through that emotional phase. And I mean sometimes I do see her, and I go, "damn," you know, she went through all that, and I cry, but I won't let her see it. But, I don't know, it was okay.

Sylvia had been somewhat offended by Morgan's remark "You're a college student, you *should* know":

I didn't like that comment! I mean, just because you're a college student, and because you're here, doesn't mean you know everything. And it was something that she just threw me off on that one, like a curve ball there, you know. It didn't affect me, it's just that I know I'm a college student, and I know I don't know everything, but what I do know, I can say something about it, whatever.

Morgan approached the group in this insistent manner rather frequently, Sylvia observed. Sometimes, she admitted, the strategy was useful, especially when Morgan would ask questions that had not yet occurred to her—that way, Sylvia explained, "if someone else asks it . . . I can answer it . . . and that's more ideas for my paper."

Still, there was an apparent mismatch between the depth of Sylvia's emotions around this topic and Morgan's insistent approach in the session. When I played the same tape back for Morgan, she commented only that she was "starting to try and talk less," and that she was fairly happy with the response: "When Sylvia said, 'Oh, okay,'" Morgan observed, "it seemed like an 'aha' experience right there." But from Sylvia's point of view, Morgan had missed the mark, interpreting her initial reply of "I don't know" as an expression of insecurity or laziness rather than the plea for time that it in fact was. While Morgan's goals were to provide "collaborative" supports for student learning and to communicate high expectations, both were undermined by the assumptions that she had already made about Sylvia's level of motivation. Her intentions notwithstanding, these assumptions diminished Morgan's curiosity about what Sylvia was trying to say, and pulled at her efforts to provide tactful, appropriate guidance.

Part of being curious about students is to attend to the many ways in which they announce their need for privacy; Sylvia was, indeed, a private young woman, and it was important that Morgan not interpret her occasional guardedness as a personal rebuff or evidence of unresponsiveness. At the same time, however, Sylvia was extremely eager to talk about many aspects of her background, and noted again and again how much she enjoyed our conversations. Had Morgan only been encouraged to ask, I suspect that she, too, would have been provided some useful insights into the subtleties of Sylvia's background and current struggles with writing.

Notes

1. Although Sylvia qualified as an EOP student on the basis of her parents' income, the family's real estate holdings rendered her ineligible for financial aid. Sylvia received academic counseling from DPU's EOP office, but she was the only focal student not receiving financial aid.

2. A study conducted by Lily Wong Fillmore (1991) suggests that such language loss and ensuing social disruption may be a quite common phenomenon among young children who are taught at school in a language other than that spoken at home.

Collaborative Activity 5.3

In small groups, consider the conflicts/tensions between Sylvia's home and school cultures. How would you characterize the differing goals, values, and beliefs in these two scenes? Examine the significance of the rhetorical interactions or situations in these scenes: Sylvia's interactions with family, friends, members of organizations, visiting high school students, classmates, her peer instructor (Morgan) and her writing teacher (Williams). What do these interactions reveal about the differing scenes of communication and about Sylvia's roles within these scenes? Be prepared to share your responses with the class.

Writing Activity 5.5

Think back on your own most recent writing/language experiences before coming to college—whether in high school, in a community college, in your home, or in the workplace—and write a page in which you describe your own transition from these scenes to the university scene. Which college classes have been an easy transition, and which more difficult? Why? Focus on your introduction to the differing expectations of the college scene, particularly the expectations for communicating in this scene—speaking, listening, reading, and writing.

While the scene of the writing course, as the profile of Sylvia shows us, is made up of various participants with diverse backgrounds and levels of preparation, there are shared goals within this scene and goals it shares with the larger college or university scene. As a smaller scene, a port of entry, located on the border of the larger scene of the university, the first-year writing course tries to teach you how to make essential academic writing choices, the kinds of choices that are expected and valued throughout the university. Of course, the specific mission and goals of a writing course will depend, among other things, on the kind of institution you are in. Nevertheless, its specific goals and approaches often take place within a shared larger scene of writing instruction.

You might not be aware that, on a national level, writing programs share objectives for writing instruction. The National Council of Writing Program Administrators (WPA)—a group of college faculty who direct writing programs and oversee the teaching of first-year writing courses—has developed a statement describing the skills and knowledge that all students should possess by the end of first-year writing. They have created these objectives with much input from writing instructors and writing program directors at universities and colleges across the country. The example below, "WPA Outcomes Statement for First-Year Composition," describes the common knowledge, skills, and attitudes that first-year writing programs at postsecondary institutions across the United States seek to cultivate.

WPA Outcomes Statement for First-Year Composition

RHETORICAL KNOWLEDGE

By the end of first-year composition, students should

- Focus on a purpose
- Respond to the needs of different audiences

- Respond appropriately to different kinds of rhetorical situations
- Use conventions of format and structure appropriate to the rhetorical situation
- Adopt appropriate voice, tone, and level of formality
- Understand how genres shape reading and writing
- Write in several genres

CRITICAL THINKING, READING, AND WRITING

By the end of first-year composition, students should

- Use writing and reading for inquiry, learning, thinking, and communicating
- Understand a writing assignment as a series of tasks, including finding, evaluating, analyzing, and synthesizing appropriate primary and secondary sources
- Integrate their own ideas with those of others
- Understand the relationships among language, knowledge, and power

PROCESSES

By the end of first-year composition, students should

- Be aware that it usually takes multiple drafts to create and complete a successful text
- Develop flexible strategies for generating, revising, editing, and proofreading
- Understand writing as an open process that permits writers to use later invention and rethinking to revise their work
- Understand the collaborative and social aspects of writing processes
- Learn to critique their own and others' works
- Learn to balance the advantages of relying on others with the responsibility of doing their part
- Use a variety of technologies to address a range of audiences

KNOWLEDGE OF CONVENTIONS

By the end of first-year composition, students should

- Learn common formats for different kinds of texts
- Develop knowledge of genre conventions ranging from structure and paragraphing to tone and mechanics

* Practice appropriate means of documenting their work
* Control such surface features as syntax, grammar, punctuation, and spelling.

Writing Activity 5.6

Write a paragraph in which you define your own criteria for effective writing. What assumptions, for example, do you have about what constitutes effective writing? What do you aim to achieve when you write? What do you think you should be learning in your writing course? Then compare your criteria (1) to the objectives in the example above, (2) to Sylvia's description of the "basic ingredients of an essay," and (3) to the criteria your teacher and your writing course have identified (via the syllabus, assignments, class discussions, etc.).

Collaborative Activity 5.4

Examine the WPA objectives in the example above in light of the scene of the writing course and the college and university scene (You might want to refer to your institution's mission statement, which you analyzed in Writing Activity 5.1, p. 189). How do the WPA objectives reveal the scene of writing courses? For example, do they reflect the role of the writing course as a kind of passport to the university? How do they reveal the scene of the college or university? Do the objectives seem to reflect the university's emphasis on the pursuit, production, and exchange of knowledge? Prepare to share your discoveries with other groups.

When college writing instructors collaborated to frame the objectives above, they attached a warning that writing is an extremely complex process and that the objectives for writing courses cannot be taught in reduced or simple ways. The next section will examine how these shared objectives of writing instruction are carried out within the multiple situations and complex and varied rhetorical interactions of the writing class scene.

The Situations of Writing Courses

The writing class scene consists of a number of situations or rhetorical interactions. Many take place in a particular setting—the classroom space—with participants (teachers and students) pursuing the common subject of writing, with the shared purpose of learning to communicate more effectively. Seeking to develop rhetorical knowledge that will be useful for different purposes and audiences, writing teachers ask students to participate in a variety of rhetorical situations, whether working in groups with other students to discuss a reading, conferring with a teacher over paper topic ideas, reading/responding to papers in a peer review workshop, or participating in the sharing of ideas in large-class discussions. In fact, to carry out the objectives of the writing course noted in the WPA Outcomes Statement, most classroom situations require active student participation, dialogue, and hands-on practice writing and communicating. Some of the rhetorical interactions—such as critical reading and conferencing—might take place outside the physical classroom, but they are nonetheless aspects of the scene of the writing course.

READING IN WRITING COURSES

Because first-year writing courses emphasize critical thinking, reading, and writing, they require that you do more than absorb and memorize material. *In writing courses, teachers ask students to interact with readings as well as with classmates and the teacher.* Academic readers inquire into the material, raise questions about it, and critically examine it—to stake out claims or positions and actively apply and construct knowledge, developing new frameworks of understanding.

One way to actively engage in learning is through **active reading**. The act of reading a text is not just an act of passively passing your eyes over the text but rather an active creation of the meaning of that text. You create meaning through the connections you make as a reader, and these connections depend on the expectations you bring to the texts as well as the questions you ask of it. Reading for your college writing course (and most other college courses) typically requires such a deliberate, engaged, and critical stance. *As an academic reader, you are expected not only to appreciate what you are reading, but also to take a position in relation to it—to examine its argument, to become aware of its assumptions, to imagine counterarguments and evidence.* In short, reading in your writing course means reading from the perspective of a writer, someone who is looking to engage the reading for ideas to apply or expand or even challenge in one's own writing. As an active reader, you should imagine yourself in *critical dialogue* with the text you are reading. Box 5.2 highlights some strategies for critical reading.

Educator Paulo Freire clarifies this active, critical engagement in learning by comparing teaching and learning to banking. The "banking" concept of education envisions students as passive "receptacles" that teachers/ bank clerks "deposit" information into; meanwhile students passively receive, file, and store the deposits. While the scenes of some of your college courses will

Box 5.2   *Strategies for Critical Reading*

1. Previewing

Before closely reading the text, begin by quickly familiarizing yourself with it, looking for clues about the scene and about where to start. Scan the text for its visual and textual features—the title, author, place and date of publication, and any headings, references, introductory notes, prefaces, abstracts, or graphics that might help you guess what type of text it is. Since particular genres encourage particular ways of reading, you can search genres for clues about the situation and scene for communicating with writers. The following questions will help you to look for signals about where to start with your reading:

- What is the genre of the text I'm about to read? What are my expectations going into the text?
- What is my purpose for reading? What reading strategies best fit my purpose?
- What clues can I learn about the situation and scene from the title, the author, place of publication, date of publication, editorial notes, blurbs, abstracts, prefaces, or introductions?
- Based on a quick scan of the textual features, what guesses can I make regarding the writer's purpose and the role designated for the reader?
- Do I have any previous knowledge of the subject, and how will this affect my reading?
- How will my values, assumptions, attitudes, and beliefs influence my reading?

2. Annotating

Annotating, the process of making notes and comments in the margins of your text as you read, is a way of entering into an active conversation with the text you are reading. Annotation helps you to read more accurately, think critically about what you read, and retain what you read. You can talk back to the writer, question points that are unclear and comment on areas of agreement and disagreement. Annotation includes marking a text, either by bracketing information, highlighting or underlining, and may include the following marginal annotations:

- *Comments* on the passage ("This is confusing" or "I'm not convinced by this argument")   *(continued on next page)*

(continued from previous page)

- *Evaluations* of the validity of points ("This source is biased" or "These numbers do not add up")
- *Questions* either asking for clarification ("What does this mean?") or challenging claims ("What is the significance of this statistic?")
- *Definitions* of terms or unknown words
- *Paraphrases* or restatements of difficult passages in your own words

3. Analyzing

Another method of active reading is **analyzing** a text, which means identifying its components and examining how these components—the writer's purpose, use of evidence, and word choice—work together to create meaning. To read effectively and analytically, you should consider the connections among a number of factors: the scene, the occasion that motivates the response, the controlling purpose, the writer's image or persona, the role you are invited to play as reader, and the textual conventions that help you and the writer play out your roles in the scene. By analyzing a text, you gain a critical perspective into how the text works to create meaning.

4. Rereading

When faced with an unfamiliar genre or challenging text, or when required to respond to a text, you will need to read it more than once. Reading critically and actively means *rereading* a text because, when you return to a text a second or third time, you often see what you overlooked the first time. Multiple readings also allow you to critically read and "reposition" yourself—to read from new perspectives and to consider the subject from your positioning in various scenes.

require their share of passively receiving information (through lectures) and filing and storing this information (through memorization), the scene of a writing course requires that you be challenged through what Freire describes as "problem posing" education. In a model of education as problem posing, teachers and students enter into dialogue with one another and with texts, with students cast in the role of "critical coinvestigators." As coinvestigators, students are called upon to critically examine material and to explore connections between their own perspectives and the course content. Instead of passively receiving knowledge, students actively construct knowledge by locating meaning in their observations and interpretations and by being actively engaged in their own learning.

DISCUSSION IN WRITING COURSES

Rather than a traditional lecture class, you are probably finding that your writing class tends to be defined more as a workshop, with situations that call for interaction, whether through class discussion, group work exchanges, or in-class writing activities. A common situation in the writing class scene is class discussion, where students and teachers are constantly posing problems and asking questions, in addition to sharing diverse viewpoints necessary for critical reflection. You may find it beneficial to pay close attention during class discussions to the teacher's questions and discussion-leading devices, which can reveal his or her assumptions or expectations. How the teacher leads the class discussion and topics/questions that he or she raises may be particularly revealing about what issues the teacher finds important. In addition, listening to the varied perspectives of the class can give you critical insight into a topic or reading as you consider perspectives that you otherwise might not have considered.

PEER REVIEW IN WRITING COURSES

One of the most important rhetorical interactions in the writing classroom is between student writers who give feedback on each other's writing, often referred to as **peer review** or *peer evaluation*. Such peer review models the collaborative nature of college and university knowledge making that we discussed earlier. Students, working either in pairs or small groups, are able to get immediate feedback on their drafts in progress and to address a real audience as they discuss their drafts face-to-face with their readers. Because peer evaluation gives writers a chance to get feedback on their drafts from someone who does not have the power of a grade over them, this situation makes for a more open and productive exchange of opinion. As a peer reviewer, it is important to exercise your critical reading and thinking skills. While you should refrain from negatively criticizing your classmate's writing, you should be willing to critique it—to respond as an interested and engaged reader who has questions, suggestions, and useful feedback to give to the writer (see the sample peer review in the following section, "The Genres of Writing Courses").

Collaborative Activity 5.5

Returning to the excerpt "Sylvia" reprinted earlier, examine Sylvia's interactions with her peer tutor (Morgan). What is the nature of these interactions? Which of the peer tutor strategies do you find effective and which do you find ineffective? To improve these peer review exchanges, what advice would you give Sylvia on her role as writer? What advice would you give to Morgan on her role as peer reviewer? In your small group, come up with a list of guidelines for writers and peer reviewers in the writing class situation that will make these interactions more productive. Your instructor may choose to compile these guidelines so that you can refer to them when you do your own peer reviews.

Writing Activity 5.7

One of the complaints of Sylvia's writing teacher is that Sylvia's writing lacks liveliness and vivid detail. However, Sylvia is unsure of how to offer "sufficient support" in her papers. After examining the excerpt from Sylvia's essay on stereotypes, write a paragraph addressed to Sylvia that gives advice on how she might provide the detail her teacher is asking for. Make concrete suggestions. How would you respond to Sylvia's explanation for her difficulty with writing, which she attributes to her "troubled linguistic background"?

The Genres of Writing Courses

Of all of the various situations and rhetorical interactions within the writing classroom, one might argue that the actual practice of writing is most significant and most influential in shaping the workshop atmosphere of the writing class scene. A popular credo of writing teachers is that "Writers learn to write by writing." First and foremost, writing classes are concerned with the subject of writing and with the shared objective of writing processes, defined in the WPA Outcomes Statement as the development of "multiple drafts to create and complete a successful text" and the use of "flexible strategies for generating, revising, editing, and proofreading." Because these processes of writing repeat themselves in writing classes, from writing assignment to assignment and from writer to writer, there are various genres that correspond to the repeated processes of writing—inventing, drafting, and revising. For instance, to respond to the situation of inventing or generating ideas, students often use the genres of freewriting, brainstorming, or clustering, which are defined as follows:

- **Freewriting:** writing continuously without stopping, leaving yourself free to discover what you think about something without editing or censoring. Typically, a writer begins with a topic, perhaps just a word or a question, and begins writing whatever comes out on that topic without stopping.

- **Brainstorming:** listing (either individually or collaboratively) as many ideas as you can think of on a topic as quickly as you can, without stopping to reread, reflect, or censor any of the things that come to mind. The basic difference between freewriting and brainstorming is the difference between connected prose and a list. You may pause while brainstorming, unlike freewriting, but do not stop to reread or reflect.

- **Clustering:** visually depicting the relationship between ideas by writing in the center of a blank page a word or phrase that captures the heart of what you are trying to write about, drawing a circle around that word, then writing down anything you think of to do with that topic anywhere on the page. When one word prompts other ideas, circle it and draw lines from that word to the other words it prompts. What you end up with is something that looks a bit like a spider web, with circles and lines linking other circles, something like an octopus with many tentacles. Below is the clustering we did while inventing the substance of Chapter 3.

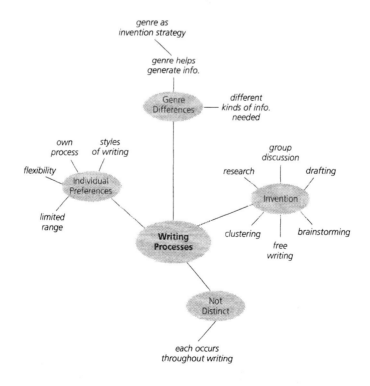

Collaborative Activity 5.6

What other repeated rhetorical strategies or genres have you employed when generating ideas for a paper? In groups, make a list of additional genres for generating ideas, and write out a brief definition of each. How do you choose when to use which genres? Share your list with the rest of the class, and be prepared to discuss how situation and scene may play a part in your choice of genres for invention.

While these invention genres respond to the situation of generating ideas, the drafting stage often results in different situations, such as interactions between students and their classmates, who give feedback on works in progress. These repeated interactions between peers or peer reviews have led to a patterning of questions and responses, the genre of the peer review sheet. An example of this genre, based on a paper a student wrote arguing against the closing of her hometown theater, appears in the example below.

Draft Workshop: Response Sheet

Writer: Sarah Lee
Peer Evaluator: Bob Evans

1. What strengths does this paper have? What is especially interesting or effective?

   You know the issue very well and you stay focused on it throughout your paper. Your personal experience is very effective.

2. State the writer's controlling idea. How well does the draft focus on this main idea? Any suggestions for improvement?

   The controlling idea is the argument that Lafayette needs to join together to save the local theater. I would develop more of your reasons why, maybe address why the town does not support the theater and why they should.

3. Given the writer's purpose, is the audience appropriate? To what extent does the writer seem to be keeping the audience in mind? What questions/arguments might the audience have that aren't addressed by the writer?

   Audience is appropriate—you may want to shift the focus a little more to those who pay for its upkeep (taxpayers, local businesspeople and leaders in the town). You could talk about the $$ a theater brings to the community/town and how much more attractive the town is to outsiders with this source of entertainment available.

4. What additional evidence—examples, details, illustrations or textual support (facts, statistics, quotations)—might strengthen the paper and support the claims being made? Where is more of the writer's own commentary, argumentation or analysis needed (as opposed to sources)?

I think you could add quotes from locals affected by the potential closing—maybe one from a teen, a child, adult, historians, etc. You could even do a survey to see how the town as a whole (or a sampling) feels about losing the theater. This way you could gain more support. You need stronger reasons than just pure entertainment—talk about sentimental/historical value more and quality of life issues?

5. Comment on the organization of the draft. How logical and unified is it? Suggestions? Is the format and genre appropriate given the audience and scene for writing? Make suggestions.

Organization is good; consistent throughout; moves the argument along logically. You may want to include a solution at the end.

6. Comment on voice and tone. Are they appropriate to audience and purpose and to the larger scene of writing?

You may want to redirect voice to be stronger and challenging. Ask residents why don't they support local business? don't they want places of entertainment? Challenge them to act!

7. What two main things should the writer focus on as he/she revises the paper?

—more concrete reasons for supporting the theater

—more citizens' voices

Writing Activity 5.8

Collect peer review sheets from your writing class (perhaps drawing on those you have received or written for your peers), and respond to the following questions regarding what this genre reveals about the classroom situation and scene. What assumptions about writing does the genre reveal? What roles for readers (peer reviewers) and writers does the genre encourage or discourage? What actions does the genre make possible, and what actions does it make difficult?

Writing Activity 5.9

Reread the WPA Outcomes Statement, and then describe how the genre of the peer review sheet reflects the writing course objectives outlined within the statement. Which of the objectives does the peer review sheet seem to be responding to most?

While the peer review sheet is a genre frequently used by students as they respond to each other's drafts, instructors have their own typical ways of commenting on and evaluating student papers. For instance, teachers often use the genre of marginal comments, similar to the marginal annotations that we defined in our discussion of critical reading. These notes typically ask questions of clarification, note points of interest, or highlight areas of confusion. Marginal comments are meant to provide a template of sorts for one reader's active response in the process of reading. Finally, teachers may make summary comments or end comments that highlight strengths of the paper and suggest possible ways to revise. These comments often correspond to particular marginal comments made throughout the text and synthesize these individual comments into overall strategies for revision.

While there are multiple genres that enable participants in the writing classroom to respond to various situations—whether generating ideas for writing, drafting, reading/responding to drafts, or evaluating writing—the most important genres are those that you will compose in response to writing assignments. Chapters 6 and 7 closely examine three genres that are commonly taught and practiced in the writing classroom scene: the *analysis paper*, the *argument paper* and the *researched position paper*. Since taking the time to understand a genre is an effective way to begin writing it, the following chapters will explore how knowledge of specific writing classroom genres can help writers decide the most effective way of negotiating the writing process and deciding on the most effective rhetorical strategies. We hope to show you that as you encounter different situations as a writer within academic scenes—whether writing a report for history, filling out a scholarship application, or writing a letter to the editor of your student newspaper—you can use your genre knowledge to determine how to act effectively within these scenes of communication.

Writing Projects

Writing Project 5.1

Observe the scene of a class you are taking. Drawing on Box 1.2: Guidelines for Observing and Describing Scenes (pp. 44–45), describe the scene, the interactions within the scene, and the genres used to carry out the class objectives. Then use these data to explain how this particular classroom scene both fits the academic scene at large (you may want to refer to Writing Activity 5.1 (p. 189), which asked you to examine your institution's mission statement) and has qualities of its own. Present your findings as a guide that helps college students who are entering this course develop a better idea of what this scene is, how it functions, and how they are expected to act within it.

Writing Project 5.2

Write a letter to your high school English teacher or to the school board explaining how your high school courses did/did not prepare you for this particular writing course. You might consider the goals and expectations of the courses, criteria for evaluation, types of assignments, types of texts (both those you read and write), use of class time, your role in the classroom, your relationship to your instructor and peers, etc.

Writing Project 5.3

Choose and then compose a genre that would effectively respond to the following situation: Explain to a group of high school students what to expect from their college writing course, and give them advice on how to prepare. You might consider the goals and expectations of the course, criteria for evaluation, types of assignments, types of texts (both those you read and write), use of class time, your role in the classroom, your relationship to your instructor and peers, etc. While this clarifies your purpose, participants, and subject, it is up to you define the setting (college fair day or a school Web site, for example) and to formulate an appropriate response—a letter, flyer, pamphlet, PowerPoint presentation, Web site, etc.—to this situation.

Writing Project 5.4

Write a critique of a genre that is used in an academic scene, and address it to your classmates and instructor for this course. The genre may be from your writing class (peer review sheet, journal) or from another course, or it may function within the larger academic scene—the syllabus, textbook, or application form (loan, scholarship, financial aid, housing).

After identifying the patterns and underlying assumptions of the genre, evaluate the possibilities and limitations of this genre in the writing course scene. You will want to draw on the Questions for Critiquing Genre in Box 4.1 (p. 161), as well as refer to the sample critiques in that chapter. Make sure to state and then develop a **claim** that evaluates some aspect of the genre's effects. Then support your claim with **evidence** taken from the genre. In the process of developing your claim, keep in mind that you will not only need to describe the effects a genre has, but also to evaluate the strengths and/or limitations of these effects. Your claim is the point you want to make about the genre, and your evidence is the features of the genre you will use to demonstrate your point. You might wish to review the discussion of claims, pp. 235–236.

Writing Project 5.5

Study what electronic genres are commonly used in academic scenes at your college or university. For example, many courses now use a class organizing technology like Blackboard or Course in a Box that include genres of discussion boards, announcements, course documents, and so on. Many courses set up a discussion list for the class. Some teachers create Web sites for their students. Select an electronic academic genre, collect multiple examples of the genre, and use Box 2.1 (pp. 93–94) to help you analyze how the genre reflects and reveals its academic situation and scenes. Your analysis, directed at an audience of your writing class (students and instructor), should explore what the rhetorical interactions reveal about this online scene.

Writing Project 5.6

Reread the "Sylvia" excerpt and compare Sylvia's transition into college to your transition into college. Once you have examined the similarities and differences in your experiences, write an essay in which you make a claim about what accounts for any similarities and differences, and then support that claim with evidence from your and Sylvia's experiences.

Writing Analyses and Arguments

In this chapter, we will focus on two genres commonly taught and practiced in college writing courses: The analysis paper and the argument paper. We will begin our inquiry into the writing course and its scene of writing by comparing the analysis paper to another genre you might already be familiar with, the five-paragraph theme. The chapter then moves into a discussion of the situations that call for analysis papers. Using a sample student paper, we describe what analysis is and how to perform it. Then we invite you to read and analyze a professional example. In the second half of the chapter, we guide you through a detailed analysis of the generic features first of analysis papers and then of argument papers. We will help you to identify the different patterns in each genre, to interpret what these patterns mean, and to develop strategies for using that knowledge to make more effective choices as you write analysis and argument papers. At the end of the chapter, we include several samples of student analysis and argument papers.

The Five-Paragraph Theme versus the Analysis Paper

If your experience in high school was similar to that of many students, then you may have learned to write a genre sometimes called the "five-paragraph theme." For those of you who did not learn it, the **five-paragraph theme** has a set structure of five paragraphs for which it is named:

An introductory paragraph, which contains a thesis

Three body paragraphs, each of which contains one supporting idea and evidence

A concluding paragraph, which summarizes the three supporting ideas and then restates the thesis

Central to the five-paragraph theme is the thesis, the **controlling idea** of a paper, which often takes the form of a three-part structure that matches the theme's organization: For example, "There are three reasons for x: First reason, second reason, third reason."

One of the primary purposes for using the five-paragraph theme is to provide a ready-made organizational structure that adapts to a variety of writing situations in high school. The genre is also easy for teachers to read, allowing them to give students more practice in writing because the teachers can assess a high number of themes in a relatively short amount of time. While the five-paragraph theme thus proves quite useful for many situations in high school scenes, few if any college situations call for a five-paragraph theme. Essay examination might use a five-paragraph structure, but in college this genre requires a level of analysis and complexity that the five-paragraph theme is not meant to handle.

Although the exact shape it takes and the way it gets communicated differ from scene to scene and genre to genre, analysis as a mode of inquiry is valued in many genres across various academic scenes of writing, including writing courses. In college-level writing courses, the analysis paper does resemble the five-paragraph theme in some of its generic features. Both genres revolve around a thesis or controlling idea; both use evidence to develop and support that idea; both include introductions, bodies, and conclusions. As a different genre, though, coming from a different scene and situation, *the analysis paper in college-level writing courses also challenges you to build on your previously learned genres in important ways.* These include:

- Developing a more complex controlling idea
- Incorporating academically authorized evidence rather than personal opinion
- Organizing from the particular controlling idea, and using more than three self-contained supporting paragraphs
- Using more complex transitions to lead readers through that structure
- Analyzing as well as providing evidence

We will discuss each of these in more detail, and we will show you an example of a text written by a first-year student who had some difficulty moving from the five-paragraph theme to the analysis paper. If you have learned in the past to write the five-paragraph theme—perhaps even come to depend on the genre—you may need to keep reminding yourself that it is *not* a genre that will work well in most college writing situations and that the analysis paper has different generic features.

Writing Activity 6.1

If you learned to write the five-paragraph theme (or something similar to it), explore the extent to which it has been helpful to you and how it has limited you. If you have not learned the five-paragraph theme, consider the "tricks" you have come to depend on in writing (for example, a pattern for writing introductions or conclusions or a way of organizing certain kinds of papers). Using the Guidelines for Critiquing Genres, Box 4.1 (p. 161), examine how these patterns, like all generic expectations, both make things easier for you and sometimes constrain what you want to do.

The Scene and Situation of Analysis Papers

Following the pattern we have established in this book and outlined in Box 2.1 (pp. 93–94), we will take you through this genre so important to writing classes and other academic scenes—in short, we will analyze analysis papers.

PARTICIPANTS, SETTING, AND SUBJECT

Since writing courses are one of the places analysis papers are written, and we described the scene of writing courses in Chapter 5, you already know much about the scene of this genre. You already know, too, much of the situation of the analysis paper, for it inhabits the same setting and involves the same participants as other writing class genres. The writer has the double role not only of author with a claim to make but also of student with learning to demonstrate. The usual readers of analysis papers, teachers and classmates, will similarly read the genre not only to learn from the analysis but also to evaluate how well the analysis paper has been written.

The subjects of analysis papers can range widely, including anything susceptible to analysis. Some common subjects and purposes of analysis papers include:

- To observe a text, activity, or event and to explain what it means and how and why it works
- To take an idea and use it to clarify and understand a concept or phenomenon
- To consider the relationship and consequences of one text, activity, or event on another
- To uncover the implicit assumptions of a text, an argument, a concept, etc.

* To identify an inconsistency in a text, activity, or event and to explain and explore its implications

For example, an analysis paper might examine how rhetorical appeals operate in a Web page, might use the concept of scene to understand a local organization, might compare the arguments of two articles in a debate, might explore the assumptions underlying the notion of individualism, or might explain apparently conflicting practices in a professional site. In short, analysis papers take as their subjects anything that merits analytic attention.

THE OBJECTIVES OF ANALYSIS

Analysis is at the heart of analysis papers, of course; it is what gives the genre its name. The place of writing classes as ports of entry helps explain the purpose of the analysis paper, for a major objective of this genre is to teach students about the kinds of analysis expected in the college and university scene. In the writing class analysis is also a major *purpose* of the situation of the analysis paper, for teachers and students use it to demonstrate students' ability to analyze and to write about that analysis.

The ability to analyze is one of the most important skills one can develop in college because analysis in its various forms is central to critical academic inquiry. Essentially, analysis involves taking something apart to understand it—the reverse of **synthesis,** or putting things together. Analysis examines how things work, why they do what they do, what they mean, and what effects they have. To analyze something is not just about taking it apart to see how it works; it is also about trying to understand how it can be improved and changed. Most important of all, analysis requires us to take a critical, more detached observational stance, one in which we withhold judgment and personal opinion as much as possible so that we can get at the internal workings and possible meanings of our object of study.

As a college student, you will be asked to write genres involving analysis in many of your courses. In a literature course, you might be asked to analyze how characters in a novel differ; in psychology, you might be asked to analyze how gender affects interpersonal relationships; in economics, you might be asked to analyze the effect of increased interest rates on the economy; in history, you might be asked to analyze how the cold war changed the balance of power in the world; and in biology, you might be asked to analyze why hatchery salmon are threatening wild salmon. Exactly how you perform these analyses will depend on the conventions and expectations of each disciplinary scene and genre. But generally speaking, in all these instances your challenge as a writer is to critically observe your subject, to take it apart and examine its workings, to read what others have said about it, and then to develop some claim or idea that helps us understand it better.

Although our emphasis in this part of the book is on academic genres, analysis is not something that only academics do only in academic scenes. We analyze all the time in order to function in the world. When we enter a scene of a party, to return to our example in Chapter 1, we analyze it in order to decide how we should act: We take it apart by looking at how people are dressed, what music is playing, what food is served, how people are communicating, etc. Then we put these elements (the clothing, music, food, style of communicating) back together in order to draw a conclusion about what these different elements mean for how we should act. This conclusion that we construct becomes the **claim** we are making about this situation. If we are later asked why we formulated this claim, we could point to the **evidence** (the clothing, music, food, style of communicating) to **support** the claim.

By and large, analysis papers in writing courses operate from a similar premise. After you have analyzed your subject and established a claim (your central conclusion or argument about the subject) that helps explain it in some way, your challenge as a writer is to support and develop that claim with evidence, evidence that will convince your readers that your observation and explanation are justified and significant. The relationship *between* the claim and evidence used to support that claim is central to the analysis paper. But this relationship is not as obvious as it may seem at first. It involves more than just compiling evidence to support a claim. That is, to write an effective analysis paper, you cannot simply string together a series of examples and facts and assume that your readers will connect these pieces back to your claim. As a writer, it is up to *you* to make the meaningful connection for your readers. *You are expected to analyze how your evidence relates to and supports your claim.*

Analysis involves making explicit the assumptions that connect your evidence to your claim. For example, imagine your first day at a new job. Based on your observations of this workplace scene, you come to the conclusion that it is a relaxed work environment. To support this claim, you cite examples from your observations such as the informal dress of your co-workers, the shared jokes and laughter among the staff, and the flexible hours. These facts are your evidence. As someone making this claim, though, you are expected to ask yourself why you connect that evidence to that claim, to make explicit your assumptions: "So what?" So what that the employees dress informally? So what that they laugh and share jokes? So what that the hours are flexible? How and why does this evidence support your claim that this is a relaxed work environment?

To answer these questions, you need to unpack some of the assumptions that connect your evidence to your claim. For example, one of your unstated assumptions is that laughter among coworkers helps to create a

relaxed atmosphere. By making that assumption explicit—that is, by showing how and why the evidence relates to the claim (how and why laughter
creates a relaxed work environment)—you are analyzing your evidence in
ways that begin to **make meaning** for your readers.

Of course, the above example is fairly obvious. It will not always be as
simple to identify and analyze how your evidence relates to your claims. We
will show you more complicated examples later in this chapter. But even in
this fairly straightforward example, we can see the basic relationship of the
analysis paper:

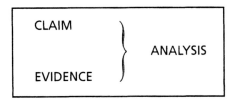

This relationship is a major part of what sets the analysis paper apart from the
five-paragraph theme. In the discussion of the student paper, taken from an
introductory writing course, that follows Writing Activity 6.2, we will exemplify analysis and illustrate the challenges some first-year students experience
when they are asked to make the transition from five-paragraph themes to college-level analysis papers. We will show how you can advance past the simple
association typical of the five-paragraph theme.

Writing Activity 6.2

Think about a recent scene you observed or situation you participated in where
you were called on to analyze an activity, event, process or object—to break something down and to understand how it works and why (it doesn't have to be a
situation that led to a written analysis). What was the scene of your analysis?
Identify the situation of the analysis—the subject, participants, purposes, and setting. What evidence did you rely on for your analysis? What conclusions did you
draw from your analysis, and how did your evidence support these conclusions?

MOVING FROM THE FIVE-PARAGRAPH THEME TO THE ANALYSIS PAPER

The following student paper begins to meet the challenges of college-level
analysis papers but remains a bit limited by its adherence to the five-paragraph theme. Since the five-paragraph theme genre does not lend itself to

the kind of analysis expected in college writing courses, the writer of this paper struggles to fully analyze the subject matter.

The writing assignment for this sample paper asks students to analyze two reviews of the same movie that were published in different magazines. Here is part of what the instructor specified in the assignment:

> The primary goal of your essay is to evaluate how well the two reviewers communicated the necessary information to their respective audiences, given the fixed form of a movie or television review.

This assignment calls for an analysis paper. It asks students to take two reviews and analyze how each communicates its information to its intended audience. To do this, students will need to take the reviews apart and examine how each one works in its specific magazine and for its target audience. Then the students will be expected to develop a claim based on this analysis and support it with evidence. Here is one student's paper in response to the assignment.

1

The motion picture <u>Terms of Endearment</u> is a comical movie with an unexpected somber ending. The film follows the relationship between a mother and a daughter and the men in their lives. A review of the movie was written in <u>Time</u> and <u>Films in Review</u>. They are two different reviews for two types of audience. <u>Time</u> magazine is geared toward a general audience, while <u>Films in Review</u> is intended for readers who are interested in the movie industry.

Kenneth L. Geist, the author of the review in <u>Films in Review</u>, and Richard Schickel, the author of the review in <u>Time</u>, take different approaches to the review of the movie <u>Terms of Endearment</u>. Half of Geist's review contained information about James L. Brooks, the director of the movie. The other half of the review was about the main characters. Schickel's review dealt mainly with the plot and the characters.

Both authors discuss the plot, but write about it differently. Geist felt that the movie was "a constantly surprising comedy which chronicles the thirty-year relationship of a

2

mother and a daughter and their wayward men." He uses difficult vocabulary intended for a well-educated reader. For example, Geist writes, "Alone and fearful of reaching fifty, Aurora surrenders to her bibulous and lecherous neighbor, Garrett, a former Astronaut, whom she had previously disdained as uncouth." When discussing the story, Geist gave away too much to the reader. He stated that Emma became infected with cancer and eventually died. When Schickel explained the same part in the story, he did not completely give the story away. Instead of saying that Emma has cancer, he refers to it as "Emma's illness." He never states that she dies.

Both Geist and Schickel discussed the director of the movie. Geist went more into depth about James Brooks than Schickel. Geist talked about what a wonderful and talented director Brooks is. He conveys this when he writes, "Brooks, the creator of such memorable television series as the <u>Mary Tyler Moore Show</u>, <u>Lou Grant</u>, and <u>Taxi</u>, has demolished Hollywood's scornful notion that t.v. craftsmen are below the salt of feature filmmakers." He also talks about Brook's gift as a screenwriter. Almost the entire article written by Geist was about Brooks. Only a small portion discussed the characters and the storyline. Schickel wrote very little about Brooks. He only talks about him in one paragraph, while Geist's main focus was Brooks. In Schickel's section on Brooks, he goes into Brook's view on what the film is about. Schickel wanted the readers to know what Brooks was trying to create.

The reviews are both well-written for their intended audience. They both contain information about the plot, characters, and the director. The review in <u>Films in Review</u> should be read if the reader has already viewed the movie and is interested in knowing about the director. Schickel's review should be read by anyone interested in the movie. He wrote an exceptional review which covered the movie well

> 3
>
> without giving the entire story away. Geist gave a lot of interesting facts about Brooks. He wrote a complete review of Brooks, but he gave away the surprise of the movie by revealing too much of the plot. Both reviews are worth reading. The one the reader chooses depends on if he or she is interested in finding out about the movie or the director.

This paper is a good example of the successes and difficulties students face when they begin writing analysis papers. The student has apparently done a fine job of analyzing the two reviews, taking them apart to examine how each differs from the other. The student also seems aware that the two reviews differ because of where they appear and for whom they are written, an awareness that is exactly what the assignment called for. But when the student writes the paper, the student runs into some difficulties, some of which are due to an overreliance on the five-paragraph theme. By doing our own analysis of this student's paper, below, we will identify these difficulties and suggest ways for you to overcome them. A closer look at the paper will further clarify the **inquiry method** of analysis, which is the primary purpose for learning analysis papers.

Here again is the introduction:

> The motion picture Terms of Endearment is a comical movie with an unexpected somber ending. The film follows the relationship between a mother and a daughter and the men in their lives. A review of the movie was written in Time and Films in Review. They are two different reviews for two types of audience. Time magazine is geared toward a general audience, while Films in Review is intended for readers who are interested in the movie industry.

The writer provides a fairly helpful introduction that gives a little bit of background for the movie and the two reviews. But, as you may have noticed, the introduction does not really explain why we are reading this paper, or why we should care about the analysis that follows. It just jumps in and takes the reader by surprise. More appropriately to the five-paragraph theme genre, the claim presented here is a fairly weak listing of points or statement of fact and fails to reflect the purpose of the analysis paper genre: To explain what these differences mean and to explore their implications.

While the introduction does make a statement about how the two reviews differ, it does not ask the **"So what?" question** that is critical to analysis papers: So what that "*Time* magazine is geared toward a general audience, while *Films in Review* is intended for readers who are interested in the movie industry?" A thoughtful reader might respond to this sentence by saying, "it's nice to know that *Time* magazine is geared toward a general audience, while *Films in Review* is intended for readers who are interested in the movie industry, but what does that have to do with this assignment?" After all, the assignment did not ask students to compare the audiences of different magazines; it asked students to compare reviews in two different magazines. By asking the *So what* question, however, the writer might be able to state a better claim, one that is more analytical and that the rest of the paper can support, perhaps something like:

Claim: Because *Time* magazine is geared toward a general audience, while *Films in Review* is intended for readers who are interested in the movie industry, the two reviews of *Terms of Endearment* address the movie differently.

Although it could still be more specific, this new claim, unlike the original, does more than just describe what is fairly obvious. It adds a level of complexity because now the writer has to connect the audiences and the reviews.

Let us now look more closely at the first supporting paragraph:

Kenneth L. Geist, the author of the review in <u>Films in Review</u>, and Richard Schickel, the author of the review in <u>Time</u>, take different approaches to the review of the movie

> Terms of Endearment. Half of Geist's review contained infor-
> mation about James L. Brooks, the director of the movie. The
> other half of the review was about the main characters.
> Schickel's review dealt mainly with the plot and the characters.

This is perhaps the weakest paragraph in the paper, but it also has a great deal of potential. In it, the writer tries to support the claim that both movie reviewers take different approaches in their reviews. As evidence, the writer cites *Films in Review*'s focus on the director and *Time*'s focus on the plot and characters. This is interesting evidence. But once again, the question is "So what?" So what that the reviewers take different approaches? So what that one focuses on the director while the other focuses on the plot and characters? Here the writer seems to be relying on the reader to make some pretty important connections, connections that are central to the paper's analysis.

Part of the difficulty here is that the writer never establishes a strong enough claim in the introduction. Without having something to prove, the evidence just sits there. The evidence needs a claim to connect back to so that it can be analyzed. If we use our new revised claim and the already existing evidence, the two would look something like this:

> **Claim:** Because *Time* magazine is geared toward a general audience, while *Films in Review* is intended for readers who are interested in the movie industry, the two reviews of *Terms of Endearment* address the movie differently.
>
> **Evidence:** The *Time* review focuses on plot and characters, while the *Films in Review* review focuses on the director.

Something is still missing, though. We still do not know how and why this evidence relates to and supports the claim. This is where analysis comes in. The writer needs to make more *explicit* the assumptions that underscore the connection between the claim and evidence. *How* does the evidence support the claim? Such analysis, when added to the claim and evidence, might look something like this:

Claim: Because *Time* magazine is geared toward a general audience, while *Films in Review* is intended for readers who are interested in the movie industry, the two reviews of *Terms of Endearment* address the movie differently.

Evidence: The *Time* review focuses on plot and characters, while the *Films in Review* review focuses on the director.

Analysis: Readers of *Time*, who make up a general audience, want to read the review so they can decide if they should go see the movie, so focusing on the plot and characters will help this general audience learn something about the movie. But for readers of *Films in Review,* who are interested in the movie industry, it is more interesting to find out who made the movie, how he or she made the movie, etc. So the fact that the *Time* review discusses the plot and characters while *Films in Review* discusses the director reflects how each review is geared toward a different audience.

Notice how the analysis we have added adds meaning to the evidence by making it *relevant* to the writer's claim. It does not rely on the reader to make the connection.

Now let us look at one more supporting paragraph from the sample paper:

Both authors discuss the plot, but write about it differently. Geist felt that the movie was "a constantly surprising comedy which chronicles the thirty-year relationship of a mother and a daughter and their wayward men." He uses difficult vocabulary intended for a well-educated reader. For example, Geist writes, "Alone and fearful of reaching fifty, Aurora surrenders to her bibulous and lecherous neighbor, Garrett, a former Astronaut, whom she had previously disdained as uncouth." When discussing the story, Geist gave away too much to the reader. He stated that Emma became infected with cancer and eventually died. When Schickel explained the same part in the story, he did not completely give the story away. Instead of saying that Emma has cancer, he refers to it as "Emma's illness." He never states that she dies.

This paragraph provides more good evidence to support the claim that the two reviews differ because of their audiences. It shows the results of the research the student has done on the two reviews and cites it effectively. And importantly, the writer begins to address the "So what?" question. Notice, for example, how the writer analyzes the first piece of evidence:

Evidence: For example, Geist writes, "Alone and fearful of reaching fifty, Aurora surrenders to her bibulous and lecherous neighbor, Garrett, a former Astronaut, whom she had previously disdained as uncouth."

So what?

Analysis: He uses difficult vocabulary intended for a well-educated reader.

By explaining how the difficult vocabulary in the Geist review is geared toward the more educated reader of *Films in Review*, the writer relates the evidence back to the main claim, which is that each review reflects its target audience.

The analysis is not sustained in the rest of the paragraph, however. Immediately following the first piece of evidence, the writer provides two more examples to show the difference between the reviews:

Evidence: When discussing the story, Geist gave away too much to the reader. He stated that Emma became infected with cancer and eventually died.

Evidence: When Schickel explained the same part in the story, he did not completely give the story away. Instead of saying that Emma has cancer, he refers to it as "Emma's illness." He never states that she dies.

Here, we return to the "So what?" question. Why do we, as readers, need to know this? How do these two pieces of evidence relate to the paper's main claim?

Writing Activity 6.3

As a writer, what would you do with these two pieces of evidence? How would you address the "So what?" question? Write up your own analysis to show how you would relate the evidence to the paper's main claim.

Finally, let us take a look at the sample paper's concluding paragraph:

The reviews are both well-written for their intended audience. They both contain information about the plot, characters, and the director. The review in <u>Films in Review</u> should be read if the reader has already viewed the movie and is interested in knowing about the director. Schickel's review should be read by anyone interested in the movie. He wrote an exceptional review which covered the movie well without giving the entire story away. Geist gave a lot of interesting facts about Brooks. He wrote a complete review of Brooks, but he gave away the surprise of the movie by revealing too much of the plot. Both reviews are worth reading. The one the reader chooses depends on if he or she is interested in finding out about the movie or the director.

In this conclusion, the writer goes beyond the typical five-paragraph theme by doing more than just restating the points of each paragraph. But the conclusion does not suit the analysis paper well because the writer loses sight of the paper's focus. The writer shifts from analysis to *evaluation*, summarizing the evidence and recommending who should read which review and why. The text would have been more successful as an analysis paper if the focus had stayed on the analysis itself, explaining the meaning of the analysis, its "So what?" For example, the writer could ask: "Okay, now that I have demonstrated that these two reviews differ in their approach to the movie because of their different audiences, what does this mean in the bigger picture? What is the result or consequence of doing the kind of analysis I just did?" *Speculating on the consequences, considering the implications, or explaining the significance of one's claim is a more effective way of concluding an analysis paper because it helps readers better understand the broader relevance of the paper they just finished reading.*

Writing Activity 6.4

Rewrite the conclusion to the sample paper above. Consider how you might more effectively keep the focus on the analysis itself. Write a conclusion that speculates on the consequences, implications, or significance of the claim the paper makes.

Our analysis of the movie reviews paper has, we hope, given you a better understanding of what analysis involves and provided some ideas about how to build on what you already know about writing. Your previous knowledge of the five-paragraph theme, with its thesis statement, creation of subpoints, and need for supporting detail, can help you adjust to the purposes of the analysis paper, with its claim, evidence, and analysis of how the claim and evidence are connected. As you move into courses in other disciplines, you will of course have to learn different notions of analysis, ones more specifically suited to the kinds of claims and evidence writers make in those scenes. Learning the analysis paper in your writing course can help you adapt to the analysis required in those scenes.

To provide you with a further example of analysis, we have included below a piece written by Rosina Lippi-Green and published in her 1997 book *English with an Accent: Language, Ideology, and Discrimination in the United States*. Although a scholarly chapter rather than an analysis paper, Lippi-Green's text demonstrates effective analysis, connecting claims to evidence and never forgetting the "So what." As you read, notice how Lippi-Green goes about supporting her overall claim that the language of Disney films perpetuates stereotypes. You might want to annotate the text (see Box 5.2: Strategies for Critical Reading, pp. 221–222), underlining the main claims and highlighting the evidence used to support those claims. You might also want to briefly summarize Lippi-Green's analysis of evidence as it relates to the claim and ask questions where you have them in the margins of the text.

Teaching Children How to Discriminate
What we learn from the Big Bad Wolf

Rosina Lippi-Green

All official institutions of language are repeating machines: school, sports, advertising, popular songs, news, all continually repeat the same structure, the same meaning, often the same words: the stereotype is a political fact, the major figure of ideology.

—Roland Barthes, *The Pleasure of the Text* (1975)

In 1933, while the US was in the depths of a severe depression, Walt Disney's animators created a short cartoon which would make an $88,000 profit in the first two years of its release (Grant 1993: 56). Perhaps this figure is not so surprising, given the statistics of the time: by 1930 there were some 20,000 motion-picture theaters in business, serving 90 million customers weekly (Emery and Emery 1992: 265). Thus the first filming of *Three Little Pigs*, a familiar story with a message of hard work in the face of adversity, was widely seen. The theme of good triumphing over evil was clearly a timely and popular one, and it is one that has not gone out of favor: this cartoon is still shown with regularity, in part or whole, on Disney's cable television channel.

One of the topics which is often discussed in relation to this particular Disney animated short is a scene included in the original release, in which the wolf—in yet another attempt to fool the pigs into opening the door to him—dresses as a Jewish peddler (Grant 1993, Kaufman 1988, Precker 1993b). He has a hook nose, wears sidelocks and a dark broad-rimmed hat similar to one worn by some Orthodox Jews, carries his wares before him, and contrives a Yiddish accent.[1] Kaufman recounts that it wasn't until the film's re-release in 1948, fourteen years later, that Disney reanimated the scene in which the Wolf appears as a Jew. This step was taken in response to communications from the Hays Office, which brought the issue of Jewish sensibilities to Disney's attention.[2] Grant reports that Disney later admitted that the original scene was in bad taste (1993: 54); nevertheless, only the offending visual representation was changed, and much later (at a date never specified clearly), "in case the Yiddish dialect of the original scene might itself be found offensive, the dialogue was changed as well. Now the Wolf spoke in a standard 'dumb' cartoon voice" (Kaufman 1988: 43–44). Even when the wolf no longer appeared Jewish, he spoke with a Yiddish accent, thus maintaining the underlying message based in anti-Semitism and fear of the other: a link between the evil intentions of the wolf and things Jewish. Grant also relates that the newer animation and dialogue still leaned on more general stereotypes and fears: "the disguised wolf no longer has Hebraic tones or mannerisms, instead saying: 'I'm the Fuller brushman. I workin' me way through college.' The syntax alone belies that statement" (1993: 54).

Sixty years later, a similar controversy would arise over the portrayal of characters in Disney's *Aladdin*, a movie set in a mythical Arabic kingdom. An offending line of dialogue in an opening song, "Where they cut off your ear if they don't like your face / It's barbaric, but hey, it's home," was partially changed in response to complaints from the American Arab Anti-Discrimination Committee (AAADC), but as the representative of the AAADC pointed out, the accents of the characters remained as originally filmed. The representative particularly objected to the fact that the good guys—Aladdin, Princess Jasmine and her father—talk like Americans, while all the other Arab characters have heavy accents. This pounds home the message that people with a foreign accent are bad.

(Precker 1993a)[3]

Is there truth to this supposition? What are children to take away from the Big Bad Wolf, and from brutal Arabian palace guards? Is it significant that they see bad guys who sound a certain way, look a certain way, and come from a certain part of town or of the world? Is this a part of how children learn to assign values on the basis of variation in language linked to race, ethnicity, and homeland? To make this point, it would first be necessary to demonstrate regular patterns which are available to children on a day-to-day basis, for as Silverstein (1992) asserts, "we are faced first-off with indexical facts, facts of observed/experienced social practices, the systematicity of which is our central problem: *are* they systematic? if so, *how*?" (322).

This chapter is about the sociolinguistic aspects of the systematic construction of dominance and subordinance in animated films aimed at children.

It is first observably true that somehow, children learn not only how to use variation in their own language, but also how to interpret social variation in the language of others. They do this with or without exposure to television and film, but in the current day, few children grow up without this exposure. The 1995 *World Almanac* reports that 98 percent of all US households, or some 94.2 million homes, have television sets; of these, 79 percent own video cassette recorders and 63 percent subscribe to basic cable. As seen in Figures 1 and 2, when children are not in front of the television set, they are avid consumers of the products of the movie industry; in 1992 over 15 million seats were occupied by children under the age of 2; those between 6 and 11 double this number.

For better or worse, the television and film industries have become a major avenue of contact to the world outside our homes and communities. For many, especially for children, it is the only view they have of people of other races or national origins.

In traditions passed down over hundreds of years from the stage and theater, film uses language variation and accent to draw character quickly, building on established preconceived notions associated with specific regional loyalties, ethnic, racial, or economic alliances. This shortcut to characterization means that certain traits need not be laboriously demonstrated by means of a character's actions and an examination of motive. It also means that these characterizations are culture- and period-bound; in this, films have much in common with fiction, and the representation of our cultures and our selves is equally worthy of study.

It must be noted at the outset that it is not my intention to condemn out of hand all use of abstraction in entertainment film, or even particularly in cartoons.

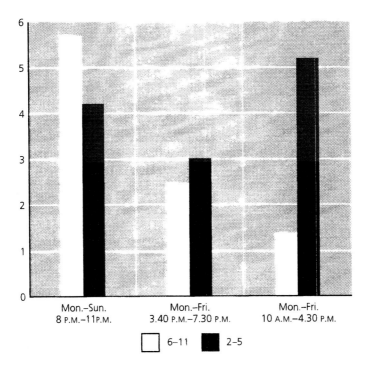

Figure 1 Average hours per week children watch television, by time period and two age groups
Source: 1995 *World Almanac and Book of Facts*

Some stereotyping may be inevitable. Whether or not all stereotyping has negative repercussions is a matter of interpretation; here I hope to show that while the practice is sometimes mild and no obvious or direct harm follows from it, there are always repercussions. For that reason alone, it would be good to be more generally aware of the way stereotypes function in film directed at children.

Talking the Talk

Any actor necessarily brings to a role his or her own native language. In many cases, the variety of English is irrelevant to the characterization and can be left alone. Often, however, the director or actor will target a particular social, regional, or foreign accent of English, perhaps because it is intrinsic to the role and cannot be sacrificed. US audiences may or may not suspend disbelief when Robin Hood speaks with a California accent, but it would be harder to cast someone with an upper-class British accent as any of the recent US presidents and not do serious harm to audience expectations and reception.

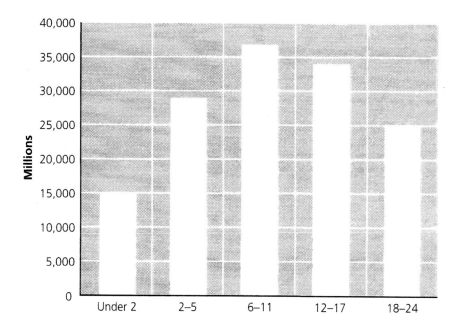

Figure 2   Movie theater attendance calculated for the year 1992, by age
Source: Mediamark Research 1993, vol. P13

In a similar way, non-native speakers of English who come to the US to make films necessarily bring their L2 accents to their work. This accent may restrict the roles they can play, or they may have roles written or rewritten to suit the immutable nature of their accents (Arnold Schwarzenegger, Gérard Depardieu, Sophia Loren, and Greta Garbo provide examples). Actors undergo accent training of various kinds in an attempt to teach them to imitate what they need for a particular role, although we have seen that even with expensive and careful tutoring not all actors are equally capable of this task, even in the limited way it is asked of them during filming.

What is particularly relevant and interesting in this context, however, is the way that actors *attempt* to manipulate language as a tool in the construction of character, whether or not they are successful. Educational programs for the training of actors for stage and screen often include classes on speech, dialogue, and the contrivance of accent. If it is possible to fool some of the people some of the time, it is still necessary to learn the skill behind this trick.

The materials used in these courses are interesting in and of themselves, because the approach often includes not just the mechanics and technicalities of one particular regional or foreign accent, but also issues of content and approach.

> Dialect actors must avoid going so far with certain speech traits that they end up creating ethnic or linguistic stereotypes . . . language or dialect background does not dictate character actions. Characters with accents must have the same range of choices available to them as characters whose speech is identical to yours.
>
> (Karshner and Stern 1990: Preface)

This is an enlightened and realistic position, certainly. Other materials prepared for actors are not always so even-handed, as seen in *Foreign Dialects: A manual for actors, directors and writers* (Herman and Herman 1943), a volume still in print:

> The Cockney Dialect: . . . The typical Cockney is often a brash little fellow. He is an inveterate heckler, and some of his favorite victims are the soap-box orators in Hyde Park. His speech is usually nasalized, possibly because of adenoid trouble which is quite prevalent in the British Isles. Often, his dialect is delivered in a whine . . . there is always a slovenliness to the pronunciation.
>
> (19)

> The Swedish Dialect: . . . the Swedes are usually more light-hearted than their Scandinavian cousins, more interested in the joys of living and eating. The Norwegians, on the other hand, are likely to be more solid and serious. The Swede likes conviviality, and the Norwegian solitary, lonely contemplation.
>
> (295)

> The Polish Dialect: . . . [Poles] are religious—especially the women—and devoutly Catholic. The Pole is industrious and will not shy from the hardest labor in the steel mills, foundries, and other heavy-duty jobs. He is a pleasure-loving person and it is this quality that leads him into the extremes of conviviality. He is not what may be called a thinking man . . . he is slow to thought, slow to speech, and slow to action.
>
> (351)

Sometimes, the contrivance of accent appears a logical and reasonable dramatic strategy. Often stories about people who come to the US from other countries lean hard on accent to establish the origin of the character (Al Pacino's Cuban-accented English in *Scarface;* Nick Nolte's Italian-accented English in *Lorenzo's Oil* or Marlon Brando's in *The Godfather;* the range of attempted Swedish accents in *I Remember Mama*). For films set in the southern US, actors are often coached long and hard on the acquisition of a second variety of US English (Vivien Leigh in *Gone with the Wind*); sometimes the attempt is not made at all (Clark Gable, Leslie Howard, and other men in the same movie).

Perhaps most interesting, a director often requires actors to use accents as a signal that the action and dialogue would not be taking place in English. Thus, in a Nazi concentration camp in *Schindler's List,* the commanding officer (Ralph Fiennes, who is British) speaks English with a contrived German accent to alert viewers to the fact that he would, in fact, be speaking German. There is a long list of filmed stories in which dialogue would not logically be taking place in English. Such films include *Schindler's List* (German and Polish, as well as other eastern European languages), *Papillon, Dangerous Liaisons, Impromptu,* and *Gigi* (French), *Diary of Anne Frank* (Dutch), *The Good Earth* (Chinese), *Fiddler on the Roof* (Yiddish, Russian), *All Quiet on the Western Front* (German, French), *Dr. Zhivago* and *Gorki Park* (Russian), *Kiss of the Spider Woman* (Spanish), *The Unbearable Lightness of Being* (Czech, French). Here accent becomes a signal of place and context rather than a means to quickly convey character. In such a case, it would make most logical sense to have *all* actors contrive the same French or Russian or Chinese accent.[4]

Rarely, however, is this policy consistent. In most movies, live action or animated, where accent is used as a cue to place, only some characters will speak with a contrived accent. Many possible reasons for this come to mind: Perhaps this is because not all actors are equally capable of targeting the required accent, or of temporarily disguising their own. Perhaps the director prefers no accents to partial or unbelievable ones. Or perhaps, in some cases, accent is used as a shortcut for those roles where stereotype serves as a shortcut to characterization. Actors contrive accents primarily as a characterization tool, although there is sometimes supplementary motivation in establishing the setting of the story. Below, I will consider exactly when certain accents are contrived, and perhaps more important, when mainstream US English (MUSE) is considered acceptable, or even necessary. To do this, we will consider one body of animated film in detail.

Animated Film

In animated film, even more so than is the case with live-action entertainment, language is used as a quick way to build character and reaffirm stereotype:

> precisely because of their assumed innocence and innocuousness, their inherent ability—even obligation—to defy all conventions of realistic representation, animated cartoons offer up a fascinating zone with which to examine how a dominant culture constructs its subordinates. As non-photographic application of photographic medium, they are freed from the basic cinematic expectation that they convey an "impression of reality." . . . The function and essence of cartoons is in fact the reverse: the impression of irreality, of intangible and imaginary worlds in chaotic, disruptive, subversive collision.
>
> (Burton 1992: 23–24)

There are patterns in the way we project pictures and images of ourselves and others which are available to anyone who watches and listens carefully. A study of accents in animated cartoons over time is likely to reveal the way linguistic stereotypes mirror the evolution of national fears: Japanese and German characters in cartoons during the Second World War (Popeye meets the "oh so solly" Japanese fleet), Russian spy characters in children's cartoons in the 1950s and 1960s (Natasha and Boris meet Rocky and Bullwinkle, or "beeeg trrrouble forrr moose and squirrrrrel"), Arabian characters in the era of hostilities with Iran and Iraq. In the following discussion of systematic patterns found in one specific set of children's animated film, the hypothesis is a simple one: animated films entertain, but they are also a way to teach children to associate specific characteristics and life styles with specific social groups, by means of language variation.[5] To test this hypothesis, 371 characters in all of the available Disney full-length animated films were analyzed.

Disney Feature Films

On the surface it is quite obvious that Disney films present young children with a range of social and linguistic stereotypes, from *Lady and the Tramp*'s cheerful, musical Italian chefs to *Treasure of the Lost Lamp*'s stingy, Scottish-accented McScrooge. In order to look more systematically at the way Disney films employ accent and dialect to draw character and stereotypes, it was necessary to analyze all released versions of full-length animated Disney films available.[6]

This body of animated films was chosen because the Disney Corporation is the largest producer of such films, and they are perhaps the most highly marketed and advertised of the field (Disney total advertising budget for 1992 was $524.6 million, some significant portion of which was spent directly on feature

Table 1   **The Disney films**

1938	*Snow White*	1963	*The Sword in the Stone*
1940	*Pinocchio*	1967	*The Jungle Book*
1941	*Dumbo*	1970	*The Aristocats*
1941	*The Reluctant Dragon*	1977	*The Rescuers*
1942	*Bambi*	1981	*The Fox and the Hound*
1950	*Cinderella*	1986	*The Great Mouse Detective*
1951	*Alice in Wonderland*	1989	*The Little Mermaid*
1952	*Robin Hood*	1990	*Treasure of the Lost Lamp*
1953	*Peter Pan*	1990	*The Rescuers Down Under*
1955	*Lady and the Tramp*	1991	*Beauty and the Beast*
1958	*Sleeping Beauty*	1992	*Aladdin*
1961	*101 Dalmatians*	1994	*The Lion King*

and animated films). Here I consider only full-length feature films (generally between one and a half to two hours in length) and specifically exclude short features, cartoons, and compilations of shorts grouped together for thematic reasons. Only fully animated films were included in the study, excluding those that combine live-action sequences with animation (*Song of the South, Three Caballeros*). Animated film created for an adult audience (the wartime film *Victory through Air Power* is one example) were also omitted. All characters with speaking roles of more than single-word utterances were included in the analysis.

A total of twenty-four films were viewed multiple times.[7] Each of the 371 characters was analyzed for a variety of language and characterization variables. The detailed linguistic description for each character consisted of a mix of phonetic transcription, quotes of typical syntactic structures, and marked lexical items. In cases where an actor is clearly contriving an accent, a decision was made as to what language variety was most likely intended to be portrayed. That is, a poorly imitated British (or other foreign) accent was still counted as such for the creators and (most) viewers. For example, in *Aladdin*, one of the minor characters, a thief, speaks primarily mainstream American, but also has some trilled *r*'s—definitely not a feature normally associated with American English. This character's accent was still classified as mainstream American, however, since only one atypical feature appeared in his phonology. Another character whose speech exhibits features from two or more dialects is Cogsworth, the butler/clock *in Beauty and the Beast*. He speaks with a contrived British accent in which some American features crop up unpredictably; thus, though it is not an accurate imitation of a middle- or upper-class British dialect, for the purposes of this study it must be classified as such.

After a brief consideration of the findings of the quantitative analysis more generally, I will concentrate on three aspects of language use in Disney films. These are the representation of African Americans; the way that certain groups are represented (particularly lovers and mothers); and finally, using French accents as a case study, the way that even positive stereotyping can be negative and limiting.

The whole mouse and nothing but the mouse

Of the 371 characters with speaking roles in the twenty-four movies examined, 259 or 69.8 percent are male. Female characters make up the other just over 30 percent. A look at the way female and male characters are deployed, overall, indicates that within the proportions established, they are equally distributed as major and minor characters. Female characters are almost never shown at work outside the home and family; where they do show up, they are mothers and

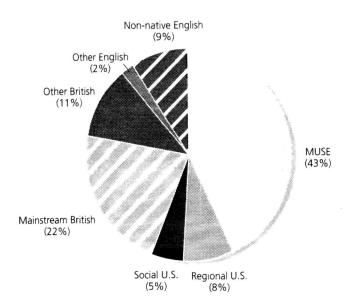

Figure 3   371 Disney animated characters by language variety used

princesses, devoted or (rarely) rebellious daughters. When they are at work female characters are waitresses, nurses, nannies, or housekeepers. Men, conversely, are doctors, waiters, advisors to kings, thieves, hunters, servants, detectives, and pilots.

It is certainly and demonstrably the case that the universe shown to young children in these films is one with a clear division between the sexes in terms of life style and life choices. Traditional views of the woman's role in the family are strongly underwritten, and in Disney films, whether they are filmed in 1938 or 1994, the female characters see, or come to accept, their first and most important role in life as that of wife and mother. What does an examination of language use have to add to this observation? What do characters, male and female, speak?

For the most part (43.1 percent) they speak a variety of US English which is not stigmatized in social or regional terms, what has been called MUSE throughout this study. Another 13.9 percent speak varieties of US English which are southern, or urban, or which are associated with particular racial, ethnic, or economic groups. Mainstream varieties of British English are spoken by 21.8 percent (Figure 3).

While 91 of the total 371 characters occur in roles where they would not logically be speaking English, there are only 34 characters who speak English with a foreign accent. The tendency to use foreign accents to convey the setting of the story is confirmed by these distributions; there are twice as many

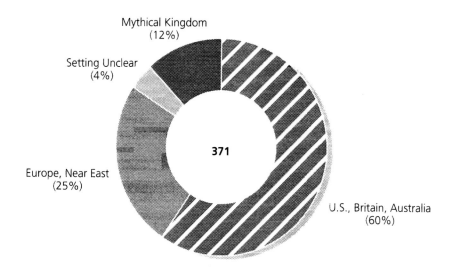

Mythical Kingdom
(12%)

Setting Unclear
(4%)

371

Europe, Near East
(25%)

U.S., Britain, Australia
(60%)

Figure 4   371 Disney animated characters by story setting (percentage figures rounded up)

characters with foreign-accented English in stories set in places like France and Italy.

The Lion King, set in Africa, is certainly a case of a story in which the logical language would not be English. This is acknowledged, indirectly, in the names of the characters, many of which are derived from Swahili. The good-natured but dumb warthog is called Pumbaa, or *simpleton;* Shenzi, the name of the leader of the hyena pack, means *uncouth.* However, the only character who actually uses traces of Swahili and a contrived Swahili accent is Rafiki (Swahili, *friend*), the wise and eccentric baboon who fulfills the role of spiritual guide.

Figure 3 indicates that some 90 percent of all the characters speak English natively, with an American or British English accent. However, Figure 4 makes it clear that 60 percent of all the characters appear in stories set in English-speaking countries; thus, a significant number of English-speaking characters appear in stories set abroad (sometimes these are "Americans abroad" as in Donald Duck in search of treasure; sometimes these are characters who are not logically English speaking, given their role and the story, as in all the characters in *Aladdin*). In Figure 5 three *language settings* are considered: stories set in English-speaking lands, those set in non-English-speaking countries, and finally, those set in mythical kingdoms where it would be difficult to make an argument for one language or another as primary (*The Little Mermaid,* for example, at times seems to be in a Mediterranean setting). Since a contrived foreign accent is often used to signal that the typical or logical language of the setting

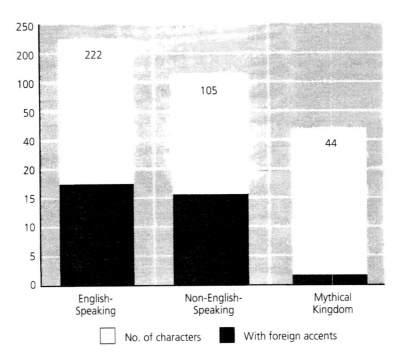

Figure 5   371 Disney animated characters by language spoken in the country in which the story is set, and the number of characters with foreign-accented English

would not be English, it is not surprising to see that the highest percentage of characters with foreign-accented English occurs in the second type of language setting. But it is also significant that even more characters with foreign accents appear in stories set in the US and England.

The breakdown of characters by their language variety becomes interesting when we examine that variety in relationship to the motivations and actions of the character's role. Disney films rely heavily on common themes of good and evil, and with very few exceptions they depend also on happy endings. Characters with unambiguously positive roles constitute 49.9 percent of the total; those who are clearly bad or even evil, only 19.4 percent. The remainder are divided between characters who change significantly in the course of the story (always from bad to good) and those characters whose roles are too small and fleeting for such a judgment to be made (86, or 23.2 percent of the total), as seen in Table 2.

Female characters are more likely to show positive motivations and actions (Figure 6). Unlike male characters who sometimes are bad and then become good, bad females show no character development.

Table 2   **371 Disney animated characters by major language group and evaluation of character's actions and motivations[8]**

	Positive	Negative	Mixed	Unclear	Total %
			Motivations		
US	122	33	11	42	208 56.1
British	53	28	11	37	129 34.8
Foreign	10	11	6	7	34 9.2
Total %	185 49.9	72 19.4	28 7.5	86 23.2	371 100.0

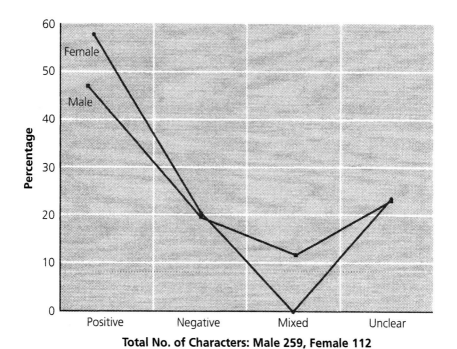

Total No. of Characters: Male 259, Female 112

Figure 6   371 Disney animated characters by gender and evaluation of actions and motivations

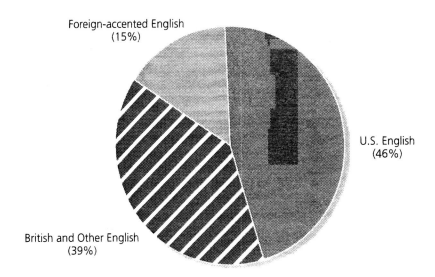

Figure 7   72 Disney animated characters with negative motivations and actions, by major language group

The pie chart in Figure 7 would first seem to indicate that there is no relationship between non-native English accents and the portrayal of good and evil. There are 72 characters who are truly bad, in major and minor roles. They include the poacher and would-be child-murderer Percival McLeach in *The Rescuers Down Under* with his contrived southwestern accent and idiom ("purty feather, boy!" "I whupped ya'll!" "Home, home on the range, where the critters 'r ta-id up in chains"), and the whip-and-cleaver wielding Stromboli of *Pinocchio*, with his threats of dismemberment, incredible rages, and florid, contrived Italian accent. Of these evil 72, however, a full 85 percent are native speakers of English; almost half are speakers of US English. Bad guys with foreign accents account for only 15 percent of the whole.

Taken in context, however, the issue is more complicated. In Figure 8, which compares positive, negative, and mixed motivations (the marginal characters have been removed for the sake of this discussion) by major language groups, it becomes clear that the overall representation of persons with foreign accents is far more negative than that of speakers of US or British English. About 20 percent of US English speakers are bad characters, while about 40 percent of non-native speakers of English are evil.

Additional interesting patterns come forward when we examine the representation of specific languages linked to national origin, race, or characterization.

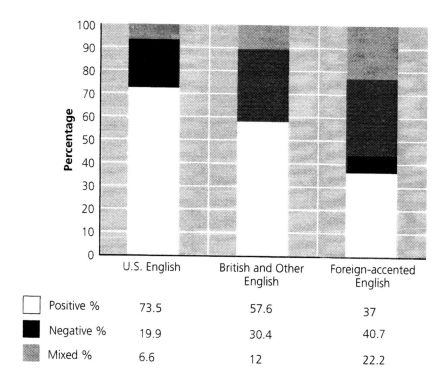

	Positive %	Negative %	Mixed %
U.S. English	73.5	19.9	6.6
British and Other English	57.6	30.4	12
Foreign-accented English	37	40.7	22.2

Figure 8   285 Disney animated characters of positive, negative, or mixed motivations and actions, by major language group

Beasts and beauties

With the 1967 release of *The Jungle Book,* the relationship between voice, language, and characterization entered a new realm in Disney film. This was the first feature in which actors were cast on the basis of voice recognition. Actors and musicians who had already established a personality and reputation with the movie-going public were drawn, quite literally, into the animation and storytelling process. This strategy was not greeted with enthusiasm by all film critics:

> Animating full-bodied, expressive characters is what men like Thomas, Kahl, Johnston and Lounsberry do best. Other artists provide a handsome backdrop and add dazzling animation effects. But breathing heart and soul into a film is not so easily accomplished. *The Jungle Book* lacked this quality, and substituted for it a gallery of characters whose strongest identity was with the stars who

provided their voices. The animators enjoyed working with people like George Sanders, Louis Prima, and Phil Harris, and incorporated elements of their personalities into the animated characters. Audiences naturally responded, so the animators felt justified in continuing this practice. "It is much simpler and more realistic than creating a character and then searching for the right voice," [producer] Reitherman contended.

(Maltin 1987: 74–75)

This additional complication to the use of accent and dialect in the building of character and stereotype is relevant to a discussion of the representation of African Americans by means of language in Disney films.

Especially in more recent years, Disney has engaged African American actors to provide the voices of major characters in their animated films. Sometimes these actors speak MUSE, as is the case with James Earl Jones speaking the role of the father in *The Lion King*. Sometimes they fluctuate between MUSE and AAVE, drawing on rhythmic and lexical items for dramatic and comic effect. This is the case with Whoopi Goldberg's performance as one of the evil hyenas, also in *The Lion King*. Sometimes these actors seem to be using their own variety of English with little embellishment, as was the case when Pearl Bailey spoke the part of Big Mama in *The Fox and the Hound*. Table 3 gives an overview of all the characters in these films who use, to a greater or lesser extent, AAVE. Additional AAVE-speaking characters seem to have flitted in and out of the abduction scene in *The Jungle Book;* however, they were not included in the analysis because the speaking roles were too small to be sure of the variety of English used. It needs to be stated quite clearly that this list does not represent the sum total of all African Americans who had speaking roles in the movies examined, but only those who chose or who were directed to use AAVE for a particular part.

While the 161 MUSE speakers appear in proportions of 43.1 percent humanoid, 54.4 percent animal and 2.5 percent inanimate creatures (such as the talking teapot in *Beauty and the Beast*), all AAVE-speaking characters appear in animal rather than humanoid form. Given the low overall number of AAVE speakers, however, it is hard to draw any inferences from that fact. The issue is further complicated in that every character with a southern accent appears in animal rather than humanoid form. Further examination of unambiguously positive and negative characters indicates that a full 43.4 percent of 90 characters in human form show negative actions and motivations while only 18.6 percent of the 156 animal characters are negative.

Perhaps more disturbing than the issue of human versus animal form is the way in the world which is cast so clearly for those African Americans who are speakers of AAVE. The stereotypes are intact: the male characters seem to be unemployed or show no purpose in life beyond the making of music and pleas-

Table 3 **Disney animated characters who use AAVE part or all of the time**

Name	Actor (where credits available)	Humanoid or animal	Film	Role evaluation	Typical language of setting
Dandy	Cliff Edwards	crow	Dumbo	Mixed	English
Fat	Jim Carmichael	crow		Mixed	English
Glasses	Hall Johnson Choir	crow		Mixed	English
Preacher		crow		Mixed	English
Straw Hat		crow		Mixed	English
King Louie	Louis Prima	primate	Jungle Book	Mixed	Hindi*
Big Mama	Pearl Bailey	owl	Fox and Hound	Positive	English
Scat	Scatman Crothers	cat	Aristocats	Mixed	French
Shenzi	Whoopi Goldberg	hyena	Lion King	Negative	Swahili*

*The category "typical language" is based on the country in which the story is set. Most of the movies are set in the US, thus the typical language is English. *The Jungle Book* is set in India, and *The Lion King* in Africa. The typical languages of these stories could be any one of many native languages spoken in those places; I have chosen one of the many possible languages in such cases.

ing themselves, and this is as true for the crows in *Dumbo* as it is for the orangutan King Louie and his crew of primate subjects in *The Jungle Book*. Much has been made of King Louie and his manipulation of the only human being in this story; singing in the scat-style made popular by African American musicians, he convinces his audience that he has one goal in life, and that is to be the one thing he is not: a human being, a man. African American males who are not linguistically assimilated to the sociolinguistic norms of a middle and colorless United States are allowed very few possibilities in life, but they are allowed to want those things they don't have and can't be.

The two female characters are also controversial, but for very different reasons. Pearl Bailey's Big Mama must be seen as a stereotype of the loving, nurturing mammy, but one with a mind of her own. Whoopi Goldberg, who voices the part of one of the hyenas in *The Lion King*, slips in and out of AAVE for comic and dramatic effect. It must be noted that she is the only African American actor to do so in this film, a film which included—for Disney—an unusually high number of African Americans. We never hear AAVE from James Earl Jones as the King. None of the characters, whether they speak MUSE or AAVE, show any clear connection to things African, with the exception of the wise baboon, Rafiki, who occupies a special but peripheral role in the film's story.

In general, children who have little or no contact with African Americans are exposed to a fragmented and distorted view of what it means to be black, based on characterizations which rest primarily on negative stereotype linked directly to language difference.

Lovers and mothers

Romance is a major plot device in many of Disney's animated films. Of the twenty-four stories examined here, thirteen depend in part or whole on the development of a relationship between a male and a female character which has not to do with friendship, but with love and mate selection. Those characters who are young and in potential search of a mate or love interest provide some of the most interesting material in these films overall. There has been much commentary in the popular press on the physical portrayal of young men and women in extreme and unrealistic terms, for both sexes. Doe-eyed heroines with tiny waists and heroes with bulging necks and overly muscular thighs have been roundly criticized, with little effect. There is little or no discussion of the *language* spoken by lovers, however.[9]

In spite of the setting of the story or the individual's ethnicity, lovers speak mainstream varieties of US or British English (Table 4), with some interesting

Table 4   **Lovers and potential lovers in Disney animated films**

Language variety	Film	Male	Female
Mainstream US	*Beauty and the Beast*	Gaston	(no mate)
		The Beast	Belle
	Rescuers	Bernard	—
	Rescuers Down Under	Bernard	—
	Cinderella	Prince Charming	Cinderella
	Sleeping Beauty	Prince Philip	Aurora
	Little Mermaid	Prince Erik	Ariel
	Snow White	Prince	Snow White
	Lion King	Simba	Nala
	Lady and the Tramp	—	Lady
Socially marked US	*Lady and the Tramp*	Jock	—
	Aristocats	O'Malley	—
Non-US English	*Robin Hood*	Robin Hood	Maid Marion
	Rescuers Down Under	Jake	(no mate)
	101 Dalmatians	Pongo	Perdita
		Roger Radcliff	Anita Radcliff
Foreign-accented English	*Rescuers*	—	Miss Bianca
	Rescuers Down Under	—	Miss Bianca
	Aristocats	—	Duchess

exceptions. Of the male characters in Table 4, only two can be said to be logically and certainly speakers of US English: Bernard, who appears twice (*The Rescuers* and *The Rescuers Down Under*), and Jock (*Lady and the Tramp*). All the other characters would be speakers of British or Australian English, or of languages other than English. The languages of the four princes (from *Cindrella, Snow White, Sleeping Beauty,* and *The Little Mermaid*) are debatable: the Disney version never specifies where these magical kingdoms are located (whether in the country of the story's origin or elsewhere).

Two of the male romantic leads speak socially marked varieties of US English: in *The Aristocats,* O'Malley (voiced by Phil Harris, a popular entertainer and singer of his day and cast on the power of voice recognition) does nothing to change or disguise his own English, which is rich in those characteristics which are often thought of as "working class" (simplified consonant clusters, double-negative constructions, and other stigmatized phonological and grammatical features). This is also the case with Jock from *Lady and the Tramp*. Both of these characters are prototypical rough lovers, men with an edge who need the care and attention of good women to settle them, and both are rewarded with such mates—females who speak non-stigmatized varieties—because they prove themselves worthy. There are no male romantic leads with foreign accents.

There is even less variation among the female romantic leads. There are no rough, working-class equivalents of O'Malley and Jock. In fact, of the seven females who speak MUSE, only one is an unambiguous case of a character who would logically speak US English: Lady of *Lady and the Tramp*. The use of a typical or logical language for the part and background of the character is clearly less important in this case than a consistent portrayal of an ideal lover and potential mate which stresses the lack of "otherness."

However, there are two female characters (one of whom occurs in two movies, *The Rescuers* and *The Rescuers Down Under*) with foreign accents, but they are both voiced by the same woman, Eva Gabor. The Gabor sisters were widely known and recognized in US culture in the 1950s and 1960s for their glamor and demanding behavior in many highly publicized affairs with rich men. They were recognizable on the basis of their Hungarian accents, and they brought with them a set of associations about sexually aware and available females that resulted in typecasting. The roles that Eva Gabor voiced for Disney were thus of elegant, demanding, and desirable females, and could be seen not so much as characters with foreign accents as one of the Gabor sisters in full costume. Perhaps Disney's hope that the public would associate the character on the screen with the public image of the actress voicing the part overrode more logical considerations. It was noted by at least one critic, however, that it made little sense to have the character of *The Aristocats'* Duchess, a pure-bred Persian cat living in France, speaking with a Hungarian accent.

Table 5   **The language of mothers and fathers in Disney animated films**

Language	Mothers	Fathers
MUSE	15	8
Socially marked US	0	0
Regionally marked US	0	1
Mainstream British	2	8
Socially or regionally marked British or other English	2	4
Foreign-accented English	1	1

To be truly sexually attractive and available in a Disney film, a character must not only look the idealized part, but he or she must also sound white and middle-class American or British.

In a similar way, mothers and fathers are most likely to have mainstream accents of US or British English, again with some interesting exceptions. As seen in Table 5, only two of these characters speak English with a foreign accent, although what would follow logically from the story setting is that eleven of these mothers and fathers would not be native speakers of English. Another thirteen characters appear in stories where the logical language might or might not be English. This applies particularly to the retelling of fairy tales in magical kingdoms (*Cinderella, Sleeping Beauty, The Little Mermaid*).[10] The two foreign accents which are evident are Gepetto's (contrived) Italian-accented English in *Pinocchio,* and once again Eva Gabor as the glamorous Duchess in *The Aristocats.* The only US-English-speaking father character with an accent which might be stigmatized is Gramps of *The Rescuers,* who is part of a larger group of stereotypical southerners with contrived accents.

Eva Gabor's voicing of the Duchess is the only instance in any of the movies where a mother takes on a romantic lead. Otherwise, in Disney movies parenthood and romance do not intersect. However, there are a great number of single-parent families overall. Of the twenty mothers, nine are widows or become widows in the course of the story, or have no husband in evidence; five are step- or substitute mothers and are unmarried; and in two cases the question of paternity is never raised, perhaps because it could not be answered in a way Disney considered suitable for children's entertainment. This is the case in *The Aristocats,* but more particularly in *The Lion King,* where Mufasa is the undisputed dominant male of his pride, and would thereby have fathered both Simba and Nala, who grow into adulthood and become mates. The fathers, in a similar way, are often widowers or simply without wives: this is the case for eleven of the twenty-two.

There are few married couples with major roles in any film. Mr. and Mrs. Darling make only small appearances in *Peter Pan,* which is also the case for the mother and father in *Lady and the Tramp* and for Colonel Hardy and his wife Winifred in *The Jungle Book.*

Perhaps most interesting is the fact that mothers who speak non-US varieties of English have a little more latitude in social and regional variation in their language. This may be because the non-mainstream varieties of British English are not poorly thought of by US English speakers, who do not distinguish, for the most part, between stigmatized varieties of British English (Geordie, Midlands, Cockney, etc.) and those with more social currency.

Lovers in Disney films marry, and sometimes at a very tender age. But young or middle-aged married couples with growing families are seldom if ever seen. And while young lovers are presented in idealized form both physically and linguistically, in later life stages these same kinds of characters are not quite so narrowly drawn. The picture of motherhood portrayed in these animated films excludes careers and work outside family and home, and clings very closely to language varieties associated with middle-class norms and values. When seen at all, mothers are presented without a hint of ethnicity, regional affiliation, color, or economics. Fathers, often comic or droll characters, have in their language (as in work, preoccupations and interests) a wider set of choices available to them.

Francophilia Limited

It is not hard to elicit stereotypes of the French, because this is not a national origin group which is seen in negative terms. Because there are good—or neutral—things to say, it is perhaps easier to say them:

> despite, or possibly because of, their civilized natures, the French people retain a childish eagerness for fun and frivolity as well as for knowledge. There is an impishness about many of them which is captivating. They are curious, like most children, and this curiosity leads them into experimenting with such things as piquant sauces for food . . . it can be said of the French . . . that when they are good, they are very, very good—but when they are bad, they are—Apaches.
>
> (Herman and Herman 1943: 143)

Aside from the clearly racist final comment which has to do not with the French, but with a Native American tribe, this view of the nation is not overtly negative. It is condescending, certainly, and narrow, but it does not call France a nation of idiots or a kingdom of evil (as the Herman and Herman volume does not hesitate to do in other cases).

There are two films which are set directly in France: *The Aristocats* and *Beauty and the Beast,* with a total of thirty-eight characters appearing in both stories. There is a wide range of characterizations, excessively evil and good,

Table 6   **Characters with French-accented English in Disney animated films**

Setting	Character	Role	Film
France	Lumiere	maitre d', steward	*Beauty and the Beast*
	Stove	chef	
	Cherie	chambermaid	
	Unnamed	milkman	*Aristocats*
	Unnamed	chef	
Elsewhere	Louis	chef	*Little Mermaid*
	Unnamed	waiter	*Rescuers*

moody, generous, silly, drunken. Male characters include lawyers, aristocrats, barkeepers, vagabonds, inventors, booksellers, hunters, and servants. *Beauty and the Beast* takes place in an active, busy rural village; *The Aristocats* primarily in Paris. There are children and old people, lovers and villains. Of all these thirty-eight very diverse characters, all of whom would logically be speaking French, there are a total of five who indicate this by contriving a French-accented English. In other films, two additional characters appear with French accents, as seen in Table 6.

Of these seven characters, one is female (Cherie, a feather duster), and her primary purpose seems to be as a romantic foil for the character Lumiere; her only line, having been pursued behind the draperies by him, is "Oh no! I've been burnt by you before!" There are other beautiful and charming women and girls in *Beauty and the Beast,* but none of them are coquettish, and none of them have French accents. The subtle but unmistakable message is quite a simple one: there may logically be thirty-eight characters before us who are French, but the truly French, the prototypical French, are those persons associated with food preparation or presentation, or those with a special talent for lighthearted sexual bantering. If a personality is established at all, there are two basic personality types available to them: irascible (the chef in *The Little Mermaid,* and his counterpart in *The Aristocats*); and the sensual rascal.

Is this a terrible picture to give children? After all, there are no truly "French"—linguistically, culturally, truly French—characters who are criminal, who threaten children, who are lazy or conniving. But there are also no French who are surgeons, rock singers, who teach school or drive a cab, or who are elderly. Rich people and aristocrats, in France or elsewhere, speak with British accents no matter what their logical language. The domain of life experience for things French is as narrow, if not as overtly negative, as that for AAVE speakers.

The cultural stereotypes for specific national origin groups are perpetuated in a systematic way in these stories created for, and viewed primarily by, children.

Summary

Close examination of the distributions indicates that these animated films provide material which links language varieties associated with specific national origins, ethnicities, and races with social norms and characteristics in non-factual and sometimes overtly discriminatory ways. Characters with strongly positive actions and motivations are overwhelmingly speakers of socially mainstream varieties of English. Conversely, characters with strongly negative actions and motivations often speak varieties of English linked to specific geographical regions and marginalized social groups. Perhaps even more importantly, those characters who have the widest variety of life choices and possibilities available to them are male, and they are speakers of MUSE or a non-stigmatized variety of British English. These characters may be heroes or villains, human or animal, attractive or unattractive. For females, on the other hand, and for those who mark their alliance to other cultures and places in terms of language, the world is demonstrably a smaller place. The more "negatives" a character has to deal with (gender, color, stigmatized language, less favorable national origin) the smaller the world. Even when stereotyping is not overtly negative, it is confining and misleading.

That's Entertainment

Disney films are not the only way in which we perpetuate stereotypes on the basis of language. The manipulation of language variety and accent to draw character is an old tool, but it is seldom a completely benign one. Stereotyping is prevalent in television programming and movies: situation comedies (*Beverley Hillbillies, I Love Lucy, Sanford and Son, All in the Family, Molly Goldberg, American Girl, Ma and Pa Kettle, Green Acres, Andy Griffith*) in particular provide numerous examples, which need to be examined more closely.

Language and accent as symbols of greater social conflict are also found in serious dramatic efforts, on television and film. The 1993 film *Falling Down* provides a disturbing example. In that film, a middle-class worker portrayed as beleaguered by inner-city life loses his temper with an irascible convenience-store clerk; the episode begins when the protagonist asks the price of an item. The following is from the script:

> *The proprietor, a middle-aged ASIAN, reads a Korean newspaper . . . the Asian has a heavy accent . . .*
>
> ASIAN: eighdy fie sen.
> D-FENS: What?
> ASIAN: eighdy fie sen.

D-FENS: I can't understand you . . . I'm not paying eighty-five cents for a stinking soda. I'll give you a quarter. You give me seventy "fie" cents back for the phone . . . What is a fie? There's a "V" in the word. Fie-vuh. Don't they have "v's" in China?

ASIAN: Not Chinese, I am Korean.

D-FENS: Whatever. What differences does that make? You come over here and take my money and you don't even have the grace to learn to speak my language . . .

(Smith 1992: 7–8)

Here, accent becomes a very convenient and fast way to draw on a whole series of very emotional social issues, and all of them in a spirit of conflict, from immigration and the rights and responsibilities thereof, to greater issues of dominance and subservience, race and economics. The scene is very believable; many have had or observed such exchanges. The protagonist, clearly a man on the edge of socially acceptable behavior, is also portrayed as someone pushed to that edge by the pressures of inner-city life. He is overtly cruel and condescending and racist; but, somehow, he is also seen as not completely wrong.

In this film, a foreign accent becomes the signal of what has gone wrong with us as a nation, and his dismay and his anger, while excessive, are cast as understandable. From Charlie Chan to this owner of a corner store, our understanding of Asians—all Asians—has been reduced to a series of simple images. They are inscrutable, hard-working, ambitious, intelligent but unintelligible people, and they make us uncomfortable.

Even films which are made specifically for the purpose of illuminating and exploring racial and other kinds of social injustice are not free of the very subtle effects of standard language ideology. A close examination of Spielberg's *Schindler's List* (1993) shows a great deal of consistency in the use of accent: "The accents of individuals reflect their position in World War II Poland. That is, German characters are given—by and large—German accents, and Jewish characters generally possess Yiddish accents" (Goldstein 1995: 1). Even here, however, the suppression of variation for some characters has been noted, this time falling along lines not of color or religion, but of gender. In an initial exploration, Goldstein found that the more sexually available and attractive a female character was, the less distinctive her accent.

Following this pattern, the German women who were wives and mistresses—and therefore the most sexually available women in the movie—did not have strong German accents [while] the older and less attractive Jewish women had heavier and thicker Yiddish accents . . . linguistic accent seems to be part of what is deemed attractive about [some] women.

(1995: 6)

These patterns held true for males as well: conservative Jews had stronger Yiddish accents; the worst of the prison guards, brutish Nazis, had the heaviest German accents (ibid.). It seems that even the highest standards in film making cannot be free of the social construction of language. And perhaps there is nothing that can or should be done about this process in its subtlest form. It is, after all, part of the social behavior which is of interest to art as the representation of the human condition.

What children learn from the entertainment industry is to be comfortable with *same* and to be wary about *other,* and that language is a prime and ready diagnostic for this division between what is approachable and what is best left alone. For adults, those childhood lessons are reviewed daily.

Notes

1. "Ethnic stereotypes were, of course, not uncommon in films of the early Thirties, and were usually essayed in a free-wheeling spirit of fun, with no malice intended. By the time the film was reissued in 1948 . . . social attitudes had changed considerably" (1988: 43). Kaufman's construction of the original caricature (Jews as wily and untrustworthy business people) as harmless is one which it is hard to take on good faith, given the general climate of anti-Semitism prevalent in Europe and the US in the 1930s.
2. In 1930, the Motion Picture Producers and Distributors of America (MPPDA) created a self-regulatory code of ethics. The office charged with this duty was put under the direction of Will H. Hays, and went into effect on July 1, 1934. The Hays Office outlined general standards of good taste and specifically forbade certain elements in film. The code specified that "no picture shall be produced which will lower the standards of those who see it. Hence the sympathy of the audience should never be thrown to the side of crime, wrong-doing, evil or sin." The specific regulations included "Revenge in modern times shall not be justified"; "Methods of crime shall not be explicitly presented"; "The sanctity of the institution of marriage and the home shall be upheld"; "Miscegenation (interracial sexual relationships) is forbidden." The Code specifically addressed the inadvisability of caricaturing national-origin groups or portraying them in offensive ways.

    In 1968 a rating system was put into effect, and the Code was no longer used.
3. Other interviews with AAADC representatives were further reported in the same paper·

    > Although they are Arabs, Aladdin and Princess Jasmine, the heroes, talk like Americans. Merchants, soldiers and other ordinary Arabs have thick foreign accents. "This teaches a horrible lesson," says [the representative]. "Maybe they can't redub it now, but we asked them to please be sure there is no accent discrimination in the foreign-language versions."
    >
    > (Precker 1993b)

4. Sometimes a cast is a combination of those who must contrive the accent and those who are native speakers of the language in question, and bring that L2 accent to their performance, as was the case with *Gigi.*
5. It might be argued that many aspects of animated films are actually aimed at the adults who watch films with children, and that the children themselves are less likely to comprehend the stereotypes. The small body of studies in this area indicates that while children's attitudes toward particular language varieties are not fully developed until adolescence, they do begin forming as early as age 5 (Rosenthal 1974, Day 1980). Giles *et al.* (1983) found that significant changes occurred between the ages of 7 and 10 in children's attitudes toward different language varieties.
6. The first round of analysis was conducted as a graduate-level seminar project in social dialectology. The students who contributed to the analysis at that stage were Carlson Arnett, Jennifer Dailey-O'Cain, Rita Simpson, and Matthew Varley. The results of that project were presented as a poster at the 1994 "New Ways of Analyzing Variation" conference at Stanford University. The data presented here represents a second viewing of all films originally studied as well as the addition of three films not included in the original study: *The Lion King, The Aristocats,* and *Snow White.*
7. In the pilot study, each participant watched at least four films, although most had seen more than these initial four. To aid in the consistency of language characterization as well as coding for other

variables, three films were viewed and coded as a group. Subsequently, I reviewed all films and checked the original coding.

8. Standard tests of correlation of the relationship of a character's nationality to his or her motivation (positive, negative, mixed) were shown to be highly significant at levels better than .001.

9. Characters of an age to pursue a partner who do *not* do so in the story line are usually portrayed as awkward, fat, or ugly (examples include the stepsisters in *Cinderella*, the witch-like Cruella de Ville in *101 Dalmatians*, LaFou in *Beauty and the Beast*).

10. Other cases were also ambiguous. Whether Colonel Hardy and his wife Winifred, the military elephants in *The Jungle Book*, are logically speakers of an Indian language or of English could be debated. The same problem applies to this determination for the Indian Chief in *Peter Pan*.

Works Consulted

Burton, J. (1992) "Don (Juanito) duck and the imperial-patriarchal unconscious: Disney studios, the good neighbor policy, and the packaging of Latin America." *Nationalisms and Sexualities*. A. Parker, M. Russo, D. Sommer, *et al.*, eds. New York: Routledge: 21–41

Day, R. (1980) "The development of linguistic attitudes and preferences." *TESOL Quarterly* 14: 27–37.

Emery, M. and E. Emery (1992) *The Press and America: An interpretive history of the mass media*. Englewood Cliffs, NJ: Prentice-Hall.

Fairclough, N., C. Harrison, C. Creber, *et al.* (1983) "Developmental and contextual aspects of children's language attitudes." *Language and Communication* 3(2): 141–146.

Goldstein, E. (1995) "Analysis: accent in Spielberg's *Schindler's List*." Unpublished ms.

Grant, J. (1993) *Encyclopedia of Walt Disney's Animated Characters*. New York: Hyperion.

Herman, L. and M. S. Herman (1943) *Foreign Dialects: A manual for actors, directors and writers*. New York: Theatre Arts Books.

Karshner, R. and D. A. Stern (1990) *Dialect Monologues*. Toluca Lake, CA: Dramaline Publications.

Kaufman, J. B. (1988). "Three little pigs—big little picture." *American Cinematographer* (November): 38–44.

Maltin, L. (1973) *The Disney Films*. New York: Crown.

—— (1987) *Of Mice and Magic: A history of American animated cartoons*. 2nd revised edition. New York: Plume Books.

Precker, M. (1993a) "This Aladdin is rated PC." *Dallas Morning News*. October 2. Dallas: 5c.

—— (1993b) "Animated debate." *Dallas Morning News*. July 12. Dallas: 1c.

Rosenthal, A (1974) "The magic boxes: preschool children's attitudes toward Black and Standard English." *Florida Foreign Language Reporter* 12: 55–62, 92–93.

Silverstein, M. (1992) "The uses and utility of ideology: some reflections." *Pragmatics* 2(3): 311–324.

Smith, E. R. (1992) *Falling Down*. Script revision dated March 17, 1992. Film (1993) directed by J. Schumacher. Arnold Kopelson Productions in association with Warner Bros. Inc.

Collaborative Activity 6.1

Working with your group, identify three claims that Lippi-Green makes and some of the evidence she uses to support each claim. Then locate passages in the text where she offers analysis, showing the assumptions behind her linking of the evidence to the claim. Be sure to keep your notes, since you may return to this chapter for a later writing assignment.

Writing Activity 6.5

Lippi-Green's analysis relies heavily on visual rhetoric or the visual presentation of ideas (see Chapter 3 for further discussion of visual presentation). Notice how she includes charts, graphs, and tables to illustrate and extend her points. Notice, too, how those visual elements are integrated into the text. Does she refer to them in the body of her chapter? Does she give them captions or labels? Discuss how those visual elements help Lippi-Green support her claims and help her readers understand her analysis. What are the effects of using graphic illustrations and visuals to present evidence? What claims do they reinforce? What concepts or relationships do they clarify? How do they build credibility or ethos?

Generic Features of the Analysis Paper

With some understanding of the scene and situation of the analysis paper, including its defining purpose of teaching and practicing analysis, we now turn to *describing* the patterns in the generic features of analysis papers. As you may have had a chance to discover for yourself in doing your own genre analysis in Chapter 2, performing such an analysis of the analysis paper can help us understand not just what the expected features are but why they are what they are—how the features of the genre function in and what they can tell us about the scene of the writing course. Such a critical knowledge of conventions and their underlying assumptions will enable you to write analysis papers more effectively and confidently because you will be more informed about the choices you can make.

Compared to genres such as the resumé, the brochure, the lab report, the complaint letter, and the obituary, the analysis paper is a more flexible genre. Although certain assumptions and expectations exist, writers have more room to maneuver within them. This flexibility is why we ask you to remember that the rhetorical patterns and strategies we are about to describe are not meant to *prescribe* how you should write an analysis paper. We will in turn consider

- Content
- Rhetorical Appeals
- Structure
- Format
- Sentences
- Words

CONTENT

Whatever the writing assignment—to uncover the assumptions of a text, or to take an idea and use it to explore another concept, or to explain what a text, activity, or event means and how it works—writers of analysis papers will typically establish a claim that is central to the paper and develop it with evidence and analysis which explains how the evidence relates to the claim. Indeed, what can be called the "content" of the analysis paper *is* its analysis of the subject. More specifically, the content consists of the idea that the writer has formulated about his or her given subject, an idea that he or she has developed into an issue or problem that can be addressed and supported. As such, the most typical and significant move writers of analysis papers make is to turn the results of their observations and analysis into an issue/problem that becomes the paper's claim. That is, *they turn their study of a subject into an interpretation of the subject.* The introductory section of analysis papers, usually one or two paragraphs, tends to be devoted to making this move toward the claim.

Because they know that they will eventually have to construct a claim based on that subject—one that uncovers some of its assumptions, explains its meaning, and/or examines how it works—writers select subjects that lend themselves to analysis. For example, consider a claim such as "The HBO series *The Sopranos* has attracted a great deal of criticism from some Italian-American groups recently because of its negative stereotypes." While interesting, this claim is ultimately not analyzable. It just states a fact that does not require analysis to examine its meaning. A more appropriate claim would present an idea about *The Sopranos* that requires evidence and analysis to support it:

The Sopranos exploits negative stereotypes of Italian Americans as gangsters.

While this claim is more analyzable, requiring the writer to examine how *The Sopranos* exploits stereotypes, it still needs to stand up to the "So what?" question writers are expected to ask themselves in analysis papers. So what that *The Sopranos* does this? Why is the writer making this claim? A more effective claim, based on the "So what?" question, might be the following:

Claim: By exploiting negative stereotypes of Italian Americans as gangsters, the highly acclaimed HBO series *The Sopranos* contributes to the perpetuation of this stereotype.

With this claim, the writer not only has something to analyze (to uncover how the show exploits stereotypes), but also has a reason for performing the analysis (to show how such stereotyping leads to further stereotyping). The content of an analysis paper, then, concentrates on a subject that lends itself to analysis, develops a controlling idea that makes a central claim about that subject, and uses analysis to support that claim with evidence.

Collaborative Activity 6.2

After reading the sample analysis papers, on pages 302 to 319, decide with your group what the controlling idea (central claim) of each paper is. Then assess how effective that claim is for an analysis paper. What makes the subject analyzable? How well does the claim lead to analysis of the supporting evidence? How well does it pass the "So what?" test?

RHETORICAL APPEALS

Nor surprisingly, since they are grounded in the logical process of analysis, analysis papers rely heavily on *logos* (the appeal to logic and reasoning) over *pathos* (the appeal to emotion) and *ethos* (the appeal to the writer's credibility). By presenting evidence and making logical points, analysis papers appeal to the readers' reasoning rather than to their emotions or the writer's character. To reinforce this emphasis on the subject, on the logic and the evidence, *writers of analysis papers work toward projecting an image of themselves, an ethos, of a rational person who is examining the evidence objectively.* They take an observational, distant stance in relation to the evidence. They tend to stand back and engage it objectively. Although personal testimony can be used as evidence in some cases, generally writers of analysis papers rely on a critical examination of observed facts such as, for example, what politicians actually say, what advertisements actually contain, and how a certain event coincided with another. There is little room in the body of analysis papers, therefore, for writers to engage in making value judgments or recommendations. Writers withhold such evaluations in order to examine how something works, what it means, and why.

Withholding evaluation does not mean, however, that writers of analysis papers do not have a stake in the analysis. In fact, the writer's presence is most evident in analysis papers when he or she tries to make use of the evidence, examine its meaning, and comment on its relevance. In this way, the writer takes an *active* position, directing the readers' attention to aspects of the evidence that he or she wants them to notice. In some cases, writers will simply write: "Notice how this ad uses the color red to create an atmosphere of seduction." Writers will also guide readers to their point of view in less direct ways:

1. Announcing what the evidence means ("This quote is an excerpt from a letter written in response to a debate over illegal immigration, and exemplifies the Democrats' use of discourse to gain sympathy toward illegal immigration.")

2. Breaking the evidence down into parts that reflect the writer's claim ("The next aspect is that of the woman's posture.")

3. Explaining the meaning of the evidence ("So, in this advertisement Skyy Vodka has used the desire for sex and high status to make their product seem like it will improve people's lives." and "Hence, the sentence assumes more than one meaning. Literally, it instructs the student to avoid interfering with the work of others in the class. The syntax of the sentence also suggests . . . .")

Personal opinion and judgment can also be inferred indirectly from the writer's word choice. Phrases such as "the child's authority is sacrificed" and "the daunting presence of the principal" carry the force of the writer's opinion and appeal subtly to the reader's emotions. So while logos appears to dominate the analysis paper, subtle appeals to emotion and a credible ethos that treats judgments as facts contribute to the effectiveness of the paper.

Collaborative Activity 6.3

In small groups, examine the sample analysis papers on pages 302–319, and assess how each balances logos, pathos, and ethos. In addition to seeing the emphasis on logos, find places where the writers appeal to readers' emotions, where they reveal their judgments, and where they establish their credibility. How well does each writer use the three appeals, given the expectations for analysis papers? Critique the emphasis on logos in these papers. Would any of them be improved by greater use of emotional appeals or by the personal experience of the writers? If so, how?

STRUCTURE

In keeping with this logical emphasis, analysis papers are structured around a controlling idea that is a central claim and use an introduction-body-conclusion general structure. In general, analysis papers use

1. Introductions to assert their claims

2. Body paragraphs to develop and support those claims with evidence

3. Conclusions to reassert their claims and open out to new implications or extensions of the controlling idea

In terms of structure, then, the analysis paper appears to be organized by sections rather than paragraphs. Unlike the five-paragraph essay, which is paragraph driven, with each paragraph made up of its own self-contained subclaim and support, *the analysis paper is organized by sections, each of which may contain more than one paragraph that works toward developing the central claim.* The introductory and concluding sections may contain more than one paragraph that accomplishes their goals, and the body of the paper is divided into multiple sections (each consisting of one or more paragraphs), with each section trying to accomplish its own goal within the larger structure of the paper.

This typical structure for academic papers suits its academic scene, of course, while still allowing flexibility to suit the wide range of subjects that analysis papers may treat. More specific organizational patterns vary from one paper to the next, as the central claim shifts. Yet the organization of an effective analysis paper will always reflect not some predetermined order (like five paragraphs, or compare ABABAB) but rather an order that makes sense for the logic of the analysis. The unique organization comes from *the unique logic of the central claim.*

The Introduction

Introductions of analysis papers move from the subject being studied to the claim being asserted. They set up the central claim that will constitute the controlling idea. Writers use different strategies to make this move in their introductions. Very often, they will begin with an opening sentence that makes a general observation about the subject, something such as: "Psychology is defined as the study of the mind"; "People's prejudices are often used to sell products, and many times these prejudices involve women"; and "Throughout the history of the United States, immigration has played a major role in the country's population growth." These opening sentences serve to transport the reader into the "world" of the paper and its subject of study. They also help set up the background that often follows, which adds more information about the observations. For example, the observation regarding prejudice is followed by more specific examples of how advertisers use prejudice to sell products; in addition, the observation regarding immigration in the United States is followed by a brief discussion of what immigration is and how Democrats and Republicans treat it. By helping to frame each paper, these introductory backgrounds not only set up the claim that follows, but they also give readers the impression that they are walking into the context of the claim, almost as if they are discovering the claim for themselves.

Typically, the next move that writers make in the introductory section involves establishing and defining some kind of issue or problem that their claim will address and develop. In analysis papers, the background information not only creates a context for the analysis but also sanctions it. That is, writers frequently use the background information to justify the analysis they are about to perform. For example, in the sample analysis paper about women in advertising, pp. 302–307, the writer uses the background information (which describes how advertisers use gender prejudices to sell products) to justify and make possible the analysis of various advertisements. The resulting claim is:

Claim: This combination of status and sex can be powerful, and companies know how to use these ideas to their full advantage to sell their product.

The rest of the paper explains how. In this example, the writer uses the introduction to create a context that establishes the authority and the opportunity for her analysis. That analysis becomes the claim that her paper will develop and support.

The rhetorical pattern of introductions thus typically looks something like this:

1. Provide background on the subject

2. Use that background to justify/authorize the analysis

3. Establish a claim based on that analysis

This pattern shows how writers of analysis papers use introductions to create the conditions in which their analyses take place, conditions that not only position their analyses, but also make their analyses possible. Rhetorically, writers often move through this pattern by first describing their subject in seemingly straightforward ways and then using that description to sanction their analysis based on that description. For instance, notice how the writer of the following excerpt uses the introduction to move rhetorically from describing the more obvious functions of grade school, using simple declarative sentences, to establishing a claim that analyzes the less obvious functions of grade school:

Grade school is a place children go to be taught the most basic skills for living a normal, happy life. Children will learn multiplication, division, cursive writing, spelling, and reading all in a normalized environment. They will also learn how to interact with others, listen attentively, and speak with confidence. . . . **Beneath all of this educational prepping lies a complex structure of surveillance, control, and centralized authority. A vast system of educational control has been laid out for children to enter into at a very young age.**

The sentences in bold represent the paper's central claim and controlling idea, which analyzes how grade school is a system of surveillance and control. In this case, the writer uses the subordinating clause "Beneath all of this educational prepping" to shift from the more obvious background description to the less obvious workings of grade school. Rhetorically, the writer uses this clause to literally uncover the workings of her subject. In the remainder of the paper, the writer analyzes this central claim.

The Body: Developing and Supporting Claims with Evidence

What is commonly referred to as the "body" of an analysis paper contains the set of paragraphs in which writers develop and support their central claim (what constitutes the controlling idea in analysis papers) in an order that makes sense for that particular claim. Typically, writers develop their idea by breaking down the central claim into its constituent parts. For example, in the immigration paper we discussed earlier, the writer's central claim is as follows:

Claim: In their attempts to gain public support, both Republicans and Democrats use language techniques to shape public opinion about illegal immigration.

As the claim suggests, the writer will be analyzing how politicians use language to affect public opinion. In the body paragraphs that follow the introduction, the writer breaks down this central claim into two parts, one that focuses on Republicans and one that focuses on Democrats. Here are the two resulting subclaims:

Subclaim A: In their attempt to gain public support, Republicans use language techniques to dehumanize illegal immigrants as well as blame them for economic difficulties.

Subclaim B: In contrast, Democrats tend to hold a more sympathetic view towards illegal immigration, as demonstrated in their language.

In this case, the writer separates the two subclaims and devotes two paragraphs to supporting each, so that the organization looks like this:

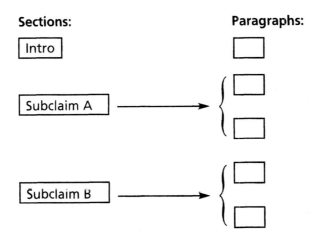

Precisely how many subclaims a writer uses, how he or she organizes them, and how many paragraphs he or she devotes to each one will depend on the demands of the central claim, on the nature of the evidence, and on the writer's strategy. (For example, it would have been just as strategically feasible for the above writer to combine subclaims A and B and devote each supporting paragraph to comparing how Republicans and Democrats talk about immigration.) Whatever organizational strategy a writer chooses, the pattern of development in analysis papers involves unfolding the central claim into its constituent parts, organizing them in some kind of order, and then supporting these parts with evidence and analysis.

The body sections present the evidence, analyze it, and guide the reader through its complexities. The typical pattern of development in analysis papers follows the analytical arrangement we described earlier:

1. The writer first sets up the piece of evidence with some brief background information that describes its context and often also explains its relevance

2. Then the writer presents the actual evidence in as much detail as possible by describing it, summarizing it, quoting from it, and so on

3. The evidence is then followed by analysis, in which the writer extracts the most relevant aspects of the evidence, explains and clarifies it, and then connects the evidence back to the claim it is trying to support

Here is how this pattern works itself out in the immigration paper:

Subclaim: In their attempt to gain public support, Republicans use language techniques to dehumanize illegal immigrants as well as blame them for economic difficulties.

Evidence: The governor of California, Pete Wilson, is one of the strongest voices in the drive to stop illegal immigration. He states: "While our educated citizens find themselves without work, illegal aliens are continuously entering the country, taking jobs, which our brothers and sisters rightfully deserve."

Analysis: Notice in this quote that Wilson dehumanizes illegal immigrants, making them seem subordinate to U.S. citizens. By using the word "alien," Wilson paints the picture of grotesque, scary beings in the minds of his readers. . . .

As you can see from this pattern, after establishing the first subclaim, the writer introduces the evidence by contextualizing it, letting readers know who Pete Wilson is. Then the writer quotes directly from Wilson, a Republican, using Wilson's own words as evidence. After that, the writer begins to analyze the evidence by pulling from it the relevant parts and explaining them in such a way that they will relate back to and support the subclaim. Such a pattern of claim-evidence-analysis is typical of analysis papers, but the pattern can unfold in various ways. For example, some writers choose to compile an entire paragraph's worth of evidence and then analyze that evidence in a separate paragraph, while other writers opt to begin with the analysis and then turn to the evidence as proof. A prescribed way of unfolding this pattern does not exist; how writers do that depends on their subject, readers, and other factors related to their specific context and strategy.

Writing Activity 6.6

Outline the structure of one of the sample analysis papers on pages 302–319. Use whatever numbering system works for you, but write out in sentences the paper's central claim and the subclaims in order. Under one of the subclaims, note how the writer moves between subclaim, evidence, and analysis, as we did in our analysis of the immigration essay's pattern.

The Conclusion

In the final section of the analysis paper, the conclusion (which can be one or more paragraphs long), the writer typically employs what is sometimes referred to as a "closing to open" strategy. Writers will often close the paper by reiterating their subclaims and showing how, when they are reconnected, they prove the central claim. In this way, they create the impression that the paper has come full circle, that the analysis has been synthesized. They also typically return to the question of "So what?" and extend the significance of their claim. Writers will sometimes consider the implications and consequences of their analysis and how it might be relevant in a larger sense to the lives of readers. Yet another concluding strategy involves writers qualifying their own conclusions by pointing out some shortcomings in their analysis that will need to be addressed in future research. (An effective analysis paper is not—indeed cannot be—the final word on a subject. So do not be afraid to expose some of your paper's shortcomings in your conclusion. Indeed, by acknowledging the paper's shortcomings, writers anticipate and, in an important sense, diffuse their readers' potential concerns.) In some cases, writers will also conclude by calling for further analysis, in so doing asking readers to apply what they have just read to other subjects and once again pointing out the significance of both their subject and their claim.

Collaborative Activity 6.4

Compare the ways the sample analysis papers introduce or conclude their papers. First, describe how each moves among the rhetorical parts we describe above. Then evaluate which ones your group finds most effective, and explain why. If your group does not like any of the introductions and conclusions especially well, explain the special challenges of introductions and conclusions and consider the ways the generic conventions may be limiting what writers believe they can do in those sections.

FORMAT

Analysis papers use formats common to academic papers: Typed, double-spaced, each page numbered, paragraphs indented, with a title and a heading indicating the writer's name, course number, and date. Some teachers specify other format requirements. Such formatting marks the paper as an academic one, suitable to the scene of a classroom and indicative of the role of the submitting student and the evaluating teacher. It also indicates the relative uniformity expected of academic assignments, with plain white paper, black ink, and a serious font. Because the types of assignments, subjects analyzed, and nature of the central claims can be so varied, the length of analysis papers varies widely.

An essential part of the analysis paper's format is the nature and use of transitions, the signals to the reader of the logical move being made from one part of the paper to the next. Writers of analysis papers use transitions as the rhetorical glue that holds the sections together and guides the reader through them. Because analysis papers in writing courses generally do not rely on subheadings in their formatting (as other academic genres such as lab reports do), the use of transitions becomes critical in guiding readers through the stages of analysis. Since the logic of the analysis is the basis for the structure, transitions in analysis papers typically explain the logical connection between parts. These logical connections are usually relatively complex; as a result, transitions in analysis papers tend to require sentences to explain the link, not just the simple transitional words like *however* (simple contrast) or *next* or *first* (simple continuation) that five-paragraph themes rely on.

Writers also use transitions to introduce evidence throughout the body. Evidence loses some of its force if it is just presented as one piece of evidence after another. The use of transitions enables the writer to explain the relevance of the evidence before it is presented, so that readers know what they are about to encounter. Some strategies used to introduce evidence include:

- Contextualizing it ("This example is an excerpt from . . .")
- Drawing attention to it ("Notice how this example . . .")
- Announcing what it means ("The following is a good example of how . . .")
- Breaking the evidence into parts ("Another aspect of the example that is telling is . . .")

Introducing evidence creates the "pointing out" effect that is so common to analysis papers.

The writer uses transitions to keep the reader's attention focused on the evidence as well as to justify further analysis. As such, transitions are one of the key ways that writers can communicate their perspectives to readers in analysis papers, where the focus is not so much on the readers as it is on the subject under scrutiny. Writers seek subtle ways to "talk" to the reader while remaining focused on the subject, as in this example: "The meaning of this sentence may seem obvious [i.e., to you the reader]. However, the language of the sentence requires closer scrutiny for true clarity." As illustrated in this example and the ones above, writers of analysis papers use transitions as signposts to direct readers from one section of the paper to another as well as to focus readers' attention on certain evidence.

Writing Activity 6.7

Examine the format of the sample analysis papers on pages 302–319. What characteristics do they share in terms of layout and appearance? Next, examine three paragraphs from one of the sample papers, and explain how the writer uses transitions to guide the reader through the stages of analysis. Look for transitional words and signposts—signals for logical connections or for pointing out evidence—and explain the effect of these transitions on the reader. Finally, indicate places where stronger transitions are needed and provide examples of what those transitions might look like.

SENTENCES

The sentences in analysis papers reflect the emphasis on *logos* and the complex relationships of analysis. Sentence structures tend to include more complex sentences, ones that show logical relationships among assertions ("By realizing that the creation of this perfect world is in fact unreal, the consumer can become more aware of the intent of the advertising and its effects on the society." or "The company is counting on men assuming that since women like Skyy Vodka, then men who drink Skyy Vodka will attract the right sort of people, and the people around a man will either raise or lower his status."). Sentences also tend to be **declarative,** assertions of facts and the ways things are ("The American culture is incredibly diverse." or "Both Democrats and Republicans use discourse to gain support."). The more distanced, observational stance of analysis papers is reflected rhetorically in these declarative assertions, as it is in the tendency to rely on forms of the verb *be (am, is, are, was, were, being, been)*. Sentences structured around *be* verbs assert a static existence, that this is just the way things are ("There are strict rules concerning the proper use of these comments, rather like the proper format for writing a letter." or "Authority is prevalent in every aspect of grade school." or "The Skyy Vodka ad is a good example of this combination of sex and status being used to draw men into believing that a product will put excitement into their everyday lives."). Writers of analysis papers tend to present evidence as objectively as possible in order to give the impression that they are showing what is already there, although perhaps what is there is hidden from view.

WORDS

Writers of analysis papers typically employ objective tone and distanced voice through the words they choose. Along with the use of the word *be,* the words seem to give the impression of pointing out what the writers are observing. Sentences such as the following are used strategically to create this "pointing out" impression with words like *another, typical, many have, example* ("Another interesting usage of syntax by programmers is . . ." or "A typical example of this language is contained in the following sentence." or "Many schools have turned to cameras for an extended version of surveillance." or "This ad is probably the best example of the idea that women are presented as possessions.").

To maintain their credibility, writers will often use qualifying words to modulate their claims and signal their careful presence. For example, writers will typically add qualifying words such as *seems, usually, can be seen as, in many ways,* or *may also.* Such qualifiers let the writer indicate that the analysis is not the absolute final word on the subject but is rather an idea which, while based on solid evidence and inquiry, is nonetheless subject to disagreement. Rhetorically, writers use such qualifications to protect against overgeneralizations and to establish their credibility as careful thinkers.

Examine one paragraph from one of the sample analysis papers on pages 302–319 for the types of sentences and words used. Can you list examples of declarative sentences, complex ones, ones using a form of *be* as a verb, words that are pointers, abstract, and qualifiers? How would you characterize the kinds of words and sentences the writer uses? How well do these achieve the desired tone or effect?

Interpreting the Generic Expectations of the Analysis Paper

What we have just described are some general patterns commonly found in analysis papers. Writers, of course, employ multiple variations on these patterns, so any attempt to devise strict directions based on these patterns will be doomed to fail. Yet the patterns and expectations are clear enough to enable us to move to the next step of genre analysis: Interpreting what these patterns reveal about the situation and scene of the analysis paper. What do the generic features we just described tell us about the scene of writing (the writing course) in which the analysis paper is used? What assumptions underscore these features? And how can we identify some of these assumptions so that we can eventually use them to make more informed writing choices?

In analyzing the generic patterns of analysis papers, we are basically engaged in the same activity that writers of analysis papers are engaged in—trying to establish and develop a claim based on the evidence we have identified. We have collected the evidence about analysis papers, and now we have to ask ourselves, "So what?" What does this evidence mean?

As it turns out, just as with most analysis papers, a number of legitimate claims can be developed based on the patterns we have found in analysis papers. For example, we could claim that the patterns reveal how the analysis paper positions the writer as a critical observer. Similarly, we could claim that the purpose of analysis papers is to engage or focus on a subject more than a reader, so that the reader takes on the role of onlooker. Or we could be a bit more cynical and claim that the analysis paper breeds a kind of passivity in which writers and readers interpret how things work and why, instead of acting on them, using them, or trying to change them. There are, of course, other claims we could make as well, each of which we would be able to support with evidence we identified in our genre description. For our genre analysis here, we will focus on the claim that the analysis paper encourages an observational stance or attitude, one that is generally highly valued in academic inquiry. Such a stance focuses attention on the subject under study rather than on the reader or writer. In writing analysis papers, students are invited to participate in a form of inquiry that inducts them into the habits of mind that are common across the university: That habit of mind includes a critical sensibility that seeks to complicate what may appear simple and obvious, an unwillingness to accept things as they appear, and a desire to uncover the assumptions behind how things work and why.

To support this claim, we turn to the evidence we have gathered from the genre itself. The most obvious way in which writers of analysis papers establish an observational stance involves the way they approach and present their subject. We noticed this in the introductions, where writers begin analysis papers by describing their subject in fairly objective ways—defining what it is and/or providing some background about it. Rhetorically, the gesture here is one of placing the subject of study before the writer's and readers' eyes—and so presenting it for examination. Words like *notice* and *this example shows* create a pointing out effect that positions the writer at a critical distance from the subject so that he or she can analyze it objectively. The emphasis on logos makes it seem as though the logic is making the case rather than the writer, just as the logical transitions lead the reader through the reasoning as though it is inevitable. When the writer establishes the claim in an analysis paper, it thus seems as if the claim emerged out of the subject of study and logic itself rather than what is actually the case—that the writer has constructed the claim.

To end our analysis, we might restate and then extend our claim's implications. By privileging such an observational stance, analysis papers reflect the academic scene's valuing of the subject of study over the writer or reader. While resumés focus on the writer and argument papers focus on the reader, analysis papers encourage the writer to act as though the *subject* is all that matters. Just as the Patient Medical History Form encouraged doctors to focus on physical symptoms to the exclusion of the emotional, analysis papers encourage students to focus on the logical to the exclusion of the emotional or personal. The genre of the analysis paper also follows a fairly linear, Western form of logic (claim/evidence/analysis) and instills in students the distanced, impersonal, critical habits of mind valued by the college and university scene.

Writing Activity 6.9

Now that you have identified the patterns and underlying assumptions of the genre of analysis papers, examine the strengths *and possible limitations* of this genre. Drawing on the Questions for Critiquing Genres in Box 4.1 (p. 161), adapt the questions to the genre of analysis papers and determine what you see as the effects of the genre, including its strengths and weaknesses.

Drawing in part on your findings in the Writing Activity above, discuss in groups what other claims one might make on the basis of our analysis of the analysis paper. You might consider one of the alternatives we presented on page 284 or one of your own. How would you use the evidence to support that claim?

Questions to Guide Writing Analysis Papers

Now that you have a better understanding of what analysis papers typically do and how they reflect and reveal the scene of the writing course in which they are used, how can you turn that understanding into practice? In Box 6.1, we help you apply that genre knowledge to your own writing. In helping you use this genre knowledge to make more informed writing choices, we draw on the following boxes: Box 3.1: Questions for Inventing (p. 108), Box 3.2: Questions for Drafting (p. 117), Box 3.3: Questions for Detecting Dissonance Based on Genre (p. 124), Box 3.4: Questions for Revising (p. 139), and Box 3.5: Questions for Presentation (p. 146). Applying these questions to what you now know about the analysis paper will enable you to negotiate the writing process more effectively.

Analyzing the Argument Paper

Our purpose in describing the analysis paper in such detail, from its generic features to interpreting these features, is not just to teach you how to write better analysis papers, though of course we hope more effective writing is one result. We also wanted to model for you how to analyze an academic genre so that you could analyze other academic genres as you encounter them. For you to practice doing such analysis yourself, we next will invite you to work with your classmates to perform your own analysis of another commonly used genre in writing courses, the argument paper. Knowledge of this genre will further expand your familiarity with your writing course's scene of writing as well as reinforce your developing skills as a genre analyst and writer.

Box 6.1   *Questions for Writing Analysis Papers*

Inventing

1. In what way does my writing assignment call for an analysis paper? What appears to be the instructor's purpose in making this assignment? What specifically about analysis am I being asked to learn or practice? What am I being asked to analyze? How am I being asked to analyze it?

2. What subjects might I choose that would lend themselves to analysis? What do I already know about the subjects I might analyze? What thoughts do I already have about the meaning of the subject and the claims I might want to make?

3. What kinds of information do I need to gather to provide evidence for my analysis? Where will I find the information I need for my analysis (library research, Internet research, interviewing people)?

4. Am I finding something I consider important or interesting? Am I working toward a claim that matters to me?

Drafting

1. How does the assignment direct my drafting? Will I be working alone or collaboratively? Has the assignment specified stages of drafting, so that I will need to have sections ready to submit to my instructor at specified dates? Do I need to have a draft ready for peer review at a particular time?

2. What central claim will I be making in this paper to serve as my controlling idea? What has my analysis led me to understand? Is it one all my evidence links to? Does it answer the "So what?" question?

3. How should I structure my paper? How shall I introduce and conclude my paper? How shall I organize the body?

   Introductory Section:

   - How should I describe my subject?
   - What can I say about the subject that will make it worthy of analysis?
   - How can I move from my subject to my claim about the subject?

   (continued on next page)

Body Section:

- What are the components of my central claim, the parts that I need to demonstrate?
- What subpoints have I developed that support my central claim?
- In what order should I arrange those subpoints? What organization follows from my central claim?

Concluding Section:

- In what ways has the evidence I have analyzed fulfilled the promise I made in my claim? How can I bring the parts of my analysis back together again?
- How can I extend my claim? Are there any parts of the analysis that are not accounted for by my claim? If so, what are these? Is there evidence in my analysis that leads me to qualify my original claim? What is it? What are the implications of my analysis? What does it mean in the larger scheme of things? Does it ask us to rethink some of our assumptions? Does it challenge us to change the way we think and act?

4. How can I appeal to my readers' reasoning? What do my readers already know about this subject? What do I need to write to sound credible, like a rational mind objectively explaining the subject?

5. As I draft, am I using complex transitions to link the evidence to analysis and the analysis to my central claim? Am I guiding my readers through the organization with transitions? Am I remembering to introduce, present, and analyze the evidence? Am I explaining how the evidence relates to my claim?

6. Now that I see how my analysis is connecting to my central claim, do I need to reconsider my central claim? Am I having to force the evidence to support it, or is my evidence supporting subpoints that fit comfortably with my central claim? Do I agree with what I'm claiming? Am I saying what I wanted to say?

Revising

1. What am I trying to accomplish as I revise this draft? Does the goal that the draft tries to achieve fit with the general goals of analysis papers? How well does my draft meet the goals I was trying to achieve—the goals promised in the introduction and the central claim?

(continued on next page)

2. What do readers expect from analysis papers? Has my draft met these expectations? Is it logical and based in reasoning and analysis? Do I seem rational and credible? How well have I guided readers through my reasoning so they see the connections I'm making between evidence and claim? Which reader expectations have been met and which have not?

3. In what ways does my draft seem like other analysis papers, and in what ways does it seem different? Review the description of the genre's features on pages 271–283. Does the draft follow the pattern described for content, structure, format, sentences, and words? If not, have I deliberately varied from those expectations, either to respond to something specific about my task or to resist the genre's expectations?

4. What additional evidence would be helpful to support my claim? How can I get that evidence? What else do I still need to add to my draft?

5. Does my organization of the body make sense for my central claim? Do parts need to be expanded? Deleted? Moved around to fit together more logically?

6. Have I used sentences and words that seem distanced and objective? Have I qualified my statements appropriately?

7. Have I edited the last version carefully for the conventions of Standardized Edited English, including grammar, usage, punctuation, and spelling? Have I cited any sources I used according to the citation system my instructor specified?

8. Have I formatted my text appropriately, using complex transitions, typing it neatly, adding a title and heading? Do my paragraphs look like an appropriate length to be well developed, or should I combine some paragraphs?

Reading the Scene and Situation of Argument Papers

Like analysis papers, argument papers reflect the goals and assumptions of writing courses. Remember that one objective of writing courses is to prepare students for writing in other academic scenes; many of the genres in writing courses thus are designed to teach skills that are valued in the college and university. Not surprisingly for the scene, then, one of the assumptions behind the argument paper is that argumentation, like analysis, is a rhetorical skill that applies in a variety of contexts. While the argument paper may appear most specifically in writing courses, the skills of argumentation on which it is based—clearly stating a claim and supporting that claim with logical and convincing reasons that are appropriate to a given audience—extend beyond the writing course. In fact, in one way or another, most academic genres require writers to construct and develop arguments.

In academic scenes, particularly the scene of the writing course, arguments often take the shape of what we are calling "argument papers," but they also often appear as problem-solution papers, proposals, letters to authorities, or editorials. Editorials are also common, of course, in journalism courses; in business courses, arguments may take the form of a recommendation report, a genre in which writers recommend a course of action such as "Why small businesses should invest in advertising." In public and workplace scenes, argument genres include complaint letters, letters to the editor, letters of application, resumés, and proposals. Complaint letters, for instance, work to convince a given audience to refund a defective product while resumés work to convince an employer that the job applicant is the right person for an advertised position. Exactly how arguments take shape and why they are used depend on the scene of writing and the genre.

Analysis papers and argument papers share many aspects of the writing course situation: Common settings (classrooms), participants (teachers and students), and even in some ways the same subjects (issues, texts, events, people). Their purposes, however, are distinctly different. As we discussed in the last sections, analysis papers involve making claims about their subject of study, with writers trying to arrive at a better understanding of their subject through analysis (for example, how the television show *The Sopranos* exploits negative stereotypes). Argument papers also involve analysis of a subject, but their goal extends beyond understanding the subject. *In an argument paper, the writer takes a stand in relation to the subject* (like why viewers should boycott the television show *The Sopranos*) and may use analysis to clarify or support the claim or to explain the link between the claim and evidence. For example, when writing an argument that the residence hall should adopt a more flexible visitation policy, the writer would need to analyze the advantages and disadvantages of the policy and explain each part of the proposed policy and how it is workable. *In argument papers, analysis is not the end but rather the means to an end, which usually involves trying to convince readers of something.*

While the subjects of argument papers can range widely and cover any issue that is debatable or controversial, the subjects and purposes of argument papers tend to be reader-focused, as reflected in the following purposes of argument papers:

- To convince readers of an issue of concern
- To propose that readers should/should not do X or issue a call for action
- To argue that a problem exists and the writer/reader needs to solve it
- To illustrate to readers how one event/issue brings about another
- To evaluate an issue/problem and persuade readers to accept those evaluations
- To establish criteria and to argue that X meets or does not meet the criteria

Although the primary purpose of arguments is always to convince someone of something, different argument genres have distinct purposes. For example, a letter to an authority typically aims to convince the authority to take some action: For the chancellor of the university to support construction of a new laboratory building, for a representative to vote for a specific bill, for a local business owner to hire more students. An *academic* argument paper seeks not to convince someone to do something (the intention to gain a high grade always simmers beneath the surface, but that goal is achieved by achieving the more explicit purposes of the assignment). Rather, an academic argument paper seeks to convince the reader that the writer's position is sound, credible, a reasonable position based on an interpretation of the evidence. Not only your teacher but also your classmate readers need to be persuaded that you have considered the issues carefully and honestly and that your position reflects a logical and complex understanding of the topic.

Writing Activity 6.10

Compare the argument papers on pages 320–332 with the various argument genres that we have studied in previous chapters: Editorials (Chapter 1), complaint letters (Chapters 2 and 3), and brochures (Chapter 3). You might also want to look ahead to the argument genres in later chapters, such as the letter of application and resumé, proposals, and reports (Chapter 9) or the letters to the editor and editorials (Chapter 10). After examining these argument genres, write 2 to 3 paragraphs in which you explore how these different genres respond to different situations (subjects, purposes, settings, and readers). What role does scene (the writing course scene vs. scenes outside the writing course) play in shaping these differing argument genres?

ROGERIAN AND CLASSICAL ARGUMENT

Part of persuading your readers in all arguments involves addressing "opposing arguments," finding ways to deal with the positions that other people take that might not agree with your own. How you deal with others' positions depends in many ways on the readers and purposes in your particular argument (for example, are you trying to persuade someone to change his or her mind or just to consider an issue not yet recognized?). It also depends on your view of how people are persuaded.

Two common approaches to argument reflect two different perspectives on how to persuade people. One perspective, based in classical rhetoric and a tradition of classical argumentation, treats opposing arguments as things to be countered, dismissed, proven false, or minimized. Another perspective, based in part in a therapy developed by the psychologist Carl Rogers, treats opposing arguments as sources for common ground, as things to be set beside the writer's position in order to find where the two positions can overlap or where a third position can be found that permits both arguments to persist.

Classical argumentation, the basis for much academic writing, derives from ancient rhetorical studies of the art of persuasion. *Based mostly on deductive reasoning, the argument begins with a direct statement of the claim (controlling idea), followed by reasons and evidence to support the claim. In order to explore an argument from various angles, the writer then takes opposing views into account and identifies probable counterarguments*—positions directly opposed to the claim. For example, if you want to argue that school uniforms should be mandatory in your local high school, you might follow this claim with reasons that support this assertion: The reduction of peer pressure and social stigmatization, an increased sense of community, and a safer and more productive learning environment. Following a classical argumentation approach, you would also think through opposing arguments and reservations, and would anticipate probable objections, such as concerns about increased conformity and the loss of individual expression. Particularly if you are aiming your argument at readers who are uninformed or undecided on your issue, the classical approach—focusing on arguments both for and against—is an effective strategy.

In Rogerian argument, writers seek to understand what others believe in order to find places where opposing positions can agree. One position need not be defeated in order for the other position to win, to use the war metaphor so common in discussions of argument. And people need not change their basic beliefs in order to find points of agreement from which to build a common understanding. Suppose, for example, that you want city commissioners to permit a homeless shelter, while neighbors of the proposed shelter want commissioners to deny the permit. Working to understand the neighbors' concerns might enable you to share their view, to see that the shelter needs to be operated in such a way as not to disrupt the neighborhood. Your argument to the commission might then include not only the reasons a homeless shelter is needed, or even the desirability of that particular location; it might also and more effectively include the ways the shelter can be established to direct homeless traffic away from the neighborhood, to increase security at the shelter, and to disband if it proves harmful to its surroundings after a trial period. If the neighbors also adopt a Rogerian perspective and attempt to understand your position, they might argue more effectively not only that the shelter might harm the neighborhood but also that a shelter could be established in another location to serve that needy population. In both cases, acknowledging the legitimacy of the others' arguments leads not to defeating the others but to finding positions that can meet the beliefs, values, and goals of all sides.

This Rogerian view of argument seems especially appropriate in situations where the participants need to cooperate or where solutions must serve multiple interested parties. Even issues that are firmly entrenched into opposing sides—issues like abortion, capital punishment, or gun control—might be moveable only through Rogerian approaches to find common ground: The common concern over the welfare of mothers and children, for example, or the common desire to keep our society both safe and free.

Some believe that all arguments should take Rogerian approaches in order to build a kinder, gentler argument. Others believe that Rogerian argument is less effective in situations where altering your position might weaken it too much, where encompassing the concerns of others might mean encompassing beliefs or values that you do not wish to support even in minor ways, or where the opposing arguments are weak and do not merit inclusion. Some also believe that people are best persuaded through clear opposition of viewpoints, through strong contestation that demonstrates that one position is superior to another. This more traditional view of argument, as we discussed earlier, often takes the form of a classical argument structure, one that argues its points through defeating the points of its opponents. Opposing arguments are countered through proving the opposing position either false, misguided, or unimportant.

Not surprisingly, these two approaches to argument (Rogerian and classical) often appear in different argument genres. More likely to use Rogerian argument are problem-solution papers and proposals that appeal to a shared vision or common set of values in order to convince readers to implement the solution or adopt the proposal; editorials and argument papers that appeal to a wider range of potentially uninformed or undecided readers more commonly use classical argument. Either can appear in any argument genre, however, for these approaches reflect just as much the beliefs of the writer as they do the expectations of the situation. Some people tend to argue to defeat, while others tend to argue to negotiate. If you can gain an understanding of and facility in both Rogerian and classical argument, you will be the most flexible and most likely to be able to adapt to different situations.

Writing Activity 6.11

Do you tend to favor either Rogerian or classical argument? Does one approach tend to convince you more than another? Can you think of a time when you changed your mind, or when you were able to change someone else's mind? Which argument approach was used then?

Collaborative Activity 6.6

In small groups, generate a list of campus problems or issues of concern at your institution. Then choose one issue from the list, and construct a claim that is arguable. Decide who would be the most appropriate audience to hear your claim, and then sketch out (in outline form) two approaches to the argument: (1) the classical argument approach (including reasons to support your argument and refutations of opposing arguments) and (2) the Rogerian approach (identifying common ground and areas of agreement). Based on your topic and audience, which approach seems more effective? Why?

Collaborative Activity 6.7

As a class, discuss with your instructor his or her objectives in using argument papers in a writing course. (If your teacher prefers that you learn how to write another argument genre and provides a different set of samples of that genre, you can conduct all of the Collaborative Activities in this section on an argument genre other than the argument paper.) Using Box 1.2: Guidelines for Observing and Describing Scenes (pp. 44–45), as well as the questions on situation from Box 2.1: Guidelines for Analyzing a Genre (pp. 93–94), first work in small groups to decide what questions you should ask the class and instructor in order to better understand the scene and situation of argument papers. Then conduct your discussion as a class, assigning individuals in your group the tasks of asking questions and recording answers. After the discussion, reflect on what you learned about argument papers; then synthesize and compile these reflections into a guide sheet or "tip" sheet (your teacher may choose to compile these into one set of guidelines).

To help you build on your knowledge of analysis and apply it to argument papers, we now invite you to conduct your own genre analysis of argument papers. We include several samples of argument papers on pages 320–332, all written by students in first-year writing courses. Working with your classmates, use these samples to work through your analysis. Along the way, you will have an opportunity to identify patterns in the genre, to interpret what these patterns mean, and to develop strategies for using that knowledge to make more effective writing choices when you write argument papers.

Describing Generic Features of Argument Papers

With some understanding of the scene and situation of argument papers, the next step in trying to gain a more critical understanding of the genre involves identifying and describing its generic features. What follows is an explanation of the features that you will examine in greater detail when you perform your analysis of the argument paper, along with a few hints to get you started.

CONTENT

Similar to an analysis paper, the content of an argument paper revolves around a central claim—an argument that the writer has formulated about his or her subject. The claim stakes out the writer's position on the subject and generates the direction and content of the argument. For example, a **causal claim**, such as "Violent behavior in children is caused by the violence they encounter through playing video games," will likely begin by providing examples of violent themes and images in video games and will then go on to examine the cause/effect relationship among these themes and images and violent behavior in children. Claims may also be **evaluative**, based on values, beliefs, or personal judgment. For example, the claim that "*The Godfather*" is the most accomplished film about mob life ever made" is a claim that makes a value judgment. Typically, evaluative arguments will go on to define specific criteria by which to develop and support this claim. Finally, some claims may make **recommendations** and may convince the readers to carry out a solution to a problem, change or adopt a policy, or take a particular action. A claim based on a recommendation, such as "The minimum wage is too low and needs to be raised," indicates the direction and content of the argument, which will go on to define the problem caused by minimum wage falling behind cost of living and then define a solution and specific plan for enacting the solution, as well as providing justification for the solution.

To argue any of the above claims successfully, you will need to develop the body of the argument with convincing evidence and reasons. One popular method for developing arguments is the **Toulmin method.** The twentieth-century British philosopher Stephen Toulmin wrote a treatise on argumentation entitled *The Uses of Argument* (1958) that describes a method for evaluating the reasonableness of arguments. Toulmin's approach, based on a courtroom model, has been modified to apply to writing arguments as well as analyzing them. According to this approach, all arguments consist of (1) a claim that is controversial or debatable, (2) reasons to support or justify the claim, (3) evidence and data (personal experience, anecdotes, facts, authorities) to support the reasons, and (4) warrants—analyses or assumptions that link the evidence and support to the claim. The following example illustrates this method of developing arguments:

Claim: Schools should reduce the size of classes.

Reason: Students benefit from more one-on-one interaction with teachers.

Evidence: Studies link individualized attention to better grades and performance on standardized tests.

Warrants: Better grades and performance on standardized tests are things we should strive for.

In this case, the **warrant**—the value, belief, or principle that the audience has to hold if the soundness of the argument is to be accepted or *warranted*—is that grades and standardized tests are accurate markers of student learning and hence anything that can help us improve performances in these areas should be supported. Another possible warrant might be that one-on-one interaction between teacher and student is indeed beneficial to learning—another assumption of the above argument. If this link is not assumed, the writer may need to provide additional analysis and explanation that establishes the validity of this warrant and makes this connection.

As you examine the argument papers on pages 320–327, concentrate on the subjects that lend themselves to argument and examine the central claim made about that subject and the use of reasons, evidence, warrants, and analysis to support the claim. You might consider to what extent the type of claim dictates the direction and content of the argument.

RHETORICAL APPEALS

Whichever approach you take toward others' positions, you will argue most effectively by appealing to your readers' interests and concerns through *logos, pathos,* and *ethos.* Arguments use all three types of appeals, although they may emphasize one type over the others. You may find that argument papers in writing courses depend heavily on logos, on the reason and logic that best supports the writer's position. The persuasiveness of the writer's position may also depend on ethos—the credibility, authority, and trustworthiness of the writer. And since many arguments are based on values or beliefs, arguments also heavily rely on pathos or appeals to the audience's values, beliefs, and emotions. Effective arguments convince readers through a combination of logic, emotion, and the credibility of the writer. As you read the sample argument papers, examine the use of appeals, and consider whether certain types of claims lead to an emphasis on a particular appeal.

STRUCTURE

While the structure of argument papers will depend upon your purpose, audience, approach (classical or Rogerian), and the nature of your claim (causal, evaluative, or recommendation), many academic papers follow the classical argument form or some variation of this. Classical rhetorician Aristotle came up with a four-part structure for argument consisting of an introduction, statement of the claim, proof of the claim, and conclusion, and this was later modified into a six-part structure:

1. Introduction—an attention-grabber or memorable scene

2. Background/explanation of the issue

3. Statement of the claim (the thesis or controlling idea)

4. Presentation of the reasons to support the claim

5. Summary of and refutation of opposing views

6. Conclusion (summary or call to action)

As you examine the sample papers, notice how they either follow or modify this structure. Consider how differing claims dictate different structures.

FORMAT

Similar to the analysis paper, the argument paper functions for the writing course scene and uses the same format common to academic papers: Neatly typed, double-spaced, each page numbered, paragraphs indented, with a title and a heading indicating the writer's name, course number, and date. You may want to consult our previous discussion in this chapter of the analysis paper format and consider whether or not the discussion of transitions applies to the argument paper as well. As you read the sample papers, you might also consider how various features of layout and format of the paper could make the information more accessible and improve readability.

SENTENCES AND WORDS

When trying to convince readers through your use of language, paying close attention to your construction of sentences and choice of words is crucial. To create a serious and credible ethos, most writers of argument papers will adopt a fairly formal style with sentences that are longer and more complex. In addition, to appeal to emotion, writers will often use descriptive language or words that carry a powerful emotional impact. However, to maintain ethos, it is important to avoid using words that might manipulate readers through their powerful emotional overtones or through slanted or biased language. For example, an argument on abortion that refers to "baby killing" may risk alienating readers, as would an argument for pay equity among men and women that refers to "feminazis" or an argument supporting drilling for oil in the Alaskan Wildlife Refuge that refers to "environmental wackos." Such emotionally laden terms often defeat the purpose of reasoned and logical argument. As you read the sample argument papers, consider the use of words that seem especially powerful and persuasive as well as any that seem to detract from the argument or from the writer's credibility.

Collaborative Activity 6.8

Take a close look at the sample argument papers we have included on pages 320–332. Then, using the questions outlined in step 3 of Box 2.1: Guidelines for Analyzing Genres (p. 94), describe the features we have been discussing in more detail. If your teacher does not assign another approach, to make the process more manageable we suggest the class divide the work and compile results:

1. Divide the class into six groups.
2. Assign each group one of the types of features in Box 2.1—content, rhetorical appeals, structure, format, sentences, and diction.
3. Have each group work through the sample argument papers, studying the type of feature assigned. They should look for similarities across all the papers. For example, the group working on content, using the questions in Box 2.1, seeks patterns in what kinds of content is included and excluded, what kinds of examples and evidence are used, and how the content is treated in all the papers.
4. Ask each group to report their results to the class as a whole, either in written or oral form. Since features can overlap, be sure to allow members of other groups to contribute their insights into the patterns they see.

Writing Activity 6.12

Since you will all later need the information about generic patterns of the argument paper, write your own record of the patterns of generic features that the class discovers. You might wish to create a list of features, a brief manual that compiles lists and examples from the sample papers, or a discussion of the features like the one we provided for analysis papers. You might also want to incorporate some of the information about the scene and situation of argument papers that you gathered in Collaborative Activity 6.7 (pp. 294–295).

Interpreting Generic Expectations of Argument Papers

To construct some ideas about what the patterns you discovered mean, we suggest that you again work with classmates to develop multiple interpretations. Working in the same groups that described the patterns, or the method your teacher assigned you instead, work through the questions outlined in step 4 of Box 2.1: Guidelines for Analyzing Genres (p. 94). Analyze what the patterns you have just described mean. In general, you are seeking answers to the following questions:

- What do the patterns tell us about the scenes of the writing course or college and university in which they are used?
- What do they reveal about the situation of the argument paper, including the assumptions and expectations of the people who use them?

Remember, your goal in performing this kind of analysis is to uncover the underlying assumptions of the patterns and to develop a claim based on them. The patterns themselves thus become the subject of your analysis. They are the evidence you will use to support your claim. Therefore, look carefully at these patterns as you try to answer the questions in step 4 of Box 2.1.

After your group has worked its way through those questions, discuss what claims your group might make about the situation or scene of the argument paper. Select your strongest claims to present to the class as a whole, and discuss as a class what evidence supports each of the claims. You might wish to compare your claims to the claim we made regarding the analysis paper in the section, "Interpreting the Generic Expectations of the Analysis Paper" (p. 284). Keep in mind that such analyses are always open to multiple interpretations, not one right or best answer. Your goal is to understand as much as you can about the argument paper by exploring as many possible interpretations as the evidence supports.

Writing Activity 6.13

Select a claim about the argument paper that you find most promising or interesting, either one presented to the class or one of your own devising. What sort of insight does it reveal into the purpose and meaning of the genre? After developing your claim, explain how the evidence (the patterns your class identified in the argument paper) supports your claim.

Collaborative Activity 6.9

In small groups, trade the claims about the argument paper that you worked with in Writing Activity 6.13, and evaluate those claims. Drawing on the questions for critiquing genres in Box 4.1 (p. 161), formulate at least three new claims about the limitations and possibilities of the genre of the argument paper and how it succeeds and fails as a genre.

Writing within the Generic Expectations of Argument Papers

Now that you have read the scene, situation, and features of the argument paper genre, you can better understand the choices you can make as a writer of argument. Think not only about what you would need to write in order to meet reader expectations but also about where you found variation in the genre—where you might make different choices in order to achieve different purposes or to challenge the genre. In general, as you turn to writing the genre, you want to discover answers to the following questions about inventing, drafting, and revising argument papers:

- Based on what I know about the argument paper, what strategies should I employ during the invention stage? What kind of subject should I seek? How should I approach my subject? What kind of controlling idea should I develop? What kind of research should I do? What kind of stance should I take in relation to it?

- What drafting strategies should I use? That is, what choices should I be making as I work to persuade my reader? What appeals should I emphasize? How should I be organizing the introductory section, the body section, and the concluding section? What are some typical strategies I could use to present evidence? What should my paper be sounding like?

- What revising strategies would be most appropriate for me to use? That is, how should I target my revisions? What expectations do I need to make sure I have met?

Asking yourself such questions based on your knowledge of the genre will enable you to make more informed and effective choices as a writer of argument papers in your writing course.

Writing Activity 6.14

Using the "Questions for Inventing," "Questions for Drafting," "Questions for Detecting Dissonance Based in Genre," and "Questions for Revising" outlined in Chapter 3, make a list of the questions you need to ask as you write an argument paper. You might wish to use Box 6.1: Questions for Writing Analysis Papers (pp. 287–289) as a guide to how to apply the general questions of Chapter 3 to what you have learned about the argument paper.

Collaborative Activity 6.10

Compare with your classmates your questions for writing argument papers. Work to compile one set of questions that contains the best of all your lists. Be prepared to share your compiled set of questions with the class.

In the next chapter, we will work with you to analyze one other academic genre common to many writing courses, the researched position paper, a form of argument paper. With the understanding of these three academic genres—the analysis paper, argument paper, and researched position paper—you should be well prepared to write effectively in your writing course. You should also have learned how to apply genre analysis in academic scenes so that you can encounter any academic situation in the future, read its scene and generic features, and make writing choices effective for that situation.

Samples of Analysis Papers (as submitted by students without further editing)

1.

Women in Advertising

Crystal A. Sison

People's prejudices are often used to sell products, and many times these prejudices involve women, whether it be women as objects to be desired or as possessions to be guarded. Two types of products that use these prejudices are cigarettes and alcohol; companies create ads that have thin, beautiful women as prizes for men if they smoke certain cigarettes or drink certain alcohol. In all three of the ads that I deconstructed the women are objects, things that have been won and that raise the status of the person who possesses them. Along with this idea of women as status symbols is the use of sex to sell products; if a company promises a man he will get sex if he buys their product then the product will be more attractive to the man. This combination of status and sex can be powerful, and companies know how to use these ideas to their full advantage to sell their product.

The Skyy Vodka ad is a good example of this combination of sex and status being used to draw men into believing that a product will put excitement into their everyday lives. In this ad there is a beautiful woman who looks like she was just at a fancy party and is now ready to relax with a glass of vodka and the man that she met that night. The draw of this advertisement can be seen in its promise of high status and its sexual implications: her look, her posture, and the red curtains. The first aspect of the ad that makes the reader think of sex and status is the woman's look. the evening dress that she is wearing, her make-up and her hair. This look that she has makes her seem sophisticated and alluring and many men are drawn to this; some even associate this look with wealth and prestige which are two extremely coveted things. The next aspect is that of the woman's posture, the way she is holding up her shoes and her Skyy Vodka and the way that she is tilting her head. She seems to be inviting the man to get closer to her, to get comfortable, to take off his shoes and lie down. Her tilted head seems to be asking, almost daring the man to do things that the reader can only speculate on. The final aspect of the sexual implications are the red curtains in the background; red is usually associated with sexual women, women who draw attention and are ready to act impulsively and have a good time. Red was chosen for a specific reason; it was not a random color picked out of the blue. The color is there to set the mood and send a message; this woman is ready to have a good time. The curtains can be seen as a barrier or a door which probably leads to a room and maybe even a bed; it suggests something hidden or taboo, the attitude that people sometimes take with sex.

The Skyy Vodka woman could go a long way for the man who possesses her. She is blond, thin, beautiful, and sophisticated: dressed in evening wear instead of raggedy clothes, drinking vodka as opposed to coarse beer, she could blend well in elite social circles. The man who can say that she is his will gain respect among his peers, people will envy him. The company is counting on men assuming that since women like Skyy Vodka, then men who drink Skyy Vodka will attract the right sort of people, and the people around a man will either raise or lower his status. So, in this advertisement Skyy Vodka has used men's desire for sex and high status to make their product seem like it will improve their lives.

An ad that is similar in some ways to the Skyy Vodka ad is the one for Kool Cigarettes; it is similar in that there is a beautiful woman whose attention is focused on a man whose life has improved because of the product being advertised; it is dissimilar in that they are portraying a different way of life. In this advertisement the company projects a different style than Skyy Vodka, a life that could be considered more realistic and therefore more obtainable than the one portrayed by the vodka ad. A beautiful woman in a bar dressed casually is different from a sophisticated, sexy woman alone in a room; it can be less intimidating while remaining appealing to most people. It may be believable that of all of the men in the bar the woman has noticed the man holding the pack of Kool Cigarettes. In the ad the woman's gaze is directed to the place where the man's head would be if his body was actually in the picture; the reader understands that she is attracted to the man even though only his hand is shown, this leaves most of the attention to be focused on the package of cigarettes in the foreground. The readers focus on the product while being able to imagine themselves as the man she is attracted to; they are able to do this because the man has no real physical characteristics.

The caption of the ad reads, "B Kool," and this pretty much explains the attitude the company wants to portray to the reader; you will be cool if you smoke Kool Cigarettes, and if you are cool you raise yourself in the eyes of your peers. Why should it matter if a man is cool enough to attract beautiful women? It all comes back to women being objects and

Sison 4

possessions for men, and if men strive to possess beautiful women this advertisement gives them ideas on how to do this, smoke the right cigarettes.

The final ad that I looked at was for Camel Cigarettes and it is in a different format than the Skyy Vodka ad and the Kool Cigarettes ad; this ad was created for a contest that Camel is having and this one happened to be the "Temperamental Hollywood Mega Star" contest. This ad is probably the best example of the idea that women are possessions; the prizes do not actually include the women that are pictured but the reader gets the idea that if you win the women are included in the package. The reader gets this idea from the fact that there are six women in skimpy clothes watching his expensive sports car sink to the bottom of his pool and laughing about it. This would normally not be funny at all but the women know that the man is rich and so they laugh not caring since they know he has more money. This ad is supposed to be humorous and the company would say that people should not take it seriously but they would not have created the ad to look like it does if they did not think it would make people want to win their contest. A man would want to win this contest because of what he will get, not just the prizes listed but prestige and women who like a man because of his money, women with no real purpose but to look good on the arm of the man who has won.

Both this ad and the Kool Cigarettes ad are designed for a different audience than the Skyy Vodka ad; cigarettes are considered more of a product of the common person, the middle and lower classes, while vodka is not something that just anyone drinks; one would usually think of beer or wine when they think of the common people, not vodka. These three ads cater to different people and it shows in their different approaches to selling their products. Nevertheless all the

Sison 5

ads are using men's craving for status and sex, just on different levels.

All three advertisements that I looked at were linked by the women that were in them and the men that they were made for. Susan Douglas talks about some of the stereotypes that women have do deal with in her essay, "Narcissism as Liberation":

> Aside from the impossible standards of perfection they imposed, these buns of steel urged women to never stop and to be all things to all people: to be both competitive workaholics and sex objects, to be active workers in control of their bodies and passive ornaments for the pleasure of men, to be hard-as-nails super-women and vulnerable, unthreatening, teenage beach bunnies. (130)

One can see in this some of the prejudices that are used in cigarette and alcohol ads; the "sex objects" and the "passive ornaments for the pleasure of men" are perfect examples of what women in these ads are supposed to be. This advertising can create misconceptions that can affect how people live their lives. Many of today's stereotypes come from advertising as we each strive to be the perfect man or the perfect woman of today's society; we do this even though most people are never able to live up to this ideal.

Sison 6

Works Cited

Douglas, Susan. "Narcissism as Liberation." <u>Ways of Reading: An Anthology for Writers</u>. Eds. David Bartholomae and Anthony Petrosky. Boston: St. Martin's Press, 1996. 117-33.

2.

Villasin 1

The Media's Emotional Narrative:
Jésica Santillán vs. Duke University Hospital
Marie Villasin

In "Sentimental Journeys," Joan Didion defines the "master narrative" as a story that becomes excessively indulged in emotion. She exemplifies this "master narrative," which she also calls the "preferred narrative," with the infamous 1989 New York City incident of a jogger who is brutally attacked in Central Park. Didion describes other narratives that compete with or oppose the preferred narrative. All of these narratives are notorious for removing certain information and emphasizing other information. The recent death of seventeen year old Jésica Santillán reflects the media's form of story-telling with master narratives. She was the victim of

Villasin 2

an organ mix-up by doctors at Duke University Hospital. According to *Time*, "Jésica's story had all the makings of the American miracle." A second transplant was performed as soon as organs were made available, but the organs come too late. However, receiving two rare heart and lung transplants affects other patients who desperately need the organs also. An emotional and fearful narrative has erupted from this incident in the midst of other numerous malpractice lawsuits that the media has publicized. Through their use of rhetoric, I contend the media sentimentalizes Jésica Santillán's story by emphasizing her innocence and accentuating the errors of the hospital, while downplaying the competing narrative concerning the ethical dilemma of repeat transplants.

The media used certain descriptions and symbols to portray Jésica Santillán as pure and childlike. *Newsweek* describes Jésica as "a small, frail child, barely over five feet and not much more than 80 pounds," and includes a quotation from a family friend: "She was skin and bones" (Adler 22). The fragility of this child is conveyed in this description. A child that is helpless and fragile possesses the quality of innocence. Even though Jésica was seventeen years old, the news coverage often referred to her as a child: "And for one little girl who used to like to dress up in her chunky-heeled shoes and go shopping at Wal-Mart . . ." (Adler 25). This childlike attribute the journalists used in reports also contributed to her immaculate image. Another characteristic that the media utilized in its sympathetic reports was the religious piety of the Santillán family. A caption underneath a photograph of Magdalena, Jésica's mother, reads "A devout Catholic, Jésica's mother has spent the past several weeks in prayer" (Adler 21). Religious practices are often identified with purity, especially in the United States. The reporters exploit the Santillán's unwavering faith in God to illustrate

Villasin 3

their innocence which is also identified with Jésica. The media puts emphasis on particular aspects of Jésica and her family to illuminate her innocence. This immaculate image facilitates the media's goal to generate sympathy from its audience of readers.

Similar to its attempts of creating Jésica into a symbol of purity, news coverage dramatized Duke University Hospital's mistake. The doctors in charge of her care became Jésica's opposing force in this master narrative. The narrative displayed the hospital as the harmful character in Jésica's story, whereas she stood as its image of innocence. Since Duke University Hospital is considered one of the top hospitals in the country, the exaggerated narrative explained the fall of a prestigious institution: "[Duke University Hospital's] once gleaming reputation has taken a beating. How could its surgeons have erred so egregiously" (Kher 61)? The media emphasizes the hospital error with the word "beating," stirring up images of a horrific error that cost the hospital everything. In addition, the media includes several statements from Mack Mahoney, Jésica's benefactor. His statements are used more often than statements from the hospital, producing an emotionally driven narrative striking against the medical institution:

> Mahoney says Duke officials misled Jésica's parents, who barely speak English, about the gravity of Jésica's condition. 'Dumb Mexicans--that's how they saw [the Santilláns],' he growls. He says he had to fight the hospital to make it admit--and attempt to fix--the mistake. He also claims that Duke officials refused to let him see the girl when they learned he was taking her story to the press. Says the hospital's CEO . . . 'I think we have been honest and forthcoming with the family and will continue to [be] so. (Kher 61)

Villasin 4

In this paragraph, four out of the five statements the reporter includes focus on Mahoney's description of the incident. Furthermore, this paragraph alone creates a significant impact on readers. The writer's use of the word "growl" to describe Mahoney establishes his animosity towards the hospital. Another sentimental phrase depicts the hospital's approach to the Santilláns as a Mexican family, producing strong feelings against the hospital in a time when racial equality and political correctness are encouraged. The media chose to incorporate these emotional statements to help readers feel what the victims of this incident were feeling. This sentimentality reinforces the negative qualities of the hospital which is continually affirmed in this narrative.

Although a successful master narrative has developed from this contrast of good and evil, the master narrative also exclude opposing narratives that weaken its argument. The competing narrative questions the appropriateness of allowing Jésica to receive two heart and lung transplants. Dr. Arthur Caplan explains this dilemma: "[The doctors] feel a special obligation when they made a mistake that is causing the death of this patient. Now they are trying to rescue her. This makes perfect sense, but it isn't the best national policy" (cited in Stolberg 23). As a professor of bioethics, he responds to the master narrative by arguing "that if there were another patient waiting whose situation was as dire as Ms. Santillán's, that person had a higher claim to the organs, because statistics show that a second transplant is generally less successful than the first" (Stolberg 23). Dr. Caplan expresses his opposing minority view of not giving Jésica a second transplant. However, his opposing viewpoint is quickly followed up by statements supporting the master narrative, "I'd argue she never got the first transplant," said Dr. Joseph J. Fins . . . [Some medical professionals] said it only seemed fair that Ms.

Santillán had been given a second chance" (Stolberg 23). Even though this article touches on the opposing narrative, it skims over the argument providing more support for the master narrative. The closing statement of the article ends with: "[Jésica Santillán] is a 17-year-old girl who no one wants to see die" (Stolberg 23). This quotation promotes Jésica Santillan's master narrative by implying that the second transplant is necessary and also exhibits a sentimental quality. This ethical dilemma exists but most of the news coverage omits this information or in the case of the article, the reporter diminishes the impact of the competing narrative with countering statements to call attention to the master narrative.

With persuasive writing, the media develops Jésica Santillán's story into an emotional narrative by highlighting her innocence and highlighting the medical mistake of a well-respected hospital. As an argument designed to invoke feelings from the public audience of the media, the master narrative neglects to include or expand upon other competing narratives that could weaken the sentimentality of Jésica's narrative. The media creates a dualism between the Santilláns and Duke University Hospital. Jésica's naivety and the hospital's blunder are both asserted to build this dualism of good and evil, thus sentimentalizing an incident for the media's audience. Constructing narratives is a necessity for the media because it tailors to consumers. Using emotion and glorifying incidents make events more interesting to consumers, allowing the media's survival in a consumer-based, capitalist society. In Joan Didion's essay, the victim of the incident was sentimentalized as the ideal, middle upper-class woman and conflated with the spirit of New York City. Her brutal attack was used as a scapegoat for New York City's problems, displaying how master narratives can serve multiple purposes. Humans have biases and emotions; consequently, the media cannot avoid sentimentalizing stories into narratives.

Villasin 6

Works Cited

Adler, Jerry. "A Tragic Error." <u>Newsweek</u> 3 Mar. 2003:
    20–25.

Barnard, Anne. "Relief turns to shock for family of teen
    given wrong organ type." <u>Boston Globe Online</u>. 19
    Feb. 2003
    <http://www.boston.com/dailyglobe2/050/nation/
    Relief_turns_to_shock_for_family_of_teen_given_
    wrong_organ_type>.

Buncombe, Andrew. "Teenage Girl Facing Death After
    Organ Blunder at Top U.S. Clinic." <u>The
    Independent</u> 20 Feb. 2003. <u>Expanded Academic ASAP.</u>
    Gale Group Databases. University of Washington
    Libraries, Seattle, WA. 25 Feb. 2003 <http://ww.info-
    trac.galegroup.com>.

Griffin, Lisa. "Retransplantation of Multiple Organs: How
    Many Organs Should One Individual Receive?"
    <u>Medscape</u> (2002): 92-96. 20 August 2002 <http://
    www.medscape.com/viewarticle/439666_print>.

Kher, Ulmesh, and Paul Cuadros. "A Miracle Denied." <u>Time</u>
    3 Mar. 2003:61.

Stolberg, Sheryl Gay, and Lawrence K. Altman. <u>The New
    York Times</u> 21 Feb. 2003:5. <u>LexisNexis Academic</u>. Reed
    Elsevier Inc. University of Washington Libraries, Seattle,
    WA. 25 Feb. 2003 <www.lexisnexis.com>.

3.

Media Hype

Erin Thurston

"Ordinarily trade policy is b-o-r-i-n-g. Its complexity makes it largely incomprehensible, even to some reporters covering it. It does not usually produce graphic TV footage. If it does, the impact on public opinion and public policy will depend on how the events come across" (A Page). The potential exists in the media to create a well-informed society. However often times stories are presented with a central theme, around which facts are manipulated to further a specific argument. The theme chosen usually has little to do with the real issues of the event. The media's coverage of the protests against the World Trade Organization last winter presented a narrow view of the issues the protests raised. The event, intended as a peaceful protest, morphed into the media-coined "Battle in Seattle." The issues thus changed from the environment, the threat of globalization and human and labor rights, to tear-gas, rubber bullets and billy-clubs. We looked to place blame for Seattle's looted stores and graffittied buildings rather than confront more complex issues of global trade. As a result, we came to associate the terms tear-gas, bobby-club, rubber bullets and anarchy with police, protesters, Seattle and the WTO.

The media has the potential to greatly influence their readership with the information they choose to present. With any piece of writing, there will always be a voice, whether slightly or largely biased. The responsibility of the media is to inform the public solely with reliable facts. However, the handpicking of facts and interpretation of selected ideas creates a biased view disguised as news (based on the integrity of the source medium). Joan Didion, in her essay entitled "Sentimental Journeys," using New York as her model discusses the function of a sentimental narrative in the media.

Thurston 2

> The insistent sentimentalization of experience, which is to
> say the encouragement of such reliance, is not new . . . A
> preference for broad strokes, for the distortion and flatten-
> ing of character and the reduction of events to narrative,
> has been for well over a hundred years the heart of the
> way the city presents itself . . . 8 million stories and all the
> same story, each devised to obscure not only the city's
> actual tensions of race and class but also, more signifi-
> cantly, the civic and commercial arrangements that
> rendered those tensions irreconcilable. (Didion 121-2)

The transformation of an event to a narrative takes away the
triviality of the event by narrowing the story. This narrowing
discards the more complex and rectifiably difficult problems.
The sentimental approach of the media clouds the real issues
of an event.

The sentimental narrative expressed by the local Seattle
media was one of remorse for the vandalized state of "our
beautiful city" and the violence that occurred on its streets. The
article entitled "Gas, Broken Glass and a City in Dismay" per-
sonifies Seattle as a gentle, innocent creature that had been
sheltered from the cruelties of the world before the arrival of
the WTO. "The world had arrived on our doorstep, but had we
really wanted its visit?" (Keene). The narrative produced is one
similar to the rape of a young girl. Taking into account loss of
innocence, being taken advantage of and forced to deal with
the consequences of an unwanted event, the narratives of
Seattle and the young girl are interchangeable. A victimized city
created rather a strange headline for trade protest. The media
portrays Seattle as a victim violently and forcibly brought into
the dealings of the WTO and its opposition:

> In the 24 hours between Monday's big pot party down-
> town and yesterday's real-deal riot, Seattle's sense of itself

Thurston 3
seemed to mature and change. Whatever intrigue or tolerance people might have felt about hosting thousands of
demonstrators during the World Trade Organization's
meeting quickly wore off under a haze of tear gas and
vandalism. (Keene)

The use of the word "riot" injects into the readers' mind a
sense of severe and violent upheaval. The article depicts the
protests as an unwanted event burdening Seattle and creating a nuisance in city's daily grind. The sentimentalized Seattle
not only created a haze around the protest but also injected a
false perception of the event into the public's mind.

    With the attention on violence and a sentimentalized
Seattle, the real issues of the day were completely lost. The
Seattle Times predicted the week prior that this would happen. "Seattle is a stage, but important messages about labor
rights, environmental quality and social justice will be lost
when the first brick smashes through a window"
(Impassioned). The focus changed from peaceful protests to
violence and a victimized Seattle, which returns the American
public to their comfort zone in that the public is easily con-
solable. Society doesn't know how to deal with the issues
presented by the protests, but violence is portrayed daily in
the media, making it a graspable issue.

    With headlines such as "Police Fire Pepper Spray at
WTO Protesters"(CNN), "Seattle Police Charge as Protesters
Challenge Curfew National Guard Troops Head to City"(CNN)
and "WTO Protests a Throwback to 60's: Civil Unrest Has Not
Reached the Level Seen in Seattle Since Baby Boomers
Witnessed the Riots of the Mid-60's" (Vancouver Sun), violence presents itself as the primary issue in the media's
accounts of the protests. All of these headlines contain negative connotations toward the protests. Implementing the

Thurston 4

National Guard suggests that the city was completely out of control when in actuality only a very small percentage of people were causing a disturbance.

"The narrative comforts us, in other words, with the assurance that the world is knowable, even flat" (Didion 127). By portraying the protests as riots, the public's attention is turned to violence. In turn, "Seattlites" outraged by the destruction began jumping into action to save their city by cleaning up after the vandalism. Television reporters were on hand to broadcast "what Seattle is really all about: kindness." The false narrative of "a once beautiful city in shambles" produced by the media allows the public to ignore the real issues. "The imposition of a sentimental or false, narrative on the disparate and often random experience that constitutes the life of a city or a country will be rendered merely illustrative, a series of set pieces, or performance opportunities" (Didion 131). Most Seattlites see the city's only problem as a random happening that can and must be quickly fixed and discarded from the mind. The false impression of vandalism as the main tragic consequence allowed Seattle's problems to be solved just as soon as the damages were repaired.

Cleaning up graffiti may make citizens feel better about the issues being presented to us by the media, but the media presents a rather limited scope of the protests. The WTO makes decisions that have a large impact on the environment, foreign relations and humans. In the Venezuelan Gas Case, the Environmental Protection Agency chose to use the U.S. industry average for gasoline refineries as a starting point to measure foreign refineries. U.S. standards are much higher and the WTO established that U.S. rules are "discriminatory" and the EPA would have to change its standard based on the rules outlined by the WTO (WTO Score). Europe wants nothing to do with America's hormone-treated beef, however the

Thurston 5

WTO has ruled that Europe cannot discriminate by banning altered beef. The United States chooses not to import shrimp caught by methods that kill endangered sea turtles. The WTO responded by "declaring a blanket ban on unilateral trade controls designed to protect the environment"(WTO Score). The WTO cares that every country is able to trade freely and to them the costs, the environment and human safety, are irrelevant. These rulings violate each country's individual freedom to determine what is best for themselves and the world. All of these issues are of great importance and complexity, but the media ignores them. The media's failure to address the more complicated issues of the WTO reflects the media's, as well as our own, intrigue toward violent headlines.

The media's narrativization of violence as the core of Seattle's problem with the WTO obscures the underlying theme that global destruction (the environment, human rights violations, etc.) is created by our selfishness. We consume the products of moral-less corporations and are self-indulgent in our consumption (especially Americans). Hardly any American consumers buy solely out of need. Retail is about want, greed and image. Most Americans don't care that American companies are moving overseas for the purpose of avoiding U.S. environmental laws and exploiting factory workers. What they care about is finding a balance between dirt-cheap prices and quality, in other words, a sweatshop-made product. The sweatshop workers are basically sentenced to die as slaves to corporations: given the minuscule amount (usually below a living wage) the workers are paid. They'll never be able to escape the cheap labor trap created by greedy corporations. Humans don't like to hear of other humans suffering. The information causes discomfort for not helping the situation in addition to guilt for the large gap in physical well being. Yet another potentially heart-wrenching narrative, capable of

Thurston 6

social and political action (if depicted accurately and not sug-arcoated), passed over for tear-gas.

The media chooses not to raise the underlying narratives. By focusing on violence and Seattle's "sad state," the media dismisses the real issues. So why is the looting of Starbucks more story-worthy than the environment or exploited work-ers? What is so enticing about violence? It's a regurgitated narrative; we know the story. We are not really disturbed by the media-hyped riots; we've seen it all before; in Los Angeles, Miami and Washington DC. The media's common usage of the violence narrative (presented to the public nearly everyday) keeps the public within their realm of "disbelief" though they are actually hardly altered from any previous mindset.

The majority of the public does not understand the WTO. It brought disruption to Seattle making it a dangerous and complicated subject better left ignored and condemned for violent demonstrations. The media plays off of the Public's fascination with violence because it sells well and is easily explained. Didion cites William R. Taylor of the State University of New York at Stony Brook in his discussion of "popular New York stories. . . . These stories, with their 'focus on individuals' plights', their 'absence of social or political implications' and 'ideological neutrality,' provided a 'miraculous form of social glue" (Didion 124). The dismissal of the ideology suggested by the WTO controversy allowed for the social union of Seattlites through the creation of a community narrative. With the focus on the false narrative of violence plaguing the inno-cent Emerald City, the social and political questions that should have been raised were either briefly mentioned in the ends of articles or simply ignored altogether. The media wrongly portrays events by emphasizing tangent ideas that in turn inspire a false solution. An unbiased story is hard to come by. What did you read in the paper this morning?

Thurston 7

Works Cited

"A Page One Issue?" <u>Human Rights for Workers Bulletin</u> 08
    October 1999. <http://www.sensor.com/wr-wto.htm&
    ti-- Human+Rights+for+Workers+October+8,+1999
    &top=>

Didion, Joan. "Sentimental Journeys." <u>Academic Discourse:</u>
    <u>Readings for Argument and Analysis</u>. Ed. Gail Stygall.
    New York: Harcourt, 1999.

"Impassioned, Peaceful WTO Protests Welcome." <u>The</u>
    <u>Seattle Times</u> 21 November 1999. <http:archives.
    seattletimes.com/cgibin/texis/web/vortex/display?slug=
    proted&dat=19991121>

Karon, Tony. "A WTO Primer A Look at the World Trade
    Organization and the Issues in Seattle." <u>Time Daily</u>
    <u>Online</u> 02 December 1999. <http: //info seek. go.
    com/-.@win---search&sv-- M6&IK=noframes&nh=
    IE5&qt--Time+Nlaga.zine&oq=&url=http%SA//cgi.
    pathfinder.com/time/&top=1 486>.

Keene, Linda. "Gas, Broken Glass and a City in Dismay."
    <u>The Seattle Times</u> 01 December 1999. <http://archives.
    seattletimes.com/egi- bin/texis/web/vortex/
    display?slug=mood&date=19991201>

Mulgrew, Ian. "WTO Protests a Throwback to '60's: Civil
    Unrest Has Not Reached the Level in Seattle Since
    Baby Boomers Witnessed the Riots of the Mid-
    1960's." <u>The Vancouver Sun</u> 02 December 1999.
    <http://www.vancouversuncom>

Barrett, Katherine and Greg Leteure. "Police Fire Pepper
    Spray at WTO Protesters." CNN 30 November 1999.
    <http://cnn.com/US/9911/30/WTO.02>

"Seattle Police Charge as Protesters Challenge Curfew."
    CNN 1 December 1999. <http://cnncom/
    US/9911/30/WTO.05>

"WTO Scorecard WTO and Free Trade vs. the Environment
    and Public Health: 4-O." <u>Friends of the Earth</u>.
    <www.foe.org/international/wto/scorecard.pdf>

Samples of Argument Papers (as submitted by students without further editing)

1.

Stringer 1

Best-Interest or Self-Interest?

Stacy Stringer

Webster's New Riverside Dictionary defines feminism as: "advocacy of the political and socioeconomic equality of men and women" (257). According to Suzanne Gordon, Webster's is mistaken. She wants her readers to believe that the original feminist movement "sought to balance work with love, hierarchy with healing, individualism with community" (2) and that it strived to unite our nation's people in warm, empathetic harmony. She boasts about transformative feminist's "value of relationships, interdependence, and collaboration" (2). However, the underlying and somewhat incriminating goal of "transformative" feminism, which Gordon explains and advocates, is to completely restructure society, change the landscape of the masculine world and create a nation which will satisfy only their own desires. Also in her essay, Gordon divides feminism into two harsh, illdefined, black and white categories without any regard for the shades of gray in between. She criticizes what she refers to as "adaptive" feminists as being women who have "joined men in denigrating the care-giving activities that they used to protect, preserve, and defend" (6). Her criticisms do not radiate the value of interdependence and collaboration. Unfortunately, what Gordon seems to overlook is the fact that the goals of her transformative feminists cannot become reality unless these women recognize and respect the adaptive feminists and their accomplishments.

    If Gordon looked at the feminist movement realistically, she would realize that the women she refers to as "adaptive" feminists have already accomplished much of what they set out to do. They have gotten a foothold in the job market and gained (not all but most of) the respect they deserve for being highly intelligent, capable human beings. Furthermore, their aspirations of becoming doctors or lawmakers did not stem solely from the desire to break into the male dominated work force and reconstruct it, but simply from the idea that they should be able to set their own standards and create their own happiness without anyone, male or female, placing restrictions on them.

At the same time that these women have been striving to make their dreams a reality, they have continued to function as nurturing, care-giving individuals. Contrary to Gordon's implied belief that a woman cannot possess both adaptive and transformative qualities, many of the women who have chosen to pursue their career in a competitive workforce bring compassion and caring with them. For example, female legislators may be more apt than men to favor a bill based on its benefits to women, children, or the elderly. Furthermore, due to the caring nature Gordon speaks so highly of, they will likely look at how a law will effect society rather than how it will benefit themselves. Also, it is often argued that female gynecologists are better than males at understanding and sympathizing with the pains of labor or the mental anguish of having an abnormal pap smear. Being women, they cannot (and do not) deny the instincts which are inherent to almost all females of any species and besides this, many find this to be not only helpful in their work, but desirable. They choose to let their feminine instincts influence their actions and guide them in the decisions they make in their careers.

However, regardless of their admirable accomplishments, Gordon still reprimands the adaptive feminists for being women who "pay lip service to the work of their more

Stringer 3

care-oriented sisters" (5). She makes unfair generalizations about ambitious competitive women:

> For equal-opportunity feminism, then, the ultimate goal is traditional American success--making money; relentlessly accumulating possessions; capturing and hoarding power, knowledge, access, and information; grasping and clinging to fame, status and privilege; proving that you are good enough, smart enough, driven enough to get to the top, and tough enough to stay there. (5)

These criticisms only serve as a weak cover for her hostile feelings toward her more goal-oriented "sisters." Is it possible that her ill-will toward these women stems from her bitterness of being among the "women who have been left behind"? (6) It is sad that she cannot overlook the benevolent differences between the two groups of feminists and begin to recognize the bonds that unite all women in sisterhood. Women, as a whole, should appreciate and encourage any actions whatsoever which bring respect to the female gender. This cannot be done by taking sides, placing blame or favoring extremes.

It would only benefit the women of the transformative movement if they could stop harboring bad feelings toward the ambitious tendencies of the adaptive feminists and begin to exercise the interdependence they so highly value. Even if we were to embrace transformative feminism as the ultimate goal, it is hard to imagine the transformation ever taking place without the drive and determination displayed by adaptive feminists. Is Barbara Eden supposed to fold her arms and nod her head and suddenly, transformative feminism in all its glory will be upon us? How is this "transformation" to take

Stringer 4

place? Gordon does not tell us. Consequently, I will argue that even if one abhors the aggressive tendencies of the modern adaptive female, it is impossible to change society's standards by taking on a passive role as transformative feminists have done. It is common knowledge that if one wants to overthrow a power structure of any kind, one must first seek out and obtain the power to do so.

In conclusion, adaptive feminism, however unsatisfactory it may appear to Gordon, has far more to offer society than transformative feminism's wishlist. To Gordon's credit, she is accurate in pointing out the many strengths of the modern female. We are a competent, intelligent, and yes, caring gender to which society owes much gratitude. Nonetheless, many scholars have pointed to the duality of each human existence, the vigor within, as well as the abilities to feel and to care for others. Going too far in one direction, as Gordon has done, robs the modern woman of a vital aspect of her being and fails to recognize all that she has accomplished.

2.

Perrin 1

Definition of Family
Christopher Perrin

American society is far from static. Everyday, the definitions of American values, families, beliefs and attitudes are changing. As society changes, many things become more important. Among these things is the importance of television. Where once TV was little more than an entertainment, it is now a way of life for millions of Americans. However, certain things become more important to Americans, other elements of American society have become less important. A key element that has lost its importance is the "traditional" definition of the family unit. No longer do Americans think that a family should be two parents, one or more children and possibly a grandparent or other relative. The definition has become more liberal; families can now be one parent and children, grandparents and children or sometimes two parents of the same sex and children. Also, Americans do not look at the happy families pictured in <u>Leave It To Beaver</u> and <u>Father Knows Best</u> or even <u>The Cosbys</u> and think that they represent the "normal family." Today, Americans can turn on the television and see television programs that offer a much more accurate picture of their own family. For better or for worse, because of the constantly changing definition of the family, television programs such as <u>Roseanne,</u> <u>Married With Children</u> and <u>The Simpsons</u> represent a "normal" family. To prove this point, I will first examine the definition of a "normal" family and then I will examine three of the most heavily criticized television families to show how they represent a normal family.

First, the definition of a normal family needs to be discussed. In any discussion of a normal family, one thing must be remembered. There is no such thing as a normal family. A normal family never existed, nor will it ever. The definition of the family unit in the United States has never been a constant. Even during the fifties, a decade which brought about the famous Cleaver family, the traditional family did not mirror the family seen on <u>Leave It To Beaver</u>. Throughout history up until today, the family should be seen as a support system or an institution to help satisfy the needs of its members.

These needs are basic to human survival and include the need for food and water, shelter, physical security and some emotional support and development. This theory of what a traditional family should provide is supported by Thomas Maslow's hierarchy of needs. Maslow stated that to reach the peak of self actualization, an individual must first satisfy physical needs, then security needs, then love needs, esteem needs and then that individual can become self-actualized. By using the definition of the family unit I have provided, physical, security, love and esteem needs are all provided by the family.

While the family is providing these needs, the family does not have to be a happy family or even be considered "functional." Many times, even a dysfunctional family can provide these needs to its members. The family will have its share of problems, of course, but oftentimes these problems do not hamper the development of its units. For example, in a separated family, that is one where the parents openly do not live together but are not yet divorced, the family members can still receive physiological needs, the parents will still buy food for their children and will have one way or another to feed themselves, the parents usually continue to love their children and the children often harbor affection for their parents. Thus, even though the family is considered dysfunctional, it can still offer support for the children and through the children for the parents. However, it is important to note that I do not believe all dysfunctional families fit the definition. Households where one member abuses another member physically or sexually do not meet the definition for the family because in these families, love and emotional support can hardly ever exist when one or more members are abusive. Therefore, in this paper, I refuse to condone abusive families and I refuse to label them normal or functional.

Now that the definition for a family is set, it is time to see how the television families mentioned above successfully satisfy the definition of a normal family. First, the television show <u>Roseanne</u> does satisfy the conditions provided for a normal family. The family in the television series is the normal, two-parent family with three children. The criticisms of this show include the horrible treatment of the children by Dan and Roseanne and the lack of morals in the children. However, the children in the television show are well provided for, they have never been thrown out on to the street, and <u>Roseanne</u> episodes try to teach their children the difference between right and wrong and other ethical issues. I remember one episode when the eldest daughter moved out and Roseanne was in tears over the loss of her daughter. Basically, while Roseanne and Dan do not treat their children very well, they always provide for their offspring and show love for them.

The next program I will review is <u>Married With Children</u>, starring the Bundy family. Again, critics of this program argue the Bundys do not love their children, do not even have food in the house and teach their children that lying, cheating and valuing money over all else is alright. However, this is not the case. These television situation comedies make fun of the traditional family unit, but if the critics were to watch this program, they would see the Bundy family does meet the definition of the family. First, the Bundys are never poorly fed. They always find some food, whether that be the single box of bon bons in the freezer, in which case the family goes out to eat, or if the family goes to eat at the nudie bar, the Bundys are always fed. Plus, the family always has a roof to sleep under. Even though Al is only a shoe salesman, he can afford a four bedroom, three story household for his family. Thus, the physical needs of the family are provided for by the

family. In addition to physical needs, the Bundys provide emotional support to the family unit. Al is often concerned with
the activities of his children, especially if they can make him
money. One time, Al donated ten pints of blood to make
money to cover his daughter's debts. Yes, that is ten pints of
blood, the doctors found a hidden pint in his brain. Al and
Peg often fight, but every family has its fights every now and
then. While they fight, Al and Peg also have many good times
during the episodes, even if that does mean ordering pizza
late at night. The family atmosphere of the Bundys is not
always totally kind, but they do care for each other and provide for each others' physical and emotional needs.

    The final television show I will address is the The
Simpsons. The Simpsons have come under heavy fire for the
reasons that have caused the other shows to be criticized, but
The Simpsons have the added stigma of being a cartoon,
but at the same time it addresses many adult issues. The
Simpsons are criticized because Homer, the father, rarely ever
treats his children well and Bart, the third grader, often says
"I'm Bart Simpson, who the hell are you?" and uses other
foul words. While it is true that the cartoon characters in The
Simpsons should not use bad words, the criticism about the
quality of parenting of the Simpson parents should not be
criticized as harshly. The Simpsons are actually, at times,
model parents. They love their children immensely, provide
for their physical needs at all times. Marge, the mother,
always prepares dinner for her children and Homer provides a
roof over their heads and money when Bart needs it. Marge
is more than supportive of Lisa, the second grader's, academic and musical hobbies as she never misses a quiz bowl or
music recital and often drags Homer and Bart along. Like
father and son, Homer and Bart often think on the same
wavelength. In one episode, Bart and Homer have a psychic

link to one another, and in another episode Bart meets
Homer at the door and they both blurt "Monster Truck Rally."
Maggie, the baby of the family, is cared for primarily by
Marge, but Homer does have pictures of his youngest plas-
tered all over his workplace and he cares for her greatly. In
the episode where the children are taken away by the social
welfare office, which occurred because of misperceptions on
the part of the welfare office, Marge and Homer are totally
distraught over the loss of their children, and Bart and Lisa
desire only to be taken back to their home. In addition to
love, the Simpson children receive emotional development
from their parents, also. In one episode, Homer will not let
Bart go to the Itchy and Scratchy movie and he turns out to
become Chief Justice of the Supreme Court, after having a
successful wrecking crew business. Also, Lisa attends college
in England and loves her family enough to turn down the
man of her dreams for the Simpsons. Finally, Homer and
Marge offer each other much emotional support. Many
episodes center around the steps that Homer takes to save
his marriage with Marge, like snuggling and going to marriage counseling, and the things that Marge does to stay with
Homer, such as going to the nuclear power plant instead of
going to the Fiesta Terrace for a romantic interlude with the
bowling pro.

    Times are changing and society is changing along with
them. Gone are the days of families huddling around the
radio to listen to a program and gone are the conceptions
that every family should and does mirror the family from
Father Knows Best. The traditional, more conservative notion
of the two-parent, several child and a pet family has been
replaced by a much more liberal definition of what a family
can be and still maintain its status as a family. No family is
alike, but a group of people can be a family if they provide

Perrin 7

for the physical and emotional well being of their members. Because no family is alike, the families seen on television can and do represent what some American families are. Whether this is good for society or not, if the family members are taken care of physically and emotionally, then the family has served its purpose.

3.

Bohannan 1

Keep the Doors Open

Rebecca S. Bohannan

Today, our society is being faced with many powerful issues dealing with education. The issues are broad and individual. For example, violence in schools interferes with education; costs for a college education are outrageously high. One issue that is receiving a great deal of attention today is open vs. closed admission policies in public universities. Currently, the University of Kansas is an open admissions school. It is not only important but a must for KU to continue an open admissions policy in order to provide equal and necessary educational opportunities to the citizens of Kansas.

One individual who strongly opposes open admissions is Vanderbilt professor, Chester E. Finn, Jr. In his article, "Raising the Stakes," he argues that closed admissions policy will force students to work harder in school and will improve the entire structure of education from kindergarten through high school. He believes the possible reformation of education

Bohannan 2

would be like a "domestic desert storm" (11). Also, he hopes for a uniting of universities and the economy to enforce higher expectations and standards for graduates. Many of these reforms have enormous positive potential; however, enforcing closed admissions policy is the wrong direction to take on this issue.

Undoubtedly, many problems accompany this discriminatory policy. Finn's plan for closed admissions would force high school students to focus solely on academics. However, academics aren't the only part of education. High school is a chance for students to become involved in their school as well as to learn. Students can choose to participate in sports, fine arts, clubs, organizations, plays, musicals, community services, etc. All of these activities give students a chance to develop strong social and team-working skills which are both necessary skills for today's work force. Employees need to be able to communicate with and motivate other employees. They must also be able to work together to ensure quality of goods and services. Besides developing social skills, these extracurricular activities give students who are more involved with the school a higher self-esteem. Students who are more involved with the school and have a strong self-esteem aren't likely to drop out. Also, extracurricular activities look terrific on scholarship applications. Universities want to reward students who are eager to be involved in their academic surrounding. If a closed admissions policy is enforced at KU, then more students of this state might be forced to drop these extra-curricular activities. In doing so, they might be forced to lose a vital part of education.

It is important to consider the possible effects from the pressure of closed admissions policies. Sadly enough, many students who struggle with school or feel like a failure would more likely give up or quit. High schools would receive a

Bohannan 3

dangerous increase in the number of dropouts. These dropouts would consider the idea of passing college entrance exams to be a dream. Students who work very hard and diligently in school but don't always receive the highest grades will be left behind. When discussing this issue Finn states, "high schools would no longer need to provide gobs of remedial education because they wouldn't be enrolling hordes of people who need it." In essence, Finn's plan for closed admissions will completely exclude slower learners from Kansas schools.

Possibly, some students may not realize their academic potential until they are in a serious academic atmosphere like college. They too deserve the chance to discover that potential. Professor Jeff Beasely, KU teacher, was one of these cases. He ignored academics in high school but he still decided to come to KU. He did extremely poorly academically his freshman year. However, because of open admission policies he was given the chance to transform, and now is an outstanding professor. Reasons like these are perfect examples of why the continuance of open admissions is so important.

Open admission policies are quite beneficial for several reasons. This policy allows students the chance to change. No one should be denied the opportunity to pursue a career because they were immature and foolish at times in high school. Open admissions provides this kind of equal opportunity to remedial and to successful students alike. Students who have done very well in pre-secondary school are rewarded by being able to take honors courses at the university. Americans are accustomed to many freedoms, and freedom of education needs to be one of them. Students need the freedom to attend college and shape their minds. They need to be able to better themselves in order to get

Bohannan 4

good jobs. Open admissions policy secures this freedom for all students. These are reasons why open admission policies cannot be ignored or overlooked. Can our country afford to start closing doors on our students? Can we risk the devastation of telling them "you aren't good enough and we won't allow you to become good enough?" If we can, then the education problems will only become more overwhelming. Students will miss out on extracurricular activities, dropout rates will increase, and students will be denied freedom of education. That is why this university must continue to open the door to success by opening its doors to all.

Writing Projects

Writing Project 6.1

Write an analysis paper for your teacher and classmates, using one of the three prompts below:

a. Select a text from the readings in Chapter 5 (DiPardo) or 6 (Lippi-Green) and analyze the writer's assumptions. What claims does the writer make, and what assumptions does the writer make to connect the evidence to those claims? On what basis does the writer make the argument he or she makes?

b. Lippi-Green, in her chapter on Disney films, examines the language of the films to claim that Disney films teach children to discriminate. Apply Lippi-Green's analysis to your own analysis of the language of a different genre of films (perhaps war films, romances, comedies, science fiction, horror films, kung-fu films, action films, or any other set of films with enough in common to be considered a type). Make a claim about the significance of the language used in those films.

c. Analyze the Web site of an advocacy organization—that is, one that takes a clear stand on a controversial public issue. Some examples of advocacy organizations include the Democratic, Republican, and Libertarian parties, Greenpeace, Amnesty International, the National Rifle Association, or the

National Humane Society. Examine the use of visuals as well as language to see how the organization advocates its view. You will, of course, need to make a claim based on what you discover in your analysis.

Writing Project 6.2

If you wrote an analysis of the language of a different genre of film in Writing Project 6.1b, turn that analysis paper into an argument paper. Building on the findings from your analysis, make an argument that tries to convince readers to take a position on the subject (for example, whether you think readers should protest the films) using evidence to support your argument.

Writing Project 6.3

Write an argument paper for your teacher and classmates on one of the two topics below:

a. Respond to Lippi-Green's chapter on the effects of the language used in Disney films. Is there another way to interpret the evidence she finds? Is there other evidence you could offer that leads to a different claim?
b. Write an argument paper on a topic of your choice. Be sure to select a topic suitable for argument papers, according to what you learned in your genre analysis.

Writing Project 6.4

Write a critique of either the analysis paper or argument paper, and address it to your classmates and instructor for this course. You may want to draw on the Questions for Critiquing Genre in Box 4.1 (p. 161), as well as refer to the sample critiques in that chapter. Make sure to state and then develop a *claim* that evaluates some aspect of the genre's effects. Then support your claim with *evidence* taken from the genre. In the process of developing your claim, keep in mind that you will not only need to describe the effects a genre has, but also to evaluate the strengths and/or limitations of these effects.

Writing Project 6.5

Use analysis or argument to explore a topic of your choice. Based on your analysis or argument, decide on a claim you want to make about the topic, who you would want to hear your claim, and what purpose you want to achieve. Then choose a genre that lets you make your claim for that situation. For example, you might write a guest column for the campus newspaper analyzing its minimal coverage of women's sports or an editorial arguing for more coverage of women's sports. Or you might write a review analyzing the recent movie shown on campus or write a proposal to the student activities board or student council arguing that they bring in more independent or art films.

7 Writing Research-Based Genres

The previous two chapters have helped you understand some scenes of academic writing and the genres used within them, particularly those of the first-year writing course. Both analysis papers and argument papers often use **sources**—that is, they respond to or draw from information and ideas in texts written by other people. An analysis paper might analyze a particular article and/or cite research about a subject, and an argument paper might well include facts found in various other sources to support the writer's argument. Some assignments in first-year writing courses, though, have finding and using sources as a *primary purpose*, as one of the primary learning goals for the writing task.

These research-based writing assignments can require a wide range of kinds of research, from books to observations. They also can ask for a wide range of genres, from a traditional academic research paper to a proposal to city hall. Despite their range, these research-based writing assignments in first-year writing courses typically have common purposes and expectations that arise from the place of the writing course in the academic scene.

In its broadest sense, **research** is called for in any situation where you must find information you do not already know. You are doing research when you look up a word in a dictionary, when you check the newspaper for the latest price of a stock, when you search the Internet for music to download, and when you ask your friends if they have seen a movie you are considering seeing. In college or university scenes, research usually entails gathering information from multiple sources about one subject, and research projects present your conclusions based on that information. The sources of information vary, from traditional library books and articles to literary works to interviews and surveys to experimentation in the laboratory. Thus, writing assignments for research projects in writing courses vary widely in the kinds of sources they ask students to use and the kinds of subjects they investigate.

This chapter will explore the general purposes of research-based writing assignments in writing courses, and will analyze in detail one particular genre, the researched **position paper**, in which writers conduct substantial research into a given subject in order to discover and articulate their position on it. First, we will examine the role of research in academic scenes and in the first-year writing course scene in particular. Then we will explore various types of research and types of research genres, helping you learn how to choose a genre in which to carry out your research, in case you have the chance to choose what use you make of the research you conduct. In the last half of this chapter, we will help you analyze and write the researched position paper, one common kind of research-based writing assignment that may help enlighten you about how research is presented in many academic scenes.

Writing Activity 7.1

Describe a form of research you have done outside of your courses—research on buying a DVD player, a computer, or even a car; research on movies, restaurants or concerts; research on colleges or universities; research on trip destinations, etc. What were the objectives of your research? What techniques for researching did you use, and what sources did you consult? How did your research factor into your decision making or into the action you took?

Research in Different Academic Scenes

While this chapter will focus on research-based assignments as they function for the writing classroom, it is important to keep in mind as you move beyond this writing course that the label "research paper" is used in other courses. One survey of teachers at a large, public university found that what teachers called "research papers" ranged from responses to a single source to thorough reviews of secondary sources to complex primary research. Research projects for other courses may reflect various notions of how you go about using research to discover what you think. While all academic disciplines share some common assumptions about the importance of reasoning and logic, of critical examination of ideas, and of the power of knowledge, they differ in which ideas they consider interesting, how they examine those ideas, what knowledges they seek, and how the genres of research-based writing are used to accomplish special purposes.

In your science courses, you may be asked to write a **research report,** a detailed presentation of your laboratory research following the **scientific method** (introduction, methods, results, discussion). Or you may be assigned to write what is called a **research review,** an analysis of existing scientific studies, used in both the natural sciences and the social sciences. In some courses in the social sciences, like psychology, sociology, or anthropology, you might be asked to work within the genre of the **case study report,** a genre that reflects these disciplines' interest in observing human behavior (individual "cases") and follows a format that reflects the scientific nature of these observations (with headings that usually follow a format of reviewing the literature, setting the context for the study, presenting the research questions, and sharing the results and their implications). These are just a few of the research-based genres that reflect differing approaches to and methods of research based on differing disciplinary objectives.

The writing-class research projects you do are meant to prepare you for the various research activities you will encounter in different academic scenes, because they draw on highly valued research skills and because they reveal vividly the value many academics place on information, analysis, and multiple perspectives as the sources of truth. As we focus on research-based writing within the writing course scene, we will examine how these genres, while particular to the writing course scene, also share assumptions and methods with other academic scenes.

Collaborative Activity 7.1

Describe a research assignment that you carried out in any of your high school courses or in another course in college. Explain the subject of your research, the type of research methods used, and the format for presenting your findings. Then, in small groups, share your findings. Look for any shared research objectives among the assignments. What accounts for these similarities? How are the differences in the assignments a result of the different academic scenes and situations?

Research within Writing Courses

A primary purpose for writing teachers assigning research projects and for students writing them is for students to learn the process of conducting and presenting scholarly research. This motivation reflects one of the shared objectives of writing courses: To teach and develop skills relevant to other college-level courses, and, in turn, to reflect the shared objective of colleges and universities to produce and disseminate knowledge. As genres functioning within the scene of the writing course, then, research-based writing assignments share some common assumptions and traits that derive from the values and beliefs of colleges and universities about the nature of knowledge and truth.

Research projects assume that what you already know can be supplemented by testing your beliefs, examining what happens in the world, and discovering what others know. It is not enough to think something; you must test or examine that thought against evidence or information. Although the kinds of sources expected in research vary from one academic discipline to the next, in all disciplines writers participate in careful, critical inquiry and conduct studies to answer important questions, to solve problems, to prove cases, to argue positions, and to stake out new claims for knowledge. As a result, as you carry out research in your writing course, a port of entry to other academic scenes, one of the goals is for you to learn skills pertinent to research in other disciplines.

As interpreted by the writing course, good academic research is not just gathering information to support preconceived ideas. Rather, good research is *discovery*:

- Pursuing all relevant perspectives, even those that may seem to contradict others' ideas or your own
- Gathering all the relevant information, even information that might be hard to find
- Examining the logic and assumptions behind what people claim, even claims that you may believe yourself

Good research results in new knowledge but also in new understanding of old ideas. Good research can confirm and support long-held beliefs as well as challenge traditional assumptions. Drawing conclusions based on evidence and information, based on a full knowledge of a subject, is the academic model of educated judgment. In academic scenes, a well-formed conclusion must be well-informed. In writing courses, then, research-based writing assignments ideally have a common purpose: They help writers and readers discover consciously and analytically what they think.

LEARNING TO CONDUCT RESEARCH THROUGH DIFFERENT GENRES

Of the wide variety of genres that research-based writing assignments can encompass, the researched position paper is the one we will describe in some detail in the latter part of this chapter. Increasingly, though, teachers in writing classes are assigning a number of different genres in order to help students learn the research process. You might be asked to write an analysis of a scene based in ethnographic observation as well as library sources. You might be asked to write a case study or research review, modeled after research projects in the social and natural sciences. You might be asked to create a Web site, explaining some subject from multiple perspectives. Or you might be asked to venture into the kinds of public discourse we will explore in the last chapter of this book. You might be asked to use research to write a letter to the editor, a proposal to a person in authority, a guest editorial for your local newspaper, or a letter to your congressional representative. Some writing courses tie research to service-learning projects, with library sources combined with personal experience and reflection. You might write an investigative report for your local media, a brochure for a local organization, a flyer supporting a cause, or a letter soliciting donations of time or money. Research supports so many different kinds of writing that teachers and students can learn the values and skills of research while simultaneously exploring diverse genres and their situations.

As with all writing assignments in the academic scene, as we discussed in Chapter 5 and will discuss further in Chapter 8, *your first task in research-based writing assignments is determining what the assignment requires and what range of choice you have.* You may even be able to select your genre, based on what you want to achieve through your research. For example, if you are interested in researching domestic abuse, you might research how extensive a problem it is among college women and write a letter to your college's Dean of Students proposing new awareness programs in the dorms, or research how extensive the problem is on your campus and write an investigative editorial for your campus newspaper, or survey students in the dorms and create a skit to demonstrate common scenarios for getting out of abusive situations, or research what federal programs exist to rehabilitate abusers and write a letter to your representatives urging more money for such programs. You can use research to support all of these genres and their situations.

Writing Activity 7.2

Select a subject that you can imagine researching, and describe how particular focuses of that research could lead to different genres. If you do not have a subject in mind yet (we discuss selecting subjects in the next section), you might want to use one of these subjects: The nature or availability of homeless shelters, the effectiveness of recycling programs, how people treat animals, the prevalence of fast-food chains, drinking on college campuses, the value of general education courses.

Writing Activity 7.3

When have your ideas about something changed because of new information? For example, can you remember a time when you learned a fact or statistic that surprised you and made you rethink what you believed? Or a time when someone you respected said something that made you think about a belief differently? Or when you met someone who changed your expectations of people in that person's group?

DEVELOPING APPROPRIATE SUBJECTS TO INVESTIGATE

All academic research is expected to help writers discover something new or explore other possibilities for established beliefs: Selecting as a subject to investigate something that you care about can take you beyond just fulfilling an assignment into truly productive, perhaps exciting, research. The world of possible writing subjects becomes narrower in specialized courses and in courses where the writing assignment is more specified, but, even if your assignment is highly specified, you will have room to shape the subject toward your interests. One of the sample papers in this chapter (pp. 408–413), "In Case of Emergency, Please Wait," though written for a general writing course, responded to an assignment that required the writer to incorporate observation of a scene. Within that specified assignment, the writer chose the emergency room as a place to observe, a place that presumably interested him more than others. With a highly specified writing assignment, the challenge might be to find a subject within the specifications that engages the writer's own major concerns and is interesting to the writer as well as to the reader. With a more general assignment, such as the researched position paper, the challenge is to decide on a subject that interests both the writer and reader out of all possible research subjects.

In addition to meeting the assignment's requirements and being interesting, good subjects for research projects should be *manageable*. What makes a subject interesting and manageable, of course, depends on the assignment and the genre that might be required. If you must write a letter to a legislator, for example, your subject will need an angle that will interest that legislator and lend itself to a letter from a constituent. If you must write a case study, you will need to choose a case with significance for your teacher and class and one that you can manage in the time allotted. When you choose your own genre as well as subject, you can begin with what interests you and then find a situation that lets you reach readers who share your interests. But, even then, you will need to consider how to define your subject in a way that will both be interesting to your readers and fit within the generic expectations. If you choose to write a guest column for your school newspaper, for example, your subject will need to interest current students but also be narrow enough to address in a relatively short space.

Engaging the Writer and the Reader

Making your subject interesting depends on your readers as well as your own preferences. In specialized scenes and more specialized research genres, interesting subjects often emerge from unsettled questions in a field of knowledge. Psychologists continue to debate the role of nature and nurture in human personality, for example, so subjects addressing that issue tend to be interesting to other psychologists. The role of English as an international language interests linguists since its role continues to develop and change over time. Literary scholars are interested currently in the literary qualities of unrecognized minority writers, so explorations of particular writers are interesting subjects to them. Even within the general writing course, different assignments will specify different situations, which will have different participants, and these participants will find different subjects interesting. In one writing class, the students and teacher might be reading articles and essays about the value of a liberal education. In another writing class, the participants might be especially interested in political issues, or issues of cultural diversity, or local places, or personal histories. What is interesting depends on the writers and readers, the particular participants in the particular writing scene and situation.

One study of what interested professional readers of proposals in a scholarly field identified specific traits that made the proposals interesting, and we can similarly identify, in a general way, what "interesting" means for a writing subject. An interesting research project subject

* Engages the writers' and readers' major concerns
* Is alive (that is, it involves an issue that has not already been settled)
* Has room for something more to be said

These qualities also reflect the writing course's interest (and the interest of academic scenes) in critical questions, logical debate, and multiple perspectives. That a subject involves *major concerns* will be revealed in part by the existence of published sources on the subject: If others have written about the subject, others have found it interesting in the past. That a subject *remains alive* is suggested by some of those sources being relatively recent and by their representing different versions of the subject, not all agreeing on one perspective. That a subject has *room for something more to be said* is more difficult to judge at first and may require becoming better informed about the subject before deciding, but most engaging and alive subjects have plenty of room for new contributions.

Subjects that leave little room tend to be emotionally loaded ones where positions have hardened into two sides, with the two sides simply restating their positions repeatedly. For example, abortion is a subject of major concern and one that is certainly still alive, but sources on the subject tend to repeat their positions pro and con based on the same evidence others have offered before them. For the subject to have room for new contributions, some new perspectives or information might need to develop. The debate over research using stem cells, for example, opened more room on the subject of abortion because newer stem cell research and abortion share some common principles. A subject with no room for anything new today, then, might become a good subject tomorrow with a different perspective added.

The challenge in writing class research projects is usually finding a sufficiently narrow subject that interests both the readers and you. Your major concerns might range from doing well in school to being a good parent to helping reduce homelessness. Your teacher and the other students probably have widely ranging major concerns; finding something that will engage many of those readers requires connecting your subject to common human needs and aspirations rather than to specialized interests. What are major concerns for most people, and how can your subject link into those concerns? Many subjects suitable for writing course research projects remain alive and open to new things being said; the world is full of unsettled questions and pressing issues, and many smaller or less noticed subjects remain relatively unexplored.

Left free to choose a subject for a writing course research project, writers often begin with what interests them and see if it would suit the scene of academia and what this scene values and emphasizes. Since academics typically treat knowledge as something gained from gathering and critically assessing information, a subject appropriate for a research project should be one about which you *can* gather information and which involves some critical issues. You need to have published sources to draw from, since research-based writing assignments aim to develop your thinking through interaction with other sources. Teachers often advise students to check for published sources before settling on a subject. Checking sources also indicates quickly how interesting the subject is—whether it has engaged the concerns of others, whether it is still an alive subject, and whether there is room for something more to be said on the subject.

Writing Activity 7.4

Consider the subjects of the research projects on pages 408–438. Assess how interesting each subject is for what you know of its context: Does it engage major concerns of the writer? Of the reader? Is the subject alive? Was there room for something more to be said?

Collaborative Activity 7.2

Using the criteria of how engaging, alive, and "roomy" they are, assess for yourself and then discuss with your classmates how interesting you find each of the following subjects for a general writing course (if you decide you would need to seek sources before deciding, make note of that): Getting along with a roommate, nutritional value of campus food services, campus diversity, Title IX, Internet music piracy, the death penalty, safety on campus, raising the minimum wage, the effects of technology on learning, the amount of traffic at a local intersection, controversies stemming from the 2000 presidential election, airport security, legalizing marijuana, reality TV shows, the chemistry of stem cell lines.

Manageability

You may have noticed, in the last activities, that some subjects might be interesting but might not be manageable for one reason or another. The scene of research-based writing assignments in writing classes usually requires that they be completed within the length of one course, for one thing, but some subjects might require more research than can be completed in a few months (the effects of technology on learning might be such a subject). The purpose of the assignment requires that you thoroughly gather information on the subject, but some subjects might have more information than one person could master in one term (the death penalty might be such a subject) or not enough information to use (the subject of getting along with a roommate might not have enough published about it). Some subjects might need a type of research that you might not feel qualified to conduct (the amount of traffic at a local intersection probably needs such research). Others might be covered by research beyond your level of understanding (the chemistry of stem cell lines perhaps). Look again at the sample research projects (pp. 408–438), and note their length. While the length of research projects varies (and your teacher may well specify a length), the expected length determines what subjects will prove manageable. Again, manageability depends on the particular scene: What is manageable for a senior psychology major writing her research thesis is unmanageable for a first-year student completing a researched position paper in four weeks.

A research project in a general writing class typically has some limits:

- It must be researched in a matter of weeks
- You are probably at most only generally knowledgeable about the subject
- You need to use secondary and perhaps primary sources (a distinction to be defined below)

Again, previewing published sources on a possible subject can help you decide whether a subject is manageable or not.

Because research projects often require weeks of work on one issue and require becoming thoroughly knowledgeable about, critically analyzing, and concluding about one subject, writers suffer if they don't choose a subject that sustains their interest, and the resulting written product suffers as well. If research projects are meant to help writers, as well as readers, to discover what they think, they present an opportunity to investigate something with genuine curiosity, to learn about something the writer will be pleased to understand better, and to test or reconsider important ideas or beliefs. Writers of research projects can choose subjects that interest them first, then select those that are also manageable and interesting to others in their scene and situation.

Writing Activity 7.5

Look again at the subjects mentioned in the previous activities, and decide which ones might not be manageable for a four-week paper (of about 5–7 pages) in a one-term first-year writing course. Working within those general subject areas, generate a list of alternative subjects that might be manageable as well as interesting (for example, instead of the chemistry of stem cell lines, research the possible benefits of stem cell research for Huntington's disease).

Writing Activity 7.6

Generate a list of at least ten possible subjects that you might find interesting for a research project assigned in your own writing course. From those ten potential subjects, select five that you think might also be appropriate for the particular readers you will have. Finally, shape each of those five into a subject that you think might be manageable as well. To help you complete this task, refer to the questions for evaluating research subjects listed in Box 7.1.

Box 7.1 *Questions for Evaluating Subjects for Research-Based Writing Assignments*

1. Is the subject appropriate to the scene?
   - Does the subject lend itself to logical analysis and critique?
   - Have multiple perspectives on the subject been published?
2. Is the subject interesting to the writer?
   - Does it engage your major concerns?
   - Is it likely to hold your interest for part of a semester or quarter?
3. Is the subject interesting to potential readers?
   - Can it engage the readers' major concerns?
   - Is it still alive (that is, does it involve an issue that has not already been settled)?
   - Can you create room for something more to be said?
4. Is the subject manageable?
   - Is it narrow/broad enough to fit the page requirement?
   - Do you have enough time to research it?
   - Is there enough published information on the subject? Too much?
   - Does it require some primary research? If so, are you capable of doing that research?
   - Can you understand the secondary sources on the subject?

USING PRIMARY AND SECONDARY RESEARCH

Doing research enables writers to put their own ideas together with others' ideas, to assess whether facts and evidence support the writers' ideas and to discover new perspectives which might complicate and change the writers' thinking. Some writing assignments for research projects lead students to research subjects new to them, ones about which they have no preconceptions or established beliefs. With a new subject, forming a judgment based on research requires, first of all, becoming well-informed. Often, though, students are assigned or choose to research subjects they already know something about. For such subjects, the challenge is not only to become better informed, but also to remain open to learning from the research, including the possibility of changing their minds. Becoming well-informed and learning about a subject may involve researching facts and statistics, studying others' analyses of the same subject, developing new information about a subject, or all of the above.

Writing course research projects range widely in what kinds of research they require. Typically, they require students to gather information from published books and articles and, sometimes, from Internet sources. Increasingly, research-based writing assignments require students to conduct *primary* as well as *secondary* research. **Primary research** is the design and execution of an investigation that *creates new information.* Examples of primary research include experiments, surveys, case studies, ethnographies, and examination of what are called primary texts, texts that themselves serve as evidence, like old newspapers, archives, or literary texts. **Secondary research** involves gathering information that *others* have generated, primarily through published sources like books, journals, newspapers, and magazine articles, and through Web sites. *Although primary research is often described as creating new information, both primary and secondary research create new knowledge since even the use of secondary sources requires synthesizing disparate perspectives and bits of information into your own new understanding.*

PRIMARY RESEARCH   SECONDARY RESEARCH

Conducting:	*Reading:*
Lab experiment	Library book
Case study	Journal article
Clinical experiment	Magazine article
Survey	Web site
Interview	Pamphlet
Archival research	Encyclopedia
Literary interpretation	Newspaper article

Within the scene of the writing class, the particular *situation* of your research project—your purpose for research as well as your subject and its setting—may help determine the kinds of research that will be most useful. For example, some subjects and purposes, by their very nature, might require primary research. Researching the controversial renovation of a historic neighborhood in your town might require you to examine old buildings and old documents; researching high school cliques might call for ethnographic observation of members of the clique and their interactions; and researching the Harlem Renaissance poets would almost certainly require interpretations of primary texts.

As you move from the writing class scene into more specialized disciplinary scenes, you will learn more about how to conduct primary research from the professors in these fields. In order to study how differently people speak, for example, you might need to learn how to record people's speech, learning a different alphabet and how to elicit casual speech, which reflects specialist knowledge within the discipline of linguistics. Learning how to conduct a chemistry experiment requires learning experimental design and chemical properties. Learning to do primary research in any discipline requires developing research skills that are particular to that scene.

Because the writing course functions as a port of entry into other academic disciplines, you can in your writing course begin practicing some of the general primary research methods that we discussed in Chapter 1. Some research methods—such as ethnographic observation, interviews, and surveys—cross several disciplines, so writing courses sometimes use those methods in their research projects; we did this in Chapter 1 when we asked you to observe and describe a scene (see Box 1.1, p. 40, and Box 1.2, pp. 44–45, for example).

If you are dealing with a very current research subject or a local issue on your campus or in your community, you may not be able to find what you need in the library or on the Internet and may need to observe the scene, conduct interviews with people involved, or conduct your own survey (keeping in mind the ethical concerns we noted in Chapter 1, including seeking permission for your observations, gaining consent from those you observe, and maintaining confidentiality). For example, a research project on campus recycling might require you to observe the number of recycling bins on campus and the use of those bins. Or researching the city's controversial proposal to build a mall downtown might require you to interview a city official to get up-to-date information as the plan progresses. In the sample papers in this chapter, we have included a sample survey that Julie Ann Predny used in researching her feature article (see p. 424).

Even in situations that call for primary research, most researchers also conduct secondary research and review what others have written on their subjects in the past. The line between primary and secondary research can sometimes blur a bit. Research projects on literary subjects, for example, typically require careful examination of primary literary texts as well as taking into account what other critics have said, but some projects might be strictly biographical or historical and require only secondary research. Research projects on language use (similar to the sample we will be reading and analyzing in Collaborative Activity 7.3) may require primary gathering of data on how people use language, as well as comparing that data to what others have recorded in secondary sources.

Like primary research, secondary research also varies by discipline, and the details of secondary research must be learned within specific disciplines. Researchers in different disciplines will obviously consult different sources, and the nature of those sources will differ as well. A student in political science or law might consult government documents while a geography student will consult maps or atlases. However, as students in the writing course scene—participants with various majors and diverse interests—you should also be aware that there are both general references for locating secondary sources (such as *The Reader's Guide to Periodical Literature* or Expanded Academic ASAP) and specialized references for locating secondary sources, such as indexes (the *Social Sciences Index, Art Index, Engineering Index,* or *Humanities Index*), encyclopedias *(Encyclopedia of World Architecture, Encyclopedia of Philosophy, Encyclopedia of Psychology)*, or databases (like ERIC for education, MATHFILE for math, or Psyclit for psychology). These references will give you access to resources on specific subjects and will help you locate the specialized books, periodicals, and journals of a particular discipline.

Although disciplines have their own specific resources for locating secondary sources, your writing course will probably make use of some *generalized strategies and skills* for finding and using secondary sources in all disciplines. Common sites of secondary knowledge exist, including public and school libraries, professional organizations, and the Internet; these are what writing courses usually draw on for their research projects. Even if primary research is involved, research projects in writing classes typically are less discipline-specific than are those in specialized courses; their subjects, sources of knowledge, and write-ups tend to interest a more general audience and draw heavily on secondary research. As you become more familiar with specific disciplines throughout your college and professional life, you will learn further about resources and strategies for conducting secondary research as well as primary research in your field. Understanding the kinds of research used in writing classes should prepare you to learn that more specialized research.

Writing Activity 7.7

Read the sample paper "In Case of Emergency, Please Wait" (pp. 408–413). List the sources of information used in the paper, and label each source as primary or secondary research (primary research will not be listed in the list of references at the end of the paper). Describe briefly the different effects of each kind of source: Is one kind more convincing than another to you? Does one kind establish different kinds of points from the other? Why might one use one kind of source or another?

What does one gain from each? Are some sources more specialized than others? What is the effect of citing a specialized source?

___

In the following article linguists Penelope Eckert and Sally McConnell-Ginet draw on various kinds of research to explore the language and social identities of high school social groups (such as "jocks" and "burnouts"). In order to describe the social interactions of high school students, the students' labeling of each other, and their styles of speech (as they relate to class and gender differences), Eckert and McConnell-Ginet must draw on primary research, such as interviews with the students of Belten High. However, since their study is limited to one group of high school students, the authors must also **ground their findings** in secondary research—published sources that synthesize multiple perspectives and add bits of information and understanding to their own study. As you read their study, notice how the authors use both student voices and the voices of experts to advance their findings. Notice also the different effects primary and secondary research have, both in the way evidence is visually presented in the text and in how you as a reader relate to that evidence. Based on these effects, think about strategies you might use to visually present the results of your research.

Constructing Meaning, Constructing Selves
Snapshots of Language, Gender, and Class from Belten High

Penelope Eckert and Sally McConnell-Ginet

During the course of their lives, people move into, out of, and through communities of practice, continually transforming identities, understandings, and worldviews.[1] Progressing through the life span brings ever-changing kinds of participation and nonparticipation, contexts for "belonging" and "not belonging" in communities. A single individual participates in a variety of communities of practice at any given time, and over time: the family, a friendship group, an athletic team, a church group. These communities may be all-female or all-male; they may be dominated by women or men; they may offer different forms of participation to women or men; they may be organized on the presumption that all members want (or will want) heterosexual love relations. Whatever the nature of one's participation in communities of practice, one's experience of gender emerges in participation as a gendered community member with others in a variety of communities of practice.

It is for this reason that we (Eckert and McConnell-Ginet 1992a, b) argued for grounding the study of gender and language in detailed investigations of the social and linguistic activities of specific communities of practice. Following the lead of a number of feminist social theorists (see, e.g., Bem 1993; Butler 1993; Connell 1987; Thorne 1993; di Leonardo 1991), we warned against taking gender as given, as natural. A major moral we drew is that the study of sex differences in language use does not automatically give insight into how gender and language interact in particular communities of practice. Rather, we proposed, the social and linguistic practices through which people construct themselves as different and as similar must be carefully examined.

Gender constructs are embedded in other aspects of social life and in the construction of other socially significant categories such as those involving class, race, or ethnicity. This implies that gender is not a matter of two homogeneous social categories, one associated with being female and the other with being male. Just as important, it also implies that no simple attributes of a person, however complex a combination is considered, can completely determine how that person is socially categorized by herself or by others, and how she engages in social practice. Suppose, for example, we categorize someone as a heterosexual middle-class African American professional woman. The attributes that make up this particular characterization—*heterosexual, middle-class, African American, professional,* and *woman*—all draw on reifications that emerge from and constitute conventional maps of social reality. These reifications structure perceptions and constrain (but do not completely determine) practice, and each is produced (often reproduced in much the same form) through the experience of those perceptions and constraints in day-to-day life.

Language is a primary tool people use in constituting themselves and others as "kinds" of people in terms of which attributes, activities, and participation in social practice can be regulated. Social categories and characterizations are human creations; the concepts associated with them are not preformed, waiting for labels to be attached, but are created, sustained, and transformed by social processes that importantly include labeling itself. And labeling is only part of a more complex sociolinguistic activity that contributes to constituting social categories and power relations among members of a community. How people use language—matters of "style" that include grammar, word choice, and pronunciation—is a very important component of self-constitution. How people talk expresses their affiliations with some and their distancing from others, their embrace of certain social practices and their rejection of others—their claim to membership (and to particular forms of membership) in certain communities of practice and not others. And within communities of practice, the continual modification of common ways of speaking provides a touchstone for the process of construction of forms of group identity—of the meaning of belonging to a group (as a certain kind of member). It is a resource for the orientation of the community and its participants to other nearby communities and to the larger society, a resource for constructing community members' relation to power structures, locally and more globally.

To give concrete substance to these abstract musings, we will examine some social and linguistic practices within several communities of practice related to one another and to a particular institution, a public high school in suburban Detroit. Our data come from Penny's sociolinguistic study[2] of a speech community as defined by that high school, which we shall call Belten High. For this study, Penny did three years of participant-observation in the early 1980s, following one graduating class of six hundred students through their sophomore, junior, and senior years. (More detailed reports on various aspects of this project appear in, e.g., Eckert 1988, 1989, 1990b). Her research yielded a taped corpus of about three hundred hours of speech, including one-on-one interviews, group discussions, and a variety of public events. The original study did not focus on gender issues, and the fact that so much material relevant for thinking about gender construction emerged anyway is testimony to its pervasiveness in this community's practices. In this chapter, we draw on eighty of the one-on-one interviews, emphasizing phonological variation (in particular, pronunciation of certain vowel sounds) and sample stretches of students' talk with Penny about social categories and socially relevant attributes. We use a combination of linguistic and ethnographic data to give a partial picture of how gender, class, and power relations are being mutually constructed in this particular setting. What kinds of identities and relations are the students making for themselves and for others? How does this construction of their social landscape happen? How do different communities of practice get constituted and what is their relation to one another and to the institution of the school? Being female or male, athletic, studious, popular, a cigarette smoker, a beer drinker; staying out all night; wearing certain kinds of clothes and makeup; owning a car; using a certain vocabulary and style of speech; engaging in heterosexual activities such as cross-sex dating; wearing a constant smile; using illicit drugs—constellations of such attributes and activities constitute the raw materials from which the social categories of the school are constructed. It is the significance attached to these constellations and their constituents—their socially recognized meaning—that turns them into socially relevant categories mediating power, affiliation, desire, and other social relations.

Who lunches with whom? Who talks to whom about what? Who touches whom and how (and where)? Who controls which resources? Who is admired or despised by whom? When the answers to such questions depend systematically on people's being classified as belonging to one category rather than another, the social categories involved can interact with communities of practice in two ways: (1) they often form the basis for the formation of category-exclusive communities of practice, defined by their mutual orientation to the school and engaged in finding a mutual life in the school based in this orientation; and (2) the categories themselves and the opposition between them can become the object of practice, defining a larger but more loosely connected community of practice focused on conflict over the practices of everyday life in the shared space community members inhabit. Thus, communities of practice can overlap in significant ways. What makes them all communities of practice is not any shared attributes of their members but the orientation of those members to joint participation in some endeavor, and in a set of social practices that grow around that endeavor.

Schooling in Corporate Practice

The U.S. public high school is designed to dominate and structure the lives of the adolescent age group—not just to provide academic and vocational instruction but to provide a comprehensive social environment. The school organizes sports, musical and dramatic groups, social occasions such as dances and fairs, some social service such as canned-food drives, and governing activities in the form of such things as class offices and student government. These activities are not simply organized by the school for the students. Rather, the school provides the resources and authority for the students themselves to organize these activities, and institutional status and privilege for those who do the organizing. Although an organizational framework with adult supervisors is provided—for example, athletic teams have coaches, bands and choirs have directors, clubs have faculty sponsors—students themselves play substantial organizing roles (e.g., as team captains or club officers).

It is important to emphasize that although participation in this extracurricular sphere is optional, it is also expected. Extracurricular activities are viewed as integral to one's participation in school, and indeed, one's extracurricular career constitutes an important part of an entrance dossier for colleges and universities. The school is the community in which adolescents are expected to participate—a community extracted from the larger adult-dominated community that it serves. It is seen as a community designed especially for—and in the interests of—adolescents, and adolescents are expected to base not only their academic lives but their informal social lives in that institution.

Adolescents who do not embrace this community are, therefore, seen as deviant, as "not caring."

Students are expected to compete for control of roles and resources in the production of extracurricular activities, and to base their identities and alliances in this production. This leads to a tight student hierarchy based on institutional roles and on relations with others (both student and adult) in institutional roles—in short, a hierarchy based on control of aspects of the institutional environment, and on the freedoms and privileges associated with this control. Those who participate in this hierarchy are not simply participating in individual interesting activities; they are building extracurricular careers and engaging in a corporate practice that has as much to do with visibility in and control over the school environment as with the content of the individual activities that constitute their careers.

For students participating fully in the extracurricular sphere, then, social status is constructed as a function of institutional status, personal identities are intertwined with institutional identities, and social networks are intertwined with institutional networks. Embedded as they are in a mobile hierarchy, social relations are competitive, and they change with institutional responsibilities, alliances, and status. Students are constrained to monitor their behavior carefully in order to maintain a "responsible" public persona, and to focus their interactions on the network of people in the same school and even the same graduating class who are engaged in this endeavor. In this way, the school offers an introduction into corporate practice. Of course, corporate status and its concomitant freedoms and privileges come at a price. Participating in this hierarchy requires a certain acceptance of the institution's rules and values as articulated by the ultimate institutional authorities, the adults who occupy official positions in the school.

In schools across the United States, communities of practice develop around participation in parts of the extracurricular sphere (a cheerleading squad, a "popular" crowd, a class cabinet), and a broader overarching community of practice develops around engagement in the extracurricular sphere and the mutual building of extracurricular careers. Participants build careers in the extracurricular sphere and achieve a merging of their personal and school networks, their personal and school-based identities. This is a community based on an adolescent version of corporate, middle-class social practice. Although this specific community of practice arises in response to the school institution, it is based to some extent in communities that have been emerging since childhood. Indeed, across the country, the students involved in the school's corporate affairs tend to be college-bound and to come from the upper part of the local socioeconomic range. Many of them have already learned aspects of corporate practice at home, both through exposure to their own parents' participation in such practice and through the middle-class family practices and values that support corporate practices. (For example, middle-class parents generally do not encourage their children to "hang out" in the neighborhood but to cultivate friendships through school; and they commonly discourage their children from having a best friend in favor of having a more fluid network.)

At the same time that these students base their activities, networks, and identities in the corporate sphere of the school, others reject the school as the basis of social life. Indeed, in polar opposition to the corporate community of practice, there is a community of practice based on autonomy from the school. These students base their social lives not in the school but in the local neighborhoods and in the urban–suburban area more generally. Their friendships are not limited to the school or to their own age group, and their activities tend to arise from their alliances rather than vice versa. These students are largely from the lower end of the local socioeconomic hierarchy and embrace, strongly and consciously, working-class norms of egalitarianism and solidarity. They consciously oppose the norm of corporate practice in the school, and they reject the institution as a locus of identity and social life. Because they are bound for the work force immediately after high school, furthermore, the extracurricular sphere has no hold on them as qualification for future success; rather, it appears to them as a form of infantilization and as a hierarchy existing only for its own sake. Their focus is more on the local area and its resources for entertainment, excitement, and employment; they reject environments developed especially for their own age group and seek to participate in what they see as the real world. Furthermore, in this rejection of the school's adolescent environment, they seek independence from adult control over everyday life, their bodies, activities, and consumption practices. This latter oppositional category always has a name: *hoods, greasers, stompers, stoners, grits* (depending on the region and the era) and, in the school in question, *burnouts* (or *burns*) or *jellies* (or *jells,* from *jellybrain*). The two main local names reflect the symbolic status of controlled-substance use for the oppositional category in this particular school at this particular time. These names are used by all in the school, and embraced by those to whom they apply as well as to those who choose to apply it to others. On the other hand, the activities-oriented category in schools is not always given a name, a point we will discuss in the next section. The group may, however, be called something like *collegiates, preppies, soshes* (from *socialite*), or, as in the school in question and other schools around the region, *jocks,* drawing on the symbolic status of athletic achievement for this social group.

In general usage, *jock* designates a committed athlete, and the prototypical jock is male. Except for the jocks themselves, students in Belten High use *jock* to designate a network of girls and boys who achieve visibility through their committed engagement in school-sponsored activities. (As we explain in the next section, this labeling dispute connects to the absence of a name for the activities-oriented category in some schools.) Although sports do provide the surest route to jockdom, especially for boys, other activities also confer that status.

The name *jock* points, then, to one important way in which school corporate culture constructs male dominance. The male varsity athlete is seen by the school institution as representing the school's interests, and this gives him institutional status and privilege. Interscholastic competition affords boys' varsity athletics the most direct way of establishing and defending the school's status and honor. Thus, the status that a boy gains in varsity sports is connected directly to the luster he brings to the school—not to himself personally. This is a useful lesson to learn. Achieving individual status through one's efforts on behalf of an institution—being able to identify one's own interests with institutional interests—is a hallmark of much successful competition in adult corporate practice.

Athletics is also the route that boys are expected to take to prominence. In a conversation with Penny, a group of male athletes extolled the skill, "coolness," and hard work of a male student-government officer. But they pointed out that he had had no choice but to seek a key student office because he wasn't athletic. In general, male athletes see nonathletic activities as an aside: as something one can do casually—because they require no special skill—but possibly as one's civic duty. And the status associated with varsity athletics can be a tremendous advantage for a star athlete who chooses to seek student office, an advantage that can overturn the candidacy of a nonathlete with a long history of experience and service.

Although male varsity athletes can count on their accomplishments to establish their value to the community, their status, there are no parallel accomplishments in school that lend the same kind of status for girls. Because sports still do not yield the same payoff for girls as for boys (in the section "Sports and Toughness" we discuss some of the reasons for this, and also note some changes in progress), the domain in which girls are expected to achieve prominence is already designated as second-best. Girls may receive recognition through prominence in student government, through cheerleading, or through participation in musical or dramatic activities. But for both girls and boys, achieving recognition through these activities seldom if ever evokes the kind of vicarious pride of schoolmates that gives good athletes their special distinction. The female supportive role is formalized in high school in the pairing of such activities as girls' cheerleading and boys' varsity athletics, and in the feminization of organizational activities such as holding bake sales, organizing dances, and the like. Girls tend to do the majority of the behind-the-scenes work for school activities; boys predominate in top managerial roles (class president, student-body president, and so on).

Thus, in a number of ways school corporate culture continues students' education in the male dominance that is characteristic of most American institutions and American society at many levels. It also continues and indeed intensifies education in what Rich (1980) dubbed "compulsory heterosexuality." High school brings an institutionalization of traditional gender arrangements, heterosexuality, and romance. The institutionalization of the heterosexual couple is embodied formally in the king and queen of the high school homecoming and prom. Heterosexuality and romance are also publicly constructed in high school through formal activities like dances and informally in the status of dating and in each class's "famous couple." When the yearbook depicts a "cutest couple," the relation between social status and success in the heterosexual marketplace is made visible.

Although adult corporate practice does not recognize the "cutest couple" in an institution, socializing outside the workplace is still largely driven by business and professional alliances and organized around heterosexual marriage partners. The support role of female cheerleaders for male athletes is succeeded by wifely hosting and presumptive willingness to follow wherever a husband's career trajectory leads. But there are signs of rupture in this conflation of the personal and the institutional in both adolescent and adult practice, and it is driven by ongoing larger-scale changes in gender relations. Just as girls are beginning to reject cheerleading at boys' sports events in favor of playing on their own teams, corporate wives' own careers are making them unavailable to host dinner parties. Gender transformations have begun to challenge the all-encompassing character of corporate practice, albeit on only a small scale. And in a few places, openly gay or lesbian high schoolers are beginning to resist the heterosexual imperative of traditional mixed-sex schools. For example, a group of Los Angeles high schoolers recently organized an alternative "gay prom," which was reported nationally. Fifteen years ago gay and lesbian students were not "out" at Belten High. We don't know to what extent this may have changed, but it is a safe bet that when the yearbook depicts a "cutest couple," they still won't be of the same sex.

The names of the categories that correspond to *jock* and *burnout* at Belten High, and the specific styles and activities that signal their opposition (use of controlled substances, leisure activities, clothing, musical tastes, territorial specialization, and the like), vary regionally and locally and change through time. But it is close to universal in U.S. public high schools for two opposed social categories to arise that represent some kind of class split and that constitute class cultures within the school. And so far as we know, the construction of these cultural groups always interacts in interesting ways with the construction of gender identities and relations (although of course the nature of that interaction may vary significantly). In most U.S. schools, race and ethnicity also enter into the interaction, but in this particular virtually all-white school such social dimensions are salient only inasmuch as they provide the overarching discourse within which whiteness is constructed and differentiated. Indeed, everything that we have discussed and will discuss is at the same time part of the construction of white hegemony.

The jocks and the burnouts arise as class-based communities of practice in response to the school institution. Each is based in the endeavor to build a way of life in and out of school that makes sense and that provides the means to construct valued identities. The jocks emerge out of many students' shared desire to build lives within the school institution and to develop identities and careers based in the extracurricular sphere. The burnouts emerge out of many students' need to find ways to exist in the school that neither implicate them in corporate practice nor cost them their participation in the institution, ways that at the same time allow them to foster a strong sense of identity and participation in their own broader community.

The jocks' and burnouts' opposed orientations to the school, to institutions, and to life are the terrain for daily struggle over the right to define school, adolescence, values. Both categories seek autonomy, but in different places. Jocks seek autonomy in the occupation of adultlike roles within the institution, in building individual identities through school-based careers, and in benefiting from the kinds of institutional freedoms and perks that are the rewards for participation in these careers. Burnouts seek autonomy in the avoidance of adult-run institutions, in laying claim to adult prerogatives, and in the development of networks and activities in the local community, which will be the site of their adult lives. The jocks work the center of the school institution; the burnouts work its margins.

Because it is so basic to life in school, the jock-burnout opposition comes to define the landscape of identities at Belten. Those who are neither jocks nor burnouts commonly refer to themselves as *in-betweens,* and nuances of identity throughout the school are described in the same terms that construct these two categories. Thus, the jock-burnout opposition constitutes the dominant discourse of identity in the school, and one could say that orientation to that opposition engages almost every student in the school in an overarching community of practice. But although both communities emerge from strongly held and positive values, they do not emerge as equal within the school. The jocks embody the institution—their personal relations are inseparable from formal institutional relations and their activities are inseparable from school activities. This bestows an institutional legitimacy and function on their activities and their alliances, including their heterosexual alliances, that stand in stark contrast to the illegitimate status accorded to burnouts' activities and alliances. The coconstruction of social category and gender is indeed intimately connected to the construction of institutional power, a power in which girls and boys do not share equally.

Labeling, Conflict, and Hegemony

Gender and social category are not constructed independently of each other, nor do they exist independently of practice; rather, they are continually coconstructed in the course of day-to-day practice. In the same way, labels do not exist independently of the social practice in which categories are constructed; the use of labels is not simply a matter of fitting a word to a pre-existing category. Rather, labels arise in use in relation to real people in real situations: people label as they chat, make observations and judgments about people, point people out to others, challenge people, and so on. It is through such activities that labels are endowed with meaning. We have already referred to some students as *jocks,* others as *burnouts.* But this is misleading inasmuch as it obscures the very important fact that labeling is a socially significant and contested practice within the school and is part of the continual construction of the categories it designates. The use of the term *jock* or *burnout,* and of terms related to the salient issues around which these categories are constructed (e.g., *slutty, cool, snobby*), is part of the process of constituting categories and identities.

Students coming into the school see the institution as unchanging—they see institutional roles waiting to be filled. But they see their participation or nonparticipation in the school as a creative endeavor. Even though there have "always been" jocks and burnouts, girls and boys, students coming into high school are actively and mutually engaged in constituting selves within the constraints of what has, in their view, always been—and engaging with those constraints in the process.

The jocks and the burnouts seek to define right and appropriate practices, given their relation to the institution of school. Each sees the other community of practice as embodying wrong and inappropriate practices. For the burnouts, the jocks are "about" competition, hierarchy, advantage, elitism, ambition, image-building. Girl jocks especially are seen as phony, as obsessed with popularity. For the jocks, the burnouts are "about" drugs, trouble, hedonism, lack of ambition. And girl burnouts are often seen by jocks as sleazy, if not slutty. This conflict about category "content" can present itself as a dispute over what category labels "really" mean, but of course words as such are never the real issue. The real issue is the normativity of particular practices and the deviance of others. In the following sections, we will examine labeling practices as part of the construction of social category and gender (along with other aspects of identity such as class, age, and so on). We begin with the issue of what it means to have a label at all.

Because of the deep ideological nature of the split between jocks and burnouts, it is not surprising that the terms *jock* and *burnout* are used differently by people in different places in the school. As we have noted, jocks resist accepting this label—or indeed any label—as a name for a social category defined by extracurricular orientation. Jocks, and particularly male athletic jocks, promote exclusive use of the term *jock* to refer to someone as an athlete. This is illustrated by the following response by a male varsity athlete to Penny's question, which calls the very term into question (*I don't know really . . . what that means*):[3]

> (1)   DO YOU CONSIDER YOURSELF A JOCK? Somewhat I guess, yeah. Just—I don't know really what, you know, what that means. Just, I play sports and stuff I guess, you know.

In accepting a self-designation *jock* purely on the basis of athletics, jocks reject any "derivative" meanings. This has more than one effect. Although "playing sports and stuff" might in principle be socially no more consequential than preferring apples to oranges, the status of *jock* is not a socially neutral one. The jock (male) athletes' use of the term *jock* to refer to someone as "simply" being involved in sports suppresses the connection of that involvement to social status, membership, and opportunities. At the same time, given that within the school this term is used to refer to a more generally powerful group in the institution, laying claim to it for athletes alone can have the effect of emphasizing the centrality of athletes to the institution. This latter effect depends, of course, on others' use of the term as a label for the socially dominant activities-oriented group.

The relation between corporate participation and athletics is brought home particularly in the following quotation from one of the outstanding athletes in the school. He had been participating in an independent soccer league, in which the level of play was far above that in the school; here he explains why he gave up the league to play for the school:

> (2)   WHEN YOU HAVE A TEAM LIKE THAT WHY DO YOU GO INTO HIGH SCHOOL SOCCER? I don't, well, because—because that's—it's—you know, you want to play—recognition, I don't know. We should have stayed but what you do is, when—you—there's high school sports, more people are apt to play that than play in another league, you know, because you have the recognition, scholarships, like that.

In spite of the male athletes' insistence on the narrow meaning, most people in Belten do not use the term *jock* to refer to a person in school simply as an athlete. Rather, they use it to talk about a community of practice: all the people, female and male, who build their lives around school activities. In example (3), a burnout boy directly challenges the equation of jockdom and participation in sports proposed by the (athletic) jock:

> (3)   I—well—some kids uh who went out for football in seventh grade turned into jocks. Pretty much. But it doesn't—you can—it doesn't make you a

jock if you go out and play a sport. Because I played in football in junior high and I wasn't considered a jock. I used to get high before the games.

Being an athlete doesn't make you a jock if you don't adhere to jock values. Here we see that jocks ought not to get high—or at least not be so overt in their defiance of school regulations (the ambivalence of jocks in relation to substance use is discussed in the section "Sports and Toughness.")

Only one male jock in the corpus explicitly admitted that the label could legitimately cover more than athletes. He was a former class president and a talented musician but not an athlete. Note that he does not call himself a *jock* but does acknowledge that athleticism is not all there is to jockdom:

(4)   You get your super jocks that—hell they play track and basketball and baseball, and I'm sure those people are going to—"Hey, jock!" That's their middle name practically. But, um, I think you don't have to play sports to be a jock.

In fact, this boy, a leading singer in the school, recognizes that he is frequently referred to as a *choir jock*. The choir, which travels internationally, is a prestigious activity in the school and is similar to sports in bringing recognition to the school through competition with representatives of other schools. As described by two different choir members, students have specified a difference between a member of the choir and a choir jock: a choir jock is a choir member who gets involved in more than just the singing:

(5)   . . . that's that clique. That's what everybody knows about, the concert choir jocks . . . I guess it's the officers, you know, the people that are involved, like Dan Smart, our president. I don't know, he's, you know, he's always involved in choir. Then there's Cheryl Smith. Herbie Jackson, he's always, you know, that's his highlight of our school.

(6)   IS THERE A CROWD OF PEOPLE THAT ARE CHOIR JOCKS? Oh, yeah. Definitely. We always talk about them, Kim and I. . . . We're not involved in choir that much. Yeah I mean we go to a few activities once in a while, but we don't make sure we attend all of them.

But why do so many jocks protest being labeled as members of a social category? Why do they keep trying to explain their being called *jocks* as just a matter of describing athleticism, a socially neutral attribute? A plausible explanation lies in the near-hegemony jocks achieve during the course of the transition from junior high to the senior year of high school. That ascendancy is threatened by being seen as such; jocks' interests require obscuring the social processes that subordinate nonjocks generally and burnouts in particular. It is important for jocks not to see themselves as denying others access to valuable resources by exclusionary processes. It is also important for them to constitute as normative the activities on which their community of practice centers and from which they reap advantage, with those not so engaged defined as socially deviant and thus directly responsible for any disadvantages they may suffer in the school. If the dominant category is not even labeled (and, as we noted earlier, in many schools it is not), then its distinctive interests are somewhat easier to ignore, its hegemonic control over social values and institutional norms more readily established. Two category labels in direct opposition reflect a live ongoing social struggle.

The jocks' status became unmarked in the course of junior high school. The jock and burnout categories reportedly emerged in seventh grade as apparently equal rivals, with core people in them pursuing different activities and espousing different values. In the following quotation, one burnout girl describes the original split in junior high as just such a matter of competing values and choices; she notes explicitly that category labels were used by each group to "put down" the other:

(7) Yeah, OK, there was, you know, kids that got high and smoked and thought they were really cool like us ((laughter)) and then the other ones that didn't party or anything, were always getting into sports and being goody-goodies and, you know, all that stuff so we just started putting down those people, calling them *jocks* and everything, and they call us *burns,* and that was just going on for a while, while we were all at [junior high].

A self-designated "in-between"—a girl with primary burnout connections and interests but also with many jock ties and interests—describes quite poignantly the regulative power of the polarized labeling and the conflicts, internal and public, that those labeling practices helped produce:

(8) That's—that's where all the—the jock/burn or the jock/jelly thing started. Because I didn't hear anything about it in elementary school. But once I hit [junior high], you know, that's all you heard was, "She's a jock," "She's a jell," you know. And that's all it was. You were either one. You weren't an in-between, which I was. I was an in-between ((laughter)) because here I was, I played volleyball, now what, three years. Baseball, I'll be going on my eighth year, OK? So, I get along really good with, quote, jocks, OK, and I get along really good with jellies, because I'm right—I'm stuck right in the middle. And in my ninth-grade and tenth-grade year, that kind of tore me apart a little bit too. Because I didn't—my parents wanted me to make a decision. "Now which way are you going to go?"

Near-hegemony had, however, been achieved by the beginning of high school. Early on in her fieldwork, one of the burnout boys asked Penny whether she'd yet talked to any "normal" people, reflecting his (perhaps wry) admission of being relegated to deviant status. With apparently less ironic distance, a girl who is a star athlete and a popular jock denies hearing people insult one another by labeling. Rather, according to her, the categories keep enough distance that there is no call for such activity:

(9)   The jocks sort of stayed to themselves, and the burnouts stayed to themselves and everybody else kind of stayed to themselves too. So you really—if you didn't have to you didn't mix.

She then responds to Penny's query as to whether she thinks of jocks and burnouts as separate groups:

(10)   The burns, yes. Well, not so much in high school. Like jocks—you're not really aware of it.

Though jock hegemony is not total, there is every indication that jocks often manage to present themselves and be taken as the "unmarked" or "default" category, of which "you're not really aware." Only the opponents of the institution are seen as taking a stand with respect to the institution. Although jocks are highly visible, many no longer see themselves as actively orienting toward institutional values in opposing burnouts. Rather, their own attitudes and choices seem "normal" or inevitable in the absence of some kind of social pathology. They no longer see burnouts as in serious conflict with them, presumably at least in part because they now are more or less sure that burnouts will never "lead" them, will not be in controlling positions. In the following example, a jock girl from a burnout neighborhood talks about being the only jock at the bus stop:

(11)   But, you know, it doesn't really bother me, I just figure ((laughter)) who cares what they think of me, you know, they're not—they're no uh, you know, president, that they can cut me down.

Early on in the process of constructing institutional affiliation and opposition and the other aspects of class and gender practice found in the school, jock ascendancy was being asserted more directly, according to this jock boy:

(12)   There was like—at least once a week it was, "Jocks, are going to fight jells after school," you know. DID THEY REALLY? DID YOU GET INTO FIGHTS OR WAS IT JUST A LOT OF TALK? Never. Talk. They started it every time. We'd about kill them. Because we had the whole football team, and they wanted to fight the football team. You know. DO YOU REMEMBER WHICH GUYS WANTED TO GET IN FIGHTS? None of the guys on the football team, really, you know—they didn't care.

The quotation reveals an awareness of *jock* as a category label used in conflict. It also indicates the speaker's bravado and (retrospective) claim of fearlessness.

We now turn to the matter of this focus on physical prowess in constructing class-based male social relations.

Sports and Toughness: Category Meanings and Male Power

Although the jock boy quoted in example (12) asserts that physical strength was concentrated in jock hands, the jock–burnout split really became visible and contentious when some excellent athletes among the burnouts refused to play on school teams (cf. example (3)). Both jock and burnout boys staunchly asserted that their group could beat the other in any physical contest, whether a game or a fight.

As a number of writers have observed (see, for example, Connell 1987 and Segal 1990), practices aimed at developing and displaying confidence and superior physical strength and skill play a central role in constituting a hegemonic masculinity in the United States and many other Western nations. *Hegemonic* here implies not pervasiveness in fact but power as a (partly fantasy) ideal of manliness. The body aimed at is muscular and tough, able successfully to withstand physical attacks and to defend others against them, able to win in attacks on others. Competitive sports are a primary arena in which such a masculinity is constituted, at least as an ideal.

Organized sports continue to enter into the practices constituting adult masculinities. Even relatively inactive men watch and talk about football games every week of the season. A number of writers have noted the prominence of sports metaphors in business talk, politics, and other areas of corporate life. That "level playing fields" have generally not been thought of as having females running down them is clear. The "locker-room talk" that prototypically occurs among teammates before and after games constructs women as men's sexual prey. Male camaraderie excludes women and includes other men as fellow "tough guys," to be slapped on the back, playfully punched around in certain contexts.

Such kinds of talk and bodily demeanor are, of course, not confined to the corporate world but are part of many male-dominated workplaces. The form in corporate lunchrooms is different from that in factory cafeterias, but a "macho" style of masculinity and male-male interaction rooted in sports and, more generally, physical toughness is common. Indeed, working-class men are often taken as exemplary of this ideal. Jobs that institutionalize force, strength, and even violence—such as building trades, police and prison work, military combat—are low on the class hierarchy but high on the scale of hegemonic masculinity.[4]

Although the burnouts in this school are certainly not the super-tough gang members that are so frequently studied in the city, they are urban-oriented and pride themselves on their relation to the streets: to fights, encounters with the police, the criminal justice system. Much of the early oppositional behavior between jocks and burnouts in elementary school involved contests of physical prowess, both athletic and combative challenges. The burnouts were viewed as "tough," and the jocks were hard-pressed to maintain their own prowess in the face of the burnout challenge.

Hegemonic masculinity emphasizes the possibility of physical force. It has been a central symbolic component in constructing heterosexual men as different from both women and homosexual men—in principle able to beat up either. Of course, both women and gay men have begun to challenge this view of straight men's superiority in physical strength, as attested by the enormous increase, in recent years, in female participation in organized sports and such activities as body-building and by the emergence of the "clone" style among gay men since the gay liberation movement began. But a focus on physical strength remains prominent in constituting heterosexual masculinity and, albeit in different ways, in constructing the picture of a prototypical jock and a prototypical burnout.

For the jocks, then, this physical prowess centers on participation in school-sponsored sports, violence that is tamed and put into service for the institution. The notion that jocks have tamed their violence is a crucial aspect of a more general emphasis on the control of one's urges that is an important component of corporate practice. This control is seen as requiring additional strength and autonomy. (In the section "Snobs and Sluts" we discuss how this control translates into control of sexual urges for jock girls.)

Although girls' varsity athletics is increasing in importance at Belten High as elsewhere, it still has not achieved the same institutional importance as boys'. This is only partly because girls' sports are less well attended and thus girls are less able to bring glory to the school and vicariously to those who identify with it. It is also important that the association of the athlete with physical prowess conflicts with feminine norms, with notions of how a (heterosexual) girl "should" look and behave. Heterosexual femininity is constructed as directly contrasting with the superiority in physical strength embodied in hegemonic masculinity. Too much athleticism and physicality in a girl suggests a "butch" style of femaleness. Thus, it is problematic for an athletic girl to refer to herself as a *jock* because of the "unfeminine" image that the label implies. In example (13) an accomplished female athlete who is part of the popular crowd denies being a jock:

> (13) . . . like there's some girls that play baseball and basketball and track, and they're just always—they play football and they just do everything, you know, the real, you know, girl—you can tell, they walk down the halls pushing each other, and, you know, That kind of jock. Yeah, yeah, those

kind you know? I wouldn't call my- myself a jock, I'd say. I can be athletic or something like that, but, like people don't call me *jock,* you know.

The disassociation of femininity and athletic prowess presents a powerful double bind for girls, for varsity sports are seen as the ultimate demonstration of accomplishment (and as a kind of accomplishment with greater institutional status than a superb artistic performance). The association of sports with accomplishment is commonly contrasted to other visible school activities, particularly those that are associated with female status, which are seen as relying on popularity. This emerges in the conversation of both female and male jocks, as in the following female athlete's observation, when discussing whether it is necessary to know the right people in order to participate in many activities in high school:

(14)   You can't say that for the team sports and stuff—you have to be good. But it is nice to know those people, and to be in the committees and stuff you still have to be interviewed, but if you're interviewed by kids and they like you, you're probably in. The uh student council, that's—if you know a lot of people, that's just like popularity, sort of. Yeah. I don't know if it is all popularity, but—

Being the girlfriend of a star male athlete is at least as sure a route to female achievement in the jock network as being a star athlete oneself (and perhaps less risky, given the possibility of jeopardizing success in the heterosexual marketplace through being too athletic). We discuss jock girls' pursuit of popularity in the next section. Popularity draws not on the athleticism and physicality associated with prototypical male jockdom but on its visibility.

For burnouts, the labels at Belten focus on substance use rather than physicality. But being a burnout invokes an orientation away from school and toward urban streets and the toughness to walk them freely, to be able to protect oneself in a fight. The image is decidedly not feminine. Although burnout girls can fight, they do not gain the same status as burnout boys for doing so. On the contrary, being tough in a fight is seen as somewhat admirable for boys and men, but girls' (and women's) fighting is quite generally looked down upon and viewed in terms of kicking and scratching rather than "real punchouts." Further, and more important, although girls can fight among themselves, and a few do, they cannot and do not fight boys. Thus, they cannot walk the urban streets with the same sense of personal autonomy that boys can. Burnout girls remain vulnerable to male violence. They cannot really establish their anti-institutional burnout status through being skilled fighters who need not fear others' attacks on their persons. They can, however, draw on other components of burnout toughness to constitute themselves as true "burns." In the next section, we discuss the important place of "coolness" in burnout girls' construction of themselves.

Popularity and Coolness: Category Meaning and Female Agency

The fundamental meaning of being a jock is orientation toward the institution and the possible rewards for ascending its hierarchical structures. The fundamental meaning of being a burnout is resisting the institution and its regulative constraints. These fundamental category meanings are, as we have already seen, overlaid with many other issues. In particular, girls are effectively barred from the practices most central to establishing category membership: the pursuit of athletic achievement, on the one hand, and of urban toughness on the other. They must therefore engage in other practices to construct their identities as jocks or as burnouts. The pursuit of popularity for jock girls and of coolness for burnout girls allows them to constitute themselves actively as embodying the same basic meanings as the prototypical category members, their male peers. Going out with a jock boy helps the jock girl achieve popularity; going out with a burnout boy or, even better, someone already out of school, reinforces the burnout girl's claim to coolness. Jock girls are not the only ones pursuing popularity; burnout girls do not monopolize coolness. But popularity and coolness do play central roles in constructing class-based ways of being female. We will start with popularity, but coolness enters in almost immediately as connected to burnout popularity in junior high.

Popularity is a complex that combines some kind of likability and good personhood with visibility, community status, and a large number of contacts. The pursuit of the latter three are integral parts of corporate practice, necessary for gaining control of (and strategically dispensing) resources. Inasmuch as the jocks embody the school institution, their networks in some sense define the school community. Thus, their institutional positions not only lend them opportunities for visibility, contacts, and status but center them in a community circumscribed by the school. A burnout or in-between may well have as many social contacts as a jock, but to the extent that these contacts extend outside the school, they remain "unfocused" and do not contribute to a communally constructed visibility. Furthermore, even if one's many ties are in the school, to the extent that they do not include those in power in the school, they cannot provide the opportunities for visibility that contribute to school popularity.

Burnout girls do sometimes talk of themselves or others in their network as "popular." The rubric, however, is always applied in the past tense when the girls are reminiscing about early junior high and the days when burnouts were still in active competition for school-based prominence. Although this prominence was being constructed within the school population, its focus was not on access to school resources but on access to activities outside and "around" school. A girl whom all the burnouts point to as having been popular in junior high, for example, explains why her crowd was the "big shit crowd":

(15) I just think that we used to have a lot of fun, you know, and a lot of—you know, I mean things going outside of school, you know, and a lot of people, you know, looked up at us, you know—"it's really, cool," you know, "I wish I could."

Another burnout girl tells Penny why she wanted to hang out with this same crowd during junior high school:

(16) HOW DID YOU GET TO BE FRIENDS WITH THOSE PARTICULAR PEOPLE? Um, popularity. They—they were the popular ones. . . . By ninth grade, they were the popular ones and, you know, I wanted to be known, I wanted to be known by the guys, and I wanted to be known by this—and I started, you know, hanging around them.

Popular burnouts were highly visible in school as people to hang around if one wanted to join in their fun and "cool" activities outside school. Coolness, as we will see later, is quite overtly aspired to, and the early burnout popularity was as well. In response to Penny's query about how she started hanging around the popular burnouts in junior high, the speaker we just heard above explains:

(17) Um, well, if I'd hear about, "Well, we're all going over to so-and-so's house tonight," you know, I'd say, "You think you guys'd mind if I came along?" you know, and, you know, just slowly, you know, I started to get to know them. I was—I'm not shy but I'm not outgoing either. I'm in-between. So I could really, in a way, ask them, and in a way, try to be accepted. That's why I think I started smoking cigarettes. That's when I started drinking beer, and all of that stuff.

In the following quotation, a burnout girl talks about two other burnout girls who set out intentionally to become popular in junior high. The speaker is an admirer of Joan, the second girl she mentions, and considers her attempts to become popular to be funny but not reprehensible:

(18) I know that one girl, Sally Stella, she's a—I don't know, she was just trying to make friends with everybody so she could be really popular, you know? And she thought she was so beautiful, and she had so many friends, and— I don't know—and Joan Border, like—you know, she can talk to anybody, and she was making a lot of friends too, like—it was like they were competing or something, her and Sally . . . trying to see who could get the most friends and ((laughter)) I don't know.

In junior high school, when the jocks had not yet come to dominate status in the school, they and the burnouts were two separate visible popular crowds competing to define "the good life" in school. Both participated in school activities—burnout girls were cheerleaders, burnout boys played on school teams, and both burnouts and jocks attended school dances and athletic events. However, the two categories engaged in these activities on very different terms. The burnouts viewed school activities as opportunities to "party," and their mixing of school activities with "illicit" activities eventually disqualified them from participation. At the same time, the school's insistence on monitoring these activities as a condition of participation led those who had not been sent away to back away. One might say that the issue of popularity—prominence within the school as someone to hang out with—was closed for the burnouts when they left junior high. This analysis is articulated by two burnout girls:

(19) Girl 1: Well, nobody's really popular
    Girl 2: anymore
    Girl 1: Yeah, but like they were popular then.
    Girl 2: Then they were, yeah.
    Penny: WHAT DID THAT MEAN?
    Girl 1: To have them be popular?
    Girl 2: They were the coolest.
    Girl 1: Yeah. They were the ones that had girlfriends and boyfriends first. They were the ones to try everything new out first. They hung around all the junior high kids first. And uh, that's—
    Penny: THEY WERE THE ONES EVERYBODY WANTED TO BE WITH?
    Girl 1: Yeah, yeah, every time I tried to be with them.

But by high school, the burnouts are firmly oriented outside the school and many refer to jocks in general as *the popular crowd*. Just as jockdom is denied as a social category by those in it, so is the pursuit of popularity by jock girls. In example (20) a girl on the outskirts of the central jock crowd talks about an upwardly mobile friend who left her group to try to get in with the right people:

(20) WHO DO YOU SUPPOSE SHE THOUGHT WERE THE RIGHT PEOPLE? Um, the popular, the jock people, I think. That's what I think.

Yet, the pressure to deny an interest in popularity for girls aspiring to jock success is so strong that some will use the term *jock* to mask a concern with popularity, as shown by this extract in which the girl spoken of in example (20) is (on a different occasion) talking with Penny:

(21) My girlfriends, we kind of tend towards the—I don't know, I—and none of my girlfriends are going out with, um,—I don't, I don't like to label people, but, burnouts. We, I guess we, we mainly go ((laughter)) out with, I guess, the, the athletes, the jocks and stuff. And, um, or the, um, the—I wouldn't say popular crowd, but, you know.

As we discuss further below, jock girls need to be circumspect about their interest in popularity, but jock boys have a different orientation. For jock boys, popularity is overwhelmingly viewed in terms of contacts, visibility, and community status. For them, it is clearly tied up with institutional influence, as shown in one class president's discussion of the inevitability of wanting to be popular. He articulates the separation between popularity and likability:

> (22) It starts in sixth grade, I think. You—you want to be popular because you're the oldest in the school. You want people to know you. And then once you get into junior high, you just have to be. I mean just—not because—see, you want to because you—you feel it's the right thing to do. You want to—you know, it's a big thing to be popular, but a lot of people want to be popular for the wrong reasons. They want to be popular because they think it's going to get them friends, or, uh, they think things will be easier if they're popular. But it's not like that. In fact, it could backfire. You—you create a lot of resentment if you become popular for the wrong reasons.

This boy has a clear sense of the connections among popularity, contacts, and institutional effectiveness. He displays the sense of institutional responsibility that won him his position and that indeed made him an unusually effective student-government officer. One should become popular because "it's the right thing to do"; it doesn't bring one friends or make life generally "easier." The following jock boy told Penny that although there is no formula for becoming popular, the sine qua non is getting to know people:

> (23) I think—be really outgoing you know, and don't just stay with one group of friends, you know—if you just stay really—if you don't ever go out and talk to anybody else, then, you know, nobody's never going to know who you are or anything if you're just really—stay home all the time, so—be outgoing, I think.

Jock boys will admit to the pursuit of prominence—high visibility—as a means to the end of playing a leadership role in the school, winning in the competitive governance game. Still, prominence achieved through selection to the all-state football team takes much less social effort; achieving for the school is all that is necessary for people to "know who you are" and is much less risky than having to take active steps to get to know people. (We discuss some of these risks in the next section.) Above all, this prominence is clearly based on skill and achievement, not on looks, charm, or some doubtful social "manipulation."

For girls, institutional success derives less from individual achievement than from the kinds of relations they can maintain with others. In the adult corporate world, wives still frequently derive status from their husbands' occupations, secretaries from the institutional positions of their bosses. School-based prominence for girls depends very heavily on ties of friendship or romance with other visible people. The pursuit of popularity for girls involves a careful construction of personhood, although this is not generally acknowledged (Eckert 1990a). Hence the cultivation of attractiveness, both beauty and a pleasing personality, becomes a major enterprise, to which cultivation of individual accomplishment typically takes a back seat. This enterprise, we might point out, is supported by a multibillion-dollar teen magazine industry aimed specifically at adolescent girls, providing them with the technology of beauty and personality (see Talbot.). The adult successors are women's magazines and self-help books (including those to help with communication; see Cameron, forthcoming). Thus trained, women are far more likely than men to be obsessed with being the perfect spouse, the perfect parent, the perfect friend—the perfect person, the most loved and liked. They are far less likely to be obsessed with being the highest-paid CEO or the winningest lawyer or the world's top theoretical linguist—the top star in an openly competitive "game." Personal ambition is not, of course, completely out of the question for girls and women. Feminist challenges over the past 150 years to give middle-class women access to educational and occupational equity have opened some alternative routes for women's success. For adolescent girls, as for women in later stages of life (Holland & Eisenhart 1990), however, such ambition has an uphill battle to wage against the "attractive-person" obsession.

The following description by a "second-tier" jock girl of what constitutes popularity and her account of her fear of really popular people foreground the importance (and fragility) of a carefully constructed persona and especially one that the "right" boys will find appealing:

> (24) I think personality has got to be the number one, you know—personality is probably the most important. If you've got a really good personality, you know, make people laugh all the time, then you're pretty much popular. Good looks is probably second runner up, real close up there! BUT WHEN YOU'RE TALKING ABOUT PERSONALITY . . . YOU SAY YOU GOT TO MAKE PEOPLE LAUGH AND SO ON, BUT WHAT ELSE IS—Well, just so that when you're around them you feel comfortable and not, you know, really tense or anything— That's probably the best. ARE THERE PEOPLE THAT MAKE YOU REALLY TENSE? Yes ((laughter)) LIKE WHO? Um, boys in particular. Really popular ones. I get really tense around them. I'm not—I don't know. The boy atmosphere is just kind of ((laughter)) I've really been close to girls all my life. I've really had really close friends, so it's kind of hard for me—I get really tense around people like that. But—even still—really popular people, I'm still really tense around. Maybe I'll say something wrong, maybe, you know, I'll do something wrong, and then they'll hate me, and then ((laughter)) you know.

What is essential for jock girls is approval from those already prominent, especially but not only boys. To be seen by those able to grant entry to the inner circle as desiring such entry is to jeopardize the chances of getting it.

Coolness, we have already seen, is central to burnout girls' popularity when being the center of a visible crowd in the school is still an issue. But even after concern with such popularity is left behind, coolness persists as the core of burnout status for girls. Coolness is a kind of toughness without the added implication of physical power associated with male burnouts. Coolness is a viable alternative to institutional popularity: it asserts independence of institutionally imposed norms, willingness to flaunt the injunctions of authorities and claim all the privileges of adulthood if and when one so desires. Treating conservative or conventional (especially, in this case, school-centered institutional) norms with disdain is one way to constitute oneself as cool, to stake out the territory of burnout status. Just as institutional status is essential to social status for a jock, female or male, coolness is essential to social status for a burnout, female or male. And although a burnout girl may not have access to full burnout status through fighting or other displays of physical toughness, she can be cool, verbally and emotionally tough. In example (25) a burnout girl describes how she and another friend gained status during junior high as the "biggest burnouts":

(25) But like we got along with everybody and uh we partied every day and that was the cool thing. And uh we'd smoke in school and that was cool. We used to get E's in classes [a failing grade], that was cool. You know? So, I don't know. I guess that's how.

Coolness stands in stark opposition to the jock girls' squeaky-clean image and their concern with being liked by the appropriate people and respected as "responsible" school citizens. But of course jock girls are not cowering goody-goodies, and this opposition poses a threat to their own sense of autonomy. Thus, just as burnout girls view the quest for popularity as part of their childish past, jock girls relegate the pursuit of coolness to childhood. The only time a jock girl mentioned coolness in the entire corpus of interviews was in accounting for burnouts' behavior in junior high school:

(26) Most of the people that were in junior high doing these kind of things ended up in high school ((laughter)) doing them even worse, so ((laughter)). WHEN DO KIDS START DOING THAT? Probably fifth and sixth grade when you think you're really cool—that's your cool age. Seventh—sixth, seventh, and eighth grade is your cool age, and everybody thinks, "Hey, I'm really cool, man! I'm gonna smoke! I'm gonna be real cool!" So that's what—where it starts probably.

Here, disparagingly, smoking is seen as putatively "cool" because it represents defiant assertion of adult privilege. Notice, however, that the speaker in example (26) stresses the immaturity of those vigorously pursuing coolness, implying that their claims to adult-style autonomy are sham. She is implicitly defending herself against charges of sheeplike obedience by constituting herself as having been able to uphold norms when "everybody" was urging defiance.

Jock girls are the only ones who do not embrace the notion of coolness. Burnout boys, and the more-partying in-between boys, talk occasionally about coolness as something to be cultivated, as in example (27), when an in-between boy told Penny why he could give up cigarettes at any time:

> (27) Because I don't need them. I only do them for, you know, the coolness.

And burnout girls talk with humor, but not with shame, about coolness's affecting their decisions, as shown in example (28):

> (28) I would have liked to done cheerleading or volleyball or something. AND WHY DIDN'T YOU? Some of it was uncool, you know, it was kind of uncool for—because I was considered a big burnout. ((laughter))

Just as jock boys want to insist on their physical toughness, a fair number find coolness appealing. For American boys, there are tensions in jock status connected with the need to assert a certain independence of institutionally imposed strictures on activities while at the same time using the institutional resources for enhancing their personal status. It is important for them to be seen as independent actors who are not institutionally ruled. Being labeled *squeaky-clean* can suggest a meek deference to school (or parental) regulations, whereas there can be a positive value attached to coolness—a stance of disregard for others' assessments, a willingness to engage in practices adults have forbidden, an assertion of disregard for possible negative judgments from others, a kind of social courage. So, although jock boys do not speak of actively pursuing coolness, apparently because they don't want to appear to be "trying," they do sometimes speak of it as a desirable quality and one that influenced their choice of friends in junior high. At the time of this study in Belten High, smoking, alcohol consumption, and (other) drug use were of great importance for defining burnout status. As we have already noted, the name *burnout* and the more local name *jell* or *jelly* (from *jellybrain*) refer directly to drug use. And burnouts, both girls and boys, freely define themselves in these terms. After all, drug use is a powerful symbol of their rejection of adult authority and their assertion of adult autonomy. Thus, although drug use in itself does not establish someone as a burnout any more than athletic skills confirm jock status, it is important for the burnouts to try to hold the jocks to squeaky-cleanness and to reserve drug use for themselves. If one can violate institutional norms and still reap all the institutional privileges, it becomes hard to see what is gained by eschewing institutionally endorsed roads to success. Thus, the well-known fact that many jocks drink and that a number of jock boys do some drugs leads some to assert that such people are not actually jocks, or that the category itself no longer exists (again suggesting its becoming unmarked as discussed earlier). This is illustrated by another quotation from the girl who described herself as "'in-between" in example (8):

(29) I've come to believe that there isn't such a thing in Belten, or anybody that I've met, that is a jock. Because I know for a fact that my volleyball ((laughter)) team, after games and after tournaments, we'd have parties, and we'd be drinking. And some of us, you know, I—I play volleyball, and I smoke, and there's a few others that do. And I thought back, and I said, "You guys are supposed to be jocks, what's the problem here?" ((laughter)) you know. And they said, "Hey, you know, we have a good time too," you know.

The opposition that locks jocks and burnouts into these quite divergent identity practices extends its terms into both communities of practice as well. Within the broader jock network, there is a good deal of diversity in behavior: there are clusters of girls who are truly squeaky-clean, and there are clusters of girls who party. The salience of partying in the jock–burnout split leads many jocks to refer to this latter partying cluster as *kind-of burnout.* Similarly, among the burnout girls, there are degrees of "burnout-ness."

The main cluster of burnouts is an extensive neighborhood-based network that goes back to early childhood. The girls and boys in this cluster originally engaged in school activities in junior high school, until, as discussed earlier, their noncorporate orientation came into obvious conflict with school norms. Quite distinct from this large cluster is another, smaller, cluster that is not neighborhood-based but consists of a group of girls who got together in junior high school. These girls were never interested in school activities in junior high except for attending dances, from which they were quickly excluded for drinking and getting high, and they pride themselves on being quite "wild" in comparison with the rest of the burnout girls. They stand out from other burnout girls as extreme in dress, demeanor, substance use, illegal behavior, and so on. One of these girls, in describing the social organization of space in the school courtyard, which constitutes the smoking section and the burnout territory, demonstrates the strategic nature of labeling. (The speech in parentheses in this quotation is directed to passersby.)

(30) OK, us, you know like the burnout (yeah, 'bye—wait, bum me one) the burnout chicks, they sit over here, you know, and like jocky chicks stand right here. . . . And then there's like um the guys, you know, you know, like weirdos that think they're cool. They just stand like on the steps and hang out at that little heater. (Say, hey!) And then the poins are inside in the cafeteria, because they're probably afraid to come out in the courtyard.

In this quotation, by referring to a group of burnout and in-between girls who smoke as *jocks,* the main group of burnout boys as *weirdos,* and other in-betweens and all the jocks as *poins* (from *poindexters),* the speaker positions herself and her friends in relation to the rest of the school population. She is defining her group as normative burnouts, and it is not surprising that others have referred to them, in turn, as *burned-out burnouts.*

There are many fault lines in the neat divisions we have made between jocks and burnouts, and many in the school find identification with either group deeply problematic. Some of the strongest disapproval of jocks by nonjocks and of burnouts by nonburnouts is reserved for what are seen as typically female modes of seeking popularity and asserting coolness.

Snobs and Sluts

A major character flaw that many in the school associate with jocks is being stuck-up or snobby. Boys can, of course, be snobs. But it is far easier for boys than for girls to achieve institutional prominence without drawing the charge of being stuck-up. The easiest way is simply to shine on the football field. But not all boys have this option. The successful class president quoted in example (22) clearly saw the potential for others' resentment when one cultivates promi-nence. He recommends inclusiveness and tolerance of others as the best strategy for not raising others' hackles:

(31) . . . if you're not snobby about it, the people tend to—you t- you tend to overcome, and win a lot more people if you become popular but still at the same time not too snobby. I try to talk to a lot of people now, and like right now, you know, because—because I'm president of the class, there's a lot of people that, sort of like, may know me by name or something, but there's not like really a—a group of people I won't talk to. Because a lot of people, they'll say, "Well, I don't like to talk to people in the courtyard" ((burnouts)), you know. YEAH. RIGHT. That's just the way it is. But I don't see what's wrong with it. It's not like you're s- you're- you're becoming one. Which is not, you know—what they do, it doesn't bother me. If they want to do what they do with their life, it's fine. And you shouldn't distinguish between certain types of t- people. You should just want to relate to as many people as possible.

But for jock girls, pursuit of a wide range of contacts carries with it a threat to the persona they struggle so hard to develop. To talk to a burnout girl "in the courtyard" is indeed to run the risk of "becoming one." Why? Because, as we have said in many different ways, jock girls are judged primarily by their associ-ates and only secondarily by their achievements. For boys, in contrast, the achievements come first. It is overwhelmingly girls who describe other girls as excluding people, as pursuing recognition by the school's stars at the expense of those who are outside the star circle. This is how one burnout girl accounts for not trying out for cheerleading in ninth grade (note that this is not the same girl quoted in (28)):

(32)   DID YOU GET INVOLVED IN ACTIVITIES AND STUFF LIKE THAT? Um, ninth grade, I was involved in volleyball, because that's when it started. Um, dances, here and there. I just went to talk to people. I wasn't dancing or nothing. I went to listen to the band and that. Um, uh, I can't say I really went to any basketball games or anything like that. DID YOU GO OUT FOR CHEERLEADING OR ANYTHING LIKE THAT? Now that started in the ninth grade. And that's when I—well, how—[I don't] really know how to explain how I felt. I felt that at that time, I didn't have to do that to be popular. And I thought, "Hmm, cheerleaders—everybody's going to look up at them, and they're going to, you know ((laughter)) they're going to be stuck-up, and I don't want to be known as a stuck-up cheerleader," and—so I steered away from that. I wanted to be one though. YOU WANTED TO BE ONE—That's—that's what was, that—I did, you know, because I knew I'd enjoy it. And I thought, "Well, look at the ones that were last year. All the girls look down on them. 'She's a stuck-up cheerleader,'" you know. So—

Here a quintessentially jock activity for girls—cheerleading—is equated with being seen as stuck-up (and thus to be avoided whatever its other attractions might be). In example (33), a burnout girl describes how she assumes jocks view people like her:

(33)   I think of like jocks as like sort of higher up, you know, so you think that you know, they'd be saying, "Hey," you know, "let's get rid of these like diddly little people," you know?

The management of social visibility, as we have seen, preoccupies girls seeking status as jocks. It does not, however, endear a jock girl to those who are not welcomed to her orbit, or to her old friends whom she has no time for because she is so busy networking. Even for a girl who cares only about her status among the activities-oriented crowd, the twin projects of cultivating a pleasing personality and pursuing prominence are hard to balance successfully. If the pursuit of prominence is too evident, even other institutionally minded people may well reject as stuck-up and snobby the personality thereby produced. Likability within the jock crowd cannot be sacrificed, because one needs social ties of friendship or romance for success as a jock girl: one must be someone others want as a friend or sweetheart, Good personhood ought to make others feel welcome, not excluded.

Girl jocks, then, face considerable difficulty. They must regulate their social alliances with care in order to attain the social visibility they need. But this regulation tends to involve excluding many, which leads naturally to charges of being a snob. Being a stuck-up snob, however, is inconsistent with the pleasing personality the successful jock girl needs. And of course the good personhood the jock girl constructs is itself seen as laudable, a special kind of achievement compared implicitly to the not-so-good personhood of others who have not made the same effort to seek such goodness. Such invidious comparisons, however silent they may be, also tend to lead those put down by them to view jock girls' pride in their personae as more evidence of their being stuck-up. Thus, part of burnout girls' explicit rejection of popularity by the time they reach high school derives from their despising what they see as the snobbery and sense of superiority of jock girls. But that is not the only reason for their rejection of popularity.

Part of the presentation of a corporate being is as a person who is "in control" of both her professional and her personal affairs. In the interests of presenting an image of corporate competence, jocks uniformly hide personal and family problems from their peers (see Eckert 1989). In addition, they strive to maintain an image of control over their "urges," and for jock girls, this involves importantly a control over their images as heterosexual beings. Burnouts, on the other hand, emphasize "being yourself" and value the sharing of problems. And while burnout girls do not necessarily flaunt heterosexual engagement, they certainly are not concerned with presenting an abstemious image, a concern that would be decidedly "uncool."

It is important to emphasize that it is above all the heterosexual image that is at issue in this opposition rather than sexual behavior itself. Although a jock girl's unpublicized engagement in sexual relations with a boyfriend may be considered her own business, any appearance of promiscuity is not. Indeed, anything that contributes to such an appearance, including styles of hair, dress, and makeup, as well as demeanor, will be seen as "slutty" and can seriously threaten a jock girl's status, costing her female friends as well as the possibility of being judged an appropriate public partner for a jock boy. One jock girl even considered dating too many boys to be dangerous for one's reputation:

> (34) Well, maybe there's some, I don't really know, that go out with a different guy every week. Because I—I don't—I don't think that's so much true, because you can—that—that would kind of give you a bad reputation ((laughter)) I think. I don't know. I'd leave a little space in between.

To be labeled a *slut* is to fail in the school's corporate culture. It is not surprising, then, that jocks view the prototypical burnout girl as slutty, and that burnouts view the prototypical jock girl as phony and uptight. The crucial difference is not so much in sexual behavior but in the fact that burnouts, in opposition to jocks, are not concerned with sluttiness—either in image or in behavior. Burnout girls view so-called slutty patterns of dress and demeanor as simply personal characteristics, which they may or may not think problematic, but certainly not as making someone an unsuitable friend. *Slut* is a category label that fuses gender and class.

Both burnout and jock girls actively construct their social statuses and they do so in ways that allow them to cooperate with their male peers in constituting the basic social orientation of their respective categories: resistance to institutional norms in the one case and participation in the hierarchical institutionally sanctioned practice in the other. In both cases, however, the girls lack access to the full repertoire of practices that can constitute category status for boys. And the practices open to girls in each category are highly likely to evoke great hostility from girls in the other category. Burnout girls vigorously reject the relation-cultivating popularity so important to jock girls; they hate the snobbiness and "holier-than-thou" attitudes that they associate with it. Jock girls in turn are contemptuous of the lack of "self-control" associated with coolness. They see coolness as all too easily leading to sluttiness, which they roundly condemn—and work hard to keep at bay.

Burnout girls and jock girls construct strikingly different solutions to the dilemma created for them by the overarching gender structures they all experience, structures characterized by male dominance and heterosexist preoccupation with sexual differentiation. And each group judges the other's strategic moves in response to these constraints very harshly. One result is that the overall differences in normative patterns of practice between burnout and jock girls are far greater than those between burnout and jock boys. After junior high, opposition—and conflict—between burnouts and jocks centers on opposition—and (primarily) symbolic conflict—between burnout and jock girls. This is reflected with startling clarity in patterns of phonological variation, to which we now turn.

Pronouncing Selves

The depth of the jock–burnout opposition in Belten High is borne out by differences in speech between the members of the two categories: differences in vocabulary, in grammar, in pronunciation. But more important, these speech differences are not simply markers of category affiliation. They carry in themselves complex social meanings, like tough, cool, slutty, casual, or mean, and these meanings are part of the construction of categories like those labeled by *female, male, jock, burnout*. Finding these meanings through correlations between the use of linguistic variables and indicators of social practice is a major challenge for sociolinguists. In this section, we focus on several phonological variables that enter into the construction of social identities in Belten

High, and that simultaneously are part of what constitutes a "Midwest," or Detroit, or Michigan accent. The production of linguistic styles is part of the production of identities, and local and regional pronunciations provide some of the resources that can be put to stylistic use.

The following discussion focuses on two vowels that have symbolic significance in this community. The symbolic significance is associated with recent innovations in pronunciation, innovations that reflect sound changes in progress:

- (uh) as in *fun, cuff, but* (phonetically [ ]), is moving back so that it comes to sound like the vowel in *fawn, cough, bought* [ ].
- The nucleus [a] of the diphthong (ay) as in *file, line, heist* raises to [ʌ] or [ɔ], so that the diphthong may sound more like the diphthong in *foil, loin, hoist.*

For each of these vowels, pronunciations in the stream of speech will vary from the conservative to the innovative with several stages in between. Most speakers in the community use the full range of pronunciations, generally within the same conversation. However, speakers will vary in the frequency with which they use the more conservative and more innovative pronunciations. It is in the speaker's average pronunciation or in the strategic use of one or the other pronunciation that this variability comes to have social meaning.

The changes described for the vowels above represent linguistic changes in progress, and certain social principles about such changes have emerged over the years (see Chambers 1995; Labov 1972, 1994). In general, sound change originates in locally based, working-class communities and spreads gradually upward through the socioeconomic hierarchy. In this way, new sound changes tend to carry local meaning and to serve as part of the local social-symbolic repertoire. This means that the speech of locally based working-class groups will generally show more of the innovative variants discussed above than that of middle-class groups in the same community. Middle-class speakers, on the contrary, are more likely to avoid clearly local pronunciations inasmuch as they are engaged in corporate institutions that strive to transcend local resources and loyalties. It is to be expected, then, that burnouts, with their heightened locally based identities and loyalties, might use more of the advanced variants for these vowels than do the institutionally identified jocks.

Gender, on the other hand, does not correlate quite as consistently with linguistic variables as class does. Female speakers quite regularly lead in sound change, but there are cases in which they do not.[5] More interesting, gender commonly crosscuts class, so that although working-class women may lead working-class men in a particular sound change, middle-class women may lag behind middle-class men in the same change. Such patterns can emerge only from a co-construction of gender and class, and this co-construction emerges quite clearly in the speech of the students of Belten High.

Table 1 **Correlation of Backing of (uh) with Combined Sex and Social Category**

Female jocks	Male jocks	Female burnouts	Male burnouts
.43	.40	.62	.54

Table 2 **Extreme Raising of the Nucleus of (ay) with Combined Sex and Social Category**

Female jocks	Male jocks	Female burnouts	Male burnouts
.38	.28	.79	.50

In across-the-board correlations of (uh) and (ay) with sex and social-category membership, we find that although the backing of (uh) as in *fun, cuff,* and *but* correlates only with social category, with the burnouts leading, the raising of the nucleus in (ay) *(file, line, heist)* correlates only with sex, with the girls leading. Are we to stop with these correlations, and declare that the backing of (uh) "means" burnout and the raising of the nucleus in (ay) "means" female? Are they markers of gender and category membership or are they symbolic of some aspects of social practice and identity that are part of what jocks and burnouts, and females and males, are about? In fact, when we dig deeper, we will see that these data reflect a great complexity of social practice.

Tables 1 and 2 show figures for correlations of speakers' sex and social-category affiliation (as assigned on the basis of network positions and descriptions by self and others) with the backing of (uh) and the raising of (ay).[6] The correlations in these and subsequent tables are significant at the .001 level, indicating the minimum likelihood that the correlations could be the result of chance. In each table, a probability value is shown for each group of speakers. The absolute numbers are not important, only their relative values; innovative pronunciation is most frequent among the group of speakers for whom the number is highest, least frequent among those for whom it is lowest. When we tease apart sex and social-category membership in the data for (uh), as shown in Table 1, we find that within each social category, the girls lead the boys, although particularly among the jocks this lead is not large enough to be significant in itself. We also find that the burnouts' lead over the jocks is somewhat greater among the girls than among the boys. Correlations for extreme raising in (ay) show a pattern similar to those for the backing of (uh), as shown in Table 2.

Table 3 **Correlation of Backing of (uh) with Combined Sex and Social Category, Separating Two Clusters of Burnout Girls**

Female jocks	Male jocks	Main Female burnouts	Burned-out female burnouts	Male burnouts
.41	.38	.53	.65	.52

Table 4 **Extreme Raising of (ay), Combining Sex and Social Category, Separating Two Clusters of Burnout Girls**

Female jocks	Male jocks	Main Female burnouts	Burned-out female burnouts	Male burnouts
.42	.32	.47	.93	.54

What can be drawn from the tables is that whatever distinguishes jocks and burnouts also distinguishes boys and girls within those categories; or whatever distinguishes boys and girls also distinguishes jocks and burnouts within those sex groups. One would be hard pressed to establish whether the backing of (uh) or the raising of the nucleus in (ay) is associated with femaleness or burnout-ness. And indeed, what distinguishes gender from sex is that femaleness and maleness cannot be imagined independently of other aspects of identity, such as jock- and burnout-hood.

If these vowels serve to construct meaning in the high school, and if category and gender interact in as complex a way as shown in the earlier sections, we might expect to find some of this complexity reflected in the vowels as well as in labeling practices. Let us turn to the division among the burnout girls discussed earlier, in which burned-out burnout girls distinguish themselves from the "jocky" burnouts. It turns out that these girls are overwhelmingly in the lead in the use of innovative variants of both (uh) and (ay).

Table 3 separates the burned-out burnout girls from the "regular" burnout girls. Although the "regular" burnout girls still back (uh) more than the jock girls, the burned-out burnout girls are far more extreme. A similar pattern shows up for the raising of the nucleus in (ay), in which the burned-out burnouts are overwhelmingly in the lead (see Table 4).

Vowels such as these do not simply fall into a neutral linguistic space. Consider the following segment of conversation with a burned-out burnout:

(35) . . . we used to tell our moms that we'd—uh—she'd be sleeping at my house, I'd be sleeping at hers. We'd go out and pull a all-nighter, you know ((laughter)) I'd come home the next day, "Where were you?" "Jane's." "No you weren't." Because her mom and my mom are like really close—since we got in so much trouble they know each other really good.

Interactions are situations in which social meaning is made. When this girl says to Penny, for example, "We'd go out and pull a all-nighter," raising the nucleus of (ay) in *all-nighter* so that it clearly sounds like *all-noiter,* Penny associates what she perceives about this girl in general, and what the girl is saying in particular, with this element of linguistic style. Presumably, in speaking to Penny in this way, the speaker presents herself as a burned-out burnout—as someone who gets around, does pretty much what she wants, gets in trouble, has fun, doesn't clean up her act too much for an adult like Penny, and so on. In the course of this mutual construction, the variable (ay) takes on meaning—perhaps not in isolation, but at least as a component of a broader style. In their extreme speech, then, the burned-out burnout girls are not simply using phonetic variants with a meaning already set and waiting to be recycled. Rather, their very use of those variants produces a social meaning. They are simultaneously creating meaning for (ay) and for being burned-out burnouts. Thus, as in the labeling discussed in the earlier sections, the use of phonetic variation and the construction of identities are inseparable.

Conclusion

Belten High provides some glimpses of communities of practice at work. Their members are engaging in a wide range of activities through which they constitute themselves and their social relations and project their future life histories. Language, gender, and class are all produced through such social practices. These practices have locally distinctive features, but they show patterns reflecting the influence of a larger society and its institutions. They also reflect a historical location with its particular pasts and prospective futures.

Readers may wonder just which communities of practice exist. Do girls and boys form separate communities of practice? Do jocks and burnouts? What about in-betweens? Jocky jocks? Burned-out burnouts? Does the student body of the whole high school constitute a community of practice?

Questions like this miss a critical point about communities of practice. they are not determined by their membership but by the endeavors that bring those members (and others who have preceded or will succeed them) into relations with one another (which may or may not be face-to-face), and by the practices that develop around, and transform, these endeavors. So certainly most—perhaps all—of the student-body members belong to a community focused on the issues of school-sponsored curricular and extracurricular activities or other practices involving students that occur at school or are relevant to what is going on there. The practices toward which community members are oriented focus on the issues we have briefly discussed, some high-level and others more mundane: how and whether to compete in the school-based hierarchy; how and whether to participate in the heterosexual marketplace; relation to school and family authority; post–high school prospects; who to hang out with during school; what to do directly after school (and with whom); what to do in the evenings and on weekends; where to eat lunch; whether to use drugs; what to wear; how to talk; and so on. Athletic boy jocks and burned-out burnout girls, for example, have different forms of membership in this large community of practice. And in the process of pursuing these different forms of membership, they attend to communities of practice of their own, based on and constituting specific places and points of view within the larger community.

We do not actually have to worry about delimiting communities of practice in advance. Rather, we look at people and the practices mediating their relations to one another in order to understand better the raw materials through which they constitute their own and others' identities and relations. There is no community focused on linguistic practice, no community focused on gender practice, no community focused on class practice. As we have seen, seeking popularity (or refusing to), aspiring to coolness (or refusing to), and similar practices of various kinds are saturated with implications, at one and the same time, for language, gender, and class. And the constitution of socially significant communities—both their membership and the actual content of the practices that make them into a community—has an ongoing history.

We have explored two aspects of language use at Belten: labeling and other kinds of talk about social categories and relations; and variation in the pronunciation of certain vowels. The first gives us a perspective from linguistic content on how gender and class practices and the struggles centered on them proceed. Social labeling discriminates among people and is used as a weapon to divide and to deride. Attempts to define and delimit what labels mean are really attempts to delimit what people and the social structures they build can or should be like. Unequal power in general social processes translates into unequal power in succeeding in definitional projects.[7] The prize, of course, is not controlling what this or that word means; but controlling the immediate direction of this or that aspect of social life, perhaps continuing existing social structures and relations or perhaps transforming them in some way. Social talk helps in the process of institutionalizing power and gender relations, and it helps give local force and bite to larger-scale social constructions.

Investigations of phonological variation offer a way to view similar phenomena but at a different level. Actual uses of language always have a formal aspect as well as content, and form always enriches (and sometimes contradicts) what is conveyed in social talk. Formal properties of utterances in many cases are the only source of social meaning. Of course, how one pronounces a particular vowel on a particular occasion seldom receives the same conscious attention that shapes the content of answers to questions about popularity and coolness. Nor are ordinary people as well able to say what someone else's vowels sounded like as they are to report the content of what she said. But as shown above, the low-level details of pronunciation can give a great deal of information about how people are actively constituting their own social identities and relations. And it is such subtle variations and the social meanings they express that are the stuff of which long-term and large-scale changes in conventions of linguistic practice are made.

Social talk at Belten made it clear to us that there were no separable processes constructing gender and class. Male dominance and class relations are both involved in issues of physical prowess; forms of female agency and class practices link critically to popularity and coolness; and heterosexism informs the content of class-linked femininities and masculinities. General patterns emerge only when we stop trying to partition off matters of class from matters of gender. Similarly, patterns of vowel pronunciation are clarified when we try thinking about class-gender complexes rather than class and gender as independent. Our extracts from interviews also suggest, however, the messiness of practice, its failure to fit perfectly with neat structural analyses, the social ambiguities and contradictions it embodies. Only by continuing to examine different communities of practice and the complexities within them can we really begin to come to grips with the historicity of language, gender, class, and their interactions.

Notes

1. This chapter descends directly from an invited talk we gave on July 20, 1993, at the Linguistic Society of America's Summer Institute, Ohio State University, Columbus. We thank that audience and the many others who have been interested in our ideas for their comments and questions. We thank the editors of this volume, Kira Hall and Mary Bucholtz, for their excellent advice and for their patience. Finally, we thank each other for finishing this project. As before, our names appear alphabetically.
2. This study was funded by the National Science Foundation (BNS 8023291), the Spencer Foundation, and the Horace Rackham School of Graduate Studies at the University of Michigan.
3. All quoted speech is taken from tape-recorded interviews. Penny's speech is printed in upper case. Hesitations, false starts, and so on are not edited out of these materials.
4. See McElhinny (this volume) for discussion of ways women now being hired as police officers are finding to share in normative conceptions of what it means to be a good police officer without jeopardizing their sense of themselves as "feminine."
5. See Eckert (1990a) and Labov (1991) for a piece of the debate about gender and variation.
6. The statistics in this and all following tables were calculated using Goldvarb 2, a Macintosh-based version of the variable-rule program, which is a statistical package designed specifically for the analysis of sociolinguistic variation. For information about the analysis of variation, see Sankoff (1978).
7. See, for example, McConnell-Ginet (1989) for a discussion, albeit more narrowly linguistic, of how social contexts affect definitional success.

References

Bem, Sandra L. (1993). *The lenses of gender: Transforming the debate on sexual inequality.* New Haven: Yale University Press.

Butler, Judith (1993). *Bodies that matter.* New York: Routledge.

Cameron, Deborah (forthcoming). The language-gender interface: Challenging co-optation. In Victoria Bergvall, Janet Bing, and Alice F. Freed (eds.) *Language and gender research: Theory and method*. New York: Longman.

Chambers, J. K. (1995). *Sociolinguistic theory*. Oxford: Basil Blackwell.

Connell, R. W. (1987). *Gender and power: Society, the person and sexual politics*. Stanford: Stanford University Press.

di Leonardo, Micaela (ed.) (1991). *Gender at the crossroads of knowledge: Feminist anthropology in the postmodern era*. Berkeley: University of California Press.

Eckert, Penelope (1988). Sound change and adolescent social structure *Language in Society* 17: 183–207.

——— (1989). *Jocks and burnouts: Social categories and identity in the high school*. New York: Teachers College Press.

——— (1990a). The whole woman: Sex and gender differences in variation. *Language Variation and Change* 1: 245–67.

——— (1990b). Cooperative competition in adolescent girl talk. *Discourse Processes* 13: 92–122.

Eckert, Penelope, and Sally McConnell-Ginet (1992a). Communities of practice: Where language, gender, and power all live. In Kira Hall, Mary Bucholtz and Birch Moonwomon (eds.), *Locating power: Proceedings of the Second Berkeley Women and Language Conference*. Berkeley: Berkeley Women and Language Group. 89–99.

——— (1992b). Think practically and look locally: Language and gender as community-based practice. *Annual Review of Anthropology* 21: 461–90.

Holland, Dorothy C., and Margaret A. Eisenhart (1990). *Educated in romance*. Chicago: University of Chicago Press.

Labov, William (1972). On the mechanism of linguistic change. In *Sociolinguistic patterns*. Philadelphia: University of Pennsylvania Press. 160–82.

——— (1991). The intersection of sex and social class in the course of linguistic change. *Language Variation and Change* 2(2): 205–51.

——— (1994). *Principles of linguistic change: Internal factors*. Oxford: Basil Blackwell.

McConnell-Ginet, Sally (1989). The sexual (re)production of meaning: A discourse-based theory. In Francine W. Frank and Paula A. Treichler (eds.), *Language, gender, and professional writing: Theoretical approaches and guidelines for nonsexist usage*. New York: Modern Language Association. 35–50.

McElhinny, Bonnie S. (this volume). Challenging hegemonic masculinities: Female and male police officers handling domestic violence.

Rich, Adrienne (1980). Compulsory heterosexuality and lesbian existence. *Signs* (5): 631–60.

Sankoff, David (ed.) (1978). *Linguistic variation: Models and methods*. New York: Academic Press.

Segal, Lynne (1990). *Slow motion: Changing masculinities, changing men*. New Brunswick: Rutgers University Press.

Talbot, Mary (this volume). A synthetic sisterhood: False friends in a teenage magazine.

Thorne, Barrie (1993). *Gender play*, New Brunswick: Rutgers University Press.

Collaborative Activity 7.3

Based on your reading of the article by Eckert and McConnell-Ginet, consider the following questions in your small group: How does their research situation—the purpose, subject, participants, and setting—influence the types of research they conduct? What are the effects of the primary research they conduct (the inclusion, for instance, of excerpts from taped dialogue)? What are the effects of the secondary research included? Identify the questions that guide their research, and then explain how their use of both primary and secondary research helps them to support and draw their conclusions.

Collaborative Activity 7.4

Working in the same groups as you did in the previous activity, consider how Eckert and McConnell-Ginet use visual elements in their texts. This includes their use of headings, block quotes, excerpts from transcripts, and tables. What and how do these visual elements contribute to the presentation of their research? Compare their use of visual elements with that of Lippi-Green in her chapter on Disney films that you read in Chapter 6. What can you learn about using visual elements in your own writing from these texts?

Describing Researched Position Papers

By this point you should understand what "research" means in the scene of the writing course, particularly as that scene functions as a port of entry into other disciplinary scenes. While many research-based genres in writing courses share the challenge of designing appropriate subjects and use common kinds of research, other elements of research-based genres vary too much from one genre to another to be able to discuss them in common here. Instead, we will focus on one of the most common research-based genres assigned in the first-year writing course: the **researched position paper**. Writers of researched position papers conduct substantial research into a given subject in order to discover and articulate their position on it. As such, the researched position paper requires the gathering of sources not simply as an exercise in doing research but rather as an essential part of discovering what you think.

In what follows, we will build on your understanding of the writing course scene to help you see how the researched position paper's generic features fulfill the objectives and embody the values of the academic scene. Based on such understanding of scene, situation, and generic features, you should be able to create your own researched position paper effectively and be better prepared to write research projects in courses other than writing courses.

Because they share a scene and some elements of a common situation, researched position papers share many traits with other writing course genres, especially analysis and argument papers. All three genres, of course, occur in the writing class setting, with teacher and student participants, and even similar subjects. All three genres share some resulting generic features, including an emphasis on a controlling idea (taking the form of a central claim in analysis papers), the use of evidence and analysis, organizational conventions and possibilities, and a distanced style and tone. What makes the researched position paper different from these other genres appears in its name: It draws heavily on research to establish its position. *The researched position paper reflects this valuing of research in its typical features, including content, rhetorical appeals, structure, format, sentences, and words.*

CONTENT—SELECTING SUBJECTS

Selecting a subject appropriate for a researched position paper in a writing class begins with the concerns we have already described and summarized in Box 7.1 (p. 344): Is the subject interesting, manageable, and appropriate to the scene? But selecting a good subject also involves, as always, *appropriateness for the genre*. What makes a good subject for a researched position paper differs from what makes a good subject not only for a short story, a biography, a music review, or even an analysis paper, but also for a researched case study, Web site, editorial, or letter to a representative. Researched position papers aim to have writers and readers discover what they think by critically examining the information, logic, and perspectives of others. Not all subjects lend themselves to such an academic and research-based approach. First of all, then, subjects appropriate for a researched position paper must meet some essential criteria for the genre:

- The subject must be able to be analyzed
- The subject must be able to be studied from multiple perspectives, either through multiple published perspectives or those perspectives combined with evidence and information gathered through primary research

Writing Activity 7.8

List some subjects that might be appropriate for researched position papers. These should be subjects that are interesting and manageable, about which you have yet to formulate a position. Once you have generated a list of subjects, apply the above criteria. Do the subjects lend themselves to analysis, logic, and research, providing multiple perspectives? Which subjects lend themselves more to primary research and which to secondary research? Be prepared to make a case for the appropriateness of your subjects. In order to be interesting, research subjects should not only be engaging (to readers such as your teacher) but should also engage you and cast you in the role of "critical coinvestigator," an active participant in the conversation. All of the subjects should be analyzed according to logic and should be seen from multiple points of view. They all should, in other words, suit the researched position paper genre.

RHETORICAL APPEALS—SELECTING ACADEMICALLY CREDIBLE SOURCES

Since researched position papers approach their subjects through logical analysis and critique, they rely heavily on logos over pathos and ethos (for more on these concepts, refer to Chapter 2). They focus on the subject of research and the weight of evidence and sources. In keeping with this emphasis on logic and evidence, writers work toward an image or ethos of a well-informed, knowledgeable person. And although some researched position papers may rely on pathos or appeals to readers' emotions or values (such as a researched position paper on stem cell research or euthanasia), the focus is on *logos*, which is reflected in the use of evidence and sources.

If you look at the last page of each sample researched position paper in this chapter (pp. 413–418), you will see a list of the sources each writer used. Those articles, books, Web sites, and interviews are the sources of the evidence each writer used to develop and support the writer's argument in the paper. If you look in the papers themselves, you will see that these sources provide dates, statistics, and other facts, quotations from experts and other relevant people, and opposing arguments—what one of our students calls "facts, stats, and quotes." The reasons for finding sources should be evident from our discussion so far: Researched position papers depend on sources to provide the information and multiple perspectives that should help writers and readers analyze the subject and draw conclusions about what they think.

But not just any sources of evidence will do: In order to maintain a credible ethos in such a logos-centered genre, the writer must use sources that are also centered on logos, ones that are considered reliable and credible within the particular academic scene. When writing a research project in a specialized course, you will need to learn from your teacher and librarians which journals and publishers are considered most reputable. When writing a researched position paper in a writing class, you need to use sources that are considered sufficiently "academic." Until relatively recently, readers of researched position papers expected only academic library sources—books and articles that would be shelved in a college or university library. Even popular magazines and books that might exist in public libraries were considered less reliable. While academic library sources are still required for most researched position papers, increasingly accepted as well are credible Internet sources.

Since educated, academic audiences are the researched position papers' audience, and since the research is meant to help provide information and perspectives to appeal to the rational mind of writers and readers, the sources must provide information and perspectives that will not mislead the writer and that the readers will consider credible. The kinds of books and articles found in academic libraries are likely to meet those criteria. Most library books and articles are published only after experts in their fields have reviewed the work and found them sound, so that they share the standards and values of the academic scene. The information they provide, then, has been judged reliable; you can probably trust its accuracy (for its time). Although the perspectives they provide have been judged reasonable and supportable by evidence and sound logic, however, such resources should not be used uncritically. They could be out of date or incomplete, their assumptions no longer valid. This is why you should use Box 7.2 (p. 389) to assess the credibility of your sources.

Some sources found on the Internet share academic standards for knowledge and logic and so make good sources for researched position papers, but some do not. Unlike publications in the library, anyone can post a site on the Internet, with no review of the content of that site. Once you understand the goals and values of colleges and universities, you can discern those Internet sites that academic readers (represented by your writing course instructor) would find reliable versus those academics would not find credible. Academics would seek Internet sources that come from experts in a field, people with credentials that testify to their expertise like advanced degrees or affiliations with a college or university. Academics would want those experts to be disinterested parties, that is, not to be paid by anyone with a vested interest in the issue being discussed. When scholars published in a library are not disinterested, the journal editor usually discloses that fact explicitly (for example, it is noted when a chemist's work has been funded by a drug company). Academic readers of a logos-based genre like researched position papers would look for Internet sources that support any claims with facts, logic, and research, and they would want to see the sources of that information cited. Since the Internet has become such a popular and convenient source for information, many of its sources now meet academic standards for reliability and make good sources for researched position papers.

Writing Activity 7.9

Examine the sample researched position papers (pp. 408–438), and assess how each balances logos, pathos, and ethos. In addition to seeing the emphasis on logos, find places where the writers appeal to readers' emotions, where they reveal their judgments, and where they establish their knowledge and credibility. How does the use of appeals correspond to the paper's subject and purpose? How well does each writer use the three appeals, given the expectations for researched position papers?

Collaborative Activity 7.5

Look at the lists of sources at the ends of the sample researched position papers. Which of their sources would you find in an academic library, which on the Internet? Note the titles of the books and journals and how scholarly and academically specific they sound rather than popular and general (*IEEE Intelligent Systems and Their Applications* or *New Statesman* rather than *People* or *Working Woman*). What can you tell about the Internet sources from their listings? Does anything signal how credible they are, or would you have to look them up (note, for example, if the Internet URLs end with .com or .gov for a commercial or government site or .edu or .org for an educational or organizational site). Look up on the Internet one of the cited sources. Look for how credible it appears—who sponsors the site, where does its information come from, what else makes it look academic or not? Compare notes with your classmates, and create your own guidelines for how you can tell which sources are ones appropriate to academic researched position papers.

Writing Activity 7.10

With the help of your handbook, library staff, or teacher, find six sources on one of the subjects you ended up with in Writing Activity 7.8 above—three library sources, three Internet sources. Using the questions for evaluating sources in Box 7.2, assess how credible each source would be for an academic audience of a researched position paper in a writing course.

Collaborative Activity 7.6

Bring your sources from the previous activity to class, including the URLs or, if your classroom is not computerized, a printout of the home page of each Internet site. Using the questions for evaluating sources, on the following page, compare your sources with your classmates, helping each other to judge whether they seem suitable for writing class researched position papers.

> **Box 7.2** *Questions for Evaluating Academic Credibility of Sources*
>
> 1. **Who wrote it?** What signals the author's expertise on that subject? Does the author have advanced degrees in the subject? Is the author connected to a college or university? (If you can't tell who wrote the source, be cautious.)
> 2. **Who published it?** Is the publisher a scholarly press or journal, one affiliated with a college or university? If not, is it sponsored by an organization that strives for neutrality, one that does not have an apparent political agenda? (If there is no publisher, as in some Web sites, the credibility of the author becomes essential.)
> 3. **When was it published?** If it is not within the last five years, is the subject a timeless one that will not be affected significantly by advances in research or new discoveries? (Even on timeless subjects, include more recent sources whenever possible to ensure your currency on the subject.)
> 4. **What other sources are cited?** Check the bibliography and cross references throughout. Are credible sources cited in the work? Are there names or studies that come up repeatedly in discussions of the subject by credible sources? If so, those repeated names or studies should be included in most credible sources.

Because the researched position paper so heavily stresses logos, the writer's ethos in the genre traditionally signals intellectual authority, and authority in the academic scene comes from knowledge. Ideally, in order to become thoroughly informed about the subject, writers would read every source that exists on the chosen subject. Writers of research projects in academic majors or in a narrower, more specialized discipline may indeed master all the sources on a subject they are researching. In writing classes, though, many researched position paper subjects have been written about by too many people for too long for one person to master everything, so writers typically need to narrow their subject and narrow their stance on that subject. Even in writing courses, writers need to find enough sources to feel confident that they know what they are writing about and that academic readers will accept their authority. How many sources that requires varies, of course: It depends on whether the writer is using books or articles or Web sites, it depends on the teacher's requirements, and it varies in different situations. You can look at the sample researched position papers, though, to see how many sources each of them cited at the end. You may not be able to read everything written on a subject, but you can read enough to feel genuinely informed and knowledgeable.

Part of establishing authority within the academic scene is showing that the writer understands and has considered the subject with some **complexity.** Complexity involves different things for different subjects, such as seeing implications, identifying assumptions, or countering opposing arguments, but *for all researched position papers (and most academic genres) complexity includes seeing the subject from multiple perspectives, not just the writer's.* The sample researched position papers all contain such complexity, especially addressing opposing arguments. If all the sources, then, share a common perspective, and no conflicting viewpoints are included, readers may view the writer as one-sided, undermining the writer's credibility. Remember, too, that the researched position paper's emphasis on logos comes in part from the goal of helping readers and writers discover what they think; including sources from multiple perspectives, even though embedded in a claim for one perspective, helps clarify readers' and especially the writer's judgments.

Writing Activity 7.11

Examine the researched position papers on pages 408–438 to see what kinds of complexity each explores. Where does the paper go beyond a straight statement of the author's claim or conclusion? Does the author address the implications of his or her conclusion? Are opposing perspectives addressed directly? What keeps the paper from being too simple? Once you find those areas of complexity, note whether secondary sources contribute to that complexity. Does the author cite others at those points?

Writing Activity 7.12

Add to the sources you collected in Writing Activity 7.10 two more sources that have perspectives different from the others. Find sources that approach the subject from a different angle (for example, considering economic factors while others consider only medical factors) or that hold opposing viewpoints.

STRUCTURE—INTEGRATING SOURCES WITHIN A CONTROLLING IDEA

Researched position papers are structured much like analysis papers and argument papers overall, with an introduction-body-conclusion based around a controlling idea. Like the introduction to an analysis paper, researched position papers usually begin by giving the readers an overview of the subject—setting the scene for the discussion and situating the subject and the writer's particular purpose, which is reflected by the controlling idea.

Your discovered position about the subject constitutes the researched position paper's controlling idea, and the controlling idea controls the structure of the paper, helping you decide what to include and within what framework. While the sources you find can support or challenge your ideas, they cannot tell you what to think or what to write in your researched position paper.

Academics explore an idea by testing it against what others have said and thought; they believe that knowledge and truth come from putting information together with analysis and logic, from considering all perspectives on a subject thoroughly and carefully. The purpose of the researched position paper in a writing course, then, is to have you go through the process of gathering and analyzing information so you can *discover and explain in an academically recognized way* what appears to you to be true. In short, a researched position paper's controlling idea presents what the writer has discovered through the research.

As it does in analysis papers and argument papers, the controlling idea focuses and directs the paper. For example, you might note the controlling ideas of the sample researched position papers: Each paper has a point to make, a primary purpose and idea that goes beyond "Here is what others have said or thought." With the academic scene's emphasis on an individual's thinking and ideas, it is surely not surprising that the researched position paper requires an individual's *idea* as well as information. That idea can come only from your own thinking; it will not come directly from your sources, although it may be informed by those sources. Sources provide dates, statistics, and other facts, quotations from experts, and multiple perspectives; with that input, you provide the controlling idea, the argument, the points.

Writing Activity 7.13

Examine the introductions of the sample researched position papers, and explain how they are appropriate to the scene and situation of the researched position paper. What techniques are used to introduce the paper, and which do you find most effective? Next, identify again the controlling ideas of each paper. To what extent are they framed by the introduction and to what extent do they emphasize the writer's thoughts and ideas about the subject?

The *interaction* of your ideas with information from your sources makes the use of sources especially challenging. You must structure the paper so that it integrates your sources into your own ideas, claims, and points. Most novice writers of researched position papers tend to focus too heavily on summarizing and repeating what their sources say. Readers can read the sources themselves; it is how you make use of the sources that makes your researched position paper valuable. Researched position papers **synthesize** different sources to explain something more clearly or thoroughly than any of the sources do. Or they synthesize sources in a way that creates some new insight into the subject. Or they argue for a particular perspective on the subject, using the sources to show why that perspective is the most logical and knowledgeable one. Or they add new primary research to the existing secondary research to contribute some new information or insight.

Achieving such integration requires focusing your organization and each paragraph on your own statements, reducing your sources to their minimal effective form, and signaling how the source fits into your own statement. Researched position papers focus on the writer's own statements just as analysis papers do (as we discussed in Chapter 6). The controlling idea shapes the organization of the paper, and each paragraph indicates how its idea fits within and advances that controlling idea.

For example, the first sentence of each body paragraph in a researched position paper on artificial intelligence one of our students wrote indicates how the writer transitions from one idea to another:

While most uses of artificial intelligence crowd out humans and their intelligence, the great benefits of machine intelligence in the medical field cannot be disputed.

However, artificial intelligence is not simply used for just one cause.

An illustration of machines running our institutions is the use of artificial intelligence in the workplace to train workers.

Besides being used as tools in business, machine intelligence is also being used to replace humans in specific job tasks.

In addition to its uses in business, artificial intelligence will also be utilized as a luxury item.

Even though the paper is heavily researched and uses secondary sources extensively, notice how the focus of each paragraph is the *writer's* ideas, not information from a source. Researched position papers do not need to state the point as explicitly in the first sentence of each paragraph as this one does, although such explicitness certainly keeps the reader directed toward the writer's points. But researched position papers do need to be organized around subpoints of the writer's controlling idea, not around sources.

Writing Activity 7.14

Examine the paragraph focus of one of the sample researched position papers. Outline the paper paragraph by paragraph, either by copying a primary sentence from each paragraph—one that states the writer's point—or by stating each paragraph's point in your own words. Note any paragraphs that might have unclear points or that fail to go beyond summarizing their sources. (When you have a draft of your own researched position paper, use this same outlining technique to check that you are organizing your paper around your arguments, not around your sources.)

Within the structure of each paragraph, sources need to be used in such a way that they support but do not take over the writer's own arguments. Using sources sparingly, for greatest effect, is one way to achieve that. By using them sparingly, we mean two things:

- Using only those bits of information and quotations that most directly and effectively support what you have to say
- Putting them into their briefest possible effective form

Select the sources you include carefully and thoughtfully, to provide needed information, authority, or perspective. When writers of researched position papers do include a source, they put the information into their own words (they paraphrase, discussed further under "Words," pp. 400–401) whenever possible, to keep the focus on what the writer has to say (note, however, that they still credit the source for the information). When they do include a full quotation from the source, it is usually a quotation that says something especially succinctly or vividly. If the quotation is not especially well put, it is better to put it into your own words. Remember the purpose of the researched position paper: The sources are there to help you develop your own thinking, but it is your own thinking—and words—that interest the genre's readers.

Collaborative Activity 7.7

In the sample researched position papers, find ten instances where the writers incorporated sources to support their own points—instances you think were done well. With your classmates, compare your instances and then describe what strategies you see for integrating sources effectively. What kinds of words do the writers use to introduce quotations? How do they include facts and statistics? What kinds of sentences surround the quotations they use? Based on your analysis of these examples and your understanding of the academic scene and the researched position paper genre, create a group list of suggestions for writers of researched position papers in writing classes for how to integrate their sources effectively.

FORMATS—CITING SOURCES

Most matters of form in the researched position paper are similar to that of other academic genres used in writing courses. They are typed, double-spaced, use somewhat lengthy paragraphs, and label the paper with the student's course as well as name. Researched position papers have titles that indicate the major subject and approach of the paper, and they may include headings in the body of the paper. Although other academic genres may use sources, the researched position paper depends so heavily on sources that the form they take in the paper is especially important. One feature of that form we have already discussed and will discuss further under "Sentences" and "Words" (pp. 399–401): The integration of sources within the writer's own statements. The other feature, **citation** of those sources, merits a fuller discussion of its own.

Each of the researched position papers in this chapter includes a list of citations (sometimes called a bibliography or Works Cited or References, depending on the style required by the genre) at the end, and each cites sources to show where the writer got information, a new idea, or quotation. What does the existence of this generic feature reveal about the values and beliefs of academic scenes? To academics, citing sources is not just a formality in researched position papers, or a technical obstacle to completing the paper. Instead, citing sources reflects the essence of academic values.

When you tell readers where you got your information or ideas, you are giving credit. Academics value information so much that it has become a commodity in the academic world, one requiring "credit" when taken by others. Professors can get jobs and make salaries because of what they know. They advance in their careers because of the information they provide and the new knowledge they generate, both in students and in their research fields. Similarly, researchers outside of universities and colleges are paid for their expertise and benefit from their research discoveries. Publications (articles, books, Web sites) have become *property*, owned by the writers and publishers. Such **intellectual property** is even protected by copyright laws. It is not the physical books and journals that constitute that property but their contents. When a writer takes some of that content for his or her own use, citing the source acknowledges its true ownership.

Scholars do not mind their content being used in others' papers. In fact, their reputations increase if their work is cited often. Fair use laws in the United States govern how much content a writer can take from a source and how it can be used, and they permit writers to use and cite others' content in their own papers for scholarly purposes, like researched position papers. Fair use requires that these sources must be cited, however. Taking someone's property without permission in any context is stealing. The same is true for intellectual property. Using someone else's work without acknowledging and citing the source is stealing. In the academic scene, stealing intellectual property is called **plagiarism.**

In nonacademic scenes, others' ideas and information may be treated differently, but all responsible writers make sure that readers know when work does not originate with the writer. For example, journalists often quote authorities and cite facts without giving full bibliographic information, but they do give credit to their sources (as in "According to a 2002 study by the Pew organization . . ."). In a different profession, tax accountants copy sections from tax codes without necessarily citing their source, but they know that their readers will recognize the tax code language as not the accountant's own. Similarly, lawyers draft contracts using pieces from other contracts, but all lawyers know that contracts are drafted that way, so one is rarely confused about original authorship. Different scenes have different expectations and conventions for acknowledging their sources. But in the scenes of academic researched position papers, *intellectual property is highly valued, and the explicit, elaborated acknowledgement of intellectual property is a hallmark of academic integrity.*

Since academics so highly value an individual's thinking as well as research, the property they protect includes not only facts but also ideas. An argument made, a claim asserted, an approach to a subject, a particular way of describing something—these and anything else you see in someone else's work constitute intellectual property and so must be credited to the original author. Academic plagiarism, then, includes not only copying someone else's words without using quotation marks but also not crediting the source of a fact, a metaphor, a vivid description, or a point you want to make that you got from someone else. Citing sources enables you to acknowledge your debt to other researchers even as you create your own paper with your own ideas and perspectives—your own intellectual property.

Academic citation systems have been created to streamline acknowledging sources, though they at times may seem more complicated than helpful. All citation systems have the same purpose: To tell readers the source of anything in a text not the writer's own in such a way that the readers could find the source themselves. Enabling readers to find a source requires great specificity and precision. They must be able to go to an exact place in exactly the right source to find exactly what appeared in the paper. For example, they must be able to find the specific page on which the writer found a specific statistic or the exact location and page of a Web site that included a particular expert's quotation. Such precision ensures that the source will be fully acknowledged and credited; no doubt will remain about whose idea or information appears.

Also, readers who wish to pursue an idea further or check details can do so. Scholars may sometimes find a source's idea intriguing and wish to learn more about it, even if it is a relatively minor point in the paper. They may want to check the research methods of the source, to see whether they accept the source's conclusions or whether the conclusions apply to a particular situation. When teachers ask you to use a citation system to **document** your sources, then, they are not doubting the honesty of your use of your sources but rather holding you to important academic standards and enabling your readers to pursue your subject further.

What complicates citation is that different fields and professional organizations have adopted different systems. Writers in humanities fields like English commonly use the MLA (Modern Language Association) system, while writers in social sciences fields like psychology and linguistics commonly use the APA (American Psychological Association) system. Journalists and other writers of popular articles often refer to *The Chicago Manual of Style* for their system, and professionals in other fields may have their own systems or even modifications of these three main systems. All these citation systems include mostly the same information:

- The author's name
- Title of the source
- Publisher or journal title
- Place of publication
- Date of publication
- Page number

They differ, though, in the order of that information, occasionally in some details of punctuation and abbreviations, and in how they refer to that information in the body of the paper. For example, some systems name the author in the body of the article while others name the source in footnotes or endnotes; some include the date of the source in the body but others do not. While it would be simpler if all fields used the same citation system, the different systems reflect differences in the emphases of different scenes. No matter the citation system you use, however, you should remember to record the relevant information from your sources that you will need for your works cited.

In English writing courses, the usual system is specified in the *MLA Handbook for Writers of Research Papers,* Sixth Edition (New York: The Modern Language Association, 2003). A few examples of how sources would appear in the MLA citation system appear in the text box below:

Sample MLA Style Citations

Book:

Devitt, Amy J., Mary Jo Reiff, and Anis Bawarshi. <u>Scenes of Writing: Strategies for Composing with Genres</u>. New York: Longman, 2004.

Article in a journal:

Smith, Summer. "The Genre of the End Comment: Conventions in Teacher Responses to Student Writing." <u>College Composition and Communication</u> 48 (1997): 249-68.

Chapter in a book:

Paré, Anthony, and Graham Smart. "Observing Genres in Action: Towards a Research Methodology." <u>Genre and the New Rhetoric</u>. Eds. Aviva Freedman and Peter Medway, Bristol PA: Taylor & Francis, 1994. 146-54.

Internet Web site:

Featherstone, Liza. "Wal-Mart's Female Trouble." <u>TomPaine. Common Sense: A Public Interest Journal</u> 10 Dec. 2002. 11 Dec. 2002 <http:www.tompaine.com/feature>.

Published Interview:

Brooks, Gwendolyn. Interview. <u>Literature and Belief</u> 12 (1992): 1-12.

Unpublished Interview:

Smith, Robert. Personal interview. 15 May 2003.

Notice how the citations in MLA front the author, emphasizing the role of the writer as most important. For a field that studies writing and literature, a humanistic field that values individual agency, emphasizing the author makes sense (a signaling of ownership that most scenes in the academy would share in). The date of publication comes near the end of the citation, a fact that also makes sense in a field that studies classic texts as well as newer scholarship. A study of Charles Dickens that appeared in 1942 might still be relevant and important in its insights about the literature.

Compare the emphasis on the date in the APA citation system, a system used in social science fields:

> Smith, Summer. (1997). The Genre of the End Comment: Conventions in Teacher Responses to Student Writing. *College composition and communication, 48,* 249–268.

The difference seems small: A year in parentheses appears one place or another. But that small difference represents a different perspective about currency and how quickly information becomes outdated. The APA system puts the date of publication closer to the beginning of a citation than does the MLA system, reflecting the greater importance of currency in the social sciences and sciences. That is not to say that all differences of citation systems are meaningful: Variations in uses of commas, abbreviations like "pp.," and other details may simply be conventions that have developed differently over time because of the traditional separation of disciplines. (More information on APA can be found in *Publication Manual of the American Psychological Association,* Fifth Edition (Washington, D.C.: American Psychological Association, 2001).)

Writers need to discover which citation system their particular teacher or discipline requires and then learn the conventions of that system. Consistency matters. *Follow the conventions of the appropriate citation system rigorously so that there is no chance of confusing readers.* The examples we list above cover the most common kinds of sources you might need in a typical paper. If you need to use a different citation system or have a different kind of source to credit, your grammar and writing handbook probably includes the details of the major citation systems, so you can look up what you need when you are gathering the information about your sources or editing your final paper. If not, you can find examples from the systems online (see some helpful sites on page 407). Whatever system you use, you will need a good style manual or handbook, either in paper or online, to look up details that vary from one kind of source to another.

All the citation systems, whatever their quirks and details, reveal the emphasis in all scholarship on intellectual property and on academic honesty about sources. Citation systems also reveal the emphasis in writing class researched position papers—and in the academic scene—on basing conclusions on evidence, on speaking from knowledge and information, and on considering multiple perspectives.

SENTENCES—INTRODUCING SOURCES

In general, the sentences in researched position papers follow patterns similar to sentences in analysis and argument papers. They tend to be declarative and relatively complex, especially when making transitions from one idea to the next. One kind of sentence especially important in researched position papers, though it can appear in analysis and argument papers as well, is the sentence that incorporates source material. When writers introduce material from a source, they lead the reader into the material, guiding the reader to see the relevance of the source and to see the writer's interpretation of the material.

Look at how the sample researched position papers incorporate their sources. You can see that paragraphs do not simply string sources together, one after another. Most of the text is not in quotation marks, and parenthetical names of sources do not appear after every sentence. Instead, the writer's own phrases and sentences connect those sources that are included, whether in a simple introductory phrase or a longer explanatory sentence:

As Kalman A. Toth comments, . . .

According to one psychologist, Arthur Jensen, . . .

Similar to the observations of Margaret Mead (1930) where . . .

Eliot A. Cohen illustrates the North's tenacity, . . .

This means that your genetic history, even if no true signs are visible at this time, can stigmatize you.

These phrases and explanations serve to contextualize the source, to show the reader why the source appears at this point in the paper, to indicate what significance the source's information or observation holds for the writer's own ideas. When you read a paragraph in a researched position paper, then, you can see that the sources are subordinated to points made by the writer.

Examine the sample researched position papers in this chapter, looking for sentences that introduce and incorporate source material. Find three such sentences that you think could be improved and revise them so that they more effectively lead the reader into the material, guiding the reader to see the relevance of the source and to see the writer's interpretation of the material.

WORDS—USING YOUR OWN WORDS

One important aspect of the words in researched position papers is that *most* of the words should be the writer's own words, not the words of the sources. We have discussed the importance of keeping clear distinctions between the words of your sources and your own words, in order to credit your sources appropriately. Even when using a source's idea—and giving proper credit to that source—you should work to use your own words most of the time rather than the words of your source. Conveying a source's ideas in your own words is called **paraphrasing**. Paraphrases might include a few of the same words as the source, using the same terms for a concept being discussed, for example, or using *the* or *an*, but most of the words and the sentence structure will be yours rather than the source's. Paraphrasing this paragraph, for example, you might write the following sentence:

> Paraphrasing means writing the expert's idea in your own words, and it's important to use paraphrase so that the paper sounds like your own and not someone else's (Devitt et al 400).

(Remember, of course, to credit your source with a parenthetical citation.) One strategy many find effective for paraphrasing is to read the part to be paraphrased, then turn the source over and write the idea out without looking back at the source. Removing yourself from the original in that way helps you use your own sentence structure. Paraphrasing requires more than substituting one synonym for each word. For example, compare the paraphrases below:

Original Sentence: You need to substitute your own sentence structure as well as words.

Inadequate Paraphrase: One should replace one's own syntax as well as diction.

Better Paraphrase: Paraphrasing requires changing both the sentences and the words.

The inadequate paraphrase merely substitutes synonyms for each word, while still stealing the source's sentence structure. The better paraphrase recasts the original. Typically, you will be paraphrasing an idea that covers more than one sentence, so you will not have as much trouble using your own sentences. Keep in mind your goal: To maintain the substance of the original, the idea that made you want to use this bit of the source in the first place, while making it fit your style and approach to the subject.

Your own style and approach should come through in the words you choose throughout the paper, not just when paraphrasing. All the emphasis on logos and evidence from sources might make you think that the style of researched position papers would be somewhat dull, and it can be if not done well. Researched position papers do usually adopt an academic tone—dispassionate, "objective," authoritative, knowledgeable. Their style tends to be what some consider "educated"—longer sentences, multisyllabic and abstract words. The diction is often quite specific and even concrete, though, because the level of research often leads writers to quite specific information and details. Much of that specific diction will be technical vocabulary that is explained in the paper (*DNA, genetic code, body kinesthetic, ACT scores,* and *Domino Theory,* for example).

But writers of researched position papers also argue their claims or explain their insights with conviction, and that conviction sometimes leads to more emotionally laden words. They have something to say, a controlling idea that represents their own discovery about the subject. There is room in researched position papers for a bit of pathos, appealing to readers' emotions—as long as the appeal *is backed by rational evidence*. It is in specific and concrete words that writers of researched position papers often show their convictions and appeal to readers' emotions. These words especially, but not exclusively, appear in introductions and conclusions to researched position papers, where the writer may be most strongly stating his or her point. Our sample papers include such words as *lazy, cure-all, devastating, takeover, agonizing dreaded experience, agitating, inadvertent evil look, quips, flock, misfortune, sad, disappointing reality, ashamed, infuriating.* Such emotional words reveal the writer's point of view and, if supported by the logic and evidence of the rest of the paper, can help sway readers to that perspective.

How effectively do the writers of our sample researched position papers use emotionally loaded words? Assign members of your group to examine the use of emotionally loaded words in each of the sample papers. What words does each use? How well are they balanced with more "objective" words? How well are the emotions they raise supported by the evidence of the rest of the text? If a writer uses few or no emotionally loaded words, does the writer seem to have less conviction in his or her ideas? Compare your results to refine your understanding of when you might be able to use emotionally loaded words effectively.

Interpreting Generic Features of Researched Position Papers

The generic features we have examined certainly support our original understanding of the scene behind researched position papers. The objective of teaching and practicing research leads to the researched position paper having

- Citation of sources
- Emphasis on logos
- An ethos of informed authority
- A paragraph structure built around supporting every claim with material from other sources

Some of the features of researched position papers lead us to complicate that initial understanding, though, for we see the ways that the research is subordinated to the author's own ideas:

- The controlling idea is a claim the writer makes, not a statement about the research
- The structure of the paper organizes around points in the writer's idea, not around sources
- Sentences are structured so as to integrate the source material within the writer's claims
- Sources draw from multiple and apparently conflicting perspectives, depending on the writer's ideas to address the complexity of that material

These features suggest that the college and university scene, and the writing course scene in particular, value independent thinking as well as information.

Researched position papers instill in writers not only the values of being informed about others' ideas but also the value of discovering their own ideas through the work of others. Researched position papers lead students to *join the conversation,* not just read dead transcripts of it.

Yet how students join these conversations is still carefully restricted in researched position papers. Researched position papers assume that what you already know can be supplemented by testing your beliefs, examining what happens in the world, and discovering what others know. That means that it is not enough to believe something; you must test or examine that belief against evidence or information. It is not enough to state an idea; you must demonstrate the validity of that idea in light of what others have stated before you. Your personal experience, then, is not valued as much as your reasoning since personal experience does not "prove" anything in most academic scenes.

Contrast these values of the researched position paper with other genres that value beliefs and experience—for example personal narratives, memoirs, testimonials, or sermons. Writers who want to challenge the values of this genre by including personal experience—perhaps because their motivation for studying a subject includes a personal connection—generally use that experience in an introduction or conclusion, where emotional appeals are more evident, and still maintain distance from the subject in the body. Or they might incorporate a single section that draws on personal experience to exemplify a point otherwise demonstrated by research. Similarly, impassioned tones that come from personal conviction rather than logical reasoning must be bolstered with sufficient facts and information to support the feelings in order to be considered appropriate in a researched position paper. The subjects about which writers might feel most passionate are often inappropriate for researched position papers, for they lend themselves to discussions of values, not facts, and to decisions based on beliefs, not research. The researched position paper, then, leads students to question or present their convictions only in approved, academic ways, based in logic and evidence, a form of critical inquiry that is highly valued in academic scenes.

Because even as you are carefully grounding all your ideas and convictions in evidence from your sources, you are also told to focus your paper on your own ideas and to distinguish your own ideas carefully from those of your sources, it may seem that you are getting mixed signals. You are both welcomed into a research scene as critical coinvestigators while also being told to "know your place" and to distinguish your ideas from those of published scholars. This apparent conflict reflects the academic scene's recognition of the importance of both community-generated knowledge and original research. It also reflects the student's role in the academy as both scholar and apprentice.

Collaborative Activity 7.9

What other interpretations of the researched position paper's generic features can your group think of? Are there features that we did not comment on that you have noticed in looking at our samples? Do those features suggest different interpretations? Are there interpretations you think we did not emphasize enough? What complexity can you add to how researched position papers reflect the values and beliefs of their scenes?

Collaborative Activity 7.10

Now that you have identified the patterns and underlying assumptions of the genre of researched position papers, critique the possibilities and limitations of this genre in the writing course scene. What does the genre enable students to do and learn? What limitations does it place on this learning and participation in the writing course scene and in the larger academic scene? In your group, draw on the Questions for Critiquing Genre in Box 4.1 (p. 161), and determine what you see as the effects of the researched position paper genre, including its strengths and weaknesses.

Questions to Guide Writing within Researched Position Papers

We have been guiding you through some parts of writing a researched position paper in the course of this chapter; Box 7.3 reviews and summarizes our discussion as well as adds new questions to consider when you write a researched position paper. You might also wish to review Boxes 7.1 (p. 344) and 7.2 (p. 389) on assessing the suitability of a possible subject and on assessing the credibility of sources.

With the understanding of researched position papers that you have developed in this chapter, you can approach any researched position paper assignment not as a tedious exercise in library searches and citation systems but rather as an opportunity. Researched position papers permit you to investigate something that matters to you, to see what the academic perspectives of logic, evidence, and research can help you discover about what you think.

Box 7.3   *Questions to Consider when Writing Researched Position Papers*

Inventing

1. What does my writing assignment specify about the nature of this researched position paper? What do I want to research? What ideas do I have that might be investigated through logic and evidence?
2. What possible subjects can I think of? Which of those subjects are supportable by logic and evidence? Are there multiple perspectives on those subjects? Which subjects most interest me? Which will interest my readers? Which subjects are still alive in the research, part of an ongoing discussion? Are the promising subjects manageable?
3. What kinds of research does my chosen subject and my writing assignment require? What do I already know about my subject? What do I know I will need to research?
4. Will I be able to gather the sources I need? Do I know how to conduct the primary research needed? How can I find multiple sources from multiple perspectives?
5. What databases, indexes, search engines, and other online and library resources might help me find the sources I need? How can librarians help me? What interviews, surveys, observations, or other primary research methods do I need to conduct? Who can help me develop and conduct them? How will I take notes on my secondary reading so that I can tell quotations from paraphrases and so that I have the information I will need for my citation list?
6. Does my subject still interest me? Am I still researching something that matters to me? If not, how can I shift direction to use some of the research I've done while finding an angle more interesting to me?

Drafting

1. What controlling idea have I discovered? What do I want to say that readers in the academic scene will recognize as going beyond what others have said before, either synthesizing their ideas in new ways, adding new ideas to their conversation, or adding new information from my primary research?

(continued on next page)

2. What organization does my controlling idea lead to? What subpoints do I need to make to support my controlling idea? Am I structuring around my ideas rather than around trying to fit in the research I've done?

3. How much will my readers know about this subject already, and how much will I need to explain? How can I establish my credibility with these academic readers?

4. How can I integrate my sources within my own ideas? Am I introducing and explaining my sources, contextualizing them with my own phrases and sentences? Is my tone largely rational and educated?

5. Do I still believe my controlling idea? Have I discovered a better controlling idea, perhaps one that is more complex than my original idea? If so, what new invention do I need to do before I try to draft for my new controlling idea?

Revising

1. How can I gain distance from my draft? Who would understand the subject enough to serve as a responder for me?

2. How well does my draft demonstrate that I have researched my subject well? Does my controlling idea still fit with my research?

3. Will my readers find me credible? How likely are they to understand my idea and find it logical and supported by evidence? What ideas might they have trouble understanding or accepting? How can I make it more likely that academic readers will accept what I say as valid?

4. Does my draft seem like the other researched position papers I have seen? Do I address conflicting sources and ideas? How well do I integrate my sources within my own points? Are my sentences complex enough to explain my ideas? Where could I use more emotional words to appeal to my readers' emotions? What words seem inappropriately emotional, given the evidence?

5. Do I have enough secondary sources to support my points and provide multiple perspectives without letting the sources overwhelm what I have to say? Are there other surveys, interviews, observations, or other primary research that I should add?

(continued on next page)

6. How well is my structure working? Should I reorder any of my points? Should I move evidence from supporting one point to another?

7. Have I edited carefully for Standardized Edited English so as not to undermine my credibility in this academic scene? Have I followed the appropriate citation system?

8. Are my paragraphs long enough to reflect the complexity of ideas I am examining? Have I given my paper a title? Have I used the heading my instructor prefers?

9. Have I said what I wanted to say? All that needs to be said?

Helpful Internet Sites for Research-Based Papers
in Writing Courses

Online reference works and databases and indexes that may be available through your library's Web site:

Bartleby reference resources
http://www.bartleby.com/reference/

Expanded Academic ASAP

Academic Universe (Lexis/Nexis)

National Newspaper Index

Search engines for finding online sources

http://www.lycos.com

http://www.google.com

www.altavista.com

guide.infoseek.com

Sites on evaluating sources:

"Evaluating Information Found on the Internet"
http://milton.mse.jhu.edu/research/education/net.html

"Evaluating Web Sites: Criteria and Tools"
http://www.library.cornell.edu/okuref/research/webeval.html

"The Good, The Bad, & The Ugly"
http://lib.nmsu.edu/instruction/eval.html

Sites that show citation systems:

http://www.apastyle.org (citation system for the American Psychological Association for social sciences)

University of Wisconsin-Madison Writer's Handbook
http://www.wisc.edu/writing/index.html

"Citation Style for Research Papers"
http://www.liu.edu/cwis/cwp/library/workshop/citation.htm

Samples of Research Projects
SAMPLE OF A RESEARCHED POSITION PAPER BASED IN SECONDARY RESEARCH AND OBSERVATION, APA STYLE

Elliott 1

Eugene Elliott

In Case of Emergency, Please Wait

The basic thought of having to wait is both unappealing and agitating to most people. However, when the concept of waiting is applied to emergency situations, the resulting

Elliott 2

behavior can be shocking. As Malign Akerstrom (1997) presented in her study of a Swedish emergency clinic, one of the most challenging aspects of a waiting room is "dealing with angry patients whose aggression mainly stemmed from their having to wait" (p. 504). As patients, waiting is a source of hostility primarily because we perceive waiting as a costly waste of our precious time (Akerstrom, 1997, p. 506). A key result of this hostility, from the perspective of both workers and waiters, is vented frustrations towards each other. In interviews with nursing staff, many "reported drastic physical events of aggression due to waiting" (Akerstrom, 1997, p. 508). These events were reported to include staring, derogatory remarks "about their being ugly, fat, lazy," and also indirect comments referring to the staff's incompetence (Akerstrom, 1997, p. 508–509). The professionalism of the nurses usually seemed to override the urge to take revenge. Nevertheless, sometimes the irritation becomes so great that an inadvertent evil look or stare is directed towards the patient, and "sarcastic backstage talk" takes a "veiled" form of retaliation (Akerstrom, 1997, p. 517). Through observing the emergency waiting room at Pitt County Memorial Hospital, similar behavior can be assessed, as well as other responses to the anxiety of waiting.

In one corner of the waiting room, a mother sits with her children, anxiously awaiting news of her husband's condition (he had been brought in with severe chest pain). The kids, unaware of the importance of the situation, play loudly, running and shouting despite the quiet, tense atmosphere. Already upset by the events unfolding, she suddenly screams at the little boy while grabbing the girl's arm and orders them to "sit down and shut the hell up!" This outburst attracts the attention of everyone in the room. Some people glance quickly, while others look onward out of curiosity to see what

Elliott 3

would follow. One particular nurse, obviously used to this behavior, rolls her eyes, glances at her co-worker and continues working. The children sit quietly watching television carefully looking at their mother often.

For a while thereafter, the room is fairly calm. One gentleman sits reading *Dubliners,* by James Joyce, while the other nine people watch the six o' clock news on Channel 12. Gradually, some people go to the exam rooms while still more trickle in, and the conversations grow louder, until it becomes impossible to hear the television. A baby, about four or five months old begins crying hysterically, until her mother, apparently pregnant once again, lifts her from her carseat and breastfeeds her right there where they are sitting. Quite a response erupts. A rhythmic mumbling can be heard as women roll their eyes and stare, whereas the men seem to pretend not to notice, finding something else to look at. Oddly enough, although she had registered with the triage nurse only moments earlier, she is called back almost immediately. Representative of a society uncomfortable with the display of nursing young, this is an example of how changes in values through the years have effected responses to once ordinary daily events (Mead, 1930, p. 237).

As the waiting room gets more and more crowded, one elderly gentleman paces back and forth mumbling something unintelligible to anyone else. He maintains the same path until he is finally called. Apparently his wife is currently being treated. As he leaves, another lady sitting across from me quips, "He was getting on my nerves with that pacing," apparently unaware that for the last fifteen minutes she had been thumbing nervously through every magazine on the table. Within the next couple minutes, a seating situation becomes evident. As new patients check in, the difficult decision of choosing a seat is begun. A slight division in the

Elliott 4

seating arrangement becomes noticeable, with a majority of white patients against one wall, and another section where blacks and Hispanics are sitting. Similar to the observations of Margaret Mead (1930) where ". . . men who are of kin build their houses side by side . . .", so do people of the same race sit together (p. 236). This trend continues, as each new arrival carefully scans the room and chooses his or her seat likewise.

Eventually, the effects of waiting and being confined to the crowded quarters begins to take its toll, as several people approach the nurse's station and inquire on how much longer the wait should be. Phrases such as "I don't have all damn day" and "I'm glad I'm not dyin' as slow as this place is," can be heard in quiet whisper, mostly being said to oneself. Only when a man walks in with what appears to be a popsicle stick protruding from his arm, does the monotonous chatter break as everyone stares, some cringing at the sight but continuing to look out of curiosity. Following directly behind this man, there is a hospital security guard assisting as a Greenville police officer escorts a prisoner bearing handcuffs and foot chains. Yet again a unanimous stare ensues as he checks in, then is escorted outside to wait for his name to be called.

With an almost capacity crowd, conversations can be overheard from everywhere, ranging from the purpose of someone's emergency room visit, the news, and especially how long the wait is. One younger lady who had earlier stated her problem as having been nauseous for several days, jumps up and darts towards the bathroom, vomiting just by the payphones. Seeing that she is obviously sick, a nurse helps her on back, and within three minutes a janitor is cleaning up the accident. Moments later, a gentleman whom the nurse refers to as Mr. Curry walks up to the triage desk. He had been smoking about every ten minutes for the past hour,

Elliott 5

nervously awaiting his turn. On this approach however, he yells out "Never mind, f_ this s_t" and storms out. The nurse says that she was getting ready to call his name. From this moment, the complaining was minimal. The crowd dwindles down to about five people left waiting. The new waiters watching television or reading magazines make evident the endless cycle of emergency room visits.

Emergency room waiting can be a painstaking process that tests the patience of both the hospital staff and the waiting patients. The concept of being placed in a confined area with strangers of many different backgrounds and lifestyles can be tense, especially in a critical emergency situation. Even the sincerest person can become agitated and sometimes enraged to the point of saying or doing things that he or she wouldn't do normally. This dramatic effect on human behavior is worthy of further research. Other aspects of waiting room anxiety stem from the design, decor, climate control, etc., or the lack thereof, of the particular room (Akerstrom, 1997, p. 507). Possibly examining the influence of the environment as well as attention deterring activities such as movies, games, fish aquariums and other entertaining alternatives may lead to more adequate waiting rooms with less stress and irritation. Researching the combined effects of environment and intensity of waiting situations is essential to creating more hospitable, welcoming atmospheres. Nobody really likes to wait, but waiting is inevitable in a society with so many people and their individual needs. Through further experiments and research, waiting can be transformed from an agonizing dreaded experience, into an activity that can be done with minimal agitation and anxiety.

Elliott 6
References

Akerstrom, M. (1997). Waiting—A source of hostile interaction in an emergency clinic. *Qualitative Health
Research, 7,* 504–518.

Mead, M. (1930). Scenes from Manus life. In Comely,
Hamilton, et al. *Fields of writing: Readings across the
disciplines* (4th ed.) (pp. 235–241). New York: St.
Martin's Press.

Sample of a Researched Position Paper Based in Secondary Research, Interviews, and Other Primary Research

Balta 1
Vedrana Balta
Lack of Minorities in Traditionally White
Sororities and Fraternities

It is very frustrating to know that the University of
Kansas, one of the most liberal universities in the country,
hosts such a small percentage of minorities[1] in its traditionally

[1] I would like to make some terms clear. Even though the word "minority"
stands for all non-white and non-American people as well as homosexu-
als, in this paper I will, by using this term, refer only to African Americans,
Latino, and Asian populations. The reason why I am only including these
certain groups is because they seem to represent the biggest minority
groups at the University of Kansas. Also, I will be interchangeably using
the term "Greek system" with the "traditionally white sororities and fraternities" simply because the first term is shorter than the second.

Balta 2

white sororities and fraternities. Shouldn't it be the other way around? Shouldn't minorities simply flock to all campus structures of such a supposedly accepting university? What is the reason for this abnormality? From the evidence I collected, I learned that different ethnicities are interested in the Greek system; however, only a few of them decide to pledge. But why? Even though many individuals confidently contradict this statement, I definitely argue that the cause of this misfortune is the fact that the "largest campus social structure" (Weissman) does not put many efforts into recruitment and welcoming of the minority members into its system.

We live in an extremely diversified society, a society where millions of people have come to in search of freedom, peace, liberty, or religion. The arrival of these groups of individuals had given this country a colorful, rich mix of residents and had therefore invaded the traditional white structure of early Americans. Ever since that time in history, America has strived to be promising and welcoming to all people, and especially to the minority groups.

Analogous to the example of American diversity, some people strongly believe that the Greek system at the University of Kansas has always been eager to recruit minorities to its houses. Angie Carr, the coordinator for fraternity and sorority life at the University of Kansas is, with no doubt, one of those people. With great confidence, she states that the traditionally white houses "Maximize their efforts in order to welcome and recruit African Americans, Latino, and Asian members into its 'system.'" But is this truly the case?

Based on the data regarding this subject, the validity of Angie Carr's statement cannot be verified at all. If Carr's statement were true, there would have been a much larger number of black fraternity and sorority members rather than only 11 and 6, retrospectively, out of 3,164 Greek members

Balta 3

in year 2001 (out of those students who had their pictures taken for the Jayhawker Yearbook). Furthermore, if Carr's statement were valid, last year's African American membership of 0.5% would be a mistake--not a sad, disappointing reality (Mendoza 5A).

Moreover, isn't it extremely surprising that "no individual fraternities or sororities keep minority statistics for the Greek system"? (Brubaker par 5) Why is this so? Is the Greek system as a whole maybe a little scared or even ashamed to publicize the non-presence of the non-white members in its houses? I'd say definitely yes because why else would they not keep track of the different ethnicities that have been a part of the traditional Greek system? If the recruiters did such an incredible job welcoming minority groups, shouldn't they be proud of it and also shouldn't they want other prospective students to know about the diverse environment they are choosing to live in?

This problem of extremely small numbers of minority individuals in the traditionally white sororities and fraternities was first addressed 25 years ago. On May 2, 1977, "representatives of the Interfraternity Council (IFC) presented to the University Senate Human Relations Committee a four-part plan designed to increase black participation in IFC fraternities at the University of Kansas" (Decker). This play was also intended to diminish de facto segregation as well as various racial misperceptions of that time. Yet, was this plan a true success or was it perhaps a foreshadowing of the similar problem in the future?

Well, the future then is the present now. Unfortunately, it doesn't seem like the core of this problem has changed even though the plan was proposed a quarter of the century ago! In addition to that, despite the fact that many people would like to overcome the traditional white past of the

Balta 4

Greek system at this university, the evidence, unfortunately, points that "[Greek houses are] trying to preserve the white upper class world that is changing around them" (Weissman).

Miguel Ramirez, a junior from Santo Domingo, Dominican Republic, is a perfect example of this infuriating truth. Wishing to become friends with young men of different race, culture, ethnicity, and religion than he is, Ramirez decided to join a traditionally white fraternity. Although he was, at first, extremely excited for the new experiences that this living environment had to offer, his enthusiasm gradually declined as the time went by. Even from the early beginning of the school year, Miguel started to notice that he wasn't quite clicking in with his fraternity brothers. He also noticed that his pledge brothers weren't nearly as open-minded to cultural and ethnic differences as he was when they started "looking at [him] weird" (Mendoza 5A) for simply playing his Latin music. The Dominican student, after numerous examples of feeling excluded from his "brothers" finally decided that he was mistaken about his fraternity. Soon after that, he decided to find himself new living quarters.

Of course, not all fraternities or sororities are like the one Miguel Ramirez attended. It would definitely be "unfair to label the entire Greek System as un-diverse or un-welcoming to minorities" (Weissman). Furthermore, there are many instances of minority students who have enjoyed being a part of the traditional Greek system. One such example is Tiffany Lopez, an Asian American woman, who has been a member of a traditionally white sorority throughout her entire education at the University of Kansas. This young woman openly shared that she has had an amazing experience at her sorority and that she would highly recommend it

Balta 5

to any other minority students. However, Lopez also seemed to mention that she is a very friendly, approachable individual, who is always looking for opportunities to get involved in her sorority or the university in general. Therefore, it can be logically concluded that easy-going, talkative, well-rounded persons are much more likely to fit in an unknown environment than those timid, observant kind of people, like Miguel Ramirez. Finally, it definitely seems that the outgoing individuals, no matter if they feel welcomed or not at the place where they want to be, make themselves welcomed through their easy nature. On the other hand, this isn't quite that easy for shyer people.

So, what is a possible solution to this frustrating problem? Maybe it is true that no matter what kind of recruitment the Greek system has to offer, minority members who decide to rush will "ultimately choose not to pledge one of the traditionally white fraternities [or sororities]" (Brubaker par 4). Maybe it is okay to think that it is "just more comfortable hanging out with the people of the same ethnic background" (Mendoza 5A). But how is the problem of the lack of diversity in the Greek system going to be overcome then?

No matter what the possible solutions might be, the resolving of this issue will, undoubtedly, take time. If we just think about where we stand right now in relation to the plan that was proposed 25 years ago, that will definitely give us a clue to how much time is going to go by before we make another big step regarding this issue. I wish I could just tell people to be more receptive and open-minded to all those around them; I wish I could make them see that "life after college is not all white, black, or Latino" (Carr); I wish everyone would stop being ignorant, not follow the traditions of

Balta 6

the past, and focus all of his or her attention on the future. I
wish . . .

I am afraid that I, alone, can only wish for things. But if
everyone wished my wishes and was willing to act on those
wishes, our society could definitely dissolve a great deal of
misfortunes that we have been dealing with for so many
decades.

I don't want to be pessimistic; however, I am terrified
that those wishes will still remain just wishes . . .

Balta 7

Works Cited

Brubaker, Christine. "Greek System Concerned with
Diversity." Cavalier Daily. 1 Nov. 2002
<http://www.cavalierdaily.com/CVArticle.asp?ID=389&
pid=564>.

Carr, Angie. Personal Interview. 29 Oct. 2002.

Decker, Jan. "IFC Proposes Increased Black Participation in
Frats." University Daily Kansan 3 May 1977: 8-9.

Lopez, Tiffany. Telephone Interview. 28 Oct. 2002.

Mendoza, J. R. "KU Greek System Struggles to Pledge
Minorities." University Daily Kansan 10 Dec. 2001:
A1+.

Weissman, Gary. "Race and the Greek System." Main
Street. 30 Oct. 2002 http://www.dartmouth.edu/
~mainst/2/greek.pdf.

Sample of a Feature Article Based
in Survey and Other Primary Research

In Black & White: A Look at How the Magazines Affect the Body Images of These 2 Ethnic Groups
Julie Ann Predny

Imagine flipping through the pages of any one of today's popular women's magazines--Cosmopolitan, Mademoiselle, Glamour--and coming across an article praising you; beautiful, female, **you,** perfectly perfect just the way you are with a wonderfully liberating "and don't let anyone tell you differently" message throughout. Finishing the last paragraph, you inwardly have to smile. How nice, finally, to hear those words, that you should love yourself just the way you are. You're flattered, pleased that the author would devote 2 pages to inflating your self-esteem. Now, turn the page: you're face to face with the dreaded fashion spread, 10 pages of the latest styles fluidly skimming or snugly hugging a few size-4 beauties. You wonder if it's a bad joke that the ensembles shown are the ones that will never translate well onto your soft, supple curves--or at least, 2 pages ago they were soft and supple. Now they seem to be just plain sagging and sad in the face of these vixens. Feeling a little confused? What exactly are the creators of this thing trying to tell you?

The answer is anything but clear. Is the message that yes, the editors and writers want you to know that you're fine, honey, just the way you are, but you're just not ideally what the world is looking for? This mixed message is one that gets thrown at all women. However, are some taking it more to heart than others? Past surveys conducted by mainstream magazines such as Glamour and Cosmopolitan have speculated and shown that of two of the major ethnic groups (Caucasian and African American), Caucasian women are the most harshly affected. For whatever reasons, the African American women polled seemed to take these mixed messages more in stride.

Thinking back on those results, I found myself wondering whether things had changed, even though the layout of popular magazines has stayed basically the same. To my surprise, I found that the gap between Caucasian and African American women seems to be narrowing.

The survey results from several years ago did not show that African American women were totally unaffected by the unrealistic feminine ideals that bombarded them just as frequently as they did Caucasian women; it just appeared that they didn't take it all as personally. For example, when the participants were asked to describe some of their goals for the future (5 years) the results showed that the African American women most commonly listed things like having a great career or being financially independent. Caucasian women, on the other hand, more frequently included goals such as weight loss/gain. For whatever reason, the majority of women that seemed to hold the more positive image of themselves and their bodies was comprised of African American women.

It wasn't all that difficult to speculate why this disparity may have existed. It's possible that it's due to a disparity in the ethnicity of popular models; so far there have always been invariably more Caucasian models shown than African American models. Even if you sat down and made a count of the models in *today's* mainstream magazines (as I did) you would see that Caucasian models still greatly outnumber African American models on an average of 11 to 1. African-American women may not identify as closely with the Caucasian models and have therefore been less likely to feel threatened or influenced by them. Literally, they just can't be exactly like them, so they are less likely to feel a need to try. Kara, 20 (African American), says, "A lot of magazines don't focus on the black woman's body and what looks good on her. I feel that a lot of magazines focus on the Caucasian woman."

Magazine Model Count
These numbers include women in the ads, the models, and celebrities. All are Feb. 2001 issue.

Magazine	African American	Caucasian
Mademoiselle:	8	124
Cosmopolitan:	19	147
Vogue:	10	128
Glamour:	12	146

Which inevitably brings us around to the issue of what most of these models DO look like. Dana, 20 (African American), puts it best, saying, "Most models have that boyish, thin look about them that is not very flattering at all. I believe that women were born to have curves. We are women and therefore we should look like women, curves and all." It has seemed to have been more acceptable in society for African American women to naturally be more curving in figure; Caucasian women can be as well but for some reason the pressure has been on them more heavily to strive for that "boyish, thin look." In fact, in recent years, especially with the emergence of rap songs that praise an African American woman's natural figure ("Baby Got Back" for one), it's been much more okay for African American women to retain the curves that make them obviously female. It's fairly obvious even to the causal observer that there are only a handful of African American models and celebrities who emulate Caucasian models' near-emaciated standards of beauty.

So is it still true? Do African American women suffer less from the model-mania that today's mainstream magazines are pushing? In order to investigate this further (on a smaller scale, however), I took a survey of 12 young women living in my college dormitory hall; I was lucky enough to have a fairly even split between Caucasian and African American hallmates (five African American and seven Caucasian). What I found was that the African America women were just as likely to make losing weight or worrying about their hair a top concern. Likewise, the Caucasian women had high-reaching immediate goals such as completing school and being financially independent. Both groups were able to have fairly realistic and positive perspectives.

Kara said that "I think the effect can be positive as long as you realize [that] these women aren't perfect but have had their pictures touched up." Even Dana, who replied that magazines had negative effects, felt it necessary to add "I don't feel I have to compete with them [the models] though." Jean, 20 (African American), also pointed out that "The way a woman looks at a magazine depends on her self-esteem. It may depress a woman to see a skinny model in an ad if she is not confident in herself." The most enthusiastic response came from Janelle, 30 (African American), who said "I'm very happy being me. Besides, why mess with perfection?"

The Caucasian women's responses were equally as positive, like Alison, 21, who remarked that "They [magazines] used to affect me negatively. Now all I see are hideous twigs. Gain some weight; Guys like curves." There was also the intimate response from Kate, 19, who said, "When I was younger I nearly became anorexic because I read too many fashion magazines. . . . The models, be they the products of endless airbrushing or computer imaging, present an impossible standard [to live up to]." It was heartening to see that the African American and Caucasian women surveyed both had 5-year goals that were positive and empowering. They were completely non-body related such as finishing school, pursuing higher degrees, career advancement; one girl even listed getting a puppy.

In addition to the similarity in high goals, both the Caucasian and African American women had gripes about their bodies or other physical aspects of themselves. Kristen, 20 (African American), said that she would be eager to change her weight and, if she only could, her shoe size. Most of the other African American women surveyed also seemed to want to change their hair texture. One can only speculate that this could possibly be attributed to the fact that most of the hairstyles that are popular today are meant for Caucasian hair, and simply don't work well for the typical texture of African American hair--thick, coarse, extremely curly--even with the new chemical straighteners that are available (which can be damaging and expensive if done frequently).

There was still a faint hint of the past survey results which indicated that just maybe, Caucasian women are still smarting from the effects of the mixed messages sent out by today's magazines. Alison also replied that if she could change anything about herself, it would be her self-esteem. Yet another Caucasian woman, Jenna, 22, even asserted that magazines and rail-thin models had a positive effect because "It is a motivation for us as women to always look good. These models set the standard and we try, or succeed, in surpassing it." It's doubtful that many women would agree. Although it's apparent that from the majority of the other responses, these were extremes, the fact remains that they exist all the same.

The unfortunate thing is that although magazines seem to be changing their ways (a couple have tested the waters with fashion features for sizes 12-14, while others have occasionally used an African American model as the center of a fashion spread) these changes just aren't coming fast enough for impressionable young women like Alison and Jenna, and that goes for Caucasian, African American, Asian, and Hispanic alike. The fact is that most magazines will try to attribute their constant and hypocritical use of size-4s to the fact that most of the "sample" clothes coming from designers are made only up to size 5 or 6. They will keep trying to console you with the fact that most all their models are airbrushed to perfection so that the *clothes* can stand out. In a strange way, though, that's not a bad statement when you think about it. I don't know about the rest of you, but I want the world to see *me* coming, not my dress.

SAMPLE SURVEY

ANONYMOUS SURVEY

K–G Ladies:

Please, take some time to read and complete this survey. I'll be using the responses to research an exploratory paper which will take a look at the effects of women's magazines on the body image of white/caucasion women versus the effects of them on black/ethnic women. Please answer the questions as seriously, honestly, and specifically as you can; I would like to be able to utilize some of your responses as quotes for credibility in the paper. No names are necessary, nor will they be used. If I attach names to any quotes, they will be purely fictional for privacy's sake (you can even let me know who you'd LIKE to be called!). Please complete this survey within the next few days (more like 3 than 13... I'm a master procrastinator sometimes!) and return it to Rm. K-53. Thanks in advance for your time!

Julie Ann Predny

1. Age 20 & Race white

2. Do you read magazines? If yes, please list their titles:
yes: cosmo, glamour

3. Do you feel that magazines (articles, ads, models, photos) have any effect on a woman's body image? Is this effect usually more positive or negative? Please give a brief explanation of why you feel this way.
Yes – both: it can encourage women to want to get into shape/make them more health conscious, but it can also cause some to become overly-obsessed w/ trying to look exactly like the models, instead of finding just one or two things to improve

4. Do you now, or have you ever felt that magazines affected your own feelings toward your body? Positively or negatively?
Yes – both: I used to be stick-thin & was repeatedly teased by my "healthier" friends, so they made me feel better and not so freakish. well, that figure came & went & now I find myself wishing for the days when sit-ups were not a part of my world.

5. In your opinion, which parts of magazines tend to have the most direct impact on women (articles, fashion spreads, models, ads, etc.)? Why?
Ads & fashion spreads b/c they take up so much space in the magazine & they're very eye-catching & don't take very much time to make their impact

6. When reading a magazine, what parts have the most lasting effects on you, if any (see above in parentheses)?
The parts w/ pictures (I'm a very visual person)

7. List at least 3 things that you hope to accomplish in the next 5 years of your life.
find a major/graduate, find more time for fitness, stop smoking

8. If you could change anything about yourself, what would it be?
– my nose :) ..such a crooked thing!
– not be such a procrastinator

SAMPLE OF A NEWSLETTER BASED IN SECONDARY RESEARCH

Volume 1, Issue 26
December 6, 2001

COLLEGE STUDENT'S SURVIVAL KIT

Plagiarism 101: How To Avoid It

Plagiarism 101

For the typical college student the words "mid-term" or "end-of-semester" are synonymous with unmitigated terror and panic as assignments pile up and tests are scheduled in every class. To a student overwhelmed with a 12 to 15 hour classload and multiple papers due in the same week, the only way out seems to be to just point, click and plagiarize. Don't even think about it! It's not worth failing a class or facing even worse consequences like being thrown out of school. Crunch times are a part of college life and also a part of the business world outside the walls of academe. It would be better to learn to deal with crunch times in college than in your first dream job.

Think about it. When your college hands you a degree at the end of four years, in essence the institution is saying that you possess the credentials and the knowledge necessary to be hired for a professional or managerial position. If you "earn" that degree by "cut and paste", then your degree has no real significance and you become your own victim of deceit.

What is Plagiarism?

Plain and simply, plagiarism is theft. When you use someone else's words, sentence structure, ideas, or any other part of **print or electronic**

Use the Internet — just don't abuse it.

expression, you must put them in quotation marks and cite your source(s). You must must give citations when using others' ideas, even if those ideas are paraphrased in your own words.

This issue will discuss and focus primarily on the issue of Internet Plagiarism which has become a huge problem nationwide on college campuses. This may come as a shock to some, but all the freely accessible information proliferating on the Internet is not free for the taking. There will be a price to pay if you don't cite what you find there. Please, read on...

Plagiarism and the World Wide Web

The World Wide Web is an awesome and powerful source of information, but with its accessibility has made another form of plagiarism a temptation: copy and paste and the use of Internet paper mills. The copy and paste mentality has become one of the biggest problems on college campuses today. According to a survey done by Plagiarism.org., "Almost 80% of college students admit to cheating at least once and that up to 30% of undergraduate students across the country may plagiarize on every assignment they turn in" (Harris).

Why you are here

You came to college to interact with scholars, to learn how to think critically, and to become a skilled professional in a discipline. Yes, the pressures on you are very real and they come from a myriad of directions. Students today are faced with fierce competition to maintain a high GPA for graduate schools, future job recruiters and pressure from their parents. Other causes range from poor time management, fear that your writing ability is inadequate, an overload of class hours, and uncertainty about what plagiarism includes (Harris). Buying or copying a pa-

per may seem to be the easiest way out when you feel overwhelmed with assignments, but the risk is tremendous if you are caught. Your professors know about the paper mills and are trained to notice certain dead giveaways that shout, "I have copied and pasted this paper!" Don't take the risk and don't cheat yourself out of your education.

Internet Paper Mills

There are a number of sites on the Web advertising download-able student papers (for free or for sale). Some of these sites maintain that they do not provide these papers with the intention that students will claim them as their own; rather, the papers are for research or informational purposes. Others openly acknowledge that their sites were created in order to provide students with materials for plagiarism. Whatever the intent of the creators, these sites are being used as sources for plagiarized papers.

If you are thinking about buying or downloading your next research paper, be aware that many professors know about these sites and have visited them

(familiarizing themselves with their contents). Remember too that your professor has become familiar with your writing style and can discern when text is a student's own and when it has been plagiarized (whether that text comes from the Web or not). Finally, that many of the papers available are poorly written; just because it's on the Web, or someone else wrote it, does not guarantee that it is accurate, grammatically correct or even spell-checked. In addition, the web paper could have been plagiarized in its entirety from yet another source.

Cut, Paste, Plagiarize

Cutting and pasting to create a paper from several sources is yet another plagiarism strategy. Don't believe for a minute that this is okay. These "assembly-kit" papers are often betrayed by wide variations in tone, diction, and citation style. The introduction and conclusion are often student-written and therefore noticeably different from the often glowing middle. The dead giveaways that pepper a copy and paste paper are immediately apparent to the trained eye. Don't take a chance. Do the research, write the paper, cite the sources and turn in your own honest work.

Citing Electronic Sources

If you are going to use source material from the Web (which is perfectly acceptable), you must cite your source in an acceptable format. Most English classes use the MLA style of formatting citations. Other disciplines may use the, such as psychology for example, may use the APA style of citation. Your professor will tell you which style is preferred for the class and the paper you are assigned.

Number One Rule: Buy a current edition of the MLA Handbook for Writers of Research Papers and the Harbrace College Handbook. These books will prove invaluable to you throughout your college career and may save you a lot of trouble, if you follow the guidelines in these books. In addition, barebones guidelines for the MLA documentation style can be found on the Web at: http://www.mla.org.

Reprinted here are some examples of on-line citation:

On-line Book

Wollstonecraft, Mary. A Vindication of the Rights of Women. New York: Everyman Library, 1929. [On-line] Available Telnet: gopher. wiretap.spies.com Directory:Library/Classics File:woman.txt.

On-Line Journal Article

Rosenberg, Martin E. "Dynamic and Thermodynamic Tropes of the Subject in Freud and in Deleuze and Guattari." Postmodern Culture 4.1 (1993): 32 paragraphs. [On-Line] Available Telnet: gopher. nebula.lib.vt.edu. Directory: Electronic Bookshelf/ejournals/ postmodern culture/PMCV4N1 File: rose0401.txt

On-Line Abstract

Natchez, Gladys. "Frida Khalo and Diego Rivera: The Transformation of Catasttrophe to Creativity." Psychotherapy-Patient 8 (1987):153-74. [On-Line] Abstract Available: DIALOG File: Psy-chINFO Item: 76-11344

CD-ROM Abstract

Natchez, Gladys. "Frida Khalo and Diego Rivera: The Transformation of Catastrophe to Creativity." Psychotherapy-Patient 8 (1987):153-74. [On-Line] Abstract Available: Silverplatter File: PsychLIT Item: 76-11344

All this information was taken from the fifth edition of the MLA Handbook for Writers of Research Papers which also features sections on computer research methods and other electronic resources.

Since professors may not distinguish between deliberate and accidental plagiarism, the heart of avoiding plagiarism is to make sure you give credit where it is due. This may be credit for something somebody said, wrote, emailed, drew, or implied. If you didn't write it—cite it!

COLLEGE STUDENT'S
SURVIVAL KIT

1979 Downtown Blvd
Center for Academic Excellence
Washington, D.C.
Phone: 555-555-5555
Fax: 555-555-5555
Email: center@gov.com

*The College Students
Resource Newsletter*

[
We're on the Web!
collegestudentsurvivalkit.com
]

Research it, write it, cite it!

Professor's Detection Strategies

Detection is becoming easier due to computer technology and is the latest strategy in an effort to deter the growing trend of Internet plagiarism. These detection sites utilize huge databases of online paper-mills in addition to searching millions of web pages for plagiarized material. Professors submit student's papers for analysis and if "if the service finds similarities, it notifies the teacher, who must then decide whether the similarities are coincidences, justified by proper footnotes or outright dishonesty" (Harris). These Internet services usually charge a fee by the number of students on a class, with discounts given for extra-large classes. Some detection sites include:

- Plagiarism.com at http://www.plagiarism.com. Educational materials and a software-screening program that creates a test of familiarity for a student to complete. The company says that no student has been falsely accused.

- Plagiarism.org at http://www.plagiarism.org. Online service that checks submitted student papers against a large database and provides reports of results. Also monitors term paper mills.

- Wordcheck at http://www.wordchecksystems.com. Keyword matching software. Requires local database of papers or texts to match.

- Integriguard at http://www.integriguard.com. Compares submissions against a database of other papers and Web sites.

- Eve at http://www.canexus.com/eve/index.shtml. Inexpensive software agent that searches the Web to compare a suspect paper with Internet content. Shows site and degree of match. (Virtual Salt)

Sources:

1. Gibaldi, Joseph. MLA Handbook For Writers of Research Papers. 5th ed. New York. The Modern Language Association of America. 1999. 1-293.

2. Harris, Robert. "Evaluating Internet Research." *VirtualSalt.* 17 Nov. 1997. 20 Nov. 2001. <http://www.virtualsalt.com/evalu8it.htm>.

SAMPLE OF A LETTER TO AN AUTHORITY BASED IN SECONDARY RESEARCH

February 16, 2001

Citizens of Clarksville,

As many of you already know, on January 1, 2001, five city council members were sworn into office for the first time. In an election where five of the six incumbents lost their positions, newcomers Gabriel Segovia, Marshall Ross, Phil Drew, Margie Clark, and Joe Couch won city council seats by promising lower property taxes. Now in office, these council members seek a drastic 82-cent reduction in our city's property tax rate. That the new council members won on the platform of lower property taxes speaks to the public's desire to lower these taxes. But, while the idea of paying fewer taxes on our property certainly appeals to us all, I feel that reducing our tax levels would be a terrible mistake.

As a concerned citizen of this city, I feel it is necessary to ask some questions about what our public officials are doing. I urge you, the citizens of Clarksville, to look at the answers to these questions before you make your decision; because it is only after answering these questions that we can decide whether a lower property tax rate is really what Clarksville needs.

How much is 82 cents per $100 worth to me? According to Clarksville tax code, residential property is taxed at 25% of its appraised value. The tax rate for this 25% of our property is $2.01 for every $100 of property owned. For example, if I own a house that, together with the land it was built on, is worth $50,000, I would pay $251 in property taxes. Commercial property is taxed at 40% of its value, so if my commercial property is worth $100,000, I would pay $804. So if I am lucky enough to be blessed with $150,000 worth of commercial and residential property, I would pay a little more than $1,000 in property taxes each year.

An 82-cent cut in property taxes would reduce the rate to $1.19 per $100 of property, saving the individual taxpayer a minimal amount of money. Using the hypothetical example above, I save $102 on my residential property and $328 on my commercial property for a total savings of $430. I am sure that $430 matters to anyone who pays taxes, no matter how much money they make. But is an extra $430 a year worth the sacrifices in public services that would occur after such a drastic tax cut?

How important is our tax money to the city? Our city functions on the taxes of its property owners. Our taxes pay for the police officers and firefighters who keep our homes and families safe. Our taxes pay for the upkeep of our public parks, pools, and other public recreation. Our taxes pay for the beautification of our city. In short, our city government needs our tax dollars to provide us with the public goods we want.

The city's budget for the coming fiscal year predicts revenue totaling about $53 million, 37% of which comes from the city's property tax. It seems to me that 37% of the city's budget is an important sum. It becomes more important when 22% of the city's projected budget comes from the local sales tax, beer and liquor tax, business tax, and hotel/motel tax, all of which are sensitive to the economy. If the local economy were to take a dip, the 37% of our budget provided by our property tax becomes vital to keeping the city's finances afloat.

Our property taxes become more important when we look at what they pay for. Two years ago, the city council elected to raise property taxes by eighty-two cents per $100 of property. With this increase, we have seen our city budget grow by about $14 million since 1999, and the city has done positive things with this money.

Since 1998, the number of city employees has increased dramatically. This increase has not been some bureaucratic expansion, however. The police force has increased by thirty-six, while the fire department gained twenty-five new employees. Parks and recreation will have fifteen new employees this year. These new employees who make us safe and give us valuable public goods were paid for with our property taxes.

This year alone, the police department will hire seventeen new employees, while the fire department will add eight. These new employees, along with the additional parks and recreation employees, will cost us $1.2 million, about $34,000 for each new employee. Since we will all enjoy the benefits of having the new city employees to provide us with public services, this is a price I will gladly pay.

Consider what we will get with a larger police force. Increased police presence will make our streets safer. With seventeen new officers, patrols could be expanded; and programs such as D.A.R.E., where police officers interact positively with the public, could be increased. If one of those seventeen new officers saves a life, prevents a home from being burglarized, or keeps a youth from trying drugs, then it is worth my extra $430.

Consider what the extra parks and recreation employees will do for us. Our city pools are just one place that parks and recreation employees work. Our public pools give us more than a fun summer activity for the youth of our city; they also serve as positive activity for the city's more at risk youth. With our tax money, the city can afford to hire more lifeguards, who will then be able to teach more swimming lessons to our youth. If one of those lifeguards becomes a positive role model to an at risk youth, then my extra $430 was well spent.

Another area where our tax money is well spent is capital projects. Clarksville's downtown area is in dire need of public money after the tornado of 1999. The capital projects budget, as well as the highway and streets budget will pay to rebuild the city streets of downtown Clarksville. Capital projects are also necessary if we want to revitalize our downtown area with more economic activity. If the capital projects budget is able to bring even a small amount of growth to downtown Clarksville, if my tax dollar fixes the damaged roads of downtown Clarksville, then I am more than happy to pay my $430.

After looking at the answers to my simple questions, I find it hard not to keep our property tax rate as it is. If you want a safer city, if you desire more public recreation, if you want our city to offer an exciting downtown area, then I urge you to contact the city council member from your ward and tell him or her that you are willing to pay the extra fee to make Clarksville great.

Can we afford to keep paying the current property taxes? I feel that we should all ask ourselves a more appropriate question: can we afford not to keep paying our current property taxes?

Sincerely,
James B. Weakley II

SAMPLE OF A WEB SITE BASED IN SECONDARY RESEARCH

Help Save Memphis' Music Heritage

who we are

our goals

what you can do

history lesson

contact

"my music is still in memphis, because that's where i got it, that's where i learned it, that's where i felt it."

- chips moman

Help Save Memphis' Music Heritage

who we are

our goals

what you can do

history lesson

contact

who we are

Memphis has always been known as the home of the blues and the birthplace of rock n' roll. Now, that's even the city's catch phrase. After a decade and a half of rebuilding, downtown Memphis is trying to bring people back to the hotspot of old times, and they're undoubtedly succeeding. Despite the music heritage, developers are focusing on modernizing Beale Street and downtown Memphis. They are ignoring the music traditions that Memphis is home to, and they need to realize that history can be more important than making money on a new Beale. Developers need to bring Memphis back its glory as the groundbreaking spot for rock 'n' roll.

MEMPH S

Truth?

The official Memphis Tourism logo

At Memphis Music, a large group of music-loving Memphians have joined forces in an effort to realign the focus of the investors in charge of Memphis' future. These investors need to focus on making Memphis what it appears to be – a haven for music fans. Is there any way for Memphis developers to return to the genuine blues, soul, and rock mecca it was for decades before now and still appeal to the typical consumer? We believe that the answer to that question just may be the key to making Memphis a hot commodity again.

Memphis has done a good job of representing itself in cultural and political history. There is the Civil Rights museum, dedicated to the memory of Martin Luther King, Jr. There is also the Peabody Hotel, an over 120-year-old hotel that chronicles the history of Memphis society. A. Schwab's on Beale Street refused to sell out to bulldozing developers after Beale's original clientele had dropped away, and continues to do well to this day, still reflecting its history as a general store in the early 20th century.

Cultural History:

The Peabody Hotel, the South's grandest.

Memphis has an extensive group of potential customers who could use a crash course in Memphis music history. Why won't the city take hold of this opportunity to show off the impressive history that it has waiting to be relived? We want to see the city become what it used to be, what it should be. It is our pleasure to do what we can in order to help Memphis' future blossom.

Help Save Memphis' Music Heritage

who we are

our goals

what you can do

history lesson

contact

our goals

Memphis has seen a lot of improvement in the downtown area. It is now an area that people will go to on the weekends, and has become a major hotspot for summer nights. Beale Street is as popular as ever. Developers have done a very good job of remodeling downtown to fit the new image of Memphis. They have forgotten, however, to remodel what we all know as an integral part of Memphis – the music. Memphis Music wants the city to realize that what they've accomplished is impressive, but we have some other ideas in mind.

- Bring real blues musicians back to Beale Street
- Honor the musicians of Beale Street past
- Build a museum representing the styles of music that have taken place in Memphis – the blues, the beginnings of rock and roll, and soul
- Ressurrect Mud Island's museum, chronicling cultural, historical, and musical happenings of the Mid-South
- Highlight the areas of the city that have been breeding grounds for music with plaques and/or more recognition in Memphis tourism guides
- Hold festivals in honor of Memphis music

Memphis has long been a highlight for music lovers on tour of the southeastern United States. The city boasts the 2nd largest tourist attraction in the United States – Graceland. Memphis is located in the center of at least 10 highly populated southern cities within a 400-mile radius. It attracts over 8 million tourists yearly, all willing to spend over $1.7 billion in retail. Downtown doesn't only attract those from outside Memphis. Memphis itself has 1.1 million residents, 200,000 of which live within 10 minutes of downtown, and many more within a 25-mile radius (City of Memphis Official Site).

Elvis Presley's
Graceland:

The only reason to
visit Memphis?

Dan Ball

Many tourists come while on a pilgrimage of all the important musical stops of the Mid-South, and also because Memphis is just a fun town to visit. Residents of Memphis should have enough pride in city history to bring them downtown so they can learn as much as possible. Memphis has the potential to educate so many people, and it is time to take the initiative. Memphis Music wants to do just that.

Memphis Music is also dedicated to supporting the new found success downtown. We also want to prove to the city that improving the coverage of its music history can also be a success, and bring money and prestige to what the city already has to offer. We are not builders, we are not lawyers, and we are not investors. However, we are the city of Memphis, and we will have a voice. Memphis Music is that voice, and our main goal is to use it to its very fullest.

who we are

our goals

what you can do

history lesson

contact

what you can do

Memphis Music can only do so many things. Since we are just a group of music lovers, we can't neccessarily be the movers and shakers in the fight to win back our music history. However, the little things can go a long way, so we shouldn't stand idly by as the suits behind the money make our decisions for us. After all, we are taxpaying citizens, and if we want the music back, we have to lend a hand in getting it.

So, in the spirit of joining in, here's a list of things that YOU can do to help:

- Write to city officials at this site
- Attend shows of Memphis musicians
- Write to the Commercial Appeal
  email: letters@gomemphis.com
- Write to the Memphis Flyer
  email: letters@memphisflyer.com
- Contribute to music education programs at your neighborhood schools
- Recommend musicians to play on Beale Street
- Purchase local musicians' music from local retailers
- Visit Sun Studios, Graceland, and Beale Street – explore the city for hidden treasures
- Educate yourself further through listening, watching, reading, and acting

The bottom line is that the future of our music history lies in the hands of everyone in the city. That includes you. To join us, all you have to do is contribute some of your time. It will reap rewards that we and our children will be able to enjoy for decades to come.

Help Save Memphis' Music Heritage

who we are

our goals

what you can do

history lesson

contact

history lesson

Back in the early 20th century, Beale Street was the haven for delta blues music. Incredibly talented black musicians brought their talent to downtown Memphis, what is known as the crossroads of music. For many decades, Beale Street was mainly this, a breeding ground for talent America had never experienced before.

Blues Greats:

Fred McDowell, Johnny Woods, Bukka White Nathan Beauregard, Furry Lewis, Sleepy John Estes

For a long time, America didn't know about the blues. To learn, people had to travel directly to the blues hotspots – Memphis, St. Louis, and Chicago. When recordings started becoming available, the blues left the streets of the black American and entered the living rooms of white America. During the 60's and 70's, Beale lost much of the fresh blues it used to offer. Instead, it gave Memphis a place to go on the weekends.

Take also, for example, Sun Studios on Union Avenue and Stax Records at College Street and McLemore Ave. These two record labels were major producers of soul, blues, and rockabilly hit records. Both labels were largely responsible for the immersion of American music into rock n' roll. Sun Studios boasted the bragging rights of Sam Phillips and Elvis Presley, not to mention later showcasing Jerry Lee Lewis. Elvis and Jerry Lee are widely known as two of the best rockers music has ever heard.

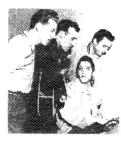

Sun Stars:

Jerry Lee Lewis, Carl Perkins, Elvis Presley, Johnny Cash

Stax was responsible for giving us the soul of the 60's and 70's. In 15 years, Stax had produced about 800 singles and 300 full albums. Plenty of well-known musicians either recorded at Stax, or really wanted to. Stax was even the fifth-largest black-owned business in America in 1974 (Soulsville, USA).

Sun Studios still stands at its original site, and offers tours and memorabilia. Stax, however, suffered a more severe sentence. The building was torn down in 1989, and a church was built in its place. Preservation of these two sites needs to be taken into better consideration.

These sites reflect the success of Memphis in the recording industry and further define the city as one that was able to start a music revolution that still exists today. The deterioration of historic music settings in the city is inexcusable and will certainly not be ignored.

Help Save Memphis' Music Heritage

who we are

our goals

what you can do

history lesson

contact

contact

You can reach us via e-mail, phone, or regular mail.

email: jherzog@utk.edu

phone: (901)754–0790

mailing address:

　　Memphis Music

　　1765 Crump Avenue

　　Memphis, TN 38107

Beale Street at night

Writing Projects

Writing Project 7.1

For the instructor of this writing course, write your own researched position paper, following your teacher's specifications for length and kinds of research. Consider using one of the subjects and the sources that you developed in the activities early in this chapter.

Writing Project 7.2

Design a research project that requires some local primary research. Select a subject that has a local connection so that you have local sources to interview, survey, or observe. Consider conducting a mini-ethnography, like our sample student research paper on the emergency room (p. 408) and the Penelope Eckert and Sally McConnell-Ginet study of high school cliques (p. 348), or consider interviewing someone whose perspective will add to what you can find in secondary sources (a local angle on a subject often benefits from interviews of local people). See our discussion of these research techniques in Chapter 1 (p. 26). If you have discovered some action that needs to be taken, write a proposal for change to someone in a position to help that change happen. Otherwise, write a researched position paper for your teacher and classmates.

Writing Project 7.3

Select a research subject that you are very interested in, regardless of how well it suits the academic scene. As you investigate the subject, work toward discovering what you most want to say about your subject, then choose a genre to write that lets you say what you want. For example, you might discover that you want to convince teenagers not to smoke, so you choose to write a pamphlet to distribute at junior high schools. Or you might discover that you are fascinated by the originators of radio, so you write a magazine feature article explaining how the true inventors failed to get proper credit. Or you might discover that one cell phone company really does offer a better deal, so you might want to create a Web site that compares the different packages and their benefits for different kinds of customers. The point of this assignment is for you to investigate something that you genuinely want to know more about and for you to select a genre that suits your purposes.

Writing in Unfamiliar Academic Scenes and Genres

The previous three chapters have introduced you to and helped you analyze several genres you will encounter in the scene of your writing course, especially the analysis paper, the argument paper, and research-based genres. Your knowledge of these genres will not only help you make more effective writing choices when writing them; it will also help you gain more access into the scene of the writing course itself by revealing its goals and assumptions as they are embedded in these genres. But as you know, especially from Chapter 5, the writing course is not the only academic scene in which you will be writing.

As you make your way through various academic scenes and situations, and as you are asked to write in their genres, you will be expected to take up and practice the goals and expectations that are embedded in them. Because they are so entrenched a part of how people interact in different scenes, situations, and genres, these goals and expectations will not always be made explicit to you. But since genres embody these goals and expectations, you can use the kind of genre analysis we have been doing in order to understand the goals and expectations of other, unfamiliar scenes of writing.

In this chapter, we will teach you *how* to apply your knowledge of scenes, situations, and genres to other academic scenes. We will start by guiding you through an understanding of different academic scenes and their common objectives as reflected in the shared features of writing assignments. Next we will describe how writing assignments themselves can help you identify disciplinary situations and their genres. Finally, we will describe how you can use genre analysis to make effective writing choices within these situations.

You can think of this movement from scene to situation to genre, which we have described throughout the book, as a series of repositionings, in which you first position yourself in the larger disciplinary scene, then in a particular situation within that scene, and then in a genre that will help you respond effectively to that situation. Each repositioning serves a different purpose and provides a different level of engagement. At the level of *scene,* you are basically trying to understand the general framework of your writing environment: what sort of place it is, who participates in it, and what their shared objectives are. In a very real sense, there is a logic to why people do what they do and write the way they do in different academic disciplines. Understanding the disciplinary scene of your course will give you some insight into this logic.

At the level of *situation,* you are engaging in a specific rhetorical interaction located within the disciplinary scene (one that reflects to some extent the shared objectives of the larger disciplinary scene). By carefully reading your writing assignment, you can access the writing situation and begin to identify your position within it, including who the readers are and what the subject, setting, and purposes for writing are. Since writing assignments will also often specify a genre for you to write, you can analyze that genre in order to make informed decisions about how to act appropriately and effectively in the situation. Such knowledge is your passport and your guide into the complex world of the college or university, helping you write with more awareness and confidence as you move from one academic scene of writing to another.

Fortunately, you do not need to start from scratch every time you move from one academic scene of writing to another. The analysis, argument, and research skills you have practiced in your writing course can serve as a foundation, a starting point, for the kinds of writing you will do in other courses. You might not, for example, be asked to write an analysis paper per se in some other academic scenes, but you will be asked to apply your analytical skills as you write different academic genres, each with different conventions and expectations.

Writing Activity 8.1

Of the skills that you have learned and practiced in your writing course, which ones have been the most valuable for you in your other courses? What makes this knowledge and these skills applicable to other courses and disciplines?

Observing Disciplinary Scenes

The first step in learning to write within an academic scene outside of your writing course is to understand that scene, and understanding a scene, as we explained in Chapter 1, involves observing and describing, in general, its participants and their shared objectives. Of course, it would take years of immersion in a discipline to understand fully its participants and their shared objectives. However, you can begin to gain some insight into academic scenes by employing the strategies for observing scenes, situations, and genres that we outlined in Chapter 1. The understanding you will gain will eventually help you make more effective choices within that scene.

Say, for example, that you are taking a course in cultural anthropology. The scene of that course takes place within the larger disciplinary scene of anthropology, which involves various participants, all of whom are involved in some shared objectives. The first step in trying to understand the scene of your cultural anthropology course, then, is to locate it in its larger disciplinary scene and to identify some of *that* discipline's shared objectives.

Use the guidelines for observing scenes in Box 1.2 (pp. 44–45) to help you identify what the discipline looks like: Where—in what places—are the shared objectives of this discipline carried out? How is the discipline organized? What are its parameters? How is it configured? Then try to identify why people participate in the disciplinary scene. Ask such questions as: What is it that brings people together in this scene? What overarching objectives do they share? What are they trying to do or trying to accomplish? Next, try to identify the situations or different interactions happening within this disciplinary scene, including who participates in the interactions, what subjects the participants deal with, where and when they interact (the setting), and their purposes for doing what they do. Finally, observe the genres being used to interact within these situations. What texts typically appear and are used repeatedly in situations within this scene? Because you may not have the time or access it takes to observe the disciplinary scene, one of the most effective ways to begin understanding a scene is by examining the typical texts or genres used in this scene, which reflect the participants' patterns of behavior or habits of communication (Refer to Box 2.1, pp. 93–94, for guidelines for analyzing genres). Another way to understand the shared objectives is by interviewing a knowledgeable member of that disciplinary scene, most likely a professor, instructor, or advanced student. (Refer to Box 1.1, p. 40, for guidelines for conducting interviews.) Once again, the questions for observing scenes that we outlined in Box 1.2 will help you develop questions you can ask your interviewee in order to gain a general understanding of the discipline of which your course is a part.

Of course, the writing you do takes place not only in a disciplinary scene such as anthropology; it takes place more specifically in the scene of your cultural anthropology course, which has it own particular participants, shared objectives, situations and genres. As we described in Chapter 5, the best place to start understanding the scene of your course is by looking at the genre of the course syllabus, which often describes the course objectives (see the discussion of analyzing syllabi in Chapter 5). Doing so will give you valuable insight into the scene of the course.

Understanding your academic scene of writing, from the larger disciplinary scene to the more particular scene of the classroom that is embedded within it, will give you a framework for making writing choices—choices that are informed by a greater knowledge of the classroom scene's underlying disciplinary goals and expectations.

Writing Activity 8.2

Select a course in another academic discipline, preferably one in which you are currently enrolled, and observe its scene, including its genres. Begin first by interviewing your instructor (or another knowledgeable member of the discipline) in order to identify and describe the larger disciplinary scene, especially the shared objectives in which the course functions, and to gather samples of its genres. To describe the scene, use the questions for observing scenes in Box 1.2 (p. 44–45) as your guide. Ask your teacher about typical texts or genres used within the discipline or the names of major journals or periodicals that you could consult. Next, analyze course genres such as your course's syllabus and textbook to identify your course's particular objectives and goals. Finally, try to identify how your particular course reflects the shared objectives that exist within the larger discipline. Speculate also on why your course may depart from the discipline's shared objectives. What do these shared objectives, along with any departures from these objectives, reveal about the scene of your course and its participants? How will knowledge of these objectives help you when you are ready to write in this scene?

Using Writing Assignments to Guide Writing in Different Disciplines

Chapter 5 described how the academic scene is a place where communication happens (a university or college campus) among groups of people (students, faculty, and staff) with shared objectives (to facilitate the pursuit, production, and exchange of knowledge). Within it participants in the various disciplines carry out their common goals through their shared patterns of communication or genres. One such genre, the writing assignment, is used repeatedly in various academic courses and disciplines. As a result, it can tell us much about these specific scenes and our performance as writers within them.

Writing assignments are presented by instructors for the purpose of accomplishing course objectives, ensuring that students are learning the course material and thinking critically about it, and measuring this learning. No matter the disciplinary scene, students are the primary readers of writing assignments and read the assignments to gain a clearer understanding of the teacher's expectations and to gain an understanding of their writing situations, including their subjects, their roles as writers, their purposes for writing and the conventions they are expected to follow. As a result, the writing assignment functions as a sort of "contractual agreement" between teacher and students for how to act within the writing situation. Some teachers treat it more formally than others, seeing the requirements of the writing assignment as more binding. But most assignments leave room for negotiation, room to enter into the shared agreement and to choose among a number of appropriate responses. These commonalties indicate that writing assignments, despite their functioning for differing disciplinary scenes, share important features, essential criteria, or keys for unlocking the assignments' expectations and giving you access to differing academic scenes and situations.

The following assignments from classes in nursing, engineering, geology, and math all share certain general qualities. These shared qualities are important to note because they reveal certain insights about writing that you can use to write effectively across many different academic scenes and situations. As you read these four assignments, look for the common qualities of all writing assignments as well as the particular differences that come from each assignment existing in a different disciplinary scene. Refer back to the questions for analyzing writing assignments in Box 5.1 (p. 198) to help guide your reading of the assignments.

WRITING ASSIGNMENT FROM NURSING
Dr. Cheryl L. Bosley, Department of Nursing, Youngstown State University

---

Journal Writing Guidelines

Journal writing is making an entry on paper each week about your clinical experiences. You are encouraged to explore and analyze your thoughts, feelings, and actions through reflection; make judgments and draw conclusions; and communicate this in your journal entry. This helps to develop reflective, analytical, and creative thinking.

When reflecting on the clinical experience, focus on the following:

1. Open-mindedness (various points of view)

2. Questioning (identifying key questions)

3. Reflecting on the information (hidden and explicit meanings)

4. Reasoning (identifying problems and solutions)

5. Examining own feelings about an issue

Credit for journal writing is calculated on the following:

1. Journal is completed weekly and turned in on time.

2. Journal is done following guidelines given in class.

3. Journal shows effort on the part of the student.

4. Journal entries reflect personal exploration and analysis.

5. Journal shows evidence of self-evaluation at midterm and final evaluation.

*No credit is deducted from journal grade for grammar, spelling, or punctuation.

*No credit is deducted from journal grade for clinical performance.

Guidelines for Journal Entries:

1. Submit 1–2 typed pages, word processor highly recommended.

2. Do not make a rough draft before writing entry.

3. Make entry very soon after clinical experience.

4. Turn in to instructor within 24–48 hours after clinical.

5. Keep focused on the objective/purpose of journal writing.

6. Do not revert to a time log or play-by-play account of daily clinical activities.

7. Make two copies and retain one for your personal notebook.

Procedure for Developing a Journal Entry

A. Think about the events of the day's clinical experience.

B. Think about the answers to these questions:

   1. What events (incidents, encounters, interactions, issues, etc.) stick out in your mind? Analyze (Evaluate, Explore) what happened.

2. What events led to the event?
3. Why did it happen?
4. How did it happen?
5. What were you thinking?
6. What were you feeling?
7. What did you do?
8. Could the outcome have been different? How?
9. Could the situation be handled differently? How?
10. What questions does this situation pose?
11. What pieces of information relate to the situation?
12. Is there any missing information that is needed in order to see the complete picture?
13. What solutions are obvious? What are other possible or alternative solutions?
14. Can you relate this to concepts and theories from lecture, text, journal articles, or other sources of information?
15. Can you relate this to anything from other past experiences?
16. What did you learn from this experience?

C. Start writing!

WRITING ASSIGNMENT FROM ENGINEERING
Dr. Daniel H. Suchora, Department of Mechanical Engineering, Youngstown State University

Design Project Write-up Guide—The Professional Report

I. General Guidelines

A. In a professional report, results are stressed. The procedure used is to be documented, however, the object of the write-up is to report results.

B. Professional reports in industry will be read and used by many people with various backgrounds. Some will be engineers and others may not. The professional report begins by stating the results and conclusions and then proceeds to give details only as necessary to reflect how the results were obtained. Do not write your reports to the instructor.

A good professional report should begin with a general statement of what was done, why it was done, the results obtained, and any conclusions or recommendations arrived at. The beginning of the report should be written to a general audience with later stages of the report getting more technical in nature. The president of a company who may be a non-engineer should be able to read the beginning of the report and get a general idea of what was done and any conclusions or recommendations reached. Engineering personnel should be addressed in the report where specific technical points are developed.

C. Use a good quality paper for your write-up.

D. The professional report is generally typewritten. A word processor should be used for much of the text portion of the report. Graphics software should be used for figures or graphs. Some sections can be neatly handwritten when their form would be difficult to handle with a word processor (sample calculations, etc.).

II. The Report

A. *Title Sheet.* The title sheet should include the title of the report, the reporter's name, and the date the report is submitted.

B. *Table of Contents.* The table of contents is optional depending on length and complexity of the report. If it is felt that the table of contents will aid the reader of the report, it should be included; however, if the report format is not complex, the table of contents can be omitted.

C. *List of Figures.* The list of figures is optional, depending upon the number of figures in the report and if listing the figures separately will aid the reader.

D. *Summary and Results.* This is the most important section of the report. It should begin with a general elementary statement of what was done, why it was done, the results obtained, and any conclusions reached or recommendations to be made. The later stages of this section should be more technical and develop and/or document techniques used to develop the results. These sections may include tables of results, graphs, or figures if inclusion of these items will aid the reader in interpreting the results.

E. As an example of some important points in regard to a professional report, consider the design of a gearbox. Obviously the gearbox will be required to transmit power under various restrictions. The beginning of the report should:

(1) Define *the Problem.* In simple terms and especially with sketches including dimensions and made to scale, clearly indicate the design

constraints. For a gearbox design this may include the gear ration required, input/output RPM, torque and/or HP capacity, space restrictions, orientation of input and output shafts, type of input and output coupling, cost limitations, operating environment, and most importantly methods by which design factors of safety are determined. Design factors of safety are best determined by following an established design code which should be clearly documented.

(2) *Design Presentation.* Next, the final design is given, including all dimensions and information necessary for a design draftsman to make detail drawings for manufacture. Following the design presentation all calculations are given documenting the design in regard to the design restrictions including required factors of safety. Always refer to the final design sketches to orient the reader to the calculations being performed. Remember that anyone with an engineering background should be able to follow your work without you present to explain it. It is generally not acceptable to present false starts you may have considered even though you may have spent considerable time on them—also remember that your report should not be in chronological order—you are presenting results and then documenting those results.

(3) Computer programs can be an important result of an engineering project. Oftentimes others will use your program to solve similar problems and hence it is extremely important that you effectively document your work. This documentation generally will appear in an appendix, however, it could appear in the Summary & Results section depending on the length and complexity of the report.

(4) Remember that you are trying to communicate results effectively. Anything that accomplishes this is O.K., even if it violates something in these or any other guidelines. Also, remember that it is not necessary to have section titles like "Define the Problem," etc.

III. Letter of Transmittal. The engineering report is generally done for someone. When giving the person your report, it is customary to attach a note or letter to the front, which serves as an introduction to the report. Typically, this note may simply state that this is the report that was requested. A more elaborate letter of transmittal may tell the reader of more advanced testing techniques which are available, etc.

IV. Closure. This set of guidelines is meant to be a general guide and, in some cases, you may not want to follow it exactly. At a particular company you may find other standards to use in writing engineering reports. However, this guide is one that many people follow.

WRITING ASSIGNMENT FROM GEOLOGY
Dr. Ray Beiersdorfer, Department of Geological
and Environmental Sciences, Youngstown State University

Rock Project Assignment

The goal of this project is for you to improve your observation and writing skills. Being able to carefully observe and communicate your observations is an important skill for everybody. The assignment is to write a report describing the building stone of a building (or monument) in the downtown area. You will be working in teams of three. Each group will submit one report, and each group member will receive the same grade. The following outline is a guide for the report and covers the details you should be thinking about. You can receive further guidance by talking to Dr. Ray after class or during his office hours.

Location: Obviously the first step is choosing a building (or monument). Although the specific building is up to you, it must have rock (not concrete or bricks) on at least part of it. Try to pick a building that is interesting to you and at a location you will feel comfortable spending an hour or two observing and describing.

Audience: An important consideration in a scientific paper is your audience. Who will be reading the paper? Assume that you work for a private/government agency and that your paper is going to be a technical report to your boss. You can further assume that the reader is familiar with basic (introductory geology level) terminology. However, be sure to explain any advanced terminology that may be unfamiliar to anyone but an expert in your field.

Prospectus: Your prospectus should be a one-page (maximum) hand- or typewritten statement that delineates the exact location of the building (or monument) that you want to describe. In addition make a first stab at determining the rock type (igneous, metamorphic or sedimentary) and include a brief description of what the rock looks like. Dr. Ray will check your prospectus to make sure you are on the right track.

Format of the Paper: The suggested format for the paper is outlined below—followed by a brief summary of the content of each section. Remember, the paper does not have to be long, but it does have to be complete. It is not necessary to submit your paper in a "clear plastic binder," but it is necessary to type it.

1) Title   4) Discussion/Conclusion
2) Introduction   5) References
3) Body

1) The title of your paper should give a potential reader a clear idea of what you will discuss. It should appear on the title page as the first page of your paper. Additional information to be included on the title page is the names and ID numbers of each group member, the class and the full date.

2) The introduction is the part of your paper which includes enough information about the building and its location that the reader will be able to find it. Any information you can gather about the history of the building (e.g., when it was built) can be included in the introduction. It is not required that you include this information, but it does tend to make the paper more interesting to the reader.

3) The body or "meat" of your paper is where you describe (in detail) the building stone. If necessary, the body of the paper can be subdivided into specific sections, using subheadings for clarity. If appropriate some of the data can be listed in tables. A hand drawing illustrating the important textural features of your building stone is required. Additional illustrations (or even a photo) are permissible but are not required. Be sure to include a scale bar of some sort in your illustrations (that is why geologists always include their hammer or people in photos, we all don't have a hammer fetish). Cite illustrations and tables at the appropriate juncture (in the text), and make sure that they have captions that clearly explain what the reader is seeing. Normally an illustration is found immediately after the page on which it is first mentioned; however, attaching them to the end of the paper is acceptable. If you use an illustration that is not your own, be sure to cite the reference.

4) A discussion/conclusion should summarize the important points of your paper. This is where you can use your creativity. How do you think the rock formed? What is the evidence to support your ideas? In which order did the minerals crystallize? If multiple interpretations can be drawn from the evidence, then determine if a preponderance of evidence favors one interpretation over another. In this section you can go beyond the facts to speculate on some aspect of your interpretation or future implications if your research were to continue. This would also be a good point in the paper to discuss the weathering that you described in the main section. How well is this rock holding up since the building was constructed? Do you see any increased weathering effects near ground level that could be attributed to ____?

5) A scientific paper normally contains many references. In this case your main reference will be your class text (especially Chapter 2, Appendix A and Appendix B). Remember, the emphasis of this project is on observing and writing down your observations. This is not a "term paper" type project. You do not have to look up a lot of information in books. However, anytime you mention an important idea that is not your own, you should immediately indicate (in parenthesis) the reference. References appear at the end of your paper in alphabetical order. Different academic disciplines usually prefer different formats for mentioning references within a paper and listing them at the end. Use the format of the Geological Society of America Bulletin. It is important that you avoid misusing reference information. Plagiarizing the work of someone else can get you in a lot of trouble. [sample references follow].

Grading: The rock project is worth 15% of the grade in this course. It will be judged on the basis of its quality of presentation, organization, prose, and scientific content. Some of the specific criteria that will be used when evaluating the papers are 1) organization, 2) use of evidence, 3) clear and accurate descriptions, 4) attention to audience, and 5) mechanics—grammar, spelling, coherence. Remember a reader is always predisposed to like a paper when it is neat, organized, and contains clear, readable illustrations. An example of the grading scheme that will be used to grade your paper is below.

Content

Accurate Descriptions	25%
Interpretation of Rock Type	10%
Accuracy of Data	10%
Insight/Original Thought	10%

Structure

Illustration	15%
Organization	10%
Referencing	5%

Mechanics

Prospectus	5%
Grammar/usage	5%
Spelling/punctuation	5%

WRITING ASSIGNMENT FROM MATH
*Dr. Anita C. Burris, Department of Mathematics
and Statistics, Youngstown State University*

Research Paper Summaries

1. Read the article "Reading Research Papers" by A. Hobbs.

2. Go to the library and find four research articles involving algebra.

Do at least one article from each of the following. The remaining two articles may be from either journal listed below or from any math journal:

The Journal of Pure and Applied Algebra
Proceedings of the AMS

Choose articles that are 2-10 pages in length, and whose title and/or abstract indicate that you may understand some of what is written in the article.

3. Write a 1-page summary of each article. Follow the basic format outlined in the Reading Research Papers article. Some general guidelines:

- It is ok if you get lost/don't understand some of the proofs. If the Theorem statements don't make sense to you, then the article you are trying may be too difficult. If an article is too difficult, choose another article.

- You do not need to turn in a copy of the article with your summary.

- You do not need to type your summaries.

- Identification information can be placed either at the bottom of the page as suggested by Hobbs, or at the top of the page.

- Summary must include any definitions and/or notations that were previously unknown to you.

- Summary need not include definitions/ notations that were previously known to you.

- Summary must include statements of all Theorems of the paper.

Writing Activity 8.3

Drawing on Box 5.1: Questions for Analyzing Writing Assignments (p. 198), describe the key features of the previous assignments from nursing, engineering, geology, and math. What has each writing assignment specified about the writing situation and its setting, subject, writers, readers, and purposes? Has the assignment specified a particular genre to respond to the situation?

By carefully reading your writing assignments, you gain insight into the nature of the subject you are being asked to write about, why you are being asked to write about it, the kind of role you are being asked to perform as a writer, what your readers will be expecting from your writing, and what sorts of conventions you will be required to follow. Such insight will help you make more effective writing choices within the situation. After completing Writing Activity 8.3, you have probably already noticed that each of the assignments helps frame a different situation within each of these scenes, in terms of the subject matter, the relations between reader and writer, and the purposes for the assignment. In addition, you have likely also noticed that each of these assignments also indicates the genre that the writer will be expected to use in responding to the situation that the assignment sets up. Both the situation and the genre that are embedded in the writing assignment reflect the differing knowledge and objectives of the disciplinary scene in which the writing assignment exists.

We will now examine the writing assignments provided in order both to explore what these assignments reveal about their different disciplines and to teach you how you can apply this knowledge to your own reading of and writing in the new academic scenes you will encounter. Remember: Writing assignments serve as a map of the situation you are about to enter into as a writer. You can use the clues embedded within writing assignments in order to start making effective writing choices based on the subjects, purposes, and settings for writing, and the roles of participants (writers and readers)—whatever the scene or situation.

IDENTIFYING DISCIPLINARY SUBJECTS, SETTINGS, AND PURPOSES

One of the goals of writing within academic scenes is for students to engage critically with the subject matter, whether the subject consists of the stone façade of a building or an algebraic theorem. The writing assignments in this chapter reveal that a discipline's purposes will closely correspond to the particular subject and setting identified by the writing assignment. For instance, in the very scientific and technical field of engineering, the purpose for the writing assignment is to "report results;" furthermore, the instructor uses the technical topic of a gearbox design to clarify the purpose and how it should be carried out. In addition, the assignment identifies a professional "industry" setting, which corresponds to the professionally written, results-oriented report. In contrast, in the highly interpersonal field of nursing, where the subject is the students' clinical experiences and where students interact with patients in hospital settings, the purpose is to "explore and analyze [their] thoughts, feelings and actions through reflection" on these interpersonal experiences. The different subjects, settings, and purposes defined by the assignments reflect the differing objectives of the course scenes.

Writing Activity 8.4

Choose a writing assignment from a course you are taking, and describe the key features discussed above. What are its subjects, settings, and purposes? How can you tell?

IDENTIFYING THE ROLES OF WRITERS

In keeping with the view of students as critical coinvestigators and participants in academic scenes, all of the writing assignments share the goal of initiating students into the disciplinary scene and inviting them to participate in its shared objectives. The details of these shared objectives, however, differ from scene to scene and reflect their different disciplines. For instance, in the engineering assignment, the fact that the writers are called on to report results to an audience of company president and a specialized audience of engineering personnel defines the role of the writer as that of a professional, and the assignment repeats the word "professional" throughout. The math assignment refers to "Proceedings of the AMS" (assuming that students will know AMS stands for American Mathematical Society) and asks students to consult an academic journal for specialists in the field, *The Journal of Pure and Applied Algebra*. The geology assignment asks students to assume that they are experts and "to explain any advanced terminology that may be unfamiliar to anyone but an expert in the field." Finally, the nursing assignment refers to specialized "clinical experience" and asks students to relate their journal experiences to "concepts and theories from lecture, text, journal articles, or other sources of information." Students are expected to fully engage in their learning and join the dialogue of this scene. They are warned that their journal entries should avoid the "banking" approach we mentioned in Chapter 5, of filing and storing information, and should not "revert to a time log or play-by-play account of daily clinical activities." In each case, writers are asked to demonstrate their expertise in the subject and to present themselves as critics, knowledgeable professionals in the field or, at the very least, professionals-in-training.

Writing Activity 8.5

Returning to the writing assignment you described in Writing Activity 8.4, what writing role does it ask you to perform? How can you tell?

IDENTIFYING THE ROLES OF READERS

Writing assignments are openings in the dialogue, spaces where you can "enter the disciplinary conversation." Entering into a conversation or joining a dialogue implies that there must be people you are addressing— listeners or participants in the conversation. While academic conversations often seem limited to exchanges between student and teacher, the academic audiences you will address are often more varied. In any setting, as you enter into a conversation, you should be aware of the other participants, whose knowledge and attitudes might affect your contributions to the dialogue. The sample writing assignments we are looking at reveal various audiences that you might be called upon to address in various academic scenes:

The Teacher as Reader

The teacher's role as reader is more complicated than it may seem. One role the teacher assumes is that of *evaluator,* in which case you should be careful to find out what the criteria for evaluation will be if they are not clearly spelled out on the assignment sheet (the assignments from nursing and geology specify these criteria for evaluation). If the teacher's criteria for responding to and evaluating your writing are not clearly specified, you can get an idea of the teacher's expectations through his or her in-class lectures, through class discussions, through discussions of writing assignments, and through the teacher's comments on your previous written work.

However, your instructors typically also take on additional roles and read/respond as *representatives of their disciplinary scene,* in which case you would have an "expert" reader in the field—one who sees how well you are conforming to the norms and conventions (vocabulary, format, organization, tone) of that scene. The engineering assignment, for example, identifies an "expert" audience consisting of "engineering personnel." The engineering professor, as a representative of the engineering personnel, will likely be reading to see how well specific technical points are developed. Even when the instructor does not specify an expert audience, the instructor is likely evaluating your work in light of that discipline's expectations and standards, essentially reading your work from the perspective of an expert.

Finally, teachers may assume the role of a *"fictionalized" reader,* perhaps even an outside reader—such as an editor of *Time* magazine or your local congressional representative. In this case, they project themselves into a role and keep in mind the values, beliefs, and interests of this audience as they read. In the geology writing assignment, students are given an imaginary audience, an audience outside the university (a boss at a private/government agency). In this case, teachers may read to gauge how well writers project an authoritative or expert tone without excluding a lay audience. The instructions that students can "assume the reader is familiar with basic terminology" while being careful to "explain any advanced terminology" will help writers formulate appropriate rhetorical strategies in responding.

Keep in mind that, in cases where you submit your writing to the actual audience (by sending your letter to your congressional representative or sending an editorial to your local newspaper), the teacher is still an audience for your writing and may have a separate set of criteria for you to meet.

Specialists as Readers

Often instructors, particularly as you begin taking courses in your major, will have you address the actual community of specialists or experts within that discipline rather then fictionalizing or impersonating that community. For instance, as a psychology major, you might be asked to write for other members of that discipline with differing levels of expertise: psychology majors, a psychology textbook, practicing psychologists in the field, or the journal *Cognitive Psychology.* These readers would expect you to follow the norms, conventions, and language use of the disciplinary scene. Here, the roles of the teacher as reader and the audience of specialists may converge, since the teacher will be evaluating from the perspective of his or her role in the discipline. The engineering assignment and the geology assignment define readers with varying degrees of specialization in the scene. In the geology assignment, the reader is a member of the disciplinary scene—although a novice member—who understands basic but not advanced terminology. And in the engineering assignment, the readers range from nonengineers who want general information about the project to engineering specialists who will understand specific technical points. These specialized audiences give writers direct experience with "entering the conversation."

The Implied Audience

Sometimes the audience in a writing assignment may be implied rather than explicitly stated. In this case, you can use what you know about the genre for writing and the writing situation to help you identify the likely readers. For instance, in the journal-writing assignment for nursing, you can assume that because the purpose is to reflect on personal experiences and examine your feelings, that you yourself may be the primary audience. However, the "guidelines" do stipulate that you will also turn the journal in to the instructor. It's important to remember that, when writing within the different academic scenes, there's *always* an academic audience, even if this audience is not specified. The math assignment, for instance, does not explicitly identify an audience, but given the instructional purpose—to read research articles on algebra and then write summaries—you can assume an academic audience, most likely the teacher as reader. The professor will be most interested in how critically you read the articles and how clearly and comprehensively you summarize the ideas in the article.

The "Academic Audience"

Some assignments also assume a general "academic audience," a general audience consisting of educated individuals who, although they may be members of differing disciplinary scenes, nonetheless share some common intellectual values. For instance, these readers will appreciate writing that is clear, focused, well organized, with claims that are well reasoned, well supported and well documented. The geology assignment alludes to this general academic audience in the "Grading" section, where it issues the following cautionary advice: "Remember a reader is always predisposed to like a paper when it is neat, organized and contains clear, readable illustrations."

Writing Activity 8.6

Returning to the writing assignment you described in Writing Activity 8.4, what audience does it specify? If no audience is specified, what audience seems to be implied by the assignment, and how can you tell? What does that choice of audience suggest about the discipline's values and objectives? How does your understanding of audience help shape your purpose and way of responding?

Keep in mind that, because the goals of academic writing are multifold, your purposes and audiences for writing can be multiple as well. For example, the engineering assignment identifies multiple readers with various levels of specialization. According to the assignment, "The beginning of the report should be written to a general audience with later stages of the report getting more technical in nature. The president of a company who may be a non-engineer should be able to read the beginning of the report and get a general idea of what was done and any conclusions or recommendations reached. Engineering personnel should be addressed in the report where specific technical points are developed." Part of the report (the introduction) addresses nonspecialists while other parts address engineering specialists. An awareness of these multiple audiences for writing will help writers organize the report and make appropriate language choices as they present their results to both expert and nonexpert readers.

Writing assignments function within the various academic scenes you will encounter in the academy, and they work to clarify your writing situation—the reasons you are writing, the subjects you are writing about, the settings you are interacting within, and the participants in these interactions. Learning how to discern the particular situations in particular writing assignments marks a critical step in learning how to make effective writing choices in different scenes and their situations.

Collaborative Activity 8.1

Trade your findings from Writing Activity 8.3 with classmates. Compare the situations embedded in each of the assignments. How do the readers and writers, subject matter, purposes for writing, genres, and rhetorical conventions differ? What can you learn about each of the disciplinary scenes as a result of their different situations and genres?

Collaborative Activity 8.2

After comparing the situations embedded in each assignment in Collaborative Activity 8.1, discuss with your classmates how a writer might go about responding to each of the situations. Based on your analysis of the readers and writers, subject matter, purpose for writing, genre, and rhetorical conventions in each assignment, what writing choices would you make in each of the situations?

IDENTIFYING THE GENRE

In addition to shaping the writing situation, writing assignments will often also specify a genre that will help you respond to that situation in an expected way. So even if the elements of a writing situation are similar from one academic situation to the next, the specific ways of responding to a situation will depend on the genre you are being asked to write.

For example, while the sample writing assignments from geology, math, engineering, and nursing share common assumptions about the value of analysis, argument, and research, the strategies and conventions people use to carry out these goals differ from discipline to discipline and from genre to genre. For instance, both the nursing assignment and the engineering assignment ask students to carry out analyses and draw conclusions. However, the engineering assignment specifies the professional genre of the report, while the nursing assignment asks students to keep a more informal journal. These differing genres reflect the differing disciplinary objectives of these scenes. Since the purpose of the nursing assignment is to get students—who are on-site performing clinical activities—to reflect on their clinical experiences and the personal role they played in the events of the day's clinical activity, the genre of the journal is an appropriate response. Likewise, since the purpose of the engineering assignment is to professionalize students and to give them experience with types of writing and the multiple audiences they will encounter on the job, the genre of the report—a genre that functions for this professional community—also makes sense.

These specified genres, as we have seen throughout this textbook, carry with them certain expectations reflective of their scenes and situations, expectations you need to read in order to respond appropriately to the assignment. For example, the *different genres use different types of evidence:* The math assignment asks students to include "statements of Theorems" and to make sense of mathematical "proofs" as part of their summary of research articles. In the scientific report on rock formation and the engineering report, students are asked to use graphics, visuals, or illustrations, which are needed to convey the pertinent textural characteristics of rock or to convey a complex technical process or design. The genre of the engineering report carries with it a specific format (title sheet, table of contents, list of figures, summary, and results) that reflects the professional role the writer is expected to assume as he or she writes for this professional community. Further, the generic patterns of the engineering report, with its use of Roman numerals and its use of matter-of-fact but technical language (such as the example of the gearbox design and "the gear ratio required, input/output RPM, torque and HP capacity . . ." etc.) reveal the values and criteria for effective writing that are asked for in the engineering report—an organized and professional report, with clear but technical descriptions.

Writing Activity 8.7

Both the engineering and the geology assignments ask for "reports." Take note of any similarities in what the two assignments ask for, and explain these similarities. Also note how their conceptions of "reports" differ, and explain how these differences might be the result of differing disciplinary objectives and values.

Collaborative Activity 8.3

Working in groups, compare the different genres that each of the writing assignments from math, geology, nursing, and engineering specifies. In what way does each of these genres respond to the situation specified by the assignment? What makes each genre appropriate for the situation? And what would a writer need to know about the genre and its relationship to the situation in order to write it effectively?

Creativity within Writing Assignments

It may seem that your role as writer within the academic scene and your ability to creatively interpret this scene are limited by the routine, scheduled performances of writing assignments—assignments that have already "blocked out" your actions and have scripted your responses. As a result, you may go through the motions but lack a real investment in your role. Surprisingly, even the most limited and restrictive writing assignments provide opportunities for choosing your rhetorical strategies and accomplishing your own purposes. Take, for example, the engineering report, with its strict set of guidelines. The instructor reminds student writers that "you are trying to communicate results effectively. Anything that accomplishes this is O.K., even if it violates something in these or any other guidelines." So even within the seemingly tightest constraints, you always have choices as writers. In this case, meeting the purpose and communicating effectively to the audience are the most important goals, but the instructor rightly acknowledges that there may be different strategies for accomplishing these goals.

Analysis, Argument, and Research in Different Disciplines and Genres

As the writing assignments also indicate, even important academic concepts such as analysis, argument, and research—concepts that you read about and practiced in Chapters 6 and 7—will vary according to disciplinary scene and will produce different genres. For instance, the social sciences—including sociology, social work, psychology, political science, economics, and anthropology—rely on analysis in much of their research, and this reliance is reflected in the various genres used within them. While the essential concept of analysis—to uncover assumptions, to examine how something works and why—functions the same way in the social sciences as it does in your writing course, social scientists use different methods and genres to conduct and communicate their analyses, which are used to study various aspects of human behavior. Social scientists tend to use more formal methods of inquiry, for example. Instead of developing *claims*, they develop *hypotheses*. Instead of *supporting* the claims with evidence as we described in the analysis paper, social scientists *test* their hypotheses through more controlled case studies and data. It might seem at first that these differences are just a matter of wording, but it is actually more than that. It reflects a somewhat different assumption about the nature of analysis, one based more on a scientific method of inquiry. Such inquiry is more systematic and more controlled, reflecting an even more detached observer than the one who writes analysis papers.

Most of the genres social scientists use reflect such assumptions. In social work courses, for instance, students are often asked to write genres that prepare them to conduct research studies. One such genre used in sociology and other social science disciplines, sometimes called a "library research report," asks students to identify and describe a research problem, one that builds on already existing research in the field. This genre calls for analysis, because it invites students to examine the relevant research in sociology—looking for gaps in the research and uncovering what has been done and what still needs to be done—and then to develop a research problem or question based on that analysis. The main purpose of this genre is to teach students how to develop hypotheses, hypotheses that they can then test later.

A closely related social work genre, often called a "Data Set Analysis," also prepares students to do background research, using analysis. The genre asks students to look at a data set such as GSS (General Social Survey—a database of statistics and demographic information about such things as homelessness, divorce rate, religious groups, etc.) and develop a research question that uses that data. For example, a student might develop a research question having to do with the relation between abortion rates and religious affiliation. In writing the data set analysis, the student would be expected first to introduce the research question and its significance. After that, the student is expected to conduct a review of the literature related to that question, in which he or she looks at what other researchers have said about the subject. Based on that review, the third step asks the student to refine his or her research question, perhaps adding a variable that other researchers have not considered, such as social class and its effect on the relation between abortion and religious affiliation. The fourth step involves developing a hypothesis based on that research question, one that the student will be expected to test (for example, "The higher a woman's social class, the less likely will her religious affiliation affect her decision to have an abortion"). The fifth step involves the actual data analysis. This is where the student turns to the data set to test the hypothesis. This step requires the student to explain what statistical technique and what variables he or she used. This is then followed by a descriptive analysis of the data, including an examination of the patterns that emerge in the data such as frequencies, averages, and means. The sixth step involves a description of the results. And the final step involves a discussion of the results, including what the data means.

Although the social work assignment involves analysis—that is, it involves taking apart the data and seeing what it means—it looks and works differently from the writing course analysis paper we described in Chapter 6. It is more systematic; for example, it uses subheadings to announce each of the steps: Introduction, Literature Review, Refined Research Question, Research Hypothesis, Data Analysis, Results, and Discussion. Yet it also shares some basic analysis qualities with the analysis paper you might practice writing in your writing course.

As such, as you make your way from one academic scene of writing to another, pay attention to how different scenes will ask you to perform different kinds of analyses in different situations and genres, and then combine what you know about analysis in general with the specific assumptions and expectations regarding analysis shared by those who participate in these specific scenes. Because these assumptions and expectations are embedded in the genres, you can use your analysis of the genre to make effective writing choices.

Collaborative Activity 8.4

Drawing on the guidelines for conducting interviews from Box 1.1 (p. 40), interview members of two different academic disciplines (preferably a teacher from a course you are taking in each of these disciplines) and ask them to explain how each of their disciplines generally defines and practices "analysis," "argument," and "research." Does each have a genre comparable to the analysis paper? To the argument paper? To the researched position paper? How do these genres differ in how they perform an analysis? What do their arguments look like? What counts as research and what is involved in doing it? What other genres are used for carrying out analysis, argument, and research? When you have collected your answers, report to the class how analysis, argument, and research are defined and used in the genres of each of the disciplines.

Working in the same group as in Collaborative Activity 8.4, collect samples of one of the genres you learned about from each of the two disciplines you analyzed in that activity. Using genre analysis, describe how each of the two disciplinary genres makes use of analysis, argument, and/or research. Use the information you gathered from your interviews to help you interpret how the two genres reflect how each of their disciplines defines analysis, argument, and/or research. Make sure to keep a record of your findings because you might need to refer back to them in response to Writing Project 8.2 at the end of this chapter.

Practicing How to Analyze and Write an Unfamiliar Academic Genre

In previous activities you surveyed the scene of a course and accessed your situation by examining the writing assignment. The next set of activities asks you to analyze a genre that you might be asked to write in a particular discipline in order to make effective writing choices in the situation. To analyze the genre that is specified for you in the writing activity, follow the guidelines for analyzing genres in Box 2.1 (pp. 93–94) as well as the process we suggested for analyzing the argument paper in Chapter 6 (p. 289). Your goal is to identify and describe the features of the genre, to interpret what these features mean, and then to use that interpretation to make more effective and informed writing choices when writing the genre. The following three writing activities will guide you through this process.

In groups with common interests, select an academic discipline such as economics, psychology, history, biology, etc. Then select a genre that is commonly used in that discipline. To help you in selecting a genre, ask members of that discipline for guidance. For example, ask a faculty member or an advanced student to tell you what genre is most common to his or her scene of writing. Use the questions from step 2 of Box 2.1: Guidelines for Analyzing Genres (p. 93) to find out about the scene and situation in which the genre is used, including who uses it and for what purpose. Then ask the interviewee where you can find samples of the genre. The faculty member or student might be able to show you some samples or to direct you to a place in the library where you can find samples.

Collaborative Activity 8.7

Once you have collected samples of the genre, use steps 3 and 4 of Box 2.1 to guide your analysis of the genre. Identify and describe the genre's most common features, and then interpret what these features mean. Then, in your group, draw on the questions for critiquing genres in Box 4.1 (p. 161), and determine what you see as the effects of the genre, including its strengths and weaknesses.

Collaborative Activity 8.8

Based on your genre analysis in the previous two writing activities, develop a list of strategies for writing the genre, moving through the stages of the writing process as well as the parts of the genre itself. To help guide you, use the questions for invention, drafting, and revising in Chapter 3 (pp. 108,117, and 139) as well as the guiding questions we suggested in the "Writing within the Generic Expectations of Argument Papers" in Chapter 6 (p. 300).

In this chapter, we have moved from the general to the specific: from the scene to the situation to the genre. Because scene, situation, and genre interact, you can use your knowledge of one to inform your understanding of the other. Such knowledge will serve you well as you write within different academic scenes.

Writing Projects

Writing Project 8.1

Select one of the writing assignments from math, geology, engineering, or nursing reprinted in this chapter and write instructions, addressed to students who will be given the writing assignment in the future, explaining what they need to know in order to respond effectively to the assignment. Conduct research in order to describe the disciplinary scene in which the assignment appears, explicate the assignment in order to explain the specifics of the writing situation, and then analyze the genre that the writing assignment specifies. Once your research is complete, present your findings as instructions to future students about how they can use this understanding of scene, situation, and genre to make effective writing choices in response to the assignment.

Writing Project 8.2

In Collaborative Activity 8.5, your group described and compared how two genres from two different disciplines make use of analysis, argument, and/or research. In a 4- to 6-page analysis paper (refer to Box 6.1 on pages 287–289 for guidelines for writing analysis papers) written to your writing course instructor, analyze how each of these genres differs from either the analysis paper, the argument paper, or research paper that we discussed in Chapters 6 and 7. Note any similarities and differences, and then analyze what these similarities and differences reveal about each of these scenes, including the scene of the writing class.

Writing Project 8.3

Drawing on the guidelines for conducting interviews from Chapter 1 (p. 40), interview someone who conducts research in a discipline outside of English (an advanced student, a graduate student, an instructor or professor). Find out as much as you can about the disciplinary scene (including its participants, their shared objectives, research methods, and assumptions—refer to the guidelines for observing scenes in Box 1.2, pp. 44–45), its situations (the particular rhetorical interactions that happen within the scene, involving particular participants, subjects, settings and purposes for interacting—refer to the guidelines for observing situations in Box 1.2), and the genres it uses to respond to these situations (including where and when the genres are used, why, and by whom—refer to the guidelines for analyzing genre in Box 2.1, pp. 93–94). If possible, analyze samples of some of the genres used (including their rhetorical and linguistic patterns) and study secondary sources, including textbooks or manuals on writing in that discipline if they exist. Then choose a genre suitable for communicating your research findings on the writing done in that particular discipline and on how the writing reflects that scene. The genre you choose—whether a researched position paper, a Web site, or brochure (see Chapter 7 for further guidelines for presenting rescarch)—should be appropriate to an audience of teachers and majors in that field.

Writing Project 8.4

In Writing Activity 8.4 and then in Activities 8.5 and 8.6 that followed it, you selected and analyzed a writing assignment from another course in order to identify and describe its writing situation. Now is your chance to make use of this insight and respond to the assignment. Determine what genre the writing assignment specifies, analyze it, critique it, and then write that genre according to the situation and expectations of the assignment. When you are done, write a memo to your writing course instructor explaining (a) the choices you made and why you think they are appropriate and effective given the situation and genre; and (b) any changes you made that varied from the assignment and your evaluation of the limitations or failures of the genre.

Reading and Writing Beyond Academic Scenes

III

Reading and Writing within Workplace Scenes

9

In Part II we examined the ways in which genres can give you access to academic scenes and can help you perform successfully within its various situations. While we focused primarily on the situations and genres of the writing course scene, the previous chapter, Chapter 8, explained how you can use your genre knowledge to participate effectively in other college classes and disciplinary scenes. In Part III you will have a chance to extend this knowledge to scenes beyond the academy. In the same way that you have used genres as rhetorical maps to help guide your exploration of academic landscapes, you can also use genre knowledge as you travel beyond academic scenes to navigate the sometimes unfamiliar terrain of workplace and public scenes. In this chapter we will focus on how your participation in the genres of the academic scene can prepare you to participate in workplace scenes.

We often refer to **workplace scenes** as altogether different from academic scenes, particularly when we speak of leaving college to "enter the workforce" or "join the real world" (suggesting that the academic world is somehow not "real"). Indeed, from your current vantage point, you may have difficulty envisioning how your writing course (or, for that matter, the writing you do in other courses) could possibly prepare you for the various situations you will encounter in the workplace. For instance, you might wonder how your knowledge of writing argument and analysis papers will translate into the knowledge you will need to perform in particular workplace scenes and situations. Yet, despite the distinctions we make between university and workplace scenes and between academic writing and nonacademic writing, there are connections between these two scenes of writing. One connection is *genre*. The skills you have learned and practiced in your writing course—how to analyze genres and how to use that analysis to make effective writing choices—can transfer to your ability to read and write your way into various workplace scenes.

Writing Activity 9.1

In a couple of paragraphs, describe your career interests and the type of job you ideally envision yourself having after graduating from college. Or, if you already have a career and are returning to college, explain how you hope to advance your career. What type of workplace scene do you see yourself participating in after college, and what role do you envision having in this scene? Speculate on the communication skills you might need to succeed in this job. What types of writing situations do you anticipate encountering within this scene, and what kinds of writing do you anticipate doing? Then speculate on the ways that the communication skills you have learned in this or other writing courses might be useful for either getting a job or performing successfully on the job.

Comparing Academic and Workplace Scenes

Like academic scenes, workplace scenes are places in which communication happens (corporations, office buildings, job sites) among groups of people (employers, employees) with some shared objectives (to successfully carry out the work of the organization). To help them accomplish their shared objectives, the participants within workplace scenes draw on typical rhetorical ways of responding to repeated situations—that is, genres.

For instance, just as faculty use the genre of the syllabus to communicate course goals and expectations for their students, employers might distribute handbooks or training materials to their incoming employees in order to communicate the company's goals and expectations. And just as the college or university has applications for admission, enrollment cards, financial aid forms, and so on, workplaces have similar genres that respond to repeated activities, such as job application forms, contracts, benefits forms, and brochures—genres that help them carry out their daily "business." Both scenes also rely on genres that enable internal correspondence—like memos from administrators to faculty or from employees to managers—as well as external correspondence, like letters or newsletters to "investors," whether company shareholders or university alumni. Some of the genres we mentioned—such as letters, memos, and brochures—cross borders of academic/nonacademic scenes, in a general way. Other genres are unique to particular scenes. But whether they appear in academic or workplace scenes, or are unique or shared, all of these genres have something in common: They help their users accomplish their shared objectives and carry out the "work" of the organization or institution.

COMPARING PURPOSES

Within a typical workplace scene, you will likely find multiple smaller scenes. Large companies might include public relations departments, payroll offices, billing departments, offices of accounting, research and development departments, or marketing divisions, each with its own various situations involving particular subjects, settings, participants and purposes. Within these workplace situations, the purposes for writing tend to emphasize less the writer's understanding of the subject matter (analysis of/exploration of a subject), which is common in academic writing, and more the reader's ability to understand the information and act on it—to use the information to accomplish some goal. *Like some academic writing (reports, reviews of literature), workplace writing is information-oriented; on the other hand, unlike most academic writing, workplace writing is also very often action-oriented.* In other words, the purpose of most workplace writing situations is to produce a result or to bring about change.

Yet even as they tend to share this information and action orientation, the purposes behind workplace situations are as diverse as the workplace scenes themselves: to solve a problem, explain a procedure, instruct someone on how to carry out a process, or request resources or funding for a project. And for each of these varied situations, there are genres used to accomplish these actions and communicate this information. Whether an information-oriented letter sent to customers explaining a product recall from a public relations department or an action-oriented proposal sent to directors requesting that they hire a new staff member, workplace genres reflect the shared objectives of workplace scenes.

COMPARING AUDIENCES

Because there are multiple situations and genres within workplace scenes, there are also multiple *audiences.* Many technical writing and business writing textbooks that focus on workplace writing instruction draw a distinction between the audiences in academic situations and the multiple audiences or "users" of texts in workplace situations. In academic situations you often address a single person, your teacher (and, sometimes, your peers). However, in workplace situations, you communicate with a wide variety of people with differing levels of expertise and with different professional concerns based on varying positions in the organization. For instance, in your workplace you might have readers who are located within your organization—either within your own group or department or in other departments or divisions located elsewhere in the organization. Or you might be addressing readers outside of the organization (an *external* audience).

In addition, because of the action-oriented nature of workplace documents, your readers will also be the actual users of the document and will play different roles that are often defined as **primary and secondary reading roles.** The *primary* audience uses the information and makes decisions based on it, while the *secondary* audience consists of individuals more indirectly affected by the decisions or actions. For example, a writer creating a brochure on company benefits must first consider the readers of that document, including prospective employees (the likely primary readers), current employees (the secondary readers who are also affected), readers in the personnel office (additional secondary readers), and perhaps even external readers consisting of the insurance providers. Each of these readers will read the document for different purposes, with prospective employees thoroughly combing the document to survey the coverage or perhaps even to determine whether the benefits package warrants accepting a job with this particular organization. Current employees, on the other hand, might just scan the document, reading only those sections that pertain to a situation whereby they need to review a benefits policy. Other readers, such as personnel officers who handle benefits and claims, as well as insurance providers, will read to discern the accuracy and clarity of information.

COMPARING WRITERS

In addition to the multiple readers of workplace documents, *multiple writers* may participate in this process as well. ***Writing a document in the workplace will often be collaborative in nature, with more than one person shaping the document.*** Businesspeople and professionals often find themselves working in groups or teams on various writing projects. Philip C. Kolin in *Successful Writing at Work* estimates that "in the world of work, 90% of all businesspeople spend some time writing as part of a collaborative team." The models of collaboration in the workplace reflect the importance of team efforts that draw on diverse talents and experience as well as the value placed on the efficiency of completing a written project. Some corporations may follow a **division-of-labor model,** in which employees with individual areas of expertise (writers, graphic designers, technical consultants) will be assigned various roles on the same project, working independently on their parts. This model draws on the specialized expertise and unique interests and knowledge of employees. Workplaces may also follow the **integrative model,** in which all employees work together cooperatively on the same project, researching together and writing together. This process works well for lengthy projects that would take too long for just one person to write on his or her own.

With the input of so many individuals, how does a writer in the workplace create a coherent document with a coherent persona or voice? The workplace writer's task is often to bring together all of the voices and merge them into a voice that reflects the company's persona. In much academic writing, writers seek to use ethos to create an individual voice or a credible and authoritative persona, but in workplace writing the credibility of the *company* takes precedence over the credibility of the writer. Therefore, despite the multiple readers and writers who participate in the situations and genres of a workplace scene and who may bring varying perspectives, these participants' work is driven by the goals, values, and needs of the overarching workplace scene. In some ways, we might say that workplace writing is "authored" by and on behalf of the company or business.

Successfully merging the voices of multiple writers and incorporating the input of multiple readers have been made easier by the technologies that have shaped workplace writing. With networking capabilities—such as the ability to share files over local area networks and to carry out electronic editing of texts—technology has had a noticeable effect on collaboration, drafting, and revision strategies. In addition, electronic communication, such as e-mail, has become an essential tool of almost every workplace and, due to its quickness, efficiency, and convenience, has transformed the traditional genres of letters and memos. Through such electronic communication, members of a workplace can communicate with individuals in their own organization, employees in branch organizations, or with employees and customers across the country or around the world. Furthermore, with the use of the Internet, many workplaces are using Web sites to advertise their products and services to a broad audience.

Collaborative Activity 9.1

In small groups, compare and contrast two of the same genres but from different scenes—one from a workplace scene and one from the academic scene. For instance, your group could compare a company's employee handbook to your college's student handbook. Or your group could compare Web sites, newsletters, brochures, letters, memos, reports, or proposals from the workplace scene with their generic counterparts in the academic scene. Your group may want to draw on the sample workplace genres (the proposal and report) at the end of this chapter and then bring in an academic proposal or report to compare. As your group compares and contrasts the genres and their situations, respond to the following questions: How are the subjects, settings, and purposes of the genres similar or different? Are there differences in the roles for participants (readers and writers)? How are these differences reflected in the content, rhetorical appeals, structure, format, sentences, and diction? How are the differences in both rhetorical interactions (situations) and rhetorical strategies related to differences in scene (academic vs. workplace)? How do you explain any similarities between the genres? Be prepared to report your findings to the class.

Learning the Language of Workplaces

Workplaces are complex scenes made up of various situations. They encompass groups of people who, while occupying differing levels of power and carrying out different responsibilities, share objectives and follow a set of common practices for communicating with one another and with external audiences. Part of learning the genres used by your workplace includes learning the specialized languages that different workplaces adopt.

The **specialized language use** within a workplace—the jargon, technical terminology, and unusual uses of familiar words or phrases—may at first present an obstacle to new members of the organization. However, you will soon find that specialized language serves specific functions in the scene and reflects the shared objectives of its participants. Students have observed this specialized language use in the jobs they currently hold. For instance, consider the following excerpt from a paper entitled "Restaurant Lingo," written by a student who works as a waitress:

> If you walked into a restaurant and were told that the fate of the free world depended upon your fixing the problem of the unannounced 86 of miss mud to satisfy the C.U.S. at table 44, would you know what to do?

Most of us who are outsiders to this scene would probably not know what to do, to answer the writer's question. But, as the writer explains, in a scene where food must be delivered to waiting customers in a timely fashion, it's necessary to use what she calls a "micro language" of shortened words and phrases. So "miss mud" is used for Mississippi mud pie, C.U.S stands for "corporate undercover shopper" (a person hired to evaluate the services), and "86" refers to an item the restaurant has run out of. This specialized language helps the participants interact with each other in the various situations that occur in the workplace scene. Sometimes the language—like yelling "full hands in" or "full hands out" when coming through the swinging kitchen doors—serves a particular function, such as preventing accidents. However, other times the language is used to separate insiders from outsiders, or, as the writer of "Restaurant Lingo" observes, "to separate the staff from the venue patrons." She describes a sticky situation where a problem occurred with one of the wait staff, and the manager was able to tap on this individual's shoulder and ask the person to "check on the C.U." As the writer explains, "This meant they [management] wanted to see you privately as soon as you were finished with what you were doing. This was done so that the customer was not alarmed in any way, and also to make sure not to unnecessarily embarrass the server." In this case, the shared language not only helps the workplace scene function effectively and efficiently in its various situations, but it also reflects the overarching value the scene places on the enjoyable dining experiences of restaurant patrons.

Another student, who worked during the summers as a bricklayer, reflected on how the shared language and common terminology of his workplace scene enabled participants to carry out their actions and defined the roles of participants in the different situations of that scene. The following is an excerpt from his paper entitled "The Wonderful World of Masonry Construction":

> Since speed is crucial for the masonry community to get as many bricks laid as possible, terminology must be short and efficient. For example, when a bricklayer needs cement, he yells, "Mud!" This is much faster than yelling, "I need some cement!" Yelling "Mud!" is also easy for the laborer to understand when he is standing far away. This avoids the time-consuming hassle of the laborer walking over to the bricklayer to ask what he said since the laborer is often far away from the bricklayer.
>
> Terminology is also used to emphasize the professional aspect of masonry construction. Long-time members, or professionals, use their terminology to separate themselves from non-members and beginners. For instance, professionals refer to the objects that cement is placed on for a bricklayer to use as "mudboards." On the other hand, non-members often call mudboards "tables" or "plywood things."

Here again, we see how the shared language of this workplace scene serves a practical function in terms of saving time and making the work more efficient. In addition, as the second paragraph illustrates, the shared language also reflects the professionalism of the scene and clarifies the roles of the participants, distinguishing the experts in the scene or "long-term members" (who use the correct technical term "mudboards") from the nonexperts or "beginners" (who call them "plywood things"). In this way, the language serves not only as a means of communication but also as a means of identification.

Just as workplace scenes have regularized forms of speaking—such as calling out "Full hands in!" or "Mud!"—they also rely on regularized forms of writing, or written genres, to accomplish their goals and get their work done efficiently. For example, if an employer had to write up a new contract from scratch each time an employee was hired, this would quickly become a very time-consuming activity. However, because this situation recurs, there is a genre—the contract form—that personnel directors can follow (while making minimal changes like names, positions, and salaries). The workplace is made up of many recurring situations, like people leaving for other jobs or people traveling to meetings and conferences; and various genres, such as the resignation letter or the trip report, respond to these situations. As a result, like the common language described in the students' restaurant and masonry workplaces, the written genres of a workplace scene reflect its shared objectives and can help us understand more fully the different interactions within its situations.

Writing Activity 9.2

Consider a job you've had or are currently holding, and describe any specialized ways of speaking or writing in that scene. Or, if you currently don't have a job, interview a friend with an off-campus job and ask him or her to describe any special terminology, jargon, shorthand, or slang that workers use to communicate in different situations. Does the communication between workers differ from the communication between workers and managers? Are there different ways of communicating with people outside the organization (the public, other clients, other businesses)? Give a few examples of the specialized language of this workplace, and in a paragraph or two, explain how this specialized language helps carry out the group's actions and reflects the goals, attitudes, or values of the workplace.

Using Genres to Gain Entrance to Workplaces

Genres are the way that work gets done in workplace scenes. There are genres that help carry out internal correspondence, like memos, and genres for external correspondence, such as letters. There are instructions and manuals for carrying out procedures and processes and proposals for offering solutions to problems. There are also various reports to explain progress on a project, to detail a business trip, to provide information, to test the feasibility of an idea, to evaluate a procedure, or to carry out research and development. *Genres help their users do the communicative work of the scene and, as a result, the goals and assumptions of a workplace scene are embedded in its genres.* As we saw earlier with academic scenes, situations, and genres, we can use genres to gain access to the workplace—to its rituals and behavior. In what follows, we will first show you how to use genre knowledge of the resumé and the application letter to gain access to workplace scenes. Then, we will perform a more detailed genre analysis of another common workplace genre, the proposal. This analysis can serve as a model

THE GENRE OF THE RESUMÉ

for how you can use genre analysis to understand other workplace genres, such as reports, to both uncover the goals and assumptions of the workplace and make more effective writing choices within workplace scenes of writing.

The Genre of the Resumé

For many of you, the first nonacademic genre that you will need to know in order to gain entry into the workplace scene is the **resumé**, which is a concise summary of your qualifications for a job. Many of you are probably already familiar with this genre and may have already written a resumé. (Refer to the discussion of the resumé in Chapter 4 for a brief history and critique of the genre.) This genre is used by most workplaces and professional organizations and reflects the qualities that employers look for and the information that companies need to make hiring decisions. The purpose of the resumé is to highlight your accomplishments and abilities and to show a prospective employer that you are the best qualified for the job. Like other workplace genres, the resumé is reader-based rather than writer-based. In other words, the focus is not on what the writer knows (as in much academic writing) but is instead based on what readers need to know to make their decisions and to carry out their hiring actions. Therefore, it might be helpful to *think of your resumé as an argument—an attempt to persuade your audience that you are the best-qualified candidate for the job* and to motivate your readers to hire you (or at least interview you).

While the highly ritualized and oft-repeated situation of applying for jobs has led to well-defined conventions within the resumé genre, these conventions can vary depending on the specific workplace scene. For example, an engineering company might be very conservative in its expectations of what the resumé should look like and might expect a neatly typed document printed on white or buff paper and following a standard format. However, for an advertising agency, and ad executives who have more artistic and less scientific and technical backgrounds, writers might be able to use more creativity, perhaps printing the resumé on colored paper, adding creative designs and even graphic illustrations. As with any writing act, it is necessary to read your scene before shaping your response.

While various scenes may call for creative variations in response to the situation of applying for a job, the resumé—because it is a regularized form of communication in the workplace that achieves the shared objective of hiring the most qualified applicants—has developed definite patterns. You can observe these patterns in the sample resumé shown here. (We have included an additional sample student resumé on page 509 for you to refer to.)

ERIN FULLERMAN

5226 Southside Avenue
Austintown, Ohio 44514
(330) 799-9XXX
Fullerman@xxx.com

• CAREER OBJECTIVE

Seeking an elementary teaching position.
(Certified grades K–8)

• EDUCATION

Bachelor of Science in Education, May 1999
Youngstown State University, Youngstown, OH.
Minor: English Literature
Dean's List: Two Semesters

• TEACHING EXPERIENCE

Student Teaching I & II. Washington Elementary School,
Youngstown, OH. 3rd grade, Spring 1999
Observed, graded papers, created and taught two units in
English literature, and tutored students in different areas.

Field Experience in Teaching. Harold Hirsch School,
Youngstown, OH. Grades 1–5, Fall 1998.
Tutored students one-on-one, coordinated school program,
made teaching aids.

Teacher. Tabernacle Presbyterian Church, Youngstown, OH.
Grades 2 and 3, Fall 1998–99.
Prepared lesson plans and materials for each session

• ADDITIONAL WORK EXPERIENCE

Assistant Manager, Morrie's Clothing Store, Berlin Lake, OH,
Fall 1997

Waitress, Pete's Landing, Austintown, OH, Summer 1997

Salesclerk, Helene's Department Store, Youngstown, OH,
Summer 1996

• UNIVERSITY ACTIVITIES

Student Senate Councilwoman
English Club
Gamma Phi Delta Sorority

• REFERENCES

Available upon request at the Career Planning and Placement
Center, YSU, Youngstown, OH 44555. (330) 865-9XXX.

Resumés like this one always begin with the contact information of the applicant (name, address, phone number, e-mail address), reflecting the practical need for workplaces to contact you regarding an interview or possible job. This information, particularly your name as an applicant, is usually featured rather prominently (in boldface type or larger type) to draw attention to yourself—the product being "marketed" to prospective buyers/employers.

CONTENT

Because prospective employers are most interested in qualities that are relevant to the position, resumés share common subject matter, including sections on education and employment. The *education section* includes a listing of degrees, institutions granting the degrees, and dates when degrees were obtained—in order to ensure that you have the necessary credentials for the job (or will have them by the time the job begins). This information on education is also necessary because it may affect your pay scale as an employee and the level at which you are brought in. In addition to the education section, there is also an *employment section,* which gives names, dates, and locations of employers as well as the positions/titles held and duties performed. Once again, this information reflects the reader-centered nature of the resumé. The employer will be interested in your relevant job experiences and will want to determine whether you have the skills needed to perform successfully on the job.

While all resumés include education and employment information, some may also include *personal information,* such as hobbies, community service, and relevant organizations and activities. The fact that personal sections are optional demonstrates that employers generally value the level of experience and expertise you bring to the job over your personal interests or qualities. However, some employers will want to get a sense of you as a person and to gauge how well you interact with others (for example playing team sports may indicate that you can also be a "team player" on the job). Keep in mind that you should use the scene to help you decide what information is appropriate to include. For instance, if you are applying for a job as a layout editor, it would be appropriate to include your work on the yearbook staff. On the other hand, your playing in a rock band might be relevant only to particular jobs—such as jobs with a record store or in the music industry. The writer of the sample resumé on page 478 includes her membership in the English Club (which is relevant to her minor in English literature), her role as a student council member (which shows leadership capabilities that may be useful to her goal of getting a teaching job), and her membership in a sorority (which demonstrates her ability to work and interact well with others).

Finally, resumés include a list of *references* or an indication of where references might be obtained. This acknowledges that the brevity of the genre allows only so much information but that employers may want to contact other individuals to learn more about the applicant.

RHETORICAL APPEALS

The kinds of information included, as just described, make it clear that ***ethos is the most critical of the rhetorical appeals in a resumé***. Logos certainly matters: The potential employer needs facts and information to assess your qualifications for the job, and without the right qualifications no amount of ethos can persuade the reader that you should be hired. But in the end what your resumé is selling is you, and you use ethos to persuade readers that you can be believed, that your qualifications are what you say they are, that your references will say good things about you. All of the qualifications that you list are part of establishing your ethos. So is the care you take with presentation, as we will describe below. Like most workplace genres, resumés make little use of pathos, for readers' emotions rarely form the basis of business decisions (another indicator of what workplaces tend to value). Using logos and ethos, your resumé must convince readers that you are qualified for the job, a credible applicant, and someone whom the employer can see doing good work for the company. The sections of a resumé not only provide the information needed, in other words, but also establish your credibility.

STRUCTURE

The organization of the sections of a resumé, as in the example above, responds to the situation of applying for a job—both the purposes of the writer who wants the job and the needs of the workplace audience who will be making the hiring decisions. To clarify their purposes for seeking the job and to immediately clarify for readers that they are interested and qualified, many resumé writers will open with a brief statement of objectives, for example, "Objective: Seeking an elementary teaching position." This sets the context for the substance of the document—sections on education and employment that justify and develop the stated objective. And, logically, references come last because the process of contacting references is likely the last step in the review process, following the employer's determination of whether or not the the applicant is worthy of further review.

The organization of the education and employment sections depends on the writer's circumstances. For instance, for an individual right out of college who has had little work experience, it might make more sense to organize educational background before employment history, perhaps indicating relevant coursework or internship experiences. But for someone who has been out of college for many years and has gained a lot of on-the-job experience, organizing the employment section first would better highlight this experience. In addition, the resumé may follow different rhetorical strategies and may be structured either chronologically or analytically. It is most common to organize information chronologically, using time as the organizing factor for each section of the resumé. Most sections move in *reverse chronological order*, beginning with the most recent degree or most recent job, in order to highlight your most recent experience (see earlier sample on page 478).

In the **analytical resumé** (also referred to as the *bullet resumé* or the *functional resumé*), job applicants include a section on skills or abilities in order to highlight specific skills and accomplishments (see the sample at the end of the chapter, page 509). For individuals whose educational and job experience might not fully reflect their relevant skills and abilities to carry out the job they are applying for, the analytical resumé may be appropriate.

LANGUAGE AND FORMAT

The rhetorical and linguistic features of the resumé and the visual appearance or format also reflect the situation. The resumé is brief, usually 1–2 pages long, so that employers who receive multiple applications can quickly sort through the candidates who are qualified and those who don't meet the qualifications. Because of this need for brevity, descriptions of qualifications may be stated in short phrases or fragments, such as the following description of job duties:

DUTIES:
* Managed 15-person communications department
* Produced company newsletter
* Oversaw annual printing budget

Rhetorically, the use of such phrases not only reflects the emphasis that the resumé places on brevity but reflects something else, too. It suggests that when writers describe themselves in the resumé, they literally *become* the work that they have done. That is, the verbs of the sentences which describe what the applicant does (*Managed, Produced*, and *Oversaw*) take the place of the subject (the actual person who does the action). In this way, the style of the resumé reflects the importance the workplace puts on actions and the way that workplaces combine the work and the worker. While this deviation from standard usage is perfectly acceptable and even necessary for preserving the brevity and concision of the genre and reflecting the values of its users, the resumé should otherwise be completely free of grammar, punctuation, usage, and spelling errors that could cast doubt on your professionalism and on the accuracy of information presented.

The format used is instrumental in portraying a sense of professionalism (contributing to your ethos) and in making information stand out or easier to locate. Writers may use boldface type or use a larger typeface for their names, in order to make the resumé memorable. Keeping in mind the reader-based focus of the genre—the emphasis on the ease of finding information and improving the document's readability—writers may use bold, underline, italics, or different typefaces to distinguish between, for instance, places of employment and positions held. The use of headings and white space also helps readers quickly locate important information, since readers (the prospective employers) may be reviewing hundreds of resumés and will need to move through them fairly quickly. Ultimately, the formatting and layout of the resumé, just like in other workplace genres, reflect the value organizations place on the visual rhetoric of a text. The format and design of the document not only make it more appealing and interesting to readers but also help readers navigate complicated information (like instructions, descriptions of objects and processes, or large amounts of data).

Collaborative Activity 9.2

Examine the two sample resumés in this chapter (the one earlier in this chapter and the one on page 509). In small groups, describe the content, rhetorical appeals, structure, format, sentences, and diction of the resumés, and make a list of similarities/differences (refer to step 3 of Box 2.1, page 94 for guidance in describing generic patterns). Evaluate the effectiveness of each resumé. To what extent are any differences based on the differing "objectives" of each resumé? What can you infer about the scenes and situations for which each of these resumés was written? What differing choices would you make and why?

Writing Activity 9.3

Based on your examination of the sample resumés and your responses to Collaborative Activity 9.2, critique the genre of the resumé. In addition to drawing on the guidelines for critiquing genres (Box 4.1, p. 161), you might also refer to

Randall Popken's critique of the resumé (p. 159). Consider how the genre of the resumé both enables its users to represent themselves and limits this representation. Does the genre create inequalities among its users and privilege certain objectives, values, and actions?

The Job Application Letter

Within workplace scenes, the resumé is not the only genre that enables participants to respond to the situation of applying for a job. A companion genre, **the job application letter,** has as its purpose to highlight significant aspects of the resumé and to elaborate on qualifications in greater detail than is appropriate to the resumé. It is a chance to

Tell the story of the writer's career so far

Create a stronger persona

Make a stronger ethical appeal than the depersonalized resumé achieves

To that end, job application letters must frame that story and shape that persona to meet the needs not of the writer but of the potential employer. The sample job application letter shown here is a companion to the resumé we discussed previously. (Another sample job application letter can be found on page 511.)

5226 Southside Avenue
Austintown, Ohio 44514

January 13, 1999

Sylvan Learning Center
Nation Job Network
601 SW 9th Street
Des Moines, Iowa 50309

To Whom It May Concern:

Please consider my application for the full-time employment opportunities for teaching, which were posted on the Internet on the Nation Job Network. I will graduate this spring from Youngstown State University with a Bachelor's degree in Elementary Education and with a minor in English Literature. I am certified to teach grade levels K–8.

Throughout my studies at Youngstown State University, I completed many hours of fieldwork and required observation. I recently finished my student teaching experience at Washington Elementary under the supervision of Ms. Ollis. During this time I wrote and taught many lessons and also volunteered my time after school to tutor children in the classroom. I also had the privilege to write and direct a play the students performed during the holiday season.

During the Fall of 1998, I was asked by the Director of Children's Services at Tabernacle Presbyterian Church to teach second and third grade Sunday school, where I learned how to write and teach lesson plans for various activities. I also volunteered at Harold Hirsch School for the mentally handicapped; there I dressed as the Easter Bunny for a school program, and I also volunteered my time working one-on-one with the students.

Over the past few years I have worked not only with children but also the public. I have worked in sales and in restaurants, and this has given me the experience to deal with and communicate with the public. I have also had the responsibility of carrying out managerial duties, such as the handling of money and training of new employees. Whether working with children or as a server at a restaurant, I feel that I have gained good organizational and motivational skills as well as communication skills.

I have included detailed information about my background in the enclosed resumé. I would appreciate your consideration of my application for this position. I feel that I would be an asset to the Sylvan Learning Center. If you have any questions, please feel free to call or e-mail me at (330) 799-9XXX or Fullerman@xxx.com. Thank you for your consideration.

Sincerely,

Erin Fullerman

CONTENT

The job application letter is part of the argument the writer makes for why he or she should be interviewed or hired. Together the job application letter and resumé form a persuasive argument, with the letter establishing the *claim* for a position and the resumé providing *supporting evidence* for the claim. *To be a successful argument, the letter makes a claim that the qualifications of the resumé (the evidence) fit the particularities of the job, emphasizing and applying the most significant evidence from details of the resumé.* For instance, the writer of the application letter shown here highlights the details that are most relevant to the teaching job she desires, including her most recent student teaching experiences, and provides concrete illustrations of the experiences she gained in tutoring, making lesson plans, and directing a school play.

The content of the letter reflects its purpose within the situation of applying for a job: to convince the reader/employer that the writer is the most qualified person for the position. Because the purpose of the letter is to appeal directly and specifically to the needs of the audience (the prospective employer), effective letters highlight those qualities featured in the job ad, without repeating qualities already listed on the resumé. The writer of the above letter includes specific details (such as writing and directing the school play and dressing up as the Easter Bunny for a school program) not included on the resumé.

RHETORICAL APPEALS

Since the situation of the letter is the same as that of the resumé, it is not surprising that the same kinds of rhetorical appeals are used in both. But the job application letter, even more than the resumé, emphasizes ethos over logos. Here, the facts do not speak for themselves. Instead, the writer creates an image of a good employee, sounds like someone good to work with, and connects the evidence of qualifications to the job in a way that makes the reader believe that the applicant should be interviewed or hired. The voice and persona of the letter are critical, but they are difficult to achieve: somehow sounding confident but not cocky, qualified but not arrogant. Notice that the writer of the application letter says that she "had the privilege" of writing and directing the school play, and she uses the phrase "I feel" to qualify her strongest claims about her abilities. Yet she still asserts those abilities directly to show readers what a credible person she is, and she details her greatest accomplishments that suit the job she is applying for.

STRUCTURE

The structure of the letter roughly corresponds to the structure of the resumé, with its introductory objective followed by discussion of employment and education and then closing contact information. After beginning the letter by identifying the position and explaining the writer's interest in it (usually with phrasing such as "Please consider my application for the full-time employment opportunities for teaching, which were posted on the Internet on the Nation Job Network"), the letter may then go on to highlight the aspects of the writer's educational background and previous work experience that make the writer uniquely qualified for the job. Somewhere toward the end, the letter usually informs the employer of availability for an interview and contact information (the writer above invites prospective employers to call or e-mail her). All of this information is directed at the reader's needs, at the ways that the writer's story of his or her career meshes with the job description.

LANGUAGE AND FORMAT

Just as a story follows a particular format, you will notice that the letter of application above and the one later in this chapter follow certain conventions of correspondence, such as including an inside address, dating the letter, and beginning with a salutation, such as "Dear Sir or Madam" or "To Whom It May Concern." (See the discussion of the business letter format for the complaint letter, Chapters 2 and 3.) This format not only creates a professional persona but also appeals to the reader's needs and expectations of professional correspondence.

To further appeal to the readers' needs and engage them in the narrative, and to build the desired ethos, letters of application project what is commonly called a "you attitude." This means writers put themselves in the reader's position and signal awareness that the readers and their needs are of the utmost importance. In other words, the reader's needs (not the writer's) control the content, structure, and choice of sentences and words. For instance, in the above letter of application, the writer focuses not only on experiences that are directly related to the teaching position (such as her student teaching and volunteer work at an area school), but she also connects her experience in sales and service positions with the job by focusing on the organizational and communication skills she developed. She ends by reminding readers that she "would be an asset" to their organization. Writers, then, should approach their qualifications in terms of how and why they are valuable to a particular employer, connecting the writer's story to the reader' needs and interests.

Writing Activity 9.4

Examine the sample application letters in this chapter (pp. 483 and 511). What rhetorical and linguistic patterns do you see? (Again, refer to step 3 of Box 2.1, p. 94, for guidance in describing a genre's patterns.) How much room does the genre of the application letter leave for personal creativity? For instance, in the case of the job application letter, are there other responses that might be effective? In what scenes or situations?

Collaborative Activity 9.3

How do the rhetorical and linguistic patterns of the application letter compare and contrast to the resumé? What do these patterns allow the applicant to do that the resumé does not? How much does this have to do with the resumé's visual layout? What does the resumé's visual design allow the applicant to do that the application letter does not?

The Interactions of Genres in the Workplace

Once you are hired you will find that workplaces have entire networks of genres that interact to carry out their communicative actions. For example, when you submit a proposal requesting funding for a project, your boss may ask you to do a report on the feasibility of the project. When you write up the report for your boss, you might attach a memo that quickly summarizes the main points of the report. Your boss will then send the proposal on to his or her manager, who may request to see a PowerPoint presentation that quickly highlights the main components of the project and benefits to the company. Once the project is approved, you might be asked to collaborate with other writers in creating a manual explaining the new procedure and, a year later, to do a follow-up report evaluating the implementation of your proposed plan. In addition, if your project requires purchasing equipment or materials, you will need to get bid proposals from suppliers and fill out purchase requisition forms. In order to participate in the workplace scene, you must recognize and understand its interrelated network of genres and their corresponding situations so that you can participate more fully in its communicative interactions. Since genres allow work to get done in a workplace, learning how and why these genres function can help you perform more successfully on the job.

In the sections that follow, we will draw on the genre of the proposal to explore the ways in which you can use your knowledge of genre to understand the various workplace situations and to make more informed choices as writers and as participants in the workplace scene. While you may not need to write a proposal (though it is a common genre), learning how to apply genre analysis in the workplace scene may help you approach writing various workplace genres with confidence.

Analyzing the Genre of the Proposal

In Part II of this book, on academic writing, you analyzed the genre of the argument paper. This genre has much in common with the genre of the proposal, which shares its persuasive aim and reader-centered approach. *A proposal makes an argumentative claim, convincing readers that a problem exists and documenting that problem.* But while an argument paper may stop with influencing a reader's belief or supporting an opinion, the proposal makes a **motivational argument**, one that recommends a specific course of action. You have probably routinely encountered situations that call for proposals, whether written or not, situations where you see a problem and are called upon to solve that problem or come up with a reasonable plan of action. You may have needed to resolve a conflict with a roommate, significant other, friend, or family member; or a policy of your school, living unit, or other organization needed to be changed; or you wanted to start a new practice that would make things go more smoothly.

As an example, let's say that you are running into difficulties completing your writing assignments for this class and others without the use of a computer to draft, revise, and print out copies to turn in. As a result, your plan is to propose to your parents or extended family that they buy a computer for you. You will need to document the problem by convincing them of the large number of writing assignments you face this semester and in upcoming semesters. You will also need to consider all of the alternatives, such as the availability of computer labs on campus, and address these alternatives—perhaps by arguing that the facilities are overcrowded and that you can rarely find an open terminal. Finally, in order to anticipate objections, like the cost versus benefits, you will need to show your readers that the benefits outweigh the costs. You might argue that a computer would not only teach you valuable technological skills that will better prepare you for a job, but also that it would increase your productivity, thereby improving your grades and post-college opportunities. In addition, you could argue that it is a tool you can continue using beyond college. Your aim, then, is not just to convince your audience (your parents or extended family) that the computer is a useful tool but to motivate them to take action—to purchase a computer. The combination of all these factors shapes your writing situation.

Writing Activity 9.5

Describe a situation in which you had identified a problem and proposed a solution or plan of action for resolving the problem (keep in mind that your proposal might not have been written). How did you support your claim that a problem exists? What alternatives did you consider? What objections did you anticipate or respond to? How did you consider your audience when making the proposal? Was your proposal successful in solving the problem? Why/why not?

Individuals routinely do this kind of problem-solving when they write proposals in workplace scenes. By once again drawing on the guidelines for analyzing genre (Box 2.1, pp. 93–94), we can examine the patterns of this genre and analyze what those patterns reveal about the workplace scene, including its participants—their values, beliefs, and goals—and the actions performed through the genre. The goal is not only to enable you to effectively write proposals (a genre that you will find in academic and public scenes, not just workplace scenes) but also to demonstrate how the analysis of workplace genres can give you insight into the scene's shared objectives and its various situations.

THE PROPOSAL AND ITS SITUATIONS

While proposals as a genre share the goal of persuading readers to approve of a proposed plan or to follow a recommended course of action, they are written for different purposes, by and for many participants, on many subjects, and in many different settings. Various situations prompt a proposal

- From an employee to a supervisor seeking authorization to purchase a new printer and scanner
- From a company to clients/potential customers offering a product or service
- From a small business to a large corporation or agency requesting funding to conduct research or carry out an investigation
- From a department head to a division director requesting permission to hire a new staff member

- From an engineering firm to corporations of government agencies requesting a contract to design or build power plants or water treatment facilities

The nature of each of these proposals depends upon the situation to which it responds—what subject it is addressing, who is writing and reading it, where and when it is written, and why it is written. Proposals can be initiated by readers (*solicited proposals*) or by writers (*unsolicited proposals*). Proposals that are solicited usually respond to another genre known as the **Request for Proposal** or **RFP.** Because most workplaces cannot themselves provide all of the products and services that they need, they may ask for other interested businesses or prospective suppliers to submit proposals. For instance, the maintenance and cleaning at most workplaces is contracted out to other companies. To get the best deal, most workplaces require that prospective suppliers—in this case, suppliers of janitorial services—submit a proposal that makes the case that they deserve the contract.

In addition to proposals that are submitted to organizations outside of the writer's workplace scene, many proposals are *internal*—usually correspondences between employees who want to make change and those (supervisors, managers) who can enact these changes or at least approve them. As an employee, you may see a problem and decide to develop a persuasive argument for addressing the problem, thereby benefiting the company by improving employee morale, increasing productivity, or lowering costs. For instance, discouraged by the fact that your workplace recently acquired costly new equipment that is not being used, you might propose that employees attend a training session. Or seeing problems with the amount of overtime that a number of employees claim each month, you might propose a better system for tracking overtime. To save paper, you might propose that all internal memos be delivered via e-mail rather than hard copy. To increase employee morale and strengthen community, you might propose an employee picnic or end-of-year party.

While you may have a number of ideas and plans of action that you wish to propose, it is most likely that you, alone, will not be writing the proposal. Many proposals, like much of writing that goes on in the workplace, are the results of collaboration among a number of people in the workplace. Particularly for longer proposals, there may be a division of labor, with one individual carrying out research on the problem, another looking at the resources needed to implement the solution, another developing the budget, and another working out a schedule for implementing the solution. Since proposals often affect many people, multiple writers not only make the work more manageable but also draw on broader expertise and convey greater support for what is being proposed.

In addition to multiple writers, a proposal will typically have multiple audiences, since many departments and programs may be affected and different levels of approval may be needed. A proposal requesting additional hiring in a department may go from a staff member to a department supervisor who may read it, add his or her own thoughts, and send it on to a division director or manager. The proposal may also be routed to other relevant readers, such as personnel staff or human resources workers who need to be notified of potential ads they will need to place. The situation of the proposal, then, often involves multiple readers and writers and has as its overarching purpose to argue for a change in a workplace.

Writing Activity 9.6

Describe the situation of the sample proposal included at the end of this chapter, pages 513–515 ("Edison After-School Assistance Program"). Begin by identifying the scene for this proposal. What seem to be the shared objectives of the groups of people communicating in this scene? Can you identify the setting for this rhetorical interaction (proposal) happening within the scene? What is the subject being discussed? Who is participating in this interaction, and what are their purposes? Finally, explain how the responses to the above questions might have shaped the writer's choices of content, rhetorical appeals, structure, format, sentences, and diction.

The rhetorical strategies and conventions that writers use to write proposals—external or internal—will vary according to the situation and scene. For instance, a proposal to make every Friday "Jeans Day" may be more informal than a proposal requesting time and resources to study the effects of carpal tunnel syndrome on office workers. While proposals can vary in length, format, and tone, common patterns emerge from this regularized form of workplace communication. You can get a first glimpse at these patterns by taking a look at the sample proposal shown here.

The "Proposal for Desktop Publishing System Improvements" was written by a graphic artist, a staff member in the communications department of a large engineering firm. The proposal addresses multiple audiences, including the graphic artist's immediate supervisor, the art director; the director of the communications department; and the head of the division. Drawing on this sample genre (we have included an additional sample on page 513), we will describe the typical patterns that emerge and analyze what they reveal about how the workplace functions, the roles of readers and writers, and the values and beliefs of participants in the workplace scene.

PROPOSAL FOR DESKTOP PUBLISHING SYSTEM IMPROVEMENTS

PURPOSE

Following is a proposal for improvements to our desktop publishing system. After carefully analyzing our current setup and workflow, this proposal presents the best investment in maintaining and enhancing our publishing system. The proposed setup eliminates our shortage of appropriate workstations and moves all of the artists in the department onto the same computer platform. This plan also takes into account personnel, workflow, and how to most effectively utilize new and existing equipment. Ultimately it provides a good "step up" for the entire graphics staff. The basic recommendation is to add three new G4 Macintosh pre-press workstations and a few minor software upgrades for our existing Macs. The total cost will be about $23,500. With these additions to our existing network, we should be well-equipped for many years.

BACKGROUND

Our existing desktop publishing network consists of three PowerMac design stations (PowerMacs) and one pre-press production/scanning system (the G3 PowerMac) — shared by six graphic artists. Only the G3 has the power for color pre-press work, and it is being used as a layout workstation, scanning station, file server, and backup. A Windows/Pentium computer and an old Pentium 2 Ventura station contribute slightly to the overall production picture. Basically the entire graphics department is competing for use of the one G3 Macintosh, which is our one adequately equipped computer for the type of work we are now doing. Approximately half of the department's graphics work requires using the G3, resulting in significant "downtime" for designers and difficulty in meeting deadlines.

There are two fundamental problems with our current setup and workflow:

1. We are short one workstation (five artists and four computers). With every project now being produced electronically, it is impossible to "share" computers and maintain a good workflow.

2. The entire graphics staff needs a "step up" in computer capability.

   • The newsletter, *Highlights*, is now produced with fully digital production, and the Pentium machine is incapable of handling the scans and graphics involved. Plus, the docutech connection from Windows has never been properly established.

   • We need to eliminate the 10-year-old Ventura system. It is obsolete and incompatible with the rest of our software. We need to phase the system out.

   • The three art directors would benefit from having more powerful computers—capable of running PhotoShop and driving larger, high-resolution monitors. They are presently splitting "powertime" on the G3 with the other graphic artists.

OBJECTIVES

Industry Compatibility—The #1 Advantage

Basic compatibility with vendor's Macintosh equipment will eliminate costly outside services.

• The Communications Department will have direct access to millions of dollars of cost efficient, high-end printing technology through service bureaus.

• Files for high-resolution output could be transferred via modem, eliminating time-consuming trips to service bureaus to deliver a disk.

• Brochures could be produced directly from the Macintosh, eliminating tedious paste-ups and costly pre-press color services.

A Wide Range of Uses

While the existing Ventura system is limited to basic print production, the Macintosh equipment will have a wide range of graphics applications.

- Brochure Design/Production: Efficient production of mock-ups and proofs (shorter start-to-finish production time); dynamic computer generated graphics, charts, maps, etc.; accurate color proofing, fast revision; efficient pre-press; fewer software limitations for improved overall design quality

- Video: Incorporation of computer graphics and scanned still photography into video productions; computer animation of engineering renderings, in-house production of titles and digital video effects; conversion of video images to digital computer format for use in brochures

- Photography: Ability to scan any photo on file for use in brochure mock-ups and color proofs; conversion of scanned photo images to video; creation of a file library of scanned images

Compatibility with Operating Groups
and Affiliates through Ethernet Networking

The addition of a Macintosh system in the Communications Department will establish compatibility with other offices and affiliates using existing Macintosh software and will

- Allow Communication's Macintosh computers to access other existing Macintosh computers and printers on the company ethernet network.

- Easily connect future design stations to share printing resources.

- Permit access to future Macintosh systems in other business units (new and existing systems will be able to share Communication's scanners, etc.).

PROPOSED PLAN
This plan involves adding three new PowerMac workstations. Rearranging existing equipment will provide every designer with a "step up" from the present situation while eliminating production bottlenecks. It will also allow us to shift all graphics work to the Macintosh and eliminate our three-platform production setup (Ventura, Windows, and Macintosh). Having individual workstations and upgraded system software will improve productivity by eliminating the "share-time" situation—five designers all needing to use the same computer (the Quadra). Plus, we will be fully networked with each other, the printshop, other marketing departments, and e-mail.

The following steps are suggested:

1. Add three new pre-press design stations (new G4 DP800s).
Three new G4 systems will provide each of the three art directors a pre-press capable computer to produce client communications. These workstations will be configured to match a typical computer used by the pre-press vendors who do our photo-retouching and page assembly. The advantages these workstations provide is more power to run software, better monitors to view documents, and full compatibility with pre-press vendors.

2. Shift existing hardware.
Use old design stations (existing PowerMacs) to replace Windows and Ventura systems and to provide everyone his/her own workstation. The PowerMacs are not high-powered computers by today's standards, but they will work very well for production of employee communications materials and black & white ads.

3. Keep G3 as a dedicated scanning/photo-retouching station.
This centrally-located machine will no longer have to be shared for design work. All designers and photographers will have access to scanners, tape backup, etc. without interrupting someone else's work.

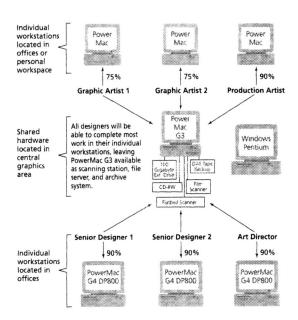

4. *Keep Windows Pentium to support PC graphics users.*
There is still a need for a Windows PC, especially for graphics
conversions. We often use it to save Mac-produced logos and
other graphics in file formats needed by other departments'
visual arts groups. The old Pentium will be our link to the main-
frame network for our timesheets, Bisnet, and the other
Windows computers in our department. We can also use it to
run Ventura as we phase out projects that are on that system.

MATERIALS
Software Upgrades

Mac OS X offers many improvements over the 3-year old system software we are currently using.

Freehand is one of our most-used graphics packages for
logos, charts, maps, diagrams, etc. The 10.0 upgrade has new
features and will keep us current with outside vendors.

PhotoShop is used to enhance photo scans or create montages, etc. The latest version has several improvements.

COSTS
Hardware and Software

Improvements for Communications
Department Desktop Publishing System

Software and RAM Upgrades:
System X (for existing computers)

4 @ $150.00	$600.00
Freehand 10: 4 @ $150.00	$600.00
PhotoShop 6: @ $150.00	$150.00
512 MB RAM upgrades for G3's:	
3 @ $350.00	$1050.00

UPGRADES TOTAL: **$2,400.00**

Pre-Press Design Stations (3):
Macintosh G4 DP800, 1.2 Gb

Ram/80 Gig Hard Drive	$3,500.00
22" Trinitron Display	$1,000.00
Video Card	$150.00
Extended Keyboard	$150.00
External Firewire drive	$200.00

HARDWARE TOTAL
(3 @ $5,000.00):   **$15,000.00**

Software:

QuarkXPress 4+	$590.00
PhotoShop 6+	$590.00
Freehand 10+	$390.00
Office+	$300.00
ATM	$60.00
HDtoolkit	$35.00

SOFTWARE TOTAL
(3 @ $1,965.00):   **$5,895.00**

GRAND TOTAL
(three Mac DP800s + software upgrades):   **$23,295.00**

CONTENT AND RHETORICAL APPEALS

Whether the goal of a proposal is to obtain funding for a project or to change a policy, *proposals share two basic elements: the statement of the problem and a recommended solution.* Since the subject matter or content of the proposal is related to your work—a situation in your office or an office policy or procedure—you will be familiar with much of the information you will need to include. However, since your goal is to persuade readers to approve your plan of action, your content should reflect this reader-centered focus. In other words, you should focus less on your concerns and more on what readers need to know to make their decision.

In addition, because workplace arguments are typically decided on the basis of logical appeals, you must include factual evidence and documentation both for your argument that a problem exists and for your proposed plan to solve the problem. Both of these arguments should be supported with evidence that relates to the reader's organizational or professional needs and is accepted as valid by the workplace participants. The content and rhetorical appeals, therefore, must be relevant to the needs, values, and attitudes of your readers and their organizations. For example, in the "Proposal for Desktop Publishing System Improvements," the writer's request for improvements to the desktop publishing system must convince not only the readers within the communications department but also the readers beyond that department who participate in the larger workplace scene. Therefore, the writer must present evidence that relates to the organizational needs of these multiple readers. For this reason, in the *Objectives* section, the writer refers to "a wide range of uses" for the equipment both within the department and with "other offices and affiliates." The writer not only includes evidence of how the proposed system would save time on projects in the communications department but also provides evidence of how the computers will increase networking capabilities with other computers and printers on the company's ethernet network (see the third point, "Compatibility with Operating Groups and Affiliates through Ethernet Networking," under the heading "Objectives").

STRUCTURE

In order to convince readers that a problem exists and that the solution directly addresses the problem, proposal writers will strategically structure their points. The proposal typically begins with an *Introduction or statement of Purpose,* which briefly states the request and plan of action. For instance, in the sample above, the writer summarizes the plan, clearly states the recommendation—to "add three new G4 Macintosh pre-press workstations and a few minor software upgrades for our existing Macs"—and even forecasts the cost, which comes at the end of the proposal. This gives busy workplace readers a quick overview of the proposal. This opening section, *Purpose,* functions much like the controlling idea of an analysis or argument paper by stating the main points or central claims and forecasting what's to come.

The description of the proposal's Purpose is followed by a more detailed *Background* section, also called *Problem* or *Statement of Need.* In this critical section of the argument, writers must logically persuade readers of the problem at hand, making it seem significant to them. For example, the writer of the "Proposal for Desktop Publishing Improvements" refers to issues that readers will take seriously—significant "downtime" caused by lack of equipment and "difficulty meeting deadlines" (and thus difficulty satisfying potential clients or customers). The writer supports the claim— that there are "fundamental problems with the current setup and workflow"—with facts and evidence. He notes that the department is "short one workstation (five artists and four computers)," that the 10-year-old system is "obsolete and incompatible with the rest of our software," and that three art directors are currently splitting their time on the one powerful computer.

Once readers are persuaded that there is a problem, the writer must convince them that the proposed action will meet their needs. As a result, the description of the problem is followed by a section of *Objectives,* which serves as a transitional section between problem and solution, linking the problem to the proposed course of action. The separation of objectives from the solutions enables readers to evaluate the aims of the project separately from the writer's particular plan for achieving those aims. Once again, these objectives should reflect the reader's needs, both short- and long-term. As a result, the writer cites immediate short-term results of purchasing equipment that will "eliminate costly outside services" and increase the efficiency of production of brochures, video, and photography. The third objective reflects the long-range objective of "Future design stations [that] can be easily connected to share printing resources" as well as "access to future Macintosh systems in other business units."

The heart of the proposal is the *Plan* or *Solution*—the clear and specific course of action or the plan for achieving the objectives stated previously. In this section, writers must convince readers that they have a "feasible" plan for carrying out the solution, one that—given all of the alternatives—is best suited to addressing the problem. Knowing that readers will appreciate specificity, the writer in the previous sample proposal outlines four steps for implementing the plan (in the section "Proposed Plan") and justifies the solution by appealing to the common values of the readers—the valuing of increased productivity and application to the greater good and more efficient functioning of the organization.

To convince readers that the plan is feasible, and to establish their credibility, writers need to have a clear method or set of procedures for implementing the course of action. Readers will judge the effectiveness of the proposal based on

The method for conducting the project

The qualifications of people involved in the project

The materials and equipment that are appropriate for carrying out the project

The acceptability of the timeframe for completing the project

The cost-effectiveness of the project

Therefore, proposals may have some combination of sections called "Methods," "Personnel," "Materials," "Schedule," and "Cost." In our sample proposal, the writer's Proposed Plan clearly indicates the methods that will be used to implement the new equipment, and this implementation doesn't require any personnel; furthermore, a schedule of implementation is not really relevant. As a result, only sections on Materials and Costs are included. (For an example of a proposal that includes sections on Personnel and Schedule, see the sample proposal on p. 513.)

Since the bottom line of most workplaces is cost, this section usually comes last. Because readers are being asked to invest money, time and/or resources, most proposals include a *Cost* section that details the budget and justifies expenses, with the purpose of persuading readers that the cost of the proposed action is worth the benefits accrued to the company. Putting the Cost section last serves a rhetorical purpose. Before telling readers *what* they will be investing, you tell them *why* they should be investing. If a proposer makes a particularly convincing case, by the time the reader of the proposal reaches the end, he or she should be able to recognize the soundness of the investment.

The structure of the proposal, then, follows a typical organizational pattern of moving from most important to least important points. The proposal begins with the most important information—the statement of the problem, the objectives, the proposed solution and the methods for carrying out the solution. The other smaller details—materials, personnel, schedule and cost—vary in terms of how they are organized but always come after the description of problem/solution. Obviously it is necessary to convince readers that there is a problem and a workable solution before persuading them that you have the resources to carry out the plan.

FORMAT

The structure of the proposal and each of the sections described above are easier to follow due to the *format of the document*—the visual elements of a text, such as font size, typeface, margins and spacing as well as the textual markers such as bulleted and numbered lists. The sample proposal uses boldface headings with all caps to announce each section (separated by spacing) and to create a visual hierarchy of information for the reader to follow. These features help direct the reader's attention to each section and make the information more easily accessible should readers need to check back on things like Cost or Personnel involved. These attributes of format can also be used to emphasize or highlight important points. For instance, in the sample proposal the writer uses a regular typeface to list the costs of individual programs and technologies but uses boldface type to indicate the totals and to cue the readers, since this bottom line is what the readers will be more interested in. These features of format not only increase readability and make the information easier to find, they also add a certain amount of credibility as the professional presentation translates to a professional ethos.

VISUAL PRESENTATION

In addition to format, the visual rhetoric of the document is important. This includes graphic illustrations, such as icons, photographs, drawings, charts and graphs, diagrams, and tables. Visuals are often more powerful than words, especially when communicating with non-native speakers, when conveying safety information (like using a red stop sign to indicate safety comments), or when conveying complex data or complicated processes. In many workplace documents, visuals such as graphics, tables, and charts are sometimes included to help the reader process complex information and conceptualize it more readily. In the sample proposal on page 496, the writer uses a diagram to illustrate the setup of the new equipment and the new workflow created among the six individual workstations; this allows readers to envision the specific uses of the new equipment and its particular function. By better understanding the proposed action and actually visualizing where the new equipment will be located (indicated through the use of the desk icons) and how the equipment will be shared among the artists and designers (indicated by the use of arrows), readers may be more willing to accept the writer's request.

STYLE

The reader-centered nature of the proposal is also reflected in the distanced, professional voice of the writer or writers. This professional ethos is apparent in the way that proposal writers often use passive sentence constructions such as "Brochures could be produced" and "The proposal has been designed." The professional tone is also reflected in the use of technical terms or workplace jargon, with reference to "high-resolution output" and "pre-press vendors." Because the proposal is making an argument and may even be competing with other proposals (and is most certainly competing for money and resources), the tone must also be confident and authoritative. The weight of facts and evidence creates this authority. However, the facts and evidence that support the claims for both a problem and a solution appeal to the reader's needs and values, thus maintaining the "you attitude" that is central to many reader-based workplace genres.

Writing Activity 9.7

Because they make claims about problems, support these claims with evidence, and argue for solutions, proposals are similar to the argument papers you described and analyzed in Chapter 6. Drawing on what you discovered from your work in Chapter 6 and from your own knowledge of argument papers, compare and contrast proposals and argument papers in more detail. What similarities do they share? How do they differ? How does the nature of the argument change as you move from one genre to the next? What does one genre allow you to do that the other one does not? In particular, how do you account for the differences in the format and visual presentation of the argument paper vs. the proposal?

Interpreting Generic Features of the Proposal

Having described the content, structure, and textual features of the proposal, we will now explore what these rhetorical patterns reveal about the genre and the workplace scene in which it is used. The genre features we just described can give us insight into the assumptions and expectations of participants in the workplace scene. Exploring the significance of the repeated rhetorical features of the proposal marks the final step in our genre analysis and can give us a more critical understanding of the function of the proposal in the workplace and the identities, activities, and values of its users.

We have learned that the genre of the proposal performs valuable actions. External proposals allow workplaces to "sell" themselves and to market their goods and services, thereby increasing profits. The value placed on profitability to the workplace also underscores the internal actions that proposals perform. The internal proposal that we have studied, for instance, seeks to better utilize the skills of the staff and "eliminate costly outside services," thus appealing to this corporate value of cost-efficiency. Proposals like this one, which are initiated from within a workplace scene, allow participants in that scene to carry out specific actions—to bring about change, solve problems and, in general, to create a better workplace environment. Whether they seek to improve employee morale, increase efficiency of procedures, or better utilize the company's resources, the outcome usually benefits the company and its productivity, thereby reflecting the values placed on profitability.

In addition, the persuasive function of the proposal genre, with its documentation of the problem and researched solutions, reflects the emphasis on competition in the workplace—the need to come up with the best plan and to get the boss's approval. It is no accident that those writing the proposals are usually low to mid-level employees while the readers/decision makers occupy managerial or director positions, thus reflecting and reinforcing the hierarchical structure of the workplace scene. Obviously, those with more status have more say in how resources are used while those with less status compete for the resources available.

The competition among proposal writers for limited resources is further reflected in the focus on the readers' or organization's needs. For instance, in the sample proposal, the writer repeatedly refers to the benefits to worker and workplace productivity and increased efficiency. With the emphasis on how the workplace rather than the writer (or the writer's coworkers) benefits from the proposed plan, the professional ethos of the workplace is valued over the writer's character or voice. Passive sentences play a significant role in shifting the emphasis from an individual to the collective. In fact, while as a writer you might be responsible for writing a proposal in your workplace, chances are very good that the proposal may not even bear your name as an author. Chances are even better that the document will be cowritten by several employees. This reflects the value the workplace scene places on seeing an employee as a "team player" as well as the valuing of "professionalism," shown in writing from a professional rather than a personal persona.

The valuing of the workplace readers (usually upper management) over the individual writers (usually mid to lower-level employees) is also reflected in the systematic and strategic patterning of sections. The division of the proposal into Purpose, Background, Objectives, etc. represents a reader-centered focus, which is also reflected in the concern with the visual presentation of the text, such as the use of headings, typeface, graphics, etc. All these techniques serve to increase readability and put the focus on how readers—busy managers and directors—can access information more easily.

Collaborative Activity 9.4

In a small group, compare the proposal on page 492 with the one on page 513 ("Edison After-School Assistance Program"). Compare the scenes and situations of the proposals. Then make a list of any similarities in features, and, in a separate list, note any differences in the two proposals. What do you think accounts for the similarities? How do the differing scenes and situations account for differences? Prepare to share your findings with the rest of the class.

Writing Activity 9.8

Based on your examination of the sample proposals and your responses to Collaborative Activity 9.4, critique the genre of the proposal. Drawing on the guidelines for critiquing genres (Box 4.1, p. 161), consider how the genre of the proposal both enables its users to represent themselves and limits this representation. Does the genre create inequalities among its users and privilege certain objectives, values, and actions?

Writing Proposals

You should now have a better understanding of the shared features of proposals as well as of the shared objectives and assumptions of the workplace scenes and situations in which they function. We will now turn to how you can apply this genre knowledge to your own writing of proposals—to how you can make more informed writing choices. Consider the following sets of questions, which we have adapted from Chapter 3 to the genre of the proposal.

As a writer, you can use your genre knowledge to choose the most effective writing processes and to make the most effective writing choices. Your understanding of the proposal and its patterns of communication helps you make more effective rhetorical decisions about inventing, drafting, and revising; furthermore, your understanding of these patterns of communication gives you access to patterns of behavior within the workplace scene, patterns that will enable you to reflect critically on why you are making certain writing choices. Next, we invite you to perform your own analysis of another commonly used genre in workplace scenes, the report. Knowledge of this genre will further expand your familiarity with workplace scenes and your ability to participate effectively within them.

Box 9.1 *Guidelines for Writing Proposals*

Questions for Inventing Proposals

- What is the scene of writing behind this proposal? What kinds of proposals tend to be accepted? What do I want to accomplish in the proposal? Who will I need to write to? What kinds of information will my readers need in order to be convinced?
- What is the nature of the problem that I see? What are my first ideas of how I might solve the problem?
- What do I already know about the nature of the problem and how it might be solved? What kinds of information will I need to gather to assess the problem? To see if my proposal is feasible?
- What research will I need to do? Who will I need to talk to? Will I need to bring others in on the proposal?
- Where will I find the information I need? What alternative proposals should I consider?
- As I discover information, do I still believe that a problem exists and that my solution is the best one? If I still see a problem, what better solution could I propose?

Questions for Drafting Proposals

- Given what I know about the proposal and its scene and situation, what strategies for drafting will be most effective? Should I draft with others? When should I draft different sections?
- What is my plan? What exactly am I proposing to have happen? How exactly do I think that proposal will fix the problem?
- Do I need the usual Statement of Problem, Objectives, Proposed Solution, and Methods? Should I add any parts, like Discussions of Materials, Schedule, or Cost?
- How can I convince my readers to accept my proposal? What evidence should I be including to convince them it is needed and feasible? Am I appealing to what matters most to readers and my company?
- Am I including enough specific information? Am I using visual elements, like bullet points, headings, and graphics, to make the information easy to read and follow?
- Do I still believe my proposal is the best solution? After drafting the description of the problem, do I still see it as a real problem? Does my plan still solve it? *(continued on next page)*

Questions for Revising Proposals

- Is this a significant proposal (involving significant money or important to the company's future) so that I should revise extensively? Is this informal enough that I can give it to my reader after only a brief revision?
- If a significant proposal, which of my colleagues might read the draft and suggest how I can make it more persuasive?
- Does my plan define a problem and argue for a solution? How well does my draft achieve those goals? Where does it fail to achieve those goals?
- How likely are my readers to approve my proposal? What in my proposal might keep them from approving it?
- In what ways is my draft similar to other proposals? Does my draft follow the description in this chapter of the proposal's content, appeals, structure, format, and language? Where it differs, have I made a deliberate choice because the situation or scene of my proposal calls for a different approach? If not, how can I change my draft to fit the genre of the proposal more closely and get my proposal approved?
- What information should I include that I have not yet included? What details will my readers still want to know? What other information will my readers need in order to be convinced of the need or feasibility of my proposal?
- Have I edited my proposal carefully for Standardized Edited English?
- Does my proposal look like other proposals? Does it use elements of format to clarify information (bulleted lists, headings, spacing, typeface and type size)? Is each section an appropriate length? Have I included visual elements (graphs, images, figures) to help my readers process the more complicated information?
- Have I said what I wanted to say? All that needs to be said?

Analyzing the Genre of the Report

The more you can learn about the genres that circulate within and make possible the work that people do within workplace scenes—both in terms of their features and in terms of what their features reveal about them—the better prepared you will be to participate in the life of your workplace. This is why we will now invite you to perform your own genre analysis of another workplace genre, the **report**. Before your supervisors approve your proposal, they may ask you to carry out a *fact-finding report* or a *cost/benefit report*. If a proposal is approved, you may be asked to write a *progress report* on the status of the project. And once the project or course of action is complete, you may be asked to write a *project report* or *completion report*. While each of these reports has purposes and functions according to their differing situations and so have some different genre features, ***they all seek to inform workplace readers about a subject.***

The reports that you will be called upon to write in workplace scenes are similar to reports that you have written in academic scenes: book reports, lab reports, research reports, etc. Like these academic reports, workplace reports seek to inform individuals about a subject—to convey the results of research or interpret information for an audience. Reports in the workplace come in many varieties and are usually distinguished according to length and scope—for instance, short vs. long reports, or formal vs. informal reports. Short reports are fairly routine and provide information about planned, ongoing, or recurring events—progress reports, sales reports, trip/travel reports. Long reports are more intensive and in-depth explorations of a problem or idea, with wide-ranging and long-term implications.

In contrast to the action-oriented purpose of the proposal, the report is more *information-oriented.* The informational, fact-finding nature of the report means that it often precedes or accompanies a proposal. The writer of the "Proposal for Desktop Publishing System Improvements," for example, was asked by his boss to write a cost-justification report that would accompany his proposal. This sample report (a short report written as a memo to his boss) can be found on page 516.

Collaborative Activity 9.5

Examine the sample report on pages 516–517 (and bring in any samples of the genre from workplace scenes that you have access to). Then, using the division of labor we suggested for analyzing the argument paper in Chapter 6 and following the guidelines for analyzing genres, Box 2.1 (p. 93), identify and describe the workplace situations in which the genre is typically used, and then describe the patterns of this genre's features. Do you see any patterns in the content and rhetorical appeals covered in reports? Is there a structure or format that is typical of this genre? How would you describe the sentences and diction used? After making a list describing these patterns, analyze what they reveal about the workplace scene in which reports are used, and share your preliminary findings with the class.

Collaborative Activity 9.6

Having described the report in the previous activity in terms of its patterns, and having analyzed what these patterns might tell us about how and why people within workplace scenes write reports, work in groups to develop a list of writing tips writers could use to make effective choices when writing reports. What do writers need to keep in mind? What content and organizational strategies might be useful for writers to use? On the textual level, what kinds of sentence, word, and stylistic choices can and should writers make? What writing strategies and questions can you suggest for writers as they go through the process of writing their reports? Refer to Box 3.1: Questions for Inventing (p. 108), Box 3.2: Questions for Drafting (p. 117), Box 3.4: Questions for Revising (p. 139), and Box 3.5: Questions for Presentation (p. 146), and adapt these questions to the writing of reports.

As this chapter has demonstrated, by studying workplace genres, we can learn much about the situations that occur in the workplace, including the people who interact within them, their purposes, their ways of dealing with their subject, and their beliefs and assumptions. For example, a professor of rhetoric and writing at the University of Arkansas-Little Rock, Roger Munger, studied the "run reports" of emergency medical technicians and found that this genre helped EMTs perform their duties and not only enabled them to reflect on their actions but also to change their practices. The run report is a preprinted form with space for EMTs to describe the nature of the emergency and explain what action, if any, they took during the ambulance run. Munger's analysis of the run report suggests that the genre allowed EMTs to review their past actions, make sense of those actions, recall missed steps of patient care and, in general, to learn from these past experiences, thus affecting their future actions. According to Munger, "how workers are allowed to document information seems to affect how they perform their professional duties."* This genre analysis demonstrates that workplace genres both shape and are shaped by workers' actions. This potential for genres to accomplish actions and to bring about change is a topic we will continue to explore in the next chapter on public scenes and genres.

---

*Munger, Roger. "Emergency Medical Technician Run Reports: A Study of Genre, Practice, and Reflection." *Business Communication Quarterly* (June 1999): 116–120.

Samples of Workplace Genres
SAMPLE RESUMÉ

ALLISON PENDLETON
509 Meadowcrest Street, Apartment 4,
Freeport, Missouri 65033
(314) 743-7XXX

EDUCATION   **Northeast Missouri State University,**
Kirksville, Missouri
Bachelor of Science in Psychology,
GPA 3.7/4.00, May 1997

WORK EXPERIENCE
Science Peer Advising Services Coordinator (Division of Science, NMSU)
- Selected by faculty to be the first peer advisor coordinator
- Coordinated a group of 22 upper-class science majors as peer advisors
- Trained science peer advisors to assist in Leadership Conference for 200 incoming freshmen
- Established a peer advisement office for the 1996-97 academic year
- Provided a liaison service for students and faculty concerning student questions, class enrollment, and major/career exploration
- Organized a pre-registration workshop
- Counseled students in areas of academic and career concerns
- Participated in developing the first structured tutorial program for non-science students in science courses

Scientific Research Assistant (Division of Science, NMSU)
- Assisted professor of Biology in mitochondrial research

- Used the Statpak statistics program in analyzing data
- Utilized Framework, MS Word, Excel and Database programs in keeping records, making reports, creating agendas and writing letters

Counselor Assistant (Academic Planning Services, NMSU)
- Assisted with enrollment of 250 incoming new students
- Compiled student information for faculty
- Proctored the Toledo test to incoming science students
- Hosted approximately 150 students and their parents
- Resolved problems on student schedules
- Used various Windows/PC and Apple computer systems and software

Related Work Experience
- High School Summer Research Program Staff
- Testing Assistant
- General Psychology Assistant Instructor
- Residence Hall Desk Worker

UNIVERSITY ACTIVITIES
- Student Senate Councilwoman
- NMSU Homecoming Committee Secretary
- Gamma Phi Delta Sorority
- Admissions Student Ambassador/Student to Assist Recruitment

REFERENCES available upon request

SAMPLE LETTER OF APPLICATION

4332 Euclid Boulevard
Cleveland, Ohio 63231

April 30, 2000

Ms. Faye Reynolds
Personnel Manager
Weston Publishing Company
1500 Briarcliff Drive
Pittsburgh, Pennsylvania 44562

Dear Ms. Reynolds:

I am applying for the position of layout editor that was advertised in the April 15 edition of the *Tribune Chronicle*. Next month I will graduate from Clarkson University with a degree in journalism and an emphasis in desktop publishing. My journalistic training and experience with layout design and editing qualify me to be a productive member of the editorial department at Weston Publishing.

While attending Clarkson University, I took a wide range of courses in magazine and newspaper design and editing, feature writing, editorial and opinion writing, and professional editing. As part of my minor in desktop publishing, I also took classes in related areas such as graphic design, computer science, advertising and public relations. In a number of my classes, I acquired experience using computer layout and graphics programs and am proficient in PageMaker, QuarkXPress, Illustrator, Corel Draw and PhotoShop.

Through my work experiences, I have had the opportunity to apply the knowledge and skills gained during my education. I am currently working in the public relations department of a local retirement home, where I am responsible for the layout and design of the monthly newsletter as well as local newspaper advertisements. In addition, I worked for two years in the Alumni Office at Clarkson University, where I was responsible for editing and layout of the quarterly alumni magazine. Other related experiences include proofreading and editing for the school yearbook and page layout design for the student newspaper.

I would welcome the opportunity to talk with you about the position and my qualifications. Please call me at (650) 987-6XXX to set up an appointment. I look forward to hearing from you.

Sincerely,

Lisa Taylor

SAMPLE PROPOSAL

PROPOSAL

Edison After-School Assistance Program

Introduction

We are proposing to implement an after-school program to aid Edison Junior High students in academic achievement and the transition to the high school setting. The proposal has been designed to help students in the academic areas of math, science, and English and draws on the use of high school students as peer tutors.

Problem

Edison Junior High is experiencing increased failure rates in courses and on standardized tests. Particularly in the areas of English, math, and science, many students are struggling to keep up with the course objectives and are falling behind. The scores in math, science, and English are lagging behind those of other schools in the area.

Objectives

The objectives for this program include the following:
- To help each student to successfully complete each course on his or her first try.
- To make the transition from junior high to high school smoother both academically and socially.
- To reduce failure rates at the junior high level, thereby promoting academic success at the high school level.
- To improve teacher and student relations.
- To improve student self-confidence and self-esteem.
- To improve teaching strategies.

Proposal

We propose to install an after-school program in Edison Junior High School. The program will take place three days a week after school and will assist students in math, English, and science. The program will be mandatory for any student with a D or below. Any student with a C or above is welcome to join the program voluntarily. The program will be two hours long with the second hour being voluntary for all students. Some transportation will be provided after the first hour by way of busing and car pools.

Method

During the first hour teachers will review the assignments and work done in that day's class. This review can be done through quizzes and worksheets as well as an additional class lecture on the material and one-on-one work with the student. The second hour will be held in the computer lab and will involve applications and possibly computerized competitions between the students.

Personnel

Teachers will have the option of teaching these after-school programs. They will be paid $2,500 for teaching these classes, and if the program is picked up after the trial period, the fee will go up to $3,000.

Along with the teachers there will be peer tutors from the high school level as well. The students from the high school level can help increase the teacher to student ratio and therefore give the students more one-on-one time in the class. The peer tutors will not only give the students more academic help but will also provide a friendly face that the junior high student can look forward to once they are in high school.

Schedule

We propose this program for one school year. The children initially involved will be children with D averages from the previous year. Halfway through the first nine week period any student that has a D or below average will be enrolled in the classes. If at the end of the year the teachers, students, parents, and administrators are satisfied with the progress of students in this program, then the program can be continued.

At the end of the trial period there will be several methods of evaluating the course: questionnaires to students and parents; teachers' evaluations of the program. In addition, administrators may monitor the program throughout the year.

Proposed Budget

Major items to consider:	Estimated cost:	Potential resources:
Planning and Development		
Staff time	600.00	Parent/Teacher Organization
Printing/publicity	400.00	Local Business Donations
Development staff	1,500.00	Parent/Teacher Organization
Sub-Total:		
Start-up costs	$2,500.00	
Operation		
Instructional staff salaries	7,500.00	Federal grants
Office supplies	150.00	Parent/Teacher Organization
Transportation	10,000.00	Federal grants
Subtotal:		
Operating Costs	$17,650.00	
TOTAL COST	**$20,150.00**	

SAMPLE REPORT

TO: Robert Luckert, Director of Communications
FROM: Doug Wright, graphic designer
SUBJECT: Macintosh Production Cost Savings Report
DATE: January 24, 1996

As you requested, following are estimated cost savings that can be attributed to the Macintosh-based publishing system that we have requested. Projecting cost savings by using Macintosh equipment is complicated because of the varying characteristics of each printed piece and the many different ways a design/idea can be executed. However, to produce two identical brochures—one on Ventura and one on Macintosh, utilizing all the shortcuts available in high-end production—bottom-line savings will occur in two areas:

- Production Costs
- Outside Services
- Time and Labor Costs

Production Costs
The chart on the next page show bottom-line cost savings using Macintosh for the production of major brochures. Note that this represents only a portion of Communications' actual work.

Outside Services
Extra colors/graphics would be available at no outside charge (would be generated on the computer instead of by the printer):

- Halftones (B&W photos)
- Color builds
- Artwork enlargements/reductions
- Blended colors/gradations
- C.O.B. photos
- Blending/manipulating photos

Projects:	Ventura	Macintosh	Total Savings
Eight 6-page brochures:	$65,920.00	$54,720.00	$11,200.00
Five 12-plus page brochures:	$70,400.00	$61,200.00	$9,200.00
Three issues of *Solutions*:	$91,740.00	$84,900.00	$6,840.00
Annual Review:	$47,358.00	$42,680.00	$4,678.00
Ten full-page color ads:	$5,100.00	$4,000.00	$1,100.00
Ten B&W ads:	$2,300.00	$150.00	$2,150.00
Smitty's/JF Graphics costs:	$4,100.00	$.00	$4,100.00
TOTAL:	**$286,918.00**	**$247,650.00**	**$39,268.00**

Time and Labor Costs

Other more immeasurable savings would be related to the added capabilities of the Macintosh software and the reduced time and labor for designers.

- *Start-to-completion time* on any given project would be greatly reduced, because the designer is able to complete more of the tasks in-house on Macintosh equipment without waiting for outside services.
  —Task is done right the first time
  —Travel time or delivery time is eliminated
- *Faster experimentation of design options* would be possible (could be designed on-screen instead of manually producing different mock-ups).

Recommendation

This report projects cost savings in the areas of production of materials, use of outside services and time/labor. With the addition of the Macintosh equipment requested, the Communications Department will save nearly $40,000 each year in production costs for major brochures alone. The purchase of the proposed Macintosh system would be well suited to support the firm's graphics needs in a cost-effective, timely manner.

Writing Projects

Writing Project 9.1

Drawing on the guidelines for interviewing in Box 1.1 (p. 40), interview an individual who works in the same field that you plan to enter (at least at this stage of your academic career). Or, if you have already worked or are currently working in your chosen field, interview another person working in your field whose job responsibilities, title, and position differ from your own. Find out what types of writing go on in his or her workplace situations and the various purposes and audiences for this writing. How much time does this individual spend writing on the job? What function does the writing serve, and what purpose does it accomplish? Do writers in this workplace seek input from others? Does your interviewee have any advice on communication skills that college students such as yourself would need in order to succeed at this job? In addition to the interview, seek answers to the above questions by consulting manuals and guides for writing in that field. When you have completed your research, write a researched position paper (see Chapter 7) on what you have learned about writing in that workplace scene. Address your paper to an audience consisting of your instructor and classmates.

Writing Project 9.2

For this project, choose a workplace scene, and with the permission of the person who oversees the workplace, observe the patterns in people's habits of behavior and communication within this scene (see Box 1.2: Guidelines for Observing and Describing Scenes, p. 44). Keep a notebook to record the actions and language use you have observed. What actions are being performed, and how does language help perform these actions? How would you describe the communicative interactions among workers? In addition to observing the workplace scene, you might also interview members of this scene or collect sample writings from the workplace—any forms, mailers, brochures, flyers, etc. Once you have collected this information on your workplace, present your findings in the genre of your choosing, and use your selection of genre to help you shape an appropriate situation for your writing, including your setting and audience. For example, you might write a short manual for prospective employees of this workplace, or you might write a guide or report for college majors who might be interested in this workplace.

Writing Project 9.3

Create your own resumé based on a job that you are currently qualified for (a job on or off campus) or for a summer job; or find an advertisement for the job you would like to have upon graduating—your ideal position. Write a resumé that summarizes your qualifications for that job. If you are writing for a hypothetical situation (your ideal job), you may project some qualifications (expected date of completing your degree, any required internships, etc.). After writing a 1–2 page resumé, attach a memo, addressed to your instructor, that reflects on and explains the choices you have made in writing your resumé. A **memo**, short for memorandum, is a type of internal correspondence in an organization, often used to request information or to respond to such a request. The conventional format for a memo includes two sections: the heading and the body. The heading specifies the date (DATE), name of recipient (TO), name of the writer/sender (FROM) and the subject (RE or SUBJECT). The body of the memo quickly gets to the main point and presents the message.

In formulating your message, you should consider the following questions: In what way does your resumé stick to the expected conventions? In what way does it (if indeed it does) differ? What organizational choices did you make? How and why did you decide to present the content? What kinds of word choices did you make? What effects do you think your choices will have on prospective readers? What limitations does the genre of the resumé impose on its users, and what are the effects of these limitations?

Writing Project 9.4

Write a letter of application to accompany the resumé that you wrote for the previous writing project. Keep in mind that a letter of application, like a resumé, is an argument of sorts—a "sales document." Write a 1–2 page letter that documents your qualifications and draws on evidence and concrete illustrations to convince your readers that you are the best-qualified candidate for the job. After completing the letter, write a memo to your instructor that explains how the letter you wrote relates to and complements the resumé. What did the letter allow you to do (and how) that the resumé did not?

Writing Project 9.5

Write a proposal that addresses some problem in either a job you have now (or had in the recent past) or in the academic "workplace." For instance, one student, who was an assistant manager at a pizza parlor, wrote a proposal for dealing with chronically late employees and recommended that management implement a point system for penalizing bad behavior and rewarding good behavior. Another student, a desk clerk in a residence hall, proposed that desk clerks be given pass keys to let in locked-out residents after hours instead of having to contact a resident assistant. In order to convince readers that there is a problem, remember to document and support your claims. In addition, to argue convincingly for your solution, remember to present a solution to the problem clearly, to consider all alternatives, and to anticipate objections. Your proposal should clearly state your purpose, define the problem, clarify the objectives of the proposal, and define a solution; it may include any of the following: the method for carrying out the solution, materials /equipment needed to implement the solution, personnel needed to carry out the plan, or a schedule for implementing the plan. Your proposal should also include any costs, if applicable.

Writing Project 9.6

Drawing on your responses to Collaborative Activity 9.5, write a genre analysis paper on the subject of the report. In an analysis paper written to your instructor and classmates, make a claim about what the genre of the report tells us about the people who use it and the scene in which it is used (refer to Box 6.1, p. 287, for guidelines for writing analysis papers). Be sure that your paper has a controlling idea that indicates what you think the genre reveals about some aspect of the situation or scene: how people behave, their goals and beliefs, or the actions they perform. Your controlling idea will also need to be supported with specific examples and explanations taken from your analysis of the genre.

Reading and Writing within Public Scenes

10

Perhaps no other scene so fully depends on its genres as does the **public scene.** Other scenes share locations (like schools and universities), share common objectives and values (like the belief in logic and reason), and may even share participants who see each other regularly as they go about their lives day to day, as is often true in workplaces. But where does the public scene exist? What values do all members of the public share? How many members of the public scene see each other in a week, a month, or even a year? For what we are calling public scenes, genres go far toward helping to identify their members, define their common situations, and shape their shared values. In many ways, genres serve as the sites in which members of the public communicate and interact with one another.

In this chapter, we will examine the nature of this public and explore a wide range of public genres, analyzing them for what they can tell us about how and why people communicate and behave in public scenes of writing. We will begin by describing how some public genres appeal to a specific public while others appeal to a more general public. Then we will focus on a segment of the public called the public sphere, in which people interested in political issues and issues of policy engage in rational debate. We will describe the genres, called civic genres (genres such as letters to the editor, editorials, pamphlets, and petitions), people use in order to shape public opinion and effect social change within the public sphere. As we will see, participating in civic genres can range from trying to influence a large, general public to having one's say within smaller groups with common interests. Having an impact on society, using writing to serve a public good, can even include contributing your writing talents to groups who need your services. This chapter, then, applies genre analysis and writing to scenes and situations in the world outside of work and school to see how people communicate information to broad audiences and to influence public actions. Such knowledge of how and why public genres work will serve you well as you use these genres to participate within public scenes of writing as a writer and a citizen.

The Public and Its Genres

Grocery lists, letters to friends, diaries and journals, voice mail messages—these and many other genres help us go about our day-to-day lives and interact with important people in our lives. The genres we are interested in for this chapter are ones that work within broader scenes than work, school, or those that include only friends and family. The focus is on genres that address what some have called a **general public**—nameless people who need some information the writer has or whose opinion somehow matters to the writer or the scene.

Of course, various situations call for conveying information to as broad a public as possible. When a couple is married, many genres are used, including toasts, invitations, thank-you notes, and, of course, the ceremony. The traditional wedding scene is not just a private affair, however; it also includes situations that call for public broadcasting of the information, often through a wedding announcement in the newspaper. The significance of this public announcement is evident in the fact that gay couples are increasingly demanding, and gaining, the right to announce commitment ceremonies in the newspapers just as heterosexual couples do. Similarly, informing is a primary purpose of many articles in newspapers and magazines and many Web sites, genres designed to convey information to a broad public. Think about a news report on the most recent business scandal, a feature article on postpartum depression, or a Web site for the National Parks or Wildlife Service. Genres conveying specific information to a general public include dictionaries and other reference works, billboard advertisements, brochures from local services like health centers, bus schedules, and other written and electronic sources of information that a general public may need.

Unlike the academic genres we explored in previous chapters, the scenes that use these public genres are at most loosely defined. There is no well-defined group of dictionary-users as there is a group of molecular biologists, for example. The readers of news reports are a vague group compared to the readers of lab reports. It is in the very nature of public genres that the "public," the participants in the scene, constitutes a shadowy community.

HOW PUBLIC GENRES DEFINE PUBLIC SCENES AND SITUATIONS

Perhaps even more so than in workplace and academic scenes, in public scenes genres help to constitute their own situations (settings of interactions involving certain participants, subjects, and purposes). *The nature of particular public genres helps to define who reads and writes them.* Although it is intended as a public broadcast of a marriage, for example, the wedding announcement in the newspaper is not read by everyone, not even by all newspaper readers. The newspaper article reporting last night's baseball game similarly is read only by a subset of the general public. Both genres define their publics by signaling the nature of their readership and defining the subject matter, purposes, and settings in which this readership interacts. They do so by such features as the kind of information included and the language used. Compare the two texts reprinted below, one a wedding announcement and one a game report. Pay special attention to what information is included and what is omitted, and note any special language used, including terms you might not know.

Wedding announcement

Lee-Audus

Jenny Lee, Eudora, and Ryan Audus, Lawrence, were married Aug. 11, 2001, at Trinity Episcopal Church in Lawrence with the Rev. Robert Lord officiating.

The bride is the daughter of Donna and Joseph Ketchum, Eudora, and Ronald Lee, Linwood. The groom is the son of Kenneth and Cheryl Audus, Lawrence.

Julie Avila was matron of honor. Aaron Kabler was best man.

Bridesmaids were Kristi Durkin, Maribeth Orr and Carly Audus. Groomsmen were Nathan Knust, Shawn Ferguson and Vicente Avila.

Alexis Avila and Jacqueline Black were flower girls. Dawson Kabler was ring bearer. Jafferty Costello was candlelighter.

A reception followed at Liberty Hall in Lawrence.

The bride is a graduate of Eudora High School and Kansas University, where she earned a bachelor's degree in business administration. She is an associate financial representative for Northwestern Mutual, Fairway.

The groom is a Lawrence High School graduate. He received a bachelor's degree in sports management from KU and is a product manager for TouchNet, Lenexa.

The couple live in Fairway.

Source: Lawrence Journal-World, Saturday, November 10, 2001, 2D.

GAME REPORT

Arizona Denies New York Fourth Straight Crown

By Ben Walker
Associated Press Baseball Writer

Phoenix — The final World Series comeback belonged to the Arizona Diamondbacks, and it was the greatest of all.

Luis Gonzalez hit an RBI single to cap a two-run rally off Mariano Rivera in the bottom of the ninth inning, and Arizona stunned the New York Yankees, 3-2, in Game 7 on Sunday night.

"We went through sports' greatest dynasty to win our first World Series," said pitcher Curt Schilling, who shared the MVP award with fellow ace Randy Johnson.

The Yankees were only two outs from their fourth straight championship and fifth in six years when it suddenly fell apart.

Tony Womack tied it with an RBI double and, after Craig Counsell was hit by a pitch to load the bases with one out, Gonzalez blooped a soft single to center field.

Rivera, who had saved 23 straight postseason games, could do nothing but watch the ball fall in to end the Yankees' run.

"That's baseball," Rivera said. "There's nothing I can do about it."

The Yankees were trying to become the third team in history to win four titles in a row. The Bronx Bombers did it from 1936-39 and from 1949-53.

"We're obviously disappointed in the result, but not the effort," Yankees manager Joe Torre said.

Owner George Steinbrenner sounded the same tone.

"I'm proud of my team. We played our hearts out. It was a very tough loss. I will be a gracious loser," he said. "We'll be back. Mark that down. We'll be back. I'm not a good loser."

What began as a November duel between Schilling and Roger Clemens climaxed with the Diamondbacks winning the title in just their fourth year of existence.

It was the fastest rise in history, breaking the mark of five years set by the 1997 Marlins. That Florida team was the last to win when trailing in the ninth inning of a Game 7, doing it against Cleveland.

The Diamondbacks bounced back from two of the toughest losses in Series history. They dropped Games 4 and 5 at Yankee Stadium, blowing two-run leads in the bottom of the ninth both times.

Randy Johnson, 38, earned the victory in relief. He also won Game 6 on Saturday night, a 15-2 romp.

Johnson was 3-0, making him the first pitcher to win three times in a Series since Detroit's Mickey Lolich in 1968. The Big Unit won five times in this postseason.

Johnson, Schilling and several Arizona old-timers, including Gonzalez, Mark Grace, Matt Williams and Mike Morgan, won their first championship ring.

"They have a great ballclub over there, but this team was relentless," Gonzalez said. "This is probably going to go down as one of the best World Series ever."

Arizona's Bob Brenly became the first manager to win the championship in his first year since Ralph Houk did it with the Yankees in 1961.

"I felt that we outplayed them," Brenly said.

The Diamondbacks outscored New York 37-14 in a Series in which the home team won every game, just the third time that has ever happened.

The Yankees, the team that would not give up, nearly won it for the city that would not give in. A highly motivated bunch, they showed extra resolve after the Sept. 11 terrorist attacks in New York.

"That was the greatest Game 7 ever," said New York City Mayor Rudolph Giuliani, who went to the

Diamondbacks locker room to offer his congratulations to them. "As a Yankees fan, I wish it turned out differently."

The Yankees were a home run swing away from elimination in the first round against Oakland, and lost the first two games at Bank One Ballpark.

But back in the desert, they looked lost.

Alfonso Soriano's solo homer off Schilling put New York ahead 2-1 in the eighth. Rivera, the most dominant reliever in postseason history, set down the Diamondbacks in the bottom half.

Then in the ninth, Arizona rallied.

Grace led off with a single and Rivera threw away Damian Miller's bunt for an error, putting runners at first and second.

Jay Bell bunted into a force play at third, but Womack lined a tying double to the right-field corner. Counsell, who scored the winning run in Game 7 with Florida in 1997, was hit by a pitch.

With the infield in, Gonzalez hit it hard enough for a game-winning single that set off fireworks, pounding music and deafening cheers.

Rivera had pitched six scoreless innings in the Series before Arizona won.

"That was the one guy we wanted to stay away from the whole World Series," Gonzalez said. "We got him the one time it counted."

The Yankees fell to 5-6 in deciding Game 7s of the Series.

Schilling was nearly untouchable at the start. The first pitcher to start three games in a Series since Minnesota's Jack Morris in 1991, he once again showed no ill effects from working on three days' rest.

Schilling allowed only one hitter to reach through six innings, and even that guy did not last long on the bases.

Paul O'Neill, playing his final game before retiring, was thrown out trying to stretch a double into a triple in the first.

But given a 1-0 lead in the sixth on Danny Bautista's RBI double, Schilling gave it back.

A strange wind started swirling through the ballpark to start the top of the seventh. Maybe it was a precursor of what was to come because moments later, Arizona had blown its edge.

Schilling retired 16 straight hitters before slumping. Derek Jeter led off with a single and O'Neill followed with a single in front of center fielder Steve Finley.

One out later, Tino Martinez tied it with an RBI single.

Clemens, pitching the biggest game of his great career, worked out of several early jams. The Diamondbacks caught up to him in the sixth after Finley led off with a single.

Bautista was next, and many people thought the man with five RBIs in Saturday's 15-2 romp would bunt. Brenly once again crossed up his critics and let Bautista swing away, and it worked.

Bautista hit a drive into the left-center gap, and Clemens simply stood on the mound with his right hand on hip, watching the play unfold.

Clemens was pulled after 6 1/3 innings with 10 strike-outs. He left without a Game 7 victory, the only thing missing on his Hall of Fame resume.

Notes: Yankees outfielder David Justice played in the previous two Game 7s and lost both times, with Atlanta in 1991 and Cleveland in 1997. He singled as a pinch-hitter in the eighth. ... All 50 players on the rosters appeared in at least one Series game.

Source: Lawrence Journal-World, Monday, November 5, 2001, 1C, 3C.

What differences in the kinds of information provided did you notice? Both genres include facts about what happened and names of participants, but the facts and the styles differ in obvious ways.

The wedding announcement includes information about who performed various roles, gives the family background of the bride and groom, and identifies the locations of the ceremony and reception. What information is not included? In the past (and still in some forums), wedding announcements also included descriptions of what the wedding party wore, how the locations were decorated, and what food was served. No wedding announcements, no matter how unconventional, describe what family tensions reared up in the seating arrangements, state how many times the bride had been married before, or quote the parents on whether or not they approve. In the wedding announcement genre, such information is not considered appropriate or relevant to the situation of announcing a marriage publicly.

Compare the information included in the game report: scores at various points, including at the end, players who performed especially well or poorly, descriptions of key plays, comments by the coaches. Unlike wedding announcements, game reports do tend to refer to tensions between the teams, give past records of the participants, and quote the coaches on whether or not they approve of their players' performances. But game reports rarely report the family lineage of the players (unless the player is related to another known athlete). In turn, wedding announcements do not describe critical moments during the ceremony. Out of all the possible information one could include about a given event, whether a wedding or a game, each genre selects particular kinds of information as appropriate to the scene and situation of writing.

DEFINING SPECIFIC PUBLICS

The kind of information included suggests the kind of audience, narrowing the readership from a completely unspecified general public to the particular public that reads the genre. Readers of wedding announcements may never see each other, but they share a common interest in local society as reflected in the genre they all read. Readers of game reports may well share the game experience as well, but, whether or not they attended the game, they share a common interest in that sport and that team and in the details of how a game played out. Those commonalities are partly *defined* by the genre they all read.

The narrowing of the public appears clearly in the language used. You probably noted the terminology used in the two examples you examined.

The game report uses words known well by those who follow the sport: two-run rally, RBI, MVP, load the bases, blooped a soft single, for examples just in the first paragraphs. The wedding announcement uses its own technical terminology: matron of honor, groomsmen, ring bearer, candlelighter, for examples. To be a reader of each genre, a member of its public, you must be willing and able to learn and use that vocabulary. Of course, anyone may be an actual reader of a particular text. You may read your first wedding announcement when someone else shows you the announcement of the wedding of someone you know. You may read the report of a game that was your first experience in the sport, or you may read the report of Game 7 of the 2001 Arizona-New York World Series because you watched that particular game, even if you do not usually watch, much less read about, baseball. But such an occasional reader will not get the full implications of a genre meant for a special readership. Reflected in particular kinds of content and language, each public genre defines its audience from among the entire general public to create a particular public.

Collaborative Activity 10.1

Bring to class an example of a public genre other than wedding announcements and game reports. Make sure it is a genre written for an audience broader than family and friends and other than academic or workplace audiences. Compare the genres brought in by your group, using Box 2.1 (pp. 93–94) to help you describe the kinds of information they include, the way they present this information, and the kinds of language they use. In doing so, try to characterize the particular public each genre defines.

DEFINING MORE GENERAL PUBLICS

While wedding announcements and game reports obviously appeal only to some readers within a general public, some other genres seem to define a broader public audience. Although readers must have general knowledge of the world, newspaper articles on the front page, for example, do not seem to require the technical knowledge that wedding and sports genres do. News reports tell *all* readers of the paper what has been happening in the world. Similarly, editorials comment on significant issues for general readers. Letters to the editor speak to all newspaper readers. Crossword puzzles offer a daily game, and comics offer daily amusement that any newspaper reader could understand. Advertisements announce sales. Ann Landers gives advice. Each of these genres is available to anyone who can pick up a copy of the newspaper and who can read—a truly general public. Along with newspapers, forums like magazines and Web sites commonly include such public genres.

Even though these genres seem more accessible than wedding and sports genres, these genres, too, define particular publics and reflect particular situations. First of all, not all newspaper readers read every genre, not even the front-page articles or the comics. Only those interested in the kind of news reported on the front page read those articles, and children may read only the comics. Some readers skim the first lines of news articles and read only a few articles in full. *These facts of readership, parts of the genres' situations, influence how the genres are written.* News articles report the most essential information in the first few sentences so that some readers can skip the rest and still have basic knowledge. Most comics use language easily understood by children as well as adult readers. Other such apparently general genres as editorials select subjects and presume background knowledge so as to define a narrower readership. Some editorial writers concentrate on international or political issues, for example, and feel no need to identify world leaders or explain long-standing or significant political debates. Other editorial writers focus on home or family issues, defining a readership with different knowledge and interests. Even the "general public" of the newspaper, then, divides into more specific publics based on common interests, and the genres help to define those more particular publics.

Not only do different genres within a newspaper appeal to different segments of the public, but also different newspapers reach different regional publics. The *Des Moines Register* does not reach the same national public as the *San Francisco Chronicle*, and neither reaches the same national public as the *New York Times* or *USA Today*. And some members of the general public do not read newspapers at all. Some might be members of a magazine-reading public, others might listen to television or radio talk shows, and still others might surf the Internet. In short, many "general publics" exist, just as we saw that many academic scenes exist. When we speak of the public, then, we need to acknowledge that no public includes everyone and that even the broadest-seeming genres reflect particular situations and create their particular publics.

Writing Activity 10.1

Make a list of all the public genres you read (or watch or hear) that other people also follow. Which ones are accessible to a more generalized readership and appeal to a broader, more "general public"? What signals the genre's availability to a general public? Which ones define narrower publics with particular knowledge and interests? How are these particular publics defined by the genre and by its particular situations (subjects, settings, participants, and purposes)?

Civic Genres and Public Participation

One particular set of public genres works to define a public that is interested in political and policy issues and tries to influence public opinion in order to improve society. These kinds of public genres that try to shape public opinion and effect societal change are part of what are called **civic genres**. Before we examine some particular civic genres, we need to examine the shared objectives of their public scene and to consider some of the debates about its validity and importance.

SHARED OBJECTIVES BEHIND CIVIC GENRES

Letters to the editor, editorials, guest columns, speeches, pamphlets, and petitions are all genres that address a large public in order to persuade people to agree with the writers. Some of these civic genres, like petitions and most pamphlets, also are meant to change behavior as well as minds. Petitions persuade people to sign but then are delivered to someone in authority who can effect change more directly. Writers of pamphlets typically want to persuade people to send money or change their lifestyles as well as to believe in the rightness of the pamphlet writer's cause. A letter to the editor might urge people to take action, or it might just urge people to believe differently (or to affirm their prior beliefs).

Often civic genres have no intention of changing people's behaviors *directly* or of making them do something immediately. Instead, writers of these texts want people to agree with the writers, perhaps to change their minds about an issue, perhaps to understand new arguments in favor of the writers' positions. Many of these writers mainly want to influence public opinion.

What good does it do just to influence public opinion instead of persuading people to take some action? Writers of civic genres believe that public opinion matters to the people who can make change happen. Built into the scene in which civic genres are used is the belief that government representatives and other people in positions of power care what "the public" thinks (and the dependence on public opinion polls reflects this), so influencing what the public thinks is influencing what people in power will do. This belief, of course, is built into representative governments and organizations that rest on democratic principles. If a public consensus can be developed, then the public's representatives in the state and organizations will need to follow that consensus. *Writers of civic genres presume that a public consensus—and hence public policy—should be based in rational discussion of significant public issues.* Editorials, letters to editors, speeches, and columns participate in the public, rational debate that should help us discover what is best for our common interest.

Writing Activity 10.2

Bring to class an example of a civic genre—a pamphlet, petition, flyer, letter to the editor, editorial, or any other genre that seeks to influence public opinion. Describe the public scene that is being targeted. What seem to be its common interests and shared objectives? Is the genre trying to change the minds of readers or their behavior or both?

PARTICIPATING IN THE PUBLIC SPHERE

Civic genres participate in what some scholars call the **public sphere.** In somewhat simplified terms, the public sphere is a forum for rational debate among all members of a group about issues of general concern. The public sphere is not a single location, like a town hall or an editorial page or an electronic discussion list. It includes all these locations and any others where people debate public issues in rational ways. The public sphere must also allow any person to voice any opinion about an issue, as long as the issue is generally relevant and the opinion is based in reason. And all people must have access to these forums, whether as speakers, writers, readers, or listeners. Through the use of civic genres that emerge from and shape these forums, individuals can participate in rational discussions of significant issues, thereby shaping the public opinion that represents the greatest good for the society at that time and place.

In some ways, this model of the public sphere is an idealized one, a model of what we wish would be in a perfect democratic world. It is also somewhat limited. In fact, the public debate about an issue often leaves out many people and many opinions. Public debate is not always rational, and the hallmarks of Western logic may dominate other ways of making significant arguments. Feminists in the 1960s and 1970s, for example, argued that the personal is political, an argument that leads among other things to basing rational argument in personal experience as well as public logic.

Also, everyone does not have equal access to the forums and genres of the public sphere. Vigorous public debate can silence less aggressive opinions, as you may have experienced in the classroom when heated debate leads to some participants dominating the conversation. In every society, too, some people have more power than others, and their opinions tend to be broadcast and listened to more than others'. Some entire groups may be underrepresented in the public sphere. Historically, members of minority groups have not received equal access to most public forums or public genres, and poorer members of society tend not to be those who are in a position to or can afford to write letters, circulate petitions, or offer guest columns.

Even if we somehow solved the problem of unequal access, some scholars would question whether there is such a thing as a general public or a "public sphere" that is common to everyone in a society. What forums exist in which *everyone* participates, so that public opinion can reflect a common general debate? Certainly the media—books, newspapers, magazines, radio, television—link us to others in society in ways that appear to create a space for general debate; however, even these forums may be limited in the public opinions represented. The word *media* is the plural form of *medium*, which comes from a Latin word meaning "middle," reminding us that media forums like television and radio are *mediated* experiences. In other words, what stories a newspaper decides to cover depends upon what stories the editorial board finds interesting or important. By functioning as gatekeepers and imposing their perceptions of significance on the audience, journalists and editorial boards can narrow and limit full public participation. In addition, not everyone reads a daily newspaper, much less contributes to one. Not everyone watches television, and not everyone is permitted to speak on the television stations that are widely watched. Some of the most widely shared genres—perhaps television shows, advertisements—are very restricted in who gets to produce them. While they may draw on and provide common cultural references, they do not allow the kind of access required for participating in shared public debate.

Writing Activity 10.3

Drawing on the sample civic genre that you examined in Writing Activity 10.2, critique the possibilities and limitations of the genre. Drawing on Box 4.1: Questions for Critiquing Genres (p. 161), consider whose needs are most and least served by the genre and how the genre enables and limits its users' actions. Does the genre create inequalities or privilege certain ways of doing things?

Collaborative Activity 10.2

In groups of three, assign each member of your group to bring to class a different newspaper published on the same date. You might choose to have one person bring a large national daily (like the *New York Times, Wall Street Journal,* or *Washington Post*), another your regional/local paper, and another either an independent or alternative paper from your city or a daily from another town/city (which you can find online or in the library). Analyze the similarities and differences in what the papers report. Do the papers reflect a shared public sphere, or do they define particular publics (or both)? What counts as news in each one? What different perspectives does each paper take on similar subjects? What opinions and points of view are left out? Examine any differences in coverage of politics, sports, entertainment, crime, etc. What do these forums indicate about their readerships or publics? What do the similarities or differences you noted tell you about the differing assumptions and expectations of these public forums?

What does this debate about the existence and accessibility of the public sphere mean? We believe that it makes it all the more important for us to speak up when the opportunity arises, to participate in the genres of civic discourse, to make our voices heard whenever and wherever we can, and to make a point of listening to as many different voices as possible. While access to the public sphere may be uneven, you can use the civic genres to which you *do* have access (like letters to your senator or congressional representative, letters to the editor, petitions, etc.) to influence public actions. Drawing on the rhetorical strategies of civic genres, you can carry out social actions and work to be heard and to hear others. For public debate and consensus to work in imperfect civic scenes, in which access and representation are unequal, everyone must participate in multiple public groups of differing memberships and participate in multiple public genres in order to obtain a more informed understanding of and to participate more fully in the issues. Read a daily newspaper or two, listen to multiple news shows on television and radio, seek out Web sites from a wide range of reputable sources, attend forums sponsored by groups you don't belong to and on subjects you don't usually consider. Read or listen to every source critically, knowing that the debate on each issue is larger than a single source. In a diverse and large society, the public sphere will be diverse and large and will require good citizens to work to be well-informed and to participate in public debate through public genres.

Writing Activity 10.4

List all the public forums you listen to or read, including newspapers and magazines but also Web sites, discussion lists, and radio and television shows. Note which of those sites use genres that allow the public to respond (for example, a Web site that includes a bulletin board, a newspaper that accepts letters to the editor, a radio show that has a call-in component). How do the genres in these public forums both enable and limit participation and response?

Collaborative Activity 10.3

Compare the list of public forums and genres that each member of your group has access to (listed in the preceding activity). Note how many forums many of you share and how many different forums appear among your lists. Discuss whether the particular publics of each forum overlap or are relatively distinct. Discuss also how you could broaden the range of publics you participate in, what different kinds of forums you could find, and how you could go about finding them.

Collaborative Activity 10.4

Compile for the class a list of public forums that your group believes include multiple public groups, use genres that allow the public to participate, and encourage rational debate. Annotate that list by describing for each forum its particular public and how someone could contribute to the forum's debate. What are the various genres that emerge from these forums and shape the goals of these forums? How might you change these genres to increase participation and debate?

Examples of Civic Genres

The genres through which people participate in the public sphere thus have significant objectives and can lead to significant change, even though they do not necessarily advocate that readers/listeners take a specific action and even though they might not reach everyone involved in an issue. A letter to the editor, guest column on an editorial page, or political Web site participates in a large, dynamic dialogue, with one text responding to others on the same issue so that people can see the issue more clearly in all its complexity. It is each citizen's responsibility not only to listen to this dialogue but also to join in. Democracy depends on citizens who speak up at public forums, contribute to discussion lists, write letters to the editor, offer columns to newspapers, magazines, and Web sites that are read by a public audience. If public consensus develops from public debate involving multiple voices, good citizens need to contribute their voices and opinions so that the common interest can be discovered.

In case you think your voice is too small or faint to be heard, consider the case of John, a student at one of our universities. Having researched the low pay of campus workers for an argument paper in his writing class, John discovered that campus workers were paid $5.65 per hour, well below the average wage for workers statewide ($9.50 per hour), and were not provided full benefits. To try to make a difference, John decided to join the Living Wage Campaign, an organized effort on the part of faculty, students, and staff to support campus workers. To assist in this effort, John turned his paper into a flyer that he posted on and off campus, attempting to inform and shape public opinion and to motivate individuals to lend their support to the campaign, including marching in campus protests. Unlike some other scenes in which genres might have immediate effect, like proposals in workplace scenes and syllabi in academic scenes, civic genres don't often have immediate, visible effects in their public scenes. Nonetheless, John's work may help to influence public opinion as others read his flyer. In any case, his rhetorical contributions enable people to become better informed through his participation in the public debate.

You may have opportunities to participate in many different public genres. Some groups publish newsletters, for example, that they distribute widely. Others develop Web sites containing essays or thought pieces. Some create pamphlets that broadcast the group's stances. Some organize town meetings or panels or run discussion lists. As you become more active in civic organizations, you will need to learn the particular genres used in their scenes of writing. Each offers a somewhat different response to somewhat different situations, of course, so you can use the genre analysis you have been learning in this book to understand and produce effective examples of the new civic genres you encounter. To help model how you can use genre analysis to understand and write civic genres more effectively, we will now guide you through detailed analyses of two civic genres: the letter to the editor and editorials, or guest columns.

Analyzing Letters to the Editor

One civic genre potentially available to all of us is letters to the editor. They are not really written for the editor at all. Rather, *they are written to the particular public that reads that publication, to express someone's point of view and try to persuade others to see things the same way.*

Many kinds of publications accept letters, including magazines and newspapers as well as some online journals and regularly published newsletters. Let's begin with the examples of the genre. We will then help you analyze the situation and features of letters to the editor.

Below are all of the letters to the editor that appeared in one issue of one town's newspaper. We include *all* the letters so that you can see some range of what this genre encompasses without our selecting particular types of letters. As you read these letters, look for the underlying scenes and assumptions as well as the common situation and generic features.

LETTERS TO THE EDITOR
(*LAWRENCE JOURNAL-WORLD*, NOVEMBER 8, 2001)

1. Truck traffic

To the editor:

Keep trucks out.

We voted to reduce traffic on 23rd Street. To do this all through traffic should be encouraged to use I-435. As for traffic on 31st street, we need traffic lights, turn lanes and limited zoning. We should not be pawns for politicians or the trucking industry, including the future Richards-Gabauer truck/rail exchange.

Steve King,
Lawrence

2. Driving passion

To the editor:

I read several excellent letters in J-W recently that had comments about the traffic congestion in Lawrence and how KDOT's solutions would damage the wetlands.

To find sensible solutions, we need to look at history to see what caused this mess. The automobile, notwithstanding its shortcomings, is at the top of the list of what people want, whoever they are and wherever they live.

High taxes designed to discourage car ownership have not had much effect, nor has the battle with urban traffic. People still drive under the most adverse conditions, or they move out when conditions become unbearable, then we have urban sprawl.

Federal, state and local governments in the U.S. subsidized the roads that accommodated the automotive revolution. However in Europe, public transit and the railways have received the subsidies, which public policy has been hostile or indifferent to the automobile. Perhaps that is because they don't have oil barons at the head of the government.

According to a recent study by Detroit Wayne State University, many suburban commuters now spend more than three hours in traffic each week day. Once home, they can't stop, except to switch hats, becoming taxi drivers, fetching children and running errands. According to author Tony Hiss, the average American family makes 14 car trips a day. More and more time in the car becomes almost intolerable when it occupies up to 30 hours and requires some 90 drives each week. People are no longer driving; they are driven.

Lawrence needs to maintain its unique character. Citizens need to join neighborhood groups to promote walking through neighborhoods to visit with neighbors.

Lester C. Marsh
Lawrence

3. Slap in the face

To the editor:

The recent firing of two Allen Press employees for wearing Halloween paraphernalia is one of the most boneheaded and ridiculous moves I've ever seen a company make. As a business owner with over 100 employees on my payroll, I am saddened to realize that there are still bosses who behave and think in such intimidating and threatening ways.

At my company we have a laissez-faire attitude toward dress. I myself am guilty of wearing, dare I say, shorts, T-shirts and sandals in the summer, and I encourage my employees to do likewise. Halloween should be a time of fun for everyone. Unfortunately Allen management's only contribution to the mirth was a regressive, sick slap in the face directed at its employees.

Donald Phipps,
Lawrence

4. Trickle-down trick

To the editor:

We are gradually sliding into a recession, and lowering interest rates alone clearly hasn't helped much.

The cause of this recession seems evident. Obviously it is NOT a shortage of investments. Our factories, our retail stores, our transportation facilities, our service establishments, they all are laying off workers—over 415,000 in October alone—clear evidence that our economy is currently producing well below capacity. Why? Basically because consumers, economically insecure, have reduced their spending.

Now the president is proposing a "stimulus package" that, in professional lingo would be referred to as "supply side economics." What he proposes is a series of new tax cuts that would benefit primarily the wealthy (tens of thousands of dollars for the ones earning more than a million dollars a year), in the expectation that they will then invest it, which in turn will create jobs, and make the economy blossom again (I like to refer to it as feeding the horse so that the sparrows may eat). Now let me ask you: Honest, if you were in business and had an extra $50,000 or so, would you invest it in expanding your enterprise if you already can't sell the goods you have for sale? Does that make any sense to you?

Wouldn't it make more sense to place more purchasing power into the hands of those who do not have enough and would need and use this money for immediate consumer purchases? We could, for instance pay unemployment compensation for an additional three or six months to those who have lost their jobs without any fault of their own, or we could raise the minimum wage of workers that keeps them below the poverty level. Then, when these individuals spend their money and buy the goods that are for sale producers will have the incentive to produce more; and if they need to make more investments, they'll surely do so by using their own money or borrowing through bond sales from the public or, otherwise, from a bank.

Makes sense doesn't it? But try to sell that idea to those who believe that the way to go is to make the rich richer, and then some of it will surely trickle down to the poorer.

Harry G. Shaffer,
Lawrence

5. A rigid fiefdom

To the editor:

Regarding the recent flap about the firing of two employees at Allen Press, the company indeed has the right to fire employees because they don't adhere to the company's dress policy. Moreover, employees of the company have a right to seek employment elsewhere, and the company's customers have the right to seek another firm to do business with.

Allen Press' policy regarding dress reminds me of a recent excerpt I read in a book about the Taliban. A government official in Afghanistan issued an edict that women had to wear quiet shoes under their head-to-toe burqas. Failure to do so would result in serious penalties including beating or whipping. I am thankful that we are much more civilized here in the U.S. Over here, one might lose one's livelihood for not adhering to some draconian policy, but at least we're not beaten or whipped.

U.S. and Afghan societies have something else in common. Both countries have at their hearts institutions whose beginnings are rooted in the Middle Ages. The fundamentalist interpretations of the Koran that the Taliban adhere to trace their beginning to the first millennium. Capitalism as we know it, owes much of its roots to Europe of the Middle Ages. We have been given some freedoms, but being employed by a large company has some parallels to serfdom. One need not think independently, nor express oneself. Just do the job and take the shekels paid. Companies preach empowerment, and send their employees to seminars about teamwork, then fire them because they wore a Halloween button.

I haven't had any dealings with Allen Press, and only know of them from the story I read. I hope that this incident represents an exception in the way they deal with employees. If it isn't, I hope at least some of their employees have the opportunity to find a less rigid fiefdom to serve.

Tim Bowles,
Olathe

6. A sorry state

To the editor:

Terry Allen's dismissal only illuminates the sorry state of Kansas football. Rarely in collegiate athletics is a head coach fired while a season is in progress, regardless of how poorly a team is competing. College athletics, while driven by and dependent on revenue, should ultimately be about learning and it is hard to see how this late season dismissal helps the University of Kansas. Allen's firing will have little if any consequence on recruiting, and fans are not likely to flock to the remaining two home games to cheer on the Jayhawks because the message from the administration is that this season is officially a wash.

While that comes as no surprise to most, Allen's dismissal goes not only against the spirit of college athletics but against KU's institutional mission as well. This late-season move serves little more than a three-week headstart in the search process for a new coach. Regardless of the outcomes of the final games, the 2001 Jayhawks are Terry Allen's team and this move should have come at the end of the season.

I do not know Terry Allen, but by all accounts, he seems to be a decent, well-respected individual who was not met with success during his tenure at KU. And this does not distinguish him from any KU coaches in the recent past.

While a new era in KU football may loom on the horizon, the real shame lying beneath another losing season and another head football coach is that two varsity sports, men's swimming and tennis, were sacrificed last winter to pave way for increased spending for football. Dr. Bohl and the KU Athletic Department have a rare opportunity to correct a mistake and reinstate these programs that represented the best of the University of Kansas: scholarship, leadership, and athletic excellence.

Andrew Poggio,
Iowa City, Iowa

7. Credit is due

To the editor:

What a slap in the face to all teaching librarians to find out in the Friday Journal-World that they are considered non-instructional personnel. I would dare to say that the people conducting this audit have not been in very many school libraries in Lawrence.

The librarian at my school spends most, if not all, of her day instructing groups of students. She is the central figure in all of our curricular studies, and is not just shelving books, as some people seem to think. I invite these people to visit Quail Run library any day of the week and see just what non-instruction really is!

Michele Trompeter,
Lawrence

Writing Activity 10.5

Choose one of the letters to the editor and try to reconstruct, as best you can, the writer's scene and situation. What shared objectives, values, beliefs, and assumptions are reflected in the editorial? What is the writer's purpose for writing? How does he or she transform a reported action into a significant public issue? What assumptions does the writer seem to make about audience?

Collaborative Activity 10.5

Using the samples provided and Box 2.1: Questions for Analyzing a Genre (pp. 93–94), work with your group to do an initial analysis of the genre of letters to the editor. Write a one-paragraph description of the scene of letters to the editor; then describe the situation of this genre—the readers, writers, purposes, subjects, and settings. Follow that paragraph with an initial list of generic features that these letters seem to have in common, despite their differences.

Some of the details of the letters you analyzed reflect the particular newspaper these letters were written for. Every forum has a policy on what letters they will accept. The *Lawrence Journal-World* states its "Letters Policy" as follows:

Letters Policy

The Journal-World welcomes letters to the Public Forum. Letters should be 350 words or less, be of public interest and should avoid name-calling and libelous language. The Journal-World reserves the right to edit letters, as long

as viewpoints are not altered. Shorter letters are preferred and generally receive greater readership.

Letters must bear the name, address and telephone number of the writer.
Letters may be submitted by e-mail to:

letters@ljworld.com

This letters policy appears in small print at the bottom of the editorial page
in this newspaper. Other forums have similar statements that specify length,
relevant subjects, and other details that make a letter more or less publish-
able in that forum. Note that the policy recognizes the place of letters to the
editor in the public sphere, specifying that letters should be of public interest. The importance of rational debate may be suggested by the prohibition
against name-calling and libelous language. This policy is not unusual, but
each forum is different, so it is important to check the policy before writing
a letter. Such policies are essential parts of the genre's situation.

By now, you have become so practiced at doing genre analysis that you
probably handled the last group activity easily, recognizing the scene and
situation in the genre and describing the genre's features. Rather than
repeating the analysis you are capable of doing, then, let's concentrate on
some of the more subtle features important to this particular genre, ones
you probably noted but that deserve closer examination.

PUBLIC ISSUES

The letters reproduced here cover a range of subjects, including traffic congestion, the practices of a local business, the economy, college football, and
the instructional value of librarians. These subjects did not simply occur to
the writers as good subjects to write about. Each letter arose in response to
someone else's action, usually an action reported in the newspaper. The
newspaper story may have reported what happened, from its own perspective; the letters to the editor help turn those actions into debatable issues,
ones that merit attention in the public sphere.

The general subjects become public issues in part through the actions of
the letter writers. (We note, too, of course, that the newspaper's way of
reporting the story initially may contribute to making an issue of what
happened.) The last letter, "Credit is due," illustrates this move to public
issue most obviously. The newspaper had referred to librarians as non-
instructional personnel, and the letter writer "makes an issue of it" by writing
a letter complaining and explaining the instructional role of librarians.

Other readers might not have noticed the wording or the implications,
but one reader writes a letter to turn that wording into an issue of some
public significance. Similarly, the newspaper had reported on the firing of

employees for wearing Halloween-themed attire, and that act had become a private issue for the employees, who were considering filing suit. The act becomes a public issue, though, as people like the two letter writers here critique that action and what it represents of significance for the larger public. The fourth letter, "Trickle-down trick," responds to a less local action, the president's economic proposals, and "takes issue" with that plan. In writing a response to that plan, the letter writer creates a space for debating the president's proposals; the writer assumes that legislative actions need not simply be accepted but merit public review and discussion. He brings the action as an issue into the public sphere.

In the case of each letter, someone's reported actions have prompted the letter as a response, but *it is the writing of the letter that has transformed the reported action into a significant public issue.* This transformation of a reported action into a significant public issue is one of the rhetorical strategies a writer must make when writing a letter to the editor.

Civic discourse has as one of its major roles the enabling of public debate about actions affecting the public interest. Any subject that has potential significance for society can become a public issue. The public may not be in a position directly to enforce traffic laws, change a business's dress codes, implement economic policies, keep a football coach, or hire more librarians. However, through civic genres such as letters to the editor, the public can call attention to the actions of those in power and to their beliefs and values (as well as the writer's own) and can sway public opinion to support or discourage their actions.

Writing Activity 10.6

Think of three subjects or actions that you might help "make an issue out of" by writing a letter to the editor. (You might think of issues for your campus newspaper as well as subjects of local and national significance.) List the actions your letters would respond to, and for each one state in a sentence the stance you would take to turn the action into an issue of public significance.

OPENINGS AND CLOSINGS

To sway public opinion, writers must not only call attention to an issue but must also get readers' attention. As you surely noted in your description of their situation, letters to the editor appear in a cluster on one or two pages, competing with each other and often with editorials for attention. Since newspaper readers are often in a hurry and selective (and newspapers prescribe a certain length for letters to the editor), letters have to grab their attention and have to try to make their point quickly and directly. Many readers will not read the entire letter. To be persuasive in such a situation, letters to the editor usually begin (after the obligatory "To the editor:") with a clear, direct assertion of the writer's position. Look at the openings of our sample letters, isolated below:

1. Keep trucks out.

2. I read several excellent letters in J-W recently that had comments about the traffic congestion in Lawrence and how KDOT's solutions would damage the wetlands.

3. The recent firing of two Allen Press employees for wearing Halloween paraphernalia is one of the most boneheaded and ridiculous moves I've ever seen a company make.

4. We are gradually sliding into a recession, and lowering interest rates alone clearly hasn't helped much.

5. Regarding the recent flap about the firing of two employees at Allen Press, the company indeed has the right to fire employees because they don't adhere to the company's dress policy.

6. Terry Allen's dismissal only illuminates the sorry state of Kansas football.

7. What a slap in the face to all teaching librarians to find out in the Friday *Journal-World* that they are considered non-instructional personnel.

You probably have no doubt of the writer's opinion, even if the issue is a local one you might not fully understand (like traffic on 23rd Street, for example). The one exception is letter 2, whose opening raises the subject but does not take a stand. Would you be likely to continue reading letter 2? Not only does the letter not make clear the writer's position, but also it does not grab the reader's attention. The other letters begin with a strong statement, sometimes the strongest statement of the entire letter. Imagine a newspaper reader scanning the letters quickly: The reader immediately knows what positions are being argued and can choose which to read further.

Writing Activity 10.7

For each of the three issues you created in the last exercise, write at least three different opening sentences that might start your letter to the editor.

Letters to the editor usually end as they open, with a powerful statement of the writer's stance. Since readers typically scan the beginning and then the ending of a text, the closing statement gives the writer another shot at catching readers. Examine the last sentence of each letter to the editor below:

1. We should not be pawns for politicians or the trucking industry, including the future Richards-Gabauer truck/rail exchange.

2. Citizens need to join neighborhood groups to promote walking through neighborhoods to visit with neighbors.

3. Unfortunately Allen management's only contribution to the mirth was a regressive, sick slap in the face directed at its employees.

4. But we try to sell that idea to those who believe that the way to go is to make the rich richer, and then some of it will surely trickle down to the poorer.

5. If it isn't, I hope at least some of their employees have the opportunity to find a less rigid fiefdom to serve.

6. Dr. Bohl and the KU Athletic Department have a rare opportunity to correct a mistake and reinstate these programs that represented the best of the University of Kansas: scholarship, leadership, and athletic excellence.

7. I invite these people to visit Quail Run library any day of the week and see just what non-instruction really is!

Notice that these final statements not only deliver a strong assertion of the main point but also do so more elaborately than the opening. The sentences are longer, the arguments more fully fleshed out. The closing comes at the end of the letter, after all, after the writer has had a chance to argue the point, offer details, and perhaps persuade the reader. The last sentence is the last chance to have an impact on the reader, to make a logical, emotional, or personal appeal that might sway readers to the writer's point of view.

Collaborative Activity 10.6

Analyze and describe the kinds of appeals (logical, emotional, ethical) used by the closing statements of each letter. Discuss why the writers might have chosen these appeals for the ending.

LENGTH AND DETAIL

The *Journal-World*'s letters policy states a maximum length of 350 words and states that shorter letters gain more readers. So is shorter always better? No. If that were the case, the best letter would read simply, "No," or "Yes," or "Keep trucks out." While writers want their letters to be read, they also want to persuade those readers. Persuasion takes argument and detail.

The first letter on truck traffic, in fact, may be too undeveloped to persuade anyone. It states the writer's ideas (direct through traffic to an interstate and change 31st Street), and it offers a reason (reduce traffic and resist what politicians and trucking industry want). If you already agree with the problem, already are inclined to resist what politicians and industry want, and already want more restrictions on 31st Street, you are likely to agree with this letter. If you agree with the problem but had not thought of those proposed solutions, this letter may give you a new idea to consider. But if you agree with the problem but not with slowing down traffic on 31st Street, this letter offers little to persuade you otherwise. Such a short letter, in other words, works best for confirming readers' prior ideas or for raising new ideas. To persuade a wider public of the rightness of those ideas, a letter to the editor generally needs to offer more argument and evidence.

Compare the approach of the two longer letters, on the economy and on the firing of the football coach. Each offers reasons for the writer's stance and explains those reasons. The economy letter also offers some statistics as evidence of his point (and to enhance his ethos, his personal credibility). The drawback, of course, is that the letters require of readers more concentration and time. But neither letter is too long: Neither letter is so long that even those interested in the issue would not read the whole letter. Remember the scene and the readership of newspapers. The general public who reads this newspaper may scan the first sentences of the letters; the particular public of people interested in each issue is likely to read all of the letters on those issues. Good letters to the editor balance the need to reach as large a readership as possible with the need to persuade readers of the rightness of the writer's position.

Collaborative Activity 10.7

Compare the length and detail of the two letters on the employees fired for wearing Halloween paraphernalia. In what ways is each letter most effective? How well does each letter balance logos, pathos, and ethos? How might each letter be improved? Which letter do members of your group find most persuasive? Why? (Notice how your prior beliefs about dress codes and the roles of employees influence which letter you find persuasive.)

CONCISENESS AND VIVIDNESS

Within newspapers, the situation to which letters respond calls for brevity and engagement. Therefore, crafting concise sentences and using precise and vivid words is especially critical in letters to the editor. Each word of the 350 words maximum (or whatever the length your forum specifies) must count, both literally and figuratively. Letters must also grab readers' attention, and lively words can help do that.

Letters to the editor often use powerful words, ones packed with meaning and carrying an emotional punch. In our sample letters, the word *boneheaded* might have stood out because of its strong judgment, but this and other letters carry similarly powerful, though perhaps more subtle, words to make their points. Words that are both precise in meaning and lively in effect include *pawns, battle, oil barons, mirth, regressive, sick, flap, edict, draconian, serfdom, shekels,* and *sacrificed*. Phrases with impact include *athletic excellence, slap in the face, dare I say,* and *feeding the horse so that the sparrows may eat*. Statements including these less common, less everyday words and phrases hold the readers' attention more and carry emotional as well as logical weight. They also, of course, influence what readers think of the writer, the writer's ethos. Do you respect the thinking of someone who calls an action boneheaded? Do you admire his directness? Do you appreciate the knowledge of someone who compares the dress code to Taliban policies of burqas and shekels, or do you resent his trivializing of important international struggles? In short, writers must take care to make their letters lively and intriguing while conveying the most persuasive image of the writer and considering the effect on readers.

Writing Activity 10.8

Look back at the openings you wrote for your possible letters. Rewrite them to use more precise and vivid words wherever possible.

Collaborative Activity 10.8

Working through each letter, describe how the writer's choices of words and arguments affect how readers perceive the image of each writer. Based on these discussions, have each group member write a one-paragraph profile of one of the writers. What sort of persona do the writer's choices of words, phrases, and arguments help create? Who, that is, emerges from the language of the letter? And how does that constructed persona shape the way you as a reader might respond to the letter?

In such a situation requiring brief but persuasive statements, concise sentences help such vivid word choices stand out. Notice how the sentences in the letters consist of content-filled words, even those that are not especially vivid. "Keep trucks out" models the most concise sentences, ones with substantive words only. Of course, most English sentences require some emptier words like *the, have, of, in,* or *is,* but writing concisely pares sentences of as many of those emptier words as possible. Looking back at the first sentences of each letter, you can see how relatively few empty words appear. Compare "Terry Allen's dismissal only illuminates the sorry state of Kansas football" to a wordier version: "It seems to me as I consider the situation that the dismissal of one Terry Allen as the coach of the football team at the University of Kansas may be something that illuminates the state of football at the University of Kansas to be that of a sorry one." The livelier words are still present, but they are buried under a mass of verbiage.

Strategies for Revising Letters to the Editor

Your goal when you revise a letter to the editor is to pare your sentences down to the most *precise and lively language* possible. Knowing some stylistic tricks can help you revise your sentences for conciseness. The few we will describe especially apply to letters to the editor: picking specific verbs, reducing phrases to words, and finding agents and actions.

PICKING SPECIFIC VERBS

Verbs control sentences. Because of how English sentences operate, your verb choice will determine much of the rest of your sentence. So focusing on your verb choice can help you strengthen your sentences. When you act to shape public opinion through a letter to the editor, you should use *strong verbs* that convey specific actions or precise meanings: for example, *struggle, perpetrate, dismantle, rejoice, illuminate.* Weaker verbs are more general, vaguer, or more static: for example, *seem, have, do, show, be.* The weakest verb in English is a form of *be,* like the *is* in this sentence. Forms of *be* include *am, is, are, was, were, be, being, been.*

Some of these forms of *be* and other weak verbs appear in verb phrases along with other, stronger verbs: for example, *am battling, has been perpetrating, did insist, might be depicting.* With other strong verbs present, uses of *be* do not significantly weaken your assertions. When a form of *be* serves as the *main* verb of a sentence, however, the sentence describes little action, just mere existence: being. Forms of *be* state equation: Something IS something else. When a form of *be* serves as your main verb, then, you miss an opportunity to emphasize a livelier action. You don't need to study grammar to learn to reduce your dependence on forms of *be* as main verbs. Knowing the forms of *be*, you can search your drafts for those forms and, whenever you find one, ask whether it appears with a strong verb and, if not, consider revising the sentence to use a stronger verb.

Writing Activity 10.9

Find at least three examples of what you consider to be strong verbs in the sample letters to the editor. What is the effect of these verbs on the writer's message, audience, and/or persona? Now see if you can find at least three examples of weak verbs. Substitute stronger verbs and once again analyze the effect on writer, reader, and message.

You may have noticed in some of the sentences you revised for the last activity that potentially powerful verbs may lurk around weaker verbs. "It is a good idea to discuss the consequences first" can become "The committee should discuss the consequences first." One trick for revising weak sentences is to spot stronger potential verbs nearby (or "To revise weak sentences, spot stronger potential verbs nearby").

To revise for such conciseness, you must be willing to abandon some words in your initial draft for tighter statements. Again, it pays to remember the *scene* and *situation* in which letters to the editor function. A word limit typically imposes tight restrictions. Every word counts. The more words you can eliminate through tighter sentences, including by choosing stronger verbs, the more your message can persuade.

Writing Activity 10.10

Look back at the *weak* verbs that you identified in the last activity. Do any of them have potentially stronger verbs near them? If so, revise the sentences to use the stronger verb that's lurking. If not, see if any other sentences in the letters contain potential verbs and revise those sentences to change the verbs. What different effects do you achieve with each revision?

FINDING AGENTS AND ACTIONS

The next revision technique to give your letters to the editor conciseness and liveliness requires closer examination of your meaning and often more extensive revision, but it pays off with greater persuasive power. As you seek more specific verbs for each sentence, search also for verbs with *more vivid actions, and find people who perform those actions.* Then rewrite the sentence to make those people perform that action.

> **Rewrite** "The parking lots on campus should not be oversold"
>
> **To** "The parking board should not oversell the parking lots."
>
> **Rewrite** "There should be a general discussion about the possible solutions to the parking problems on campus"
>
> **To** "Students, faculty, and staff should discuss how they can solve the parking problems on campus."
>
> Even more substantively, **rewrite** "Something should be done to make parking on campus more available to students"
>
> **To** specify who should do what: "The parking board should designate more parking lots for students," or "Students should demand more parking."

Making most of your sentences emphasize agents (those who do the action) and actions increases the impact of your statements, especially in a genre like letters to the editor where brevity and liveliness matter. Of course, this impact is not desirable in all scenes of writing and their genres. In genres such as lab reports and resumés, for instance, de-emphasizing the agent helps emphasize the *action:* ("Twelve ounces of nitrate were added to the solution" or "Managed large budget"). In the genre of the letter to the editor, however, readers are attracted to people doing things, so readers will more likely read your letter if it emphasizes agents and actions. This revision technique also gives life to ideas, animates the abstract, and turns thoughts into deeds just as you, through the public genre of the letter to the editor, turn thoughts into actions.

Writing Activity 10.11

In the sample letters to the editor, find at least three examples of what you consider to be places where agent and action were emphasized. What is the effect of this emphasis on the writer's message, audience, or persona? Now see if you can find at least three examples of places where the writer did not emphasize agents and actions. Rewrite those sentences, and once again analyze the effect on writer, reader, and message.

Even in letters to the editor, of course, a writer sometimes might not want to emphasize actions and agents. Perhaps the writer wants to emphasize a static state or is defining an abstract concept, for example, as in "Deflation is a steady decline in prices." Or perhaps the agent matters less than the consequences, as in "The football team has been defeated in 24 games over the last three years." Good reasons justify agent-less or action-less sentences.

However, some writers misuse the ability to disguise actions and agents, and you should take care to avoid such misuse yourself. For example, pointing a finger at an unidentified agent raises anger and anxiety without solution: "Our rights have been taken away, and we will soon be reduced to buying music on the black market." Disguising the agent can wrongly enable parties to avoid taking responsibility for their actions, as in "The coach was fired midseason, and that decision should be supported." Especially in public genres and civic discourse, including letters to the editor, we can best conduct reasonable debate about issues if we clarify the agents and actions involved. Public consensus should develop not by obscuring but by clarifying issues.

REDUCING PHRASES TO WORDS

Some writers of academic genres adopt a style heavy in phrases that sound important but convey relatively little substance. Academic writing situations may seem to encourage such phrases, for they lend an air of significance and learnedness to even the emptiest statements—a strategy some weaker scholars might substitute for becoming knowledgeable about their subject. Writers guilty of inflated phrases must work especially hard to eliminate them in such genres as letters to the editor where brevity matters more than an intellectual tone.

In revising letters to the editor, look to eliminate phrases where a word will do. You can get to know some common inflated phrases and their one-word substitutes, such as the following ones:

INSTEAD OF THIS PHRASE	USE	THIS WORD
in the event that		if
at the time that		when
at the present time		now
has an effect on		affects
due to the fact that		because
think about		consider

Other inflated phrases are less common but develop in a particular subject. Watch out for phrases that describe something for which a single word exists. The examples below illustrate the type of phrase, not the particular phrases you might find in your own letters.

INSTEAD OF THIS PHRASE	USE	THIS WORD
the people who work for the business		employees
a place where people could feel safe		a refuge
the last thing that was mentioned		the latter
broke an idea into parts		analyzed
living in the same house		cohabiting

Expanding your vocabulary through reading and remaining alert to new words will help you access appropriate words for what you want to say, but you can eliminate many wordy phrases simply by paying attention to the problem. If you reread the sample letters to the editor, written by ordinary citizens, you will find very few inflated phrases. The scene—defined in part by journalistic editorial guidelines, practical considerations such as space, readers' habits of scanning letters, and rhetorical effects such as the need to make a strong, immediate, and persuasive impression—calls for tight, concise prose, and these letter writers comply.

Writing Activity 10.12

Return to the sample letters to the editor, looking this time for inflated or wordy phrases. If you find any, rewrite them for brevity. What are the effects of your rewrite on the letter's message, audience, or persona?

Writing Activity 10.13

Return to the opening sentences you wrote for potential letters to the editor in Writing Activity 10.7. Draft a paragraph to follow one of the openings you wrote. Then revise that paragraph for conciseness and vividness, including using strong verbs, emphasizing actions and agents, and reducing phrases to words. What is the effect of the changes you made? How do they better reflect the situation for writing?

Collaborative Activity 10.9

Trade the paragraph you wrote in the preceding activity with a classmate. See if you can shorten your classmate's paragraph at all, either by using the techniques we have described or by any other means. Then compare the two versions of each paragraph: What kinds of revisions did your partner find that you would like to do yourself in the future? Did either of you shorten the paragraph too much? Is it possible for a letter to the editor to be too concise? Does one version respond better to the situation for writing? Why?

The same general principle applies to all of the ways we have recommended you revise your sentences in letters to the editor: Revise for clarity, to reduce obscurity or obfuscation. But remember your goal is more important than technique. You seek to grab and hold your reader's attention and to give your brief argument maximum persuasive power. If more words better achieve those goals, then use more words. In most letters to the editor, though, fewer well-chosen words will overpower more, less thoughtfully chosen words. Qualities of effective letters to the editor include:

- Conciseness and vividness
- Attention-grabbing opening sentences
- Powerful closing sentences
- Sufficient detail and appropriate length
- Significant public issues

By attending to these generic features, you can address the public scene, participate in civic genres, and contribute to the developing of public consensus in the public sphere. Your writing can make a difference in our common public life.

Analyzing Editorials

Another genre that can contribute to public discussion is the editorial. Newspapers and magazines often use the title "guest column" for an editorial written by someone other than a member of the editorial staff. We will use the term *editorial* from now on to describe both guest columns and editorials.

The editorial shares many traits with academic analysis and argument papers as well as researched position papers, so it might at first seem hard to distinguish them. All of these genres present rational discussion of a significant issue, focus on a controlling idea, draw from reliable and credible sources, organize logically, and develop ideas with specific details. But consider the scene and situation of the editorial in contrast to that of the academic genres. Editorials speak to a public audience, not to a teacher or necessarily well-educated audience. The editorial writer has greater flexibility in defining a particular public, as we discussed earlier in this chapter, by his or her choice of subject, purposes, setting, and language; the academic writer usually has an assigned audience. The editorial writer can also often *choose* a public forum, whether a campus newspaper, an organization's newsletter, or an individual Web site, for example, further defining the editorial's audience.

Most significantly, perhaps, the *purpose* of the editorial differs from that of the academic genres that appear similar in form. Researched position papers and analysis papers aim to advance understanding of and knowledge about a significant subject in the academic scene; they need to demonstrate the reasonableness of their assertions and offer the writer's reasoned perspective. They need not persuade their readers to believe what they believe, even if they offer an argument. In addition, analysis papers and researched position papers take a more objective, critical stance rather than an invested persuasive stance. Editorials, on the other hand, like letters to the editor, participate in the ongoing discussion of the public sphere in order to help shape public consensus. To be effective, rather than critically examining and supporting an academic argument, editorials need to provide especially telling arguments or support, and they need to change some people's minds. This fundamentally persuasive purpose for editorials, along with the broader public nature of its audience and forum, leads to a fundamentally different genre.

Read the three editorials reprinted below (and refer to the editorials on drilling in the Arctic National Wildlife Refuge in Chapter 1) and try to identify common features. Remember the kinds of generic traits we have analyzed throughout this book, including the type of content of the genre, its organization, choice and use of detail, style, and tone (for guiding questions to help you identify genre features, see Box 2.1, pp. 93–94). Note especially how the texts reveal their common scene, described in our preceding paragraph, and also how each defines its particular situations and particular publics.

SAMPLE EDITORIALS
1. Editorial by Robert Chamberlain, University Daily Kansan,
October 10, 2001

Feminists Ignore Half the Problems

For some people, October means baseball. For others, it means Halloween. For me, it means an avalanche of sexism and questionable methodology. In fact, the first ominous pebbles began tumbling down Mt. Oread* in the form of a hysterical column by Shay O'Brien about the "domestic violence epidemic."

According to this piece, the age group with the highest rates of abuse, women ages 16 to 24, experienced "rates of domestic victimization at 19.6 per 1000." In the general population of women, the rate is about "240 women every day." Pretty scary, huh?

But let's look at them again. In the group most likely to be abused, less than two percent of women encounter domestic violence. Moreover, assuming what the column reports is true, in the general population only about one-tenth of one percent of women ever encounter domestic violence. Not exactly an epidemic.

But that's only the beginning. Given that abuse rates are 10 times higher for women age 16 to 24, it stands to reason that something is unique about the group. I would say it is their proximity to 16 to 24-year-old men. Given that young men are both disproportionately likely to commit violent crime and also more likely to hang around young women, I would say that the underlying cause of abuse isn't societal indifference. In fact, abuse is only symptomatic of a larger social problem: the plight of young men in our country.

* [nickname for the University of Kansas]

Unfortunately, the women's movement is uninterested in helping young men. Thus, while you're sure to hear that women are far more likely to attempt suicide, you won't hear that men are far more likely to succeed. You won't hear that prostate cancer affects slightly more men than breast cancer does women. You won't hear that even though women aren't "natural" homemakers they are overwhelmingly given custody of the children in divorces.

You won't hear about all this because so-called Third Wave Feminists still adhere to Second Wave ideologies and tactics. This October, feminist activists will undoubtedly trot out the same old tired (and inaccurate) numbers about 1 in 4 women being raped and a 27 percent wage gap between the genders. Personal experience will continue to trump careful analysis in academic gender debates. And silly references will still be made about an invisible, oppressive patriarchy that selectively subjugates women to advance the interests of men.

However, in order to really make a difference in solving the problems it identifies, feminism must move past gendered analysis. Disenfranchised young men, a phenomenal gap between the wages of workers and managers, and an underclass that goes without enough food, health care, and opportunity for advancement aren't gender-specific issues. Yet in our community there are those who select issues only on the basis of their effect on a single gender. In Women's Studies 201, I learned a label for this sort of selection criteria: sexist.

Unfortunately, this sexism is insidious because it is well-meaning. The sexist activists are by and large good people who want to make our community better. But they fail to realize that unless the old models of single gender activism are rejected the only debate that can ensue will be the standard gender bickering that has occurred for the past 20 years.

I fearlessly predict that for the vast majority of Third Wave Feminists at KU this article will be filed in the "Robert Chamberlain is sexist and we don't like him" archive. However, I sincerely hope that a select few will read it and take it seriously. It is only through the efforts of these motivated post-feminist scholars that a broader new movement for social justice will coalesce. And it is this movement that offers the best hope for our abused women, our forgotten men, and our nation as a whole.

2. *Editorial by Amer G. Zahr (*The Michigan Daily, *November 26, 2001)*

Fraternities and a Heightened Rape Culture

I must say I was quite disturbed. As I was walking through the Diag in the beginning of the school year, during the first waves of the fraternity rush period, I saw an interesting banner. It encouraged rushing for Chi Psi, a campus fraternity, using the attractive slogan, "Chi Psi, The Gentleman's Fraternity." Better yet, the black banner with white writing also included a white cutout of both the Playboy bunny and the Déjà Vu logo (a "gentleman's club" chain).

What we had here was the laying of a foundation for a fraternity culture that is, at best, passively encouraging male dominative roles or, at worst, outright misogynistic. Should we be surprised after seeing such a banner, embodying such an attitude, that campus women have reported being raped at the local Beta house a few weeks ago? Should we be surprised that Scot Boeringer, in a 1996 article titled "Influences of Fraternity Membership, Athletics, and Male Living Arrangements on Sexual Aggression," asserts that there exists more significant use of intoxicants and non-physical verbal coercion in obtaining sex by fraternity members? Should we be surprised that the journal *Gender and Society* published a study in which interviews with fraternity members found a tendency to give alcohol to women on the theory that women who were drinking would be less resistant to sexual advances? Should we be surprised that Peggy Reeves Sanday, in her book *Fraternity Gang Rape*, argues that alcohol is a tool that men in fraternities are taught to use to "work a yes out" of unwilling women? Should we be surprised that in their article, "Fraternity and Sorority Membership and Gender Dominance Attitudes," Linda Kalof and Timothy Cargill found a substantial difference in dominance attitudes among Greek and non-Greek students, concluding that affiliation with Greek organizations is associated with traditional male dominant-female submissive attitudes?

Colby Nordheimer, a woman who was raped at a fraternity party at the University of Arizona, gave an interview to the *Arizona Daily Wildcat* in 1996. When asked how much fraternity culture played into her being assaulted, Nordheimer replied, "I am a Greek ... I don't think all fraternity men are rapists necessarily, but I do think that at times, there's a certain disrespect for women. It becomes a game, and sometimes they cross the line without necessarily knowing they've crossed it."

So what exists here is a number of studies and personal accounts showing that an overall American rape culture is highly and disproportionately prevalent in the campus fraternity environment. But this must concern us here in Ann Arbor to an even higher degree. Our university, unfortunately, holds the fraternities to no standards and to no accountability. Our university almost pretends like the frats don't exist, except for, of course, the Office of Greek Life. The office is located in the Michigan Union, and like other organizations, reapplies for office space every year. They are, however, unlike other groups, in no danger of ever losing their space. They employ a director, an assistant director and an administrative coordinator. They also house the four governing boards of the Greek community. It is a quite sophisticated operation. One would think that if such an organization were so prevalent in the Union's student organization office space, and such a visible presence on campus and in many students' lives, that our administration would hold them to the same types of standards as we hold other students and other organizations.

In my own view, the fraternities perhaps create as much benefit as other entities, while creating much more trouble. They are comparable to no student groups. A fraternity, to me, actually, is much more like a bar. They are cut from the same cloth. Frats encourage social interaction between members. Bars do the same (have you ever seen *Cheers*?). Frats cater to students. So do bars. In fact, I would suppose that many more students visit bars than ever visit frats. On the side of vice, frats are a hub for underage drinking. Bars house underage drinking, but much less, since they check identifications and use stringent standards since they are actually held accountable for allowing underage drinking. Back on the side of benefit, frats, like other students groups, carry out many community service activities, helping the local community. Bravo. Well, bars do the same thing. In fact, bars help the community not only by creating a social outlet, but also by creating a countless number of jobs for students as waiters and waitresses, line cooks, hostesses, bouncers, etc. That's community service if I ever heard of it.

In the end, frats=bars. The Union houses an Office of Greek Life. For fairness' sake, it should also house an Office of Bar Life. Greek Life representatives visit resident adviser training sessions to explain how they will relate to students' lives. Representatives from local bars should be afforded the same privilege. I don't see why not.

My proposal is that we treat the bars as we treat the frats. Now, another idea may be to treat the frats as we treat bars. In other words, we could treat the frats as if they don't exist. Sure, students can join them, and participate in all their virtues and vices, but not on the University's penny. Close down the Office of Greek Life. Let them seek private space to lease.

Or, finally, and probably most practically, our administration should create standards and regulations that the fraternities must live up to. And it must create real sanctions that make frats think twice before they create the kind of environment they are currently encouraging. Unfortunately, in the current context, it does not seem we are making any progress in stopping fraternities from egging on a dangerous misogynistic attitude, and viewing themselves as an untouchable "gentleman's club."

3. Editorial by Nick Woomer (The Michigan Daily, *November 28, 2001)*

Dancing on the Grave of the Protestant Work Ethic

It's Wednesday, a week after the start of Thanksgiving break, and (thankfully) politeness doesn't require you to ask everyone you have a conversation with "so how was your break?"

Every year, the responses are similar: "Pretty bad, I've got a bunch of work to do for this one class of mine and I'm still working on my personal statement for law school. . . . " "It was great, I saw a lot of my old high school friends at the bar and basically just chilled for a few days before things get real stressful again. . . ."

Generally, the lousy breaks aren't really "breaks" at all —just lulls in the school year that allow you to catch up on work. The good breaks tend to be the exact opposite— some quality time spent with friends and/or family, good conversation, good food, and reading material of one's choosing.

The lesson here is hardly a profound one: For most people, work = bad, and leisure = good. It's a simple, almost universally acknowledged truth and yet most Americans now regard the traditional 40-hour workweek as a luxury. The average American today works longer, harder and for less real income than ever before.

In the same way that the health care industry has con-vinced most Americans that any single-payer health care system will be a dystopian bureaucratic disaster ("Ever been to Canada? Talk about hell on earth. . . ."), Americans have somehow been convinced—although I suspect the so-called "Protestant Work Ethic" shares a big part of the blame—that work is some sort of end-in-itself.

Apparently it's harder to convince the French that obvious facts are, in fact, not true. Not only does everyone in France have access to health care (even those lazy poor people), but they also have a 35-hour workweek. And no, the country isn't on the verge of collapse; in fact, things over there are going just fine thank you.

By almost all accounts, the 35-hour workweek (or, rather, the 1,600-hour work year), which was adopted in 1998 by Lionel Jospin's government and now affects almost 50 percent of France's work force, is changing life there— dramatically. The legislation has caused affected employees to have between 11 and 16 extra days off per year. Now, more French people have more leisure time, and they're using it to go on more vacations (2000 saw an 18 percent jump in camper van purchases) and—this should please all you "family values" people—they're spending more time socializing with their friends and family. More people are working too; in June France's state planing commission estimated that the 35-hour workweek was responsible for creating one in six new jobs.

French employers have also seen the benefits of a reduced workweek—well-rested, happy workers are much more productive workers who make fewer mistakes and are less likely to mouth-off to customers. On the other hand, French employers (especially in capital-intensive industries) are trying to compensate for higher overhead costs—you lose money when you invest in machines that aren't being worked by someone—by cutting breaks and pushing employees to work at an uncomfortable pace. As a result, French labor ministry research indicates that only about 59 percent of those affected by the reduced work-week think it has made their lives better.

So, given its not-quite-overwhelming success, should we just give up on the reduced workweek? There's evidence that the problem isn't that 35 hours a week is too little, but that it's too much. An 8/8/01 column in the *Ottawa Citizen* cited an experiment in Finland where the traditional 8-hour workday is divided into two six-hour shifts. Even though they're required to pay workers for working eight hours a day, Finnish employers aren't losing money because the increased service hours, productivity and reduced overhead costs offset the cost of paying workers for two extra hours of work. Similar experiments are being conducted all over Europe.

According to Bruce O'Hara, the *Citizen* column's author, "the work-time issue has had so much attention in Europe that my guess is that some time in the next five years, at least one city or region will pilot-test a 28-hour workweek built around two community-wide shifts. I further predict that the model is so practical that it will quickly become the norm across Europe."

What the European and hypothetical experiments in shorter workweeks indicate (at the very least) is that it may be more than possible to significantly improve people's social lives at little or no economic cost. It's time to take a critical look at America's fabled "Protestant Work Ethic," do an economic cost-social benefit analysis, and start enjoying life.

Collaborative Activity 10.10

Analyze the editorials included in this chapter according to Box 2.1: Questions for Analyzing a Genre (pp. 93–94), and compile an initial list of the features of editorials you first notice—the patterns that they seem to share.

Because editorials appear in a wide range of settings and define many different publics, one editorial can appear quite different from another. Columnists like Ellen Goodman and Leonard Pitts, Jr., who often write about family issues or how issues affect women and minorities, may include their personal experiences with an issue or tell stories from other people's lives. The particular publics they define appreciate the human emphasis and find individual stories persuasive. Columnists like Molly Ivins or George Will, who often write about national political issues, tend to include statistics or quotations from experts or politicians to support their arguments, appealing to a different particular public. Yet all four write editorials, texts whose purpose is to persuade people to their way of thinking through rational argument about significant public issues.

RHETORICAL APPEALS

One of the markers of this persuasive genre, and one of the ways it differs from the academic genres we've described, is its use not only of logical but also of emotional and personal appeals (logos, pathos, and ethos). As you will recall, logos is appealing to an audience's rational mind, to the persuasiveness of logical and rational arguments; pathos is appealing to an audience's emotions, persuading readers by making them feel the writer's position, whether through sympathy, compassion, anger, or any other appropriate emotion; and ethos is appealing to an audience's belief in the personal qualities of the writer, persuading the readers that the writer should be believed or agreed with on this subject. In appeals from ethos, writers may try to convince readers that they are credible because of their expertise, sympathetic because of their experiences, or believable because they are in positions of power, for example. In the academic and workplace scenes, logical appeals are depended on heavily, but in the public sphere the most effective arguments draw on all three kinds of appeal.

Collaborative Activity 10.11

Reread the editorials above, and find places where each writer uses each of the three kinds of appeals. Make note of any areas where the appeals overlap (for instance, where an ethical appeal to the writer's credibility is based on identification with the audience or rational arguments/evidence).

Writing Activity 10.14

Describe which kinds of appeals you tend to find most effective, using these editorials for examples. If an editorial writer persuades you, do you tend to believe the writer because of who he or she is (ethical), because of how she or he makes you feel (emotional), or because of the rational arguments and evidence offered (logical)? (Of course, we all respond to all three kinds of appeals, but many of us gravitate toward one kind or another. Knowing which appeal you prefer can remind you not to depend too heavily on your own preference but to include other appeals that other readers might find persuasive as well.)

SUBJECTS, LANGUAGE, AND FORMAT

In addition to using all three appeals in their common situation, editorial writers share common types of subjects, ways of beginning and ending their texts, ways of integrating evidence and details, and even some aspects of style, tone, and voice. Effective editorialists who wish to persuade the widest range of readers do not denigrate their readers, for example, or ignore the arguments of people who disagree with them. Some use humor and some are stern, but they all choose words carefully, with attention to precision and vividness, necessary qualities for their persuasive purposes.

Writing Activity 10.15

Find at least three editorials from different forums. Analyze your editorials using Box 2.1: Questions for Analyzing a Genre (pp. 93–94). Adding this information to that generated in Collaborative Activity 10.10, write a 1-page description of the editorial genre for your classmates.

Writing Activity 10.16

Drawing on your analysis of editorials in Writing Activity 10.15, write a 1-page critique of the editorial genre. To help you critically consider the possible limitations of this genre and the effects of these limitations, consult Box 4.1: Questions for Critiquing Genres (p. 161).

Collaborative Activity 10.12

Bring to class the editorials you gathered from different forums. Compare the descriptions you each wrote, and find points of similarity and difference among your analyses. Compile a list of generic features of the editorial that encompasses all the editorials your group gathered. Then discuss what the features of this genre reveal about the public scenes in which the editorial functions and about the individuals (writers/readers) who participate in that scene—their beliefs, assumptions, and expectations.

Collaborative Activity 10.13

Based on the analysis of editorials that you have done in the last several activities, write a list of writing tips for making effective choices when writing editorials. What do writers need to keep in mind? What content and organizational strategies might be useful? How should writers of editorials use the three kinds of rhetorical appeals? On the textual level, what kinds of sentence, word, and stylistic choices can and should writers make? Then, what writing process questions can you suggest for writers as they write their editorials? Refer to Box 3.1: Questions for Inventing (p. 108), Box 3.2: Questions for Drafting (p. 117), Box 3.4: Questions for Revising (p. 139), and Box 3.5: Questions for Presentation (p. 146), and adapt these questions to the writing of editorials.

Writing for Specific Publics

We have emphasized in this chapter writing in the public sphere at large, in forums that anyone can access like Web sites, magazines, or newspapers. We also noted that not everyone reads these forums and that each genre in fact defines a more particular public as its audience, a public of people interested in the same subjects or issues. Those people with common interests sometimes form smaller political groups, organizations of people banded together to try to influence public opinion and public policy toward the group's common interest. Organizations such as the National Organization for Women, the NAACP, the National Rifle Association, and Amnesty International are common ones with which you might be familiar. These smaller publics, too, try to influence public opinion in the public sphere. Some scholars in fact believe that most public policy results from negotiations and compromises among these groups, rather than from a broader public consensus in the public sphere. Another way to have some impact on society and its policies, then, is to become active in organizations that represent your interests. There, too, genres exist to help you have that kind of impact.

Many of the genres used in these more particular publics share situations and even names similar to those of the broader public sphere. Organizations' newsletters often include letters to the editor and guest columns, for example. Speeches and messages to electronic discussion lists serve both broad publics and special interest groups. The scenes of these special interest groups differ significantly to the extent that their participants represent a much narrower public and probably agree with the writer on some significant values and beliefs. The audience of such a specific public is much more homogenous, then, than the audience within most civic or public scenes. When you decide to join the conversation in a smaller political scene, then, you will need to adapt your understanding of the genres to these different audiences, whose beliefs will be more clearly defined.

Another significant way you can use writing to improve society is to contribute your writing talents and skills to a public organization. You can offer to write newsletter copy, a pamphlet or brochure, letters to potential donors or volunteers, advertising copy, news releases. Local organizations and local branches of national organizations, in particular, can often use help broadcasting their message to the larger public. Organizations even need to write letters to the editor or guest columns sometimes, especially to clarify misconceptions that might have appeared in a public forum or to ask for a community's support. One of our students volunteered for an organization that promotes education about the Bill of Rights and was asked to write a newspaper guest column to inform people. His column even gained him an invitation to serve on a televised panel about the Bill of Rights. When you write as a representative of an organization, of course, you are under some different strictures to represent *their* views and not just your own; this situation is similar in some ways to the situations common in workplace writing. To contribute your writing talents to an organization, you often need only to offer. If one organization does not need your help, another probably will. Seek out organizations whose purposes and values you support, of course, whether that is the local humane society, the campus recycling group, or your neighborhood association.

In short, your writing does matter in society. If you write to broadcast your wedding to the public, you are keeping others informed. If you write to persuade others that campus parking rules must change, you are contributing to public debate and helping to shape public opinion. If you write for smaller organizations, you advance a public cause and contribute their interests to the rational debate of the public sphere. If you choose not to write anything public, that choice, too, matters. Choosing not to participate in the debate about public issues leaves others to make decisions for you, permits the actions of authorities to go unchallenged, and undermines our democratic society and representative government. We earn our society by participating in it as good citizens.

Writing Projects

Writing Project 10.1

Write a letter to the editor, perhaps based in one of the issues you developed as you worked through this chapter. Be sure to specify the scene (which newspaper, magazine, or Web site). If an article or letter exists that shows the action your letter responds to, give your teacher a copy of that source, too. Seriously consider sending your letter to the forum for publication. After you write your letter to the editor, write a memo to your teacher explaining the writing choices you made and how these choices respond to the demands of your writing situation (the setting, the subject, the readers, and your purposes for writing) and to the demands of the scene (especially the objectives and constraints of the particular newspaper, magazine, or Web site).

Writing Project 10.2

Choose a newspaper, magazine, or Web site, and write an editorial in response to one of the following prompts. When you are finished drafting the editorial, write a memo explaining how the choices you made as a writer respond to the demands of the scene, situation, and genre of editorials.

a. Respond to one of the editorials included in this chapter or the editorials on drilling in the Arctic National Wildlife Refuge from Chapter 1. Assume that the editorial originally appeared in your local or campus newspaper.

b. Write an editorial on an issue of your choice for a specific publication (your campus or local newspaper would be accessible forums). If you wrote a researched position paper for Chapter 7, consider writing an editorial based on that research.

c. Critique one of the civic genres, arguing that the genre has limitations as a forum for public discourse. Remember that the audience of an editorial will not have the background in genre analysis that you have, so you will have to explain your argument and offer evidence that your readers will understand.

Writing Project 10.3

Write a public text in a genre that we have not analyzed in this chapter, choosing from one of the prompts below. Be sure to collect samples of the genre and analyze the genre to understand its scene and features before you write.

a. Choose an organization whose cause you support and write a pamphlet explaining its purposes and services to the public. (If possible, choose an organization related to the subject of the research paper you wrote for Chapter 7.)

b. Contact a local organization and offer to write whatever kinds of text they might need. If they need a genre with which you are unfamiliar, use the genre analysis you have been learning to understand the scene, analyze the features, and write in this genre.

c. Write a text in any other public genre that you can analyze (you might have genres you analyzed for group activities early in this chapter). If your actual situation does not fit the genre (a wedding announcement when you are not married, for example), imagine yourself in the situation and create the necessary details.

Credits

Chapter 1

Classified ads, *The Seattle Times*, December 11, 2002. The Seattle Times Company, 2003. Reprinted with the permission of The Seattle Times Company.

Bob Ferris, "New Technologies But Still the Same Messy Business," TomPaine.com, April 3, 2001. Reprinted by permission.

Elizabeth Morrison, "My Opinion: The Shortsightedness and Exploitation of Oil Drilling," *The Digital Collegian*, November 17, 1993. © 1993 Collegian Inc. Reprinted by permission.

Bernie W. Stewart, "Alaska Environmental Bugaboos," *Drilling Contractor*, Sept./Oct. 1999. Adapted and reprinted with permission from *Drilling Contractor*, the official magazine of the International Association of Drilling Contractors.

Stephanie Smith, "Ethnography of a Greyhound Track: A Study on Social Stratification and Diehards," from *Field Ethnography: A Manual for Doing Cultural Anthropology* by Paul Kutsche, © 1998. Reprinted by permission of Pearson Education, Inc., Upper Saddle River, NJ.

Chapter 2

Perri Klass, "Learning the Language," *A Not Entirely Benign Procedure: Four Years as a Medical Student*. Copyright © 1987 by Perri Klass. Used by permission of G.P. Putnam's Sons, a division of Penguin Group (USA) Inc.

William Murdick, "Sample Complaint Letter," *The Portable Business Writer*. Copyright © 1999 by Houghton Mifflin Company. Used with permission.

Judith S. VanAlstyne, "Sample Complaint Letter," *Professional and Technical Writing Strategies: Communicating in Technology and Science*. Reprinted by permission of Pearson Education, Inc., Upper Saddle River, NJ.

Michael H. Markel, "Sample Complaint Letter," *Technical Communication,* 5e. Copyright © November 1997 by Bedford/St. Martin's. Reprinted with permission of Bedford/St. Martin's.

Nicole Rebernick, "The Genre of Restaurant Menus: A Comparative Analysis." Reprinted by permission.

Menu, Sicily's Italian Restaurant, Knoxville, Tennessee.

Menu, Bela Roma Restaurant, Knoxville, Tennessee.

Chapter 3

Cathleen Ceremuga, "Writing Situation Analysis (for informative paper, 'Meeting Spindles')." Reprinted with permission.

Cathleen Ceremuga, "Meeting Spindles, or Interning at the Philadelphia Children's Zoo." Reprinted with permission.

Chapter 4

Theresa Devine-Solomon, "For the Bride or Groom." Reprinted with permission.

Amy J. Weishaar, "Changing Forms." Reprinted with permission.

Randall Popken, "Resume-in-Letter," from "The Pedagogical Dissemination of a Genre: The Resume in American Business Discourse Textbooks, 1914–1939," *JAC: A Journal of Composition Theory,* 19.1 (1999): 91–116. Reprinted with permission.

Randall Popken, "Free-Standing Resume from 1924," from "The Pedagogical Dissemination of a Genre: The Resume in American Business Discourse Textbooks, 1914–1939," *JAC: A Journal of Composition Theory,* 19.1 (1999): 91–116. Reprinted with permission.

Chapter 5

Anne DiPardo, "Sylvia," *A Kind of Passport: A Basic Writing Adjunct Program and the Challenge of Student Diversity.* Copyright 1993 by the National Council of Teachers of English. Reprinted with permission.

"WPA Outcomes Statement for First-Year Composition," http://www. english.ilstu.edu/Hesse/outcomes.html. Reprinted with permission of the Council of Writing Program Administrators.

Chapter 6

Rosina Lippi-Green, "Teaching Children How to Discriminate: What We Learn from the Big Bad Wolf," *English with an Accent: Language, Ideology, and Discrimination in the United States* (London: Routledge, 1997). Reprinted by permission of Taylor & Francis Books Ltd.

Index

E-mail, 104
  developing genres of, 174
  messages, 105, 113
Embedding, 71, 72, 176
Emoticons, 104, 174
Encyclopedia of Philosophy, 347
Encyclopedia of Psychology, 347
Encyclopedia of World Architecture, 347
Engineering Index, 347
English with an Accent: Language, Ideology, and Discrimination in the United States (Lippi-Green), 245
ERIC database, 347
Essay examinations, 112
Ethnography, 26
  techniques of, 37
"Ethnography of a Greyhound Track: A Study on Social Stratification and Diehards" (Smith), 27–36
Ethos, 273, 297, 565–566
Evaluative claims, 295–296
Evidence, 74, 160, 385
  analyzing, 236
  developing and supporting claims with, 277–280
  different types of, in different genres, 459
  in proposals, 498
  rational, 401
  resumé qualifications in job application letter, as, 485
  from sources, grounding ideas in, 403–404
  strategies for introducing, 282
  to support thesis, 232
  use of transitions to introduce, 281–282
  weight of facts and, in proposals, 502

Fair use laws, 395
"Feminists Ignore Half the Problems" (Chamberlain), 557–559
Field Ethnography: A Manual for Doing Cultural Anthology, 26
Five-paragraph theme
  versus analysis paper, 231–232
  moving from, to analysis paper, 236–237
  structure of, 231–232
Format, 66, 96
  of analysis papers, 281–282
  of argument papers, 298
  citing sources in researched position papers, 394–399
  identifying, 71
  of job application letters, 486
  of proposals, 501
  of resumé, 481–482
  subjects, language, and, in editorials, 566–567
"For the Bride or Groom?" (Devine), 154–158
Fountain (Duchamp), 149
"Fraternities and a Heightened Rape Culture" (Zahr), 559–562
Freewriting, 25, 224–225
Freire, Paulo, 220, 222
Functional resumé. *See* Analytical resumé

Game report, 524–527
General public, 522
Genre analysis
  complaint letter sample, 64–66, 70–73
  defined, 63
  guidelines for, 93–94
  learning, 50
  menus used in, 81–90
  practicing, 80, 92
  sample, 73–79
Genre critique, 151–152
  examples of, 153–160
  forms of, 152

from, to change, 163–164
importance of, 152–153
performing your own, 160–162
questions for, 161
"The Genre of Restaurant Menus: A Comparative Analysis" (Rebernik), 74–79
Genres
  academic. *See* Academic genres
  acting with, 21–23
  analysis, argument, and research in different types of disciplines and, 460–462
  anticipating processes behind different, 102–103
  changing, 162–164, 174
  civic. *See* Civic genres
  controversy around power of, 181–182
  creating new, 180
  creative choices within, 148–149
  critiquing and changing, 148–182
  defined, 7, 22, 24
  different types of evidence in different, 459
  drafting with, 111–116
  expectations of, 22–23
  identifying, 458–459
  identifying rhetorical and linguistic patterns of, 65
  interactions of, in workplace scenes, 487–488
  interrelationship of purpose and, 95
  inventing with, 105–111
  invention strategies for other, 107–108
  learning patterns of, 96
  learning to conduct research through different, 337–338
  making choices writing within, 148
  proposals, 488–502
  the public and its, 522–530
  putting back together of, 23–25
  questions for detecting dissonance based on, 124
  reading, 48–50
  reading scenes and situations through, 58–60
  from reading to analyzing, 63–64
  reports, 506–508
  research-based, 335–336
  resumé, 477, 479–482
  revising old, to develop new ones, 175, 176, 177–178
  revising with, 118
  as rhetorical maps, 469
  roles of, in writing processes, 100–104
  samples of workplace, 509–517
  script or pattern of, 92
  as social scripts, 58–59
  strategies for identifying, 42–43
  from thinking critically to critiquing, 150–162
  understanding limitations of, 162
  using
  workplace, 139
  of writing courses, 224–228
  written in hypertext, 178–179
Goodman, Ellen, 565
Graphics, 142
Guided responses, 120

Harlem Renaissance, 345
Humanities Index, 347
Hyper-reading, 179
Hypotheses, 461, 462

I, Rigoberta Manchú (Manchú), 181–182
"In Black & White; A Look at How the Magazines Affect the Body Images of These 2 Ethnic Groups" (Predny), 419–424
"In Case of Emergency, Please Wait," 339, 408–413
Individual Education Plan (IEP), 180